**INSTRUCTORS...**

Dalhousie University
Department of Economics
6214 University Avenue
PO Box 15000
Halifax, NS
Canada    B3H 4R2

Would you like your **students** to show up for class **more prepared**?
  *(Let's face it, class is much more fun if everyone is engaged and prepared...)*

Want an **easy way to assign** homework online and track student **progress**?
  *(Less time grading means more time teaching...)*

Want an **instant view** of student or class performance?
  *(No more wondering if students understand...)*

Need to **collect data and generate reports** required for administration or accreditation?
  *(Say goodbye to manually tracking student learning outcomes...)*

Want to **record and post your lectures** for students to view online?
  *(The more students can see, hear, and experience class resources, the better they learn...)*

 With **McGraw-Hill's** *Connect*,

## INSTRUCTORS GET:

- Simple **assignment management**, allowing you to spend more time teaching.
- **Auto-graded** assignments, quizzes, and tests.
- **Detailed visual reporting** where student and section results can be viewed and analyzed.
- Sophisticated **online testing** capability.
- A **filtering and reporting** function that allows you to easily assign and report on materials that are correlated to learning objectives and Bloom's taxonomy.
- An easy-to-use **lecture capture** tool.
- The option to **upload course documents** for student access.

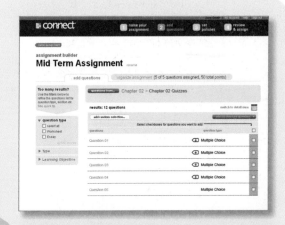

# PRINCIPLES OF
# MICROECONOMICS

## FOURTH CANADIAN EDITION

### Robert H. Frank
Cornell University

### Ben S. Bernanke
Princeton University (affiliated)
Chairman, Board of Governors of the
Federal Reserve System

### Lars Osberg
Dalhousie University

### Melvin L. Cross
Dalhousie University

### Brian K. MacLean
Laurentian University

McGraw-Hill
Ryerson
Connect. Learn. Succeed.

Principles of Microeconomics
Fourth Canadian Edition

ISBN-13: 978-0-07-040144-0
ISBN-10: 0-07-040144-6

1 2 3 4 5 6 7 8 9 10 QDB 1 9 8 7 6 5 4 3 2

Printed and bound in the United States of America.

Care has been taken to trace ownership of copyright material contained in this text; however, the publisher will welcome any information that enables them to rectify any reference or credit for subsequent editions.

Sponsoring Editor: *James Booty*
Marketing Manager: *Jeremy Guimond*
Developmental Editor: *Daphne Scriabin*
Editorial Associate: *Erin Catto*
Supervising Editor: *Jessica Barnoski*
Photo/Permissions Research: *Daphne Scriabin*
Copy Editor: *Julie van Tol*
Proofreader: *Simpson Editorial Services*
Production Coordinator: *Sheryl MacAdam*
Cover Design: *Greg Devitt*
Cover Image: *JG Photography/Alamy*
Interior Design: *Greg Devitt*
Page Layout: *Laserwords Private Limited*
Printer: *Quad/Graphics Dubuque*

**Library and Archives Canada Cataloguing in Publication**

Principles of microeconomics / Robert H. Frank . . . [et al.].—4th Canadian ed.

Includes bibliographical references and index.
ISBN 978-0-07-040144-0

   1. Microeconomics—Textbooks. I. Frank, Robert H.

HB172.P75 2012        338.5        C2011-906897-4

# ABOUT THE AUTHORS

**Professor Frank** is the Henrietta Johnson Louis Professor of Management and Professor of Economics at the Johnson Graduate School of Management at Cornell University, where he has taught since 1972. His "Economic View" column appears regularly in *The New York Times*. After receiving his B.S. from Georgia Tech in 1966, he taught math and science for two years as a Peace Corps Volunteer in rural Nepal. He received his M.A. in statistics in 1971 and his Ph.D. in economics in 1972 from The University of California at Berkeley. During leaves of absence from Cornell, he has served as chief economist for the Civil Aeronautics Board (1978–1980), a Fellow at the Center for Advanced Study in the Behavioral Sciences (1992–93), Professor of American Civilization at l'École des Hautes Études en Sciences Sociales in Paris (2000–01), and the Peter and Charlotte Schoenfeld Visiting Faculty Fellow at the NYU Stern School of Business in 2008–09. Professor Frank is the author of a best-selling intermediate economics textbook—*Microeconomics and Behavior*, Eighth Edition (Irwin/McGraw-Hill, 2010). His research has focused on rivalry and cooperation in economic and social behaviour. His books on these themes include *Choosing the Right Pond* (Oxford, 1995), *Passions Within Reason* (W. W. Norton, 1988), *What Price the Moral High Ground?* (Princeton, 2004), *Falling Behind* (University of California Press, 2007), *The Economic Naturalist* (Basic Books, 2007), *The Economic Naturalist's Field Guide* (Basic Books, 2009), and the *Darwin Economy* (Princeton, 2011), and have been translated into 22 languages. *The Winner-Take-All Society* (The Free Press, 1995), co-authored with Philip Cook, received a Critic's Choice Award, was named a Notable Book of the Year by *The New York Times*, and was included in *BusinessWeek*'s list of the 10 best books of 1995. *Luxury Fever* (The Free Press, 1999) was named to the *Knight-Ridder* Best Books list for 1999.

Professor Frank has been awarded an Andrew W. Mellon Professorship (1987–1990), a Kenan Enterprise Award (1993), and a Merrill Scholars Program Outstanding Educator Citation (1991). He is a co-recipient of the 2004 Leontief Prize for Advancing the Frontiers of Economic Thought. He was awarded the Johnson School's Stephen Russell Distinguished Teaching Award in 2004 and 2010 and the School's Apple Distinguished Teaching Award in 2005. His introductory microeconomics course has graduated more than 7,000 enthusiastic economic naturalists over the years.

**Professor Bernanke** received his B.A. in economics from Harvard University in 1975 and his Ph.D. in economics from MIT in 1979. He taught at the Stanford Graduate School of Business from 1979 to 1985 and moved to Princeton University in 1985, where he was named the Howard Harrison and Gabrielle Snyder Beck Professor of Economics and Public Affairs, and where he served as Chairman of the Economics Department.

Professor Bernanke was sworn in on February 1, 2006, as Chairman and a member of the Board of Governors of the Federal Reserve System. He has also been appointed to a second term, which expires January 31, 2014. Professor Bernanke also serves as Chairman of the Federal Open Market Committee, the System's principal monetary policy-making body. He was appointed as a member of the Board to a full 14-year term, which expires January 31, 2020. Before his appointment as Chairman, Professor Bernanke was Chairman of the President's Council of Economic Advisers, from June 2005 to January 2006.

Professor Bernanke's intermediate textbook, with Andrew Abel and Dean Croushore, *Macroeconomics*, Seventh Edition (Addison-Wesley, 2011), is a best-seller in its field. He has authored more than 50 scholarly publications in macroeconomics, macroeconomic history, and finance. He has done significant research on the causes of the Great Depression, the role of financial markets and institutions in the business cycle, and measuring the effects of monetary policy on the economy. Professor Bernanke has held a Guggenheim Fellowship and a Sloan Fellowship, and he is a Fellow of the Econometric Society and of the American Academy of Arts and Sciences. He served as the Director of the Monetary Economics Program of the National Bureau of Economic Research (NBER) and as a member of the NBER's Business Cycle Dating Committee. In July 2001, he was appointed editor of the *American Economic Review*. Professor Bernanke's work with civic and professional groups includes having served two terms as a member of the Montgomery Township (N.J.) Board of Education.

**Lars Osberg** is currently McCulloch Professor and Chair of the Department of Economics at Dalhousie University, but he began life in Ottawa. As an undergraduate, he attended Queen's University in Kingston and the London School of Economics and Political Science. After two years working for the Tanzania Sisal Corporation as a CUSO volunteer, he went to Yale University for his Ph.D. His first book was *Economic Inequality in Canada* (1981), and the most recent is *The Economic Implications of Social Cohesion* (2003). In between, there were eight others. He is also the author of numerous refereed articles in professional journals, book chapters, reviews, reports, and miscellaneous publications. His major fields of research interest have been the extent and causes of poverty and economic inequality, with particular emphasis in recent years on social policy and the implications of working time, unemployment, and structural change. Among other professional responsibilities, he was president of the Canadian Economics Association in 1999–2000. Recent papers can be found at http://myweb.dal.ca/osberg/.

**Melvin Cross** received an Associate of Arts degree from Dawson Community College in 1968, a B.A. from the University of Montana in 1970, an M.A. from Simon Fraser University in 1972, and a Ph.D. in economics from Texas A&M University in 1976. He is an Associate Professor and Graduate Coordinator in the Department of Economics at Dalhousie University, which he joined in 1975. He held an adjunct appointment in the School of Resource and Environmental Studies, and was an Associate Fellow in the Foundation Year Program of the University of King's College from 1991 to 2002. Professor Cross has taught as a visitor at Queen's University, the University of Sydney, and Carleton University. His teaching and research interests are in the economics of natural and environmental resources and the history of economic thought. He has taught principles of economics throughout his career. He is an author or co-author of articles in the *Canadian Journal of Fisheries and Aquatic Science*, *Canadian Public Policy*, *History of Political Economy*, *Marine Resource Economics*, and other journals. He is Past President of the Atlantic Canada Economics Association, having served as Vice-President during 2007–09, and then President in 2009–11.

**Brian K. MacLean** is Professor of Economics at Laurentian University in Sudbury, Ontario, where he has been Chair of the Department of Economics and Director of the Institute for Northern Ontario Research and Development. He was born and raised in Charlottetown, Prince Edward Island, speaks Japanese as a second language, and has been a visiting professor at Hokkaido University in Sapporo, Japan, and Saitama University, just outside of Tokyo, where he returns each summer to deliver a series of lectures. His publications include the prescient edited volume *Out of Control? Canada in an Unstable Financial World* (Lorimer, 1999). His recent research includes topics such as the implications for other economies of Japan's experience of countering the aftermath of a major asset price bubble and the implications for macroeconomics of the global financial crisis and recession. He has served on the Executive of the Canadian Economics Association, as the CEA liaison with the Canadian Women Economists Network, and has been a Steering Committee member of the Progressive Economics Forum for more than a decade.

# BRIEF CONTENTS

# CONTENTS

## Chapter 6   Production, Cost, and the Quest for Profit: The Supply Side in the Long Run   160

## Chapter 7   Economic Surplus and Exchange   183

## Chapter 9  Thinking Strategically  260

## Chapter 10  Externalities and Property Rights  284

## Chapter 11   The Economics of Information   310

# PREFACE

Feedback from users of the previous editions supports our conviction that there is a different and better way to introduce beginning students to economics. In its bare bones, the philosophy of this text rests on two pillars: (1) the repeated application of a set of core economic principles to real world problems and (2) an active, student-centred approach to learning.

## THE FIRST PILLAR: REPEATED USE OF CORE PRINCIPLES

The best way to teach introductory economics—or to introduce virtually any subject, for that matter—is to show students the many practical implications of the core ideas of the discipline. Of course, if we asked a thousand economists to provide their own lists of core ideas, we would get a thousand somewhat different lists. But we suspect that almost all the lists would start with much the same basic problem, that of scarcity, and would use much the same basic principle, that of comparing costs and benefits.

- **The Scarcity Problem:** Although we have boundless needs and wants, the resources available to us are limited. Having more of one good thing, therefore, usually means having less of another.
- **The Cost–Benefit Principle:** An individual (or a firm or a society) will be better off if, and only if, the extra benefits from taking an action are greater than the extra costs.

From this basic starting point, five other important principles follow:

- **The Principle of Relevant Costs:** The "opportunity cost" of a decision is the goods that have to be foregone because of that decision. Moreover, in considering whether to produce or consume more of a good, what matters is the cost of one more unit (i.e., marginal cost).
- **The Principle of Comparative Advantage:** Total output is largest when each person concentrates on the activities for which his or her opportunity cost is lowest.
- **The Principle of Increasing Opportunity Cost:** In expanding the production of any good, first employ those resources with the lowest opportunity cost. Only when all of the lowest-cost resources are employed does it make economic sense to use resources that have higher opportunity costs.
- **The Efficiency Principle:** Economic efficiency occurs when total economic surplus is maximized. Efficiency is an important social goal because, when the economic pie grows larger, everyone can potentially have a larger slice.
- **The Equilibrium Principle:** A market in equilibrium leaves individuals no incentives to change their behaviour, but it may not exploit all gains achievable through collective action.

Our point is not that this is the best short list, but rather that the introductory course will be taught most effectively if it begins with a well-articulated short list of some principles, illustrating and applying each principle in many different contexts.

# THE SECOND PILLAR: ACTIVE LEARNING

Our second guiding principle has been that active learning by students—"student-centred" learning, in the jargon—is an essential part of an effective learning process. By "learning," we do not mean being able to answer a test question the next day. By the time they reach university, many students have become quite good at quick memorization—and at forgetting "useless stuff" equally rapidly. Even the brightest students never fully internalize a concept unless they actually use it repeatedly. We think it is useful for instructors to ask themselves, "What do I want my students to retain from this course, five, ten, or twenty years from now?" Our reading of research in education indicates that long-term retention depends on students both seeing the value of a concept and *actively* using it. Therefore, throughout the book we use a number of devices to foster active learning.

1. **Worked Examples:** New ideas and concepts are not simply asserted, as in most books. Instead, they are introduced by means of simple examples, usually numerical, which are developed step-by-step in the text. These examples display the reasoning process used to reach the economic conclusion or insight, and they provide a model for the student to apply when working exercises and problems.

---

### EXAMPLE 6.3

#### Does owning the land make a difference?

Continue with the previous example, but suppose Bernard's Uncle Warren, who owns the farmland Bernard has been renting, dies and leaves Bernard that parcel of land. If the land could be rented to some other farmer for $6000/year, is Bernard better off to remain in farming?

As shown in Table 6.3, if Bernard continues to farm his own land, his accounting profit will be $16 000/year, or $6000 more than before. But his economic profit will be the same as before (–$1000/year) because Bernard must deduct the $6000/year opportunity cost of farming his own land. The reduction of $6000 in explicit costs is exactly offset by an increase of $6000 in implicit costs. If others have preferences like Bernard's together with similar outside employment opportunities, then the normal profit from owning and operating a farm like his will be $17 000/year; that is, the opportunity cost of the land and labour provided. But, since Bernard earns an accounting profit of only $16 000, he will again be better off if he abandons farming for the managerial job.

---

2. **Exercises:** Following many examples, and indeed throughout each chapter, we pose exercises in the running text that challenge the student to test and extend his or her understanding of the ideas being discussed. Answers to these exercises are provided at the end of the chapter, allowing immediate feedback.

---

**GM and Ford must both decide whether to invest in developing a new engine. Games 1 and 2 below show how their profits depend on the decisions they make. Which of these games is a prisoner's dilemma?**   EXERCISE 9.2

|  |  | Game 1 Ford | | | | Game 2 Ford | |
|---|---|---|---|---|---|---|---|
|  |  | Not invest | Invest |  |  | Not invest | Invest |
| GM | Not invest | 10 for each | 4 for GM 12 for Ford | | GM Not invest | 4 for GM 12 for Ford | 5 for each |
| GM | Invest | 12 for GM 4 for Ford | 5 for each | | GM Invest | 10 for each | 12 for GM 4 for Ford |

---

3. **Anecdotes and Illustrations:** Active learning is more likely to take place when students are engaged and motivated. We begin almost every chapter with an anecdote that motivates the discussion, and we illustrate the ideas with memorable cartoons, photographs, and original line drawings. Most important, we have striven to minimize jargon and engage the student with direct, friendly writing. (For examples see Chapter 6, p. 163 and Chapter 8, p. 221.

4. **Recap Boxes and Summaries:** To keep students focused on the forest as well as on the trees, at strategic points in each chapter we have provided "recap boxes." Recaps summarize the main ideas of the previous section. The recap box summations are reiterated in numbered end-of-chapter summaries, which are designed to review the most important concepts presented in each chapter.

---

**RECAP**

### THE PRICE-TAKING FIRM'S SUPPLY CURVE

The price-taking firm faces a fixed market price for its product, meaning that it can sell any quantity it wants at the market price. As a result, market price is also marginal revenue. In the short run, the firm must consider whether to operate or to shut down. If it is worthwhile to operate in the short run, the firm chooses the level of output that maximizes its profits.

A price-taking firm will maximize profit by choosing the output level for which marginal cost is equal to the market price of its product (provided market price exceeds minimum average variable cost, as will be shown). When it chooses its output level, the firm simultaneously chooses the number of workers it will employ. Provided that it has decided to produce and not shut down, the price-taking firm's supply curve is its marginal cost curve,[2] which is upward sloping in the short run because of the law of diminishing returns. Adding the supply responses of all such firms in a market provides the market supply curve.

---

5. **Core Principles Icon:** Throughout the book, whenever one of the core principles is discussed, a small icon appears in the margin. Each core principle is thereby reinforced many times.

---

COST–
BENEFIT

**The Cost–benefit Principle:** A rational decision maker will take an economic action if, and only if, the extra benefits from taking the action are greater than the extra costs.

---

6. **Review Questions and Problems:** Questions for review at the end of each chapter encourage the student to test his or her understanding of the main ideas of the chapter. End-of-chapter problems are carefully crafted to help students internalize and extend core concepts.

In keeping with the active learning principle, we have integrated the discussions of public policy issues into the relevant theory chapters. Both the First and Second editions had a separate "Economics of Public Policy" chapter. This changed with the third edition, where we first presented the relevant theoretical discussion, and then immediately showed how useful these concepts are for an important public policy issue. We have retained this pattern in the fourth edition. For example, Chapter 10 on the theory of externalities and property rights is integrated with a discussion of global climate change, a presentation of the marginal abatement cost approach to pollution reduction, and an analysis of the merits of a carbon tax or "cap and trade" system for reducing $CO_2$ emissions. There is no better way to keep students motivated and interested in economics than by showing *immediately* how economics can be used to help solve current and significant social problems.

# ECONOMIC NATURALISM

Economics is all around us, every day. Economics is fascinating because of its power to explain. As part of the active-learning approach, we encourage students to become "economic naturalists" who employ basic economic principles to understand and explain what they see around them in the "laboratory of life."

Studying biology enables people to observe and marvel at many details of the natural environment that would otherwise have escaped notice. For the naturalist, a walk in a quiet wood becomes an adventure. In much the same way, studying economics can enable students to see the world in which they live and work in a new light. Beginning with Chapter 1 and then continuing throughout the text, Economic Naturalist examples show students the relevance of economics to their world—how economics can help them to understand (and perhaps improve) the world they live in. The following are just a few examples of questions raised:

1. Why are some places littered with beer cans and wrecked cars while others are not?
2. Why do some movie theatres offer discount tickets to students?
3. Will a higher tax on cigarettes curb teenage smoking?
4. Why does Lady Gaga earn millions more than singers of only slightly lesser ability?
5. How does comparative advantage arise and why might countries not take advantage of it?
6. Why does London, England, impose a tax on every vehicle that enters the central business district during business hours?

Once students realize that they can pose and answer such questions on their own, they often are hooked. The excitement of discovery provides its own motivation. A student who tastes this excitement is much more likely to use economics long after completing an introductory course. We cannot claim that every student who uses our text will continuously improve his understanding of economics throughout the rest of his life. However, we do believe that our book will help an instructor come closer to this ideal, and even modest progress toward the ideal is a worthy objective. Our students will journey deep into the twenty-first century. What an instructor accomplishes in the classroom may prove to be the most enduring part of her professional legacy.

---

**ECONOMIC NATURALIST** 1.1

**Why are some places littered with beer cans and wrecked cars while others are not?**

Arriving in the U.K. from Nova Scotia in the summer of 2001, a visiting economic naturalist was surprised to see how much the back alleys of British towns were littered with discarded beer cans and how many abandoned cars could be seen at the side of English roads. Why did the U.K. have these problems of littering when Canada did not?

The beer can litter problem has an easy explanation—in the U.K., there was no system of deposits on beverage containers, so they were often thrown away after they were emptied, and aluminum cans accumulated at the roadside and in back alleys. Although aluminum can be recycled, scrap yards did not pay enough per can

---

# EVIDENCE MATTERS

Getting students to appreciate the power of economic theory and the importance of a few simple economic principles is a crucial goal of an introductory course. But economics would be a very simple (and dull) subject if all markets could be analyzed in terms of the intersection of two straight lines—a supply curve sloping up at 45 degrees and a demand curve sloping down at 45 degrees. If that were all there was to it, there would be hardly any point in having upper-level economics courses, because markets would be the same. If that were really the case, all problems of economic policy could be solved in the same way and from the comfort of an armchair—by anybody who had taken the one all-purpose economics course that universities (or high schools) would teach.

However, practicing economists know that much of the intellectual fascination of economics comes from the variety of contexts in which economic principles are useful as well as from the interplay of theory and data. As instructors, we think that in an introductory text it is a big mistake to not let students in on this interplay, in part because many students (particularly the brighter ones) are turned off by the unrealism of a one-size-fits-all approach. Hence, we return continually to the theme that "evidence matters." For example, in Chapter 4 we now present empirical estimates of the price elasticity of demand for a variety of commodities, and we show in Chapter 7 how the costs, in lost economic surplus, of rent controls depend crucially on the elasticity of demand and supply. Only data can tell us if any effects are large or small. A key refrain running through the text is that of respecting the empirical evidence.

# WHAT IS NEW AND IMPROVED IN THIS EDITION

We have revised all of the chapters in *Principles of Microeconomics*. In some places, clarity is improved by cutting: we have reduced the number of pages, but the number of chapters remains at fifteen. However, we have added important topics.

## CHAPTER 1: WHY STUDY ECONOMICS?

- In the first three editions, Chapters 1 to 3 were identical in the micro and macro-economics halves of the text, in order to emphasize the common elements in micro and macroeconomics. A central objective for the fourth edition of the textbook has been to revise these chapters. They still emphasize the common elements, but the introductory chapters for *Microeconomics* have been differentiated somewhat from those for *Macroeconomics*. Thus, the opening chapters introduce both macroeconomics and microeconomics more effectively. Chapter 1 achieves this objective through a number of revisions. The revisions include a reorganization that moves the discussion of macroeconomics vs. microeconomics to the beginning of the chapter from the end of the chapter in the third edition.
- The new structure is:

  - 1.1 Economics as a Subject
  - 1.2 Scarcity, Rationality, and the Cost–Benefit Principle
  - 1.3 Three Important Decision Pitfalls
  - 1.4 Economic Theories and their Evaluation
  - 1.5 Economic Naturalism
  - 1.6 What Will be Produced, How, and For Whom?

- The restructuring keeps a strong emphasis on the cost–benefit principle (optimization) through simple examples while conveying to students more of a flavour of what economics is about—how it relates to real-world public policy concerns they may have, and how it relates to other university subjects.
- The new section 1.1 on Economics as a Subject brings forward the micro vs. macro discussion from section 1.7 of the previous edition, discusses economics as a social science, and, as part of explaining economics as a subject, it mentions Adam Smith, Alfred Marshall, and John Maynard Keynes as key figures in the development of economics. We do not emphasize the history of economic

thought in the textbook, but Smith, Marshall, and Keynes do come up in later chapters of both micro and macro.

- Related to economic methodology, the revised chapter sticks to positive economics in terms of the statement of the cost-benefit principle and the applications chosen in the sections prior to the section on economic methodology. In other words, we do not employ welfare economics before first explaining what it is and how it differs from positive economics.
- The chapter's learning objectives are keyed to the chapter sections, end of chapter summary, review questions, problems, and answers to in-chapter exercises. This pattern continues through all the chapters.

## CHAPTER 2: COMPARATIVE ADVANTAGE: THE BASIS FOR EXCHANGE

- The new Chapter 2 gives almost no attention to international trade. Material on international trade has been moved to Chapter 15, "International Trade and Trade Policy." This change shortens Chapter 2 and moves the more subtle components of comparative advantage to the final chapter.

## CHAPTER 3: SUPPLY AND DEMAND: AN INTRODUCTION

- The opening section of the chapter has been streamlined and a sharper distinction has been made between questions about what a society produces and questions about the distribution of a society's produce among its members.
- The distinction between the supply curve and quantity supplied, and the distinction between the demand curve and quantity demanded, has been clarified. Chapter 3 now includes definitions of quantity supplied and quantity demanded.
- The phrase *ceteris paribus* now appears in Chapter 3. It was not included previously. Discussion of the phrase is used to highlight the role played by the assumption that along any given supply curve or any given demand curve, influences other than price and quantity are held constant. This makes it easier to show how the demand and supply curves can shift if other things are not held constant.
- Four algebraic boxes appear in Chapter 3. The boxes provide an alternative to verbal and graphic descriptions of supply and demand. The first box provides a linear supply curve, and the second box, a linear demand curve. Box 3 provides an equilibrium solution to a supply-and-demand problem. Box 4 links changes of intercept values to shifts of the supply and demand curves. The boxes were chosen instead of an appendix in order to divide the algebra into separate, small pieces that can be comprehended more easily. The boxes also make it easy for instructors who want to skip the algebra to do so. At the same time, readers are less likely to ignore material in boxes than material in an appendix at the end of the chapter. The algebraic boxes partially address requests to add material to the appendix at the end of Chapter 1 while simultaneously keeping the new algebraic material closer to where it can be used. They also address requests from some instructors to include the algebra.

## CHAPTER 4: DEMAND: THE BENEFIT SIDE OF THE MARKET

- The principal changes in Chapter 4 are editorial, intended to tighten and clarify the exposition.
- The introduction to Part 2, "Competition and the Invisible Hand," now emphasizes that perfect competition is not a model that fits all markets, and that other models will be introduced later in the textbook.
- The subsection, "Price Elasticity Changes along a Straight-Line Demand Curve," has been moved to Appendix 4A, "'Average' Price Elasticity of Demand: The Arc (or Midpoint) Formula." Material in the subsection, "Price Elasticity of Demand and Total Expenditure," has been condensed and moved to Appendix 4A.

## CHAPTER 5: PRODUCTION AND COST: THE SUPPLY SIDE IN THE SHORT RUN

- Much of the rewriting in this chapter is intended to clarify the exposition and to be more succinct.
- We have revised the subheading, "Price equals marginal cost: Profit Maximization and the Seller's Supply Rule," to "Profit Maximization and the Seller's Supply Rule." (The subheading appears in Section 5.2. "Price equals marginal cost" is the profit-maximizing rule for perfect competitors only. It does not apply to other types of firms; hence the revision.)

## CHAPTER 6: PRODUCTION, COST, AND THE QUEST FOR PROFIT: THE SUPPLY SIDE IN THE LONG RUN

- The revisions to Chapter 6 aim at clarifying the exposition and shortening it where possible. We have made no major changes to the content or pedagogy of the chapter.
- It is pedagogically useful to distinguish accounting profit from normal profit and economic profit. However, accounting profit is a term that economists introduce into economics textbooks for the purpose of teaching economics. Reviewers have remarked that accountants do not use the term accounting profit. Net income appears in profit-and-loss statements, and is the accounting concept closest to what economists call accounting profit. However, economists do not define accounting profit carefully enough to ensure that it is synonymous with net income. We have retained the term, accounting profit, because it is pedagogically useful (for teachers of economics). We also have revised the text in the subsection, "Three Meanings of 'Profit,'" in order to recognize that the term, accounting profit, is not consistent with accounting standards.

## CHAPTER 7: ECONOMIC SURPLUS AND EXCHANGE

- Several graphs that appear in the 3rd Canadian edition have been deleted and sections of the running text revised in an effort to shorten Chapter 7. Because the term "efficiency" has several possible meanings, it can be confusing to students. When we mean that an outcome maximizes "economic surplus," we are careful to say that it is a "surplus-maximizing outcome," thus making the exposition more precise and keeping the focus on economic surplus.

## CHAPTER 8: MONOPOLY, OLIGOPOLY, AND MONOPOLISTIC COMPETITION

- Some reviewers noted that the title of Chapter 8 was misleading because it included little about oligopoly. A short section on oligopoly from the fourth U.S. edition has been adapted and added to Chapter 8.
- The new title of Part 3, where markets other than perfect competition are introduced is, "The Real World is an Imperfect Place." The new title of Chapter 8 is "Monopoly, Oligopoly, and Monopolistic Competition."
- We have added Table 8.1 "The Spectrum of Market Structures," to summarize characteristics of monopoly, oligopoly, monopolistic competition, and perfect competition.
- Because network economies are presented as a type of economies of scale, the subsection, "Network Economies," now follows immediately after the subsection, "Economies of Scale."
- In previous editions, postal services have provided an example of a monopoly granted by government. We have deleted postal services and replaced it with the monopoly of fur trade granted by the Britain to the Hudson's Bay Company late in the 17th Century. (Canada Post now faces competition from a number of close substitutes.)

## CHAPTER 9: THINKING STRATEGICALLY

- Changes to Chapter 9 are mainly editorial, though there are some exceptions.
- The last paragraph of the introduction to Chapter 9 emphasizes to a greater degree than previously that game theory plays an important role in analyzing oligopoly. It also provides a connection with Section 8.8, "Oligopoly."
- We have changed Example 9.10, "Remote Office Game," to emphasize the question of how much money would be sufficient to overcome the pangs of guilt associated with dishonesty.
- Modifications to the subsection, "Preferences as Solutions to Commitment Problems," emphasize that widely observed social norms and norms of honesty can overcome commitment problems.

## CHAPTER 10: EXTERNALITIES AND PROPERTY RIGHTS

- Chapter 10 now provides a stronger emphasis on greenhouse gas (GHG) emissions and climate change. Editorial changes tighten the wording of the chapter.
- Figure 10.2, "Scenarios for GHG Emissions from 2000 to 2010," and a short discussion of the figure are new. This is in keeping with the greater emphasis Chapter 10 now places on climate change.
- A short, new paragraph provides a discussion about rules governing the use of equipment and technical innovations on Formula 1 racing cars. The rules provide a way of controlling positional externalties.

## CHAPTER 11: THE ECONOMICS OF INFORMATION

- Editorial changes clarify and tighten wording, and shorten the chapter.
- Revisions to Chapter 11 include updated data concerning provision of healthcare. These data appear in Section 11.4, which we have renamed "Imperfect Information and Health Care."

## CHAPTER 12: LABOUR MARKETS

- We have updated and revised figures, numbers, and references where appropriate. Also we have edited some sections to tighten and clarify the writing.
- Section 12.1 now includes a derivation of a labour demand curve.
- Figure 12.1 is new. It and supporting text distinguish movement along a labour demand curve from a shift of a labour demand curve. Subsequent figures have been renumbered.
- Revisions to Section 12.2, "Monopsony and Imperfect Competition in Labour Markets," extend and clarify the discussion of monopsony.

## CHAPTER 13: INCOME DISTRIBUTION

- Chapter 13 includes a number of editorial revisions that are intended to clarify and tighten the text.
- Data on income, income distribution, welfare payments, compensation for CEOs, etc., have been revised to the most recent figures available as of June 2011.
- A new Figure 13.3 replaces the previous Figure 13.3, "Percentage Change in Family Taxable Income, Canada, 1982–2004." The new Figure 13.3 is divided into two panels. Panel (a) of the new Figure 13.3 retains the single panel of the old Figure 13.3. Panel (b), "Top 1% Income Shares, Canada, 1920-2007," is new.
- A new "Economic Naturalist" links the potential importance of tax revenue from natural resource extraction to the ability of governments to deliver old age pensions that could reduce poverty.

## CHAPTER 14: PUBLIC GOODS

- Revisions to Chapter 14 consist primarily of updating data and references and editing to improve clarity. There are no major revisions to this chapter.
- Data in the subsection, "Private Provision of Public Goods," that concern charitable donations have been updated.
- Data in the subsection, "Human Rights as Public Goods," have been updated. These data concern expenditures on health care.
- Data in section 14.5, "Local, Provincial, or Federal," that concern federal spending and provincial spending as percentages of Canadian GDP have been updated.

## CHAPTER 15: INTERNATIONAL TRADE AND TRADE POLICY

- Comments concerning a chapter on international trade in *Principles of Microeconomics* have ranged from: "Why include international trade in *Microeconomics*? It belongs in *Principles of Macroeconomics*," to: "If a microeconomics textbook does not include a chapter on international trade, I will not adopt it." We have decided to include the chapter in the fourth edition.

## THOROUGHLY MODERN MICRO

Pedagogy is extremely important because a text that does not communicate effectively is pointless. But the decision about *what* to teach is at least as important as the decision of *how* to teach it. Because we believe that a central concern of economics is efficiency, we have devoted extensive space to the concept of economic surplus. Introduced in Chapter 1 and applied repeatedly in Chapters 2 to 5, this concept is developed more fully in Chapter 7 than in any leading introductory text. Throughout the book, the concept of economic surplus underlies our ongoing argument in support of economic efficiency as an important social goal. We stress that maximizing economic surplus aids in the achievement of *all* goals, both public and private—while also noting that if society is to preserve the institutions that enable economic surplus to be maximized, some agreement about the equity of the distribution of economic returns is essential. Our book also balances theory and empirical evidence, We emphasize, from start to finish, both the implications of economic theory for individual decision making, and the importance of empirical evidence on the actual magnitude of theoretically predicted impacts. Chapter 1, for example, starts by discussing three widespread and important pitfalls: the tendency to ignore opportunity costs, the tendency not to ignore sunk costs, and the tendency to confuse average and marginal costs and benefits. Chapter 7 notes that the impacts of rent controls on both the amount and the distribution of economic surplus depend partly on the elasticity of supply for of apartments. Throughout the book, we call students' attention to situations in which economic theory can help them analyze individual and social choices.

An introductory course in economics should offer something for two types of students: an understanding of the world around them for those who will never take another economics course, and preparation for some of the ideas that will be encountered in more advanced courses for continuing students. We are troubled that many people receive postsecondary degrees without ever having been exposed to ideas like the prisoner's dilemma or the tragedy of the commons. These and other simple applications of game theory have enormous power to explain events in the world. They are also ideal vehicles for illustrating several of the core ideas of economics—ideas that are hugely important in modern courses in microeconomic theory, industrial organization, and international trade, among other things. In Chapter 9, we introduce students to the principles of games and strategic behaviour in a highly intuitive way that does not rely on formal mathematics. We develop a limited number of simple principles that have proved entirely accessible to first-year students. In our experience, students are delighted to learn that these few principles can explain, among other things, why urban highways are too crowded (unless a congestion tax is charged), why the concentration of $CO_2$ in the atmosphere is increasing, and why the National Hockey League has a helmet rule. Similarly, Chapter 11 develops some of the key issues in the economics of information. These ideas have had an enormous influence on other areas of economics (e.g., macroeconomics, labour, health, and development). In Chapter 12 we show how these ideas help to explain discrimination in the labour market, and in Chapter 11 we highlight their importance for understanding Canada's current debates on public policy in health care.

## ORGANIZATION OF TOPICS

*Principles of Microeconomics* is divided into four parts. Part 1, which has common elements with Part 1 of *Principles of Macroeconomics,* is composed of three chapters. Parts 2–4 are composed of four chapters each. Many Canadian examples are used to illustrate microeconomic principles and policies, and some are noted in this preface. Part 1 introduces students to the most basic ideas of economics, including the core principles that are used throughout the book. Chapter 1 begins by confronting a basic question: why study economics? It focuses on how economic analysis can help us solve practical problems, using the ideas of scarcity, tradeoffs, costs, and benefits.

Chapter 1 includes the fundamental notion that the desirability of any action depends on its marginal costs and benefits. Following Chapter 1 is a brief Appendix that reviews the basic mathematical tools—working with equations, graphs, and tables—that students will need for the course. Chapter 2 introduces the ideas of specialization and gains from trade. Finally, Chapter 3 provides an introductory overview of supply-and-demand analysis—the discussion starts with the example of the market for hamburgers in Toronto, but the generality of a supply and demand approach is emphasized by using the examples of housing, tennis balls, French fries, and airfares. Chapter 15 deals with how supply and demand pertains to markets that have macroeconomic implications, such as markets for foreign exchange.

Part 2 explores in detail the concepts of demand, supply, economic surplus, and efficiency in the context of perfect competition. Building on the introduction to supply and demand in Chapter 3, Chapter 4 shows how people spend their limited income in rational ways. This chapter also discusses price elasticity of demand and its uses. An appendix on indifference curves follows Chapter 4. Chapter 5 turns to the sellers' side of the market, showing how upward-sloping short run supply curves follow from profit-maximizing decisions by producers. Chapter 6 clarifies how the quest for profit can drive competitive firms to minimize the long run average cost of production. Finally, Chapter 7 develops the concept of economic surplus and explains Adam Smith's crucial insight: when demand and supply curves fully reflect social benefits and costs, competitive markets maximize economic surplus.

In our revision of this text, we have paid close attention to the excellent comments and critiques provided by a panel of referees and early users. Since most Canadian courses in principles of microeconomics develop short-run and long-run cost curves, Chapter 5 includes a section that shows how the law of diminishing marginal returns shapes the graphs of short-run marginal and average costs, and how average fixed cost decreases as output increases. Chapter 6 provides a discussion of how, in a perfectly competitive market, entry and exit cause firms to operate at minimum long-run average cost. Graphs of long-run average cost are included. Some instructors may prefer to de-emphasize cost curves in order to reinforce basic applications of opportunity cost. Chapters 5 and 6 are designed so that instructors who prefer to concentrate on other topics can omit detailed treatments of cost curves.

Part 3 studies markets that depart from the ideal of perfect competition. Chapter 8 examines the implications of monopolistic, oligopolistic, and monopolistically competitive markets. When only a few producers exist in a market—and in many other noncompetitive situations—behaviour often takes on a strategic component, so Chapter 9 introduces some elementary tools of game theory and demonstrates their applicability to a variety of economic situations. Chapter 10 considers the effects of externalities. We show that elementary game theory—including the ideas of the prisoner's dilemma, the arms race, and the tragedy of the commons—is quite useful for analyzing many situations with externalities. We discuss the implications of excessive use of carbon-based fuels for climate change and present an analysis of how either a carbon tax or a cap-and-trade permit system can efficiently reduce carbon emissions. Chapter 11 examines incomplete and asymmetric information. The examples of the "lemons" problem in the used-car market and statistical discrimination between young males and females in the market for automobile insurance provide clear evidence of the relevance of economics to issues that our target audience is likely to have experienced.

Finally, Part 4 uses the tools that have been developed in Parts 1 through 3 to approach some issues of applied economics and economic policy, in a Canadian context. For example, about 70 percent of employed Canadian women work in nursing and related health occupations, teaching, clerical, administrative, sales, and service positions. Chapter 12 tackles differentials in pay by using tools developed earlier—human capital investment, marginal productivity, imperfect information, and positional externalities—and includes a discussion of occupational segregation as well as Canadian policies that attempt to deal with it. Chapter 13 considers the benefits and pitfalls of government policies to redistribute income and reduce poverty. As well, we note Canada's success in reducing poverty among senior citizens, and we examine the complexities of designing adequate policies for children and for Canadians of working age. Although many introductory texts gloss over the distinctions between federal, provincial, and municipal governments, Canada is a federal state, with a relatively high degree of decentralization (compared to other federal states); examples in Part 4 present this reality. Chapter 14 discusses public goods and taxation, as well as broader issues concerning the government's role in the economy. It also notes that total program spending by the provinces now greatly exceeds that of the federal government, and we examine the reasons that this pattern has emerged. Chapter 15 ends the textbook with a discussion of international trade. It develops comparative advantage as the principal argument for trade. The chapter also uses supply and demand to analyze the effects of tariffs, quotas, and other impediments to trade, and to identify who wins and who loses as a result of such impediments. Chapter 15 also shows how the laws of supply and demand can be used to understand movements of exchange rates. By closing with applications of comparative advantage and supply and demand, Chapter 15 forms a link with Part 1, where these concepts were first introduced.

In all the chapters, we emphasize the importance of differences between markets and how such differences imply that no one public policy can solve all social problems.

## COMPREHENSIVE LEARNING AND TEACHING PACKAGE

### FOR THE INSTRUCTOR

### INSTRUCTOR RESOURCES

McGraw-Hill Ryerson has made every effort to include the support material that is most critical for you and your students.

McGraw-Hill Connect™ is a web-based assignment and assessment platform that gives students the means to better connect with their coursework, with their instructors, and with the important concepts that they will need to know for success now and in the future.

With Connect, instructors can deliver assignments, quizzes, and tests online. Nearly all the questions from the text are presented in an auto-gradeable format and tied to the text's learning objectives. Instructors can edit existing questions and compose entirely new problems. They can track individual student performance—by question, assignment, or in relation to the class overall—with detailed grade reports, and they can integrate grade reports easily with learning management systems such as WebCT and Blackboard and much more.

By choosing Connect, instructors are providing their students with a powerful tool for improving academic performance and truly mastering course material. Connect allows students to practice important skills at their own pace and on their own schedule. Just as important, students' assessment results and instructors' feedback are all saved online—so students can continually review their progress and plot their course to success.

Connect also provides 24/7 online access to an eBook—an online edition of the text—to aid them in successfully completing their work, wherever and whenever they choose.

## KEY FEATURES

### SIMPLE ASSIGNMENT MANAGEMENT

With Connect, creating assignments is easier than ever, so you can spend more time teaching and less time managing. You can:

- Create and deliver assignments easily with selectable end-of-chapter questions and test bank material to assign online
- Streamline lesson planning, student progress reporting, and assignment grading to make classroom management more efficient than ever
- Go paperless with the eBook and online submission and grading of student assignments

### SMART GRADING

When it comes to studying, time is precious. Connect helps students learn more efficiently by providing feedback and practice material when they need it, where they need it. Connect will:

- Automatically score assignments, giving students immediate feedback on their work and side-by-side comparisons with correct answers
- Access and review each response; manually change grades or leave comments for students to review
- Reinforce classroom concepts with practice tests and instant quizzes

### INSTRUCTOR LIBRARY

The Connect Instructor Library is your course creation hub. It provides all the critical resources you'll need to build your course, just how you want to teach it. You can:

- Assign eBook readings and draw from a rich collection of textbook-specific assignments
- Access instructor resources, including ready-made PowerPoint presentations and media to use in your lectures
- View assignments and resources created for past sections
- Post your own resources for students to use

### EBOOK

Connect reinvents the textbook learning experience for the modern student. Every Connect subject area is seamlessly integrated with Connect eBooks, which are designed to keep students focused on the concepts key to their success. Connect can:

- Provide students with a Connect eBook, allowing for access to the textbook anywhere at any time
- Merge media, animation and assessments with the text's narrative to engage students and improve learning and retention

- Pinpoint and connect key concepts instantly by using the powerful eBook search engine
- Manage notes, highlights, and bookmarks in one place for simple, comprehensive review

## LYRYX ASSESMENT FOR ECONOMICS (LAECON)

Based on *Principles of Microeconomics* by Frank, Bernanke, Osberg, Cross, and MacLean, Lyryx Assessment for Economics is a leading-edge online assessment system, designed to support both students and instructors. The assessment takes the form of a homework assignment called a *lab*. The assessments are algorithmically generated and automatically graded so that students get instant grades and feedback. New labs are randomly generated constantly, providing the student with unlimited opportunities to try a type of each question. After they submit a lab for marking, students receive extensive feedback on their work, thus promoting their learning experience.

### FOR THE INSTRUCTOR

The goal of Lyryx is to enable you to use these labs to generate course marks instead of having to create and mark your own labs. The content, marking, and feedback have been developed and implemented with the help of experienced instructors in economics. After registering your courses with us, you can then use LAECON content to create your own unique labs by selecting problems from our bank of questions and setting deadlines for each one of these labs. You have access to all your students' marks and can view their best labs. At any time, you can download the class grades for your own programs.

### FOR THE STUDENT

LAECON offers algorithmically generated and automatically graded assignments. Students get instant grades and instant feedback—no need to wait until the next class to find out how well they did! Grades are instantly recorded in a grade book that the student can view. Students are motivated to do their labs for two reasons. First, because their results can be tied to assessment, and second, because they can have their grade recorded. Instructors know from experience that students who do their economics homework will be successful in the course. Recent research regarding the use of Lyryx has shown that when labs are tied to assessment, even if worth only a small percentage of the total grade for the course, students WILL do their homework—and MORE THAN ONCE!! Please contact your iLearning Sales Specialist for additional information on the Lyryx Assessment Economics system. Visit http://laecon.lyryx.com.

## SUPERIOR SERVICE

**Superior Service**   Service takes on a whole new meaning with McGraw-Hill Ryerson and *Principles of Microeconomics*. More than just bringing you the textbook, we have consistently raised the bar in terms of innovation and educational research—both in economics and in education in general. These investments in learning and the education community have helped us to understand the needs of students and educators across the country, and allowed us to foster the growth of truly innovative, integrated learning.

**Integrated Learning**   Your Integrated *i*Learning Sales Specialist is a McGraw-Hill Ryerson representative who has the experience, product knowledge, training, and support to help you assess and integrate any of our products, technology, and

services into your course for optimal teaching and learning performance. Whether it's helping your students improve their grades, or putting your entire course online, your *i*Learning Sales Specialist is there to help you do it. Contact your *i*Learning Sales Specialist today to learn how to maximize all of McGraw-Hill Ryerson's resources!

**Course Management**   McGraw-Hill Ryerson offers a range of flexible integration solutions for Blackboard, WebCT, Desire2Learn, Moodle, and other leading learning management platforms. Please contact your local McGraw-Hill Ryerson *i*Learning Sales Specialist for details.

**Tegrity**   Tegrity is a service that makes class time available all the time by automatically capturing every lecture in a searchable format for students to review when they study and complete assignments. With a simple one-click start-and-stop process, you capture all computer screens and corresponding audio. Students replay any part of any class with easy-to-use browser-based viewing on a PC or Mac. Educators know that the more students can see, hear, and experience class resources, the better they learn. With Tegrity, students quickly recall key moments by using Tegrity's unique search feature. This search helps students efficiently find what they need, when they need it across an entire semester of class recordings. Help turn all your students' study time into learning moments immediately supported by your lecture. To learn more about Tegrity watch a 2-minute Flash demo at http:// tegritycampus.mhhe.com, and speak with your local *i*Learning Sales Specialist.

**Create Online**   McGraw-Hill's Create Online places the most abundant resource at your fingertips—literally. With a few mouse clicks, you can create customized learning tools simply and affordably. McGraw-Hill Ryerson has included many of its market-leading textbooks within Create Online for eBook and print customization as well as many licensed readings and cases. For more information, please visit www.mcgrawhillcreate.com.

**CourseSmart**   CourseSmart brings together thousands of textbooks across hundreds of courses in an eTextbook format providing unique benefits to students and faculty. By purchasing an eTextbook, students can save up to 50 percent off the cost of a print textbook, reduce their impact on the environment, and gain access to powerful Web tools for learning, including full text search, notes and highlighting, and email tools for sharing notes among classmates. For faculty, CourseSmart provides instant access to review and compare textbooks and course materials in their discipline area without the time, cost, and environmental impact of mailing print examination copies. For further details, contact your iLearning sales specialist or visit www.coursesmart.com.

### Instructor's Resources

- **Instructor's Manual** This manual is extremely useful for all teachers, but especially for those new to the job. It offers suggestions for using the Test Bank, and the Economic Naturalist cases. It supplies sample syllabi with assignments, sample exams, and supplemental material. For each chapter, it provides an overview, an outline, teaching objectives, additional Economic Naturalist discussion questions, answers to textbook questions and problems, homework assignments with answers, and sample quizzes with answers.
- **Computerized Test Banks** The test banks (micro and macro), updated by David Sabiston of Mount Royal University, ensure maximum flexibility in test preparation, including the reconfiguring of graphing exercises. The test banks contain more than 5000 multiple-choice questions categorized by Learning Objective, Learning Level (knowledge, comprehension, application, analysis), Type (graph, calculation, word problem), and Source (textbook, Web, unique).
- **PowerPoint Slides** Rafat Alam of Grant MacEwan University has updated this package of dynamic slides including the important illustrations in the textbook.

# ACKNOWLEDGEMENTS

Our thanks first and foremost go to James Booty our Sponsoring Editor and to Daphne Scriabin our Developmental Editor. The entire team at McGraw-Hill Ryerson deserves credit for keeping the project moving in a timely fashion. We also thank Julie van Tol and Suzanne Simpson Millar for their close and accurate copy editing, and we are grateful for the outstanding work of the McGraw-Hill Ryerson production team: Supervising Editor, Jessica Barnoski; Production Coordinator, Sheryl MacAdam; and Designer, Greg Devitt.

We would also like to express our sincere thanks to Teresa Cyrus for the close reading and perceptive comments provided in her technical reviews of the manuscript. We also thank the following teachers and colleagues, whose thorough reviews and thoughtful suggestions led to innumerable substantive improvements:

Rafat Alam, Grant MacEwan University

Khyati Antani, Humber College

Aurelia Best, Centennial College

Janice Compton, University of Manitoba

Dilip Das, Conestoga College

Sigrid Ewender, Kwantlen Polytechnic University

Bruno Fullone, George Brown College

Michael Hare, University of Toronto

Matlub Hussain, Dawson College

Rosmy Jean Louis, Vancouver Island University

Robert Jefferson, Wilfrid Laurier University

Barbara Mann, Centennial College

Amy Peng, Ryerson University

Norman Smith, Georgian College

Amy Sopinka, University of Victoria

Brennan Thompson, Ryerson University

Gary Tompkins, University of Regina

Angela Trimarchi, University of Waterloo

Steven Wald, York University

Carl Weston, Mohawk College

# DEDICATION

For Ellen    **R. H. F.**

For Anna    **B. S. B.**

For Molly    **L. S. O.**

For Anna, Nathan, and Thomas, in memory of Carmelita    **M. L. C.**

For Kathleen and Vera, in memory of Ken    **B. K. M.**

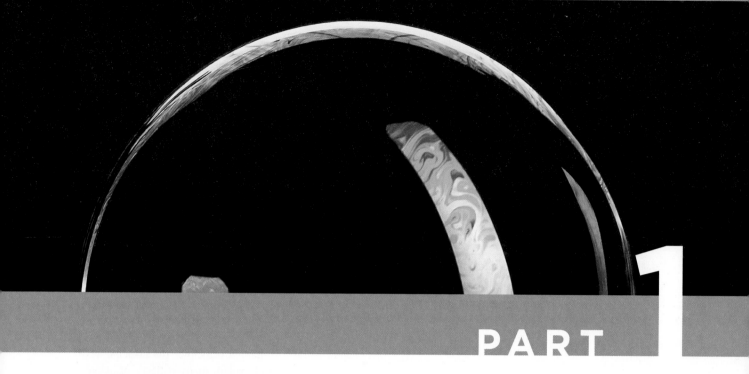

# PART 1

# INTRODUCTION

How many students are there in your economics class? Why has the average class size in Canadian universities increased over the last twenty years? Why does global fossil fuel consumption continue to increase? What policies might be effective in dealing with its implications for the atmosphere's concentration of $CO_2$ and the resultant global climate change?

Why were summer jobs so much easier to get in 2008, before the financial crisis and recession, than they were a year or two later? What determines the ups and downs of the unemployment rate?

To answer these questions, and many others, you need to know something about economics. And as a discipline of thought, economics is both as old as the hills and as young as last minute's newsflash. Human societies have always depended on a division of labour to produce the goods and services needed to sustain life, and for almost as long, people have tried to figure out how the allocation of tasks works and how it could be made to work better. In today's global economy, the range of commodities, the diversity of jobs necessary to produce them, and the complexity of mechanisms of coordination that make our division of labour work are massively more complicated than they were in caveman days. But the same big questions are always there. How can we explain how much is produced and who gets what share? Can we increase total production and improve the division of that output?

Because societies have changed, economics has evolved over time. This text discusses some ideas that have been around for a long time, because the problems they address have long been with us. It also discusses some concepts that are relatively new, because the world has new problems and because some problems have only recently been solved. As an academic discipline, economics is both a subject matter and a *way of thinking* about the world. Over many years, economists have developed principles and models that are useful for understanding a wide range of situations, and the range of issues analyzed by economists has grown enormously. Economic analysis helps us understand practical problems with immediate impacts on our living standards (such as changes in rents and the real estate market) and complex issues with long-term impacts on the world's ecology (such as trends in pollution and greenhouse gas emissions). A major objective of this book is to help you learn these principles and models and how to apply them to a variety of issues.

The three chapters of Part I introduce the subject matter of economics and demonstrate how economists use models to clarify the essentials of a situation. Chapter 1 provides an overview of what economics is all about and shows that comparing the cost and benefit of choices is a useful approach to economic decision making. Chapter 2 analyzes specialization among individuals in the production of goods and services. A high degree of specialization requires not only trade but also the widespread use of money, prices, and markets, which can be illustrated with the circular flow of income and expenditure. Finally, Chapter 3 presents an overview of the model of supply and demand, perhaps the best-known model in economics.

# CHAPTER 1
# Why Study Economics?

## LEARNING OBJECTIVES

When you have completed this chapter, you will be able to:

**LO1** Define economics, microeconomics, and macroeconomics.

**LO2** Identify John Maynard Keynes, Alfred Marshall, and Adam Smith, and state briefly the influence of each of them on economics.

**LO3** State and explain the problem of scarcity and its relation to opportunity cost.

**LO4** Explain how a rational decision maker applies the cost–benefit principle.

**LO5** State how three pitfalls can undermine rational economic decisions.

**LO6** Explain how data are used to evaluate economic theories.

**LO7** Distinguish positive economics from welfare economics.

**LO8** Define an economic naturalist.

We begin this chapter by explaining the subject matter and characteristics of economics. We include a discussion of the evaluation of economic theories. The organizing idea of this chapter is the cost–benefit principle. The principle will help you understand and explain many patterns of behavior you observe in the world around you. Understanding the principle can help one to avoid three pitfalls that can plague decision makers in everyday life. We will identify and explain these pitfalls. Chapter 1 concludes with a discussion of "economic naturalism" and two basic ways of organizing economic activity. Economic naturalism is a term that indicates an ability to use basic economics to help make sense of observations we encounter in everyday life.

## 1.1  ECONOMICS AS A SUBJECT

Because humans are curious, people have been trying to explain what makes an economy work for a very long time. The "origins" of economics as a system of thought are thus lost in antiquity. Nevertheless, a useful starting definition was provided by the British economist Lionel Robbins back in 1932: "Economics is the science which studies human behaviour as a relationship between given ends and scarce means which have alternative uses."[1]

This definition is useful partly because it is pretty broad. Many people are familiar with the economists who comment on television about the latest trends in financial markets, but economics is much more than that. Among the professors who teach in the economics department of your university, you will find a wide range of research interests: remedies for global recession, social programs to deal with poverty and income insecurity, funding alternatives for health and for university and college education, measures to combat global climate change, economic development strategies for low-income countries and regions, and many, many others.

A somewhat more modern definition of **economics** is, "the study of how people make choices under conditions of scarcity and the results of those choices for society." Both this and Robbins's definition refer to scarcity, which simply means that choices among alternatives are necessary. If one chooses to purchase a motorcycle, the same

**economics** the study of how people make choices under conditions of scarcity and the results of those choices for society

---

1  Lionel Robbins, *An Essay on the Nature and Significance of Economic Science*, 2nd ed. (London: Macmillan, 1940).

funds cannot be used to pay for a holiday in Europe. A student who enrolls for a course and wants to attend lectures cannot take a job during class times. The idea that choices among mutually exclusive alternatives are very often necessary is central to economics.

## ECONOMICS: MICRO AND MACRO

Present-day economics has two main branches: microeconomics and macroeconomics. Economists use the term **microeconomics** to describe the study of choices individuals make under scarcity, and the implications of these choices for the behaviour of prices and quantities in individual markets. **Macroeconomics**, by contrast, is the study of the performance of national economies and of the policies that governments use to try to affect that performance. Macroeconomics tries to understand the determinants of such things as the level of national output, the unemployment rate, and the inflation rate. This text will focus on microeconomics, while a companion text emphasizes macroeconomic analysis.

A century ago, there was no distinction between macroeconomics and microeconomics. For a remarkably long time, the nineteenth century textbook, *Principles of Economics* (1890), by **Alfred Marshall** dominated the teaching of economics.[2] Marshall's influence on microeconomics continues to the present day. Part of the reason for his continuing impact is the power of his "methodological individualism." Marshall insisted that one should always attempt to explain why *individuals* behave as they do, and that uncritical acceptance of broad generalizations about groups or types of people simply hampers the understanding of human behavior. Marshall's economics is microeconomics. Much of the first few chapters of the book you now are reading can still be traced to the work of Marshall.

Macroeconomics as we know it today emerged with the publication of **John Maynard Keynes's** *The General Theory of Employment, Interest and Money* in 1936, which provided a new framework for thinking about the Great Depression of the 1930s. During the 1930s, the failure of much of the industrialized world to recover from depressed output and high unemployment was something that previously accepted theories could not explain satisfactorily. Macroeconomics thus started to develop as a main branch of economics in response to a widespread perception that new ways of thinking about the economy as a whole were needed.

At the introductory level in universities and colleges, students typically study microeconomics in one term (using this text or another like it) and macroeconomics in another term (using the companion text). If they go on to major in economics, students will take additional core courses in microeconomic and macroeconomic theory at a more advanced level, courses in quantitative methods such as mathematics and statistics for economics, and a variety of courses in fields such as public finance, labour economics, health economics, international trade, international finance, development economics, environmental economics, money and banking, industrial organization, urban economics, or history of economic thought. Some fields such as health economics and environment economics make much use of microeconomic theory, whereas other fields such as international finance and money and banking tend to make more use of macroeconomic theory.

## ECONOMICS AS A SOCIAL SCIENCE

One distinguishing feature of economics as a social science is that economic theories are often expressed as abstract models. Indeed, two years after the publication of his *General Theory of Employment, Interest and Money*, John Maynard Keynes described economics as a "science of thinking in terms of models joined to the art of choosing models that are relevant to the contemporary world."[3]

The term *model* is used to express the idea that thinking clearly about the economy involves abstracting from unnecessary detail; that is, selecting key features of reality to

**microeconomics** the study of individual choices under scarcity and the implications of these choices for the behaviour of prices and quantities in individual markets

**macroeconomics** the study of the performance of national economies and the policies that governments use to try to improve that performance

**Alfred Marshall** (1842-1924) an economist of the nineteenth and early twentieth centuries who published *Principles of Economics* (1890) and whose influence on economics continues to this day

**John Maynard Keynes (pronounced "Kains")** (1883–1946) a British economist whose *The General Theory of Employment, Interest and Money* (1936) is widely regarded as the seminal work in modern macroeconomics

2  You can read five of the six books of Alfred Marshall's *Principles of Economics* online at http://socserv2. socsci.mcmaster.ca/~econ/ugcm/3ll3/marshall/prin/index.html.

3  Quoted in Robert Skidelsky, *Keynes: The Return of the Master* (Toronto: Penguin Canada, 2009), p. 58.

focus on and ignoring the rest. We need to do this because our minds simply cannot keep track of all possible bits of information, and only some of it is important. When we go to the supermarket, for example, there is music on the public address system and we may have conversations with other shoppers and store employees, but does that determine what we buy? To analyze grocery sales, economists will focus on the prices and quantities of commodities purchased, because economists assume that these are the really crucial variables. Models, in other words, are based upon assumptions. Sometimes models are expressed with mathematical equations (e.g., when presented in specialized publications for academic economists), but in introductory textbooks such as this one, the models are mostly expressed with a combination of words, tables, and graphs.[4] An **economic model** can be defined as a representation of economic reality that highlights particular variables and the relationships among them.

In addition to the frequent use of abstract models to express theories, another distinguishing feature of economics has been the tendency of economists to assume in their theories that human beings are rational. In economics, a **rational decision maker** has clear objectives and behaves logically to achieve those objectives.

In most market situations this is taken to mean that the decision maker is self-interested and acts to realize his or her self-interest.[5] This self-interest assumption can be found in *The Wealth of Nations*, probably the most influential economics book ever written, where, in 1776, **Adam Smith** famously declared, "It is not from the benevolence of the butcher, the brewer, or the baker that we expect our dinner, but from their regard to their own interest."[6]

Rational decision making can be applied by use of the cost–benefit principle. This principle is derived at the level of microeconomics but has applications in both microeconomics and macroeconomics. The cost–benefit principle represents an approach to making choices, and the need to make choices stems from the scarcity problem.

**economic model** a representation of economic reality that highlights particular variables and the relationships among them

**rational decision maker** someone with clear objectives who behaves logically to achieve those objectives

**Adam Smith** (1723–1790) Scottish economist who wrote *The Wealth of Nations* (1776), probably the most influential economics book ever written

## RECAP

### ECONOMICS AS A SUBJECT

Economics is the study of the production, exchange, and distribution of goods and services. Economics includes both microeconomics and macroeconomics. Microeconomics studies individual choices in individual markets and the consequences of that behaviour, especially at the level of particular markets or industries. Macroeconomics, by contrast, studies the performance of national economies and of the policies that governments use to try to affect that performance.

Three particularly important figures in the history of economics are Adam Smith (1723–1790), the author of the enormously influential *The Wealth of Nations* (1776); Alfred Marshall (1842–1924), whose *Principles of Economics* (1890) greatly contributed to the spread of neoclassical microeconomics throughout the English-speaking world; and John Maynard Keynes (1883–1946), whose *The General Theory of Employment, Interest and Money* (1936) revolutionized thinking about macroeconomics.

Economics is a social science and as such belongs to a group of disciplines including political science, sociology, and psychology. One distinguishing feature of economics as a social science is that economic theories are often expressed as abstract models. Another distinguishing feature has been the greater tendency of economists over other social scientists to make the assumption that human beings are rational—that is, have clear objectives and behave logically to achieve them.

4  An example of a specialized publication for academic economists is the *Canadian Journal of Economics*.

5  Note that we are careful not to say that individuals always are purely self-interested. Many important issues (such as the raising of children) cannot plausibly be analyzed solely with reference to purely self-interested behaviour. The "clear objective" that a rational, altruistic person pursues may be the benefit of others.

6  Adam Smith, *The Wealth of Nations* (New York: Random House, 1969 [original 1776]), Book 1, Chapter II, p. 14. Also found at http://socserv.mcmaster.ca/~econ/ugcm/3ll3/smith/wealth/wealbk01.

# 1.2 SCARCITY, RATIONALITY, AND THE COST-BENEFIT PRINCIPLE

If we could always have whatever we wanted, for free, right now, we would never have to choose—all we would ever have to say is "more please," and we would get it. Unfortunately, the real world is not like that. Most things have a cost in time or money or other resources, all of which we have in only limited amounts. As we noted earlier, scarcity means that we have to make choices. More of one good means choosing less of another.

That such trade-offs are widespread and important is a central problem of economics. We can call this the **scarcity problem**, because it is the simple fact of scarcity which makes trade-offs necessary. Another name for the scarcity problem might be the "no-free-lunch" idea, which comes from the observation that even a lunch that is given to you takes time to eat—time you could have spent doing other useful things.

**The Scarcity Problem:** Because material and human resources are limited, having more of one good thing usually means making do with less of some other good thing.

Trade-offs require that choices be made. If people have to make economic choices because resources are scarce, how will they make their choices? Microeconomics commonly assumes that decision makers act rationally. It further argues that this is the most useful assumption to make when analyzing economic decisions. Economic decision makers, it is often assumed, will compare costs and benefits and take an action only if the benefits to them exceed its costs to them. More precisely, a rational decision maker will take an economic action if, and only if, the extra benefits from taking the action are greater than the extra costs. We call this statement the **cost–benefit principle**. It is one of the core principles of economics.

**The Cost–benefit Principle:** A rational decision maker will take an economic action if, and only if, the extra benefits from taking the action are greater than the extra costs.

## APPLYING THE COST–BENEFIT PRINCIPLE

The cost–benefit principle is a fundamental tool for the study of how rational people make choices. Often, the major difficulty in applying the cost–benefit principle is coming up with reasonable measures of all the relevant benefits and costs, especially the costs. To illustrate how the cost–benefit principle is applied, we begin with a very simple example that puts you in the role of the decision maker.

### EXAMPLE 1.1

#### Will you walk downtown to save $10 on a $25 computer game?

Imagine you are about to buy a $25 computer game at the nearby campus store when a friend tells you that the same game is on sale at a downtown store for only $15. If the downtown store is a 30-minute trip away, where will you buy the game?

Application of the cost-benefit principle leads to the prediction that you will buy the computer game downtown if the benefit of doing so exceeds the cost. The benefit of taking any action is the dollar value of everything you gain by taking it. Here, the benefit of buying downtown is exactly $10, since that is the amount you will save on the purchase price of the game. The cost of taking any action is the dollar value of everything you give up by taking it. Here, the cost of buying downtown is the dollar value of the time and trouble of making the trip. But how do we estimate that dollar value?

One way is to perform the following hypothetical action. Imagine that a stranger has offered to pay you to do an errand that involves the same trip downtown (perhaps to drop off a letter for her at the post office). If she offered you a payment of, say, $100, would you accept? If so, we know that your cost of walking downtown and back must be less than $100. Now imagine her offer being reduced in small increments until you finally refuse the last offer. For example, if you agree to walk downtown and back for $9 but not for $8.99, then your perceived cost of making the trip is $9. Thus, an economist applying the cost–benefit principle would predict that you would buy the game downtown, because the $10 you save (your benefit) is greater than your $9 cost of making the trip. On the other hand, suppose that your cost of making the trip is greater than $10. In that case, the cost–benefit principle predicts that you would buy the game from the nearby campus store.

Note that if the time it would take to walk downtown and back has a value to you of more than $10, it is perfectly rational to decide *not* to save $10 on the computer game. Economists know that money isn't everything. But in order to compare the sizes of benefits and costs, we need some common unit of measurement. Economists often use dollar values (that is, in economies such as Canada's where the dollar is the currency) to measure costs and benefits because they are a convenient and comparable unit. This, however, does not imply that we will always choose the alternative that costs the least or saves the most money.

## OPPORTUNITY COST

Suppose, for example, that the time required for the trip downtown is the only time you have left to study for a difficult test the next day. Or suppose you are watching one of your favourite movies, or that you are tired and would love a short nap. In such cases, we say that the **opportunity cost** of making the trip, the value of what you must sacrifice to walk downtown and back, is high and you are more likely to decide against making the trip.

**opportunity cost** the value of the next-best alternative that must be foregone in order to undertake an activity

In this example, if watching the last hour of the movie is the most valuable opportunity that conflicts with the trip downtown, the opportunity cost of making the trip is the dollar value you place on pursuing that opportunity—that is, the largest amount you would be willing to pay to avoid missing the end of the movie. Note that the opportunity cost of making the trip is not the combined value of *all* possible activities you could have pursued, but only the value of your *best* alternative, the one you would have chosen had you not made the trip.

Throughout the text, we will pose exercises like the one that follows. You will find that pausing to answer them will help you to master key concepts in economics. Because doing these exercises is not very costly, the cost–benefit principle indicates that it is well worth your while to do them!

**EXERCISE 1.1**    **You would again save $10 by buying the game downtown rather than at the campus store, but your cost of making the trip is now $12, not $9. Where does the cost–benefit principle predict that you will buy the game?**

## EXAMPLE 1.2

### What is the opportunity cost of selling flowers on the sidewalk?

Suppose that you are a flower seller, with a stock of cut roses that will wilt by tomorrow morning. If you do not sell them tonight, their value tomorrow will be zero. You can think of two possible places to sell your flowers: on the sidewalk outside your home or downtown in an upscale, romantic restaurant, where you can embarrass people into buying flowers for their dates. However, to get into these restaurants, you must give the restaurant owner a $25 payment, plus you must sacrifice time (which you value at $10) and pay a $5 bus fare to travel downtown—a total travel cost of $15. Suppose that you expect to sell all the flowers in about an hour wherever you are, and you expect to get about $50 for your flowers if you sell downtown. You do not have anything else to do during the time you will spend selling flowers. What would be the opportunity cost of selling them on the sidewalk? What is the least revenue from sidewalk sales that would make selling on the sidewalk your rational choice?

By selling on the sidewalk, you give up the net return that you could get by selling downtown. If you had sold the flowers downtown, you would have gotten a net return of $10 ($50 revenue minus the $25 payoff, minus $15 in travel costs). So the opportunity cost of selling the flowers on the sidewalk is $10. You are better off selling on the sidewalk only if you expect to make more than $10 at that location. (Notice that this example does not specify how you got the flowers—whether you grew them yourself, bought them in the marketplace, or received them as a gift *does not matter*. The important thing is that the flowers will wilt by tomorrow and be valueless, hence the opportunity cost of the flowers themselves is zero.)

Notice from Example 1.2 that opportunity costs can be either *explicit* or *implicit*. An explicit opportunity cost requires an outlay or payment. For example, a payment of $25 to a restaurant owner for access to the customers is an *explicit* opportunity cost. The $25 cannot be used to purchase something else. The $5 for bus fares is also an explicit opportunity cost. An implicit opportunity cost does not involve an actual payment. If it uses up your time to make a trip downtown and you would pay $10 to avoid the trip, then the trip downtown has an implicit opportunity cost of $10 even though you do not actually pay anyone $10. The total opportunity cost of any action is the sum of explicit and implicit opportunity costs.

**RECAP**

## SCARCITY, RATIONALITY, AND THE COST-BENEFIT PRINCIPLE

The resources available to us, including time, are limited. Scarcity means that we have to make choices—having more of one good thing usually means having less of another. Cost-benefit analysis is an approach to making choices, and the cost-benefit principle can help us predict the choices made by economic decision makers.

The cost-benefit principle holds that a rational decision maker will take an economic action if, and only if, the extra benefits from taking the action are greater than the extra costs. Applying the cost-benefit principle is facilitated by measuring all benefits and costs in a common monetary unit such as dollars. The measurement of all relevant costs is aided by the concept of opportunity cost. The opportunity cost of an activity is the value of the next-best alternative that must be foregone to perform the activity.

# 1.3 THREE IMPORTANT DECISION PITFALLS

Rational people will apply the cost–benefit principle most of the time, although probably in an intuitive and approximate way, rather than through explicit and precise calculation. Knowing that rational people tend to compare costs and benefits enables economists to predict their likely behaviour. Yet researchers have identified situations in which people tend to apply the cost–benefit principle inconsistently. People sometimes tend to ignore certain costs that are relevant to a decision at hand, for example, and sometimes they are influenced by costs that are irrelevant.

Three of the most commonly encountered and important pitfalls concern opportunity costs, sunk costs, and the difference between average and marginal costs. In these situations, the cost–benefit principle may not predict behaviour accurately, but it proves helpful in another way, by identifying specific strategies for avoiding bad decisions.[7]

---

7  The examples in this section are inspired by the pioneering research of Daniel Kahneman and the late Amos Tversky. Kahneman was awarded the 2002 Nobel Prize in economics for his efforts to integrate insights from psychology into economics.

We will examine these three important decision pitfalls in this section. Knowing these pitfalls will help you to deepen your understanding of what economists mean by rational behaviour.

## PITFALL 1: IGNORING OPPORTUNITY COSTS

Opportunity costs are like dogs that fail to bark in the night.

Sherlock Holmes, Arthur Conan Doyle's legendary detective, was successful because he saw details that most others overlooked. In *Silver Blaze*, Holmes is called on to investigate the theft of an expensive racehorse from its stable. A Scotland Yard inspector assigned to the case asks Holmes whether some particular aspect of the crime required further study. "Yes," Holmes replies, and describes "the curious incident of the dog in the nighttime." "The dog did nothing in the nighttime," responds the puzzled inspector. But, as Holmes realized, that was precisely the problem. The watchdog's failure to bark when Silver Blaze was stolen meant that the watchdog knew the thief. This clue substantially reduced the number of suspects and eventually led to the thief's apprehension.

Just as we often don't notice when a dog fails to bark, many of us tend to overlook the implicit value of activities that fail to happen. As discussed earlier, however, intelligent decisions require taking the value of foregone opportunities into account. What is not stated may be as important as what is explicitly stated.

The opportunity cost of an activity, once again, is the value of all that must be foregone in order to engage in that activity. If buying a computer game downtown means not watching the last hour of a movie, then the value to you of watching the end of the movie is an implicit cost of the trip. Many people make flawed decisions because they tend to ignore the value of such foregone opportunities. In order not to overlook implicit costs, economists often translate questions like, "Should I walk downtown?" into ones like, "Will I be better off if I walk downtown or watch the end of the movie?"

As the next example makes clear, even people who seem to know they should weigh the pros and cons of the actions they are contemplating sometimes don't have a clear sense of how to measure the relevant costs and benefits.

## EXAMPLE 1.3

### Will you walk downtown to save $10 on a $1020 laptop computer?

You are about to buy a $1020 laptop computer at the nearby campus store when a friend tells you that the same computer is on sale at a downtown store for only $1010. If the downtown store is half an hour's walk away, where will you, as a rational decision maker, buy the computer?

Assuming that the laptop is light enough to carry without effort, the structure of this example is exactly the same as that of the earlier example about where to buy the computer game—the only difference is that the price of the laptop is dramatically higher than the price of the computer game. As before, the benefit of buying downtown is the dollar amount you'll save, namely, $10. And since it's exactly the same trip, its cost also must be the same as before. So if you are perfectly rational, you will make the same decision in both cases. Yet when real people are asked what they would do in these situations, the overwhelming majority say they would walk downtown to buy the game but buy the laptop at the campus store. When asked to explain, most of them say something like, the trip was worth it for the game because you save 40 percent, but not worth it for the laptop because you save only $10 out of $1020.

This is faulty reasoning. The benefit of the trip downtown is not the proportion you save on the original price. Rather, it is the absolute dollar amount you save. Since the benefit of walking downtown to buy the laptop is $10, exactly the same as for the computer game, and since the cost of the trip must also be the same in both cases, the net benefit from making both trips must be exactly the same. And that means that a rational decision maker would make the same decision in both cases. Yet, as noted, most people choose differently.

**For someone living in Toronto, which of the following is more valuable, all else equal: saving $100 on a $2000 plane ticket to Tokyo or saving $90 on a $500 plane ticket to Ottawa?**

EXERCISE 1.2

The pattern of faulty reasoning in the decision just discussed is one of several decision pitfalls to which people are often prone. In the discussion that follows, we will identify two additional decision pitfalls. In some cases, people ignore costs or benefits that they ought to take into account, while on other occasions they are influenced by costs or benefits that are irrelevant.

## EXAMPLE 1.4

**Is it rational to use your frequent-flyer coupon to fly to Vancouver for winter break?**

With winter break at the University of Alberta only a week away, you are still undecided about whether to fly to Vancouver and then go to Whistler with a group of classmates. The round-trip airfare from Edmonton to Vancouver is $500. All other relevant costs for the vacation while at Whistler will total exactly $1000. The maximum you are willing to pay for the vacation is $1350. You could travel to Whistler by paying $500 to fly from Edmonton to Vancouver or by using a frequent-flyer coupon to pay for the flight. Your only alternative use for your frequent-flyer coupon is for your plane trip to Ottawa the weekend after winter break to attend your brother's wedding. (Your coupon expires shortly thereafter.) If the Edmonton–Ottawa round-trip airfare is $400, is it rational for you to use your frequent-flyer coupon to fly to Vancouver for winter break?

The *cost–benefit* criterion tells you to go to Vancouver if the benefits of the trip exceed its costs. If not for the complication of the frequent-flyer coupon, solving this problem would be a straightforward matter of comparing the maximum price you would pay for the week at Whistler (your benefit from the trip) to the sum of all relevant costs. And since your airfare and other costs would sum to $1500, or $150 more than what you are willing to pay for the trip, the rational choice is not to go.

But what about the possibility of using your frequent-flyer coupon for the trip? Using it for that purpose might make the flight to Vancouver seem free, suggesting you would reap a net benefit of $350 by making the trip. But doing so would also mean you would have to pay $400 for your airfare to Ottawa. So the opportunity cost of using your coupon to fly to Vancouver is really $400. If you use it for that purpose, the cost of the trip still exceeds its benefit and it still fails the cost–benefit test. In cases like these, you are much more likely to decide rationally if you ask yourself, will my benefit be greater if I use my frequent-flyer coupon for this trip or save it for an upcoming trip?

## PITFALL 2: FAILURE TO IGNORE SUNK COSTS

Pitfall 1 occurs when people ignore opportunity costs. In another common pitfall, the opposite is true: people are influenced by costs that really are not opportunity costs. *The only costs that are relevant to a decision about whether to take an action are the costs that we can avoid by not taking the action.* As a practical matter, however, many decision makers appear to be influenced by **sunk costs**—costs that are beyond recovery at the moment a decision is made. For example, money spent on a nontransferable, nonrefundable airline ticket is a sunk cost.

Because sunk costs must be borne *whether or not an action is taken,* they are irrelevant to a rational decision of whether to take the action. Suppose, for example, that you have invested $300 000 in a small manufacturing shop that is still incomplete and worthless in its current state. Things have not gone well, and it will cost another $290 000 to finish the job. But due to a new technological development, you could start a new,

**sunk cost** a cost that is beyond recovery at the moment a decision is made

equally valuable manufacturing shop from scratch for only $275 000. If one of the two options, finishing off the original shop or starting a new shop from scratch, is rational, which one is it? The key to this decision is that the original $300 000 has already been spent. That money is gone; it is a sunk cost. For the same return, you can either invest an additional $290 000 or invest an additional $275 000. Starting a new shop from scratch is the rational choice.

**EXERCISE 1.3**

**Indian Summer, an Indian restaurant in Northern Ontario, offers an all-you-can-eat lunch buffet for $9.99. Customers pay $9.99, and no matter how many times they refill their plates, there is no additional charge. One day, as a good-will gesture, the owner of the restaurant tells 10 randomly selected guests that their lunch is on the house. The remaining guests pay the usual price. If all diners are rational, will there be any difference in the average quantity of food consumed by people in these two groups?**

## PITFALL 3: FAILURE TO UNDERSTAND THE AVERAGE-MARGINAL DISTINCTION

As we have seen, rational economic decisions take proper account of opportunity costs. Because sunk costs are not opportunity costs, sunk costs are irrelevant to economic decisions and are not counted when the cost–benefit principle is applied. Further, accurate application of the cost–benefit principle is not possible if marginal costs and benefits are confused with average costs and benefits.

The cost–benefit framework emphasizes that the only relevant costs and benefits in a rational decision about whether to change the amount of an activity are *marginal costs* and *benefits*. Economists define the **marginal cost** of an activity as the increase in total cost that results from carrying out one additional unit of the activity. Similarly, the **marginal benefit** of an activity is the increase in total benefit that results from carrying out one more unit of the activity. In many contexts, however, people seem more inclined to compare **average costs** and **average benefits**—total cost or benefit per unit of activity.

To see the importance of the average-marginal distinction, suppose that you are a sales manager in charge of deciding whether to assign a newly hired salesperson to one sales region or another. Suppose also that you wish to assign the new salesperson in a way that maximizes sales. What data would help you to make your decision? A sales manager not familiar with the average-marginal distinction might be satisfied with obtaining data on average sales per salesperson in the two regions. The sales manager might then assign the new salesperson to the region where sales per salesperson (i.e., average sales) are highest. But it is not necessarily the case that the region with higher average sales is the region where an additional salesperson will add the most to total sales. In fact, average sales are not useful in determining where to send the new salesperson. Perhaps the new salesperson will add little to total sales in the region with higher average sales because the region is nearly saturated. If the region with lower average sales in underserved, a new salesperson in that region might significantly increase total sales. The relevant question concerns how much the new salesperson will add to total sales in one region versus another. The average sales per salesperson in each of the two regions are not relevant.

**marginal cost** the increase in total cost that results from carrying out one additional unit of an activity

**marginal benefit** the increase in total benefit that results from carrying out one more unit of an activity

**average cost** total cost per unit of activity

**average benefit** total benefit per unit of activity

**EXERCISE 1.4**

**The average-marginal distinction is also relevant to understanding income tax systems. Suppose that the first $9999 of income is not taxed at all. If your income reaches $10 000, however, the tax rate on each dollar of income above $10 000 is 15 percent. All income you earn in excess of $50 000 is taxed at 50 percent. How much tax would you pay if your income is $10 500? if your income is $20 000, or $120 000? What is your average income tax rate at each income level? What is your marginal tax rate?**

The conclusion that some costs, especially marginal costs and opportunity costs, are important while others, like sunk costs and average costs, are irrelevant to economic decisions is implicit in our original explanation of the *cost–benefit principle* (an action should be taken if, and only if, the extra benefits of taking it exceed the extra costs). Yet, the pitfalls of (1) ignoring opportunity costs, (2) considering sunk costs, and (3) confusing average with marginal cost are so important that we enumerate them separately. As a result, a core principle worthy of repeated emphasis emerges:

**The Principle of Relevant Costs:** In considering whether to produce or consume more of a good, what matters is the cost of one more unit (marginal cost).

COST-
BENEFIT

RELEVANT
COSTS

---

*RECAP*

**THREE IMPORTANT PITFALLS**

1. **The pitfall of ignoring opportunity costs.** When performing a cost-benefit analysis of an action, it is important to account for the full opportunity cost of the action. The opportunity cost of an action is the value of the next best alternative that is foregone by taking the action.

2. **The pitfall of not ignoring sunk costs.** When deciding whether to perform an action, it is important to ignore sunk costs—costs that cannot be avoided even if the action is not taken.

3. **The pitfall of using average instead of marginal costs and benefits.** It is a mistake to increase an activity simply because its average benefit is greater than its average cost or to reduce an activity simply because its average benefit is less than its average cost. The cost–benefit principle states that total benefit can be increased by increasing the amount of an activity if, and only if, the benefit of one more unit of the activity is greater than its cost. Likewise, total benefit can be increased by decreasing the activity if, and only if, its marginal benefit is less than its marginal cost.

---

# 1.4 ECONOMIC THEORIES AND THEIR EVALUATION

In economics, how do we know if a theory is useful? How do we evaluate a theory? Should we be concerned about the realism of the assumptions behind our theories?

## ALL ELSE EQUAL

In the real world, many things can happen, at the same time, for many different reasons; therefore, one concept that is absolutely essential for evaluating theories is that of "all other conditions being held constant." When economists, or other social scientists, make predictions, these are seldom unconditional. In, for example, our discussions earlier in this chapter of going downtown to save money when purchasing a computer game or a computer, or to sell roses, we never mentioned the weather. In the real world, a sudden blizzard or thunderstorm is likely to change people's decisions, but, implicitly, we assumed that the weather did not change. Typically, our predictions are "all else being equal," which is similar to the prediction you were asked about in Exercise 1.1. In that exercise, the cost of a trip downtown increased from $9 to $12, and you were asked to say what the cost–benefit principle would predict about where you would buy the computer game. In essence, you were asked to say what would happen if one condition (the cost of a trip downtown) changed while other relevant conditions stayed the same. Scientific theories are generally like this; they predict what will happen if there is change in one variable (or possibly a few variables) while all other variables stay the same.

Similarly, in Example 1.2, application of the cost–benefit principle leads to the prediction that you will sell the flowers on the sidewalk if you can obtain more than $10 by selling there. But if rain suddenly starts to pour, you may decide not to sell roses at all. This result is not what was predicted by application of the cost–benefit principle to the original conditions. But the result is not a refutation of the theory. The prediction was based on "all else equal." It was based, among other things, on an implicit assumption that the weather would not change dramatically. Many other events could also affect your decisions; for example, you might suddenly inherit tens of millions of dollars from a rich aunt and decide that you want to fly to Paris rather than sell flowers.

**ceteris paribus** a Latin phrase meaning "all else equal"

The Latin expression for "all else equal" is ***ceteris paribus***. Although English-speaking economists these days typically only know a few Latin expressions, nearly all of them know *ceteris paribus*. You should, too.

## THE REALISM OF ASSUMPTIONS

Many newcomers to economics are concerned with the realism of the assumptions employed in economics. Some of these concerns are more justified than others. For example, people differ in terms of how well their economic decisions can be explained by assuming that they pursue the cost–benefit principle. Someone whose own decisions seem very haphazard compared to the decision making described in Examples 1.1 and 1.2 above might be inclined to question the realism of employing the cost–benefit principle for predicting economic behaviour.

Examples 1.1 and 1.2, however, were only intended to explain how cost–benefit calculations work. They were framed in terms of an individual decision maker to keep matters simple. But in economics, we are typically not concerned with predicting the decisions of a specific person. Rather, we are usually interested in predicting outcomes that involve decisions by large groups of people. In microeconomics, for example, we might be interested in predicting how an increase in the provincial tax on gasoline would affect gasoline consumption. Even in a small province, total gasoline consumption depends on the decisions of tens of thousands of automobile owners, individuals, and company truck owners. In the short run, an increase in the provincial tax on gasoline may not change the behavior of some people at all—they may already be locked into car ownership and commuting patterns that they cannot easily change quickly. Although economists would predict that gasoline consumption would decline when there is an increase in the provincial tax, many people may be unable to change their behaviour in the short run. However, if some people reduce their gasoline purchases, the prediction will be correct, and over time, as individuals replace their cars and re-evaluate where to live and work, much more change in gasoline consumption is likely. In a case such as this, the assumption that people apply the cost–benefit principle is less than fully realistic when applied immediately to all people, but it can still lead to successful predictions.

Newcomers to economics are sometimes concerned that economic models are not "realistic." But a model is a bit like a map. No map of an area can possibly replicate the area in all details. Maps necessarily abstract from reality in order to highlight the most important features of concern to the users of the map, and different maps are useful for different purposes (e.g., you may want a map marked with bicycle routes for a cycling vacation, but the public works department needs a map that marks underground wiring and pipes). Model builders ignore influences that they consider relatively unimportant in order to concentrate attention on the most important influences.

Physicists, for example, who want to predict how quickly a rock dropped from the top of a tower will hit the ground can do a fairly good job even if they ignore (i.e., assume away) the influence of air resistance. Even though the physicist knows perfectly well that air resistance has an influence, it is small enough to be ignored given the force of gravity and the density of a rock, and it makes the calculations much simpler. But if the same physicists were asked how long it would take a feather to fall to the ground, they would know that air resistance *will* make a difference in that case and must be taken into consideration. Choosing the right assumptions makes the difference between a model that performs well and one that does not. Because different assumptions often lead to different conclusions, you should always examine the assumptions upon which economic models are based.

## POSITIVE ECONOMICS, WELFARE ECONOMICS, AND EFFICIENCY

Why do people study economics? There is no single answer. For some people, the motivation is simply to understand how the economy works. But others may study economics because they want to use their understanding of economic processes in order to change economic outcomes, which implies that they should have some way to evaluate which outcomes are "better."

Our discussion of economic theory has emphasized the use of economics for prediction. Economic theories that are used to make predictions are examples of *positive economics*. **Positive economics** has two dimensions. First, it offers cause-and-effect explanations of economic relationships. Second, positive economics has an empirical dimension. In principle, data can be used to confirm or refute propositions, or hypotheses, that emerge from positive economics. In principle, data can also be used to measure the magnitude of effects predicted by positive economics. For example, data on gasoline sales can be used to evaluate whether the increase in the provincial tax on gasoline had the impact predicted by an economic model.

While economics shares with physics and other natural sciences the use of theory for predictive purposes, there is more to economics than prediction. **Welfare economics** is concerned not only with prediction or facts, but it also involves the evaluation of economic outcomes or situations according to ethical or value standards. While it may use many of the same assumptions and models as positive economics, welfare economics is not purely concerned with prediction. It is also concerned with judging whether some outcomes or situations are superior to or better than others. To judge the optimality of outcomes or situations, ethical or value standards must be used. The justification for welfare economics is the expectation that better decisions will be made if the costs and benefits of decisions are systematically tallied and evaluated according to explicit criteria.

Consider an example from microeconomics that involves welfare economics. Would it be good public policy to impose a new tax on the carbon content of fossil fuels? Positive economics enables one to make a prediction about the impact of the tax on the prices of fossil fuels, the incomes of workers and owners, the costs for those who consume fossil fuels, and the total impact on fossil fuel production. To draw a conclusion about whether the new tax makes Canadians better or worse off, however, we need to use welfare economics and combine the factual predictions of positive economics with some ethical criteria. If everybody is made better off by a new policy, the choice is simple. However, this outcome is very rare. It is far more common for some people to be made better off while others are made worse off when a policy choice is made, which implies making some judgment about whether the losses of some people *should* be outweighed by the gains of others. If the total money value of the gains is greater than the total money cost of the losses, the winners could (in principle) compensate the losers and still be better off themselves. If that compensation actually occurs, one could then say that everyone is at least as well off after the policy change, compared to before, so at least the new outcome is better than the original outcome. But full compensation is rare in reality, so ethical judgments about the distribution of gains and losses are hard to escape.

Sometimes the term positive economics is contrasted with the term *normative economics,* which is said to be explicitly concerned with issues of fairness, equity, or ethics. However, this contrast can mislead people into thinking that economics which is not explicitly concerned with issues of fairness, equity, or ethics must be positive economics.

**positive economics**
economic analysis that offers cause-and-effect explanations of economic relationships; the propositions, or hypotheses, that emerge from positive economics can, in principle, be confirmed or refuted by data; in principle, data can also be used to measure the magnitude of effects predicted by positive economics

**welfare economics**
economic analysis that is concerned not only with prediction or facts but also involves the evaluation of economic outcomes or situations according to ethical or value standards (which may be either explicit or implicit)

But whether economics is positive or not is solely a matter of whether it is restricted to issues of fact or prediction. Economic evaluations and policy statements do not become positive economics just because the ethical or evaluation standards are implicit or hidden or relatively uncontroversial.

## EVIDENCE AND FALLACIES

Whether economists are making predictions as part of purely positive economics or making statements about desirable public policy based on the predictions of positive economics, they must be concerned as natural scientists with evaluating their predictions using evidence. Often this assessment of predictions with evidence will be somewhat casual, involving, say, the comparison of two variables over time. Other times, it will be more formal and will draw upon techniques from the discipline of statistics. The branch of economics known as **econometrics** involves the application of statistical techniques to economic data and the development of rigorous statistical techniques for analyzing such data.

In making use of evidence, one of the most important logical errors is to mistake correlation for causation. Just because two variables move together or one variable precedes another does not mean that one is the cause of another. Correlation does not necessarily indicate causation. Although, for example, the United States spends considerably more per capita on health care than Canada does, Canadians have a longer life expectancy than Americans. Does this imply that spending more money on health care reduces life expectancy? Hardly![8] If two variables move together but are otherwise unrelated, we have a **spurious correlation**. Cause and effect and correlation are two very different things.

Another significant logical mistake is known as the *fallacy of composition.* The statement, "If one farmer harvests a larger crop he will be better off; therefore, if all farmers harvest larger crops, all farmers will be better off," is an example. If all farmers harvest larger crops, prices may decrease by an amount that would more than offset the benefit of larger harvests. What is true for an individual is not necessarily true for an entire group. The statement, "What is good for business is good for the country," provides yet another example. A tax reduction for large corporations may benefit their shareholders, but it does not necessarily follow that the tax reduction is good for everyone else.

The **fallacy of composition**, therefore, occurs if one argues that what is true for a part must also necessarily be true for the whole. It is the mistake of assuming that what is true for a part (such as an individual consumer or firm) is also necessarily true for the whole (such as the whole market or economy). Although the example of the farmer is a microeconomic one, the issue is particularly important in macroeconomics.

**econometrics** a branch of economics that involves the application of statistical techniques to economic data and the development of statistical techniques for analyzing such data

**spurious correlation** a case in which two variables move together but are otherwise unrelated

**fallacy of composition** the argument that because something is true for a part, it also is necessarily true for the whole

---

**RECAP**

### ECONOMIC THEORIES AND THEIR EVALUATION

Economic predictions are always subject to the *ceteris paribus* (all else equal) qualification.

Not all concerns about the realism of economics models are justified. Economic models that assume rational behaviour can lead to accurate predictions about the behaviour of large groups of people even if some people do not behave rationally. Models in economics or other disciplines cannot be perfectly realistic, but this is no more of a problem than the fact that a map is not a full-scale reproduction of the area it represents. On the other hand, the predictions of models do depend on the assumptions they are based upon, and choosing the right assumptions makes the difference between a model that performs well and one that does not.

---

8   In Chapter 11 we will see how microeconomic theory can help to explain health care costs.

Positive economics offers cause-and-effect explanations of economic relationships. In principle, data can be used to confirm or refute propositions, or hypotheses, that emerge from positive economics. *Welfare economics* is concerned with the evaluation of economic outcomes or situations and is not strictly limited to predicting what will happen. It is concerned with judging whether some outcomes or situations are superior to or better than others according to ethical or value standards that may be explicit or implicit.

As scientists, economists must be concerned with evaluating their predictions using evidence in the form of data. Formal evaluation of economic theories and predictions typically involves the application of econometrics. In evaluating statistical evidence, it is important to be aware of possible pitfalls such as the fallacy of composition and the argument that a spurious correlation implies cause and effect.

## 1.5 ECONOMIC NATURALISM

With the rudiments of the cost–benefit framework under your belt, you are now in a position to become an **economic naturalist**, someone who uses insights from economics to help make sense of observations from everyday life. People who have studied biology are able to observe and marvel at many details of nature that would otherwise escape their notice. For example, while the novice may see only trees on a walk in the woods in early April, the biology student notices many different species of trees and understands why some are already in leaf while others are still dormant. Likewise, the novice may notice that in some animal species, males are much larger and more impressive in appearance than females, but the biology student knows that that pattern occurs only in species in which males take several mates. Natural selection favours larger males because their greater size helps them to prevail in the often bloody contests among males for access to females. By contrast, males tend to be roughly the same size as females in monogamous species, where there is much less fighting for mates.

In similar fashion, learning a few simple economic principles enables us to see the mundane details of ordinary human existence in a new light. Whereas the uninitiated often fail even to notice these details, the economic naturalist not only sees them but becomes actively engaged in the attempt to understand them by using positive economics. Let's consider an example of the type of questions that economic naturalists might pose for themselves.

**economic naturalist** someone who uses insights from economics to help make sense of observations from everyday life

### ECONOMIC NATURALIST 1.1

**Why are some places littered with beer cans and wrecked cars while others are not?**

Arriving in the U.K. from Nova Scotia in the summer of 2001, a visiting economic naturalist was surprised to see how much the back alleys of British towns were littered with discarded beer cans and how many abandoned cars could be seen at the side of English roads. Why did the U.K. have these problems of littering when Canada did not?

The beer can litter problem has an easy explanation—in the U.K., there was no system of deposits on beverage containers, so they were often thrown away after they were emptied, and aluminum cans accumulated at the roadside and in back alleys. Although aluminum can be recycled, scrap yards did not pay enough per can to make it worthwhile for people to collect them. By contrast, in Canada, consumers pay a deposit on beverage containers; even if they do not bother to return their empties, the cans and bottles they discard in public places are collected and returned for the refund. Although the deposit on each container is not large, it is enough to motivate street people and children to collect them. On an hourly basis, this is a poorly paid "job," but it still pays more than the opportunity costs of their time. The deposit system means that discarded bottles and cans have, effectively, a market value.

The same idea of market value explains the problem of abandoned cars in the U.K. Typically, auto wrecking yards in Canada are willing to pay a few dollars for old cars because the steel has value as scrap iron, and there are often usable parts, even on an old heap. Driving (or towing) an old car to the scrap yard may be a sad event, but there are at least a few dollars to be had in scrap value. However, this wasn't true in the U.K. in 2001. Because there had been a decline in the price of scrap iron, and because the British government had introduced an environmental charge for disposal of tires and car batteries, disposing of old cars cost money—if done legally.

The low price of scrap iron meant that the value of the steel and parts in a car was now less than the environmental charge for disposal. Old cars became a liability rather than a small asset. Faced with this liability, some drivers in the U.K. just took off the plates and walked away from their cars (which were usually soon vandalized and stripped of anything valuable). The visiting economic naturalist observed several cars abandoned outside the front gate of an auto wrecking yard; the yard owners wanted to be paid to accept the vehicles, but the car owners had not wanted to actually pay money to dispose of their cars. Since they could just park their cars and leave, they did.

Although littering is neither legally nor ethically defensible, it is influenced by the basic cost–benefit principle. Therefore, public policy to reduce litter has to try to ensure that the benefits to individuals of reducing litter exceed their costs. In the U.K., government policy did not even try to influence that cost–benefit calculation to make it worthwhile to avoid beer-can littering, and the new environmental charges on automobiles backfired by increasing the private benefits of littering, thereby creating a new (and worse) environmental problem.[9]

## 1.6   WHAT WILL BE PRODUCED, HOW, AND FOR WHOM?

A major theme of this text is *the division of labour*—how specialization and exchange can improve consumption possibilities. Although we will discuss how *competition* among producers will work to reduce costs of production, that emphasis should not obscure the fact that the division of labour is essentially a form of *co-operation*. As societies have developed, that co-operation has become very complex—as a budding Economic Naturalist, the next time you take a plane trip you should ask yourself: how many people have to co-operate in doing their jobs right if this flight is to arrive safely? The pilot and co-pilot and air traffic controllers and the pilots of all other nearby planes are just the start; don't forget the mechanics who service the jet engines and the machinists who make the parts, plus many, many others!

Nevertheless, every society always has to answer the same basic economic questions: What goods and services will be produced? How much of each? Who will get to consume these goods and services?

For example, food and housing have to be produced if humans are to survive, and all human societies also provide people with some entertainment during their hours of leisure. But how much of our limited time and other resources will we devote to building housing, how much to the production of food, and how much to providing entertainment and other goods and services? What techniques will we use to produce each good? Who will do each specific task? Economists who are concerned about *efficiency* will ask, could we reallocate productive resources and produce more output from the same or fewer inputs?

9  For a large and fascinating collection of economic naturalist examples, see Robert Frank, *The Economic Naturalist: In Search of Explanations for Everyday Enigmas* (New York: Basic Books, 2008).

As we will see in subsequent chapters, these questions about *production* are inextricably linked to the basic question of *distribution*: Who will get more and who will get less? For example, what income will the person who stocks shelves in a grocery store earn? How much will the CEO of the grocery chain receive? Will society make provision for those who cannot work; for example, a taxi driver paralyzed in a car accident?

Since each person's income helps determine his or her demand for the goods and services a society produces, the type and amount of goods produced depends on the distribution of incomes. Production and distribution are thus simultaneously determined. But what *distribution* of income would be fair? Economists concerned about *equity* will therefore also ask, could we reallocate rewards so as to produce a fairer distribution of consumption?

## ALTERNATIVE METHODS OF ORGANIZING ECONOMIC ACTIVITY

This text will discuss how markets work, because markets play an extremely important role in organizing economic activity in modern societies. However, they are not the only possible method. Consider the economic units of ancient and medieval times. They were, by modern standards, small, isolated, and relatively self-sufficient. For example, Athens, the largest of the city states in ancient Greece, probably occupied an area less than half the size of Prince Edward Island and had a comparable population of maybe 140 000 people. In such a world, the economic matters of production, distribution, and prices were determined by central, authoritative control based on widely accepted rules, customs, and traditions. In the participatory democracy of Greek city states, citizenship was reserved for adult males. Citizens performed jury duty, worked on legislative affairs, and undertook other civic tasks. Slaves and foreigners produced goods and services. Plunder also was used to support the city state. Elsewhere, however, monarchs ruled their kingdoms with nearly absolute power.

This sketch of economic circumstances in ancient times suggests several ways of allocating economic resources. In a *command* system a central authority—the king, for example—makes most economic decisions. The Greeks also used *personal characteristics* to allocate certain occupations when they reserved some tasks for citizens and then restricted citizenship to males. If the sons and daughters of slaves also are slaves, *tradition* is being used to allocate economic tasks. As well, the ancient Greeks used *force* to allocate resources when they relied on plunder to take goods and services from non-Greek communities.

These ancient examples do not exhaust the list of possibilities. A *lottery* reallocates resources in favour of the winner and away from all others who participate in the lottery. A *queue* can be used to allocate items such as tickets for a rock concert or to ration goods on a *first-come, first-served* basis. A *tournament* allocates resources when a contest determines who wins a prize.[10] *Majority rule* can be used to decide resource allocation, as when governments allocate resources among competing uses such a health care, roads, social services, and education. *Command* is another possibility; it can be implemented on a small scale, as in ancient kingdoms or modern family enterprises, on a somewhat larger scale within corporations, or on a truly immense scale, as in the central planning of the former Soviet Union.

For much of the twentieth century, in centrally planned communist nations, a central bureaucratic committee established production targets for the country's farms and factories, developed a master plan for how to achieve those targets (including detailed instructions concerning who was to produce what), and set up guidelines for the distribution and use of the goods and services produced. However, with the fall of the Soviet Union

---

10 Prizes in athletic tournaments are one example, but a prize to motivate salespersons in a sales contest also allocates resources.

and its satellite nations in the late 1980s, only a few countries ruled by a communist party remain. Cuba, North Korea, and China are three examples. The rapid growth of markets in China makes it unclear how to classify the economy of China today. Cuba also has instituted market-based reforms, albeit it on a smaller scale. Only North Korea remains a largely centrally planned economy.

In the twenty-first century we are therefore left, for the most part, with economic systems in which production and distribution decisions are left to individuals and firms interacting in markets. In market economies, people decide for themselves which careers to pursue and which products to produce or buy. However, there are few, if any, *pure* market economies today. Modern industrial countries are more properly described as *mixed economies*, meaning that goods and services are allocated by a combination of markets, regulation, and other forms of collective control. Still, people are for the most part free to start businesses, to shut them down, or to sell them. Within broad limits, the distribution of goods and services is determined by market incentives—in particular, by the prices of commodities.

In Canada, as elsewhere, markets therefore play a crucial role in determining both what is produced and who gets what. Therefore, we need to understand how (and why) markets can often successfully answer these questions, and also how (and why) they may sometimes fail.

## SUMMARY

- Economics is the study of the economy, the production and distribution of goods and services. Economics consists both of microeconomics, which focuses on the consequences of individual behaviour at the level of specific markets, and macroeconomics, which focuses on the performance of national economies and policies to improve that performance. **LO1**

- Economics differs from other social sciences not just by its subject matter but also by a tendency to think in terms of models and a tendency to assume, unless the evidence suggests otherwise, that people behave rationally. **LO4**, **LO6**

- Three particularly important figures in the history of economic thought are Adam Smith (1723–1790), the author of *The Wealth of Nations*; Alfred Marshall (1842–1924), whose influence on microeconomics continues to this day; and John Maynard Keynes (1883–1946), who is associated with Keynesian macroeconomics. **LO2**

- The scarcity problem says that because material and human resources are limited, having more of one good thing usually means making do with less of some other good thing. **LO3**

- The cost–benefit principle says that a rational decision maker will take an action if, but only if, its benefit is at least as great as its cost. The benefit of an action is defined as the largest dollar amount the person will be willing to pay in order to take the action. The cost of an action is defined as the dollar value of everything the person must give up in order to take the action. **LO4**

- Often the question is not whether to pursue an activity but rather how many units of it to pursue. In these cases, the rational actor pursues additional units as long as the marginal benefit of the activity (the benefit from pursuing an additional unit of it) exceeds its marginal cost (the cost of pursuing an additional unit of it). **LO4**

- In using the cost–benefit framework, we need not presume that people choose rationally all the time. Indeed, we identified three common pitfalls that plague decision makers in all walks of life: a tendency to ignore opportunity costs, failing to ignore sunk costs, and a tendency to base decisions on average costs and benefits when it is appropriate to use marginal costs and benefits. **LO5**

- Predictions in economics make use of the *ceteris paribus* assumption, also known as the "all else equal" assumption. **LO6**
- As scientists, economists must be concerned with evaluating their predictions using evidence in the form of data. Formal evaluation of economic theories and predictions typically involves the application of econometrics. **LO6**
- In evaluating statistical evidence, it is important to avoid the fallacy of composition and be aware that correlation does not imply causation. **LO6**
- Positive economic analysis offers cause-and-effect explanations of economic relationships. Welfare economics is concerned with both cause-and-effect and the evaluation of economic outcomes according to ethical standards. **LO7**
- An economic naturalist has the ability to use economic principles to make sense of observations encountered in everyday life. **LO8**

## CORE PRINCIPLES

**The Scarcity Problem**
Because material and human resources are limited, having more of one good thing usually means making do with less of some other good thing. (5)

**The Cost–benefit Principle**
A rational decision maker will take an action if, and only if, the extra benefits from taking the action are greater than the extra costs. (5)

**The Principle of Relevant Costs**
In considering whether to produce or consume more of a good, what matters is the cost of one more unit (marginal cost). (11)

## KEY TERMS

Adam Smith (4)
Alfred Marshall (3)
average cost (10)
average benefit (10)
*ceteris paribus* (12)
econometrics (14)
economic model (4)

economic naturalist (15)
economics (2)
fallacy of composition (14)
John Maynard Keynes (3)
macroeconomics (3)
marginal benefit (10)
marginal cost (10)

microeconomics (3)
opportunity cost (6)
positive economics (13)
rational decision maker (4)
spurious correlation (14)
sunk cost (9)
welfare economics (13)

## REVIEW QUESTIONS

1. On what grounds does the textbook describe the Robbins definition of economics as a product of its times? **LO1**
2. Who were Adam Smith, Alfred Marshall, and John Maynard Keynes? Of Marshall and Keynes, who is associated with microeconomics and who with macroeconomics? **LO2**
3. Describe the scarcity problem and the cost–benefit principle in your own words. **LO3, LO4**
4. True or false: As a rational decision maker, your willingness to drive downtown to save $30 on a new

appliance will depend on what fraction of the total selling price $30 is. Explain. **LO5**
5. Many people think of their air travel as being free when they use frequent-flyer coupons. Explain why these people are likely to make wasteful travel decisions. **LO5**
6. Is the nonrefundable tuition payment you made to your university this semester a sunk cost? How would your answer differ if your university were to offer a full tuition refund to any student who dropped out of school during the first two months of the semester? **LO5**

7. Discuss valid and less valid concerns about the realism of economic assumptions. **LO6**

8. If a government uses cost–benefit analysis to decide whether or not to build a bridge, is the government using positive economics or welfare economics? **LO7**

9. What do the fallacy of composition and spurious correlations have in common? How do they differ? **LO7**

10. What is an economic naturalist? **LO8**

## PROBLEMS

1. State which of the following economic issues are primarily microeconomic and which are primarily macroeconomic. **LO1**
   a. The national unemployment rate
   b. The inflation rate
   c. Why cell phone service plans in Canada cost more than in Morocco
   d. Why airline fares rose significantly in 2010
   e. The causes of the global recession of 2008–2009

2. The maximum price you would pay for having a freshly washed car when you go out to dinner is $6. The smallest amount for which you would be willing to wash someone else's car is $3.50. You are going out to dinner this evening, and your car is dirty. How much net benefit would you receive from washing it? **LO4**

3. To earn extra money in the summer, you grow tomatoes and sell them at the farmers' market for 30 cents per kilogram. By adding compost to your garden, you can increase your yield as shown in the following table. If compost costs 50 cents per kilogram and your goal is to make as much money as possible, how many kilograms of compost will you add? **LO4, LO5**

| Kilograms of compost | Kilograms of tomatoes |
|:---:|:---:|
| 0 | 100.0 |
| 1 | 120.0 |
| 2 | 125.0 |
| 3 | 128.0 |
| 4 | 130.0 |
| 5 | 131.0 |
| 6 | 131.5 |

4. For each long-distance call anywhere in Canada, a new phone service will charge users 30 cents per minute for the first 2 minutes and 2 cents per minute for additional minutes in each call. Tom's current phone service charges 10 cents per minute for all calls, and his calls are never shorter than 7 minutes. If Tom's dorm switches to the new phone service, what do you predict will happen to the average length of his calls? **LO4, LO5**

5. The meal plan at university A lets students eat as much as they like for a fixed fee of $500 per semester. The average student there eats 125 kg of food per semester. University B charges $500 for a book of meal tickets that entitles the student to eat 125 kg of food per semester. If the student eats more than 125 kg, he or she pays extra; if the student eats less, he or she gets a refund. If students are rational, at which university will average food consumption be higher? At which university is more food likely to be wasted? Explain briefly. **LO4, LO5**

6. A shirt company spends $1000 per week on rent for its factory. Each shirt made at the factory requires $2 worth of cloth and $6 worth of labour and energy. If the factory produces 2000 shirts per week, **LO4, LO5**
   a. What is the average cost of a shirt?
   b. What is the marginal cost of a shirt?

   If the factory produces 3000 shirts per week,
   c. What is the average cost of a shirt?
   d. What is the marginal cost of a shirt?

7. A group has chartered a bus trip to Niagara Falls. The driver's fee is $95, the bus rental $500, and the fuel charge $75. The driver's fee is nonrefundable, but the bus rental may be cancelled a week in advance at a charge of $100. At $25 a ticket, how many people must buy tickets a week before so that cancelling the trip definitely will not pay? **LO4, LO5**

8. Sam bought a Trek bicycle for $800 instead of a Cannondale for $1000. Now he finds out that another bike store in town is selling the Cannondale for $800. Mikkel, Sam's friend, offers him $600 for his Trek. If Sam is a rational consumer, will he sell Mikkel his Trek and buy the Cannondale? **LO4, LO5**

9. Which of the following are examples of the use of positive economics and which are examples of welfare economics? **LO7**
   a. The Canadian Centre for Policy Alternatives forecasts that GDP will rise as a consequence of increased government spending to counter the recession.
   b. A cost–benefit study from the C. D. Howe Institute suggests that Canadians would be

better off if Canada were to sign a free trade deal with China.

c. A report from the Department of Finance in Ottawa argues that the current contribution rate for the Canada Pension Plan premiums is high enough to sustain the benefits paid by the plan for decades into the future.

d. A paper published in the journal *Canadian Public Policy* claims that a high estate tax in Canada would substantially reduce wealth inequality among Canadians.

10. Which of the following statements represent examples of the fallacy of composition? Which of them represent examples of spurious correlations? Explain. **LO6**

a. What is good for business is good for the country.

b. Students at schools that have introduced sex education programs have higher rates of sexual activity. Therefore, sex education programs cause students to engage in more sexual activity.

c. If one farmer produces a bigger crop, she will be better off. Therefore, if all farmers produce bigger crops they will all be better off.

d. Every year as the Christmas shopping season reaches its peak in Canada, the amount of cash circulating in the economy increases. The increased cash in the economy is the cause of increased retail spending in Canada during the Christmas shopping season.

## ANSWERS TO IN-CHAPTER EXERCISES

**1.1**  The benefit of buying the game downtown is again $10 but the cost is now $12, so your net benefit from buying it downtown would be $10 − $12 = −$2. Since your net benefit from making the trip would be negative, the rational choice would be to buy at the campus store. **LO4**

**1.2**  For a rational decision maker, saving $100 is more valuable than saving $90, all else equal. The percentage sizes of the discounts are irrelevant. **LO4, LO5**

**1.3**  If the diners are rational, whether or not they were randomly selected to have lunch on the house should make no difference in the average quantity of food they consume at the buffet. (Carefully designed experimental research, however, indicates that those who pay out of their own pocket for a buffet may fail to ignore sunk cost and feel that they must get their money's worth. They will tend to consume more than those who are randomly selected to have lunch on the house.) **LO4, LO5**

**1.4**  If income is $10,500, only the income in excess of $10,000 is taxed. Therefore, the tax paid is $0.15 \times \$500 = \$75$. The marginal tax rate is 15 percent because $0.15 is paid on taxes for each extra dollar of income in excess of $10,000. The average tax rate is $75/10,500 = 0.7 percent.

If income is $50,000, each dollar of income over $10,000 is taxed at the marginal rate of 15 percent. Therefore, the tax paid is $0.15 \times \$40,000 \times \$6,000$. The average tax rate is $6,000/$50,000 = 12 percent.

If income is $120,000, the tax payer will pay no tax on the first $10,000 plus a 15 percent tax on the amount of income between $10,000 and $50,000 plus a 50 percent tax on income over $50,000. Thus the total tax bill will be:

$$\$6,000 + (0.50 \times \$70,000) = \$6,000 + \$35,000 = \$41,000.$$

The marginal tax rate is 50 percent because $0.50 of every extra dollar is paid as taxes. The average tax rate is $41,000/$120,000 \times 34.2 percent. **LO5**

# APPENDIX 1A
# Working with Equations, Graphs, and Tables

**equation** a mathematical expression that describes the relationship between two or more variables

**variable** a quantity that is free to take a range of different values

**dependent variable** a variable in an equation whose value is *determined by* the value taken by another variable in the equation

**independent variable** a variable in an equation whose value *determines* the value taken by another variable in the equation

**constant (or parameter)** a quantity that is fixed in value

Although many of the examples and most of the end-of-chapter problems in this book are quantitative, none require mathematical skills beyond basic high school algebra and geometry. In this brief appendix we review some of the skills you will need for dealing with these examples and problems.

The ability to translate simple verbal descriptions into the relevant equations or graphs is important. You will also need to translate tabular information into equations or graphs, and sometimes you will need to translate graphical information into a table or equation. The following examples illustrate all the tools you will need.

## 1A.1 USING A VERBAL DESCRIPTION TO CONSTRUCT AN EQUATION

We begin with an example that shows how to construct a long-distance telephone billing equation from a verbal description of the billing plan.

### EXAMPLE 1A.1

**Your long-distance telephone plan charges you $5/month plus 10 cents/ minute for long-distance calls. Write an equation that describes your monthly telephone bill.**

An **equation** is a simple mathematical expression that describes the relationship between two or more **variables**—quantities that are free to assume different values in some range. The most common type of equation we'll work with contains two types of variables: **dependent variables** and **independent variables**. In this example, the dependent variable is the dollar amount of your monthly telephone bill, and the independent variable is the variable on which your bill depends; namely, the volume of long-distance calls you make during the month. Your bill also depends on the $5 monthly fee and the 10 cents/minute charge. But in this example, those amounts are *constants*, not variables. A **constant**, also called a **parameter**, is a quantity in an equation that is fixed in value, not free to vary. As the terms suggest, the dependent variable describes an outcome that depends on the value taken by the independent variable.

Once you have identified the dependent variable and the independent variable, choose simple symbols to represent them. In algebra courses, $X$ is typically used to represent the independent variable and $Y$ the dependent variable. Many people find it easier to remember what the variables stand for, however, if they choose symbols that are linked in some straightforward way to the quantities that the variables represent. Thus, in this example, we might use $B$ to represent your monthly *bill* in dollars and $T$ to represent the total *time* in minutes you spent during the month on long-distance calls.

Having identified the relevant variables and chosen symbols to represent them, you are now in a position to write the equation that links them:

$$B = 5 + 0.10T, \qquad\qquad (1A.1)$$

where $B$ is your monthly long-distance bill in dollars and $T$ is your monthly total long-distance calling time in minutes. The fixed monthly fee (5) and the charge per minute (0.10) are parameters in this equation. Note the importance of being clear about the units of measure. Because $B$ represents the monthly bill in dollars, we must also express the fixed monthly fee and the per-minute charge in dollars, which is why the latter number appears in Equation 1A.1 as 0.10 rather than 10. Equation 1A.1 follows the normal convention in which the dependent variable appears by itself on the left-hand side while the independent variable or variables and constants appear on the right-hand side.

Once we have the equation for the monthly bill, we can use it to calculate how much you will owe as a function of your monthly volume of long-distance calls. For example, if you make 32 minutes of calls, you can calculate your monthly bill by simply substituting 32 minutes for $T$ in Equation 1A.1:

$$B = 5 + 0.10(32) = 8.20. \qquad\qquad (1A.2)$$

Your monthly bill when you make 32 minutes of calls is thus equal to $8.20.

---

**Under the monthly billing plan described in Example 1A.1, how much would you owe for a month during which you made 45 minutes of long-distance calls?**

**E X E R C I S E   1 A . 1**

# 1A.2   GRAPHING THE EQUATION OF A STRAIGHT LINE

The next example shows how to portray the billing plan described in Example 1A.1 as a graph.

## E X A M P L E  1A.2

**Construct a graph that portrays the monthly long-distance telephone billing plan described in Example 1A.1, putting your telephone charges, in dollars per month, on the vertical axis, and your total volume of calls, in minutes per month, on the horizontal axis.**

The first step in responding to this instruction is the one we just took; namely, to translate the verbal description of the billing plan into an equation. When graphing an equation, the normal convention is to use the vertical axis to represent the dependent variable and the horizontal axis to represent the independent variable. In Figure 1A.1, we therefore put $B$ on the vertical axis and $T$ on the horizontal axis. One way to construct the graph shown in the figure is to begin by plotting the monthly bill values that correspond to several different total amounts of long-distance calls. For example, someone who makes 10 minutes of calls during the month would have a bill of $B = 5 + 0.10(10) = \$6$. Thus, in Figure 1A.1 the value of 10 minutes/month on the horizontal axis corresponds to a bill of $6/month on the vertical axis (point *A*). Someone who makes 30 minutes of long-distance calls during the month will have a monthly bill of $B = 5 + 0.10(30) = \$8$, so the value of 30 minutes/month on the horizontal axis corresponds to $8/month on the vertical axis (point *C*). Similarly, someone who makes 70 minutes of long-distance calls during the month will have a monthly bill of $B = 5 + 0.10(70) = \$12$, so the value of 70 minutes on the horizontal axis corresponds to $12 on the vertical axis (point *D*). The line joining these points is the graph of the monthly billing equation, 1A.1.

**FIGURE 1A.1**
**The Monthly Telephone Bill in Example 1A.1**
The graph of the equation $B = 5 + 0.10T$ is the straight line shown. Its vertical intercept is 5, and its slope is 0.10.

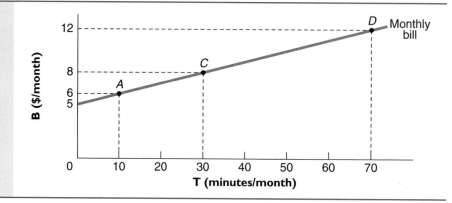

As shown in Figure 1A.1, the graph of the equation $B = 5 + 0.10T$ is a straight line. The parameter 5 is the **vertical intercept** of the line—the value of $B$ when $T = 0$, or the point at which the line intersects the vertical axis. The parameter 0.10 is the **slope** of the line, which is the ratio of the **rise** of the line to the corresponding **run**. The ratio rise/run is simply the vertical distance between any two points on the line divided by the horizontal distance between those points. For example, if we choose points $A$ and $C$ in Figure 1A.1, the rise is $8 - 6 = 2$ and the corresponding run is $30 - 10 = 20$, so rise/run $= 2/20 = 0.10$. More generally, for the graph of any equation $Y = a + bX$, the parameter $a$ is the vertical intercept and the parameter $b$ is the slope.

**vertical intercept** in a straight line, the value taken by the dependent variable when the independent variable equals zero

**slope** in a straight line, the ratio of the vertical distance the straight line travels between any two points **(rise)** to the corresponding horizontal distance **(run)**

**rise** vertical distance a straight line travels between any two points

**run** horizontal distance a straight line travels between any two points

## 1A.3 DERIVING THE EQUATION OF A STRAIGHT LINE FROM ITS GRAPH

The next example shows how to derive the equation for a straight line from a graph of the line.

### EXAMPLE 1A.3

**Figure 1A.2 shows the graph of the monthly billing plan for a new long-distance plan. What is the equation for this graph? How much is the fixed monthly fee under this plan? How much is the charge per minute?**

The slope of the line shown is the rise between any two points divided by the corresponding run. For points $A$ and $C$, rise $= 12 - 8 = 4$, and run $= 40 - 20 = 20$, so the slope equals rise/run $= 4/20 = 1/5 = 0.20$. And since the horizontal intercept of the line is 4, its equation must be given by

$$B = 4 + 0.20T. \tag{1A.3}$$

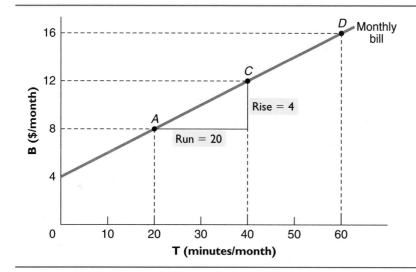

**FIGURE 1A.2**
**Another Monthly Long-Distance Plan**
The vertical distance between points A and C is 12 − 8 = 4 units, and the horizontal distance between points A and C is 40 − 20 = 20, so the slope of the line is 4/20 = 1/5 = 0.20. The vertical intercept (the value of B when T = 0) is 4. So the equation for the billing plan shown is $B = 4 + 0.20T$.

Under this plan, the fixed monthly fee is the value of the bill when $T = 0$, which is \$4. The charge per minute is the slope of the billing line, 0.20, or 20 cents/ minute.

**Write the equation for the billing plan shown in the accompanying graph on the next page. How much is its fixed monthly fee? its charge per minute?**

**EXERCISE 1A.2**

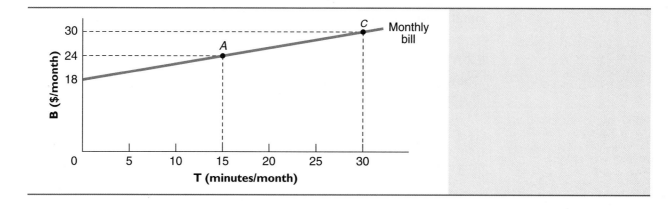

# 1A.4  CHANGES IN THE VERTICAL INTERCEPT AND SLOPE

Examples 1A.4 and 1A.5 and Exercises 1A.3 and 1A.4 provide practice in seeing how a line shifts with a change in its vertical intercept or slope.

### EXAMPLE 1A.4

**Show how the billing plan whose graph is in Figure 1A.2 of Example 1A.3 would change if the monthly fixed fee were increased from \$4 to \$8.**

An increase in the monthly fixed fee from \$4 to \$8 would increase the vertical intercept of the billing plan by \$4 but would leave its slope unchanged. An increase in the fixed fee thus leads to a parallel upward shift in the billing plan by \$4, as shown in Figure 1A.3. For any given number of minutes of long-distance calls, the monthly charge on the new bill will be \$4 higher than on the old bill. Thus, 20 minutes of calls

**FIGURE 1A.3**
**The Effect of an Increase in the Vertical Intercept**
An increase in the vertical intercept of a straight line produces an upward parallel shift in the line.

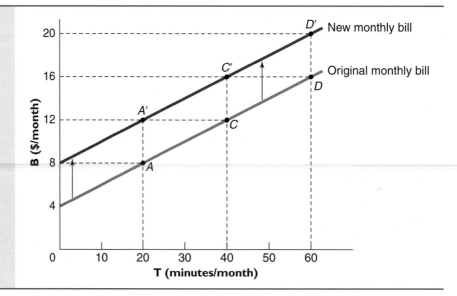

per month cost $8 under the original plan (point *A*) but $12 under the new plan (point *A′*). And 40 minutes costs $12 under the original plan (point *C*) but $16 under the new plan (point *C′*). Sixty minutes costs $16 under the original plan (point *D*) and $20 under the new plan (point *D′*).

**EXERCISE 1A.3**   **Show how the billing plan whose graph is in Figure 1A.2 would change if the monthly fixed fee were reduced from $4 to $2.**

## EXAMPLE **1A.5**

**Show how the billing plan whose graph is in Figure 1A.2 would change if the charge per minute were increased from 20 cents to 40 cents.**

Because the monthly fixed fee is unchanged, the vertical intercept of the new billing plan continues to be 4. But the slope of the new plan, shown in Figure 1A.4, is 0.40, or twice the slope of the original plan. More generally, in the equation $Y = a + bX$, an increase in $b$ makes the slope of the graph of the equation steeper.

**FIGURE 1A.4**
**The Effect of an Increase in the Charge per Minute**
Because the fixed monthly fee continues to be $4, the vertical intercept of the new plan is the same as that of the original plan. With the new charge per minute of 40 cents, the slope of the billing plan rises from 0.20 to 0.40.

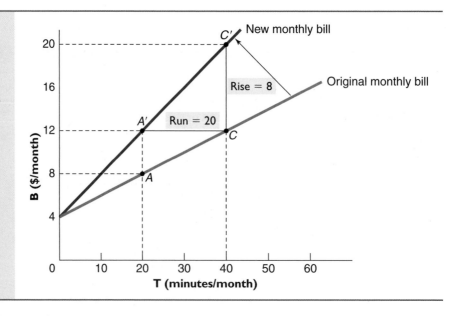

**Show how the billing plan whose graph is in Figure 1A.2 would change if the charge per minute were reduced from 20 cents to 10 cents.**

Exercise 1A.4 illustrates the general rule that in an equation $Y = a + bX$, a reduction in $b$ makes the slope of the graph of the equation less steep.

# 1A.5 CONSTRUCTING EQUATIONS AND GRAPHS FROM TABLES

Example 1A.6 and Exercise 1A.5 show how to transform tabular information into an equation or graph.

## EXAMPLE 1A.6

**Table 1A.1 shows four points from a monthly long-distance telephone billing equation. If all points on this billing equation lie on a straight line, find the vertical intercept of the equation and graph it. What is the monthly fixed fee? What is the charge per minute? Calculate the total bill for a month with one hour of long-distance calls.**

One approach to this problem is simply to plot any two points from the table on a graph. Since we are told that the billing equation is a straight line, that line must be the one that passes through any two of its points. Thus, in Figure 1A.5 we use $A$ to denote the point from Table 1A.1 for which a monthly bill of $11 corresponds to 20 minutes/month of calls (second row) and $C$ to denote the point for which a monthly bill of $12 corresponds to 40 minutes/month of calls (fourth row). The straight line passing through these points is the graph of the billing equation.

**TABLE 1A.1**
**Points on a Long-Distance Billing Plan**

| Long-distance bill ($/month) | Total long-distance calls (minutes/month) |
|---|---|
| 10.50 | 10 |
| 11 | 20 |
| 11.50 | 30 |
| 12 | 40 |

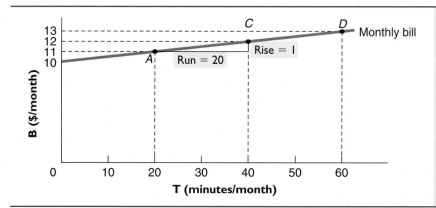

**FIGURE 1A.5**
**Plotting the Monthly Billing Equation from a Sample of Points**
Point $A$ is taken from row 2, Table 1A.1, and point $C$ from row 4. The monthly billing plan is the straight line that passes through these points.

Unless you have a steady hand, however, or use extremely large graph paper, the method of extending a line between two points on the billing plan is unlikely to be very accurate. An alternative approach is to calculate the equation for the billing plan directly. Since the equation is a straight line, we know that it takes the general form

$B = f + sT$, where $f$ is the fixed monthly fee and $s$ is the slope. Our goal is to calculate the vertical intercept $f$ and the slope $s$. From the same two points we plotted earlier, $A$ and $C$, we can calculate the slope of the billing plan as $s$ = rise/run = 1/20 = 0.05.

All that remains, therefore, is to calculate $f$, the fixed monthly fee. At point $C$ on the billing plan, the total monthly bill is $12 for 40 minutes, so we can substitute $B = 12$, $s = 0.05$, and $T = 40$ into the general equation $B = f + sT$ to obtain

$$12 = f + 0.05(40), \tag{1A.4}$$

or

$$12 = f + 2, \tag{1A.5}$$

which solves for $f = 10$. So the monthly billing equation must be

$$B = 10 + 0.05T. \tag{1A.6}$$

For this billing equation, the fixed fee is $10/month, the calling charge is 5 cents/minute ($0.05/minute), and the total bill for a month with one hour of long-distance calls is $B = 10 + 0.05(60) = \$13$, just as shown in Figure 1A.5.

**EXERCISE 1A.5**

**The following table shows four points from a monthly long-distance telephone billing plan.**

| Long-distance bill ($/month) | Total long-distance calls (minutes/month) |
|---|---|
| 20 | 10 |
| 30 | 20 |
| 40 | 30 |
| 50 | 40 |

**If all points on this billing plan lie on a straight line, find the vertical intercept of the corresponding equation without graphing it. What is the monthly fixed fee? What is the charge per minute? How much would the charges be for one hour of long-distance calls per month?**

See Connect for a brief discussion of how simultaneous equations can be used to decide which of two different long-distance billing plans is best for your purposes. As you read this book, you also will find that equations and graphs play a principal role in both microeconomics and macroeconomics. Supply and demand graphs and equations appear in Chapter 3 as only one of many examples. As Chapter 3 will show, supply and demand can be expressed as simultaneous equations in the same way that two long-distance billing plans can be expressed as simultaneous equations.

**KEY TERMS**

| | | |
|---|---|---|
| constant (22) | parameter (22) | variable (22) |
| dependent variable (22) | rise (24) | vertical intercept (24) |
| equation (22) | run (24) | |
| independent variable (22) | slope (24) | |

## ANSWERS TO IN-APPENDIX EXERCISES

**1A.1**  To calculate your monthly bill for 45 minutes of calls, substitute 45 minutes for $T$ in Equation 1A.1 to get $B = 5.00 + 0.10(45) = \$9.50$. **LO1A.1, LO1A.2**

**1A.2**  Calculating the slope using points $A$ and $C$, we have rise $= 30.00 - 24.00 = 6.00$ and run $= 30.00 - 15.00 = 15.00$, so rise/run $= 6/15 = 2/5 = 0.40$. And since the horizontal intercept of the line is 18, its equation is $B = 18 + 0.40T$. Under this plan, the fixed monthly fee is \$18, and the charge per minute is the slope of the billing line, 0.40, or 40 cents/minute. **LO1A.3**

**1A.3**  A \$2 reduction in the monthly fixed fee would produce a downward parallel shift in the billing plan by \$2. **LO1A.4**

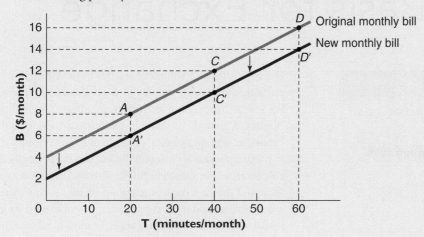

**1A.4**  With an unchanged monthly fixed fee, the vertical intercept of the new billing plan continues to be 4. The slope of the new plan is 0.10, half the slope of the original plan. **LO1A.1, LO1A.5**

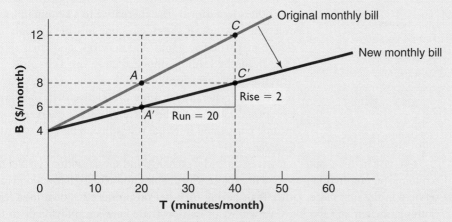

**1A.5**  Let the billing equation be $B = f + sT$, where $f$ is the fixed monthly fee and $s$ is the slope. From the first two points in the table, calculate the slope $s =$ rise/run $= 10/10 = 1$. To calculate $f$, we can use the information in row 1 of the table to write the billing equation as $20 = f + 1(10)$ and solve for $f = 10$. So the monthly billing equation must be $B = 10 + 1.0T$. For this billing equation, the fixed fee is \$10/month, the calling charge is \$1/minute, and the total bill for a month with one hour of long-distance calls is $B = 10 + 1(60) = \$70$. **LO1A.6**

# CHAPTER 2
# Comparative Advantage: The Basis for Exchange

## LEARNING OBJECTIVES

When you have completed this chapter, you will be able to:

**LO1** Explain the principle of comparative advantage.

**LO2** Demonstrate the relationship between opportunity cost and comparative advantage.

**LO3** Explain the principle of increasing opportunity cost.

**LO4** Explain how the menu of goods and services produced by an economy is determined.

**LO5** Identify factors that change an economy's menu of goods and services.

**LO6** Describe transactions of goods and services as a circular flow of income and expenditures in an economy.

During a stint as a volunteer teacher in rural Nepal, a young economic naturalist employed a cook named Birkhaman, who came from a remote Himalayan village in neighbouring Bhutan. Although Birkhaman had virtually no formal education, he was spectacularly resourceful. His primary duties, to prepare food and maintain the kitchen, he performed with competence and dispatch. But he also had many other skills. He could thatch a roof, butcher a goat, and repair shoes. An able tinsmith and a good carpenter, he could sew, fix a broken alarm clock, and plaster walls. On top of all that, he was a local authority on home remedies.

Birkhaman's range of skills was broad even by Nepalese standards. But even the least skilled Nepalese villager can perform a wide range of tasks that most North Americans hire others to perform. The alternative to a system in which everyone is a jack of all trades is one in which people *specialize* in particular goods and services, and then satisfy their needs by trading among themselves. Economic systems based on specialization and the exchange of goods and services are generally far more productive than those with less specialization, and this is a large part of the reason why income per person in Nepal is less than 6 percent of that in Canada.

Our task in this chapter is to investigate why exchange and specialization can increase economic output. In doing so we will explore why people choose to exchange goods and services in the first place, rather than having each person produce his own food, cars, clothing, shelter, and the like. We will focus first on trade between individuals in this chapter. Chapter 15 focuses on comparative advantage and international trade.

A major focus of this chapter is what economists call *comparative advantage.* Roughly speaking, a person has a comparative advantage at producing a particular good or service, let's say haircuts, if that person is *relatively* more efficient at producing haircuts than at producing other goods or services. We will see that we can all consume more of *every* good and service if each of us specializes in the activities at which we have a comparative advantage.

This chapter will also introduce the *production possibilities curve,* which is a graphical method of describing the combinations of goods and services that an economy can produce. The development of this tool will allow us to see much more precisely how specialization enhances the productive capacity of even the simplest economy.

Photo courtesy of Robert H. Frank

Did this man perform most of his own services because he was poor, or was he poor because he performed most of his own services?

# 2.1 EXCHANGE AND OPPORTUNITY COST

Time is a scarce resource, and the fact that there is never enough time to do everything implies that the opportunity cost of spending more time on any one activity is having less time available to spend on others. As the following example makes clear, this helps explain why everyone can do better by concentrating on those activities at which they perform best relative to others.

## EXAMPLE 2.1

### Will Eddie Greenspan be better off if he writes his own will?

Eddie Greenspan graduated from Osgoode Hall Law School in 1968 and was called to the bar in 1970. Today, he is one of Canada's top criminal defence lawyers. Greenspan has defended against charges ranging from drunk driving to murder, and his client list includes notables such as Garth Dzrabinsky and Conrad Black. Passionate about criminal law, Greenspan says, "I defend only innocent people because until they're convicted, everybody is presumed to be innocent," and "If they say they're innocent, they're innocent."[1] If you ever find yourself to be the underdog charged with a felony and up against a tough crown prosecutor, you will rest a little easier if Eddie Greenspan is conducting your defence.

Although Greenspan spends virtually all of his working hours defending people accused of crimes, he also is competent to perform a much broader range of legal services. Suppose, for example, that he could prepare his own will in one hour, only half as long as it would take any other lawyer. Does that mean that Greenspan will be better off if he prepares his own will?

On the strength of his talent as a litigator, Greenspan probably earns several million dollars a year, which means that the opportunity cost of any time he spends preparing his will would be more than $1000 per hour. Lawyers who specialize in property law typically earn far less than that amount. Suppose that Greenspan is able to prepare his will in one hour. Nevertheless, he engages a competent property lawyer who prepares the will in two hours and charges a fee of $700. By not preparing his own will, Greenspan can use the hour he has saved to earn $1000; he can be $300 richer if he employs the property lawyer.

Will a top lawyer make more income if he prepares his own will?

Notice two things in the preceding example. First, Greenspan's considerable skills enable him to write a will in less time than a property lawyer. Because of this, economists would say that Greenspan has an *absolute advantage* at preparing his will. A person has an **absolute advantage** over another person if he or she takes less time to perform a task than the other person does. It also follows that, compared to Greenspan, the property lawyer has an absolute disadvantage in writing wills.

Second, because Greenspan can earn $1000 per hour in trial work, the opportunity cost of his time is $1000 per hour. The opportunity cost of the property lawyer's time is $350 per hour. Because the opportunity cost of the property lawyer's time is $350 per hour, the property lawyer has a *comparative advantage* in preparing wills. A person has a **comparative advantage** over another if his or her opportunity cost of performing a task is lower than the other person's opportunity cost. As the logic of Example 2.2 below shows, it also follows that Greenspan has a comparative advantage in trial work.

Example 2.1 is not an argument that people whose time is valuable should never perform their own services. That example implicitly assumed that Greenspan would have been equally happy spending an hour preparing his will or preparing for a trial. If he was tired of trial preparation and felt it might be enjoyable to refresh his knowledge of property law, preparing his own will might then have made perfect sense! But unless he expected to gain special satisfaction from performing that task, he would almost certainly be better off if he hired a property lawyer. The property lawyer would also benefit, or else she would not have offered to prepare wills for the stated price.

**absolute advantage** one person has an absolute advantage over another if he or she takes fewer hours to perform a task than the other person does

**comparative advantage** one person has a comparative advantage over another if his or her opportunity cost of performing a task is lower than the other person's opportunity cost

1   Andy Halloway, "Eddie Greenspan: On Defence and the Law," *Canadian Business*, 31, January 2005, http://www.canadianbusiness.com (May 2008).

## THE PRINCIPLE OF COMPARATIVE ADVANTAGE

Example 2.1 indicates one of the most important insights economics can offer: when the opportunity costs of performing various tasks are different for different people, they can increase the total value of available goods and services by trading with one another. The following simple example captures the logic behind this insight.

### EXAMPLE 2.2

**Will Rikke be better off if she updates her own Web page?**

Consider the case of Rikke and Beth. Rikke can update a Web page in 20 minutes or repair a bicycle in 10 minutes. Beth can update a Web page in 30 minutes or repair a bicycle in 30 minutes. Table 2.1 summarizes the data: Rikke clearly possesses an absolute advantage over Beth in both activities.

**TABLE 2.1**
**Productivity Information for Rikke and Beth**

|       | Time to update a Web page | Time to complete a bicycle repair |
|-------|---------------------------|-----------------------------------|
| Rikke | 20 minutes                | 10 minutes                        |
| Beth  | 30 minutes                | 30 minutes                        |

Time used to update a Web page cannot be used to repair a bicycle, and vice versa. Thus, each woman incurs an opportunity cost whenever she updates a Web page instead of repairing a bicycle. If Rikke spends 20 minutes updating a Web page, she sacrifices the opportunity to use the same 20 minutes for repairing two bicycles. The opportunity cost of each Web page that Rikke updates is therefore two bicycle repairs. If Beth were to use 30 minutes to update a Web page, she sacrifices the opportunity to use the same 30 minutes to repair a bicycle. The opportunity cost of each Web page that Beth updates is only one bicycle repair. Table 2.2 summarizes the data on the opportunity costs. The left-hand column shows that Beth's opportunity cost of updating a Web page is half the amount of Rikke's. Like the property lawyer who has a *comparative* advantage over the trial lawyer in writing wills, Beth has a *comparative* advantage over Rikke in updating Web pages.

**TABLE 2.2**
**Opportunity Costs for Rikke and Beth**

|       | Opportunity cost of updating a Web page | Opportunity cost of repairing a bicycle |
|-------|-----------------------------------------|-----------------------------------------|
| Rikke | 2 bicycle repairs                       | 0.5 Web-page update                     |
| Beth  | 1 bicycle repair                        | 1  Web-page update                      |

The same reasoning will provide each woman's opportunity cost of repairing bicycles. Since it takes Rikke 20 minutes to update a Web page and only 10 minutes to fix a bicycle, each bicycle repair she does prevents Rikke from updating one half of a Web page; that is, the opportunity cost of each bicycle that Rikke repairs is half a Web-page update. Similarly, the opportunity cost of each bicycle that Beth repairs is one Web-page update. For each woman, the opportunity cost of one bicycle repair is the *reciprocal* of her opportunity cost of updating a Web page. The right-hand column of Table 2.2 shows each woman's opportunity cost of one bicycle repair. Notice that Rikke has a comparative advantage over Beth in bicycle repairs.

Suppose that the community where Rikke and Beth live wants 16 Web page updates per day. If neither person specializes, and Rikke spends one half of her eight-hour workday repairing bicycles and one half updating Web pages, she can update 12 Web pages and repair 24 bicycles. Suppose Beth provides four more updates by spending two hours on Web pages, for a total 16 updates per day between them. With her remaining six hours, Beth can repair 12 bicycles. Together, Rikke and Beth repair 36 bicycles per eight-hour day. These data are summarized in Part A of Table 2.3.

**TABLE 2.3**
**The Gains When Rikke and Beth Specialize**

| | Time spent updating Web pages | Number of updated Web pages | Time spent repairing bicycles | Number of bicycles repaired |
|---|---|---|---|---|
| **Part A: Without Specialization** | | | | |
| Rikke | 4 hours | 12 | 4 hours | 24 |
| Beth | 2 hours | 4 | 6 hours | 12 |
| Total output | | 16 | | 36 |

| | Time spent updating Web pages | Number of updated Web pages | Time spent repairing bicycles | Number of bicycles repaired |
|---|---|---|---|---|
| **Part B: With Specialization According to Comparative Advantage** | | | | |
| Rikke | 0 hours | 0 | 8 hours | 48 |
| Beth | 8 hours | 16 | 0 hours | 0 |
| Total output | | 16 | | 48 |
| Net gain with specialization | | 0 | | 12 |

Suppose each woman had specialized according to comparative advantage. In eight hours Beth would update 16 Web pages and Rikke would repair 48 bicycles. Part B of Table 2.3 summarizes these data. With specialization, 12 more bicycles are repaired, and there is no reduction in the number of Web page updates. Specialization reduces the opportunity cost of the 16 Web page updates the community wants. Therefore, specialization creates 12 additional bicycle repairs!

Rikke is *not* better off if she updates her own Web page, even though she is a faster programmer than Beth. Because she has a comparative advantage in repairing bicycles, Rikke will be better off if she specializes in repairing bicycles and hires Beth to update her Web page.

The details of Example 2.2 include the number of minutes each person needs to complete each task. However, the information necessary to compute the opportunity cost of one good in terms of another can be presented as each person's *productivity* in each task. **Productivity** is units of output per hour divided by units of input per hour. Because the information can be presented in either of these two ways, one must pay careful attention to the form in which it is presented.

Exercise 2.1 below provides data on the labour *productivity* of Mina and Barb. Like Beth and Rikke of Example 2.2, both have skills as computer programmers and bicycle mechanics. Each woman's labour is an input to a production process. Her labour productivity is her output per hour of labour time. Thus, Barb's productivity when she repairs bicycles is three repairs per hour. Barb also can update three Web pages per hour. Barb has a greater productivity in both tasks that gives her an absolute advantage over Mina in both tasks: *greater productivity* confers an *absolute* advantage. However, Barb has a *comparative* advantage in only one task because she has a lower opportunity cost than Mina does in only one task. A *lower opportunity cost* confers a *comparative* advantage. Work through Exercise 2.1 to see how to proceed when information is presented in this alternative format.

**productivity** units of output per hour divided by units of input per hour

EXERCISE 2.1

**Will Barb be better off if she updates her own Web page?**

The following table shows the productivity rates for Barb and Mina in HTML programming and repairing bicycles. Does the fact that Barb can program faster than Mina imply that Barb will be better off if she updates her own Web page?

|       | Productivity in programming    | Productivity in bicycle repair |
|-------|--------------------------------|--------------------------------|
| Mina  | 2 Web-page updates per hour    | 1 repair per hour              |
| Barb  | 3 Web-page updates per hour    | 3 repairs per hour             |

COMPARATIVE
ADVANTAGE

The principle illustrated by Examples 2.1 and 2.2 is so important that we state it formally as one of the core principles:

**The Principle of Comparative Advantage:** Total output is largest when each person concentrates on the activities for which his or her opportunity cost is lowest.

*"We're a natural, Rachel. I handle intellectual property, and you're a content-provider."*

Indeed, the gains made possible from specialization based on comparative advantage constitute the rationale for market exchange. They explain why each person does not devote 10 percent of his time to producing cars, 5 percent to growing food, 25 percent to building housing, 0.0001 percent to performing brain surgery, and so on. By concentrating on those tasks at which we are relatively most productive, together we can produce vastly more than if we all tried to be self-sufficient.

This insight brings us back to Birkhaman the cook. Though Birkhaman's versatility was marvellous, he was not nearly as good a doctor as someone who has been trained in medical school nor as good a repairman as someone who spends each day fixing things. If several people with Birkhaman's talents had joined together, each of them specializing in one or two tasks, together they would have enjoyed more and better goods and services than each could possibly have produced on his own. Although there is much to admire in the resourcefulness of people who have learned through necessity to rely on their own skills, that path is no route to economic prosperity.

## SOURCES OF COMPARATIVE ADVANTAGE

At the individual level, inborn talent can be a source of comparative advantage. For instance, some people seem to be naturally gifted at programming computers, while others seem to have a special knack for fixing bicycles. But nobody is born knowing how to fix bicycles or program computers. Actual ability, at a particular point in time, is always the result of innate ability *plus* education, training, and experience. To understand why some people, such as Eddie Greenspan, are so good at law while others are better at carpentry, we have to examine how those skills were developed.

*RECAP*↰

**EXCHANGE AND OPPORTUNITY COST**

Gains from exchange are possible if trading partners have comparative advantages in producing different goods and services. An individual has a comparative advantage when his or her opportunity cost—measured in terms of other production opportunities foregone—is smaller than the corresponding opportunity costs of his or her trading partners. Maximum production is achieved if each person specializes by producing the good or service in which she has the lowest opportunity cost (the principle of comparative advantage). Comparative advantage makes specialization worthwhile even if one trading partner has an absolute advantage in every activity.

# 2.2 COMPARATIVE ADVANTAGE AND PRODUCTION POSSIBILITIES

Comparative advantage and specialization allow an economy to produce more than if each person tries to produce a little of everything. In this section, we first examine an imaginary economy with only one person and then note how economic possibilities change as additional people join the economy. Along the way, we introduce a useful graph called the *production possibilities curve*, which is used to describe the combinations of goods and services that a particular economy can produce.

## PRODUCTION POSSIBILITIES IN A ONE-PERSON ECONOMY

We begin with a hypothetical economy consisting of a single worker (Susan) who lives on a small island. Susan's options are limited to producing sugar cane and Macadamia nuts. The more time she spends cutting sugar cane, the less time she has available for picking nuts. If she wants more sugar cane, then she must make do with a smaller amount of nuts. Knowing how productive she is at each activity, we can easily summarize the various combinations of sugar cane and nuts she can harvest each day if she makes full use of her available working time (eight hours). This menu of possibilities is known as the **production possibilities curve (PPC)**.

As the following example illustrates, constructing the production possibilities curve for a one-person economy is a straightforward matter.

**production possibilities curve (PPC)** a graph that describes the maximum amount of one good that can be produced for every possible level of production of the other good

### EXAMPLE **2.3**

**What is the production possibilities curve for an economy in which Susan is the only worker?**

Susan has to allocate her production time between sugar cane and nuts. Each hour per day that she devotes to cutting sugar cane yields 1.5 kg of cane, and each hour she devotes to harvesting nuts yields 3 kg of nuts. If Susan works a total of eight hours per day, her production possibilities curve is the graph that displays, for each level of sugar cane she cuts, the maximum amount of nuts that she can pick.

The vertical axis in Figure 2.1 shows Susan's daily production of sugar cane, and the horizontal axis shows her daily production of nuts. It is easiest to understand this graph if we start by looking at two extreme allocations of her time. If she works the full eight hours of her working day cutting sugar cane at the rate of 1.5 kg of sugar cane per hour, she would pick (8 hours/day)(1.5 kg/hour) = 12 kg per day of sugar cane and 0 kg of nuts. That combination of sugar cane and nuts is represented by point *A* in Figure 2.1, the vertical intercept of Susan's production possibilities curve.

Now suppose, instead, that Susan devoted all her time to picking nuts. Picking at a rate of 3 kg of nuts per hour, her total daily production would be (8 hours/day)(3 kg/

hour) = 24 kg of nuts (plus zero sugar cane). That combination is represented by point B in Figure 2.1, the horizontal intercept of Susan's production possibilities curve.

Because Susan's production of each good is exactly proportional to the amount of time she devotes to that good, the remaining points along her production possibilities curve will lie on the straight line that joins A and B. For example, suppose that Susan devotes six hours each day to cutting sugar cane and two hours to picking nuts. She will then produce (6 hours/day)(1.5 kg/hour) = 9 kg of sugar cane and (2 hours/day) (3 kg/hour) = 6 kg of nuts per day, which is the point labelled C in Figure 2.1. Alternatively, if she devotes two hours to sugar cane and six hours to nuts, she will get (2 hours/day)(1.5 kg/hour) = 3 kg of sugar cane and (6 hours/day)(3 kg/hour) = 18 kg of nuts per day. This alternative combination is represented by point D in Figure 2.1.

In this simple example, we have assumed that there is no change in Susan's output per hour, whether she spends more or less time producing nuts or sugar cane. This implies that Susan's production possibilities curve (PPC) is a straight line, with a constant slope. If Susan changes her allocation of time and moves from Point C to Point D, she will give up 6 kgs of sugar cane in order to produce 12 more kilograms of nuts—the slope of Susan's PPC is the ratio of vertical "rise" to horizontal "run"; that is, 6 kg of sugar cane/12 kg of nuts. *Figure 2.1 thus shows graphically that Susan's opportunity cost of an additional kilogram of nuts is 1/2 kg of sugar cane.*

How much sugar cane does Susan give up when she produces more nuts? The opportunity cost (OC) of nuts can be expressed as the following simple formula:

$$OC_{nuts} = \frac{\text{loss in sugar cane}}{\text{gain in nuts}}.$$

One could equally well express the same trade-off in terms of Susan's opportunity cost of sugar cane:

$$OC_{sugar\ cane} = \frac{\text{loss in nuts}}{\text{gain in sugar cane}}.$$

To say that Susan's opportunity cost of an additional kilogram of nuts is 1/2 kg of sugar cane is exactly equivalent to saying that her opportunity cost of 1 kg of sugar cane is 2 kg of nuts.

The production possibilities curve shown in Figure 2.1 is an example of the scarcity problem—when resources are limited, having more of one good or service generally means having to settle for less of another (see Chapter 1). Although in everyday life the "price" of a commodity is usually expressed in dollar terms, economists think of the concept of price in more general terms—what a person has to give up in order to gain something. If Susan

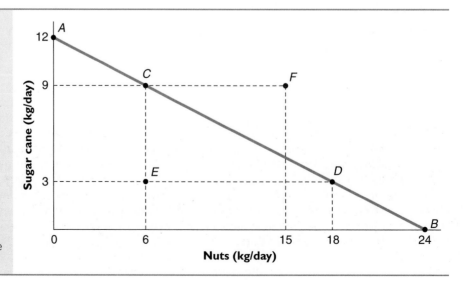

**FIGURE 2.1**

**Attainable and Efficient Points on Susan's Production Possibilities Curve**

Points that lie either on the production possibilities curve (for example, A, C, D, and B) or to its left (for example, E) are said to be attainable. Points that lie to the right the production possibilities curve (for example, F) are unattainable. Points that lie on the curve are said to be efficient, while those that lie within the curve are said to be inefficient.

wants an additional kilogram of sugar cane she can have it, but only if she is willing to give up 2 kg of nuts. The opportunity cost of producing sugar is, in effect, its price (2 kg of nuts).

Any point that lies either on the production possibilities curve or to the left of it is said to be an **attainable point,** meaning that it can be produced with currently available resources. In Figure 2.1, for example, points *A*, *B*, *C*, *D*, and *E* are attainable points. Points that lie to the right of the production possibilities curve are said to be **unattainable** because they cannot be produced using currently available resources. In Figure 2.1, *F* is an unattainable point because Susan cannot produce 9 kg of sugar cane per day *and* 15 kg of nuts.

Points that lie within the curve are said to be **inefficient,** because existing resources would allow for production of more of at least one good without sacrificing the production of any other good. At *E*, for example, Susan is producing only 3 kg of sugar cane per day and 6 kg of nuts, which means that she could increase her harvest of sugar cane by 6 kg per day without giving up any nuts (moving from *E* to *C*). Alternatively, Susan could pick as many as 12 additional kilograms of nuts each day without giving up any sugar cane (moving from *E* to *D*). An **efficient point** is one that lies on the production possibilities curve. At any such point, more of one good can be produced only by producing less of the other.

Note that in distinguishing between *attainable* and *unattainable* levels of production per day we assumed that a workday is composed of 8 working hours. In this example, we assumed Susan could work 8 hours per day because we wanted to specify a working day that could be sustained over time—that was attainable in the longer run, and not just for short periods of time. Clearly, if Susan were to work 18 hours per day, she could produce both more nuts and more sugar cane, but she could not expect to keep this up for too long, since sleeping, eating and other "personal maintenance" activities take time.

Why might Susan be at point E? It is never in her self-interest to use an inefficient technique, but perhaps she has mistakenly adopted an inferior technique (e.g. using a glove which slows her down). By switching to an efficient technique, she gets more of both goods.

## FACTORS THAT INFLUENCE THE PRODUCTION POSSIBILITIES CURVE

To see how the slope and position of the production possibilities curve depend on an individual's productivity, let's compare Susan's PPC to that of a person who is less productive in both activities.

### EXAMPLE 2.4

**How do changes in productivity affect the opportunity cost of nuts?**

Suppose Tom can harvest nuts at a rate of 0.75 kg per hour and sugar cane at 0.75 kg per hour. If Tom lives alone on an island, describe the economy's production possibilities curve.

We can construct Tom's PPC the same way we did Susan's. Note first that if Tom devotes an entire workday (8 hours/day) to cutting sugar cane, he harvests (8 hours/day)(0.75 kg/hour) = 6 kg of sugar cane per day and 0 kg of nuts. Therefore, the vertical intercept of Tom's PPC is *A* in Figure 2.2. If instead he devotes all his time to picking nuts, he gets (8 hours/day)(0.75 kg/hour) = 6 kg of nuts per day and no sugar cane. That means the horizontal intercept of his PPC is *B* in Figure 2.2. As before, because Tom's production of each good is proportional to the amount of time he devotes to it, the remaining points on his PPC will lie along the straight line that joins these two extreme points.

How does Tom's PPC compare with Susan's? Because Tom is less productive than Susan at both activities, the horizontal and vertical intercepts of Tom's PPC lie closer to the origin than do Susan's (see Figure 2.3). For Tom, the opportunity cost of an additional kilogram of nuts is 1 kg of sugar cane, which is twice Susan's opportunity cost of nuts. This difference in opportunity costs shows up as a difference in the slopes of their PPCs: the absolute value of the slope of Tom's PPC is 1, whereas Susan's is 1/2.

**attainable point** any combination of goods that can be produced using currently available resources

**unattainable point** any combination of goods that cannot be produced using currently available resources

**inefficient point** any combination of goods for which currently available resources enable an increase in the production of one good without a reduction in the production of the other

**efficient point** any combination of goods for which currently available resources do not allow an increase in the production of one good without a reduction in the production of the other

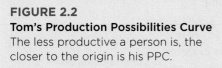

**FIGURE 2.2**
**Tom's Production Possibilities Curve**
The less productive a person is, the closer to the origin is his PPC.

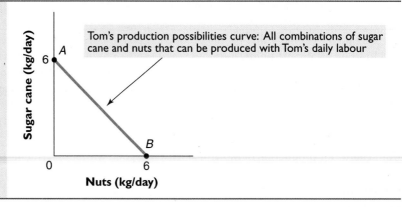

**FIGURE 2.3**
**Individual Production Possibilities Curves Compared**
Though Tom is less productive in both activities than Susan, Tom's opportunity cost of cutting sugar cane is only half that of Susan's.

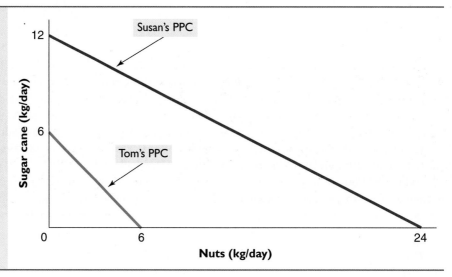

While Tom is absolutely less productive than Susan at harvesting sugar cane, his opportunity cost of sugar cane is only half Susan's. Whereas Susan must give up 2 kg of nuts to cut an additional kilogram of sugar cane, Tom must give up only 1 kg. This difference in opportunity costs illustrates the concept of comparative advantage. Although Susan has an absolute advantage in harvesting both sugar cane and nuts, Tom has a *comparative* advantage in sugar cane because his opportunity cost of cutting sugar cane is less than Susan's.

Notice that the principle of comparative advantage is a relative concept—one that makes sense only when the relative productivities of two or more people (or countries) are being compared. To cement this idea, work through the following exercise.

**EXERCISE 2.2**   **Suppose Susan's output remains the same (she can harvest 1.5 kg of sugar cane per hour or 3 kg of nuts per hour), but Tom develops his skills such that he can pick 0.75 kg of sugar cane per hour or 2.25 kg of nuts per hour. What is Susan's opportunity cost of picking a kilogram of nuts? What is Tom's opportunity cost of picking a kilogram of nuts? Where does Susan's comparative advantage now lie?**

## PRODUCTION POSSIBILITIES IN A TWO-PERSON ECONOMY

As the next examples illustrate, a comparative advantage arising from disparities in individual opportunity costs can create gains for everyone.

## EXAMPLE 2.5

### How does the one-person economy's PPC change when a second person is added?

Suppose Susan and Tom decide to live on the same island. Susan can harvest 1.5 kg of sugar cane or 3 kg of nuts per hour and Tom can harvest 0.75 kg of sugar cane or 0.75 kg of nuts per hour. If they are the only two people in the economy and each works eight hours per day, describe the production possibilities curve for the economy as a whole.

To understand the PPC for a two-person economy, we can start by asking how much sugar cane they would have if both Susan and Tom worked full-time harvesting sugar cane. The answer is 18 kg per day (12 kg from Susan and 6 kg from Tom), so point A in Figure 2.4 is the vertical intercept of the PPC. On the other hand, if Susan and Tom both worked full-time picking nuts, they would pick 30 kg of nuts per day (24 kg from Susan and 6 from Tom) – which gives us point B in Figure 2.4, the horizontal intercept of the PPC.

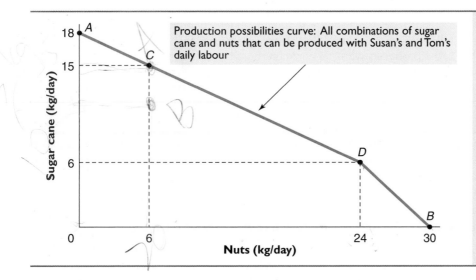

Production possibilities curve: All combinations of sugar cane and nuts that can be produced with Susan's and Tom's daily labour

**FIGURE 2.4**
**The PPC for a Two-Person Economy**
If Tom and Susan want to consume nuts, it makes sense for them to rely initially on Susan, because her opportunity cost of producing nuts is lower than Tom's. Only after Susan is fully occupied picking nuts (point D) will additional nut production start to rely on Tom.

In contrast to the PPC for the one-person economy, however, the PPC for the two-person economy is not a straight line joining the two extreme points. To see why, suppose Susan and Tom were initially devoting all their time to harvesting sugar cane, but then decide they want some nuts. If Susan starts to pick nuts, because her opportunity cost of picking nuts is only half Tom's, they can both be better off. For example, if Susan spent two hours picking nuts while Tom continued to devote all his time to sugar cane, they would lose 3 kg of sugar cane but gain 6 kg of nuts each day. Point C in Figure 2.4 represents this combination.

If Susan devotes all her time to picking nuts while Tom continues to spend all his time on sugar cane, they will be at D in Figure 2.4, which represents 6 kg of sugar cane and 24 kg of nuts per day. If they want to expand nut production any further, Tom will have to take some of his time away from sugar cane. But in doing so, they gain only one additional kilogram of nuts for each kilogram of sugar cane they lose. Notice in Figure 2.4 how the slope of the PPC changes at point D. To the right of point D, the slope of the PPC reflects Tom's opportunity cost of sugar cane, not Susan's.

**To the left of point D in Figure 2.4, what is the slope of the production possibilities curve and what opportunity cost does this slope represent?**

**EXERCISE 2.3**

The PPC for the two-person economy bends outward (is concave to the origin) because of individual differences in opportunity costs. As the following example shows, this distinctive shape represents expanded opportunities for both Susan and Tom.

## EXAMPLE **2.6**

### What is the best way to achieve a given production goal?

Tom and Susan want 15 kg of sugar cane per day and 6 kg of nuts. If their productive abilities are as described in Example 2.5, what is the most effective way of dividing their labour?

Though Tom has a comparative advantage in harvesting sugar cane, even if he spends all his time harvesting sugar cane, he can cut only (8 hours/day)(0.75 kg/hour = ) 6 kg per day. So Susan will have to harvest the additional 9 kg of sugar cane to achieve their production target of 15 kg. Since Susan is capable of harvesting (8 hours/day)(1.5 kg/hour) = 12 kg of sugar cane per day, she will need only six hours per day to harvest 9 kg. She can spend the remaining two hours picking nuts, which is exactly the amount of time she needs to pick their production target of 6 kg. In terms of their two-person production possibilities curve, this allocation of labour puts Susan and Tom at point *C* in Figure 2.4. At the optimal division of labour (point *C*), Tom specializes completely in sugar cane because his opportunity cost of harvesting sugar cane is less than Susan's. Susan, whose opportunity cost of harvesting sugar cane is higher than Tom's, harvests only as much sugar cane as is needed to complete their production target. This allocation of labour enables the desired quantity of sugar to be produced with the minimum possible sacrifice of nuts. It also illustrates **The Principle of Increasing Opportunity Cost:** when increasing the production of any good, first employ those resources with the lowest opportunity cost. Only when all of the lowest cost resources are employed does it make economic sense to use resources that have higher opportunity costs.

INCREASING
OPPORTUNITY
COST

**The Principle of Increasing Opportunity Cost:** When increasing the production of any good, first employ those resources with the lowest opportunity cost. Only when all of the lowest cost resources are employed does it make economic sense to use resources that have higher opportunity costs.

## HOW MUCH DOES SPECIALIZATION MATTER?

In Example 2.6, Tom specialized completely in sugar cane, his area of comparative advantage (lowest opportunity cost). Susan did not specialize completely in picking nuts because if she had, the two would have harvested more nuts and less sugar cane than they wanted. Given what they wanted, Tom and Susan still did better when Tom specialized entirely and Susan specialized only partially than they could have if neither had specialized, as Example 2.7 demonstrates.

## EXAMPLE **2.7**

### How much does specialization expand opportunity?

Suppose that Tom and Susan decide to avoid specialization; for example, in Example 2.6, suppose Tom had divided his time equally between nuts and sugar cane, thus producing (4 hours/day)(0.75 kg/hour) = 3 kg of sugar cane/day and (4 hours/day)(0.75 kg/hour) = 3 kg of nuts/day. Susan then devotes one hour to harvesting nuts, thus producing (1 hour/day)(3 kg/hour) = 3 kg of nuts/day. This gives Tom and Susan 6 kg of nuts, just as before, and leaves Susan with 7 hours/day to harvest sugar cane. How much worse off would they have been?

With seven hours, Susan can produce (7 hours/day)(1.5 kg/hour = 10.5 kg sugar cane/day. If Tom and Susan organize their labour this way, they will harvest the 6 kg of nuts that they want. However, they also will have 4.5 kg less of sugar than if Tom had specialized entirely. Susan and Tom would pay a higher opportunity cost than necessary to obtain 6 kg of nuts.

## A PRODUCTION POSSIBILITIES CURVE FOR A MANY-PERSON ECONOMY

The real world obviously has many millions of producers, not just one or two. But the process of constructing a production possibilities curve for an economy with millions of workers is conceptually similar. Consider again an economy in which the only two goods are sugar cane and nuts, with sugar cane again on the vertical axis and nuts on the horizontal axis. We can still ask how much sugar cane could be produced if all available workers worked full-time picking sugar cane, and this is still given by the vertical intercept of the economy's PPC. For the hypothetical economy in Figure 2.5, the maximum attainable amount of sugar cane production is 100 000 kg per day (an amount chosen arbitrarily, for illustrative purposes). The horizontal intercept of the PPC is the amount of nuts that could be gathered if all available workers worked full-time gathering nuts, shown for this same economy as 80 000 kg per day (also an amount chosen arbitrarily). Unlike the earlier examples involving one or two workers, the PPC shown in Figure 2.5 looks like a smooth curve that is bowed out from the origin. Of course, that appearance depends heavily on the scale, since Figure 2.5 is now measuring production in thousands of kilos. If we could zoom in on it, we would see that the curve is really made up of thousands of small line segments, each corresponding to one of thousands of workers. But the key point of Figure 2.5 is the same as the key point of Figure 2.4: the opportunity cost of nuts increases as the economy produces more of them. When the economy moves from *A*, where it is producing only sugar cane, to *B*, 20 000 kg of nuts per day are gained by giving up only 5000 kg per day of sugar cane. When nut production is increased still further, however— for example, by moving from *B* to *C*—the economy gives up 5000 kg per day of sugar cane yet gains only 10 000 additional kilograms of nuts. This pattern of increasing opportunity cost persists over the entire length of the PPC. In moving from *D* to *E*, the economy again gives up 5000 kg per day of sugar cane but now gains only 2000 kg of nuts per day. Note that the same pattern of increasing opportunity cost applies to sugar cane. Thus, as progressively more sugar cane is produced, the opportunity cost of producing additional sugar cane, as measured by the amount of nuts that must be sacrificed, also increases.

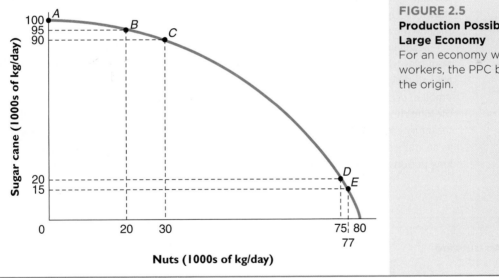

**FIGURE 2.5**

**Production Possibilities Curve for a Large Economy**

For an economy with millions of workers, the PPC bows outward from the origin.

Why is the PPC for the multi-person economy bow shaped? If some people are better at gathering nuts while others are better at cutting sugar cane, and if we start from initially producing only sugar cane and want to begin producing some nuts, which workers will we reassign? Recall Susan and Tom, the two workers discussed in Example 2.5. Tom's comparative advantage was cutting sugar cane and Susan's comparative advantage was picking nuts. If both workers were currently cutting sugar cane and you wanted to reassign one of them to gather nuts instead, whom would you send? Susan would be the clear choice, because her departure would cost the economy only half as much sugar cane as Tom's and would augment nut production by twice as much.

The principle is the same in any large multi-person economy, except that the range of differences in opportunity cost across workers is even greater than in the earlier two-worker example (Example 2.5). As we keep reassigning workers from cutting sugar cane to picking nuts, it makes sense to start by transferring the people who are not very good at cutting sugar cane. However, sooner or later we must reassign even sugar specialists like Tom. Indeed, we must eventually reassign others whose opportunity cost of producing nuts is far higher than his.

The shape of the production possibilities curve shown in Figure 2.5 illustrates the principle of increasing opportunity cost: *when increasing the production of any good, first employ those resources with the lowest opportunity cost*. This strategy will provide increased amounts of one good at the smallest possible sacrifice of other goods. In the context of our examples, using the principle of increasing opportunity cost allows each additional kilogram of nuts to be obtained with the smallest possible sacrifice of sugar cane, and vice versa.

The PPC of Figure 2.5 is a smooth curve, bowed outward from the origin, which is a contrast with the PPC of Figure 2.4 which is made up of two straight lines. Each of the two straight lines has a different slope, and the slope of each line represents a set of opportunity costs associated with one worker. Consider, for example, Figure 2.4. Susan's opportunity cost of nuts is lower than Tom's and is represented by the slope of the longer line segment. Tom's opportunity cost of nuts is represented by the slope of the shorter line segment. Because Susan's opportunity cost of nuts is lower than Tom's, the slope of her section of the PPC is shallower than Tom's. Figure 2.5 is intended to represent an economy with many thousands, perhaps millions, of workers. With many workers, individual segments of the PPC are such a small fraction of total potential output as to be indistinguishable. Therefore, the PPC in Figure 2.5 looks like a smooth curve.

## THE CAUSES OF SHIFTS IN THE ECONOMY'S PRODUCTION POSSIBILITIES CURVE

As its name implies, the production possibilities curve provides a summary of the production options open to any society at one point in time. At any given moment, the PPC shown in Figure 2.5 is a graphical representation of a fundamental trade-off confronting society: the only way people can produce more nuts is to produce less sugar cane.

Many important factors change over time, like technology or human skills or the total resources which people have to work with. In constructing the PPC, we have implicitly held all these factors constant, in order to concentrate our attention on the key economic problem of how best to allocate a given amount of resources at a point in time. However, in the long run it is often possible to increase production of all goods—indeed, this is what is meant by economic growth. As shown in Figure 2.6, economic growth can be represented as an outward shift in the economy's production possibilities curve. If maintained over long periods of time, economic growth can greatly enhance standards of living.

**FIGURE 2.6**
**Economic Growth: An Outward Shift in the Economy's PPC**
Increases in productive resources (such as labour and capital equipment) or improvements in knowledge and technology cause the PPC to shift outward. They are the main factors that drive economic growth.

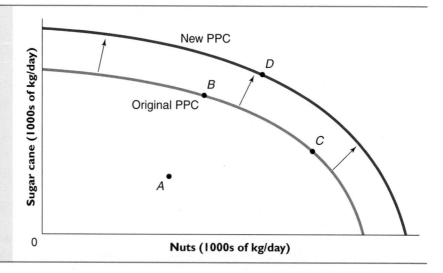

In Figure 2.6, point *A* represents an inefficient level of output. Because *A* lies within the production possibilities curve, it shows that even without changing technology or total labour force or available resources, the economy could produce more of both goods just by moving to the PPC (e.g., moving from *A* to either *B* or *C*).

Why, you may ask, might an economy ever be at point *A*? One possibility is poorly designed laws (imagine, for example, the impact on agricultural output of a law that dictated that all crops must be picked with the left hand only!). Another possibility is that some resources are involuntarily unemployed. The conditions under which recessions occur, causing labour and other resources to be idle, is an important topic in macroeconomics. Whatever the reason, if an economy is operating at any point within its production possibilities curve, it is being productively inefficient because it is not using all of its economic resources in their technically most effective way. **Productive efficiency** occurs when an economy is using all of its economic resources in their technically most effective way. Any point on a possibility curve represents a state of *productive efficiency*.

But even if both points *B* and *C* are on the PPC and are *productively efficient*, what combination of output of nuts or sugar cane would people prefer? At both *B* and *C*, more of one commodity can only be obtained at the sacrifice of some of the other. However, it might be that the economy is at point *C*, producing a relatively large amount of nuts and relatively little sugar cane, but people's tastes are such that everybody could be made happier if the economy were at *B*, with less nuts and more sugar cane. If resources can be reallocated so that people would be better off if the economy moved *along* the PPC to a different point on the curve, then the economy is in a state of *allocative inefficiency*. If it is impossible to reorganize economic resources so that at least one person is better off while nobody is worse off, the economy has accomplished a state of **allocative efficiency**.

Point *D* in Figure 2.6 is a point on a new PPC. While Figure 2.5 drew a PPC for a single point in time, Figure 2.6 draws the PPC for the economy at two points in time. With the technology and stock of productive resources available at the original point in time, *D* was unattainable. However, over time, economic growth from increases in the amount of productive resources available or from improvements in knowledge or technology that make resources more productive can shift the PPC outwards. If the PPC shifts out, the economy can produce more of both goods. Economic growth, if maintained over a long period of time, can produce dramatic improvements in the standard of living. The study of the determinants of economic growth is a major topic in macroeconomics.

**productive efficiency** occurs when an economy is using all of its economic resources in their technically most effective way.

**allocative efficiency** occurs when it is impossible to reorganize economic resources so that at least one person is better off while nobody is worse off

---

**RECAP**

### COMPARATIVE ADVANTAGE AND PRODUCTION POSSIBILITIES

For an economy that produces two goods, the *production possibilities curve* describes the maximum amount of one good that can be produced for every possible level of production of the other good. *Attainable points* are those that lie on or within the curve, and *efficient points* are those that lie along the curve. The slope of the production possibilities curve tells us the opportunity cost of producing an additional unit of the good measured along the horizontal axis. The principle of increasing opportunity cost tells us that the slope of the production possibilities curve becomes steeper as we move downward to the right. The greater the differences among individual opportunity costs, the more bow shaped the production possibilities curve will be, and the more bow shaped the production possibilities curve, the greater will be the potential gains from specialization.

Economic growth can be represented by an outward shift of the production possibilities curve. It can arise from an increase in the amount of productive resources available to an economy, from improvements in knowledge and technology, and from formation of physical capital. Small differences from one country to another in the rate at which any of these factors change will cause differences in the rate of economic growth. If the differences are sustained over long periods of time they can result in large differences in material standards of living.

## 2.3  SPECIALIZATION AND STANDARDS OF LIVING

Specialization enhances standards of living in several ways. Specialization eliminates the switching and start-up costs incurred when people have to move back and forth among numerous tasks—greater productive efficiency is the result as the economy moves to the PPC. When productive activity is organized according to comparative advantage, the opportunity cost of a given amount of output is reduced; greater allocative efficiency implies that the amount of goods and services a society can obtain from its resources is increased. The greater the differences are in opportunity costs, the greater the gains are that comparative advantage and trade make available.

Finally, specialization deepens existing skills through practice and experience, and thereby shifts out the PPC over time. These gains apply both to people and the tools or equipment they use. Specialization depends on investment in machinery and education, because highly skilled workers often need specialized equipment and education to carry out their tasks. Because only large markets can absorb the quantities of goods and services these workers can produce, specialization depends on access to such markets. Conversely, isolation, through its reduced access to large markets, greatly reduces opportunities to specialize.

### CAN WE HAVE TOO MUCH SPECIALIZATION?

As in any issue in economics, however, if we want to analyze specialization we should think about both costs and benefits. The mere fact that specialization boosts productivity does not mean that more specialization is always better than less, for specialization also entails costs. For example, most people appear to enjoy variety in the work they do, but variety tends to be one of the first casualties as workplace tasks become ever more narrowly specialized.

Drawing by Gini Kennedy

Charlie Chaplin's 1936 film, *Modern Times,* paints a vivid portrait of the psychological costs of repetitive factory work. As an assembly worker, Chaplin's only task, all day every day, is to tighten the nuts on two bolts as they pass before him on the assembly line. Finally he snaps and walks zombie-like from the factory, wrenches in hand, tightening every nut-like protuberance he encounters.

*Modern Times* was filmed nearly eighty years ago, and since then industrial engineers have realized that good job design involves finding the right balance between the benefits and costs of specialization. Modern factory designers recognize that excessive specialization will hurt the motivation of workers to produce high quality output, and may cost more in the long run, so now there is a conscious effort to avoid inefficient specialization.

# 2.4 THE CIRCULAR FLOW OF INCOME AND EXPENDITURE

We started the discussion of a production possibilities curve with the example of Susan, living alone on an island. For her, there is no trade or exchange, only her own production and consumption. In a one-person economy, there can be no gains from specialization. In the next example, which concerned a two-person economy (Tom and Susan), the PPC showed that specialization could increase total production. Moreover, exchange is simple in a two-person, two-good economy. If either Tom or Susan want to consume amounts of sugar and nuts different from what they each produce themselves, they can trade only with each other. In a hypothetical two-person, two-good economy, exchange is simple—nuts can be bartered for sugar cane or vice versa.

In a real economy, millions of people are employed in hundreds of thousands of categories of specialized jobs, and hundreds of thousands of commodities are bought and sold. Complex specialization and exchange are inextricably linked. A doctor who spends most of the day with patients must depend on someone else to grow her food, weave the cloth for her clothes and manufacture her car. Accountants and car mechanics similarly depend on someone else to produce their electricity, and teach their children and so on. In rich nations, because we all are highly specialized in our work, we all depend on the cooperation of many other individuals to obtain the things we need and desire.

The complexity of a large modern economy means that barter is rarely feasible. In our simplified two-person example, if Susan wants to trade macadamia nuts for sugar cane at the exactly the same time and place that Tom wants to trade sugar cane for nuts, then barter can work, but this "mutual coincidence of wants" is rare in a modern economy. Most of us, instead, sell our labour in return for money that we can then spend to obtain the goods and services we want, when we want them.

As we exchange goods and services for money, each of us, every day, engages in a sequence of economic transactions, every one of which can be viewed from two angles. When a student buys a coffee before class, that transaction is a purchase from the student's point of view and a sale from the coffee shop's point of view. When an employer pays a student for working a part-time job, the payment is expenditure for the employer and income for the student.

These transactions are interdependent; to stick with the previous example, students are able to buy coffee if they have the money, which they may get from their part-time jobs, and coffee shop owners need to make sales in order to have the money to pay their part time staff. More generally, labour earnings enable households to make consumption expenditures, and consumer spending provides the revenue that enables firms to hire workers and pay wages.

One way to represent visually this interdependence of spending is Figure 2.7, the *circular flow diagram*. In general, a **circular flow diagram** provides an illustration of exchange relationships in a monetary economy highlighting the mutual dependence of incomes and expenditures. Figure 2.7 can be made much more realistic, but the simplest version of the circular flow diagram is sufficient for our purposes here. It represents a very simple economy that has no government, no financial sector, and does not engage in foreign trade. In the example with Susan and Tom's production of sugar cane and nuts that we used to construct Figure 2.4, the only input needed for production was labour, and the only decision made was how much of each commodity to harvest. When goods are sold for money and money is exchanged for labour time, we have the sort of very simple economy represented in Figure 2.7.

Despite being a simplification, Figure 2.7 can represent the main idea of the circular flow of expenditure and exchange. Each transaction is represented by two flows: money (marked in red) and goods or services (marked in blue). Individuals, living in households, sell their

**circular flow diagram** an illustration of exchange relationships in a monetary economy highlighting the mutual dependence of incomes and expenditures

**FIGURE 2.7**
**The Circular Flow of Income and Expenditure**
This diagram links income and expenditure in a highly simplified model of the economy. The outer set of arrows in red indicates money or dollar flows in the economy. The inner set of arrows in blue indicates the flows of real inputs and goods and services.

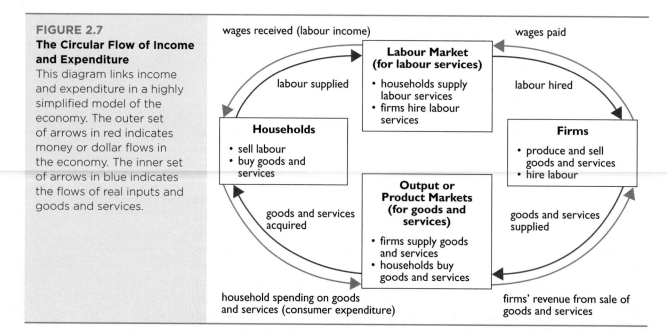

labour services to firms. Firms use the labour they hire to produce goods and services that they sell to households. The blue arrows in the upper half of Figure 2.7 indicate the flow of labour through the labour market to firms. The blue arrows in the lower half indicate the flow of goods and services from firms through markets for goods and services to households. Thus, the blue inner arrows indicate a flow of real (or physical) units. The outer red lines represent money flows.

As indicated by the red arrows in the upper half of Figure 2.7, wages and salaries are expenditures that flow from firms through the labour market to households, where they are received as income. Red arrows in the lower half show the payments flowing from households through markets for goods and services to firms. The expenditures of households are the income of firms and the expenditures of firms are the incomes of households. Because the red outer arrows represent monetary flows in the economy, in general, one party's expenditure is always somebody else's income.[2]

Two types of markets are imbedded in the circular flow of Figure 2.7.[3] Different groups of microeconomic actors interact in these markets. For example, firms hire workers in the "Labour Market" in the upper part of Figure 2.7; in Chapter 12, we will analyze how labour markets work. Goods and services are exchanged in "Output or Product Markets," which appear in the lower part of Figure 2.7. Like the labour market, the market for goods and services can be subdivided into a number of different, smaller markets. Some of these markets may be characterized by many buyers and sellers; we will discuss this type of market in depth in Chapters 4 to 7. Others may have only a few sellers and many buyers (see Chapters 8 and 9). Some markets, for example the market for lumber, may be characterized by products that can be easily graded according to quality. It may be very difficult to observe the quality of products in other markets, such as the market for used cars. These variations are considered in Chapter 11. The subject of this book is microeconomics, or the analysis of individual markets, but the contribution of the circular flow diagram reminds us that each

---

2   This two-sided nature of every transaction produces an important result. If we sum *sales* of all final goods and services and then sum *purchases* of all final goods and services, the two totals are identical. *The two sums must tally to the same number!*

3   The circular flow also could be modified to include government and international trade and markets for investment goods. We could represent each sector with its own box and an accompanying set of arrows. Each sector would have its own set of underlying microeconomic components. Our immediate task does not require the additional complexity, but the same simple principle always would remain. Every transaction has two sides—one person's expenditure always is another person's income. Therefore, the total value of expenditures must always equal the total value of receipts.

individual market is part of a general equilibrium of many markets. Because sales of goods depend on consumer expenditures, which depend on household incomes, which depend in turn on the firms' sales, each market depends indirectly on all others.

In the simplified example that began this chapter, only two goods were being produced: macadamia nuts and sugar cane. This was a very special kind of example, because the only input needed for production in a given year was the labour required to harvest nuts and sugar cane, and in the example, both the sugar cane and the macadamia trees had already been planted. In the real world, although sugar cane will grow back from its roots after being cut, it will only do so for a number of years (from 4 to 10, depending on climate and soils) before replanting is necessary. Macadamia trees have a longer productive life (up to a hundred years), but eventually they also have to be replanted. In the real world, the amount of production that is possible in any given year depends heavily on the amount of planting that has occurred in previous years. Fields of sugar cane and orchards of macadamia trees are types of capital. The formation of capital and economic growth are important topics in *macro*economics. Nevertheless, decisions about how many macadamia trees or how much sugar cane will be planted are made at the *micro*economic level.

Macadamia orchards and sugar cane fields are examples of productive assets that, if maintained, will yield crops for years to come. Buildings, roads, machinery, and many other types of structures similarly constitute assets that enhance a society's ability to produce goods and services in the future. These long-lasting assets that are produced by the economy and used as inputs to the production process are known as **physical capital**, or simply **capital goods**. Different countries have historical differences in the levels of productive assets they have formed. Differing levels of past formation of many types of productive assets constitute one important reason why the production possibilities curve, which we drew in Figure 2.6, shifts out at different rates in different countries.

**capital goods (or physical capital)** durable, long-lasting assets produced by the economy and used as inputs to the production process

 **RECAP**

Incomes and expenditures are mutually dependent. Every transaction has two sides: one person's expenditure always is another person's income. A circular flow diagram can be used to illustrate exchange relationships in a monetary economy.

## SUMMARY

■ One person has an *absolute* advantage over another in the production of a good if she can produce more of that good than the other person. One person has a *comparative* advantage over another in the production of a good if she is relatively more efficient than the other person at producing that good, meaning that her opportunity cost of producing it is lower than her counterpart's. Specialization based on comparative advantage is the basis for economic exchange. When each person specializes in the task at which she is relatively most efficient, the economic pie is maximized, making possible a larger slice for everyone. **LO1**

■ A comparative advantage may spring from differences in talent or ability or from differences in education, training, and experience. **LO1**

■ The production possibilities curve is a simple device for summarizing the possible combinations of output that a society can produce if it employs its resources efficiently. In a simple economy that produces only sugar cane and nuts, the PPC shows the maximum quantity of sugar cane production (vertical axis) possible at each level of nut production (horizontal axis). The slope of the PPC at any point represents the opportunity cost of nuts at that point, expressed in kilograms of sugar cane. **LO2, LO4**

■ All production possibilities curves slope downward because of the scarcity problem, which implies that the only way to obtain more of one good is to accept less of another. In a nut/sugar cane economy whose workers have different opportunity costs of picking nuts, the slope of the PPC becomes steeper with increasing production of nuts and movement down the curve. This change in slope illustrates the principle of increasing opportunity cost, which states that in expanding the production of any good, a society minimizes its opportunity cost by first employing those resources that are relatively efficient at producing that good. Only when all of the lowest-cost resources are employed does it make economic sense to use resources that have higher opportunity costs. **LO3**

■ The circular flow of income and expenditure emphasizes that every transaction is two-sided. One party's sale (or income) always is another party's expenditure. The circular flow also emphasizes the interdependence of the individuals who live and work in an economy. The more specialized people become, the more they must depend on each other to obtain the goods and services they want. **LO6**

■ Economic growth improves an economy's ability to produce goods and services. **LO5**

## CORE PRINCIPLES

**The Principle of Comparative Advantage**
Total output is largest when each person concentrates on the activities for which his or her opportunity cost is lowest. (34)

**The Principle of Increasing Opportunity Cost**
In expanding the production of any good, first employ those resources with the lowest opportunity cost. Only when all of the lowest cost resources have been employed does it make economic sense to use resources that have higher opportunity costs. (40)

## KEY TERMS

absolute advantage (31)
allocative efficiency (43)
attainable point (36)
capital goods (or physical capital) (47)

circular flow diagram (45)
comparative advantage (31)
efficient point (36)
inefficient point (36)
productive efficiency (42)

production possibilities curve (35)
productivity (33)
unattainable point (36)

## REVIEW QUESTIONS

1. Explain what having a comparative advantage at producing a particular good or service means. What does having an absolute advantage at producing a good or service mean? **LO1**

2. How will a reduction in the number of hours worked each day affect an economy's production possibilities curve? **LO5**

3. How will technological innovations that boost labour productivity affect an economy's production possibilities curve? **LO5**

4. Why does saying that people are poor because they do not specialize make more sense than saying that people perform their own services because they are poor? **LO4**

5. Why does every purchase of a good or service represent both expenditure and income? **LO6**

## PROBLEMS

1. Consider a society whose only worker is Helen, who allocates her production time between cutting hair and baking bread. Each hour per day she devotes to cutting hair yields 4 haircuts, and each hour she devotes to baking bread yields 8 loaves of bread. If Helen works a total of 8 hours per day, graph her production possibilities curve. **LO4**

2. Refer to Problem 1. Which of the points listed below is efficient? Which is attainable? **LO4**
   a. 28 haircuts/day, 16 loaves/day
   b. 16 haircuts/day, 32 loaves/day
   c. 18 haircuts/day, 24 loaves/day

3. Determine whether the following statements are true or false, and briefly explain why. **LO1, LO4**
   a. Toby can produce 5 L of apple cider or 70 g of feta cheese per hour. Kyle can produce 3 L of apple cider or 42 g of feta cheese per hour. Therefore, Toby and Kyle cannot benefit from specialization and trade.
   b. A doctor who can vacuum her office faster and more thoroughly than commercial cleaners is better off if she cleans her office herself.
   c. In an economy in which millions of workers each have different opportunity costs of producing two goods, the principle of comparative advantage implies that the slope of the production possibilities curve decreases in absolute value as more of the goods on the horizontal axis are produced.

4. Nancy and Bill are auto mechanics. Nancy takes 4 hours to replace a clutch and 2 hours to replace a set of brakes. Bill takes 6 hours to replace a clutch and 2 hours to replace a set of brakes. Bill and Nancy open a motor repair shop. Which of the following statements are correct? **LO1, LO4**
   a. If Nancy works only on clutches, and Bill works only on brakes, both will be better off.
   b. Bill has a comparative advantage at replacing brakes.
   c. Nancy has an absolute advantage at replacing clutches.
   d. Nancy has a comparative advantage at replacing clutches.
   e. All but one of the above statements are correct.

5. Bob and Stella are a married couple. Bob takes 10 minutes to change a lightbulb and 2 minutes to fix a broken fuse. Stella takes 3 minutes to change a lightbulb and 30 seconds to fix a broken fuse. Which of the following statements are true? **LO1, LO4**
   a. Stella has a comparative advantage at fixing fuses, because she can do it faster than Bob.

   b. Stella has a comparative advantage at changing lightbulbs and fixing fuses, because she can do both of them faster than Bob.
   c. Stella has an absolute advantage at changing lightbulbs and fixing fuses, because she can do both of them faster than Bob.
   d. Bob has a comparative advantage at fixing fuses, because Stella has a comparative advantage at changing lightbulbs.
   e. Stella has a comparative advantage at changing light bulbs.

6. Kamal and Filipe are stranded together on a desert island. The raw materials on the island are suitable only for making beer and pizza, but in unlimited quantities. What is scarce is labour. Filipe and Kamal each spend 10 hours a day making beer or pizza. The following table specifies *how much beer and pizza Filipe and Kamal can produce per hour.* **LO4**

   |        | Beer                | Pizza             |
   |--------|---------------------|-------------------|
   | Filipe | 1 bottle per hour   | 0.2 pizzas per hour |
   | Kamal  | 1.5 bottles per hour | 0.5 pizzas per hour |

   a. Draw the daily production possibilities curves (PPCs) for Filipe and Kamal.
   b. Who has an absolute advantage in making pizza? in brewing beer?
   c. Who has a comparative advantage in making pizza? in brewing beer?

   Now suppose their preferences are as follows: Filipe wants 2 beers and as much pizza as he can eat each day while Kamal wants 2 pizzas and as much beer as he can drink each day.
   d. If each man is self-reliant, how much beer and pizza will Filipe and Kamal eat and drink?
   e. Suppose the two men decide to trade with each other. Draw their joint PPC, and give an example of a trade that will make each of them better off.

7. Rework Problem 6 with the following changes: **LO1, LO4**
   a. Each individual's productivity is shown in the table that follows, *which specifies the number of hours each man needs to produce a single unit of beer and pizza.*
   b. Filipe wants 6 beers and as much pizza as he can eat each day, while Kamal wants 2 pizzas and as much beer as he can drink each day.

   |        | Production time for 1 beer | Production time for 1 pizza |
   |--------|----------------------------|-----------------------------|
   | Filipe | 5/4 hours                  | 5/3 hours                   |
   | Kamal  | 5 hours                    | 5/2 hours                   |

8. Suppose Filipe and Kamal's production possibilities curves from Problem 7 are combined. What would be the maximum number of pizzas available to Filipe and Kamal if they could buy or sell in a world market in which 1 beer could be exchanged for 1 pizza? What would be the maximum number of beers available to them? **LO2**

9. Kate and William both can produce oranges and olive oil. Kate can produce up to 10 kg of oranges per week or 5 bottles of olive oil, or any combination of oil and oranges along a straight-line production possibilities curve linking those two points. William can produce up to 50 kg of oranges per week or 1 bottle of olive oil, or any combination along a straight-line production possibilities curve linking those points. **LO1, LO2, LO3**

   a. Does the principle of increasing opportunity cost apply in either of these two economies? Why or why not?

   b. Suppose Kate and William agree that each will specialize in the production of either oil or oranges. According to the principle of comparative advantage, who will specialize in which commodity?

   c. If Kate and William agree to trade oranges and olive oil with each other, what are the maximum and minimum prices that can prevail for oranges, in terms of bottles of olive oil?

10. Jay, Kay, and Dee are marooned alone on the Greek island of Skorpios. They must find a way to provide themselves with food and drinking water. The following table shows how many hours each person takes to produce one unit of food or one unit of water. **LO2, LO4**

| | Production time for 1 unit of food | Production time for 1 unit of drinking water |
|---|---|---|
| Jay | 1 hour | 2 hours |
| Kay | 2 hours | 1 hour |
| Dee | 4 hours | 6 hours |

   a. If each person can work for 12 hours a day and each person provides only for himself or herself, draw their individual PPCs.

   b. Suppose Jay, Kay, and Dee decide to produce food and water cooperatively, so they can gain from trade. Draw their combined production possibilities curve.

   c. If the trio wants, in aggregate, to consume 15 units of food and 12 units of water, who will specialize in food production? Who will specialize in water production? Will anyone divide his or her time between food and water production?

   d. If the trio wants, in aggregate, to consume 6 units of water and as much food as possible, who will specialize in food and who will specialize in water? Will anyone divide his or her time between food and water production? How much food will be produced?

   e. Suppose production is as in part (c). Dee suggests dividing the output equally among the three of them. Assuming that the amounts of food that Jay and Kay get under this arrangement are exactly what each would have chosen if he or she had lived and worked alone, is each of them strictly better off when they share? Explain.

11. Why does each of the following transactions represent both income and expenditure? **LO6**

   a. A reckless driver pays a fine of $1000 for stunt driving.

   b. A worker receives a pay cheque on payday.

   c. A student pays the bookstore $800 for textbooks.

   d. The Canadian government spends $50 billion for new F35 airplanes

   e. A gambler wins $100 000 at the casino.

## ANSWERS TO IN-CHAPTER EXERCISES

### 2.1

|       | Productivity in programming    | Productivity in bicycle repair |
|-------|--------------------------------|--------------------------------|
| Mina  | 2 Web-page updates per hour    | 1 repair per hour              |
| Barb  | 3 Web-page updates per hour    | 3 repairs per hour             |

The entries in the table tell us that Barb has an absolute advantage over Mina in both activities. While Barb can update 3 Web pages per hour, Mina can update only 2. Barb's absolute advantage over Mina is even greater in the task of fixing bicycles—3 repairs per hour versus Mina's 1.

But, as in Example 2.2, the fact that Barb is a better programmer than Mina does not imply that Barb will be better off if she updates her own Web page. Barb's opportunity cost of updating a Web page is 1 bicycle repair, whereas Mina must give up only half a bicycle repair to update a Web page. Mina has a comparative advantage over Barb at programming, and Barb has a comparative advantage over Mina at bicycle repair. **LO2**

**2.2**   Susan's opportunity cost of picking a kilogram of nuts is 1/2 kg of sugar cane. But Tom's opportunity cost of picking a kilogram of nuts is now only 1/3 kg of sugar cane. So Tom has a comparative advantage at picking nuts, and Susan has a comparative advantage at cutting sugar cane. **LO2**

**2.3**   The slope to the left of point $D$ (in absolute value) is 1/2 kg of sugar cane per kilogram of nuts, which is Susan's opportunity cost of picking nuts. **LO2**

# CHAPTER 3
## Supply and Demand: An Introduction

In Toronto, as in any other Canadian city, the stock of foodstuffs on hand at any moment in grocery stores, restaurants, and private kitchens is sufficient to feed the city's 2.5 million residents for a week, at most. Almost no food is produced within the city, yet most of Toronto's residents have nutritionally adequate and highly varied diets. But provisioning Toronto requires millions of kilograms of food to be delivered throughout the city every day. Somehow, the system must not only deliver enough food to satisfy Torontonians' discriminating palates, but it must also deliver the *right kinds* of food: there must not be too much bacon and too few eggs, or too much caviar and not enough canned tuna, and so on. Similar judgments must be made *within* each category of food and drink: there must be the right amount of Swiss cheese and the right amounts of provolone, Gorgonzola, and feta, not too much basmati rice and not too little risotto, and a different variety of herbs and seasonings for each ethnicity of cuisine. Moreover, someone must decide how much of each type of food will be delivered to *each* of the thousands of restaurants and grocery stores in the city. Someone must determine whether the deliveries will be made in big trucks or small ones, arrange that the trucks be in the right place at the right time, and ensure that fuel and qualified drivers are available.

Thousands of individuals will play a role in this collective effort. Some people must drive food delivery trucks, rather than trucks that deliver lumber. Others must become mechanics who fix these trucks, rather than carpenters who build houses. Others must become farmers, rather than architects or bricklayers. Still others must become chefs in upscale restaurants, or at McDonald's, instead of becoming plumbers or electricians.

A great number of complex tasks must be coordinated in order to provide Torontonians with food every day. Nevertheless, the citizens of that city are able to obtain what they need fairly easily and consistently. In Canada, the overwhelmingly majority of daily decisions in the food supply chain are coordinated through markets. The remarkable fact that Torontonians are able to obtain what they need fairly easily and consistently is primarily due to the incentives that market prices establish. Yes, a grocery store will occasionally run out of flank steak, or a waiter must sometimes tell a diner that someone else has just ordered the last serving of roast duck, but such episodes remain in memory only because they are rare.

In this chapter, we will use economic models to explore how markets allocate food, housing, and other goods and services. An *economic model*, as we noted in Chapter 1, is a representation of economic reality that highlights particular variables and the relationships among them. The production possibilities curve and comparative advantage are examples of two simple economic models.

A particular economic model may work well for analyzing one type of market, but not another. For example, the market for pizzas is quite different from the market for electricity. Many restaurants in Toronto will deliver pizzas, but each house in Toronto has only one line that delivers electricity. Thus, a model designed to analyze the market for pizzas will not provide a good understanding of the market for electricity, and vice versa. Since there is often more than one economic model that could be used to analyze a particular market, economists have to choose between competing models, using evidence on the actual accuracy of each model's predictions. Nevertheless, when markets work well, they are effective in allocating a complex array of goods, services, and resources. In microeconomics, economists analyze circumstances under which markets function smoothly, but they also discuss when markets, left to themselves, cannot be expected to function well.

This chapter provides an introductory overview of how economists analyze markets with many buyers and sellers of standardized products. It uses a model based on supply and demand, two concepts that we soon will define carefully. Because a major objective of economics is to understand how markets work, subsequent chapters discuss the economic role of markets in considerably more detail. Most of microeconomics is directly concerned with analyses of individual markets, while macroeconomics focuses on national economies as entire units. Nevertheless, individual markets—labour markets, financial markets, and foreign exchange markets—also play a central role in macroeconomics. How all markets work is, therefore, a central issue for economics, even if we take as given the regulations and policies of government (e.g., food safety standards or minimum wage laws) within which markets function.

In capitalist, or market, economies, people decide for themselves which careers to pursue and which products to produce or buy. However, there are few, if any, *pure* market economies today. Modern industrial countries are more properly described as *mixed economies*, meaning that goods and services are allocated by a combination of markets, regulation, and other forms of collective control.

## 3.1  MARKETS AND PRICES

Beginning with some basic concepts and definitions, we will explore how the interactions between buyers and sellers in markets determine the prices and quantities of the various goods and services traded in those markets. By definition, the **market** for any good is the context in which potential buyers and sellers of that good can negotiate exchanges. For any good, we specify the time and the place at which it is bought and sold. So, for example, the market for hamburgers on a given day in a given place is just the set of people (or other economic actors, like firms) potentially able to buy or sell hamburgers at that time and location.

In the market for hamburgers, sellers comprise the individuals and companies that either sell or might sell hamburgers, under the right circumstances. Similarly, buyers in this market include all individuals who buy, or might buy, hamburgers. Together, they

**market** the context in which potential buyers and sellers of a good or service can negotiate exchanges

have to agree on a price if they are to make a deal. How is the market price of hamburgers determined?

Looking beyond hamburgers to the vast array of other goods that are bought and sold every day, we may ask why some goods are cheap and others expensive. Adam Smith and other early economists (including Karl Marx) thought that the market price of a good was determined by its cost of production. But although costs surely do affect prices, they cannot explain why one of Pablo Picasso's paintings sells for so much more than one of yours. Stanley Jevons and other nineteenth-century economists tried to explain price by focusing on the value people derived from consuming different goods and services. It certainly seems plausible that people will pay a lot for a good they value highly. Yet willingness to pay cannot be the whole story either. A person deprived of water in the desert, for example, will be dead in a matter of hours, but water from a municipal system sells for a fraction of a penny per litre.

Cost of production or value to the consumer; which is more significant? Writing in the late nineteenth century, the British economist Alfred Marshall was among the first to show clearly how both matter. As he put it, "We might as reasonably dispute whether it is the upper or the under blade of a pair of scissors that cuts a piece of paper, as whether value is governed by utility or cost of production."[1] Our task in the pages ahead will be to explore Marshall's insights and gain some practice in applying them. As a first step, we introduce the two main components of Marshall's analysis: the supply curve and the demand curve.

## THE SUPPLY CURVE

**supply curve** a curve or schedule showing the total quantity of a good of uniform quality that sellers want to sell at each price during a particular period of time, provided that all other things are held constant

In the market for hamburgers, the **supply curve** of hamburgers is a simple schedule, or graph, that tells us, for each possible price of hamburgers, the total quantity of hamburgers of uniform quality that all hamburger sellers together would be willing to supply per period of time at that price, provided that all other things are held constant. Notice that the definition of the supply curve refers to the *quantities* of hamburgers that sellers are *willing* to *supply* at specific prices. Although they are related, the *supply curve* and the *quantity supplied* are two different concepts. **Quantity supplied** is the total amount of a good of uniform quality that all sellers together are willing to produce and sell *at a single, specific price* during a particular period of time.

**quantity supplied** the total amount of a good of uniform quality that all sellers are willing to produce and sell at a single, specific price during a particular period of time

What does the supply curve of hamburgers look like? People will be willing to produce and sell hamburgers as long as, and only as long as, the price they receive for them is sufficient to cover their opportunity costs of supplying them (what they could have earned if they had spent their time and invested their money in some other way). Figure 3.1 provides an illustration. It portrays a single supply curve showing the relationship between *price* and *quantity supplied*. Many points lie on this single curve. Each point on a supply curve identifies a specific quantity supplied and a corresponding, specific price. Figure 3.1 indicates that if the price is $2, the quantity of hamburgers supplied will be 8000. If the price is higher, the quantity is greater; for example, at a price of $3 each, 12 000 will be supplied.

Economists know perfectly well that some hamburgers are bigger and better than others (and consequently sell for a higher price), but we want to focus on the role played by prices in the market. Hence, we simplify by making the assumption that we can draw a supply curve for a particular type of hamburger of uniform quality; for example, one made with six ounces of well-done, grade A beef and garnished with relish. We therefore think of other, similar goods (larger or smaller hamburgers, hotdogs, etc.) as being sold in other, different markets, recognizing that because these goods cater to similar wants, the markets for them are linked.

---

1  Alfred Marshall, *Principles of Economics* (1920), 8th ed., (London: Macmillan & Co Ltd, 1964), p. 290.

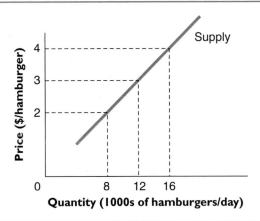

**FIGURE 3.1**

**The Daily Supply Curve of Hamburgers in Downtown Toronto**
At higher prices, sellers generally offer more units for sale. The supply curve is upward sloping.

The definition of quantity supplied also refers to a particular period of time. A quantity supplied of 8000 hamburgers per day is quite different from a quantity of 8000 hamburgers per month. Because, to be meaningful, our definition must specify the period of time during which a quantity is supplied, the label on the horizontal axis of Figure 3.1 indicates quantity supplied *per day*.

In general, people differ with respect to their opportunity costs of producing and selling hamburgers. For those with limited education and work experience, the opportunity cost of selling hamburgers is relatively low because they typically do not have a lot of high-paying alternatives. For others, the opportunity cost of selling burgers is of moderate value, and for still other people, like rock stars and professional athletes, it is prohibitively high. Because of these differences in people's opportunity costs of selling hamburgers, the daily supply curve of hamburgers will be *upward sloping* as shown in Figure 3.1, which exhibits a hypothetical supply curve for the hamburger market in downtown Toronto on a given day. (Although economists usually refer to demand and supply "curves," to keep things simple we often draw them as straight lines in our examples.)

Why is the supply curve for hamburgers upward sloping? When the price of hamburgers is low, say, $2 per hamburger, only those people whose opportunity cost of selling hamburgers is less than or equal to what they can earn in that activity will offer hamburgers for sale. For the supply curve shown in Figure 3.1, the quantity supplied at a price of $2 will be 8000 hamburgers per day, which is the total quantity of hamburgers supplied by people whose opportunity cost of selling hamburgers is $2 per hamburger or less. If the price of a hamburger were to rise above $2, additional sellers would find it worthwhile to offer hamburgers for sale. For example, at a price of $3, Figure 3.1 shows that the quantity of hamburgers supplied is 12 000 per day, while at a price of $4 the quantity supplied is 16 000. The higher the price, the more people find it worthwhile to supply hamburgers.

The upward slope of the supply curve may be seen as a consequence of the principle of increasing opportunity cost, discussed in Chapter 2. This principle tells us that as we expand the production of hamburgers, we turn first to those suppliers whose opportunity costs of producing and selling hamburgers are lowest. Only at higher prices do we turn to suppliers with higher opportunity costs.

Finally, a supply curve (or schedule) holds constant all things other than price and quantity supplied. The Latin expression *ceteris paribus* (other things constant) is often used to indicate this assumption, one which allows us to focus on the impact of price on quantity supplied. Many things could affect actual supply in the real world. If, for example, a sudden blizzard dumped a metre of snow on the city, it would be impossible for

INCREASING
OPPORTUNITY
COST

BOX 3.1

### Supply as an Equation

There are many possible ways to express economic ideas. An economic model can be explained with words, described with graphs, or represented by mathematical equations. If we choose to use the language of mathematics, the supply curve pictured in Figure 3.1 could also be written algebraically as

$$Q_s = a + bP_s.$$

Algebraically, we use $Q_s$ to mean quantity supplied in *thousands* of units and $P_s$ to mean supply price. In general, the parameter $a$ is the horizontal intercept, and the parameter $b$ is the reciprocal of the slope of the supply curve. The plus sign indicates a direct, positive relationship between quantity supplied and price. In the specific example of the supply schedule portrayed graphically in Figure 3.1, $a = 0$ and $b = 4$, so the supply curve also can be written algebraically as

$$Q_s = 4P_s.$$

If we measure quantity supplied in thousands of hamburgers per day and price in dollars, we can state the relationship between price and quantity supplied in any of three ways. Both the graphical representation of Figure 3.1 and the algebraic statement $Q_s = 4P_s$ are equivalent to the verbal statement, "If price increases by one dollar, quantity supplied will increase by 4000 hamburgers." The mathematical statement says the same thing as either the figure or the words, just more compactly.[2]

most people to get to work until the streets were plowed, and the supply of hamburgers (and much else) would be disrupted. We will ignore such possibilities and impose the assumption of *ceteris paribus* in order to show how supply and demand determine the price and quantity traded. Later, we will relax the assumption of *ceteris paribus* to see the effects of factors other than price.

## THE DEMAND CURVE

The supply curve, by itself, does not tell us how many hamburgers will be sold in downtown Toronto on a given day or at what price those hamburgers will sell. To find the prevailing price and quantity, we also need the demand curve for hamburgers in this market. The **demand curve** for hamburgers is a graph that tells us the total quantity of hamburgers that buyers want to buy at each price.[3]

Figure 3.2 graphs the daily demand for a hypothetical market for hamburgers in Toronto. It shows a relationship between *price* and *quantity demanded*. Typically, a demand curve is downward sloping. The demand curve in Figure 3.2 shows that when price is high, buyers as a group are willing to purchase fewer hamburgers. Like the supply curve, the demand curve is composed of many points. Each point on the demand curve

**demand curve** a curve or schedule showing the total quantity of a good of uniform quality that buyers want to buy at each price during a particular period of time provided that all other things are held constant

2   The reader may be perplexed by the economist's practice of placing price, the independent variable, on the vertical axis. The practice stems from Alfred Marshall, who treated quantity as the independent variable because he wanted to investigate the effect of changes in quantity on price. Such was Marshall's influence that ever since he published *Principles of Economics* in 1890, economists have placed price on the vertical axis. The work of another great economist, Leon Walras, is characteristic of practice before 1890. Walras treated price as the independent variable, and placed it on the horizontal axis. Walras may have been vexed by Marshall's influence; in his correspondence, he refers to Marshall as the "great white elephant of political economy." Marshall, *Principles of Economics*, pp. 78–85. Robert B. Ekelund, Jr. and Robert F. Hebert, *A History of Economic Theory and Method, 5th ed.* (Long Grove, Illinois: Waveland Press, Inc., 2007), pp. 383, 387–390.

3   To be truly precise, we have to specify "hamburgers of uniform quality during a particular period of time, in downtown Toronto, provided that all other things are held constant." But the key idea is fairly simple: how many would people want to buy, at each price?

identifies a specific quantity demanded at the corresponding price. Thus, a single demand curve plots many different quantities demanded and many prices. When the price is $4, quantity demanded is 8000 hamburgers per day; when the price is $3, the quantity demanded is 12 000 hamburgers per day, and so on.

**FIGURE 3.2**
**The Daily Demand Curve for Hamburgers in Downtown Toronto**
The demand curve for any good is a generally downward-sloping function of its price. At lower prices, buyers generally want to purchase more units.

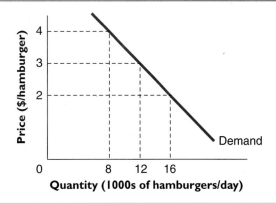

We define the demand curve in the same terms as we do the supply curve. The demand curve pertains to a good of uniform quality. Quantity demanded is specified as an amount per period of time, so the label on the horizontal axis of Figure 3.2 indicates that quantity is measured in thousands of hamburgers *per day*. Finally, the assumption of *ceteris paribus* pertains to demand just as it does to supply. A single demand curve shows the relationship between quantity demanded and price, provided that all things other than price and quantity are held constant. Therefore, we define **quantity demanded** as the total amount purchased by all buyers at a single, specific price. We will return to the question of what happens to demand when things other than price and quantity change, but first we develop the concept of market equilibrium.

**quantity demanded** the total amount of a good of uniform quality purchased at a single, specific price by all buyers during a particular period of time

---

**BOX 3.2**

**Demand as an Equation**

Demand, like supply, can be analyzed with words, with graphs, or by using equations. A linear demand curve can be represented algebraically by an equation of the form

$$Q_D = c - dP_D.$$

Quantity demanded is represented by $Q_D$, while $P_D$ represents demand price. In general, the parameter $c$ represents the horizontal intercept; that is, the quantity of hamburgers that would be consumed if the price is zero (if hamburgers were free). The minus sign indicates an indirect, negative relationship between quantity demanded and price. In the specific case of the demand curve that is graphed in Figure 3.2, the demand curve can be written as the equation

$$Q_D = 24 - 4P_D.$$

In this case, $Q_D$ represents quantity demanded in *thousands* of units, $c = 24$, and $d = -4$. Again, one could express it verbally: if price increases by one dollar, quantity demanded will decrease by 4000 hamburgers. Some people find it easiest to understand the relationship between quantity demanded and price when it is expressed verbally, while others prefer algebra or graphs. All are equally valid—they are just different ways of saying the same thing.

## MARKET EQUILIBRIUM

The concept of *equilibrium* is employed in both the physical and social sciences and is of central importance in economic analysis. We use the term equilibrium to denote a state of rest.

**equilibrium** a state of rest that occurs when all of the forces that act on all the variables in a system are in balance, exactly offsetting each other so that none of the variables in the system has any tendency to change

In general, a system in **equilibrium** has no tendency to change. In physics, for example, a ball hanging from a spring is said to be in equilibrium when the spring has stretched so that the upward force it exerts on the ball is exactly counterbalanced by the downward force of gravity. In economics, the supply curve states that when price *increases*, the quantity supplied also *increases;* the two are *directly* related. The demand curve states that when price *increases*, quantity demanded *decreases;* the two are *inversely* related. A market is said to be in equilibrium when supply and demand are exactly counterbalanced so that no participant in the market has any desire to alter his or her behaviour. In equilibrium, there is no tendency for price and quantity to change.

**equilibrium price** and **equilibrium quantity** the price and quantity of a good at the intersection of the supply and demand curves for the good

If we want to determine the final position of a ball hanging from a spring, we need to find the point at which the forces of gravity and spring tension are exactly counterbalanced and the system is in equilibrium. Similarly, if we want to find the price at which a good will sell (the **equilibrium price**) and the quantity of it that will be sold (the **equilibrium quantity**), we need to find the equilibrium in the market for that good. The price and quantity at which the supply and demand curves for the good intersect is the equilibrium. For the hypothetical supply and demand curves for hamburgers in downtown Toronto, the equilibrium price will therefore be $3 per hamburger, and the equilibrium quantity of hamburgers sold will be 12 000 per day, as shown in Figure 3.3, which combines Figures 3.1 and 3.2.

**market equilibrium** occurs when all buyers and sellers are satisfied with their respective quantities at the market price

In Figure 3.3, note that at the equilibrium price of $3 per hamburger, both sellers and buyers are "satisfied" in the following sense: buyers are buying exactly the quantity of hamburgers they want to buy at that price (12 000 per day) and sellers are selling exactly the quantity of hamburgers they want to sell (also 12 000 per day) at that same price. In this **market equilibrium**, both buyers and sellers are satisfied in that neither group faces any incentives to change their behaviour.

**FIGURE 3.3**
**The Equilibrium Price and Quantity of Hamburgers in Downtown Toronto**
The equilibrium quantity and price of a product are the values that correspond to the intersection of the supply and demand curves for that product.

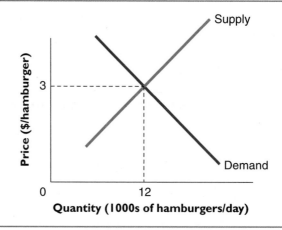

Note the limited sense of the term *satisfied* in the definition of market equilibrium. It does not mean that sellers would be displeased to receive a price higher than the equilibrium price. Rather, it means only that they are able to sell all they wish to sell at the equilibrium price. Similarly, to say that buyers are satisfied at the equilibrium price does not mean that they would not like to have a higher income or that they would not be happy to pay less than the equilibrium price. Rather, it means only that, given their incomes, they are able to buy exactly as many units of the good as they want to at the equilibrium price.

Note also that if the price of hamburgers in our downtown Toronto market was anything other than $3, either buyers or sellers would not be satisfied. Suppose, for example, that the price of hamburgers was $4, as shown in Figure 3.4. At that price, buyers want to buy only 8000 hamburgers per day, but sellers want to sell 16 000. Since no one can force someone to buy a hamburger against his or her wishes, this means that buyers will buy only the 8000 hamburgers they want to buy. So when the price exceeds the equilibrium price, sellers will be dissatisfied. At a price of $4 in this example, the quantity supplied exceeds the quantity demanded by 8000 hamburgers. Therefore, sellers are left with an **excess supply**, or **surplus**.

**excess supply,** or **surplus** the difference between the quantity supplied and the quantity demanded when the price of a good exceeds the equilibrium price; leaves some sellers dissatisfied

Conversely, suppose that the price of hamburgers in the downtown Toronto market was less than the equilibrium price, say $2 per hamburger. As shown in Figure 3.5, buyers want to buy 16 000 hamburgers per day at that price, whereas sellers want to sell only 8000. This time the buyers will be dissatisfied, because sellers cannot be forced to sell hamburgers against their wishes. At a price of $2 in this example, the quantity demanded exceeds the quantity supplied by 8000 hamburgers. Therefore, buyers experience an **excess demand**, or **shortage**.

**excess demand,** or **shortage** the difference between the quantity supplied and the quantity demanded when the price of a good lies below the equilibrium price; leaves some buyers dissatisfied

Markets for goods and services often tend toward their respective equilibrium prices and quantities provided that many buyers and sellers are competing in the market. The mechanisms by which this happens are implicit in our definitions of excess supply and excess demand. Suppose, for example, that the price of hamburgers in our hypothetical market was $4, leading to excess supply as shown in Figure 3.4. Sellers are dissatisfied because they provide more hamburgers than buyers want to buy, so they have an incentive

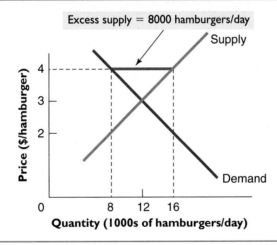

**FIGURE 3.4**
**Excess Supply**
When price exceeds the equilibrium price, there is excess supply, or surplus, which is equal to the difference between quantity supplied and quantity demanded.

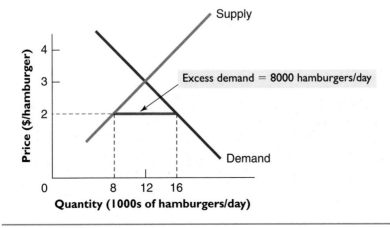

**FIGURE 3.5**
**Excess Demand**
When price lies below the equilibrium price, there is excess demand, or shortage, which is the difference between quantity demanded and quantity supplied.

to take whatever steps they can to increase their sales. A simple strategy is for them to cut their price slightly. Thus, if one seller reduced his price from $4 to, say, $3.95 per hamburger, he could attract some of the buyers who otherwise would have had to pay $4 for hamburger to sellers. Those sellers, to recover their lost business, would then have an incentive to match the price cut. But notice that if all sellers lowered their prices to $3.95, there would still be considerable excess supply in the hamburger market. So sellers would face continuing incentives to cut their prices. This pressure to cut prices will not go away until the price falls all the way to $3. At $3, excess supply is zero.

Conversely, suppose that price starts out less than the equilibrium price, say, $2 per hamburger. This time it is the buyers who are dissatisfied. A person who cannot get all the hamburgers she wants at a price of $2 has an incentive to offer a higher price, hoping to obtain hamburgers that would otherwise have been sold to other buyers. And sellers, for their part, will be only too happy to post higher prices as long as queues of dissatisfied buyers remain.

The upshot is that price has a tendency to move to its equilibrium level under conditions of either excess supply or excess demand. And when price reaches its equilibrium level, both buyers and sellers are satisfied simultaneously since they are able to buy or sell precisely the amounts they choose, given their incomes.

We emphasize that the mere fact that buyers and sellers are satisfied in this sense does not mean that markets automatically result in the best of all possible worlds. For example, a poor person may buy one hamburger each day at a price of $3, but still be hungry; in this case, he is satisfied only in the limited sense that with his available income he either cannot buy a second hamburger or prefers to buy something else.

It is also important to emphasize that the equilibrating process depends on competition among many buyers and sellers, all of whom are small relative to the size of the market. If all sellers are small, no seller has the ability to increase the price of hamburgers above the equilibrium price by restricting the quantity supplied. For example, if all sellers are small, no seller can raise the price of hamburgers to $4 by restricting the quantity to 8000 hamburgers per day. Why? Because at $4, other sellers will be perfectly willing to compete for buyers by increasing the quantity of hamburgers, while offering a somewhat lower price.

Similarly, if all buyers are small, no buyer can reduce price below the equilibrium price, say to $2, by announcing that they will pay no more than $2 for a hamburger. Why? Because at $2, only 8000 hamburgers/day will be supplied, and other buyers will compete for hamburgers by offering a somewhat higher price.

---

**BOX 3.3**

### Market Equilibrium: Supply Equals Demand

When a market is in equilibrium, no buyer or seller wants to change their behaviour, so none of the variables in the system tend to change. Figure 3.3 presents a graphical representation of equilibrium in a simple system of supply and demand—the intersection of the supply and demand curves. The intersection of supply and demand curves is the only place where quantity supplied ($Q_S$) equals quantity demanded ($Q_D$). It, therefore, identifies the equilibrium quantity, which we will call $Q^*$. Because the supply price ($P_S$) equals demand price ($P_D$) at this intersection point, the intersection also identifies the equilibrium price, which we will call $P^*$.

We can represent equilibrium algebraically by using the equations for supply and demand that appear in the previous boxes. In market equilibrium, we have that $P_S = P_D = P^*$ and $Q_S = Q_D = Q^*$. Therefore, by setting $Q_S = Q_D$ we can solve for $P^*$:

$$a + bP^* = c - dP^*.$$

The equation for supply (from Box 3.1) is on the left-hand side of the equal sign, and the equation for demand (from Box 3.2) is on the right.

Solving for $P^*$ we have that

$$P^* = \frac{(c-a)}{(b+d)}.$$

We can substitute $P^*$ into either the equation for demand or for supply to determine $Q^*$. Using the demand equation, we have

$$Q^* = c - d \times \left(\frac{c-a}{b+d}\right)$$

Therefore, the equilibrium condition states that supply is equal to demand. The equilibrium quantity is $Q^*$. By definition, $Q_S = Q_D = Q^*$, where quantity supplied and quantity demanded are represented by $Q_S$ and $Q_D$, respectively, as they were in the earlier two boxes.

If we insert the values for the parameters as stated in the two earlier boxes, we can rewrite the equilibrium condition:

$$0 + 4P^* = 24 - 4P^*.$$

Since this is one equation with one unknown, we can solve for $P^*$ and find that $P^* = \$3$. The equilibrium value for price can be substituted into either the equation for supply or the equation for demand to determine that the equilibrium quantity is 12. Remember that $Q^*$ is measured in thousands of units. Therefore, the equilibrium quantity actually is 12 000 hamburgers. The values for equilibrium price and quantity are consistent with what is shown in Figure 3.3.

As demonstrated here, an equilibrium of supply and demand involves the simultaneous solution of two equations. See Connect for additional discussion of how two simultaneous equations are solved.

## MARKETS, EQUILIBRIUM, AND FAIRNESS

When a market is out of equilibrium, it is always possible to identify mutually beneficial but unrealized exchanges. When people have failed to take advantage of all mutually beneficial exchanges, we often say that there is "cash on the table"—the economist's metaphor for unexploited opportunities. When the price in a market is below the equilibrium price, there is cash on the table, because it will always be possible for a supplier to produce an additional unit at a cost that is lower than the price buyers are willing to pay. This leads to an important result, which we will state as a core principle.

**The Equilibrium Principle:** A market in equilibrium leaves no unexploited opportunities for trade between individuals.

### Is an equilibrium solution also a fair solution?

Equilibrium and fairness are two very different concepts. Consider two societies. The first consists of a few wealthy people and many poor. The second society is more equal: almost everyone is middle class. Rich people can afford to buy mansions, middle-class people have enough income to buy small houses and poor people can only afford one room shacks. Therefore, the demand for mansions in the first society will be greater than the demand for mansions in the second society. Likewise, the two societies will have different demands for modest houses and shacks. Because the two societies have different patterns of demand, when the market for houses is in equilibrium in each society, the equilibrium combination of mansions, modest homes, and shacks in the first society will differ from the combination observed in the second society. In general, whenever the distribution of assets differs between one society and another, the equilibrium consumption of commodities will also differ. *Each different distribution of wealth will produce a different equilibrium solution for prices and quantities produced.* The equilibrium principle has nothing to say about whether any particular initial distribution of assets is fair, and thus leaves unexamined an important ethical question: is one distribution of wealth "better" than another?

**RECAP**↱

### MARKETS AND PRICES

The *market* for a good or service is the context in which potential buyers and sellers of the good or service can negotiate exchanges. For any given price, the *supply curve* shows the total quantity that suppliers of the good would be willing to sell, and the *demand curve* shows the total quantity that demanders would be willing to buy. Suppliers are willing to sell more at higher prices (supply curves slope upward) and demanders are willing to buy less at higher prices (demand curves slope downward).

*Market equilibrium,* the situation in which all buyers and sellers are satisfied with their respective quantities at the market price, occurs at the intersection of the supply and demand curves. The corresponding price and quantity are called the *equilibrium price* and the *equilibrium quantity.*

Prices and quantities tend to be driven toward their equilibrium values by the competitive actions of buyers and sellers. If the price is initially too high, resulting in excess supply, dissatisfied sellers will compete for buyers by cutting their prices to sell more. If the price is initially too low, resulting in excess demand, competition among buyers drives the price upward. This process continues until equilibrium is reached. The equilibrating process depends on competition among large numbers of small buyers and sellers.

A market in equilibrium means that all opportunities for individuals to make exchanges that are privately beneficial to both parties have been realized. If each individual starts with an initial endowment of assets and all individuals are free to make mutually beneficial exchanges, each different initial distribution of assets will in general produce a different market equilibrium of commodity production and prices. The equilibrium principle has nothing to say about whether the initial endowment of wealth is "fair."

## 3.2  EXPLAINING CHANGES IN PRICES AND QUANTITIES

If we know how the factors that govern supply and demand curves are changing, we can make informed predictions about how prices and the corresponding quantities will change. But when describing changing circumstances in the marketplace, we must take care to recognize some important terminological distinctions. For example, we must distinguish between the meanings of the seemingly similar expressions *change in the quantity demanded* and *change in demand*. When we speak of a **change in the quantity demanded**, we mean the change in quantity that people want to buy that occurs in response to a change in price. For instance, Figure 3.6(a) depicts an increase in the quantity demanded that occurs in response to a reduction in the price of tuna. When the price falls from $5 to $4 per can, the quantity demanded rises from 2000 to 4000 cans per day. By contrast, when we speak of a **change in demand**, we mean a *shift in the entire demand curve.* For example, Figure 3.6(b) depicts an increase in demand, meaning that at every price the quantity demanded is higher than before. In summary, a change in the quantity demanded refers to a movement *along* the demand curve, and a change in demand means a *shift* of the entire curve.

A similar terminological distinction applies on the supply side of the market. A **change in supply** means a shift in the entire supply curve, whereas **a change in the quantity supplied** refers to a movement along the supply curve. Why might the demand curve shift?

**change in quantity demanded** a movement along the demand curve that occurs in response to a change in price

**change in demand** a shift of the entire demand curve

**change in supply** a shift of the entire supply curve

**change in quantity supplied** a movement along the supply curve that occurs in response to a change in price

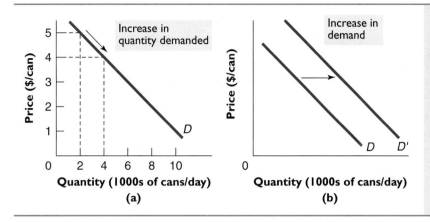

Why might the supply curve shift? Shifts in either the supply curve or demand curve happen because of changes in some of the factors we have, up until now, held constant. We can use the framework of supply and demand to analyze the implications of changes in these factors.

Alfred Marshall's supply and demand model is one of the most useful tools of the economic naturalist. Once we understand the forces that govern the placements of supply and demand curves, we are in a position to make sense of a host of interesting observations in the world around us.

## SHIFTS IN THE SUPPLY CURVE

To get a better feel for how the supply and demand model enables us to predict and explain price and quantity movements, it is helpful to begin with a few simple examples. Because the supply curve is based on costs of production, anything that changes production costs will shift the supply curve and hence will result in a new equilibrium quantity and price.

## EXAMPLE 3.1

**What will happen to the equilibrium price and quantity of new houses if the price of lumber declines?**

Suppose the initial supply and demand curves for new houses are as shown by the curves *S* and *D* in Figure 3.7, resulting in an equilibrium price of $160 000 per house and an equilibrium quantity of 40 houses per month. A decline in the price of lumber reduces the cost of making new houses, and this means that, for any given price of houses, more builders can profitably serve the market than before. Diagrammatically, this means a rightward shift in the supply curve of houses, from *S* to *S'*. (A rightward shift in the supply curve can also be described as a downward shift.)

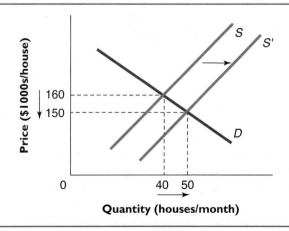

**FIGURE 3.7**
**The Effect on the Market for New Houses of a Decline in the Price of Lumber**
When input prices fall, supply shifts rightward, causing equilibrium price to fall and equilibrium quantity to rise.

If we assume that the decline in the price of lumber has no impact on incomes in the lumber industry and, hence, on the demand for homes, then a decline in the price of lumber produces a significant rightward shift in the supply curve of houses, but no perceptible shift in the demand curve. We see from Figure 3.7 that the new equilibrium price, $150 000 per house, is lower than the original price, and the new equilibrium quantity, 50 houses per month, is higher than the original quantity.

Example 3.1 involved changes in the cost of an input in the production of a good, lumber in the production of houses. We have modified the assumption of *ceteris paribus*, all other things equal, to now mean all other things equal but one (i.e., the price of lumber). As Economic Naturalist 3.1 illustrates, supply curves also shift when technology changes.

## ECONOMIC NATURALIST   3.1

### Why has the consumption of French fries increased substantially during the last 35 years?

Commercial techniques for peeling, cutting, cooking, and storing French fries are much more sophisticated now than they were 35 years ago. Today, raw potatoes are processed into French fries in a few large plants, frozen, and shipped to restaurants and consumers. Once in restaurants and homes, French fries are easily cooked. In the United States, consumption of potatoes has increased by about 30 percent since 1977, most of it because Americans are eating more French fries and potato chips.[4]

In Figure 3.8, the curves labelled *S* and *D* depict the supply and demand curves for French fries during the late 1970s. The curve *S'* represents the supply curve today. The increase in supply is the result of technological improvements in the production of French fries. As the graph shows, the equilibrium quantity of French fries has increased and the price has decreased.

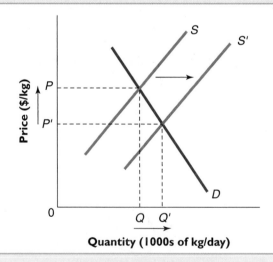

**FIGURE 3.8**
**The Effect of Technological Change on the Market for French Fries**
When new technology reduces the cost of production, supply shifts right, causing the equilibrium price to fall and the equilibrium quantity to rise.

**inputs** goods or services used in the process of producing a different good or service

Changes in *input* prices and technology are two of the most important factors that give rise to shifts in supply curves. **Inputs** are those items used in a production process to produce a good or service. In Example 3.1, lumber is an input used in the production of houses. The supply curve for houses in Figure 3.7 shifted to the right, or increased, because the price of lumber fell, thus reducing the cost of an input in building houses. Consider another example. Because petroleum is an input used in plastics production, a decrease in the price of petroleum shifts the supply curve of plastic garbage cans to the right. Garbage cans are now cheaper to produce, so there will be an increase in quantity supplied at each particular price. Generally, a reduction in the price of an input into the production of a good will increase the supply of that good. An increase in the price of an input will have the opposite effect.

**Technology** is the stock of knowledge, useful in producing goods and services, that is available to a society. An improvement in technology means that an increase in the stock of available knowledge has made it possible to produce more of at least one good or service from a given set of inputs. In the case of Economic Naturalist 3.1, the stock of knowledge concerning the production of French fries increased, causing an increase in the supply of French fries.

In the real world, many other factors can cause supply to shift. When we think about a change in something other than price and quantity, we are modifying the assumption of *ceteris paribus*. If we do this one thing at a time, we can analyze the impact of each change. For example, weather conditions have a major impact on the yield of crops and the supply of foodstuffs (and on the supply of other goods and services, too). If we introduce changes in the weather as a factor, we are allowing more than just price and quantity to change.

Expectations of future changes can also affect supply curves. Suppose that a drought causes an expectation that harvests at the end of the current growing season will be small. Suppliers are likely to withhold supplies from existing stocks on the *expectation* that whatever is withheld now can be sold at a higher price later. The supply curve for the current period will shift to the left, which is a reduction of supply. Supply in the current period is reduced, even though the existing stock of wheat is not affected by the drought. Because suppliers *expect* a smaller harvest in the future, they reduce supply now.

An increase in a subsidy can also shift a supply curve to the right, as can an increase in the number of firms serving a market. A reduction in a subsidy or the number of firms in a market would shift a supply curve to the left.

**technology** the stock of knowledge, useful in producing goods and services, that is available to a society

## SHIFTS IN DEMAND

The preceding examples involved changes that gave rise to shifts in supply curves. Next, we'll look at what happens when demand curves shift. In the following example, the shift in demand results from events outside the particular market itself.

## EXAMPLE **3.2**

### What will happen to the equilibrium price and quantity of tennis balls if court rental fees decline?

Let the initial supply and demand curves for tennis balls be as shown by the curves *S* and *D* in Figure 3.9, where the resulting equilibrium price and quantity are $1 per ball and 40 million balls per month, respectively. Tennis courts and tennis balls

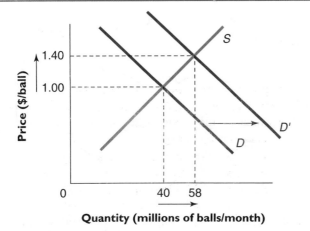

**FIGURE 3.9**
**The Effect on the Market for Tennis Balls of a Decline in Court Rental Fees**
When the price of a good's complement falls, demand for the good shifts rightward, causing equilibrium price and quantity to rise.

**complements** *a relationship between two goods such that an increase in the price of one causes a leftward shift in the demand curve for the other*

are what economists call **complements**, goods that are more valuable when used in combination than when used alone. Tennis balls, for example, would be of less value if there were no tennis courts on which to play. (Tennis balls would still have *some* value even without courts; e.g., to the parents who pitch them to their children for batting practice.) As tennis courts become cheaper to use, people will respond by playing more tennis, and this will increase their demand for tennis balls. A decline in court rental fees will thus shift the demand curve for tennis balls rightward to *D'*. (A rightward shift of a demand curve can also be described as an upward shift.)

Note in Figure 3.9 that, for the demand shift shown, the new equilibrium price of tennis balls, $1.40, is higher than the original price, and the new equilibrium quantity, 58 million balls per month, is higher than the original quantity.

## EXAMPLE **3.3**

**What will happen to the equilibrium price and quantity of overnight letter delivery service as more people gain access to the Internet?**

**substitutes** *a relationship between two goods such that an increase in the price of one causes a rightward shift in the demand curve for the other*

Suppose that the initial supply and demand curves for overnight letter deliveries are as shown by the curves *S* and *D* in Figure 3.10, and that the resulting equilibrium price and quantity are denoted *P* and *Q*. Email messages and overnight letters are examples of **substitutes**, meaning that, in many applications at least, the two serve similar functions for people. When two goods or services are substitutes, a decrease in the effective price of one will cause a leftward shift in the demand curve for the other. (A leftward shift in a demand curve can also be described as a downward shift.) An increase in Internet access is, in effect, a decline in the price of a substitute for overnight delivery for affected users. Diagrammatically, this means a leftward shift in the demand curve for overnight delivery service to *D'* in Figure 3.10.

---

**FIGURE 3.10**
**The Effect on the Market for Overnight Letter Delivery of a Decline in the Price of Internet Access**
When the price of a substitute for a good falls, demand for the good shifts leftward, causing equilibrium price and quantity to fall.

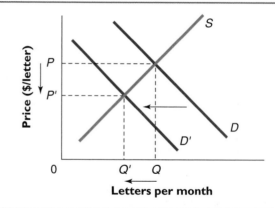

---

As the figure shows, both the new equilibrium price *P'* and the new equilibrium quantity *Q'* are lower than the initial values *P* and *Q*. More widespread Internet access probably will not put Purolator and UPS out of business, but it will definitely cost them many customers.

---

To summarize, economists define goods as substitutes if an increase in the price of one causes an increase in demand (a rightward shift in the demand curve) for the other. By contrast, goods are complements if an increase in the price of one causes an increase in demand (a leftward shift in the demand curve) for the other. The concepts of substitutes and complements enable you to answer questions like the one posed in the following exercise.

**EXERCISE 3.1**

**How will a decline in airfares affect intercity (or long distance) bus fares and the price of hotel rooms in resort communities serviced by airlines?**

## ECONOMIC NATURALIST 3.2

### When the price of oil rises, why do prices for houses in Calgary rise?

Calgary's economy is heavily dependent on the oil industry. If the price of oil rises, oil companies respond by exploring for more oil and by developing existing oil fields more intensively. As oil companies increase their activity, more people will be drawn to Calgary, some to work in the oil industry, others to supply more goods and services to the oil industry as it expands, and still others to supply goods and services to Calgary's rising population. (For example, if more families move to Calgary, more teachers will be required.) In addition, wages and salaries will tend to be bid up to attract more workers, there will be more opportunities to work overtime, and so on. Thus, individuals will tend to have higher incomes because of the oil boom. Because of a larger population and because at least some individuals will have higher incomes (and now may be able to afford to move out of apartments into houses), the demand curve for houses will shift to the right, as shown by the demand curve labelled *D'* in Figure 3.11. As a result, the equilibrium price and quantity of houses, *P'* and *Q'*, will be higher than before.

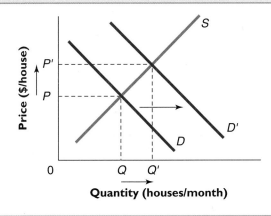

**FIGURE 3.11**
**The Effect of an Increase in the Price of Oil on the Price of Houses in Calgary**
An increase in income shifts demand for a normal good to the right, causing equilibrium price and quantity to rise.

Demand curves are shifted not just by changes in the prices of substitutes and complements but also by other factors that change the amounts that people are willing to pay for a given good or service. One of the most important such factors is household income.

As you can see above, in Economic Naturalist 3.2, two factors caused the demand curve for houses in Calgary to shift to the right when the price of oil rose: the population of the city increased, and the income of individuals increased. Either factor by itself would have caused the demand curve to shift to the right; together, they reinforce each other. When incomes increase, the demand curves for most goods will shift to the right. In recognition of that fact, economists have chosen to call such goods **normal goods**.

Not all goods are normal goods, however. In fact, the demand curves for some goods actually shift leftward when income goes up, and such goods are called **inferior goods**. When would having more money tend to make you want to buy less of something? In general, this will happen in the case of goods for which there are attractive substitutes that sell for only slightly higher prices. Ground beef with high fat content is an example of an inferior good. For health reasons, many people prefer ground beef with low fat content, and when they do buy high-fat meats it is usually a sign of budgetary pressure. When people in this situation receive higher incomes, they switch to leaner grades of meat, which causes the demand curve for high fat hamburger meat to shift leftward.

**normal good** a good whose demand curve shifts rightward when the incomes of buyers increase

**inferior good** a good whose demand curve shifts leftward when the incomes of buyers increase

**Normal and inferior goods were defined in terms of how their demand curves are affected by an increase in income. How will a decrease in income affect the demand for a normal good? an inferior good?**

EXERCISE 3.2

Preferences, or tastes, are another important factor that determines whether a given good will meet the cost–benefit test. Think about the car advertisements on TV or elsewhere that you have seen recently. A few of them convey market information; that is, they tell consumers the price or technical features of a particular brand of automobile. But the ads which feature images of beautiful women and handsome men driving through impossibly romantic scenery are all about creating brand image, thereby increasing the likelihood you will buy that particular car, at any given price. The main role of the advertising industry is to shape preferences and thereby to *shift* to the right the demand curves of consumers for the client's product.

Expectations can also influence demand. For example, if there are clear reasons to expect that the price of a product will rise in the near future, some buyers may wish to increase their purchases now, before the anticipated price rise.

## FOUR SIMPLE RULES

For supply and demand curves that have the conventional slopes (upward sloping for supply curves, downward sloping for demand curves), the preceding examples illustrate the four basic rules that govern how shifts in supply and demand affect equilibrium prices and quantities. These rules are summarized in Figure 3.12.

The qualitative rules summarized in Figure 3.12 hold for supply or demand shifts of any magnitude, provided the curves have their conventional slopes. But although it is easy

**FIGURE 3.12**
**Four Rules Governing the Effects of Supply and Demand Shifts**

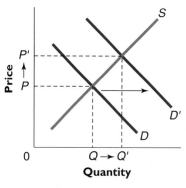

An increase in demand will lead to an increase in both the equilibrium price and quantity.

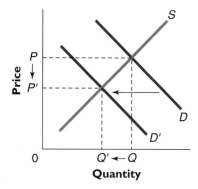

A decrease in demand will lead to a decrease in both the equilibrium price and quantity.

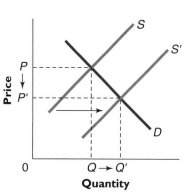

An increase in supply will lead to a decrease in the equilibrium price and an increase in the equilibrium quantity.

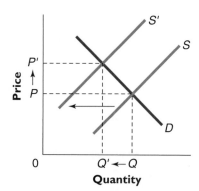

A decrease in supply will lead to an increase in the equilibrium price and a decrease in the equilibrium quantity.

enough for textbook authors to invent examples where only one thing is happening in a market, in the real world we often observe simultaneous changes in demand and supply. As the next example demonstrates, when both supply and demand curves shift at the same time, the direction in which equilibrium price or quantity changes will depend on the relative magnitudes of the shifts.

## EXAMPLE 3.4

### How do shifts in *both* demand and supply affect equilibrium quantities and prices?

What will happen to the equilibrium price and quantity of corn tortilla chips if both the following events occur: (1) researchers discover that the oils in which tortilla chips are fried are harmful to human health, and (2) the price of corn-harvesting equipment falls?

The discovery regarding the health effects of the oils will shift the demand for tortilla chips to the left, because many people who once bought chips in the belief that they were healthful will now switch to other foods. The decline in the price of harvesting equipment will shift the supply of chips to the right, because additional farmers will now find it profitable to produce corn. In Figure 3.13(a) and (b), the original supply and demand curves are denoted by S and D, while the new curves are denoted by S' and D'. Note that in both panels, the shifts lead to a decline in the equilibrium price of chips.

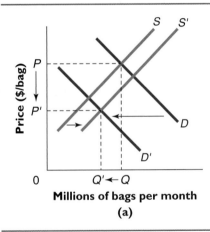

(a)

Millions of bags per month

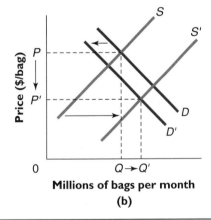

(b)

Millions of bags per month

**FIGURE 3.13**
**The Effects of Simultaneous Shifts in Supply and Demand**
When demand shifts left and supply shifts right, equilibrium price falls, but equilibrium quantity may either fall, as shown in panel (a), or rise, as show in panel (b).

But note also that the effect of the shifts on equilibrium quantity cannot be determined without knowing their relative magnitudes. Taken separately, the demand shift causes a decline in equilibrium quantity, whereas the supply shift causes an increase in equilibrium quantity. The net effect of the two shifts thus depends on which of the individual effects is larger. In Figure 3.13(a), the demand shift dominates, so equilibrium quantity declines. In Figure 3.13(b), the supply shift dominates, so equilibrium quantity goes up.

The following exercise asks you to consider a simple variation on the problem posed in Example 3.4.

**What will happen to the equilibrium price and quantity in the corn tortilla chip market if both the following events occur: (1) researchers discover that a vitamin found in corn helps protect against cancer and heart disease, and (2) a swarm of locusts destroys part of the corn crop?**

**EXERCISE 3.3**

## ECONOMIC NATURALIST 3.3

### Why do the prices of some goods, like airline tickets to Europe, go up during the months of heaviest consumption while others, like sweet corn, go down?

Seasonal price movements for airline tickets are primarily the result of seasonal variations in demand. Thus, ticket prices to Europe are highest during the summer months because the demand for tickets is highest during those months, as shown in Figure 3.14(a) (where the *w* and *s* subscripts denote winter and summer values, respectively).

By contrast, seasonal price movements for sweet corn are primarily the result of seasonal variations in supply. The price of sweet corn is lowest in the summer months because its supply is highest during those months, as shown in Figure 3.14(b).

**FIGURE 3.14**
**Seasonal Variation in the Air Travel and Corn Markets**
Panel (a): Prices are highest during the period of heaviest consumption and are the result of high demand.
Panel (b): Prices are lowest during the period of heaviest consumption when heavy consumption is the result of high supply.

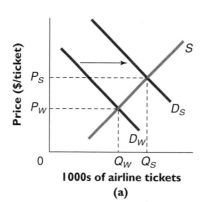

(a)

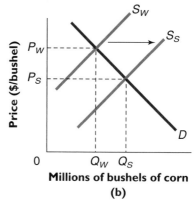

(b)

---

**RECAP**

### EXPLAINING CHANGES IN PRICES AND QUANTITIES

**FACTORS CAUSING AN INCREASE IN SUPPLY (SUPPLY CURVE SHIFTS RIGHT)**

1. A decrease in the cost of materials, labour, or other inputs used in the production of the good or service.
2. An improvement in technology that reduces the cost of producing the good or service.
3. An increase in a subsidy provided by government.
4. An increase in the number of firms.

   When these factors move in the opposite direction, supply will shift left.

**FACTORS CAUSING AN INCREASE IN DEMAND (DEMAND CURVE SHIFTS RIGHT)**

1. A decrease in the price of complements to the good or service.
2. An increase in the price of substitutes for the good or service.
3. An increase in income (for a normal good).
4. An increased preference by demanders for the good or service.
5. An increase in the population of potential buyers.

   When these factors move in the opposite direction, demand will shift left. When both supply and demand shift, it is often necessary to know the relative magnitudes of the shifts to determine if equilibrium price and equilibrium quantity increase or decrease.

BOX **3.4**

### Supply Increases: A New Market Equilibrium

In Box 3.3 we showed how algebra can be used to calculate equilibrium in a simple system of supply and demand. We can use the same algebraic system to calculate a new equilibrium when either supply or demand shifts. For this, the terms will remain defined as they were in the previous boxes.

Recall that in Box 3.1 the supply of hamburgers was represented by

$$Q_S = 4P_S.$$

Now suppose that a hamburger vendor discovers a new technique enabling him to flip six patties at one time and transfer them all to buns simultaneously with a second flip. Other vendors watch and discover they can learn the new technique quickly. Soon the six-burger flip has permeated the entire market, and vendors provide hamburgers more quickly than they did before. A technological improvement has occurred.

How can technological improvement be represented graphically? A downward shift, or a shift to the right, of the supply curve can be represented by increasing the horizontal intercept of the equation for supply.[5] This implies a new equilibrium price and quantity. Suppose the horizontal intercept increases from zero to one. The equation for supply then becomes

$$Q_S = 1 + 4P_S.$$

The equation for demand remains what it was in the previous box,

$$Q_D = 24 - 4P_D.$$

At the market equilibrium, $Q_S = Q_D = Q^*$ (equilibrium quantity) and $P_S = P_D = P^*$ (equilibrium price). We can use the supply equation, the demand equation, and the equation for market equilibrium to write

$$1 + 4P^* = 24 - 4P^*.$$

Notice that, once again, the algebra is just a mathematical expression demonstrating the same thing as the verbal statement that supply equals demand, which must be the case when the system is in equilibrium. The equation for supply, appearing to the left of the equal sign, has changed, but the expression is otherwise unchanged from what appears in Box 3.3.

Solving the expression reveals that $P^* = \$2.875$. (We can assume that vendors round their prices to $\$2.88$.) Substituting $\$2.875$ into either the equation for demand or the new equation for supply reveals that $Q^* = 12.5$. Because quantity is measured in thousands, the equilibrium quantity is 12 500 hamburgers per day. A comparison of this equilibrium quantity and price with those calculated in Box 3.3 reveals that the new quantity is larger and the new price is lower. This is consistent with the lower left-hand panel of Figure 3.12, which pertains to an increase in supply.

Changes in the values of the parameters could represent changes in either demand or supply. For example, an increase in demand can be represented by an increase in the horizontal intercept of the demand curve. A change in the slope of the demand curve can be introduced by changing the parameter that represents slope. The slope of the supply curve can be changed in the same way. Smaller or larger changes in parameters can be used to represent smaller or larger changes to demand or supply.

---

5  In Figure 3.1, the supply curve was not drawn all the way to its intercept with the vertical axis because only the empirically relevant section of the supply curve is needed. If a number of suppliers enter the market at the same time at some minimum price, but nobody enters the market at a lower price, one will observe a supply curve such as in Figure 3.1. Drawing the supply curve all the way to a negative vertical intercept implies that a negative price is possible for some quantities supplied; that is, if quantities are low enough vendors will pay people to take away hamburgers, something that is not likely to occur. The problem can be handled by stating that below some minimum positive price, no hamburgers will be supplied.

## 3.3   WHEN IS THE SIMPLE SUPPLY AND DEMAND MODEL APPROPRIATE?

This chapter has argued that a model based on supply and demand can help us to understand and predict events in many markets. If *all* markets were the same, this textbook could perhaps just stop right here, with supply and demand. It has another 12 chapters because the real world has much more complexity than the simple model of supply and demand can capture. We emphasize that we have made some important assumptions:

1. All participants in the market are so small that no single buyer or seller can influence price. Moreover, it is not possible for any buyers or sellers to form combinations that can influence price.
2. All suppliers provide an identical product. Quality is uniform. Thus, no buyer has any reason to prefer the product of one supplier over that of another.
3. All buyers know the price and quality of the product that is being supplied on the market. If information is available to one buyer or seller, it is available to all buyers and sellers.
4. Transactions can occur easily. It is not difficult for buyers and sellers to meet and conduct transactions.

Simple supply and demand models are based on these conditions. However, because these assumptions are not met in all markets, forthcoming chapters will discuss how the simple model of supply and demand has to be amended when these assumptions do not hold.

## SUMMARY

- An economic model describes results that stem from the relationships it portrays; it also provides hypotheses about what will happen if any of the variables change. The production possibilities diagram of Chapter 2 is one example of a model. The supply and demand model of this chapter is another. **LO1**

- Alfred Marshall's model of supply and demand explains why neither cost of production nor value to the purchaser (as measured by willingness to pay) by itself is sufficient to explain why some goods are cheap and others are expensive. To explain variations in price, we must examine the interaction of cost and willingness to pay. As we saw in this chapter, goods differ in price because of differences in their respective supply and demand curves. **LO2, LO3, LO4**

- The demand curve is a downward-sloping line that tells what quantity buyers will demand at any given price in a market with many buyers. The supply curve is an upward-sloping line indicating the quantity sellers will offer at any given price in a market with many sellers. The market equilibrium occurs when the quantity buyers demand at the market price is exactly the same as the quantity that sellers offer. The equilibrium price-quantity pair is the one at which the demand and supply curves intersect. In equilibrium, market price measures both the value of the last unit sold to buyers and the cost of the resources required to produce it. **LO2, LO3, LO4**

- When the price of a good lies above its equilibrium value, there is an excess supply, or surplus, of that good. Excess supply motivates sellers to cut their prices, and price continues to fall until the equilibrium price is reached. When price lies below its equilibrium value, there is excess demand, or shortage. With excess demand, dissatisfied buyers are motivated to offer higher prices, and the upward pressure on prices persists until equilibrium is reached. The equilibrating process depends on competition among many small buyers and sellers. **LO4**

- The basic supply and demand model is a primary tool of the economic naturalist. Changes in the equilibrium price of a good, and in the amount of it traded in the marketplace, can be predicted on the basis of shifts in its supply or demand curves. The following four rules hold for any good with a downward-sloping demand curve and an upward-sloping supply curve:
  - An increase in demand will lead to an increase in equilibrium price and quantity.
  - A reduction in demand will lead to a reduction in equilibrium price and quantity.
  - An increase in supply will lead to a reduction in equilibrium price and an increase in equilibrium quantity.
  - A decrease in supply will lead to an increase in equilibrium price and a reduction in equilibrium quantity. **LO6**

- Incomes, tastes, population, and the prices of substitutes and complements are among the factors that shift demand schedules. Supply schedules, in turn, are primarily governed by such factors as technology, input prices, and, for agricultural products, the weather. Changes in expectations can also shift supply and demand schedules. **LO6**

- The equilibrium principle states that a market in equilibrium leaves no unexploited opportunities for exchanges among individuals. Equilibrium is a concept of positive economics that of itself says nothing about whether one equilibrium outcome is better than another. For example, each different distribution of wealth will produce a different equilibrium solution for prices and quantities produced. The equilibrium principle has nothing to say about whether any particular distribution of wealth or income is fair. **LO5**

- The supply and demand model is not a general model of markets. It applies best to markets with specific characteristics, such as many buyers and many sellers of a uniform product. There are other models for markets with other characteristics. Macroeconomics often assumes that markets are much slower to respond to changes in demand than the supply and demand model might suggest. **LO7**

## CORE PRINCIPLES

### The Equilibrium Principle
A market in equilibrium leaves no unexploited trading opportunities for personal gain for individuals. Equilibrium is based on an underlying distribution of wealth. (However, the equilibrium principle does not say whether one equilibrium is better than another.) (61)

## KEY TERMS

change in demand (62)
change in quantity
    demanded (62)
change in quantity supplied (62)
change in supply (62)
complements (66)
demand curve (56)
equilibrium (58)

equilibrium price (58)
equilibrium quantity (58)
excess demand (59)
excess supply (59)
inferior good (67)
inputs (64)
market (53)
market equilibrium (58)

normal good (67)
quantity supplied (54)
quantity demanded (57)
shortage (59)
substitutes (66)
supply curve (54)
surplus (59)
technology (65)

## REVIEW QUESTIONS

1. Give two examples of economic models. Do economic models always give correct predictions? If not, why not? **LO1**

2. Why isn't knowing how much it costs to produce a good sufficient to predict its market price? **LO2, LO3, LO4**

3. Distinguish between the meaning of the expressions "change in demand" and "change in the quantity demanded." **LO3**

4. Distinguish between the meaning of the expressions "change in supply" and "change in the quantity supplied." **LO2**

5. Explain why, in a market suitable to analysis with the demand and supply model, a price set below the market equilibrium price would be predicted to cause a gap between quantity demanded and quantity supplied. Also, state the term or terms used by economists to describe such a gap. **LO4**

6. If supply increases at the same time as demand increases, what does the supply and demand model predict about equilibrium price and quantity? **LO6**

7. Explain why, in unregulated markets with many buyers and sellers, the equilibrium principle suggests that excess demand and excess supply tend to be fleeting. **LO4, LO5**

8. Explain why the equilibrium price and quantity in a particular market, say, for an inferior good, will depend upon the distribution of income. **LO5**

9. Why is the supply and demand model not a general model of markets? **LO7**

## PROBLEMS

1. If the market price is kept below the equilibrium price by a regulation, what does the demand and supply model predict about the gap between quantity demanded and quantity supplied? If, in the real world, there is a gap between quantity demanded and quantity supplied, does it necessarily imply that a regulation is keeping the market price below the equilibrium price? **LO4**

2. State whether the following pairs of goods are likely to be complements or substitutes. (If you think a pair is ambiguous in this respect, explain why.) **LO3, LO4, LO6**
   a.  Tennis courts and squash courts
   b.  Squash racquets and squash balls
   c.  Ice cream and chocolate
   d.  Cloth diapers and disposable diapers

3. How would each of the following affect the Canadian market supply curve for wheat? **LO6**
   a.  A new and improved crop rotation technique is discovered.
   b.  The price of fertilizer falls.
   c.  The government offers new tax breaks to farmers.
   d.  The Prairies suffer a drought.

4. Indicate how you think each of the following would affect demand in the indicated market: **LO3, LO6**
   a.  An increase in family income on the demand for winter vacations in the Caribbean.

b. A study linking beef consumption to heart disease on the demand for hamburgers.

c. A relaxation of immigration laws on the demand for elementary-school places.

d. An increase in the price of audiocassettes on the demand for CDs.

e. An increase in the price of CDs on the demand for CDs.

5. A student at the University of Regina claims to have spotted a UFO outside Regina. How will his claim affect the supply of binoculars in Regina stores? LO2, LO3, LO6

6. What will happen to the equilibrium price and quantity of oranges if the price of fertilizer used for growing oranges rises? LO6

7. How will an increase in the birthrate affect the equilibrium price of land? LO6

8. What will happen to the equilibrium price and quantity of fish if it is discovered that fish oils help prevent heart disease? LO6

9. What will happen to the equilibrium price and quantity of beef if the price of chicken feed increases? LO6

10. Use supply and demand analysis to explain why hotel room rental rates near your campus during parents' weekend and graduation weekend might differ from the rates charged during the rest of the year. LO6

11. Suppose the current issue of *The Globe and Mail* reports an outbreak of mad cow disease in Manitoba, as well as the discovery of a new breed of chicken that gains more weight from the same amount of food than existing breeds. How will these developments affect the equilibrium price and quantity of chicken sold in Canada? LO6

12. What will happen to the equilibrium quantity and price of potatoes if population increases and a new, higher yielding variety of potato plant is developed? LO6

13. What will happen to the equilibrium price and quantity of apples if apples are discovered to help prevent colds and a fungus kills 10 percent of existing apple trees? LO6

14. What will happen to the equilibrium quantity and price of corn if the price of butter increases and the price of fertilizer decreases? LO6

15. Tofu was available 25 years ago only from small businesses operating in Chinese quarters of large cities. Today, tofu has become popular as a high-protein health food and is widely available in supermarkets throughout Canada. At the same time, production has evolved to become factory-based, using modern food-processing technologies. Draw a diagram with demand and supply curves depicting the market for tofu 25 years ago and the market for tofu today. Given the information above, what does the demand-supply model predict about changes in the quantity of tofu sold in Canada between then and now? What does it predict about changes in the price of tofu? LO6

16. State whether the following statement is true, false, or uncertain and explain why: All goods and services should be provided through markets because markets in equilibrium leave no unexploited opportunities for individuals. LO5

17. Suppose that there is a single seller of electricity and that the government reduces the price that the seller is allowed to charge. Is it appropriate to apply the supply and demand model to analyze this scenario? Explain. LO7

## ANSWERS TO IN-CHAPTER EXERCISES

3.1 Travel by air and travel by bus are substitutes, so a decline in airfares will shift the demand for bus travel to the left, resulting in lower bus fares and fewer bus trips taken. Travel by air and the use of resort hotels are complements, so a decline in airfares will shift the demand for resort hotel rooms to the right, resulting in higher hotel rates and an increase in the number of rooms rented. LO6

3.2 A decrease in income will shift the demand curve for a normal good to the left and will shift the demand curve for an inferior good to the right. LO6

**3.3**    The vitamin discovery shifts the demand for chips to the right, and the crop losses shift the supply of bags of chips to the left. Both shifts result in an increase in the equilibrium price of bags of chips. But depending on the relative magnitude of the shifts, the equilibrium quantity of bags of chips may either rise, as in panel (a) of the figure, or fall, as in panel (b). **LO6**

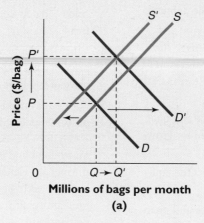

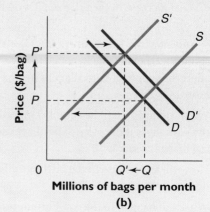

# COMPETITION AND THE INVISIBLE HAND

To understand the logic of economic processes, it is often useful to start by drawing a simple sketch that outlines the main features, and then paint a more realistic, more complicated picture of the economy over that simple outline. This text, therefore, analyzes first how things would work in an idealized, perfectly competitive economy in which consumers are perfectly informed and no firm has market power. This idealized structure is the subject of Part 2. Because many parts of the economy do not fit this idealized model very well, Part 3 will discuss how our simple model can be made more realistic, and how that affects our conclusions. But we will start simple.

In our review of supply and demand in Part 1, we accepted the law of demand, which says that demand curves are downward sloping, without further questioning. In Chapter 4, we will see that this law is a simple consequence of the fact that people spend their limited incomes in rational ways. We will also explore the concept of price elasticity, which describes the sensitivity of the quantity purchased to variations in price. In Chapter 5, our focus will shift to the seller's side of the market, and our task will be to explain why upward-sloping supply curves are a consequence of production decisions taken by firms whose goal it is to maximize profit. In Chapter 6, we will investigate the "invisible hand" of the marketplace—how economic forces guide profit-seeking firms and satisfaction-seeking consumers to an equilibrium outcome that encourages aggressive cost cutting by firms. Our agenda in Chapter 7 is to carefully develop the concept of economic surplus. We want to investigate the conditions under which unregulated markets generate the largest possible economic surplus and the circumstances under which attempts to interfere with market outcomes may lead to undesired consequences.

In Part 3, we will examine the conditions under which unregulated markets generate inferior outcomes, but before we consider what markets do poorly, we will examine what markets can do well, in Part 2.

# CHAPTER 4

# Demand: The Benefit Side of the Market

## LEARNING OBJECTIVES

When you have completed this chapter, you will be able to:

**LO1** Derive the rational spending rule.

**LO2** Use the rational spending rule to determine the optimum allocation of a budget.

**LO3** Derive a demand curve for an individual consumer by using the rational spending rule.

**LO4** Define the income effect and the substitution effect of a price change.

**LO5** Sum individual demand curves to obtain a market demand curve.

**LO6** Interpret numerical values obtained by calculating price, income, and cross-price elasticities.

**LO7** Calculate price, income, and cross-price elasticities of demand.

Many illicit drug users commit crimes to finance their addiction. The connection between drugs and crime has led to calls for more vigorous efforts to stop the smuggling of illicit drugs. But can such efforts reduce the likelihood that your laptop computer will be stolen in the next month?

Attempts to reduce the supply of illicit drugs can be seen as a leftward shift in the supply curve for drugs. If these attempts are successful, our basic supply and demand analysis predicts an increase in price. The law of demand tells us that drug users will respond by consuming a smaller quantity of drugs. But the amount of crime drug users commit depends not on the *price* or *quantity* of drugs they consume but rather on their *total expenditure* on drugs. Depending on the specific characteristics of the demand curve for illicit drugs, a price increase might reduce total expenditure on drugs, but it could also raise total expenditure.

Suppose, for example, that extra RCMP anti-smuggling efforts were to shift the supply curve in the market for illicit drugs to the left, as shown in Figure 4.1. As a result, the equilibrium quantity of drugs falls from 5000 kg to 4000 kg per day, and the price of drugs rises from $500 to $800 per kilogram. The total amount spent on drugs, which had been $2 500 000 per day (5000 kg/day times $500/kg), rises to $3 200 000 per day (4000 kg/day times $800/kg). In this particular case, then, efforts to stem the supply of drugs actually increase the likelihood of your laptop being stolen.

Other benefits from stemming the flow of illicit drugs might still outweigh the resulting increase in crime. But, knowing that the policy might increase drug-related crime would clearly be useful to law enforcement authorities.

This chapter will explore the demand side of the market in greater depth than was possible in Chapter 3. In that chapter, we merely asked you to accept as an intuitively plausible claim that the quantity demanded of a good or service declines as its price rises. This relationship is known as the law of demand, and we will see how it emerges as a simple consequence of the assumption that people spend their limited incomes in rational ways. We will also examine the conditions under which an increase in the price produces an increase in total spending—or not!

In the illicit drug example in Figure 4.1, the increase in price led to an increase in total spending. In many other cases, an increase in price will lead to a reduction in total

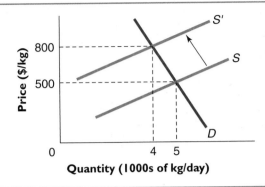

**FIGURE 4.1**
**The Effect of Extra RCMP Patrols on the Market for Illicit Drugs**
More policing shifts supply leftward and reduces the quantity demanded, but it may actually increase the total amount spent on drugs.

spending. Why this difference? The underlying phenomenon that explains this pattern, we will see, is elasticity of demand, a measure of the extent to which quantity demanded responds to variations in price.

# 4.1 NEEDS, WANTS, AND THE LAW OF DEMAND

The demand curve is a relationship between the quantity demanded and *all* costs, monetary and non-monetary, associated with acquiring a good. We can thus state the *law of demand* as follows:

**The Law of Demand:** Other things remaining equal, people will purchase a smaller quantity of any good or service they want as the price of purchasing one more unit of it increases.

As stated, the law of demand is a direct consequence of the cost–benefit principle, which says that an activity will be pursued if (and only if) its benefits are greater than its costs. Recall that we measure the benefit of an activity by the highest price we would be willing to pay to pursue it. When the price of something rises, it is more likely that the price will now exceed the highest price we are willing to pay for it. Hence we are less likely to purchase that thing.

The law of demand includes the phrase "other things remaining equal" because the cost of an activity is the sum of all the sacrifices—monetary and non-monetary, implicit and explicit—a person must make for the activity. For example, if you enjoy gourmet coffee, you may be willing to walk to the nearby coffee shop and pay $1.50 for a cup. But if that coffee shop closes and you must walk three blocks to buy a cup, still for $1.50, would you go? The money price is the same, but the total cost of the coffee (the sum of the money price and the time cost of getting it) has increased. Hence you are likely to purchase less. By stating that other things remain equal, we assume that the time cost does not change. The law of demand focuses on the relationship between money price and quantity and states that if other things, such as time cost, do not remain equal, the quantity demanded is likely to change.

COST-BENEFIT

# 4.2 CHOICES AND THE LAW OF DEMAND

In everyday language, we distinguish between goods and services people need and those they merely want. For example, we might say that someone wants a ski vacation in the Rockies, but what he really needs is a few days off from his daily routine; or that someone wants a house with a view, but what she really needs is shelter from the elements. Sometimes, of course, we hear other people protesting that they "need" something (like a third cup of coffee) which they could easily do without. However, in analyzing how

www.tfc-charts.w2d.com/learning/law_of_demand.html
Law of Demand Website

markets work, the crucial issue is how much individuals are willing and able to pay for a good. When individuals purchase a good, the good's sellers rarely know, or care, whether the purchasers regard the good as a "need" or a "want." What matters to the seller is whether or not the buyer has the money to buy the good and is willing to spend it—at the price that the seller wants to receive.

The scarcity problem reminds us that although our resources are finite our appetites are boundless. Even if we had unlimited bank accounts, we would quickly run out of the time and energy needed to do all the things we want to do. Choices are inescapable, and there are many ways to allocate our limited incomes across the myriad goods and services available for purchase. Which allocation will we choose? To answer that question, we begin by recognizing that goods and services are not ends in themselves but rather means for satisfying our desires.

## MEASURING WANTS: THE CONCEPT OF UTILITY

**utility** the sense of well-being, satisfaction, or pleasure a person derives from consuming a good or service

**util** a unit of pleasure or utility obtained from an item

Economists use the concept of **utility** to represent the satisfaction or pleasure that people derive from their consumption activities. The assumption of *utility maximization* just means that people try to allocate their incomes so as to maximize their satisfaction.

At one time, economists imagined that the utility associated with different activities could be directly measured—as in a **util** or one unit of pleasure, or utility. In his book, *Introduction to the Principles of Morals and Legislation* (1789), the eighteenth-century British economist Jeremy Bentham expressed his belief that, ultimately, it would be possible to measure the utility experienced by an individual (imagine, for example, an "utilometer" that would allow us to measure *utils*[1]). No measuring device was ever invented that could measure the pleasures of different people in comparable units. However, for the purposes of demand theory, we only need to assume that each of us knows how much utility, or pleasure, we obtain from our own consumption.

Imagine that a consumer, whom we will call Lamar, reaches the front of the line at a free ice cream stand on a hot day and wants to maximize his utility. How many ice cream cones will he ask for? Table 4.1 shows the relationship between the total number of ice cream cones Lamar eats per hour and the total utility that he derives from them, according to his own personal preferences. Utility is measured in utils per hour.[2]

As Table 4.1 shows, Lamar's total utility increases with each cone he eats, up to the fourth cone. Eating four cones per hour makes him happier than eating three, which

**TABLE 4.1**
**Lamar's Total Utility from Ice Cream Consumption**

| Cone quantity (cones/hour) | Total utility (utils/hour) |
| --- | --- |
| 0 | 0 |
| 1 | 100 |
| 2 | 150 |
| 3 | 175 |
| 4 | 187 |
| 5 | 184 |

1   The debate on the feasibility of measuring utility continues; see, for example, Daniel Kahneman, Peter P. Wakker and Rakesh Sarin, "Back to Bentham? Explorations of Experienced Utility," *Quarterly Journal of Economics*, May 1997, Vol. 112, No. 2, pp. 375–405; or Rafael Di Tella and Robert MacCulloch, "Some Uses of Happiness Data in Economics," *Journal of Economic Perspectives*, 20:1, 2006, pp. 25–46.

2   Note that the measurements in the table are stated in terms of cones per hour and utils per hour. Why per hour? Because without an explicit time dimension, we would have no idea whether a given quantity was large or small. Five ice cream cones in a lifetime is not many, but five in an hour would be more than most of us would care to eat.

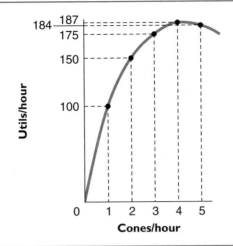

**FIGURE 4.2**

**Lamar's Total Utility from Ice Cream Consumption**
For most goods, utility rises at a diminishing rate with additional consumption.

makes him happier than eating two, and so on. But beyond four cones per hour, consuming more ice cream actually makes Lamar less happy. The fifth cone reduces his total utility from 187 utils per hour to 184 utils per hour.

We can display the utility information in Table 4.1 graphically, as in Figure 4.2. Note in the graph that the more cones per hour Lamar eats, the more utils he gets, but, again, only up to the fourth cone. Once he moves beyond four cones, his total utility begins to decline. Lamar's happiness reaches a maximum of 187 utils when he eats four cones per hour. At that point, he has no incentive to eat the fifth cone, even though it is absolutely free. Eating the fifth cone actually makes him worse off. He probably feels sick.

Table 4.1 and Figure 4.2 illustrate another important aspect of the relationship between utility and consumption—namely, that the additional utility from additional units of consumption declines as total consumption increases. Thus, one cone per hour is much better than no cones, because the first cone increases total utility by 100 utils. However, four cones per hour is only a little better than three, because the fourth cone adds only 12 utils to total utility.

The term **marginal utility** denotes the amount by which total utility changes when consumption changes by one unit. The third column of Table 4.2 shows the marginal utility values that correspond to changes in Lamar's level of ice cream consumption. For example, the second entry in the third column represents the increase in total utility (measured in utils per cone) when Lamar's consumption rises from one cone per hour to two. Note that the marginal utility entries in column 3 are placed midway between the rows of the preceding columns, indicating that marginal utility corresponds to the movement from one consumption quantity to the next. Thus, we would say that the marginal utility of moving from one to two cones per hour is 50 utils per cone for Lamar.

**marginal utility** the additional utility gained from consuming an additional unit of a good

**TABLE 4.2**
**Lamar's Total and Marginal Utility from Ice Cream Consumption**

| Cone quantity (cones/hour) | Total utility (utils/hour) | Marginal utility (utils/cone) |
|:---:|:---:|:---:|
| 0 | 0 | |
| | | 100 |
| 1 | 100 | |
| | | 50 |
| 2 | 150 | |
| | | 25 |
| 3 | 175 | |
| | | 12 |
| 4 | 187 | |
| | | −3 |
| 5 | 184 | |

$$\text{Marginal utility} = \frac{\text{change in utility}}{\text{change in consumption}}$$
$$= \frac{150 \text{ utils} - 100 \text{ utils}}{2 \text{ cones} - 1 \text{ cone}}$$
$$= 50 \text{ utils/cone}$$

**Law of Diminishing Marginal Utility:** As consumption of a good increases beyond some point, the additional utility gained from an additional unit of the good tends to decline.

This pattern of diminishing marginal utility holds true not just for Lamar but also for most consumers of most goods. If we have one bicycle or one Corvette, we are happier than we are with none; if we have two, we may be even happier—but not twice as happy, and so on.

COST-
BENEFIT

Suppose that Lamar has waited several hours in the lineup for ice cream. What will he do when he gets to the front of the line? At that point, the opportunity cost of the time he spent waiting is a sunk cost and, hence, is irrelevant to his decision about how many cones to order. And since there is no monetary charge for the cones, the cost of ordering an additional one is zero.

According to the cost–benefit criterion, Lamar will therefore continue to order cones as long as the marginal benefit (here, the marginal utility he gets from an additional cone) is greater than or equal to zero. Thus, he will order four cones.

## ALLOCATING A FIXED INCOME BETWEEN TWO GOODS

The Lamar example, so far, shows that even if a good is completely free, and even if it is the only good, he will not want to consume an infinite quantity of it. Instead, if he is a rational consumer, he will stop at the amount for which the marginal utility of the good is zero. However, a consumer's decision typically is more complicated. In the real world, a consumer must make decisions not just about a single good but about many, and the cost of consuming additional units will rarely be zero.

Suppose Lamar has a fixed income and must decide how to spend it on two different goods, each with a positive price. If Lamar is rational, will he spend all his income on one of the goods or part of it on each? The law of diminishing marginal utility tells us that if a large quantity of a good is being consumed, its marginally utility is likely to be low. If a small quantity is being consumed, the good's marginal utility is likely to be high. The law of diminishing marginal utility suggests that, instead of devoting more and more money to the purchase of a good whose marginal utility is relatively low, we generally do better to spend that money on other goods whose marginal utility is higher.

The simplest way to illustrate how economists think about the spending decisions of a utility-maximizing consumer is to work through an example like the following.

### EXAMPLE 4.1

**How many vanilla ice cream cones and chocolate sundaes will Lamar consume?**

Suppose Lamar now has to pay for ice cream at an ice cream parlour and has a fixed income of $10 per week to spend. His two favourite choices are vanilla cones and chocolate sundaes. Sundaes sell for $2 and vanilla cones for $1. The number of utils Lamar derives from consuming different amounts of each are shown in Table 4.3. If Lamar's goal is to maximize the utility he derives from spending $10 per week on ice cream, how many sundaes and how many cones will he eat?

Lamar wants to maximize the total number of utils he gets from eating two types of ice cream, cones and sundaes, on a $10 weekly budget. His spending limit, or *budget constraint,* is $10. One way Lamar can solve his problem is to list all the combinations of cones and sundaes that cost $10 per week and then choose the one that delivers the highest total utility. Suppose he spends the entire $10 on cones. At $1 apiece, that gives him 10 cones per week, yielding a total utility of 80 utils per week.

Now compare that with what happens if Lamar divides his budget between cones and sundaes. Suppose, for example, that he buys only six cones, which leaves $4 to spend on sundaes (enough to buy two per week). That gives him 80 utils/week from cones + 80 utils/week from sundaes = 160 utils/week, or twice as many utils per week as he got by spending all his income on cones. Table 4.4 shows the various combinations of cones and sundaes Lamar can buy without exceeding his $10 weekly budget constraint.

**TABLE 4.3**
**Utility from Two Types of Ice Cream Consumption**

| Vanilla cones per week | Utils/week from cones | Chocolate sundaes per week | Utils/week from sundaes |
|---|---|---|---|
| 0 | 0 | 0 | 0 |
| 1 | 36 | 1 | 50 |
| 2 | 50 | 2 | 80 |
| 3 | 60 | 3 | 105 |
| 4 | 68 | 4 | 120 |
| 5 | 75 | 5 | 130 |
| 6 | 80 | 6 | 138 |
| 7 | 84 | 7 | 144 |
| 8 | 82 | 8 | 148 |
| 9 | 81 | 9 | 150 |
| 10 | 80 | 10 | 151 |

**TABLE 4.4**
**Affordable Combinations of Cones and Sundaes**

| Cone/sundae combinations | Total utility (utils/week) |
|---|---|
| 10 cones, 0 sundaes | 80 +   0 =  80 |
| 8 cones, 1 sundae | 82 +  50 = 132 |
| 6 cones, 2 sundaes | 80 +  80 = 160 |
| 4 cones, 3 sundaes | 68 + 105 = 173 |
| 2 cones, 4 sundaes | 50 + 120 = 170 |
| 0 cones, 5 sundaes | 0 + 130 = 130 |

A glance at the table shows that Lamar's *optimal combination of goods* is four cones and three sundaes per week. His total utility from that combination is 173 utils per week—more than he'd get from any of the other affordable combinations. In other words, the **optimal combination of goods** is the *affordable* combination that delivers *maximum total utility.*

**optimal combination of goods** the affordable combination that yields the highest total utility

In Example 4.1, the combination of 8 cones per week and 4 sundaes per week gives a total utility of 202 utils per week. Why is that combination not Lamar's best choice?

**EXERCISE 4.1**

## THE RATIONAL SPENDING RULE

Remember, if Lamar really is at his point of maximum utility, he cannot become even better off just by reallocating a dollar of expenditure from one good to the other. We will soon see that in order to achieve the highest possible utility from the $10 per week he spends on ice cream, Lamar must divide his purchases between cones and sundaes so that the marginal utility of a dollar spent on cones is equal to the marginal utility of a dollar spent on sundaes. Let us refer to Table 4.3 to see if this condition is met when Lamar buys four cones and three sundaes per week.

Note that the marginal utility of Lamar's third sundae is 25 utils (the difference between the 105 utils he gets from three sundaes and the 80 utils he gets from two). And since the third sundae costs him $2, his marginal utility *per dollar* is 25 utils/$2, or 12.5 utils per dollar. Could he have gotten more utils per dollar had he spent $2 on cones instead? Spending $1 more on cones would move him from four cones per week to five, which would increase his total utility from cones by seven utils per week (the difference between the 75 utils he gets from five cones and the 68 utils he gets from four). Buying a sixth cone would increase his total utility by only five utils, for a total increase of 12 utils—significantly less than the 25 utils he sacrifices by not purchasing the third sundae. Shifting more money to cones would, thus, prevent Lamar from achieving the largest total utility possible, given his weekly budget for ice cream.

Note that when Lamar allocates his budget optimally—that is, when he buys four cones per week and three sundaes—he receives 12.5 utils per dollar from his last purchase of sundaes but only eight utils per dollar from his last purchase of vanilla cones. If this discrepancy strikes you as a problem, your economic intuition has served you well. Since Lamar is getting more bang for his buck (more utils per dollar) from the last sundae he purchases than from the last cone, it would seem that he ought to spend more on sundaes and less on cones.

The way the example is structured, however, allows Lamar to purchase cones and sundaes *only in whole-number amounts*. Spending more on sundaes would thus require a move from three sundaes a week to four. And because buying a fourth sundae would yield only 7.5 utils per dollar, which is less than he would get by spending the same amount on cones, Lamar is better off if he consumes only three sundaes.

In many real world cases, the inability to divide goods and services into fractional amounts is not an insurmountable problem. After all, if Lamar could do better by consuming, say, 3.2 sundaes per week instead of 3, he could accomplish that by consuming 32 sundaes every 10 weeks, which works out to an average of 3.2 per week.

Whenever goods can be consumed in fractional quantities, we can use the following important rule—the *rational spending rule*—to solve the consumer's allocation problem.

**The Rational Spending Rule:** To maximize utility yielded by a fixed income, spending must be allocated across goods so that the marginal utility per dollar is the same for each good.

The rational spending rule tells us that if Lamar can purchase ice cream in fractional amounts, he will continue shifting from cones to sundaes until the marginal utility per dollar he obtains from each of the two goods become equal.

The rational spending rule can be expressed as a simple formula. Also, if Lamar is rational, he will buy cones and sundaes as long as he has money for them and it increases his pleasure. Lamar will, therefore, arrange his spending so that marginal utility per dollar is the same for each good while he spends his entire budget for ice cream. If we use $MU_C$ to denote Lamar's marginal utility from cone consumption (measured in utils per cone) and $P_C$ to denote the price of cones in dollars (measured in dollars per cone), then the ratio $MU_C/P_C$ will represent Lamar's marginal utility per dollar spent on cones. Similarly, if we use $MU_S$ to denote Lamar's marginal utility from sundae consumption, and $P_S$ to denote the price of sundaes, then $MU_S/P_S$ will represent his marginal utility per dollar spent on sundaes. The marginal utility per dollar will be exactly the same for the two types—and hence, total utility will be maximized—when the following simple equation is satisfied:

**The Rational Spending Rule for Two Goods:**

$$\frac{MU_C}{P_C} = \frac{MU_S}{P_S}$$

(4.1)

The rational spending rule follows directly from the cost–benefit principle and is easily generalized to apply to spending decisions regarding large numbers of goods. In its most general form, it says that in order to maximize utility, the ratio of marginal utility to price must be the same for each good the consumer buys. If the ratio were higher for one good than for another, the consumer could always increase her total utility just by reallocating spending—buying more of the first good and less of the second.

COST-BENEFIT

## HOW INCOME AND THE PRICES OF OTHER GOODS AFFECT DEMAND

In Chapter 3, we made the plausible assumption that the demand for any good or service depends on income and the prices of other goods. As you apply the rational spending rule to work through the following exercises, you will see *why* more clearly.

**Refer to Example 4.1. How will Lamar allocate his spending between cones and sundaes if he has $14 per week rather than $10 per week to spend on ice cream?**

EXERCISE 4.2

From among the combinations of goods that are affordable, the utility-maximizing consumer chooses the combination that provides the highest total utility. Extra income stimulates demand by enlarging the set of affordable combinations; that is, by making it possible to buy more of each good than before. Since people typically have somewhat different tastes, Lamar's responses to having more (or less) income will not necessarily be the same as those of someone else.[3] In general, the market demand for a commodity is determined both by the *ability* of potential consumers to pay and by their *willingness* to pay, and both income and taste differ from one person to the next.

**Suppose that Lamar again has a budget of $10 per week to allocate between vanilla ice cream cones and chocolate sundaes. The utilities he derives from different quantities of each are, again, as given in Example 4.1, and chocolate sundaes still sell for $2 apiece. How many units of each type will Lamar buy if the price of vanilla cones is $2 rather than $1?**

EXERCISE 4.3

## THE RATIONAL SPENDING RULE AND THE DEMAND CURVE

By applying the rational spending rule to price changes, a demand curve emerges. Example 4.1 showed that, at $1 per cone, Lamar will buy 4 cones for a marginal utility of 8 utils per dollar spent on cones. With the increase in price to $2 per cone in Exercise 4.3, Lamar's marginal utility per dollar spent on the last cone drops to 4 utils and, applying the rational spending rule, he will now buy only one cone per week. As Figure 4.3 shows, the two combinations of price and quantity that result from applying the rational spending rule determine two points on a demand curve.

Notice, too, that Lamar's demand curve for ice cream cones in Figure 4.3 was based on his budget of $10/week for ice cream. If Lamar's total budget increased, we would expect this demand curve to shift. Generally, an individual's demand for a normal good will increase the larger his income is.

---

3 If the tastes of different people are different, and if income is transferred between Lamar and "somebody else," there is no guarantee that the changes in Lamar's consumption of specific goods will exactly offset the changes in the consumption of somebody else. In general, the distribution of income will affect the pattern of demand for specific commodities.

**FIGURE 4.3**
**Lamar's Demand for Vanilla Cones**
Lamar's weekly demand for vanilla cones can be derived by applying the rational spending rule to his utility schedule, which is shown in Table 4.3. The demand curve shown assumes Lamar's budget for cones and sundaes is $10/week.

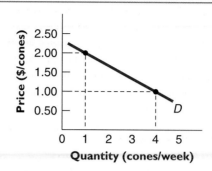

## THE INCOME EFFECT AND THE SUBSTITUTION EFFECT

If you worked through Exercise 4.3 successfully, you saw that a rise in the price of cones caused Lamar to increase his consumption of sundaes, an implication of the fact that the rational spending rule requires that the ratio of marginal utility to price be the same for all goods.[4] This means that if the price of one good goes up, consumers can increase their total utility by devoting a smaller proportion of their incomes to that good and a larger proportion to others. When the price of a vanilla ice cream cone increased, Lamar therefore decreased his consumption of cones *and* increased his consumption of sundaes—he substituted for a decrease in cone consumption by increasing his consumption of sundaes.

As well, an increase in the price of cones meant that Lamar's total income was not sufficient to purchase the bundle of goods he had previously consumed. The impact of higher cone prices on Lamar's consumption of cones therefore can be broken down into two effects: the *income effect* and the *substitution effect*.

As Appendix 4B discusses in more depth, an increase in prices can be thought of as an income loss because a price increase will reduce the purchasing power of a given, fixed income. To define the income effect of a price change, recall that before the price of a cone increased, Lamar maximized his total utility by spending $10 to purchase 4 cones and 3 sundaes per week. However, after the price of a cone rose to $2, Lamar needed $14 per week to purchase this same combination of cones and sundaes. Lamar is clearly worse off because of the price increase. His weekly budget of $10 for ice cream cannot buy as much as it did when cones cost only $1 each—Lamar's real income has decreased. The **income effect** is the change in quantity demanded of a good that occurs because a change in the price of the good changes the real income of the purchaser.

When the price of a vanilla ice cream cone increased from $1 to $2, but the price of a chocolate sundae stayed at $2, the price of cones relative to sundaes rose. But one could equally say that the price of sundaes relative to cones fell. These changes in relative prices can be expected to influence consumption, whatever the level of total income the consumer has. Suppose that after the price of cones increased, Lamar's income had been increased by enough so that, if he wanted to, he could still purchase his original consumption bundle (4 cones and 3 sundaes per week), just as he had before the price increase. Even if Lamar had been compensated in this fashion for his loss of purchasing power, such that there was no "income effect" on consumption, he still faced a change in relative prices. The rational spending rule tells us that he will reduce his weekly consumption of cones (now relatively more expensive) and increase his weekly consumption of sundaes (now relatively cheaper)—he will *substitute* the good that now has a relatively lower price for the good whose relative price has simultaneously increased, until the rational spending rule is fulfilled. When real income is held constant, the change in the quantity demanded of a good whose relative price has changed is known as the **substitution effect**.

**income effect** the change in quantity demanded of a good that occurs because a change in the price of the good has changed the real income of the purchaser

**substitution effect** the change in quantity demanded of a good whose relative price has changed while a consumer's real income is held constant

4  Strictly speaking, this only holds exactly when consumption goods can be purchased in fractional quantities.

**Suppose that when the price of vanilla ice cream cones increases from $1 to $2, Lamar is the lucky winner of a prize from a local dairy that gives him an extra $4 per week to spend on vanilla ice cream cones and chocolate sundaes. According to the rational spending rule, how many cones and how many sundaes will Lamar purchase each week?**

> **RECAP**
>
> ### CHOICES AND THE LAW OF DEMAND
>
> The scarcity problem challenges us to allocate our incomes among the various goods that are available so as to fulfill our desires to the greatest possible degree. The optimal combination of goods is the affordable combination that yields the highest total utility. For goods that are perfectly divisible, the rational spending rule states that the optimal combination occurs when the marginal utility per dollar is the same for each good. If this condition is not satisfied, the consumer can increase utility by spending less on goods for which the marginal utility per dollar is lower, and more on goods for which the marginal utility per dollar is higher.

## 4.3   APPLYING THE RATIONAL SPENDING RULE

The real payoff from learning the law of demand and the rational spending rule lies not in working through hypothetical examples but in using these abstract concepts to make sense of the world around you. To encourage you in your efforts to become an economic naturalist, we turn now to a sequence of examples.

### SUBSTITUTION AT WORK

When the price of a good or service goes up, rational consumers generally turn to less expensive substitutes. Sometimes the substitutes are quite direct, as when, for example, the price of a new Honda increases, compared to a new Ford. But sometimes substitution is more complex; for instance, when an increase in the price of gasoline causes commuters to look for an apartment closer to their work, or to shift from driving a car to taking the bus. Frequently, once you start to think about it, there are many opportunities to substitute one good for another. An especially important example is the impact of energy prices on the consumption of carbon energy sources.

Concern about reducing greenhouse gas emissions caused by the consumption of carbon-based fuels has increased in recent years, and there is ample historical evidence on the importance of gasoline prices for consumption. During the late 1970s, fuel shortages brought on by interruptions in the supply of oil from the Middle East led to sharp increases in the price of gasoline and other fuels. In a variety of ways, some straightforward and others remarkably ingenious, consumers reduced their oil consumption. They formed carpools; switched to public transportation; bought lower-powered cars; moved closer to work; took fewer trips; turned down their thermostats; installed insulation, storm windows, and solar heaters; and bought more efficient appliances.

As the next example points out, consumers not only abandon a good in favour of substitutes when it gets more expensive, but they also return to that good when real prices return to their original levels.[5]

---

5   See Valerie A. Ramey and Daniel J. Vine "Oil, Automobiles, and the U.S. Economy: How Much Have Things Really Changed?" Working Paper 16067, National Bureau of Economic Research, June 2010. Accessed at http://www.nber.org/papers/w16067.

ECONOMIC NATURALIST    4.1

### Why did people turn to four-cylinder cars in the 1970s, only to shift back to six- and eight-cylinder cars in the 1990s?

At the beginning of 1973, the price of light crude oil on world markets was about $2.10 per barrel. (Oil prices on world markets are quoted in U.S. dollars.) Major disruptions of oil supplies occurred in 1974 and 1979. By early 1981, light crude oil was selling for more than $37, and prices of other grades had increased by similar magnitudes. Prices of refined products, including gasoline, also increased dramatically. Cars with four-cylinder engines use much less gasoline than those with six- or eight-cylinder engines, which most people were driving at the time. Hence, the demand for cars with four-cylinder engines rose, while V8 engines sold poorly. After 1980, fuel supplies stabilized, though the price of gasoline continued to rise slowly. Nevertheless, by the end of the 1980s, the proportion of cars sold with six- and eight-cylinder engines was rising. Why this reversal?

To explain the reversal, we must focus on the changes in the **real price** of gasoline—that is, the dollar price relative to the average price of other items. When someone decides how big an engine to choose, what matters is not the **nominal price** of gasoline—that is, the price of it in dollar terms—but the price of gasoline *relative* to all other goods. On average, the nominal prices of all goods and services sold in Canada have been rising continually since the 1930s. (Some nominal prices have been increasing more rapidly, some less rapidly, and some have even fallen; but, on average, they have been rising.) From 1974 until early 1981, the nominal price of gasoline rose much more rapidly than the average rate of increase for all nominal prices in the economy. After 1981, the pattern began to reverse. Though the nominal price of gasoline was rising, it rose more slowly than the average rate of increase for all nominal prices. Thus, from 1974 to 1981, the price of gasoline *relative to other goods and services* was rising. After 1981, *its relative price fell sharply* and remained low until the late 1990s. In 1999, the nominal price of a litre of gasoline actually represented a lower cost in terms of other goods and services than did the 1973 price. Its real price, that is, its opportunity cost, was actually quite low. Average income also increased from 1981 to 1999. The decline in the real price of gasoline (along with rising average incomes) accounted for the reversal of the trend toward smaller engines.

Will people choose cars with large or small engines? Much of the answer depends on what happens to the real retail price of gasoline—which depends partly on trends in world energy markets and partly on taxation decisions of governments.

---

**real price** dollar price of a good relative to the average dollar price of all other goods and services

**nominal price** absolute price of a good in dollar terms

A sharp decline in the real price of gasoline also helps to account for the explosive growth in sport utility vehicle sales between 1990 and 2007. Almost four million SUVs were sold in the United States in 2001, up from only 750 000 in 1990. Gasoline has always been more expensive in Canada; nevertheless, during the 1990s it was cheaper in Canada than it had been during the 1970s. Sales of SUVs rose in Canada, too. Some SUVs, like the Ford Excursion, weigh almost 3500 kg and burn more than 23.5 litres per 100 km when driven on city streets. Vehicles like these would have been dismal failures during the 1970s, but they were hot sellers in the cheap energy environment of the 1990s and early years of the twenty-first century. The price of gasoline has an especially big impact on sales of SUVs and other vehicles that are heavy users of gasoline.

## HOW THE DISTRIBUTION OF INCOME AFFECTS DEMAND

Wealthy people generally buy different commodities than the poor do (e.g., larger houses, more expensive cars), but we need not assume that this is because the wealthy have different tastes or feel more strongly about goods like housing. A much simpler explanation is that higher incomes enable the wealthy to consume more of what they want to buy, and that what people want to buy depends in part on what they already

*"We motored over to say hi!"*

have. The very poor, for example, spend much of their income on food, but the proportion of income a person spends on food tends to fall as income rises, since other desires can be attended to once the need for food has been satisfied. At the other end of the income distribution, among the affluent, the proportion of income spent on foreign travel tends to rise as income rises. Low income earners may never travel abroad, but that is because they cannot afford to, not because they would not travel if they could afford it.

In general, the total demand for specific goods in an economy may change, not just because of changes in *average* incomes but also because of changes in the way income is distributed among people. If, for example, income is relatively equally distributed in a country like Canada, then most families may be able to afford to buy minivans, and the market for BMWs, Ferraris, and Cadillacs will be limited. If the same total income is divided more unequally, and average income remains unchanged while a larger share goes to the affluent (which means the poor and middle class get less), the structure of demand will change: fewer minivans will be sold, but sales of high-end cars will increase. In general, greater inequality implies that demand will shift downward for goods primarily consumed by poorer people (e.g., macaroni), with an upward shift in demand for the goods that more affluent people might buy (e.g., champagne).

**RECAP**

### APPLYING THE RATIONAL SPENDING RULE

Application of the rational spending rule highlights the important roles of income and substitution in explaining differences in consumption patterns among individuals, among communities, and across time. The rule also highlights the fact that real prices, as opposed to nominal prices, and income are what matter. The demand for a good falls when the real price of a substitute falls or the real price of a complement rises. Patterns of demand may differ between communities of the same average real income level if the distributions of income within those communities differ significantly.

## 4.4  INDIVIDUAL AND MARKET DEMAND CURVES

If we know what each individual's demand curve for a good looks like, how can we use that information to construct the market demand curve for the good? We must add together the individual demand curves, a process that is straightforward but requires care.[6]

### HORIZONTAL ADDITION

Suppose that there are only two buyers, Smith and Wong, in the market for canned tuna. Their individual demand curves—the amount each person would want to purchase, at each given price—have been derived by applying the rational spending rule and are as shown in Figure 4.4(a) and (b). To construct the market demand curve for canned tuna—the amount both of them together would want to buy, at each given price—we simply announce a sequence of prices and then add the quantity demanded by each buyer at each price. For example, at a price of $4 per can, Smith demands six cans per week [Figure 4.4(a)] and Wong demands two cans per week [Figure 4.4(b)], for a market demand of eight cans per week [Figure 4.4(c)].

The process of adding individual demand curves to get the market demand curve is known as *horizontal addition,* a term used to emphasize that we are adding the quantities which are measured on the horizontal axes of individual demand curves.

Figure 4.5(a) illustrates the special case in which each of 1000 consumers in the market has the same demand curve. To get the market demand curve in this case, we simply multiply each quantity on the representative individual demand curve by 1000 [Figure 4.5(b)].

**FIGURE 4.4**

**Individual and Market Demand Curves for Canned Tuna**

The quantity demanded at any price on the market demand curve in panel (c) is the sum of the individual quantities in panels (a) and (b) demanded at that price.

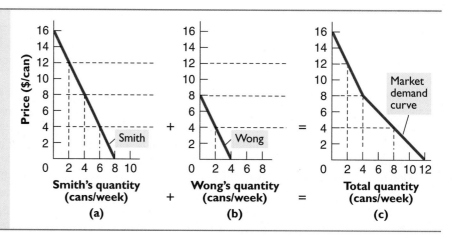

**FIGURE 4.5**

**The Individual and Market Demand Curves When All Buyers Have Identical Demand Curves**

When individual demand curves are identical, we get the market demand curve by multiplying each quantity on the individual demand curve by the number of consumers in the market.

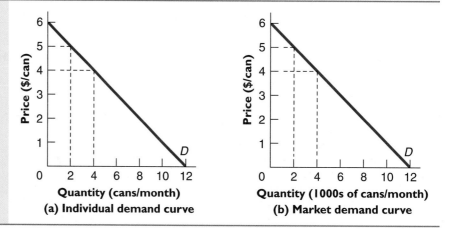

---

6  We assume that each particular good (in this case, canned tuna) is just one among many goods; i.e., it is a small part of total production. So variations in the amount of it produced have such a small impact on the incomes of households that it can be safely ignored.

## THE STRAIGHT-LINE DEMAND CURVE

So far, we have only predicted that the demand curve for a good or service slopes downward, with no predictions about the specific shape of the curve. Thus far, we have also been drawing demand curves as downward-sloping straight lines, but this is just for convenience.

In Figure 4.5(b), the vertical intercept, where quantity is zero, occurs at a price of $6. Total revenue is zero at the intercept of a straight-line demand curve with either the vertical or the horizontal axes. The economic interpretation is, therefore, if price is $6 or more, nothing will be sold and total revenue will be zero. At the horizontal intercept, price is zero and quantity is 12 000 cans per month. The economic interpretation is that, even if tuna is free, people will consume only 12 000 cans per month. But at a price of zero, total revenue will also be zero, no matter how many cans people consume.

Market demand curves may be shown not only in graphical form but in two other forms as well. The market demand relationship can be shown as a table. For example, the linear market demand curve shown in Figure 4.5(b) may be also represented as Table 4.5. It can also be represented by an equation, as is explained in Box 4.1.

**TABLE 4.5**
**The Market Demand for Canned Tuna in Tabular Form**

| Price ($/can) | Quantity (1000s of cans/month) |
| --- | --- |
| 0 | 12 |
| 1 | 10 |
| 2 | 8 |
| 3 | 6 |
| 4 | 4 |
| 5 | 2 |
| 6 | 0 |

**BOX 4.1**

### MARKET DEMAND AS AN EQUATION

Market demand can also be expressed algebraically. As shown in Chapter 3, the general formula for a straight-line demand curve is

$$Q_D = c - dP_D, \qquad (4.2)$$

where $P_D$ denotes the price of the good, usually measured in dollars per unit; $Q_D$ denotes the quantity demanded, in thousands of physical units per unit of time; $c$ denotes the horizontal intercept of the demand curve, and $-d$ is the reciprocal of the slope.[7]

To illustrate, we can write the equation for the market demand curve shown in Figure 4.6, which is the same as the one in Figure 4.5(b).

The graph shows that $c$, the horizontal intercept of the demand curve, is 12. The slope is the ratio of the vertical distance between any two points on the line (the rise) to the corresponding horizontal distance (the run). For example, if we look at the segment of the demand curve between the points labelled $A$ and $B$, the rise is $\Delta P = -1$ (since the line falls a vertical distance of 1 unit between $A$ and $B$), and the corresponding run is $\Delta Q = 2$. Thus, the slope of the demand

7  See footnote 2 of Chapter 3 for an explanation of why economists place price, the independent variable, on the vertical axis.

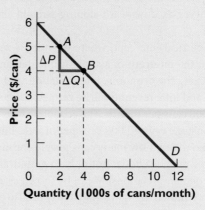

**FIGURE 4.6**
**The Market Demand Curve for Canned Tuna**

curve shown is $\Delta P/\Delta Q = -1/2$. Therefore $d$, the reciprocal of the slopes, is $-2$. Knowing both the slope and horizontal intercept of the demand curve, we also know that its equation must be

$$Q_D = 12 - 2P_D.$$

To check that this equation is indeed correct, consider whether it works for points $A$ and $B$. Does the equation hold, for example, if we let $P_D = 5$ and $Q_D = 2$? Calculations confirm that $2 = 12 - 2(5)$. Similarly, we can verify that $4 = 12 - 2(4)$.

In short, the relationship between demand and price can be expressed as a curve, a table, or an equation—all say the same thing but in different ways.

**EXERCISE 4.5**    **Find the equation of the linear demand curve for movie tickets shown in the following diagram.**

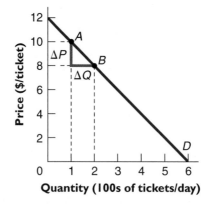

## TOTAL EXPENDITURE

Given the market demand curve for a good, the total amount consumers spend on the good will depend on the price for which it is sold. And by definition, the total daily expenditure on a good is simply the number of units bought each day, times the price for which it sells.

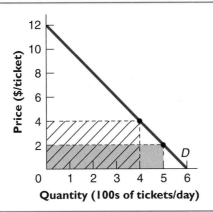

**FIGURE 4.7**
**The Demand Curve for Movie Tickets**
An increase in price from $2 to $4 per ticket increases total expenditure on tickets.

To illustrate, calculate how much movie goers will spend on tickets each day if the demand curve is as shown in Figure 4.7 and the price is $2 per ticket. The demand curve tells us that at a price of $2 per ticket, 500 tickets per day will be sold, so total expenditure at that price will be $1000 per day. If tickets sell not for $2 but for $4 apiece, 400 tickets will be sold each day, so total expenditure at the higher price will be $1600 per day.

The same point can be made in another way. In Figure 4.7, the area of the green rectangle, representing a quantity of 500 tickets/day and a price of $2, is $1000/day. The area of the rectangle containing the black lines is $1600/day. Thus, we see that the total revenue represented by the area of the rectangle containing the black lines is greater by $600/day. Notice, too, that in the previous sentence, "total revenue" has replaced "total expenditure," and recall the circular flow of income and expenditure, discussed in Chapter 3. Total expenditure for tickets by movie goers is equal to total revenue (or total receipts) received by the sellers of tickets.

Note that the total amount consumers spend on a product each day must equal the total amount sellers of the product receive. That is, the terms **total expenditure** and **total revenue** are always just two sides of the same coin.

It might seem that an increase in the market price of a product should always result in an increase in the total revenue received by sellers. But although that happened in the case we just saw, it need not always be so. When the price of a good rises, people will buy less of it, but that means the two factors that govern total revenue—price and quantity—are moving in opposite directions. So when price increases and quantity decreases, the question is, which will dominate; that is, has the quantity purchased fallen by a greater percentage than the percentage increase in price? Note, for example, that for the demand curve shown in panel (a) of Figure 4.8 (which is the same as the one we just saw in Figure 4.7), a rise in price from $8 to $10 per ticket will cause total expenditure on tickets to go down. Thus, people will spend $1600 per day on tickets at a price of $8, but only $1000 per day at a price of $10.

Panel (b) of Figure 4.8 makes the same point in a different way. The increase in price from $8 to $10 causes the quantity of tickets sold to fall from 200 to 100 per day. By itself, this causes total daily revenue to fall by $800: $8 × (−100 tickets) = −$800. The area of the green rectangle in panel (b) represents this drop in total revenue. At $10 per ticket, only 100 tickets are sold, but each of them sells for $2 more. Therefore, total daily revenue on the 100 tickets still sold must increase by $2 × 100 tickets = $200. The area of the blue square in panel (b) of Figure 4.8 represents this increase in total revenue. The net change is the sum of the two changes: −$800 + $200 = −$600/day. This is consistent with the reduction from $1600 to $1000/day shown just previously.

**total expenditure = total revenue** the dollar amount consumers spend on a product is equal to the dollar amount sellers receive

**FIGURE 4.8**
**The Demand Curve for Movie Tickets**

An increase in price from $8 to $10 per ticket results in a fall in total expenditure on tickets. Panel (a) shows the total expenditure when price is $8 per ticket and the total expenditure when price is $10 per ticket. At $8, $P \times Q$ = $8 × 200 tickets = $1600 (as shown by the lined rectangle). At $10, $P \times Q$ = $10 × 100 tickets = $1000 (as shown by the green rectangle). Panel (b) shows the reduction in total expenditure because 100 fewer tickets are sold when the price rises from $8 to $10 (green rectangle). It also shows the increase in total expenditure caused by each of the 100 tickets being sold at $2 more per ticket (blue square) when the price rises from $8 to $10.

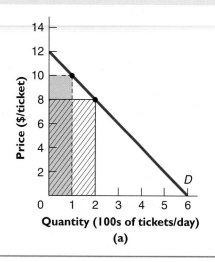
(a)

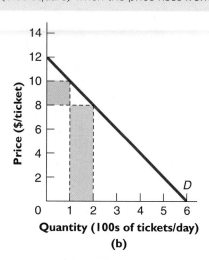
(b)

These examples illustrate a general rule: *a price increase will produce an increase in total revenue whenever the price increase is greater, in percentage terms, than the corresponding percentage reduction in quantity demanded.* Although the two price increases (from $2 to $4 and from $8 to $10) were of the same dollar value, $2 in each case, they are much different when expressed as a percentage of the original price. An increase from $2 to $4 represents a 100 percent increase in price, whereas an increase from $8 to $10 represents only a 25 percent increase in price. And although the quantity reductions caused by the two price increases were equal in absolute terms, they are very different when expressed as percentages of the quantities originally sold. Thus, although the decline in quantity demanded was 100 tickets per day in each case, it was just a 20 percent reduction in the first case (from 500 units to 400) but a 50 percent reduction in the second (from 200 units to 100). In the second case, the negative effect on total expenditure of the 50 percent quantity reduction outweighs the positive effect of the 25 percent price increase. The reverse happened in the first case: the 100 percent increase in price (from $2 to $4) outweighs the 20 percent reduction in quantity (from five units to four units).

**RECAP**

**INDIVIDUAL AND MARKET DEMAND CURVES**

To generate the market demand curve for a good, we add the individual demand curves of market participants horizontally. Although demand curves for actual goods will seldom be straight lines, they often can be well approximated as straight lines, especially when our concern is with the effects of small variations in quantity or price.

Total expenditure on a good is the product of its price and the quantity bought. Total revenue received by the seller of a good is the product of its price and the quantity sold. Because the quantity bought equals the quantity sold, total revenue must equal total expenditure.

# 4.5  PRICE ELASTICITY OF DEMAND

When the price of a good or service rises, the quantity demanded falls. But by how much?

To predict the effect of the price increase on total expenditure, we must also know by how much quantity will fall. The quantity demanded of some goods, such as salt, is not very sensitive to changes in price. Indeed, even if the price of salt were to double, or to fall by half, most people wouldn't alter their consumption of it. For other goods, however, the quantity demanded is extremely responsive to changes in price. As is shown later in Table 4.7, for example, different goods have significantly different degrees of responsiveness to price changes.

The **price elasticity of demand** for a good measures the responsiveness of the quantity demanded of that good to changes in its price. Formally, the *price elasticity of demand* for a good is defined as the percentage change in the quantity demanded that results from a 1 percent change in its price. For example, if the price of beef falls by 1 percent and the quantity demanded rises by 2 percent, then the price elasticity of demand for beef has a value of $-2$.

Strictly speaking, the price elasticity of demand is negative (or zero) because price changes move in the opposite direction from changes in quantity demanded. However, for convenience, we can drop the negative sign and speak of price elasticities in terms of absolute value. The demand for a good is said to be **elastic** with respect to price if the absolute value of its price elasticity is greater than one. It is said to be **inelastic** if the absolute value of its price elasticity is less than one. Finally, demand is said to be **unit elastic** if the absolute value of its price elasticity is equal to one.

Price elasticity is a *dimensionless* coefficient—that is, it cannot be measured in physical units since it is the ratio of the change in one variable that results from a change in the other. Also, the type of good and the units of measurement for the good are irrelevant to price elasticity.

**price elasticity of demand** the percentage change in the quantity demanded of a good that results from a 1 percent change in its price

**elastic demand** price elasticity of demand that is greater than one

**inelastic demand** price elasticity of demand less than one

**unit elastic demand** price elasticity of demand equal to one

## ELASTICITY AND TOTAL EXPENDITURE

Why does elasticity matter? Firms often have a strong interest in being able to answer such questions as, will consumers spend more on my product if I cut the price? and, will I get more revenue if I sell more units at a lower price or if I sell fewer units at a higher price? As it turns out, the answer to these questions depends critically on the price elasticity of demand.

Suppose, for example, that the business manager of a rock band knows that 5000 tickets to the band's weekly summer concerts can be sold if the price is set at $20 per ticket. Suppose the price elasticity of demand for tickets is 3. Will total ticket revenue go up or down in response to a 10 percent increase in the price of tickets?

Total revenue from ticket sales is currently ($20/ticket)(5000 tickets/week) = $100 000/week. If price elasticity of demand for tickets is 3, then a 10 percent increase in price will produce a 30 percent reduction in the number of tickets sold. This means that ticket sales will fall to 3500/week. Total expenditure on tickets will therefore fall to (3500 tickets/week) ($22/ticket) = $77 000/week, which is significantly less than the current total expenditure.[8] This example illustrates the following important rule regarding the relationship between price elasticity of demand and the effect of a price increase on total revenue:

**For a product whose price elasticity of demand is greater than one, an increase in price will reduce total revenue, and a reduction in price will increase total revenue.**

---

8  Remember that, as already noted, total revenue and total expenditure are always equal, so we can use these terms interchangeably.

Consider the intuition behind this rule. Total expenditure is the product of price and quantity. If demand for a product is elastic, the percentage change in quantity will be larger than the corresponding percentage change in price. Thus, the change in units sold will more than offset the change in revenue per unit sold.

Now let us see how total spending responds to a price increase when demand is *inelastic* with respect to price. Suppose that, in the case just considered, the elasticity of demand for tickets is not 3 but 0.5. How will total revenue respond to a 10 percent increase in ticket prices? This time, the number of tickets sold will fall by only 5 percent, to 4750 tickets/week, which means that total revenue on tickets will rise to (4750 tickets/week)($22/ticket) = $104 500/week, or $4500/week more than if price remains at $20.

As this example illustrates, the effect of a price change on total revenue when demand is inelastic runs in the opposite direction from the effect when demand is elastic:

**For a product whose price elasticity of demand is less than one, an increase in price will increase total expenditure, and a reduction in price will reduce total expenditure.**

Again, the intuition behind this rule is straightforward. For a product whose demand is inelastic with respect to price, the percentage change in quantity demanded will be smaller than the corresponding percentage change in price. Thus, the change in revenue per unit sold will more than offset the change in the number of units sold.

Finally, if demand is unit elastic, a small change in price does not change total expenditure:

**For a product whose demand is unit elastic, neither an increase nor a decrease in price changes total expenditure.**

If demand is unit elastic and the price increases, quantity will decrease by an exactly offsetting percentage; if the price decreases, quantity will increase by an exactly offsetting percentage. In both cases, price times quantity will be unchanged. Therefore, total expenditure will be unchanged.

The relationship between elasticity and the effect of a price change on total expenditure is summarized in Table 4.6, where the Greek letter epsilon, $\epsilon$, is used to denote elasticity. Remember that, although price elasticity of demand is a negative number, economists are interested in the size of a change in price relative to the size of a change in quantity purchased, and therefore express it as an absolute value. Remember, too, that total expenditure and total revenue can be used interchangeably, because one party's expenditure always is another party's revenue. This recalls the circular flow of expenditure and income discussed in Chapter 2.

**TABLE 4.6**
**Elasticity and the Effect of a Price Change on Total Expenditure**

| | | |
|---|---|---|
| $\epsilon > 1$ | Price increase causes reduction in total expenditure | Price reduction causes increase in total expenditure |
| $\epsilon = 1$ | Price increase causes no change in total expenditure | Price reduction causes no change in total expenditure |
| $\epsilon < 1$ | Price increase causes increase in total expenditure | Price reduction causes reduction in total expenditure |

COST-
BENEFIT

## DETERMINANTS OF PRICE ELASTICITY OF DEMAND

What factors determine the price elasticity of demand for a good or service? For example, if you are shopping in the supermarket and find that the price of apples has gone up, will you still buy as many? Your answer will probably depend on the following factors.

**Substitution possibilities**   If it's possible to find a different commodity to do the same job, or another solution to your problem for less money, you will be more likely to purchase the substitute instead of simply accepting a price increase. The price elasticity of demand will be higher if there are close substitutes and alternatives (you may, for example, decide to buy more bananas and fewer apples this week, if the price of apples increases and you like bananas almost as much as apples).

**Budget share**   The larger the share of your budget a good represents, the greater is your incentive is to shop around for substitutes and sales if its price increases. It may not be worthwhile to go to another supermarket for cheaper apples, but if you were buying a car, you would likely shop around. Big-ticket items, therefore, have higher price elasticities of demand.

**Time**   Some purchases cannot be delayed, and some can easily be postponed. Your current car might be working as well as it ever did but use more gasoline or look outdated. Updating to a more modern look or a more energy-efficient model, however, is costly and can be postponed for years. A person can avoid the replacement cost by tolerating a higher gas bill or an outdated appearance. For this reason, the price elasticity of demand for any good or service will be higher in the long run than in the short run.

## SOME REPRESENTATIVE ELASTICITY ESTIMATES

As the entries in Table 4.7 show, the price elasticities of demand for different products often differ substantially. In this sample, they range from a high of 2.80 for green peas to a low of 0.18 for theatre and opera tickets. This variability is explained in part by the determinants of elasticity just discussed. Patrons of theatre and opera, for example, tend to have high incomes, implying that the shares of their budgets devoted to these items are likely to be small. What is more, theatre and opera patrons are often highly knowledgeable and enthusiastic about these art forms; for many of them, there are simply no acceptable substitute forms of entertainment.

Why is the price elasticity of demand more than 14 times larger for green peas than for theatre and opera performances? The answer cannot be that income effects loom any larger for green peas than for theatre tickets. Even though the average consumer of green peas earns much less than the average theatre or opera patron, the share of a typical

**TABLE 4.7**
**Price Elasticity Estimates for Selected Products**

| Good or service | Price elasticity |
| --- | --- |
| Green peas | 2.80 |
| Restaurant meals | 1.63 |
| Automobiles | 1.35 |
| Electricity | 1.20 |
| Beer | 1.19 |
| Movies | 0.87 |
| Air travel (foreign) | 0.77 |
| Shoes | 0.70 |
| Coffee | 0.25 |
| Theatre, opera | 0.18 |

SOURCES: These short-run elasticity estimates are taken from the following sources: Ronald Fisher, *State and Local Public Finance*, (Chicago: Irwin, 1996); H. S. Houthakker and Lester Taylor, *Consumer Demand in the United States*: *Analyses and Projections*, 2nd ed., (Cambridge, MA: Harvard University Press, 1970); L. Taylor, "The Demand for Electricity: A Survey," *Bell Journal of Economics*, Spring 1975; K. Elzinga, "The Beer Industry," in *The Structure of American Industry*, Walter Adams, ed., (New York: Macmillan, 1977).

family's budget devoted to green peas is surely very small. However, there are many more close substitutes for peas than for opera and theatre.

Note that the price elasticity of demand for a category of goods will be lower than price elasticity of demand for a particular brand within the category. As stated earlier, elasticity will tend to be higher when a variety of substitutes are available. For example, Table 4.7 shows an elasticity coefficient of 1.35 for automobiles. We can expect the coefficient for Honda Civics to be significantly higher than 1.35, because a variety of other models are available as substitutes.

## USING PRICE ELASTICITY OF DEMAND

An understanding of the factors that govern price elasticity of demand is necessary not only to make sense of consumer behaviour, but also to design effective public policy. Consider, for example, Economic Naturalist 4.2, which summarizes the debate about how taxes affect smoking among teenagers.

### ECONOMIC NATURALIST 4.2

**Will a higher tax on cigarettes curb teenage smoking?**

Consultants hired by the tobacco industry have argued against higher cigarette taxes aimed at curbing teenage smoking. The main reason teenagers smoke is that their friends smoke, these consultants testified. They argued that because of this, higher taxes would have little effect. Does this make economic sense?

The consultants are almost certainly right that peer influence is the most important determinant of teen smoking. But that does not imply that a higher tax on cigarettes would have little impact on adolescent smoking rates. Because most teenagers do not have a lot of money to spend at their own discretion, cigarettes constitute a significant share of a teenage smoker's budget. For at least some teenage smokers, a higher tax would make smoking unaffordable. The price elasticity of demand is thus likely to be far from negligible. And among those who could afford the higher prices, at least some would choose to spend their money on other things rather than pay the higher prices.

If the tax deters even a small number of smokers directly through its effect on the price of cigarettes, it will also deter others indirectly by reducing the number of peer role models who smoke. And those who refrain because of these indirect effects will in turn no longer influence others to smoke, and so on. So even if the direct effect of higher cigarette taxes on teen smoking is small, the cumulative effects may be much larger. The mere fact that peer pressure may be the primary determinant of teen smoking does not imply that higher cigarette taxes will have no significant impact on the number of teens who smoke.[9]

## CALCULATING PRICE ELASTICITY

The price elasticity of demand is the percentage change in quantity demanded that occurs in response to a 1 percent change in price. For example, if a 5 percent increase in price causes quantity demanded to fall by 10 percent, the price elasticity of demand is 10 percent/5 percent = 2.0. By defining elasticity in this way, we can construct a simple formula that enables us to calculate the price elasticity of demand for a product using only minimal information about its demand curve.

9  A recent study based on Canadian data suggests that an increase in cigarette taxes is far more effective in deterring children 10–14 years of age than young people 15–19 years of age. The study reports "participation" elasticities with respect to an increase in cigarette taxes of between 1.5 and 2.0 for the first group and between 0.1 and 0.3 for the second. A participation elasticity refers to whether a person smoked or not in the previous month, and not to the quantity of cigarettes smoked. See Anindya Sen, Hideki Ariizumi, and Daciana Driambe, "Do Changes In Cigarette Taxes Impact Youth Smoking? Evidence from Canadian Provinces," *Forum for Health Economics & Policy*, 2010, 13, 2, Berkeley Electronic Press.

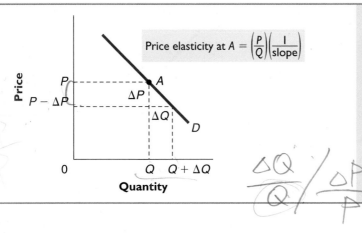

**FIGURE 4.9**
**A Graphical Interpretation of Price Elasticity of Demand**
Price elasticity of demand at any point along a straight-line demand curve is the ratio of price to quantity at that point multiplied by the reciprocal of the slope of the demand curve.

Suppose we let $P$ represent the current price of a good and $Q$ the quantity demanded at that price. Similarly, let $\Delta P$ represent a small change in the current price and $\Delta Q$ the resulting change in quantity demanded. (See Figure 4.9.) The expression $\Delta P/P$ will then stand for the proportion by which price changes when $P$ changes by $\Delta P$, and $\Delta Q/Q$ will stand for the corresponding proportion by which quantity changes. The formula for price elasticity may then be written as

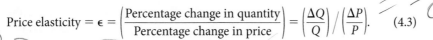

$$\text{Price elasticity} = \epsilon = \left(\frac{\text{Percentage change in quantity}}{\text{Percentage change in price}}\right) = \left(\frac{\Delta Q}{Q}\right) / \left(\frac{\Delta P}{P}\right). \quad (4.3)$$

An attractive feature of this formula for elasticity is its straightforward graphical interpretation. Thus, if we want to calculate the price elasticity of demand at point $A$ on the linear demand curve shown in Figure 4.9, we can begin by rewriting the right-hand side of Equation 4.3 as $(P/Q)(\Delta Q/\Delta P)$. And since the slope of the demand curve is equal to $\Delta P/\Delta Q$, $\Delta Q/\Delta P$ is the reciprocal of that slope: $\Delta Q/\Delta P = 1/\text{slope}$. So the price elasticity of demand at point $A$, denoted $\epsilon_A$, has the following simple formula:

$$\epsilon_A = \left(\frac{P}{Q}\right)\left(\frac{1}{\text{slope}}\right). \quad (4.4)$$

To illustrate how convenient this graphical interpretation of elasticity can be, suppose we want to find the price elasticity of demand at point $A$ on the demand curve in Figure 4.10. The slope of this demand curve is the ratio of its vertical intercept to its horizontal intercept: $20/5 = 4$, so $1/\text{slope} = 1/4$. (Actually, the slope is $-4$, but we ignore the minus sign for convenience, since price elasticity is stated as an absolute value.) The ratio $P/Q$ at point $A$ is $8/3$, so the price elasticity at point $A$ is equal to $(P/Q)(1/\text{slope})$ $= (8/3)(1/4) = 2/3$. Notice that price elasticity of demand depends on *both* the slope of the demand curve *and* the price level. In graphical terms, the price elasticity of demand depends on both the slope of the demand curve and the location of the price-quantity combination on the demand curve.

Because Equation 4.4 can be used to calculate elasticity at any point on a demand curve, it is often called the **point elasticity** formula for price elasticity of demand. As another example, consider point $B$ in Figure 4.9. Equation 4.4 gives price elasticity at point $B$:

$$\epsilon_B = (12/2)(1/4) = 3/2.$$

**point elasticity of demand**
elasticity calculated at a specific point on a demand curve

**What is the price elasticity of demand at the point where $P = 4$ on the demand curve in Figure 4.10?**

EXERCISE 4.6

**FIGURE 4.10**
**Calculating Price Elasticity of Demand**
The price elasticity of demand at point $A$ is given by $(P/Q)$ $(1/\text{slope})$ = $(8/3)$ $(1/4)$ = $2/3$.

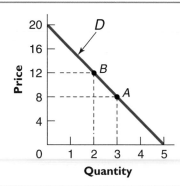

## THE RELATIONSHIP BETWEEN SLOPE AND ELASTICITY

The slope of a demand curve is *not* the demand curve's elasticity. However, it does *influence* the curve's elasticity. Figure 4.11 shows two demand curves with different slopes and, therefore, two different relationships between price and quantity demanded.

At their point of intersection, *A*, the two demand curves in Figure 4.11 have the same price and quantity, therefore, *P/Q* is the same for both curves at point *A*. Equation 4.4 tells us that even though *P/Q* for both curves is the same at point *A*, the elasticity of $D_1$ differs from the elasticity of $D_2$ because the slope of the two demand curves is different. Demand curve $D_2$ is steeper than $D_1$, which means that the absolute value of one over the slope for $D_2$ is less than the corresponding absolute value for $D_1$. Consequently, $D_2$ is less elastic than $D_1$ at the point of intersection. As a general rule, *if two demand curves intersect, the steeper curve will be less elastic at the point of intersection.*[10] The following exercise confirms this statement.

**EXERCISE 4.7**    **Refer to Figure 4.11 and use the point formula (Equation 4.4) to calculate price elasticity of demand at point *A* of $D_1$. Make the same calculation for $D_2$. Calculate the price elasticity of demand for $D_1$ when P = 1. Is $D_1$ more elastic when P = 1 than $D_2$ is when P = 4?**

**FIGURE 4.11**
**Price Elasticity and the Steepness of the Demand Curve**
Two intersecting demand curves have the same price and quantity at the point of intersection. Price elasticity of demand is always less at the point of intersection for the steeper of two demand curves.

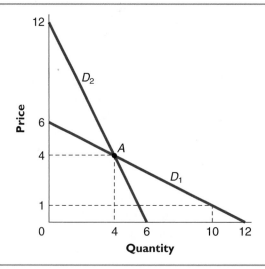

10 Please note carefully that this does not mean the steeper curve is less elastic at every point. Every straight-line demand curve is highly elastic near its vertical intercept and highly inelastic near its horizontal intercept (see Appendix 4A for more discussion of this point). Notice, too, that if two demand curves intersect, their elasticities can only be compared if they relate to goods or services measured in the same units.

## THREE SPECIAL CASES

Three special cases constitute important exceptions to the general rule that elasticity declines along straight-line demand curve.

Note that the horizontal demand curve in Figure 4.12(a) has a slope of zero, which means that the reciprocal of its slope is infinite. Price elasticity of demand is thus infinite at every point along a horizontal demand curve. Such demand curves are said to be **perfectly elastic**. A perfectly horizontal demand curve means that even a small decline in price would result in consumers demanding an infinitely large amount of the good in question, which does not seem very sensible. In practice, the price elasticity of demand may be very large, but it is not, literally speaking, infinite, and the demand curve is *almost,* but not exactly, horizontal.

**perfectly elastic** price elasticity of demand is infinite

In contrast, the demand curve in Figure 4.12(b) is vertical, which means that consumers want to consume exactly the same amount, regardless of price. While such goods may be rare, one can think of examples (e.g., rabies vaccine for people who have been bitten by a rabid dog). Price elasticity of demand is exactly zero at every point along the curve. For this reason, vertical demand curves are said to be **perfectly inelastic**.

**perfectly inelastic** price elasticity of demand is zero

Panel (c) of Figure 4.12 provides an example of a third special case, that of a demand curve that is unit elastic at every point. No matter what price is selected on a unit-elastic demand curve, total revenue always is the same—for the demand curve in panel (c), price times quantity always is $28. The area of any rectangle defined by a price-quantity combination on the demand curve of panel (c) is equal to the area of any other rectangle defined by a different price-quantity combination on the demand curve. Therefore, the demand curve of panel (c) is a rectangular hyperbola. All demand curves that are unit-elastic at every possible price are rectangular hyperbolas.

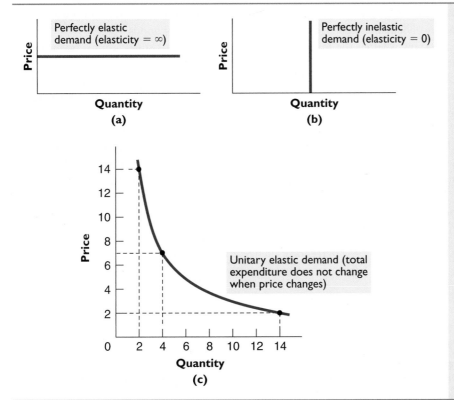

**FIGURE 4.12**

**Perfectly Elastic, Perfectly Inelastic, and Unit Elastic Demand Curves**

The horizontal demand curve in panel (a) is perfectly elastic, or infinitely elastic, at every point. Even the slightest increase in price leads consumers to desert the product in favour of substitutes. The vertical demand curve in panel (b) is perfectly inelastic at every point. Consumers do not, or cannot, switch to substitutes even in the face of large increases in price. The demand curve in panel (c) represents a case of unit-elastic demand. Regardless of the price selected, total expenditure is unchanged. In this example, total expenditure is $28 no matter what price is selected.

---

**RECAP** ↑

### PRICE ELASTICITY OF DEMAND

The price elasticity of demand for a good is the percentage change in the quantity demanded that results from a 1 percent change in its price. Mathematically, the elasticity of demand at any point along a demand curve is equal to

$$(P/Q)\ (1/\text{slope}),$$

where $P$ and $Q$ represent price and quantity and (1/slope) is the reciprocal of the slope of the demand curve at that point.

For a product whose price elasticity is greater than one, an increase in price will reduce total expenditure, and a reduction in price will increase total expenditure. For a product whose price elasticity of demand is less than one, an increase in price will increase total expenditure, and a reduction in price will reduce total expenditure.

The price elasticity of demand for a good or service tends to be larger when substitutes for the good are more readily available, when the good's share in the consumer's budget is larger, and when consumers have more time to adjust to a change in price.

---

## 4.6 INCOME ELASTICITY AND CROSS-PRICE ELASTICITY OF DEMAND

Elasticity is a concept that is used in many contexts in economics. So far in this chapter, we have looked at how the change in a good's price affects the quantity demanded, but there are many other variables that can cause a change in the quantity demanded. For example, the demand for a particular good may change if incomes change, or if the price of another good changes. Because it is useful to measure just *how much* the quantity demanded responds to changes in these other variables, economists use the concept of elasticity—the size of two percentage changes relative to each other—to quantify the response of demand to changes in income or prices of other goods.

To know whether the magnitude of a change is large or small, it must be measured relative to something else. It makes little sense to say, for example, that a $1 increase in the price of oil causes a decline of 100 000 barrels in consumption, if we do not know whether $1 is a large or a small percentage of price or whether 100 000 barrels is 0.001 percent, 1 percent, 10 percent, or some other percentage of total consumption. However, if we know the percentage change of a variable, we know the relative size of the change. Thus, an elasticity coefficient can tell us with a single number if a given percentage change in one variable causes a relatively large or small percentage change in another variable. Income elasticity and cross-price elasticity are two very commonly used elasticity coefficients.

**income elasticity of demand** the percentage change in the quantity demanded of a good in response to a 1 percent change in income

**Income elasticity of demand** is the percentage change in the quantity demanded of a good in response to a 1 percent change in income. Equation 4.5 gives the formula for income elasticity of demand:

$$\text{Income elasticity} = \frac{\text{percentage change in quantity demanded}}{\text{percentage change in income}} = \left(\frac{\Delta Q}{Q}\right)\bigg/\left(\frac{\Delta I}{I}\right) \quad (4.5)$$

where $I$ is income and the other terms are as defined previously.

**normal good** a good with a positive income elasticity of demand

Income elasticity is often used to classify goods as normal or inferior. If a good's income elasticity of demand is positive, the good is a **normal good**. As the term "normal" implies, this is by far the more usual case. Usually, when a person's income goes up, the person consumes more of a given good. But this is not always the case. Sometimes, increasing affluence enables consumers to avoid a commodity that they only purchased previously because they had little income (think day-old bread or really bad wine). If consumers buy *less* of a good as their income rises, income elasticity is *negative*, and the good is called an **inferior good**.

In Chapter 3, shifts of demand curves were used to define inferior and normal goods. Notice that definitions of inferior and normal goods made in terms of income elasticity are consistent with the definitions given in Chapter 3. There is, however, a third category of goods that can be classified using income elasticity. If the income elasticity of demand for a good is greater than one, the good is said to be a **luxury good**. If, for example, the percentage increase in the quantity of plastic surgery demanded exceeds an associated percentage increase in income, income elasticity of demand is greater than one and plastic surgery is therefore a luxury good. Defined this way, luxury goods are a subset of normal goods.

**If a 10 percent increase in income causes the number of students who buy ski vacation packages to rise by 5 percent, what is the income elasticity of demand for ski vacation packages?**

**Cross-price elasticity of demand for two goods** is the percentage change in the quantity demanded of one good in response to a 1 percent change in the price of a second good. For example, the cross-price elasticity of peanuts with respect to the price of cashews is the percentage change in the quantity demanded of peanuts arising from a 1 percent change in the price of cashews. Equation 4.6 gives the formula for cross-price elasticity of demand:

$$\text{Cross-price elasticity} = \frac{\text{percentage change in quantity good } X}{\text{percentage change in price of good } Y}$$

$$= \left(\frac{\Delta Q_X}{Q_X}\right) \Big/ \left(\frac{\Delta P_Y}{P_Y}\right), \tag{4.6}$$

where $Q_X$ is the quantity demanded of one good (e.g., peanuts), $P_Y$ is the price of another, different good (e.g., cashews), $\Delta P_Y$ is a small change in the price of $Y$, and $\Delta Q_X$ is the resulting change in the quantity demanded of good $X$.

If the price of cashews increases, the quantity of peanuts purchased will increase because people will substitute peanuts for cashews; that is, cross-price elasticity will be positive. If cross-price elasticity is positive, we say that the two goods are **substitutes**.

On the other hand, consider the relationship between the price of gasoline and the quantity of tires purchased. If the price of gasoline increases, causing people to drive less, they will wear out fewer tires. The quantity of tires purchased will decrease, and cross-price elasticity will be negative. If cross-price elasticity is negative, the two goods are **complements**.

**inferior good** a good with a negative income elasticity of demand

**luxury good** a good with an income elasticity of demand greater than one; a subset of normal goods

**EXERCISE 4.8**

**cross-price elasticity of demand for two goods** the percentage change in the quantity demanded of one good in response to a 1 percent change in the price of a second good

**substitutes** a relationship between two goods such that an increase in the price of one causes a rightward shift in the demand curve for the other

**complements** a relationship between two goods such that an increase in the price of one causes a leftward shift in the demand curve for the other

---

**ECONOMIC NATURALIST 4.3**

**Why did Maxwell's Plum in Halifax sell beer at $5.00 per mug, but give free salted peanuts to its patrons?**

In most cases, people who eat more peanuts become thirstier and drink more beer. In terms of cross-price elasticity of demand, a reduction in the price of peanuts (in this case to zero) would increase the quantity of beer consumed. Because beer and salted peanuts are complements, the sign of the cross-price elasticity coefficient is positive. The managers figured that the profits on the extra beer they sold more than compensated for the value of peanuts they gave away. If you also apply the definition of complements from Chapter 3, you know the demand for beer would increase when the price of peanuts was reduced to zero. The increase in demand not only enabled the managers to sell more beer, it increased the price they could charge, and sales were strong, even at $5 per mug. You may be able to offer similar explanations for other pricing patterns of food and beverages, computers and ink cartridges, and more.

In Chapter 3, shifts of demand curves were used to define complements and substitutes. Notice that definitions of substitutes and complements made in terms of cross-price elasticity are consistent with the definitions made in Chapter 3.

---

**RECAP**↑

### INCOME ELASTICITY AND CROSS-PRICE ELASTICITY OF DEMAND

Income elasticity of demand is the percentage change in the quantity demanded that results from a 1 percent change in income. It can be calculated by using Equation 4.5. If income elasticity is positive, the good is a normal good. If income elasticity is negative, the good is an inferior good. If income elasticity is greater than one, the good is a luxury good.

Cross-price elasticity of demand is the percentage change in the quantity demanded of one good divided by a 1 percent change in the price of another good. It can be calculated by using Equation 4.6. If cross-price elasticity is positive, the goods are substitutes; if cross-price elasticity is negative, the goods are complements.

---

## SUMMARY

- The rational consumer allocates income among different goods so that the marginal utility gained from the last dollar spent on each good is the same. This rational spending rule gives rise to the law of demand, which states that other things being equal, people will purchase a smaller quantity of the goods and services they want as the cost of purchasing one more unit of them increases. Here, *cost* refers to the sum of all monetary and non-monetary sacrifices—explicit and implicit—that must be made to engage in the activity. **LO1, LO2**

- The effect of a change in price on quantity demanded can be separated into an income effect and a substitution effect. **LO4**

- The demand curve is a schedule that shows the quantity of a good people want to buy at various prices. Demand curves can be used to summarize the price-quantity relationship for a single individual, but more commonly we employ them to summarize that relationship for an entire market. At any quantity along a demand curve, the corresponding price represents the amount which the consumer (or consumers) would be willing to pay for having an additional unit of the product. For this reason, the demand curve is sometimes described as a summary of the benefit side of the market. **LO3, LO5**

- The price elasticity of demand is a measure of how strongly buyers respond to changes in price. It is the percentage change in quantity demanded that occurs in response to a 1 percent change in price. By convention, price elasticity of demand is stated as a positive number. The demand for a good is elastic with respect to price if its price elasticity is more than one, inelastic if its price elasticity is less than one, and unit-elastic if its price elasticity is equal to one. **LO6, LO7**

- A decrease in price will increase total expenditure on a good if demand is elastic, but reduce it if demand is inelastic. An increase in price will increase total expenditure on a good if demand is inelastic but reduce it if demand is elastic. Total expenditure on a good reaches a maximum when price elasticity of demand is equal to one. **LO6**

- Goods such as salt, which occupy only a small share of the typical consumer's budget and have few or no good substitutes, tend to have low price elasticity of demand. Goods such as new cars of a particular make and model, which occupy large budget shares and have many attractive substitutes, tend to have high price elasticity of demand. Price elasticity of demand is higher in the long run than in the short run because people often need time to adjust to price changes. **LO6**

- The price elasticity of demand at a point along a demand curve can also be expressed as the formula $\epsilon = (\Delta Q/Q)/(\Delta P/P)$. Here, $P$ and $Q$ represent price and quantity at that point, and $\Delta Q$ and $\Delta P$ represent small changes in price and quantity. For straight-line demand curves, this formula can also be expressed as $\epsilon = (P/Q)$ $(1/\text{slope})$. Because we express price elasticity of demand as an absolute value, these formulations tell us that price elasticity declines as we move down a straight-line demand curve. **LO7**

- Income elasticity of demand is the percentage change in the quantity demanded of good that arises from a 1 percent change in income. If the income elasticity of demand for a good is positive, the good is a normal good. If income elasticity of demand is negative, the good is an inferior good. If income elasticity is greater than one, the good is a luxury good. **LO6, LO7**

- Cross-price elasticity of demand is the percentage change in the quantity demanded of a good that arises from a 1 percent change in the price of a different good. If cross-price elasticity is positive, the two goods are substitutes; if it is negative, the two goods are complements. **LO6, LO7**

## KEY TERMS

complements (103)
cross-price elasticity of demand
   for two goods (103)
elastic demand (95)
income effect (86)
income elasticity of
   demand (102)
inelastic demand (95)
inferior good (103)
law of demand (79)

law of diminishing marginal
   utility (82)
luxury good (103)
marginal utility (81)
nominal price (88)
normal good (102)
optimal combination of goods (83)
perfectly elastic (101)
perfectly inelastic (101)
point elasticity of demand (99)

price elasticity of demand (95)
rational spending rule (84)
real price (88)
substitutes (103)
substitution effect (86)
total expenditure (93)
total revenue (93)
unit-elastic demand (95)
util (80)
utility (80)

## REVIEW QUESTIONS

1. Why does the law of diminishing marginal utility encourage people to spread their spending across many different types of goods? **LO1, LO2**

2. Under what conditions will an increase in the price of a product lead to a reduction in total spending for that product? **LO6**

3. Why do economists pay little attention to the algebraic sign of the elasticity of demand for a good with respect to its own price, yet they pay careful attention to the algebraic sign of the elasticity of demand for a good with respect to another good's price? **LO6**

4. Why does the elasticity of demand for a good with respect to its own price decline as we move down along a straight-line demand curve? **LO6**

5. Suppose the cross-price elasticity of demand for firewood with respect to the price of fuel oil is positive. If the price of fuel oil rises, what will happen to the quantity demanded of firewood? Why? What will happen to the demand curve for firewood? Why? **LO6**

6. Large numbers of motor scooters are used for transportation in many cities in developing countries. Do you think that in developing countries motor

scooters are an inferior or a normal good? What about automobiles? Explain. **LO6**

7. What is the income effect of a price change? What is the substitution effect of a price change? **LO4**

## PROBLEMS

1. In which type of restaurant do you expect the service to be more prompt and courteous: an expensive gourmet restaurant or an inexpensive diner? Explain your answer. **LO6**

2. Mila's current marginal utility from consuming orange juice is 75 utils per 30 mL, and her marginal utility from consuming coffee is 50 utils per 30 mL. If orange juice costs 25 cents per 30 mL and coffee costs 20 cents per 30 mL, is Mila maximizing her total utility from the two beverages? If so, explain how you know. If not, how should she rearrange her spending? **LO2**

3. The following schedule shows the number of packs of bagels bought in Quebec City each day at a variety of prices.

| Price of bagels ($/pack) | Number of packs purchased per day |
|---|---|
| 6 | 0 |
| 5 | 3000 |
| 4 | 6000 |
| 3 | 9000 |
| 2 | 12 000 |
| 1 | 15 000 |
| 0 | 18 000 |

a. Graph the daily demand curve for packs of bagels in Quebec City. **LO5**
b. Derive an algebraic expression for the demand schedule you graphed. **LO5**
c. Calculate the price elasticity of demand at the point on the demand curve where the price of bagels is $3. **LO7**
d. If all bagel shops increased the price of bagels from $3 to $4, what would happen to total revenue? **LO6**
e. Calculate the price elasticity of demand at a point on the demand curve where the price of bagels is $2. **LO7**
f. If bagel shops increased the price of bagels from $2 to $3, what would happen to total revenue? **LO6**
g. Show on your graph for (a) the inelastic and elastic regions of the demand curve. **LO6, LO7**

4. Suppose chartered banks decide to greatly reduce the availability of student loans that are guaranteed against default by the Canadian government.

a. What would you expect to happen to the demand for credit cards by students? **LO5**
b. What would you expect to happen to the quantity of credit cards issued to students? To the willingness of students to incur debt at the much higher rates of interest charged on credit cards? **LO6**
c. Are credit cards a substitute, albeit an imperfect one, for student loans? What sign (positive or negative) would you expect for the cross-price elasticity of demand for credit cards with respect to interest rates charged to students for other forms of credit? **LO6**

5. Perhaps you have noticed that the baby boomers are aging. In general, their incomes have increased as they have aged. It has been reported that the quantity of wine consumed has been rising over time, but the quantity of beer has changed very little, if at all.

a. Based on this information, would you expect income elasticity of demand for wine to be positive or negative? What about beer? Explain. **LO6**
b. Would this evidence indicate that wine is an inferior or a normal good? What about beer? Explain. **LO6**
c. It is reported that for people older than 65, incomes decline and consumption of prescription drugs increases as they age. If you consider *only* this information, would you conclude that prescription drugs are a normal or an inferior good? Explain. **LO6**
d. As people age, what do you think happens to their marginal utility of prescription drugs? To their demand for prescription drugs? On taking these considerations into account, would you modify the answer you provided at (c)? Explain. **LO2**

6. Is the demand for a particular brand of car, like a Chevrolet, likely to be more or less price elastic than the demand for all cars? Why? **LO6**

7. At point A on the following demand curve, how will a 1 percent increase in the price of the product affect total expenditure on the product? Why? **LO6, LO7**

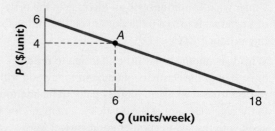

8. Suppose that the income of the average Canadian household increases because a larger percentage of women enter the labour force. What do you think will happen to demand for the following products or services? What does your answer imply about income elasticity of demand in each case? What does your answer imply about a shift of the demand curve in each case? Explain. **LO3, LO5, LO6**
   a.  raw potatoes in 10 kg bags
   b.  oven-ready French fries in 2 kg bags
   c.  skinless, boneless chicken breasts
   d.  whole, uncooked chickens

9. Would you expect the sign of the cross-price elasticity of demand for each pair listed below to be positive or negative? If the price of the first good in each case increases, what will happen to the demand curve for the second good? If the price of the first good in each pair increases, what will happen to the quantity of the second good? Is each pair a set of complements or of substitutes? Answer each of these four questions for every pair listed, and explain all of your answers in each case. **LO6**
   a.  automobiles; tires
   b.  air travel; hotel rooms
   c.  milk; soft drinks
   d.  music downloaded from the Internet; music recorded on CDs

## ANSWERS TO IN-CHAPTER EXERCISES

**4.1**  To buy 8 cones per week and 4 sundaes would cost $16, which is $6 more than Lamar has to spend. **LO1, LO2**

**4.2**  See the table below. Suppose Lamar starts with his previous optimal combination, 4 cones per week and 3 sundaes, then allocates his additional $4 one step at a time—either by spending $2 on an additional sundae or by spending that same $2 on 2 more cones. If he buys a fourth sundae for $2, he'll get 15 extra utils, or 7.5 utils per dollar. For the same money, he could buy 2 additional cones, which would give him 12 extra utils, or 6 utils per dollar. Since the first option is better, the rational spending rule tells us that Lamar will spend the first $2 of his additional $4 weekly ice cream budget on sundaes. That gives him 4 cones and 4 sundaes, with an additional $2 to spend. He can spend it either on a fifth sundae or on 2 more cones. If he buys the fifth sundae, he will get 10 extra utils, or 5 utils per dollar. If he buys 2 more cones, he will get 12 extra utils, or 6 utils per dollar. So cones are the better choice this time. Proceeding in this manner, Lamar ends up buying 6 cones per week and 4 sundaes, a combination that yields 200 utils per week. The increase in his income has increased his demand for both cones and sundaes. **LO2**

| Vanilla cones per week | Utils/week from cones | Chocolate sundaes per week | Utils/week from sundaes |
|---|---|---|---|
| 0 | 0 | 0 | 0 |
| 1 | 36 | 1 | 50 |
| 2 | 50 | 2 | 80 |
| 3 | 60 | 3 | 105 |
| 4 | 68 | 4 | 120 |
| 5 | 75 | 5 | 130 |
| 6 | 80 | 6 | 138 |
| 7 | 84 | 7 | 144 |
| 8 | 82 | 8 | 148 |
| 9 | 81 | 9 | 150 |
| 10 | 80 | 10 | 151 |

**4.3**    As we saw earlier, when the price of cones was $1 apiece, Lamar's best option was to buy 4 cones per week and 3 sundaes. But with the price of cones now $2 instead of $1, he cannot afford to buy 4 cones and 3 sundaes (they would cost him $14 or $4 more than his $10 weekly budget). So he needs to cut back, and the best place to start is with the good that delivers less marginal utility per dollar. The marginal utility per dollar delivered by the fourth cone is now only 8 utils/$2 = 4 utils per dollar, much less than the marginal utility per dollar delivered by the third sundae (which is still 12.5 utils per dollar). At 3 cones and 3 sundaes a week, he is still spending $2 too much, and the solution is to reduce consumption of cones still further (since giving up the third cone sacrifices only 5 utils per dollar, or less than he would lose by giving up a sundae). Having cut back to 2 cones and 3 sundaes, he is spending exactly $10 per week. Now suppose he cuts his cone consumption from 2 to 1. By so doing he will lose another 14 utils, or 7 utils per dollar saved. And if he then spends that $2 on an additional sundae, he'll gain 15 utils, or 7.5 utils per dollar. So Lamar's best option this time is to consume 1 cone and 4 sundaes per week, which gives him a total of 156 utils per week. **LO2**

**4.4**    Having answered Exercise 4.3, you know that when Lamar's budget for ice cream remains at $10 per week, he consumes 1 cone and 4 sundaes per week after the price of cones increases to $2. When his budget for ice cream increases by $4, Lamar has the $14 per week that is necessary to purchase his original combination of cones and sundaes. According to Table 4.3, Lamar will obtain 7 additional utils per dollar if he increases his consumption of cones from 1 to 2 per week. This is better than the 5 additional utils per dollar he will obtain if he increases his consumption of sundaes from 4 to 5 per week. Therefore, Lamar spends $2 to buy an additional cone. He still has $2 per week to spend. Table 4.3 tells us that Lamar will obtain an additional 5 utils per dollar whether he increases his consumption of cones from 2 to 3 per week or his consumption of sundaes from 4 to 5 per week. Since Lamar does not care whether he eats an additional cone or an additional sundae, let us arbitrarily assume that he consumes an additional cone. He will then be spending $14 to consume 3 cones and 4 sundaes per week. This is one less cone and one more sundae than Lamar consumed before the price of cones increased. With his real income constant, Lamar purchases one less cone. The reduction of one cone is the *substitution effect* of the increase in the price of cones from $1 to $2.

If Lamar had not received the $4 that kept his real income constant, his budget for ice cream would be unchanged at $10 per week. The solution to Exercise 4.3 shows that Lamar then would reduce his purchase of cones not to 3 but to 1. The further reduction by 2 cones is the *income effect* of the increase in the price of cones from $1 to $2. The *total effect* of the price change is the sum of the substitution effect plus the income effect (−1 cone −2 cones = −3 cones). **LO4**

**4.5**    The horizontal intercept of this demand curve is 6, and its slope is $\Delta P/\Delta Q = -2$. The reciprocal of slope is −½. So the equation for this demand curve is $Q_D = 6 - \frac{1}{2} P_D$. Notice, too, that the equation could be written as $P_D = 12 - 2Q_D$. Economists refer to this form as the inverse demand curve. **LO5**

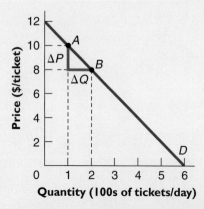

**4.6**     At point $A$ in the following diagram, $P/Q = 4/4 = 1$. The slope of this demand curve is $-20/5 = -4$, so $\epsilon = 1(1/\text{slope}) = -1/4$. By convention, elasticity is reported as an absolute value. Therefore, $\epsilon = \frac{1}{4} = 0.25$. **LO7**

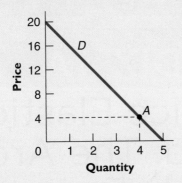

**4.7**     The point formula can be used to calculate price elasticity of demand at any point on a straight-line demand curve:

$$\epsilon = \left(\frac{P}{Q}\right)\left(\frac{1}{\text{slope}}\right).$$

The slope of a straight line is equal to the ratio of its vertical intercept to its horizontal intercept. Therefore, the slope of $D_1$ is $-\frac{1}{2}$, and the slope of $D_2$ is $-2$. By convention, we use the absolute value of slope when calculating elasticity. Elasticity for $D_1$ when P $= 4$ is

$$\epsilon = \left(\frac{4}{4}\right)\left(\frac{1}{\frac{1}{2}}\right) = 2.$$

The same calculation for $D_2$ when P $= 4$ reveals that $\epsilon = \frac{1}{2}$. *The steeper curve is less elastic at the point where the two curves intersect.*

Now calculate elasticity for $D_1$ when P $= 1$

$$\epsilon = \left(\frac{P}{Q}\right)\left(\frac{1}{\text{slope}}\right) = \left(\frac{1}{10}\right)\left(\frac{1}{\frac{1}{2}}\right) = \frac{1}{10} \times 2 = \frac{1}{5}$$

When $P = 1$, price elasticity of demand for $D_1$ is less than half the price elasticity of demand for $D_2$ when P $= 4$. Every straight-line demand curve will be highly elastic near its vertical intercept and highly inelastic near its horizontal intercept regardless of the steepness of its slope. *The curve with the steeper slope is not less elastic at every point than is the curve with the shallower slope.* **LO6, LO7**

**4.8**     Income elasticity = percentage change in quantity demanded/percentage change in income = 5 percent/10 percent = 0.5. **LO7**

# APPENDIX 4A
## "Average" Price Elasticity of Demand: The Arc (or Midpoint) Formula

### LEARNING OBJECTIVES

When you have completed this appendix, you will be able to:

**LO4A.1** Determine if demand is elastic, unit elastic, or inelastic at each point on a linear demand curve.

**LO4A.2** Determine if total expenditure is increasing, constant, or decreasing as price changes along a linear demand curve.

**LO4A.3** Calculate price elasticity of demand by using the arc formula.

## 4A.1 PRICE ELASTICITY CHANGES ALONG A STRAIGHT-LINE DEMAND CURVE

A straight-line demand curve has a constant slope: at every point along it, a one dollar change in price produces the same constant change in quantity demanded. But in *percentage* terms, a one dollar price change is small when it occurs near the top of the demand curve, where price is high. The same one dollar price change is larger in *percentage* terms when it occurs near the bottom of the demand curve, where price is low. Likewise, one unit of sales is large in percentage terms when it occurs near the top of the demand curve, where quantity is low, and small in percentage terms when it occurs near the bottom of the curve, where quantity is high. Since elasticity is the *percentage* change in quantity demanded divided by the corresponding *percentage* change in price, price elasticity has a different value at every point along a straight-line demand curve: the elasticity of demand declines steadily as we move downward along a straight-line demand curve.

Panel (a) of Figure 4A.1 illustrates how price elasticity of demand changes as price decreases along a linear demand curve. Begin with the highest price shown on the demand curve in Figure 4.A1(a), which is $6. As price decreases from $6, elasticity decreases continuously from a very high value to a value of 1 at the demand curve's midpoint, to a very low value as price approaches zero. To put it a little differently, as price decreases from $6, the demand curve, which initially is highly elastic, becomes less elastic. It reaches unitary elasticity at its midpoint and becomes highly inelastic as price approaches zero.

To see more clearly why elasticity follows this pattern, again refer to Figure 4.A1(a) and note that when price is $5, quantity demanded is 2. Suppose that if price is reduced by $1, quantity demanded increases by 2, from 2 to 4. As you can see, a 20 percent reduction of price causes a 100 percent increase in quantity. Therefore, price elasticity of demand is 5 (i.e., 100 percent/20 percent = 5). Now suppose that we start with a price

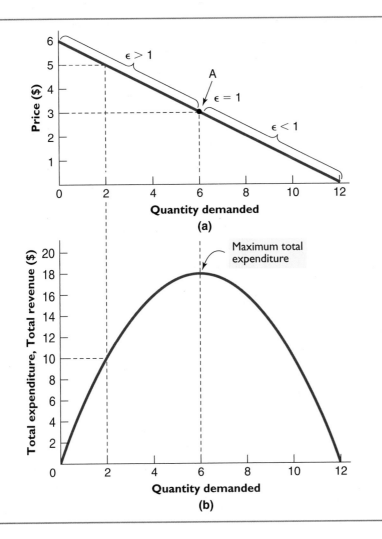

**FIGURE 4.A1**
**Price Elasticity of Demand and Total Expenditure**
Panel (a) shows price and price elasticity of demand decreasing from the upper end of the demand curve, reaching 1 at the midpoint of the curve, and continuing to very low values at the horizontal intercept. Panel (b) shows that as price decreases, quantity demanded increases, as does total expenditure, until it reaches a maximum when elasticity equals 1. Total expenditure begins to decrease as quantity continues to increase, until it reaches zero at the quantity where price is zero.

of $2. Figure 4.A1(a) shows that quantity demanded will be 8. Let us again reduce price by one dollar, from $2 to $1. Suppose that a reduction in price of one dollar again causes quantity demanded to increase by 2. This time, a reduction of $1 represents a reduction of 50 percent from the original price. And when quantity increases by 2 (from 8 to 10), the increase in quantity is 25 percent. Thus a 50 percent reduction in price causes a 25 percent increase in quantity. Therefore, price elasticity of demand is ½ (i.e., 25 percent/50 percent = ½). *As price decreases from high to low values along a linear demand curve, price elasticity of demand decreases from high to low values.*

Elasticity has a value of 1 at the midpoint of a linear demand curve. The pattern in Figure 4.A1(a) is true for all linear demand curves.

If we consider only small changes in price when calculating elasticity of demand, the beginning price will be nearly the same as the ending price. However, this is not true for larger changes. Consider Figure 4.10 (p. 100). Suppose that we begin at point *A* with a price of $8 and increase it to $12, which is the price at point *B*. What is the *percentage* change in price? The $4 price change is equal to one third of the $12 price at *B* but one half of the $8 price at *A*. Should we calculate elasticity at point *A* or at point *B*? If we use point *A*, elasticity is 2/3; if we use point *B*, elasticity is 3/2. Because *A* and *B* are two different points, the calculation of elasticity depends on which is taken as the base, and the choice is arbitrary.

**arc elasticity of demand** elasticity calculated between the endpoints of a segment of a demand curve

Because elasticity changes from point to point on the demand curve, the **arc elasticity** or midpoint formula can be used to calculate "average" elasticity for a segment of a demand curve:

$$\text{arc } \epsilon = \frac{\text{percentage change in quantity}}{\text{percentage change in price}} = \frac{\dfrac{\Delta Q}{(Q_1 + Q_2)/2}}{\dfrac{\Delta P}{P_1 + P_2/2}} \tag{4A.1}$$

where $P_1$, $Q_1$ and $P_2$, $Q_2$ are two different points on the demand curve.

When calculating elasticity at a single point, as in Equation 4.3, a *single* price and a *single* quantity are used. In contrast, Equation 4A.1 uses the *average* of prices $P_1$ and $P_2$ and the *average* of quantities $Q_1$ and $Q_2$. The common term, 2, used to calculate the two averages can be cancelled from the equation. We also note that

$$\Delta Q = Q_2 - Q_1 \quad \text{and} \quad \Delta P = P_2 - P_1.$$

Therefore, Equation 4A.1 can be simplified to

$$\text{arc } \epsilon = \frac{Q_2 - Q_1}{Q_1 + Q_2} \bigg/ \frac{P_2 - P_1}{P_1 + P_2} \tag{4A.2}$$

Equation 4A.3 provides another simple statement of arc elasticity:

$$\text{arc } \epsilon = \left(\frac{P_1 + P_2}{Q_1 + Q_2}\right)\left(\frac{1}{\text{slope}}\right). \tag{4A.3}$$

We can use Equation 4A.2 to calculate "average" elasticity over the segment of the demand curve defined by points $A$ and $B$ in Figure 4.10. We simply let points $A$ and $B$ be our first and second points, respectively:

$$\text{arc } \epsilon = \left(\frac{8 + 12}{3 + 2}\right)\left(\frac{1}{4}\right) = 1$$

The value of elasticity obtained by the arc formula is an average over the range between A and B—it is not exactly correct at either point. However, a small price change will define a small segment of the demand curve. Points A and B in Figure 4.10 would have been much closer together if the price increase had been 5 percent, not 50 percent. Therefore, elasticity would not have been nearly so much greater at B than at A. As the magnitude of the price change shrinks, the arc elasticity converges to the point elasticity. We use point elasticity when discussing price elasticity in this textbook.

## EXAMPLE 4A.1

**Refer back to Figure 4.10. What is price elasticity over the *line segment* defined by an increase in price from $P = 4$ to $P = 8$?**

To calculate elasticity for the line segment defined by an increase in price from $P = 4$ to $P = 8$, we can use the arc formula.

$$\text{arc } \epsilon = \frac{(P_1 + P_2)}{(Q_1 + Q_2)}\left(\frac{1}{\text{slope}}\right) = \frac{4 + 8}{4 + 3}\left(\frac{1}{4}\right) = \frac{3}{7}.$$

Again, elasticity is reported as an absolute value. Therefore, $\epsilon = 3/7$.

## KEY TERMS

# APPENDIX 4B
# Indifference Curves

In Chapter 4, we showed why the rational spending rule is a simple consequence of diminishing marginal utility and a fixed income. But although we worked with a numerical example and assumed that utility could be measured, we actually only have to assume that, given a choice between any two bundles or combinations of goods, *a rational consumer will rank the choices in order of preference.* We *do not need to understand or measure the utility* the consumer obtains from one bundle compared to another. The assumption that a rational consumer can rank his preferences is a weaker assumption than the assumption that utility can be measured.[1]

With this weaker, very minimal assumption we can still derive the rational spending rule, but we need two steps. First, we describe the different combinations of goods a consumer is *able* to buy, given an income and the prices of the goods the consumer wants. Second, we describe how the consumer chooses the *preferred* combination from those that are available.

## LEARNING OBJECTIVES

When you have completed this appendix, you will be able to:

**LO4B.1** Represent a budget constraint with words, graphs, and an equation.

**LO4B.2** Use indifference curves to represent a rational consumer's preferences.

**LO4B.3** Combine a budget constraint and indifference curves into a single graph.

**LO4B.4** Use the graph resulting from learning objective 4B.3 to identify a rational consumer's best affordable combination of goods.

**LO4B.5** Use a graph to separate the income effect of a price change from the substitution effect.

**LO4B.6** Derive an individual consumer's demand curve by using budget constraints and indifference curves.

## 4B.1 THE BUDGET CONSTRAINT: WHAT IS POSSIBLE

In this example, we will focus on a consumer (let's call her Jane) buying only two goods: apples and oranges.[2] As well, we limit Jane's purchasing to a single period of time and assume that she spends all her income.

Suppose Jane's income is $10 per week and apples cost $0.50 apiece while oranges are $1. Some of the combinations of apples and oranges Jane's $10 could buy are shown graphically in Figure 4B.1. Any point in Figure 4B.1 could be written as an ordered pair. For example, point *b* can be written (4, 8) to represent 4 apples and 8 oranges. The first number of the pair always represents the item measured along the horizontal axis, and the second always represents the item measured along the vertical axis. The line labelled *B* in the figure shows all the combinations, or bundles, that will cost Jane exactly $10. It

---

1   The discovery that the theory of consumer choice and demand can be based on preference orderings is considered a major breakthrough in economic theory.

2   The two-good assumption is not really very restrictive and makes it easy to use graphs. More realistically, the budgeting problem is a choice among a large number of goods. The economist Alfred Marshall proposed that the consumer's choice could be modelled as a choice between one particular named good (e.g., apples) and an amalgam of all the other goods, called a *composite good*. The composite good is all the bundles of other goods the consumer could buy with the income left after buying the named good.

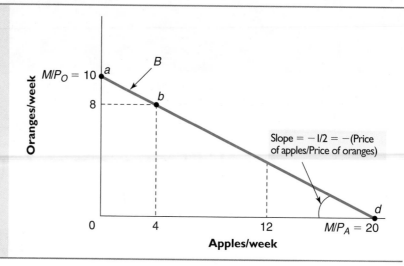

**FIGURE 4B.1**

**The Budget Constraint**

Given Jane's income and the prices she must pay, the line B describes the set of all bundles she can purchase. The cost of each bundle on B is exactly equal to her income. Its slope is the negative of the price of apples divided by the price of oranges. In absolute value, this slope is the opportunity cost of an additional unit of apples in terms of the number of oranges that must be sacrificed in order to purchase one additional apple at market prices.

**budget constraint** all commodity bundles whose total cost is exactly equal to the consumer's income; can be represented verbally, graphically, or algebraically

is called a **budget constraint**. As we will see, a budget constraint also can be specified algebraically.

We have described the budget constraint, which is Jane's income per period of time. Consumption also is an amount per period of time. Both are flows. While Figure 4B.1 provides a graphical description of the budget constraint, it also can be described algebraically.

If Jane's income is $M$, the quantity of oranges is $O$, the quantity of apples is $A$, the price of oranges is $P_O$, and the price of apples is $P_A$, spending that equals the budget constraint can be written as

$$M = P_O O + P_A A, \tag{4B.1}$$

indicating that her weekly income equals the sum of her weekly expenditures on fruit. Figure 4B.1 graphs units of oranges on the vertical axis. If we solve Equation 4B.1 for oranges $O$, we obtain

$$O = \frac{M}{P_O} - \left(\frac{P_A}{P_O}\right) A, \tag{4B.2}$$

which has the conventional form for a straight line. The vertical intercept is $M/P_O$, and $(P_A/P_O)$ defines the slope of the line. The equation for the budget constraint in Figure 4B.1 is

$$O = 10 - \frac{1}{2} A. \tag{4B.3}$$

Notice in Equation 4B.3 that $M/P_O = \$10/\$1 = 10$, which is combination $a$ of Jane's choices. Also, *the slope of the budget constraint, $(-P_A/P_O)$, gives the opportunity cost of one type of fruit in terms of the other*: Jane can obtain one more apple by giving up one-half orange or, conversely, she can obtain one more orange by giving up two apples.

## BUDGET SHIFTS DUE TO INCOME OR PRICE CHANGES

### Price Changes

The slope and position of the budget constraint are fully determined by Jane's income and the prices of the goods. Changes in any of these will result in a new budget constraint. Figure 4B.2 shows the effect of an increase in the price of an apple from $P_{A1} = \$0.50$ to $P_{A2} = \$1$. Since both total income and the price of oranges are unchanged, the vertical intercept of the budget constraint (i.e. the number of oranges Jane could buy if she purchased zero apples) stays the same. The rise in the price of apples rotates the budget constraint inward about this intercept, as shown in the figure.

**Show the effect on the budget constraint $B_1$ in Figure 4B.2 of a drop in the price of an apple from $0.50 to $0.40.**

EXERCISE 4B.1

In Exercise 4B.1, you saw that a drop in the price of an apple does not change the vertical intercept of the budget constraint. This time the budget constraint rotates outward. Note also in Exercise 4B.1 that, although the price of oranges remains unchanged, the new budget constraint allows the consumer to buy bundles that contain not only more apples but also more oranges than were in the original combinations.

**Show the effect on the budget constraint $B_1$ in Figure 4B.2 of a rise in the price of an orange from $1 to $2.**

EXERCISE 4B.2

Exercise 4B.2 demonstrates that when the price of an orange changes, the budget constraint rotates about its horizontal intercept. Note also that while only the price of oranges changed, the new budget constraint affects both the amount of oranges and apples the consumer can buy.

When we change the price of only one good, we necessarily change the slope of the budget constraint, $-P_A/P_O$. The same is true if we change both prices by different proportions. But, as Exercise 4B.3 will illustrate, changing both prices by exactly the same proportion results in a new budget constraint with the same slope as before.

**Show the effect on the budget constraint $B_1$ in Figure 4B.2 of a rise in the price of an orange from $1 to $2 and a rise in the price of an apple from $0.50 to $1.**

EXERCISE 4B.3

Note from Exercise 4B.3 that doubling the prices of both oranges and apples shifts the budget constraint both inward and parallel to the original budget constraint. This exercise is important because it shows that while the slope of the budget constraint specifies *relative prices*, it tells us nothing about how high prices are in absolute terms. When the prices of oranges and apples change by the same proportion, the opportunity cost of apples in terms of oranges does not change.

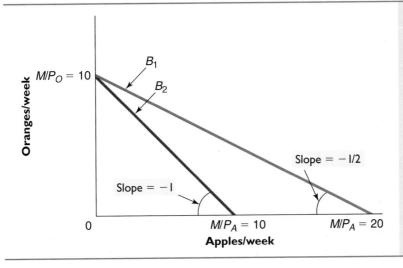

**FIGURE 4B.2**
**The Effect of a Rise in the Price of Apples**
When the price of an apple increases, the vertical intercept of the budget constraint remains the same. The original budget constraint rotates inward about this intercept.

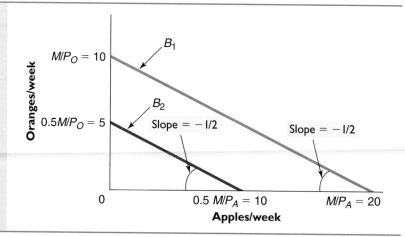

**FIGURE 4B.3**
**The Effect of Cutting Income by Half**
Both horizontal and vertical intercepts fall by half. The new budget constraint has the same slope as the old but is closer to the origin.

## Income Changes

If your money income doubled but prices also doubled, would you be any better off? The effect of a change in money income is the same as an equi-proportionate change in all prices. Suppose, for example, that Jane's income is cut by half, from $10/week to $5/week. The horizontal intercept of her budget constraint will fall from 20 apples/week, to 10 apples/week and the vertical intercept from 10 oranges/week to 5 oranges/week, as shown in Figure 4B.3. Thus, the new budget constraint, $B_2$, is parallel to the old, $B_1$, each with a slope of $-1/2$. Cutting income by half, then, has the same effect as doubling both prices, since both result in the same budget constraint.

**EXERCISE 4B.4**   **Show the effect on the budget constraint $B_1$ in Figure 4B.2 of an increase in income from $10/week to $12/week.**

Exercise 4B.4 illustrates that an increase in income shifts the budget constraint outward while keeping the slope of the budget constraint the same, just as it does with a reduction.

> **RECAP**
>
> **THE BUDGET CONSTRAINT: WHAT IS POSSIBLE**
>
> The budget constraint describes combinations of commodities whose costs are equal to Jane's income. Its position in a graph is determined by both income and prices, while its slope is determined by the relative prices of commodities in the bundle. A change in relative prices will change the slope of the budget constraint, and a change in the consumer's income will cause the entire budget constraint to shift.

# 4B.2  CONSUMER CHOICE: WHAT IS PREFERRED

The budget constraint identifies the choices that are *available*, but which combination will Jane actually select?

## THE CONSUMER'S PREFERENCES

The rational spending rule tells us how Jane will allocate spending to maximize the utility of her budget: marginal utility per dollar spent will be the same for all goods purchased. This assumes that all consumers can order their preferences. It also is reasonable to say that if two bundles have the same level of utility, Jane will know that she is indifferent between them.

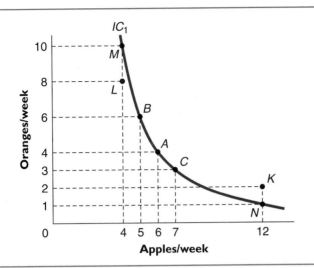

**FIGURE 4B.4**

**An Indifference Curve**

An indifference curve, such as $IC_1$, is a set of bundles that Jane prefers equally. Any bundle, such as $K$, that lies above an indifference curve is preferred to any bundle on the indifference curve. Any bundle on the indifference curve, in turn, is preferred to any bundle, such as $L$, that lies below the indifference curve.

Jane will be *indifferent* between combinations of goods when both combinations yield the same level of satisfaction or utility. An **indifference curve** plots the combinations of goods that all provide the same level of utility. The indifference curve $IC_1$ in Figure 4B.4 graphically represents the idea that Jane considers herself equally well off whether she has bundle (or combination) $A$, $B$, or $C$, or any other of the many bundles on $IC_1$.

Although Jane is indifferent between combinations on the same indifference curve, we can identify bundles that provide more or less total utility. Jane may or may not be better off with a particular combination. In Figure 4B.4 we can compare $C$ to bundle $K$, which has fewer oranges and more apples. We know that $C$ is equal in total utility to $N$ because both are on the same indifference curve. Bundle $K$, in turn, is preferred to $N$ because it has just as many apples as $N$, and one more orange. So if $K$ is preferred to $N$, and $N$ is just as attractive as $C$, then $K$ must be preferred to $C$. In general, *bundles that lie above an indifference curve are all preferred to the bundles that lie on it.* Also, we can say that bundle $A$ is preferred to $L$. Why? Bundles $A$ and $M$ are equivalent, so both $A$ and $M$ are preferred to $L$. Combination $M$ has the same number of apples as $L$, and two more oranges. Generally, *bundles that lie on an indifference curve are all preferred to those that lie below it.*

An **indifference map**, which is a graph of several indifference curves, summarizes a consumer's preferences. The farther an indifference curve is from the origin of the graph, the higher the level of utility is. Figure 4B.5 shows just four of the infinite number of indifference curves that yield a complete description of Jane's preferences. To see how she

**indifference curve** plots all the combinations of two goods that provide a consumer with the same satisfaction or utility; a consumer will be indifferent between any of the bundles that are on the same indifference curve

**indifference map** a graph of several indifference curves; the further the curve lies from the origin of the graph, the greater the level of utility it indicates

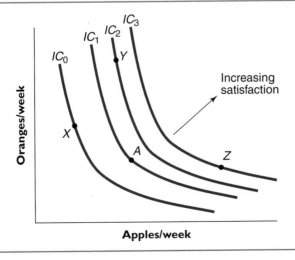

**FIGURE 4B.5**

**Part of an Indifference Map**

The entire set of Jane's indifference curves is called her indifference map. Bundles on any indifference curve are less preferred than bundles on a higher indifference curve and more preferred than bundles on a lower indifference curve. Thus, $Z$ is preferred to $Y$, which is preferred to $A$, which is preferred to $X$.

ranks any given pair of bundles, simply compare the indifference curves on which the bundles lie. Combination $Z$ is preferred to $Y$ because $Z$ is on a higher indifference curve, one further from the origin than $Y$. Notice also that we did not specify a value for the level of utility for each indifference curve. We only assume that Jane knows how to rank the bundles of goods that he or she considers.

## TRADE-OFFS BETWEEN GOODS

**marginal rate of substitution (MRS)** the absolute value of the slope of the indifference curve; the rate at which one good can be substituted for another while maintaining a constant level of utility

An important aspect of any consumer's preferences is the rate at which she is willing to replace one good with another while maintaining the same level of utility. This is known as the **marginal rate of substitution (MRS)** and is defined as the absolute value of the slope of the indifference curve; it is the rate at which she can substitute one good for another while maintaining a constant level of utility. Indifference curves are usually curvilinear in order to show a diminishing marginal rate of substitution. This implies two things: the more a consumer has of one good (a) the less an increment of that good adds to total utility and (b) the smaller is the additional increment of the second good necessary to maintain a given level of utility when a unit of first good is lost.

The slope of any curvilinear indifference curve is different at every point on the curve, indicating that *the marginal rate of substitution will be different at every point on a curvilinear indifference curve.* In Figure 4B.6 for example, the marginal rate of substitution at point $T$ is given by the slope of the tangent to the indifference curve, which is the ratio $\Delta O_T/\Delta A_T$. (The notation $\Delta O_T$ means "small change in the amount of oranges from the amount indicated at point $T$." A similar small change in the amount of apples is indicated by $\Delta A_T$.) If we take $\Delta A_T$ apples away from the bundle at point $T$, and the marginal rate of substitution at $T$ is 1.5, Jane must obtain 1.5 more oranges/week in order to make up for the loss of one apple/week if she is to maintain the same level of utility.

Notice that the MRS gives us the rate that oranges can be substituted for apples without changing total *satisfaction*, while the slope of the budget constraint tells us the rate at which they can be substituted without changing total *expenditure*. Put another way, the slope of the budget constraint tells us the marginal *cost* of apples in terms of oranges, while the MRS is the marginal *benefit* of apples in terms of oranges.

The MRS generally decreases as we move downward to the right along an indifference curve, reflecting the fact that the more Jane has of one good, the more of it she typically must be given before she is willing to give up a unit of the other good. Thus, indifference curves usually are convex, or bowed toward the origin. (See Figures 4B.4 through 4B.7.) In Figure 4B.7, note that at bundle $A$ the quantity of oranges is relatively high and the quantity of apples is relatively low. To maintain her utility, Jane must receive one additional apple/week if she sacrifices 3 oranges/week, indicating that her MRS at $A$ is 3. At $B$, the quantity of oranges is higher and the quantity of apples is lower, and she is

**FIGURE 4B.6**
**The Marginal Rate of Substitution**
MRS at any point along an indifference curve is defined as the absolute value of the slope of the indifference curve at that point. It is the amount of oranges the consumer must be given to compensate for the loss of one apple.

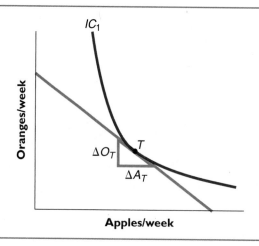

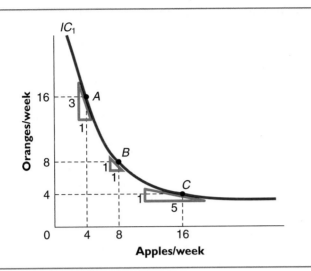

**FIGURE 4B.7**
**Diminishing Marginal Rate of Substitution**
The more oranges the consumer has, the more oranges she is willing to give up to obtain an additional apple. The marginal rates of substitution at bundles A, B, and C are 3, 1, and 1/5, respectively.

willing to give up only one orange per week to obtain one additional apple per week. Her MRS at B is 1. Finally, at C the quantity of oranges is relatively low while the quantity of apples is relative high; Jane requires 5 additional apples/week in return for giving up one orange/week—if she is to maintain the same level of utility. Her MRS at C is 1/5.

Intuitively, diminishing MRS means that consumers rarely like to consume just one thing. The more of one good an individual consumes, the more of that good she is willing to give up in return for one unit of a good of which she consumes only a little.

## USING INDIFFERENCE CURVES TO DESCRIBE PREFERENCES

Since indifference curves describe the preferences of individuals, they also differ across individuals. For example, the difference in Tom and Mary's preferences can be seen in the slopes of their indifference curves in Figure 4B.8. Point A in Tom's indifference map shows he would be willing to exchange 3 oranges for one apple. But, the same bundle in Mary's indifference map shows that she will trade only 1/3 of an orange for another apple. The difference in their marginal rates of substitution of oranges for apples shows clearly that they have different preferences.

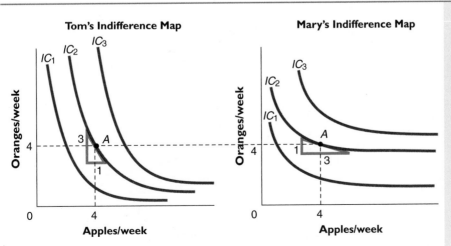

**FIGURE 4B.8**
**People with Different Tastes**
Relatively speaking, Tom loves apples; Mary loves oranges. How is this difference illustrated? At any given bundle, Tom's marginal rate of substitution of apples for oranges is greater than Mary's. At bundle A, for example, Tom would give up three oranges to get another apple, whereas Mary would give up three apples to get another orange.

**EXERCISE 4B.5**     **Consider Tom's indifference map. Explain why any two indifference curves cannot possibly intersect if Tom is rational. (The same statement applies to Mary's map.)**

## THE BEST AFFORDABLE BUNDLE

How will the consumer allocate income between two goods so that they maximize the utility of a given budget? The indifference map shows how the various bundles are ranked in order of preference. The budget constraint, in turn, tells us which bundles are affordable. The consumer's task is to put the two together and choose the most preferred bundle from the affordable choices. (Recall from Chapter 1 that even if consumers don't think explicitly about budget constraints and indifference maps when deciding what to buy, they will make decisions *as if* they were thinking in these terms, just as cyclists ride *as if* they know the relevant laws of physics.)

As an example, consider again the choices for Jane if she has an income of $M = \$10/$ week when the price of an orange is $1 and the price of an apple is $0.50; that is, $P_O = \$1$ and $P_A = \$0.50$. Figure 4B.9 shows her budget constraint and three indifference curves. Bundle $G$ is the most preferred of the five bundles shown in Figure 4B.9 because it lies on the highest indifference curve. But $G$ is not affordable, nor are any other bundles beyond the budget constraint. Choosing any bundle inside the budget constraint, however, means the consumer is not spending the entire budget. The best affordable bundle will lie, therefore, on the budget constraint and not inside or beyond it.

Which bundle along the budget constraint in our example of Figure 4B.9 is the best affordable one? It cannot be on an indifference curve that lies partly inside the budget constraint. Consider the indifference curve $IC_1$. Points $A$ and $E$ lie on both the budget constraint and the indifference curve, but it is possible to identify many points between $A$ and $E$ that are both affordable and lie above $IC_1$ and are therefore preferred over any bundle that lies on $IC_1$. In fact, the budget constraint and the indifference curve $IC_2$ are tangent at point $F$, which is the point of highest utility that Jane can afford in Figure 4B.9. With an income of $10/week, apples priced at $0.50 each, and oranges at $1 each, the combination of 4 oranges and 12 apples is the best affordable one. In general, when an indifference curve is tangent to a budget constraint, the point of tangency identifies the bundle that the consumer prefers above all other bundles that she is able to purchase. Intuitively, the consumer will find the bundle that reaches the highest affordable level of utility by moving to the highest indifference curve that can be afforded, given the budget constraint. For indifference maps that show a tangency point, that point will always indicate the best bundle.

**FIGURE 4B.9**
**The Best Affordable Bundle**
The best Jane can do is to choose the bundle on the budget constraint that lies on the highest attainable indifference curve. Here, that is bundle $F$, which lies at a tangency between the indifference curve and the budget constraint.

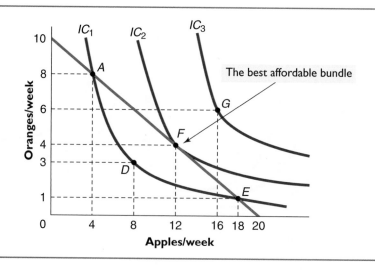

In Figure 4B.9 note that the marginal rate of substitution at *F* is exactly the same as the absolute value of the slope of the budget constraint. This will always be the case when the best affordable bundle occurs at a point of tangency. The condition that must be satisfied can be expressed in the equation

$$\text{MRS} = P_A/P_0. \tag{4B.4}$$

In the context of indifference curves, Equation 4B.4 is the counterpart to the rational spending rule developed in Chapter 4. The right-hand side of Equation 4B.4 represents the opportunity cost of apples in terms of oranges. Thus, with $P_A = \$0.50$ and $P_0 = \$1$, the opportunity cost of an additional apple is one-half orange. The left-hand side of Equation 4B.4 is $\Delta O/\Delta A$, the absolute value of the slope of the indifference curve at the point of tangency. It is the number of oranges the consumer must be given in exchange for one apple while maintaining the same level of utility. In the language of cost–benefit analysis discussed in Chapter 1, in our example the slope of the budget constraint represents the cost of apples in terms of oranges, while the slope of the indifference curve represents marginal benefit (i.e., the marginal utility of consuming an apple as compared with that of consuming an orange). Since the slope of the budget constraint is $-1/2$ in this example, the slope of the indifference curve must be $-1/2$ at the point where the budget constraint and the indifference curve are tangent. When the slope of the indifference curve is $-1/2$, one-half orange is needed to compensate for the loss of an apple. The marginal utility of one more half orange exactly offsets the utility lost when the consumer loses one apple.

If Jane were at some bundle on the budget line for which the two slopes were not the same, then it would always be possible for her to purchase a better bundle. To see why, consider point *E* in Figure 4B.9, where the absolute value of the slope of the indifference curve is less than the absolute value of the slope of the budget constraint. Suppose, for instance, that the MRS at *E* is only 1/4. This tells us that Jane can be compensated for the loss of one apple with an additional one-quarter orange. But the slope of the budget constraint tells us that by giving up one apple she can purchase an additional one-half orange. Since this is one-quarter orange more than she needs to remain equally satisfied, she will clearly be better off if she purchases more oranges and fewer apples than at point *E*. The opportunity cost of an additional orange is less than the benefit it confers. Therefore, a decision to increase the quantity of oranges and reduce the quantity of apples is consistent with the cost–benefit principle.

**Suppose that the marginal rate of substitution at point *A* in Figure 4B.9 is 1.0. Show that this means that the consumer will be better off if she purchases fewer oranges and more apples than at *A*.**

**EXERCISE 4B.6**

> ## RECAP ⬆
>
> ### CONSUMER CHOICE: WHAT IS PREFERRED
>
> An indifference curve graphs a set of bundles, each providing the same level of utility. Together, several indifference curves form an indifference map. Bundles to the northeast of an indifference curve are preferred to bundles on the indifference curve, and bundles on an indifference curve are preferred over those to the southwest of it. The consumer has no preference between bundles on the same indifference curve because they will all provide the same level of utility. The absolute value of the slope of an indifference curve is the marginal rate of substitution—the rate at which a consumer can substitute one good for another while maintaining the same level of utility. The point where an indifference curve is tangent to the consumer's budget constraint identifies the consumer's best affordable bundle. The marginal rate of substitution and the ratio of relative prices for goods in the bundle are equal at that point of tangency.

# 4B.3    INCOME AND SUBSTITUTION EFFECTS AND THE LAW OF DEMAND

Figure 4B.10 shows that if Jane has \$10/week to spend and an orange is \$1 while an apple is \$0.50, her budget constraint is line *ad* and utility is maximized at the bundle of 4 oranges and 12 apples, point *F* on indifference curve $IC_2$.

Suppose that the price of an orange declines to \$0.50, but there is no change to Jane's money income or to the price of apples. In this case, because oranges are cheaper, she now has more options. Graphically, the budget constraint facing her changes, as shown in Figure 4B.10, where the new budget constraint is line segment *a'd*. The old options are still there because the old budget constraint lies to the southwest of the new one. If Jane wanted to spend all her income on apples, the maximum consumption of apples would still be 20, point *d* in the figure, since the price of apples has not changed. But if Jane wanted to spend all of her income on oranges, the maximum possible consumption of oranges would increase from 10, point *a*, to 20, point *a'*. In fact, if Jane chooses to spend any income on oranges, she can now afford a number of bundles that were out of reach before.

With cheaper oranges, Jane's choices from among the options on the new budget constraint *a'd* will depend on personal taste, which economic theory cannot predict. However, we can predict that Jane will try to maximize her utility, and we can represent the new, higher level of utility by drawing a higher indifference curve, such as $IC_3$, which is tangent to the new budget constraint *a'd* at point *F'*. In Figure 4B.10, we have drawn the diagram so that point *F'* is at 7 oranges and 13 apples.[3] The total effect of the decline in the price of oranges in this example is to increase consumption of oranges by 3, *and* to increase consumption of apples by one. Jane is now clearly better off, since being on indifference curve $IC_3$ represents a higher level of utility than being on $IC_2$.

But how much of the change in consumption of oranges is due to the fact that they are now less expensive, and how much of it is due to the fact that Jane now has a higher real income? The decline in the price of oranges influences consumer behaviour both through a change in relative price and through a change in real income. Therefore, economists

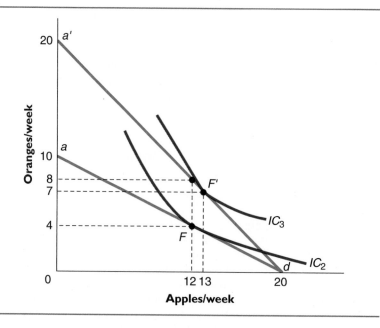

**FIGURE 4B.10**

**A Reduction in the Relative Price of Oranges**
When Jane's income is \$10/week, and the price of an orange decreases from \$1 to \$0.50, the budget constraint changes from *ad* to *a'd*. Jane consumes 7 oranges after the decrease in price, an increase of 3. At the same time, she also chooses to increase apple consumption by one.

---

3  Notice that when the set of affordable bundles increases, Jane chooses to increase her consumption of both oranges and apples. It seems reasonable to assume that consumers prefer variety, and we have chosen to draw $IC_3$ to reflect this.

have developed a way to decompose the total change in consumption into a "pure" price effect and a "pure" income effect.

A price decline for oranges means that Jane's income can cover consumption of both more apples and more oranges, as indicated at point $F'$. Because the decline in the price of oranges means that the same amount of money can now buy more goods, the *real income* of the consumer has increased. If Jane's real income had changed but prices had remained constant, consumption would have changed as well, something economists call the *income effect*. Of course, in this example real income changed because relative prices changed in the first place, but the income effect occurred because Jane became better off. This is why the **income effect** is defined as a change in quantity of a good demanded because a change in the price of the good has changed the real income of the person who purchases it, as we noted in Chapter 4.

Because oranges are now cheaper than they were, as compared to apples whose monetary price has not changed, consumers also have an incentive to substitute oranges for apples *even if total utility is unchanged*. This is called the *substitution effect*. The **substitution effect** is defined as a change in consumption that holds utility constant while there is a change in relative price.

Figure 4B.11 shows the substitution effect graphically. All points on indifference curve $IC_2$ represent bundles with the same level of utility. The original consumption point, 12 apples and 4 oranges at the original prices of $0.50 and $1, respectively, is point $F$. But imagine that the price of oranges falls to $0.50 while Jane simultaneously loses just enough money to remain on the same indifference curve while maximizing her utility. On Figure 4B.11, point $F^S$ is a combination where Jane may, at the new prices of $0.50 and $0.50, choose 10 apples and 6 oranges and remain on indifference curve $IC_2$. This illustration of a *change in consumption* of oranges that *holds utility constant while there is a change in price* is an example of the substitution effect. In general, consumers will substitute in favour of the good whose price has been reduced, as Figure 4B.11 illustrates.

The substitution effect shows the pure impact of changes in relative prices: *even if* Jane were no better off, a change in relative prices would lead consumers to shift purchases towards the now-cheaper commodity. But, in fact, the new $0.50 price of oranges does make Jane better off. In Figure 4B.12, the illustration of the pure *income effect* helps us see the impact of a change in real income while prices remain constant.

**income effect** a change in quantity of a good demanded because a change in the price of the good has changed the real income of the person who purchases it

**substitution effect** a change in consumption that holds utility constant while there is a change in relative price

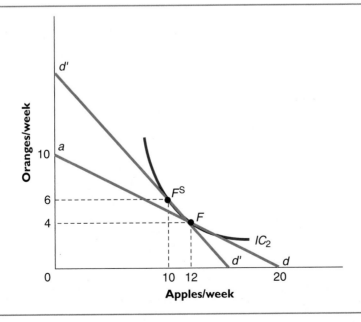

**FIGURE 4B.11**

**The Substitution Effect of a Change in Price**

After a reduction in price, money income is reduced so that Jane returns to $IC_2$, where she was before the price fell. The new budget constraint is the budget line $d'd'$. Its slope captures the new, lower price. It shows that Jane now chooses 6 oranges because of the lower price of oranges. Therefore, the *substitution effect* of the decrease in price is to increase consumption of oranges by 2. Jane also reduces the quantity of apples from 12 to 10 as she substitutes toward oranges, the good whose relative price has decreased. (The relative price of apples has *increased*.)

Suppose Jane had started from point $F^S$ on indifference curve $IC_2$; that is, she consumes 6 oranges and 10 apples, maximizing utility if apples and oranges both cost $0.50. An increase in income then puts her on indifference curve $IC_3$ while the prices of oranges and apples stay at $0.50 apiece for either. What would Jane's choices be in this case?

Point $F'$ in Figure 4B.12 shows the consumption bundle of 7 oranges and 13 apples that Jane would choose when the prices of both oranges and apples are $0.50 and income is $10. (Notice that this is the same point $F'$ that we plotted in Figure 4B.10.) She is now on indifference curve $IC_3$, a higher level of utility than $IC_2$. The change in consumption of oranges due purely to the income effect is the movement from point $F^S$ to $F'$. The pure income effect of the reduction in the price of an orange from $1 to $0.50 causes consumption of oranges to increase by one, from 6 to 7 oranges/week.

The *total price effect*, that is the change in quantity demanded that results from a change in price (in our example, the move from point $F$ to $F'$ in Figure 4B.10 or an increase of 3 oranges), is the sum of two influences—the substitution effect *and* the income effect. The substitution effect is the movement from point $F$ to $F^S$ in Figure 4B.11, an increase of 2 oranges. The income effect is the movement from point $F^S$ to $F'$ in Figure 4B.12, an increase of one orange. These two, together, make up the effect of the price change on the quantity of the good purchased: oranges, in this example.

Substitution effect ($+2$) plus Income effect ($+1$) = Total price effect ($+3$)

The change in the quantity of oranges purchased caused by a reduction in the price of an orange can also be used to plot Jane's demand curve, as in Figure 4B.13. A reduction in price, $1 to $0.50, causes an increase in quantity demanded, 4 oranges to 7, just as the law of demand states. The slope of the demand curve in Figure 4B.13 is influenced by both the substitution effect and the income effect. But sometimes we want to answer questions like, "How would quantity demanded be affected if the price of a good is changed while a consumer's utility is held constant?" We might ask, for example, "How much gasoline will a 'typical' driver purchase if the price of gasoline increases, while the consumer's level of real income remains constant?" Or, we might ask, "How does a change in the price of a good affect a consumer's real income?" For example, if the price of gasoline increases, what impact does it have on a typical consumer's real income? Indifference curves enable us to separate income effects from substitution effects and answer such questions.

**FIGURE 4B.12**

**The Income Effect of a Change in Price**
After the price of oranges decreases, the budget constraint is given by $a'd$, as in Figure 4B.10. The budget line $d'd'$ is a budget constraint that keeps Jane on the same indifference curve as before the price decrease and is identical to the $d'd'$ line in Figure 4B.11. The slopes of the $d'd'$ line and $a'd$ line are identical, because both represent the new, lower price of oranges. Therefore, the movement from $F^S$ to $F'$ represents the *income effect* of a decrease in price. Jane's real income has increased. Therefore, she chooses to increase the quantity of oranges purchased.

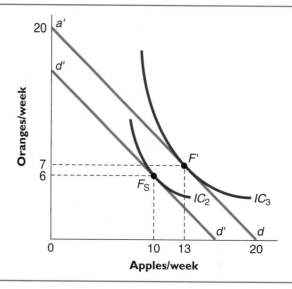

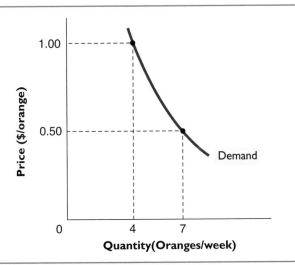

**FIGURE 4B.13**
**Total Price Effect**
When the price of an orange falls from $1 to $0.50, the quantity demanded increases by 3, from 4 to 7 oranges. The increase in quantity is the sum of the substitution effect (2 oranges), identified in Figure 4B.11, plus the income effect (1 orange), identified in Figure 4B.12.

**RECAP**

### INCOME AND SUBSTITUTION EFFECTS AND THE LAW OF DEMAND

A change in the price of a good has two effects on quantity demanded: an *income effect* and a *substitution effect.* The income effect is the change in quantity demanded of a good because a change in the price of the good changes the real income of the person who purchases it. The substitution effect is the change in quantity demanded that results from a relative price change where a consumer's utility is held constant. The total change in quantity demanded is the sum of the income effect and the substitution effect. Both effects influence the demand curve. Use of indifference curves makes it easier to separate income from substitution effects and to study the influence of each on demand curves.

## KEY TERMS

budget constraint (114)
income effect (123)
indifference curve (117)

indifference map (117)
marginal rate of substitution
  (MRS) (118)

substitution effect (123)

## PROBLEMS

4B.1 Suppose Richard's income is $M = \$1200$ per month, all of which he spends on some combination of rent and restaurant meals. If restaurant meals cost $12 each, and if the monthly rent for an apartment is $3 per square metre; draw this consumer's budget constraint with his monthly quantities of restaurant meals per month on the vertical axis and apartment size on the horizontal axis. Is the bundle (300 m²/month, 50 meals/month) affordable? **LO4B.1**

4B.2 Show what happens to the budget constraint in Problem 1 if the price of restaurant meals falls to $8. Is the bundle (300, 50) affordable? **LO4B.1**

4B.3 What happens to the budget constraint in Problem 2 if the monthly rent for apartments falls to $2 per square metre? Is the bundle (300, 50) affordable? **LO4B.1**

4B.4 When inflation happens, prices and incomes generally rise at about the same rate each year. What happens to the budget constraint from Problem 1 if

Richard's income rises by 10 percent and the prices of restaurant meals and apartments increase by 10 percent? Has Richard been harmed by inflation? **LO4B.1**

4B.5   Alisha spends all her income on two goods, $X$ and $Y$. Of the labelled points on her indifference map, which appears below, indicate which ones are affordable and which ones are unaffordable. Indicate how Alisha ranks these bundles, ranging from most preferred to least preferred. Identify the best affordable bundle. **LO4B.2, LO4B.3, LO4B.4**

4B.6   Sigmund spends all his income on two goods, $X$ and $Y$. His income and the prices of $X$ and $Y$ are such that his budget constraint is the line $AF$. Of the labelled points on his indifference map, indicate which one is the best affordable bundle. Why is it the best affordable bundle? (Hint: This problem does not have a tangency solution.) **LO4B.2, LO4B.3, LO4B.4**

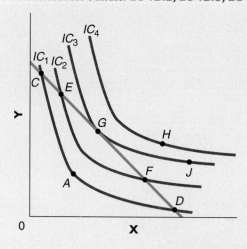

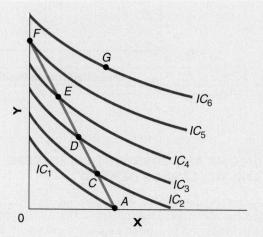

## ANSWERS TO IN-APPENDIX EXERCISES

**4B.1    LO4B.1**

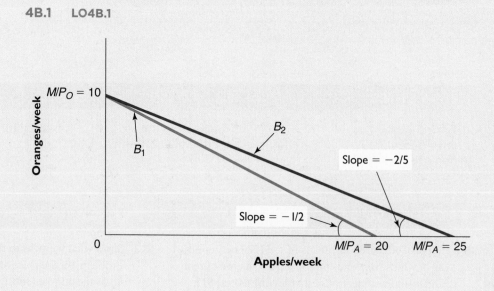

**4B.2** LO4B.1

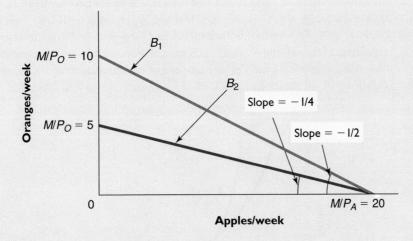

**4B.3** LO4B.1

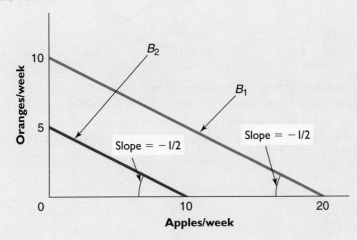

**4B.4** LO4B.1

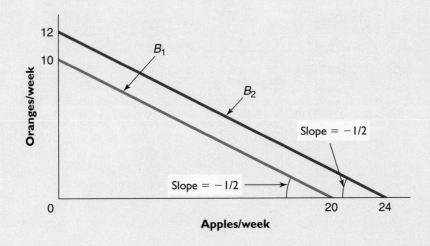

**4B.5**    Refer to the graph below. According to indifference curve $IC_2$, Tom prefers bundle $A$ to bundle $B$. $IC_2$ also shows that Tom is indifferent between $B$ and $C$ and, thus, must prefer $A$ to $C$. However, $C$ is above $IC_1$ and $A$ is on $IC_1$, so Tom must prefer $C$ to $A$. Tom cannot both prefer $A$ to $C$ and prefer $C$ to $A$. Intersecting indifference curves imply that Tom cannot consistently order preferences. Therefore, intersecting indifference curves violate a fundamental assumption of the theory of consumer choice. **LO4B.2**

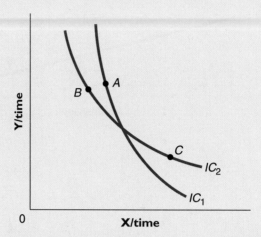

**4B.6**    At bundle $A$, Jane is willing to give up one orange in order to get an additional apple. But at market prices it is necessary to give up only one-half orange in order to buy an additional apple. It follows that Jane will be better off than she is at bundle $A$ if she buys one less orange and 2 more apples. **LO4B.2, LO4B.3, LO4B.4**

# CHAPTER 5
# Production and Cost: The Supply Side in the Short Run

In the 1970s, it took more than 50 hours of direct labour to assemble a car. In 2010, fewer than 8 hours were needed. Similar productivity growth has occurred in many other manufacturing industries. Yet in many service industries, productivity has grown only slowly, if at all. For example, the same number of musicians is required to play Mozart's *String Quartet* today as in 1800. And it still takes a barber about the same amount of time to cut someone's hair as it did a century ago.

Given the spectacular growth in manufacturing workers' productivity, it is no surprise that their real wages have risen more than fivefold during the past 100 years. But how can we explain why real wages for service workers have risen just as much? If barbers and musicians are no more productive than they were one hundred years ago, why are they now paid five times as much?

Remember that the opportunity cost of pursuing any given occupation is the most one could have earned in some other occupation. Most people who become barbers or musicians could have chosen jobs in manufacturing instead. If workers in service industries were not paid roughly as much as they could have earned in other occupations, many of them would not have been willing to work in service industries in the first place.

The trajectories of wages in manufacturing and service industries illustrate the intimate link between the prices at which goods and services are offered for sale in the market and the opportunity cost of the resources required to produce them. Whereas our focus in Chapter 4 was on the buyer's side of the market, our focus here is on the seller's side. Earlier, we saw that the demand curve is a graph that tells how many units buyers want to purchase at different prices. Our task here is to gain insight into the factors that determine the shape and position of the supply curve, which tells how many units suppliers want to produce and sell at different prices.

Although the demand side and the supply side of every market differ in several ways, there is a core similarity. Both buyers and sellers want to know if a transaction will make them better off. In the buyer's case, the question is, will I be better off if I buy another unit? In the seller's case, the question is, will I be better off if I sell another unit?

## LEARNING OBJECTIVES

When you have completed the material in this chapter, you will be able to:

**LO1** Explain how opportunity cost is related to the supply curve.

**LO2** Explain how the law of diminishing marginal returns influences marginal product and average product.

**LO3** Graph and explain the relationships among total, average, and marginal product.

**LO4** Determine the quantity of output and the number of employees that will maximize a price taker's short-run profit.

**LO5** Connect a firm's costs with its decisions about what quantity to supply and how many employees to hire.

**LO6** Graph and explain the relationships among a firm's short-run cost and product curves.

**LO7** Use a graph to represent a price taker's maximum profit.

**LO8** Explain how costs and the availability of inputs affect a firm's short-run supply curve and elasticity of supply.

COST-
BENEFIT

Both buyers and sellers use the cost–benefit criterion for answering these questions: a rational buyer will buy another unit if its benefit exceeds its cost, and a rational seller will sell another unit if its production cost is less than the extra revenue that results from selling it.

# 5.1 PROFIT-MAXIMIZING FIRMS AND PERFECTLY COMPETITIVE MARKETS

In this chapter, we will analyze the supply curve of products that are sold in markets. We will not try to analyze all the possible motivations of all the organizations that supply all types of goods and services, nor will we try to analyze all the different economic environments in which they operate. In virtually every economy, some goods and services are produced by a variety of organizations that have different motives. Churches, mosques, and temples, for example, supply religious services because their congregations believe in their doctrines. Food banks supply food because their organizers and donors want to help people in need, and karaoke singers perform in bars because they like public attention. This chapter will not examine these motivations. In this text, we will focus instead on production of goods and services that is motivated by money.

## PROFIT MAXIMIZATION FOR THE FIRM

In Canada and most other nations, *most* goods and services are offered for sale in markets and are sold by private firms whose main reason for existing is to earn *profit* for their owners. A firm's **profit** is the difference between the total revenue it receives from the sale of its product and all costs it incurs in producing that product.

In this chapter we begin by assuming that firms are *price takers*. A **price taker** is a firm that has no ability to influence the price at which it sells its product. It can decide to sell as much or as little as it wants, but the quantity it sells will not influence the market price. This model is a reasonable approximation to many markets; however, there are important markets in which firms are actually able to influence the prices of the products they sell. We will defer the study of firms that can influence the price of their products until Part 3 of this book.

A **profit-maximizing firm** is one whose primary goal is to maximize its profits. It combines factors of production to produce a good or service. **Factors of production** are the resources a firm uses to produce output. Any factor of production will fall into one of three categories: land, labour, or capital. **Land** is any land (or other naturally occurring resource) used to produce output. **Labour** is the physical or mental exertion of human beings to produce output. Durable goods produced by factors of production and then used, but not used up entirely, in a production process (e.g., buildings, machinery, and tools) are known as **capital**. An **entrepreneur** is a person who first perceives an opportunity to make a profit and then takes the necessary risks involved in organizing factors of production to realize that profit.

In addition to factors of production, firms also use *intermediate inputs* when they produce output. An **intermediate input** is an input that is used up in the production process. For example, a house-painting contractor must buy paint in order to paint a house. Because the paint is used up in producing the final output (a painted house), it is an intermediate input. Capital equipment, such as ladders and scaffolding, that lasts longer than a single period of production is considered a factor of production. Land, labour, and capital are not intermediate inputs because they retain their identities and are not entirely used up in the production process. (Note that the crucial issue is whether a factor of production is *used*. The method of payment for the factor is unimportant;

Why are barbers paid five times as much now as in 1910, even though they require about as much time to cut hair now as they did then?

**profit** the total revenue a firm receives from the sale of its product minus all costs, explicit and implicit, incurred in producing it

**price taker** a firm that has no influence over the price at which it sells its product

**profit-maximizing firm** a firm whose primary goal is to maximize the difference between its total revenues and total costs

**factor of production** resource used to produce output; falls into one of three categories—land, labour, or capital

**land** any naturally occurring resource used to produce output

**labour** physical or mental exertion by human beings to produce output

e.g., whether a painting contractor's ladders are leased or owned by the firm does not affect how much capital is used.)

## PRODUCTION BY A FIRM OPERATING IN THE SHORT RUN

Some of a firm's decisions can take much longer to implement than others—designing and building a new factory may take 12 to 18 months or longer, but new workers can usually be hired quickly, sometimes in a week or less. Thus, economists distinguish between the short run and the long run.

The distinction between the *short run* and the *long run* depends on how long it takes for a firm to change all or just some aspects of its production process. The **short run** is a period of time so short that *at least one* factor of production cannot be varied. For example, a firm operating in the short run may be able to vary the amount of labour it employs or its purchases of raw materials and other intermediate inputs, but it typically cannot vary its capital stock. We define the **long run** as a period of time long enough to make it possible for *all* factors of production, including capital, to be varied. In practice, *the distinction between the short run and the long run varies considerably from one industry to another.* The amount of time an electrical utility requires to design and build a new nuclear power generating station will be much longer than the time an owner of a pizzeria requires to order and install a larger oven. In both cases, there is a change in the capital stock, but the utility's capital is fixed for a much longer period of time.

When analyzing a firm's production decisions, it is useful to begin with short-run considerations. As an example, consider Acme Glass, a small company that makes glass bottles. For simplicity, suppose that the silica sand required for making bottles is available free from a nearby desert, and Acme's only production costs are the wages of its employees and the lease payment on its bottle-making machine. Its labour and its capital, that is, the employees and the machine, are Acme's two factors of production.

A profit-maximizing firm operating in the short run must decide how many workers to hire each day. The relationship between the number of workers and daily output is part of the information Acme needs to make this decision. Suppose that our bottle-making firm knows from experience that Table 5.1 represents the relationship between the number of workers and total daily output. We can call the known technological relationship between inputs and output a **production function**. We assume that it embodies the best currently available engineering and technical advice. There are a number of different, but equivalent, ways of describing a production function. Columns 1 and 2 of Table 5.1 represent a short-run production function (short run because we are assuming the size of Acme's bottle-making machine is fixed—in fact, everything is fixed except labour), but we could represent exactly the same relationship between labour used and output produced using graphs or mathematics.

Both *marginal benefits* and *marginal costs* must be used if we are to apply the cost–benefit principle correctly. The benefit of using more labour is the increase in output the firm obtains, and in the theory of production, an important concept is the benefit of hiring one more worker, which is called the *marginal product of labour*. The marginal product of labour is inversely related to marginal cost of production—a *higher* marginal product means a *lower* marginal cost. In what follows, we will develop this relationship in more detail.

Columns 1 and 2 in Table 5.1 determine the entries in column 3, which displays *marginal product*. **Marginal product** is the increase in total output caused by an increase of *one* unit in the variable factor of production, holding all other factors of production and technology fixed. A **variable factor of production** changes as output changes. In this example, labour is the only variable factor of production, so marginal product is about a *change* in the amount of labour employed. The bottle-making machine is the *fixed factor of*

**capital** any durable good (buildings, machinery, tools) produced by other factors of production for use in a production process

**entrepreneur** a person who perceives an opportunity to make a profit and then takes the risks necessary to organize factors of production in order to realize that profit

**intermediate inputs** any inputs that are used up in the production process

**short run** a period of time sufficiently short that at least one of the firm's factors of production cannot be varied

**long run** a period of time of sufficient length that all the firm's factors of production are variable

**production function** a technological relationship between inputs and output

**marginal product** the increase in total output caused by an increase of one unit in the variable factor of production, holding technology and all other inputs constant

**variable factor of production** an input whose quantity can be altered in the short run

**TABLE 5.1**

**Employment and Output for Acme Glass Ltd.**

| (1) Total number of employees/day | (2) Total number of bottles/day | (3) Marginal product | (4) Average product (2) ÷ (1) |
|---|---|---|---|
| 0 | 0 | | |
| | | 90 | |
| 1 | 90 | | 90 |
| | | 110 | |
| **2** | **200** | | 100 |
| | | 60 | |
| 3 | 260 | | 87 |
| | | 40 | |
| **4** | **300** | | 75 |
| | | 38 | |
| 5 | 338 | | 68 |
| | | 33 | |
| 6 | 371 | | 62 |
| | | 29 | |
| **7** | **400** | | 57 |
| **11** | **500** | | 45 |
| **16** | **600** | | 38 |
| **22** | **700** | | 32 |

**fixed factor of production** an input whose quantity cannot be altered in the short run

*production.* A **fixed factor of production** cannot be changed in the short run, so it does not change as output changes. Column 3 answers the question, how much does daily output increase when one *more* worker is hired? It shows that, if employment increases from one to two workers per day, total daily output rises from 90 to 200 bottles, for an increase of 110 bottles/day. Hence, marginal product is 110. Each entry in column 3 is determined in this way. Also, because marginal product is about a change from one amount of labour to another, each entry in column 3 appears between two corresponding entries in column 2.

In many factories, production will go more smoothly if there are enough workers to feed each machine, so there is often a range of output over which marginal product increases. If the firm has decided to remain in business, it always makes sense to add another worker if marginal product is increasing. However, beyond some point, additional workers add relatively less to total output. In our example, once output of bottles increases to more than 200/day, the marginal product of labour begins to decline. In other words, given that all other inputs and technology are fixed, beyond some point, the marginal product of labour decreases as successively more units of labour are employed in the bottle factory. Economists call this the **law of diminishing marginal returns**.

**law of diminishing marginal returns** as equal increments of one input are added, there is a point beyond which the marginal product of that input will decrease, if technology and all other inputs are held constant

If more and more labour is required to produce the same increase in bottle production, marginal product is decreasing. The pattern is highlighted by the boldface entries of Table 5.1. For example, if the daily output of bottles is to rise from 200 to 300, labour must be increased by two—from two to four employees. But to increase daily output from 300 to 400 bottles, labour must increase by three—from four to seven employees. Beyond the marginal product at seven employees, no entries appear in column 3. This is because the table adds employees one by one only until seven are reached. Adding employees one at a time makes it easy to show marginal product. However, in order to reduce the size of

Table 5.1, the next entry after seven employees is eleven employees; therefore, the increment is four employees. The additional four employees cause output to increase from 400 to 500 bottles per day, for an increase of 100. Beyond seven employees, it simplifies the table to show production of bottles increasing by increments of 100 each day and to omit entries for marginal product.

Column 4 of Table 5.1 shows *average product* of labour. **Average product** is total output divided by units of the variable factor of production, or simply output per unit of variable input. For example, the fourth entry in column 4 is calculated as 300/4 = 75. Output per unit of labour is also referred to as the average productivity of labour.

The law of diminishing marginal returns always refers to situations in which technology and at least one factor of production are fixed. In the current example, technology, or knowledge of methods of producing bottles, is fixed, as is Acme's capital (the bottle-making machine). Diminishing marginal returns often arise because, as workers are added, increasingly more workers must share the same workspace and tools. Space around the bottle-making machine will become more crowded as employees are added. If workers get in each other's way (or on each other's nerves), breakage will increase, thus requiring more visits to the first aid station and more time for removing broken glass from the work area. It is easy to believe that workers are less productive when they work under cramped, stressful conditions.

## 5.2  GRAPHING THE RELATIONSHIPS AMONG TOTAL, AVERAGE, AND MARGINAL VALUES

Figure 5.1 highlights relationships among total, average, and marginal values by graphing information from Table 5.1. Knowledge of these relationships will be helpful when we study how the law of diminishing marginal returns interacts with the principle of increasing opportunity cost. Panel (a) graphs total output of bottles/day against employees/day and thus plots the tabular production function shown in Table 5.1. Panel (a) shows total output increasing over the entire range that is plotted. Panel (b) graphs the average and marginal product of labour. Both rise to a maximum, then decrease.

Consider marginal product, which reaches a maximum at between one and two employees per day, then declines. Initially, each successive employee adds a larger amount to total output. The second employee's marginal product is greater than the first employee's. However, the third employee's addition to total output (i.e., his marginal product) is less than the second employee's. Diminishing marginal returns appear with the third employee. Thereafter, each successive employee adds a smaller and smaller amount to total output. When panels (a) and (b) are taken together, Figure 5.1 provides a picture of the relationship between total output and marginal product. Provided marginal product is positive, total output always rises as labour increases. However, the graph of marginal product shows that total output rises first by increasing amounts, then by decreasing amounts. Thus marginal product increases to a maximum and then begins to decline as diminishing marginal returns to labour take effect.

Note that the left hand broken line that is perpendicular to the horizontal axis of panel (b) of Figure 5.1 intersects maximum marginal product and extends into panel (a). In panel (a), it passes through point C, where the slope of the production function is greatest. Thus, as the quantity of labour approaches two employees per day, marginal product decreases, as shown in panel (b). Moreover, as the quantity of labour is increased beyond two employees per day, the law of diminishing marginal returns causes the slope of the production function in panel (a) to decrease. The slope of the production function can be defined as the change in output of bottles divided by the change in units of labour. Each increase of labour by one unit is associated with an increase in output of bottles; therefore, the slope of the production function is equal to marginal product. Whether one refers to panel (a) or panel (b), beyond the point where two workers are employed, diminishing

**average product** total output divided by the total number of units of the variable factor of production

INCREASING
OPPORTUNITY COST

**FIGURE 5.1**

**A Short-Run Production Function for Acme Glass Ltd.**

Panel (a) shows a production function, which summarizes the technological relationship between daily use of Acme's variable input (labour) and total daily output. It embodies the assumption that Acme uses the best available engineering and technical advice to maximize the output that can be obtained from any given combination of inputs. Panel (b) shows marginal product, which is the increase in total daily output caused when one more unit of labour is used each day. Panel (b) also shows the average product of labour, which is total output divided by units of labour. The quantity of labour where marginal product reaches its maximum is also the quantity of labour where the slope of the production function is at a maximum (point C). Diminishing marginal product of labour causes the production function to flatten as successive additional units of labour add smaller and smaller increments to total output. Point B in panel (a) aligns with maximum average product in panel (b).

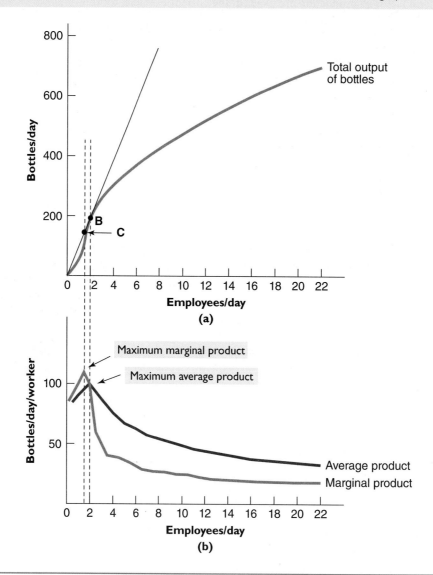

marginal returns cause successive units of labour to add smaller and smaller increments to total output. Panel (a) and panel (b), therefore, provide two different pictures of the same effect. Panel (b) also shows four elements of the relationship between average and marginal product:

1. Maximum marginal product occurs at a lower level of output than maximum average product.

2. Marginal product equals average product at maximum average product.

3. If marginal product exceeds average product, then average product is increasing.
4. If marginal product is less than average product, then average product is decreasing.

These relationships can also be seen in Table 5.1. Suppose one worker per day is employed; average product is 90. Now let the number of employees per day rise to two; marginal product is 110. Because the amount added by the additional employee exceeds the average product of 90, the output of the additional employee increases the average. As Table 5.1 shows, the average product with two employees per day is 100, 10 more than the average product with one employee. Now let the number of employees per day increase from two to three; marginal product of a third employee is 60, which is less than the average product of two employees. Thus, we expect average product to fall when a third employee is added, and Table 5.1 shows this; average product of three employees is 87. Eighty-seven, the average product of three employees, clearly is less than 100, which is the average product of two employees.

In the real world, every industry is different. Thus, short-run production functions vary from one production process to another. As a result, graphs of total output, marginal product, and average product will vary in how they are plotted. Nevertheless, Figure 5.2 illustrates the technical relationships between total output and the marginal and average product of labour. As Figure 5.2 also indicates, marginal product becomes zero and shifts from positive to negative at the point of maximum possible total output. (Note that no profit-maximizing firm would actually employ labour to the point of causing marginal product to become negative; that is, no firm would incur a cost that reduces its output.)

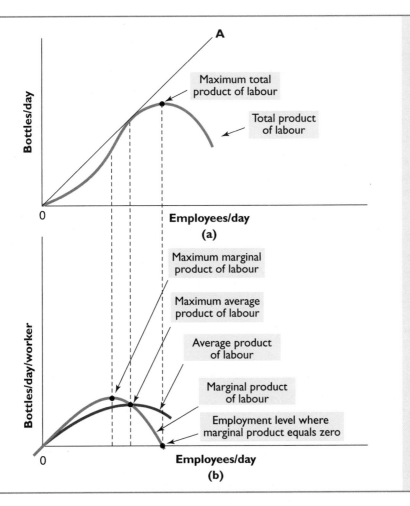

**FIGURE 5.2**

**The Relationship Between Marginal, Average, and Total Product in the Short Run**

135

changes its output

## CHOOSING OUTPUT TO MAXIMIZE PROFIT

Suppose the lease payment for Acme's bottle-making machine is $40/day, and that it must be paid whether or not Acme makes any bottles. Any cost that does not change when output changes is a **fixed cost**. For example, the cost of a *fixed factor of production* is a *fixed cost*. A fixed cost can be contrasted with a **variable cost**, which is any cost that changes as the firm changes its output. Acme's payment for its lease is a fixed cost because it does not change regardless of the number of bottles Acme makes. It also is a a sunk cost while the lease is in effect, because Acme is obliged to make lease payments for the duration of the lease regardless of any decisions it makes. For short, we'll refer to the cost of the bottle-making machine as Acme's *capital cost*. In Examples 5.1 to 5.3, we will explore how the price of bottles, the wage rate, and the cost of capital influence Acme's decisions about how many workers to hire and how many bottles to produce. Again, labour is the only variable input. The cost of labour therefore is Acme's *variable cost*.

### EXAMPLE 5.1

**If bottles sell for $35/hundred and if an employee's wage is $10/day, how many bottles will Acme Glass produce each day?**

Profit is the difference between the revenue the firm collects from the sale of bottles and the cost of its labour and capital. If the firm's goal is to maximize profit, Table 5.2 shows how the daily number of bottles produced (Q) is related to the firm's revenue, employment, costs, and profit. Columns 1 and 2 of Table 5.2 reproduce the boldfaced entries in columns 1 and 2 of Table 5.1; they represent the production function. Columns 4 and 8 of Table 5.2 compare the additional revenue obtained from selling 100 more bottles/day to the cost of making them. For this example, we will assume that bottles sell for $0.35 each and that Acme Glass can sell as many, or as few, bottles as it chooses to at that price. We will then use columns 4 and 8 to identify the daily output of bottles that maximizes profit.

**TABLE 5.2**
Employment, Output, Revenue, Costs, and Profit at Acme Glass Ltd.

| (1) Total number of employees/ day | (2) Q (bottles/ day) | (3) Total revenue ($/day) | (4) Marginal revenue ($) | (5) Total labour cost ($/day) | (6) Total fixed cost ($/day) | (7) Total cost ($/day) | (8) Marginal cost ($) | (9) Profit ($/day) |
|---|---|---|---|---|---|---|---|---|
| | | $0.35 × (2) | | $10 × (1) | | (5) + (6) | | (3) − (7) |
| 0 | 0 | 0 | | 0 | 40 | 40 | | −40 |
| 2 | 200 | 70 | | 20 | 40 | 60 | | 10 |
| | | | 35 | | | | 20 | |
| 4 | 300 | 105 | | 40 | 40 | 80 | | 25 |
| | | | 35 | | | | 30 | |
| 7 | 400 | 140 | | 70 | 40 | 110 | | 30 |
| | | | 35 | | | | 40 | |
| 11 | 500 | 175 | | 110 | 40 | 150 | | 25 |
| | | | 35 | | | | 50 | |
| 16 | 600 | 210 | | 160 | 40 | 200 | | 10 |
| | | | 35 | | | | 60 | |
| 22 | 700 | 245 | | 220 | 40 | 260 | | −15 |

Notes: Employee wage rate=$10/day
Price of bottles = $35/hundred= $0.35/bottle

To see how the entries in Table 5.2 are constructed, examine the revenue, cost, and profit values that correspond to 200 units of output (row 2). Total revenue is $70, the company's receipts from selling 200 bottles at $35/hundred. To make 200 bottles, Acme has to employ two workers (see column 1). At a wage of $10/hour, that translates into $20 of total labour cost. When Acme's fixed capital cost of $40/day is added to its total labour cost, we get the total cost entry of $60/day that appears in column 7. Acme's daily profit is total revenue − total cost = $70 − $60 = $10, the entry in column 9.

Having decided to produce 200 bottles/day, which requires two workers per day, can Acme increase its profits by hiring more workers and producing more bottles? If it produces and sells more bottles, clearly Acme's revenues will rise. However, because it must hire more labour to produce more bottles, its costs will also rise.

How can Acme decide if it will make greater profit by increasing production? To answer this crucial question, Acme must compare its *marginal revenue* with its *marginal cost*. **Marginal revenue** is the increase in total revenue obtained by producing and selling one more unit of output. We are assuming that Acme Glass has no influence on the price and that a unit of output is 100 bottles. Therefore, Acme's marginal revenue equals the price of its product, because total revenue increases by exactly the price of 100 bottles, $35, when one more unit is sold. **Marginal cost** is the increase in total cost incurred by producing one more unit of output. When Acme compares marginal revenue with marginal cost, it is applying the cost–benefit principle.

If Acme increases its daily output by 100 bottles (from 200 to 300 bottles/day), its total revenue will rise by $35/day. That is, its marginal revenue will be $35, which is the first entry in column 4. Because it must hire two more workers per day (which increases its employees from two to four) to produce another 100 bottles/day, Acme must incur a marginal cost of $20. The first entry in column 8 is $20. We see that if Acme produces and sells 100 more bottles, then it will increase its total revenue by $15 more than it increases its total cost. Therefore, its profit increases by $15/day.

**marginal revenue** the increase in total revenue obtained by producing and selling one more unit of output

**marginal cost** the increase in total cost incurred by producing one more unit of output

---

We have simplified this example by assuming that the only cost a firm incurs by increasing its output in the short run is the increase in total wages for the additional labourers. The increase in total cost to Acme when it produces *one more bottle* is the marginal cost of a bottle. Marginal cost is determined by the cost of the additional labour and marginal productivity of that labour (i.e., the marginal product of labour). Consider the decision to increase output from 200 to 300 bottles/day. Table 5.2 shows that the number of workers must be increased from two to four per day. Since the daily wage rate is $10, total cost will increase by $20/day. We can therefore write

COST-
BENEFIT

$$MC = \frac{\text{Change in total wages paid}}{\text{Change in total output}} = \frac{\$20}{100} = \frac{W}{MP_L} = \frac{\$10}{50} = \$0.20. \qquad (5.1)$$

Marginal cost is represented by $MC$, $W$ represents the daily wage rate, and $MP_L$ represents marginal product of labour. Two more units of labour, each at $10/day, are required to increase output by 100 bottles. Therefore, the increase in output is divided by two to obtain marginal product of 50.[1] Equation 5.1 tells us the marginal cost of a bottle is $0.20. This is the same as saying that the marginal cost of 100 bottles is $20.

Because a change in total wages paid to gain a unit of output is equal to a change in total costs, it follows that:

$$\frac{\text{Change in total wages paid}}{\text{Change in number of workers employed}} = \frac{MC}{\text{Change in number of workers employed}}$$

$$= \frac{\$20}{2} = \$10 = W \qquad (5.2)$$

Dividing marginal cost by the change in number of workers employed yields the wage rate.

---

1　Notice that Table 5.1 shows a marginal product of 60 for the third worker and 40 for the fourth. Equation 5.1 combines the additional output of the third and fourth workers to obtain an increase in output of 100 bottles. Therefore, marginal product in Equation 5.1 is an average of the two values shown in Table 5.1.

COST-
BENEFIT

COST-
BENEFIT

In fact, whenever marginal revenue is greater than marginal cost, the firm can increase its profit by producing and selling more output. If marginal revenue is less than marginal cost, the firm will reduce its profit by producing more output. Indeed, if marginal revenue is less than marginal cost, the firm can improve profit by reducing output. If we apply this logic, comparison of the entries in columns 4 and 8 tell us that Acme Glass will maximize profit if it increases its output to 400 bottles/day, thereby employing seven workers per day. Inspection of column 9 confirms that by producing 400 bottles/day, Acme's resulting daily profit of $30 will be the largest possible.

We have discovered Acme's profit-maximizing output by asking whether an increase in output will increase profits. A comparison of marginal revenue with marginal cost gives the answer. Suppose we had asked a different question: How many workers will Acme employ to maximize profit? To answer, we again use the cost–benefit principle and compare the marginal revenue with the marginal cost of hiring another worker. As was the case for Example 5.1, let price per bottle be $0.35 (or $35/100 bottles) and the daily wage rate be $10. Suppose Acme has hired two workers. Table 5.1 shows that marginal product of a third worker is 60 bottles/day. Because each bottle sells for $0.35, the value of a third worker's marginal product is $0.35 × 60 = $21/day. The worker's wage rate is $10/day, so marginal cost of the worker is $10/day. Thus, by adding a third worker, Acme increases its profit by $11/day. By working from Table 5.1, and continuing to compare the value of a worker's marginal product with the marginal cost of the worker, we find that Acme will maximize profits by employing seven workers. Table 5.1 shows that seven workers will produce 400 bottles/day. It should not surprise you that whether one asks for Acme's profit-maximizing output or Acme's profit-maximizing number of employees, the answer is the same: hire seven workers and produce 400 bottles/day.

## EXAMPLE 5.2

**Same as Example 5.1, except now bottles sell for $45/hundred.**

If the price of bottles rises but costs do not change, it is reasonable to expect that Acme will produce more bottles. As seen in columns 3, 4, and 7 of Table 5.3, an increase in selling price to $45/hundred increases total revenue, marginal revenue, and profit.

**TABLE 5.3**
**Employment, Output, Revenue, Costs, and Profit at Acme Glass Ltd.**

| (1) Total number of employees/day | (2) Q (bottles/day) | (3) Total revenue ($/day) | (4) Marginal revenue ($) | (5) Total cost ($/day) | (6) Marginal cost ($) | (7) Profit ($/day) |
|---|---|---|---|---|---|---|
| | | $0.45 × (2) | | | | (3) − (5) |
| 0 | 0 | 0 | | 40 | | −40 |
| 2 | 200 | 90 | | 60 | | 30 |
| | | | 45 | | 20 | |
| 4 | 300 | 135 | | 80 | | 55 |
| | | | 45 | | 30 | |
| 7 | 400 | 180 | | 110 | | 70 |
| | | | 45 | | 40 | |
| 11 | 500 | 225 | | 150 | | 75 |
| | | | 45 | | 50 | |
| 16 | 600 | 270 | | 200 | | 70 |
| | | | 45 | | 60 | |
| 22 | 700 | 315 | | 260 | | 55 |

Notes: Employee wage rate = $10/day
Price of bottles = $45/hundred = $0.45/bottle

However, costs are unaffected. Therefore, in Table 5.3 we reproduce only total and marginal cost from Table 5.2. Total and marginal cost in Table 5.3 (columns 5 and 6) are identical to total and marginal cost in Table 5.2 (columns 7 and 8). Comparison of marginal revenue with marginal cost in Table 5.3 shows Acme will maximize profits by increasing daily output to 500 bottles. This means Acme will employ 11 workers. Column 7 confirms that when 500 bottles/day are produced and sold, profits are maximized at $75/day. This example shows that the profit-maximizing firm's supply curve slopes upward.

## EXAMPLE 5.3

**Same as Example 5.1, except now the wage rate is $14/hour.**

If costs rise and the price per bottle remains at $0.35, we would expect Acme to produce fewer bottles. With a higher wage rate, labour costs are higher at every level of output, as shown in column 5, Table 5.4.

**TABLE 5.4**
**Employment, Output, Revenue, Costs, and Profit at Acme Glass Ltd.**

| (1) Total number of employees/day | (2) *Q* (bottles/ day) | (3) Total revenue ($/day) | (4) Marginal revenue ($) | (5) Total labour cost ($/day) | (6) Total fixed cost ($/day) | (7) Total cost ($/day) | (8) Marginal cost ($) | (9) Profit ($/day) |
|---|---|---|---|---|---|---|---|---|
| | | $0.35 × (2) | | $14 × (1) | | (5) + (6) | | (3) − (7) |
| 0 | 0 | 0 | | 0 | 40 | 40 | | −40 |
| 2 | 200 | 70 | | 28 | 40 | 68 | | 2 |
| | | | 35 | | | | 28 | |
| 4 | 300 | 105 | | 56 | 40 | 96 | | 9 |
| | | | 35 | | | | 42 | |
| 7 | 400 | 140 | | 98 | 40 | 138 | | 2 |
| | | | 35 | | | | 56 | |
| 11 | 500 | 175 | | 154 | 40 | 194 | | −19 |
| | | | 35 | | | | 70 | |
| 16 | 600 | 210 | | 224 | 40 | 264 | | −54 |
| | | | 35 | | | | 84 | |
| 22 | 700 | 245 | | 308 | 40 | 348 | | −103 |

Notes: Employee wage rate = $14/day
Price of bottles = $35/hundred = $0.35/bottle

Marginal cost is increased at every level of output (column 8). When marginal revenue (column 4) is compared with marginal cost, we find that 300 bottles/day is the greatest output for which marginal revenue exceeds marginal cost. Thus, Acme will maximize profit by producing 300 bottles/day. Column 9 shows that this produces a daily profit of $9, the largest possible. Acme will produce 100 bottles fewer than when the wage rate was $10/day, and it will employ three fewer workers per day.

## PROFIT MAXIMIZATION AND THE SELLER'S SUPPLY RULE

The fact that Acme's profit-maximizing quantity of output does not generally depend on its fixed costs is an immediate consequence of the cost–benefit principle, which says that a firm will increase its output if, and only if, the *extra* benefit exceeds the *extra* cost. When a firm can sell as much or as little as it chooses to produce at a given price, without being able to affect that price, we say that the firm is a *price taker*. This could happen for a number of reasons, and Chapter 7 will discuss the *perfectly competitive* product market, a particularly important instance of this. But for present purposes, we do not need to specify why the bottle-making firm is a price taker, we just need to specify that it *is;* that is, if the firm increases production by 100 bottles per day, its benefit is the extra revenue it gets, which is simply the price of 100 bottles. The cost of increasing production by 100 bottles is by definition the marginal cost of producing 100 bottles—the amount by which total variable cost and, hence, total cost increase when bottle production rises by 100 per day. The cost–benefit principle, thus, tells us that the price-taking firm will increase production as long as the price of the product is greater than marginal cost.

COST-
BENEFIT

When the law of diminishing marginal returns applies (i.e., when at least one factor of production is fixed), marginal cost goes up as the firm increases production. Under these circumstances, an additional unit of output will increase the price-taking firm's profit whenever price exceeds marginal cost. There is an important exception to this rule, which describes when a firm will be better off by shutting down. We will explore this exception shortly. After exploring the exception, we will extend our analysis to show that if output can be varied continuously, the quantity of output for which price and marginal cost are exactly equal is the quantity of output that maximizes profit.

But first, note that if Acme's capital cost exceeds $70/day and if the other circumstances portrayed in Table 5.2 pertain, then Acme will make a loss at *every* possible level of output. However, as long as Acme must pay its fixed cost, its best option is to continue producing 400 bottles every day even if its capital costs exceed $70/day. You can see this by replacing each entry in column 6 of Table 5.2 with a value of $71, and calculating Acme's losses when it produces 400 bottles per day. Compare the result of your calculations with Acme's losses when it produces nothing, and you will discover that Acme's losses are larger if it produces nothing. It presumably is better to experience a smaller loss than a larger one. If a firm in that situation expected conditions to remain the same, though, it would want to get out of the bottle business as soon as its equipment lease expired.

## A NOTE ON THE FIRM'S SHUTDOWN

It might seem that a firm which can sell as much output as it wants at a constant market price would *always* do best in the short run by producing and selling the output level for which price equals marginal cost. But there is an important exception to this rule. Suppose, for example, that the market price of the firm's product is less than average variable cost. **Average variable cost** is total variable cost divided by total output, or variable cost per unit of output. In this case, the price is so low that total revenue from sales is less than total variable cost. If the firm produces anything at all under these circumstances, it will add more to its total cost than to its total revenue. Hence, the firm will minimize its losses by deciding to produce nothing. By shutting down, it will suffer a loss equal to its fixed costs. But, by remaining open, it would suffer an even larger loss. A firm's losses need never exceed its total fixed costs. You can verify this by completing Exercise 5.1.

**average variable cost** total variable cost divided by total output; variable cost per unit of output

EXERCISE 5.1

**In Example 5.1, suppose bottles sold not for $35/hundred, but for only $5/hundred. Calculate the profit corresponding to each level of output, as in Example 5.1, and verify that the firm's best option is to cease operations in the short run.**

## GRAPHING MARGINAL COST

To plot the marginal cost curve for a specific firm, we would need to know how total cost changes for every possible change in output. In Examples 5.1 to 5.3, however, we know the firm's cost for only a small sample of production values. Even with this limited information, though, we can construct a reasonable approximation of Acme's marginal cost curve. For instance, note in Example 5.1 and Table 5.2 that when Acme expands production from 200 to 300 bottles/day, its marginal cost is $20. Strictly speaking, a marginal cost of $20 pertains neither to 200 nor to 300, but to the movement between the two. On the graph, we thus show that a marginal cost of $20 corresponds to an output level midway between 200 and 300 bottles/day; namely, 250 bottles/day, as in Figure 5.3. Similarly, when Acme expands from 300 to 400 bottles/day in Example 5.1, its marginal cost is $30, so we plot a marginal cost of $30 with the output level 350 in Figure 5.3. If we assume that marginal cost varies continuously as quantity increases, we generate the marginal cost curve shown in the diagram.

Suppose the market price facing the seller whose marginal cost curve is shown in Figure 5.3 is $35/hundred. If Acme's goal is to make as much profit as possible, how many bottles will it sell? It will sell the quantity for which marginal cost is equal to $35/hundred and, as we see in Figure 5.3, that quantity is 400 bottles/day, just as we concluded in Example 5.1.

To gain further confidence that 400 must be the profit-maximizing quantity when the price is $35/hundred, first suppose that Acme had sold some amount less than that, say, only 300 bottles/day. Its benefit from producing and selling one bottle would then be the bottle's market price, here $0.35 (since bottles sell for $35/hundred, each individual bottle sells for $0.35). The cost of producing one more bottle is equal (by definition) to Acme's marginal cost, which at 300 bottles/day is only $25/100 = $0.25 (see Figure 5.3). So by selling the 201st bottle for $0.35 and producing it for an extra cost of only $0.25, Acme will increase its profit by $0.35 − $0.25 = $0.10/day. Similarly, we can show that for *any* quantity less than the level at which price equals marginal cost, the seller can boost profit by increasing production.

Conversely, suppose Acme is currently selling more than 400 bottles/day, say 500, at a price of $35/hundred. From Figure 5.3, we see that marginal cost at an output of 500 is $45/100 = $0.45/bottle. If Acme then reduces its output by one bottle per day, it would cut its costs by $0.45 while losing only $0.35 in revenue. As before, its profit would grow by $0.10/day. The same argument can be made regarding any quantity larger than 400, so if Acme is currently selling an output at which price is less than marginal cost, it can always increase profits by producing and selling fewer bottles.

We have thus established that if Acme were selling fewer than 400 bottles/day it could earn more profit by increasing production, and if it were selling more than 400 it could earn more by reducing output. It follows that at a market price of $35/hundred, the seller maximizes profit by selling 400 units per week, the quantity for which price and marginal cost are exactly the same.

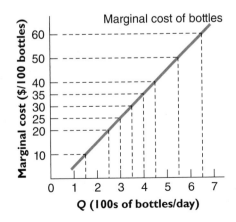

**FIGURE 5.3**
**Acme's Marginal Cost of Production**
Acme's cost goes up by $20 when it expands production from 200 to 300 bottles/day. The marginal cost of the increased output is thus $20. By convention, we plot that value at a point midway between 200 and 300 bottles/day.
Price = Marginal Cost: The Price Taking Firm's Profit-Maximizing Supply Rule
If price exceeds marginal cost, Acme can increase its profit by increasing production and sales. If price is less than marginal cost, Acme can increase its profit by producing and selling less output.

**EXERCISE 5.2**     **For a bottle price of $25/hundred, calculate the profit corresponding to each level of output, as in Example 5.1, and verify that the profit-maximizing output is 300 bottles/day.**

As further confirmation of the claim that a price-taking firm maximizes profit by setting price equal to marginal cost, note in Figure 5.3 that when the price is $45/hundred and marginal cost is equal to the price, the corresponding quantity produced is 500 bottles/day. This is the same as the profit-maximizing quantity we identified for that price in Table 5.3.

Notice that at a price of $0.25, Acme produces and sells 300 bottles each day; at $0.35, the quantity is 400 bottles/day, and so on. As price rises, Acme is increasing its output along a fixed marginal cost curve.

What happens if the price remains the same, but costs change? Table 5.4 presents this case: price is constant at $35/hundred bottles, while the cost of labour increases. This causes marginal cost to increase at each level of output. In such a case, the entire marginal cost curve shifts, as Figure 5.4 illustrates. The marginal cost curve MC in Figure 5.4 is identical to the marginal cost curve in Figure 5.3. Marginal cost data from Table 5.4 are also plotted in Figure 5.4 and labelled MC'. It is clear that when the cost of labour rises and causes marginal cost to increase, the entire marginal cost curve shifts to the left. This causes Acme to reduce its daily output of bottles from 400 to 300.

**FIGURE 5.4**
**A Shift of the Marginal Cost Curve**
Price of bottles = $35/100. Labour cost increases from $10/day to $14/day and causes MC to shift to MC'.

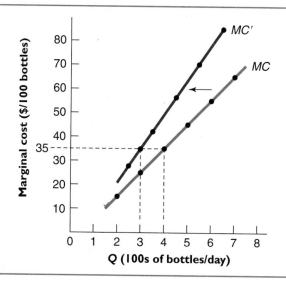

## SHORT-RUN SUPPLY WITH MANY IDENTICAL PRICE-TAKING FIRMS

The law of demand tells us that consumers make a benefit-cost comparison and buy less of a product when its price rises. And for similar reasons, producers offer more of a product for sale when its price rises. When firms are price takers, their supply curves are essentially marginal cost curves. Because the law of diminishing marginal returns implies that marginal cost curves are upward sloping in the short run, the supply curve of each firm is upward sloping in the short run. For the industry as a whole, we can get the total supply response of all firms by adding up the supply responses of all the individual firms to provide a market supply curve.

If, for example, 1000 identical bottle makers are serving the market, the short-run market supply curve shows the quantity supplied at each price as the quantity supplied by one seller multiplied by 1000. For example, at a price of $35/100 bottles, Figure 5.3 showed that one bottle maker will produce and sell 400 bottles/day. One thousand such bottle makers will, therefore, supply 400 000 bottles/day (400 × 1000). A similar calculation will show that 600 000 bottles/day will be supplied if price is $55, and so on. Because the supply curve resulting from these calculations is derived from the individual short-run supply curves of 1000 bottle makers, it is a short-run market supply curve.

Every quantity of output along the market supply curve represents the summation of the quantities individual sellers offer at the corresponding price. So the correspondence between price and marginal cost exists for the market supply curve as well as for the individual supply curves that lie behind the market supply curve. That is, *for every price-quantity pair along the market supply curve, price will be equal to each seller's marginal cost of production.*

---

**RECAP**

**THE PRICE-TAKING FIRM'S SUPPLY CURVE**

The price-taking firm faces a fixed market price for its product, meaning that it can sell any quantity it wants at the market price. As a result, market price is also marginal revenue. In the short run, the firm must consider whether to operate or to shut down. If it is worthwhile to operate in the short run, the firm chooses the level of output that maximizes its profits.

A price-taking firm will maximize profit by choosing the output level for which marginal cost is equal to the market price of its product (provided market price exceeds minimum average variable cost, as will be shown). When it chooses its output level, the firm simultaneously chooses the number of workers it will employ. Provided that it has decided to produce and not shut down, the price-taking firm's supply curve is its marginal cost curve,[2] which is upward sloping in the short run because of the law of diminishing returns. Adding the supply responses of all such firms in a market provides the market supply curve.

---

# 5.3   COSTS, PROFIT MAXIMIZATION, AND SUPPLY IN THE SHORT RUN

As we have seen, diminishing marginal returns means that marginal cost increases as the firm increases output, which also increases average cost (i.e., cost per bottle in the case of our bottle maker). But some costs are fixed (e.g., factory rent) while others (e.g., wages paid) are variable. Because marginal cost is derived from changes in the amount of variable input, marginal cost is a *variable cost*. Again, **variable cost** is any cost that changes as the firm changes its level of output, whereas fixed costs are those costs that do not change as the firm's output changes. Because total costs include fixed and variable costs, average total cost per bottle is influenced by both. In this section we will use both numerical examples and graphs to illustrate the relationships between fixed and variable costs, and between marginal and average cost.

## DIMINISHING MARGINAL RETURNS AND SHORT-RUN COSTS

Panel (a) of Table 5.5 is adapted from Table 5.1. Column 3 shows that the marginal product of a second worker is 110 bottles/day. When the wage rate is $10 per day, the cost of increasing output by 110 bottles/day is $10. Marginal cost (*MC*) is the change in total cost ($\Delta TC$) divided by the change in output ($\Delta Q$):

$$MC = \Delta TC/\Delta Q. \qquad\qquad (5.3)$$

---

2   To be exact, the price-taking firm's supply curve is its marginal cost curve as long as price exceeds minimum average variable cost.

**TABLE 5.5**
**The Law of Diminishing Marginal Returns and Short-Run Costs for Acme Glass (at a daily wage of $10)**

| | Panel (a) | | | Panel (b) | | Panel (c) | |
|---|---|---|---|---|---|---|---|
| (1)<br>Total number of employees/ day | (2)<br>Q (bottles/ day) | (3)<br>Marginal product[a] in bottles/day | (4)<br>Average product in bottles/day | (5)<br>Marginal cost ($) | (6)<br>Average variable cost ($/bottle) | (7)<br>Average fixed cost ($/bottle) | (8)<br>Average total cost ($/bottle) |
| | | | (2) ÷ (1) | $10 ÷ (3) | $10 ÷ (4) | $40 ÷ (2) | (6) + (7) |
| 0 | 0 | | | | | | |
| | | 90 | | 0.11 | | | |
| 1 | 90 | | 90 | | 0.11 | 0.44 | 0.55 |
| | | 110 | | 0.09 | | | |
| 2 | 200 | | 100 | | 0.10 | 0.20 | 0.30 |
| | | 60 | | 0.17 | | | |
| 3 | 260 | | 87 | | 0.12 | 0.15 | 0.27 |
| | | 40 | | 0.25 | | | |
| 4 | 300 | | 75 | | 0.13 | 0.13 | 0.26 |
| | | 38 | | 0.26 | | | |
| 5 | 338 | | 68 | | 0.15 | 0.12 | 0.27 |
| | | 31 | | 0.32 | | | |
| 7 | 400 | | 57 | | 0.18 | 0.10 | 0.275 |
| | | 25 | | 0.40 | | | |
| 11 | 500 | | 45 | | 0.22 | 0.08 | 0.30 |

Notes: [a] Marginal product is the increase in total output caused by hiring one more worker; however, the second-last entry in column 1 shows two more workers being hired (an increase from five to seven). Two more workers cause total output to increase by 62 bottles (from 338 to 400). Therefore, marginal product is 62/2 = 31, the second-last entry of column 3. By the same reasoning, the last entry in column 3 is 100/4 = 25. Strictly speaking, these calculations provide approximations; they are not exact.

Therefore, when output is increased from 90 to 200 bottles, the marginal cost of one bottle is about 9 cents (i.e., $9/100 bottles; note that $10/110 = $0.09). When a third worker is added, the marginal product of that worker is 60. Therefore, the marginal cost of a bottle rises to $0.17 ($10/60 = $0.17). Column 5 of Table 5.5 shows the value of marginal cost that corresponds to each value of marginal product in column 3. In each case, marginal cost is $10 (the wage rate) divided by marginal product. If additional workers add increasingly more to output (as in the first two entries of column 3), marginal product is rising. It follows (as we see in the first two entries of column 5) that marginal cost is falling.

Subsequent entries reverse this pattern because, after the second worker, marginal product declines, causing marginal cost to rise. It makes sense that the marginal product of labour and the marginal cost of production move in opposite directions—if marginal product rises, marginal cost falls; if marginal product falls, marginal cost rises.

A similar relationship exists between average product and average variable cost. Column 5 of Table 5.2 shows total labour cost at various levels of output. Since the firm's payments for labour represent the only costs that vary as the bottle maker changes its output, total labour cost is also total variable cost (*TVC*). (Of course, if the firm had additional costs, such as energy usage that varied with output, those costs also would be variable costs.) Average variable cost (*AVC*) is total variable cost divided by total output (*Q*):

$$AVC = TVC/Q. \qquad (5.4)$$

Equation 5.4 can be used to calculate average variable cost directly from columns 2 and 5 of Table 5.2. However, a slightly different method will emphasize that average product and average variable cost move in opposite directions.

Column 4 of Table 5.1 is column 4 of Table 5.5; both show values of average product. Average product is output per unit of variable input. To keep the example simple, we are assuming that labour is our only variable input, so average product in this example is output per worker. If the wage rate is $10/day, $10 is the average cost per worker. Thus, we can obtain average variable cost by dividing average cost per worker by average product:

$$AVC = \$10/average\ product.$$

Columns 4 and 6 of Table 5.5 show how, when average product rises, average variable cost falls (and vice versa). This pattern, too, is general. The law of diminishing marginal returns influences average variable cost through its effect on average product. Panel (b) of Table 5.5 displays the data on marginal cost and average variable cost that arise from the data on production provided in panel (a).

Sometimes, "a picture is worth a thousand words." Whether or not this is exactly true, the relationship between product and cost curves is shown in Figure 5.5. Panel (a) is similar to panel (b) of Figure 5.1, except that the marginal and average product curves have been smoothed. Notice, too, that panel (a) of Figure 5.5 preserves the relationship between marginal and average product that appears in panel (b) of Figure 5.2. (Figure 5.5 does not extend marginal product curve into the negative range because no profit maximizing firm would want to go there.)

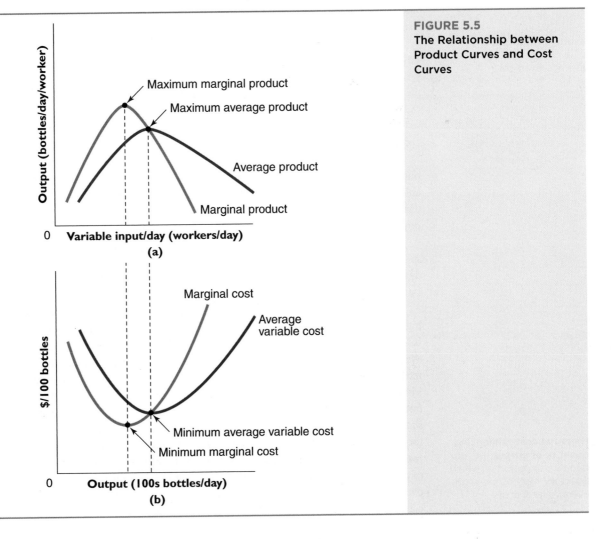

**FIGURE 5.5**
**The Relationship between Product Curves and Cost Curves**

The two panels of Figure 5.5 show that when marginal product reaches its maximum, marginal cost is at its minimum. And when average product reaches its maximum, average variable cost is at its minimum. In addition, just as marginal product intersects average product at maximum average product, marginal cost intersects average variable cost at minimum average variable cost. The two sets of curves are mirror images of each other.

To separate the effect of diminishing marginal returns from the effect of fixed cost on cost per bottle, we must add two more short-run costs to our picture. These are average fixed cost (*AFC*) and average total cost (*ATC*), which appear in panel (c) of Table 5.5. **Average fixed cost** is total fixed cost divided by total output or fixed cost per unit of output. We defined *average variable cost* earlier. Once we have included these two costs, we will discover that in the short run, cost per unit of output is influenced by two opposing trends.

Fixed costs are just the cost of fixed factors of production, which do not vary with the firm's output. Average fixed cost (*AFC*) is total fixed cost (*TFC*) divided by total output (*Q*). (See column 7 of Table 5.5.)

$$AFC = TFC/Q. \tag{5.5}$$

When Acme Glass has total fixed cost of \$40/day, this overhead is spread over an ever larger number of bottles as the daily output of bottles rises. The graph of average fixed cost in Figure 5.6 therefore approaches the horizontal axis as an asymptote. It becomes ever smaller but never touches the horizontal axis. Decreasing average fixed cost is often said to arise from "spreading the overhead." In Figure 5.6, the line representing average fixed cost is drawn as a dashed line to emphasize the fact that it is not really important in itself—it really only matters as a component of average total cost.

Total cost is the sum of variable cost and fixed cost, which implies that **average total cost** is the sum of average variable cost and average fixed cost:

$$ATC = AFC + AVC. \tag{5.6}$$

Entries in columns 6 and 7 of Table 5.5 are summed to provide average total cost in column 8, and then average total cost is graphed as a smooth curve in Figure 5.6.

Marginal cost intersects average variable cost at its minimum, which occurs at an output of 200 bottles/day. At higher rates of output, marginal cost is above average variable cost, and average variable cost is rising. Thus, beyond 200 bottles/day, the law of diminishing marginal returns means that marginal productivity is falling, which pulls down average productivity, which causes average variable cost to rise.

Average total cost depends on two opposing influences: (1) as output increases, spreading the overhead means that average fixed cost is decreasing, but (2) the law of diminishing marginal returns means average variable cost of production is increasing at rates of output greater than 200 bottles/day.

Marginal cost intersects average total cost at its minimum point, which occurs at a higher rate of output (about 320 bottles/day) than does minimum average variable cost. In Figure 5.6, as output increases from 200 to 320 bottles/day, the effect of decreasing average fixed cost on average total cost dominates the effect of diminishing marginal returns. Therefore, average total cost decreases. Beyond 320 bottles, the effect of diminishing marginal returns dominates, and therefore average total cost increases. Because output of about 320 bottles/day minimizes cost per bottle (i.e., average total cost), the *short-run cost-minimizing quantity of output* for Acme's factory is 320 bottles/day. A factory's **short-run cost-minimizing quantity of output** is the quantity of output at which it reaches minimum average total cost. When a factory exceeds its cost-minimizing quantity of output, the decrease in average total cost that is accomplished by spreading fixed cost over more and more output is more than offset by the increase in average variable cost caused by diminishing marginal returns. This causes average total cost to rise. Whether it

**average fixed cost** total fixed cost divided by total output; fixed cost per unit of output

**average total cost** the sum of average variable cost and average fixed cost

**short-run cost-minimizing quantity of output** the quantity of output at which a factory reaches minimum average total cost

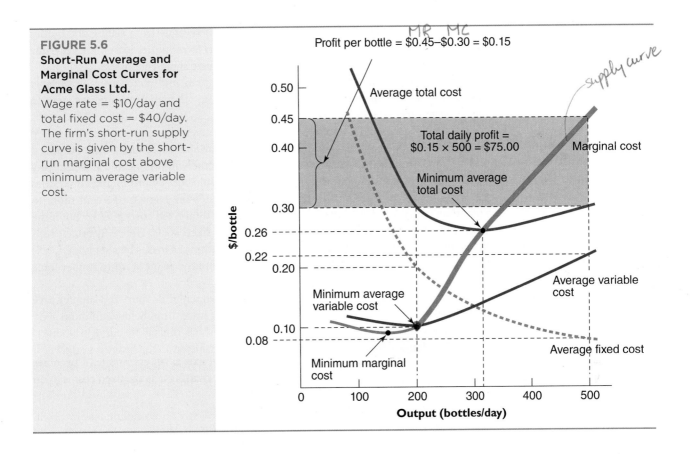

**FIGURE 5.6**
**Short-Run Average and Marginal Cost Curves for Acme Glass Ltd.**
Wage rate = $10/day and total fixed cost = $40/day. The firm's short-run supply curve is given by the short-run marginal cost above minimum average variable cost.

is profitable for a firm to exceed its cost-minimizing quantity of output depends entirely on the price of the product it sells.

Because fixed costs are spread more thinly as output increases, average total cost and average variable cost converge as output increases. (Remember that $ATC = AFC + AVC$ and that $AFC$ decreases as output increases.) Note in Figure 5.6 that average total cost is $0.30 at both 200 and 500 bottles/day. However, at 200 bottles/day, average fixed cost is $0.20 and average variable cost is $0.10. At 500 bottles/day, average fixed cost is $0.08, and average variable cost is $0.22. At the higher rate of output, average fixed cost is a smaller component and average variable cost is a larger component of average total cost.

## WHEN TO SHUT DOWN THE FIRM

If a firm's revenue from sales is smaller than its total variable costs, the cost–benefit principle tells the firm to shut down to minimize its losses. This rule can be restated in terms of the price the firm receives for what it sells. If a firm shuts down, its losses will be equal to its total fixed costs. In Figure 5.6, the lowest possible average variable cost is obtained at 200 bottles per day, where average variable cost is $0.10. Average variable cost was defined in Equation 5.4:

COST-
BENEFIT

$$AVC = TVC/Q. \qquad (5.4)$$

This can be rewritten to define total variable cost:

$$TVC = AVC \times Q. \qquad (5.7)$$

Therefore, when 200 bottles are produced, total variable cost is calculated as

$$TVC = AVC \times Q = \$0.10 \times 200 = \$20.$$

If the price per bottle drops below $0.10, Acme's revenue from selling 200 bottles drops below $20, and Acme will shut down, if it wants to minimize losses. If its revenue rises above this, Acme will operate if it wants to minimize short-run losses.

Why? Consider a price of $0.11/bottle. If the firm minimizes average variable cost by producing 200 bottles a day, each bottle sold will bring revenue sufficient to pay average variable cost plus one more penny that can be used to defray fixed costs. Acme's daily losses will be total fixed cost *less* $2. Conversely, suppose price per bottle drops to $0.09, one cent below minimum average variable cost. Each bottle produced and sold will then bring a loss of one penny, and Acme will not be able to defray any of its fixed cost. If the firm minimizes average variable cost by producing 200 bottles per day, each of the 200 bottles produced contributes on average one cent more to costs than to revenues, so Acme's daily losses will be total fixed costs *plus* $2. But if the firm shuts down, its daily losses will equal its total fixed costs. Hence, if price drops below minimum average variable cost, Acme will minimize losses by supplying nothing. The firm's **short-run shutdown point** is therefore the point of minimum average variable cost.

We determined previously that if a firm decides to operate, its short-run supply curve is its short-run marginal cost curve. Now we see that if price drops below minimum average variable cost, it will shut down; therefore, a firm's short-run supply curve is its short-run marginal cost curve above minimum average variable cost. The heavy marginal cost curve above minimum average variable cost in Figure 5.6 gives the firm's short-run supply curve. The positively sloped short-run supply curve is consistent with the principle of increasing opportunity cost.

Acme's cost curves can also be used to show explicitly an economic loss or profit. First, consider Example 5.2, which showed earlier that if market price is $0.45, Acme will produce 500 bottles each day. Cost per bottle will be $0.30 for a profit of $0.15/bottle. Thus, total profit will be $75/day ($0.15 × 500). Now consider the shaded rectangle in Figure 5.6. The rectangle's area is profit per bottle multiplied by the number of bottles: $0.15 × 500 bottles/day = $75.00/day. Thus the area of the shaded rectangle in Figure 5.6 represents profits.

**short-run shutdown point**
a firm's minimum average variable cost; if price drops below minimum average variable cost, the firm will minimize its losses by shutting down

INCREASING
OPPORTUNITY COST

---

**RECAP**

### COSTS, PROFIT MAXIMIZATION, AND SUPPLY IN THE SHORT RUN

The graphs in this section produce several results:

- The law of diminishing marginal returns means that marginal cost increases as output increases, which causes the firm's short-run supply curve to have a positive slope.

- The price-taking firm's short-run supply curve is its short-run marginal cost curve above minimum average variable cost.

- If price is less than minimum average variable cost, the firm can minimize losses by shutting down.

- Minimum average total cost occurs at a higher rate of output than does minimum average variable cost. The opposing effects of diminishing marginal returns and the spreading of fixed cost over higher rates of output cause this result.

- Whether it is profitable for a firm to exceed its short-run cost-minimizing quantity of output depends solely on the price the firm receives for its product.

# 5.4 APPLYING THE THEORY OF SUPPLY

Whether the activity is producing new soft drink containers or recycling used ones, or indeed any other production at all, the same logic governs all supply decisions of profit maximizing firms: Can I make more money if I sell one more unit? When a firm is a price taker, the gain from selling one more unit is just its sale price. The increase in costs is the marginal cost of production. Hence, to maximize profit, the firm will increase output until marginal cost is equal to the price of the product. This logic helps us understand many market outcomes; for example, why recycling efforts are more intensive for some products than others.

The acquisition of valuable raw materials is only one of the benefits from recycling. A second benefit is that, by removing litter, recycling makes the environment more pleasant for everyone. Economic Naturalist 5.1 does not explicitly discuss the benefits of reduced litter. However, such benefits may well be large enough to justify incurring extra costs in order to obtain them, as we will analyze in Chapter 10.

## ECONOMIC NATURALIST 5.1

### When recycling is left to private market forces, why are many more aluminum beverage containers recycled than glass ones?

In the case of either aluminum or glass recycling, recyclers gather containers until their marginal costs are equal to the containers' respective redemption prices. When recycling is left to market forces, the redemption price for a container is based on the price companies can sell it (or the materials in it) for. Aluminum containers can be easily processed into scrap aluminum, which commands a high price because scrap aluminum can easily be recycled into new products, and this leads profit-seeking companies to offer a relatively high redemption price for aluminum cans. By contrast, glass is easily broken, hence harder to collect, and has only limited resale value, which leads profit-seeking companies to offer much lower redemption prices for glass containers.

If the redemption price for aluminum cans is high, many people will be induced to track down these cans, whereas the low redemption prices for glass containers will lead most people to ignore those. Thus, if recycling is left completely to market forces, then we would expect more aluminum soft drink containers to be recycled than glass containers. This is, in fact, the pattern we see in jurisdictions without recycling laws. As Figure 5.7 shows, as the redemption price of aluminum containers increases, suppliers of recycling services will recycle more aluminum containers. A similar graph could be drawn for glass containers. More aluminum and fewer glass containers are recycled in jurisdictions without recycling laws, a simple consequence of the fact that the supply curves of container recycling services are upward sloping. For this reason, jurisdictions that recycle often have the same deposit system for glass and aluminum in order to provide sufficient incentive to recycle both types of containers.

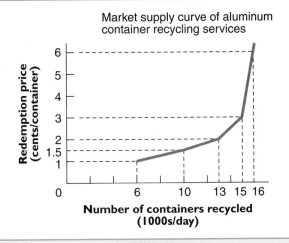

Market supply curve of aluminum container recycling services

**FIGURE 5.7**
**The Supply Curve of Aluminum Container Recycling Services**

# 5.5  THE PRICE ELASTICITY OF SUPPLY

## DEFINING AND CALCULATING ELASTICITY OF SUPPLY

On the buyer's side of the market, we use price elasticity of demand to measure the responsiveness of quantity demanded to changes in price. On the seller's side of the market, the analogous measure is **price elasticity of supply,** which is defined as the percentage change in quantity supplied that occurs in response to a 1 percent change in price. For example, if a 1 percent increase in the redemption price of glass containers leads to a 2 percent increase in the quantity supplied, the price elasticity of supply of recycled glass containers would be 2.0.

The mathematical formula for price elasticity of supply at any point is the same as the corresponding expression for price elasticity of demand:

$$Price\ elasticity\ of\ supply = \frac{\%\ change\ in\ Quantity}{\%\ change\ in\ Price} = \frac{\Delta Q/Q}{\Delta P/P}, \tag{5.8}$$

where $P$ and $Q$ are the initial price and quantity, $\Delta P$ is a small change in the initial price, and $\Delta Q$ is the resulting change in quantity. If price elasticity of supply is less than one, **supply is inelastic**; if it is greater than one, **supply is elastic.**

As with the corresponding expression for price elasticity of demand, Equation 5.8 can be rewritten as follows:

$$Price\ elasticity\ of\ supply = \left(\frac{P}{Q}\right)\left(\frac{\Delta Q}{\Delta P}\right). \tag{5.9}$$

Since $\Delta Q/\Delta P$ is the reciprocal of the slope of the supply curve, Equation 5.9 can be rewritten as:

$$Price\ elasticity\ of\ supply = \left(\frac{P}{Q}\right)\left(\frac{1}{slope}\right). \tag{5.10}$$

Equation 5.10 is similar to the expression we saw for price elasticity of demand in Chapter 4 (Equation 4.4).

Price and quantity are always positive, as is the slope of the typical short-run supply curve, which implies that price elasticity of supply will be a positive number at every point.

Generally, price elasticity of supply will change from point to point along a supply curve. (An exception occurs when a straight-line supply curve passes through the origin.)

Elasticity is not constant along straight-line supply curves that do not pass through the origin, like the one in Figure 5.8. Although the slope of this supply curve is equal to 1

**price elasticity of supply** the percentage change in quantity supplied arising from a 1 percent change in price

**inelastic supply** price elasticity of supply is less than one

**elastic supply** price elasticity of supply is greater than one

---

**FIGURE 5.8**

**A Supply Curve for Which Price Elasticity Declines as Quantity Rises**

For the supply curve shown, 1/slope is the same at every point, but the ratio $P/Q$ declines as $Q$ increases. Therefore, elasticity = $(P/Q)$ (1/slope) declines as quantity increases.

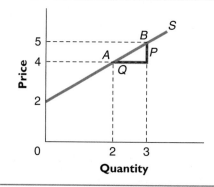

at every point, the ratio $P/Q$ declines as we move to the right along the curve. Elasticity at $A$ is equal to $(4/2)(1) = 2$ and declines to $(5/3)(1) = 5/3$ at $B$.[3]

On the buyer's side of the market, two important polar cases are demand curves with infinite price elasticity and zero price elasticity. As Examples 5.4 and 5.5 illustrate, analogous polar cases exist on the seller's side of the market.

## EXAMPLE **5.4**

### What is the elasticity of supply of seats in Rogers Centre?

Seats for athletic events sell in the market for a price, just as aluminum or corn or automobiles or any other product does. The demand for seats is a downward-sloping function of its price. For all practical purposes, however, the supply of seats in a particular stadium on a particular day is fixed. No matter whether the ticket price is high or low, the same number of seats is available in the market. The supply curve of such a good is vertical, and its price elasticity is zero at every price. Supply curves like the one in Figure 5.9 are said to be **perfectly inelastic.**

**perfectly inelastic supply curve** a supply curve whose elasticity with respect to price is zero

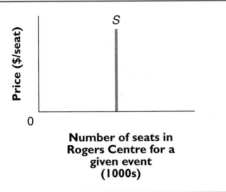

**FIGURE 5.9**
**A Perfectly Inelastic Supply Curve**
Price elasticity of supply is zero at every point along a vertical supply curve.

## EXAMPLE **5.5**

### What is the elasticity of supply of lemonade?

Suppose that it is a hot summer day and your little sister, and many children like her, are deciding whether to set up lemonade stands. The ingredients required to produce a cup of lemonade and their respective costs are listed as follows:

| | |
|---|---|
| Paper cup | $0.02 |
| Lemon | 0.038 |
| Sugar | 0.02 |
| Water | 0.002 |
| Ice | 0.01 |
| Labour (30 seconds @ $6/hour) | 0.05 |

Supposing that these proportions remain the same no matter how many cups of lemonade are made and supposing also that the inputs can be purchased in any quantity at the stated prices, draw the supply curve of lemonade and compute its price elasticity.

Since each cup of lemonade costs exactly $0.14 to make, no matter how many cups are made, the supply curve of lemonade is a horizontal line at $0.14/cup (Figure 5.10). The price elasticity of supply of lemonade is infinite.

---

3  The price elasticity of a linear supply curve that intersects the vertical axis is always greater than 1. If a linear supply curve passes through the origin, it is unit elastic. If a linear supply curve intersects the horizontal axis, its price elasticity is less than 1.

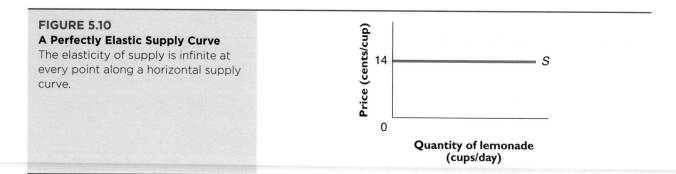

**FIGURE 5.10**
**A Perfectly Elastic Supply Curve**
The elasticity of supply is infinite at every point along a horizontal supply curve.

Whenever additional units of a good can be produced by using the same combination of inputs, purchased at constant prices,[4] the supply curve of that good will be horizontal. Such supply curves are said to be **perfectly elastic.** Because all factors of production are assumed to be variable, the example describes what happens when the law of diminishing marginal returns does not apply. For the specific production process described, the marginal cost curve is horizontal, at $0.14 cup, not upward sloping.

**perfectly elastic supply curve** a supply curve whose elasticity with respect to price is infinite

## DETERMINANTS OF SUPPLY ELASTICITY

Examples 5.4 and 5.5 suggest some of the factors that govern the elasticity of supply of a good or service. The lemonade case in Example 5.5 was one whose production process was essentially like a cooking recipe. For such cases, we can exactly double our output by doubling each ingredient. If the price of each ingredient remains fixed, the marginal cost of production for such goods will be constant, and hence they have horizontal supply curves. Again, when all factors of production can be increased, the short run and the law of diminishing returns do not apply, and so the supply curve need not be upward sloping. Example 5.5 anticipates the long run, which is discussed in Chapter 6.

Since it relates to a fixed number of items, Example 5.4 is an extreme contrast to Example 5.5 where the quantity can be changed limitlessly. The supply of seats in a stadium is almost perfectly inelastic because it cannot be altered for any particular event, regardless of what happens to price.[5]

The terms on which additional amounts of the inputs to the production process can be obtained are key to determining elasticity of supply. In general, the *more easily additional units of these inputs can be acquired, the higher the price elasticity of supply will be.* The following four factors (among others) govern the ease with which additional inputs can be acquired by a producer.

**Flexibility and Substitutability of Inputs** To the extent that production of a good requires inputs that are also useful for the production of other goods, it is relatively easy to lure additional inputs away from their current uses, making supply of that good relatively elastic with respect to price. The fact that lemonade production requires labour with only minimal skills means that a large pool of workers with widely varied skills could all equally well shift from their other activities to lemonade production if a profit

---

4  If we take very literally the assumption "inputs can be purchased in *any* quantity at the stated prices," it would imply extreme results; for example, that your sister could purchase the millions of kilograms of sugar necessary to make billions of lemonades without affecting the price of sugar. It is more realistic to think of the supply curve as being perfectly elastic over a certain range of output.

5  To be absolutely accurate, we say, "the supply of seats in a stadium is *almost* perfectly inelastic," since one can perhaps imagine, at some huge cost, tearing out existing seats in a stadium and replacing them with more, narrower seats. The ticket price would have to be extremely high for this to be profitable for a single concert, but it is conceivable. In economics, as in much else, absolute perfection is rarely observed; both perfectly elastic and perfectly inelastic supply curves are polar extremes, which are primarily useful for their conceptual clarity.

opportunity arose. Brain surgery, by contrast, requires elaborately trained and specialized labour, which means that even a large price increase would not increase the quantity of brain surgeons, except after a long time lag.

**Mobility of Inputs** If inputs can be easily transported from one site to another, an increase in the price of a product in one market will enable a producer in that market to summon inputs from other markets. For example, the supply of oil drilling services in Alberta is made more elastic with respect to price by the willingness of thousands of workers to migrate westward from Eastern Canada. The supply of entertainment is similarly made more elastic by the willingness of entertainers to hit the road. Circus performers, lounge singers, comedians, and even exotic dancers often spend a substantial fraction of their time away from home. For most goods, the price elasticity of supply increases each time a new highway is built or the telecommunications network improves, or any other development makes it easier to find and transport inputs from one place to another.

**Time** Because it takes time for producers to switch from one activity to another, and because it takes time to build new capital goods and train additional skilled workers, the price elasticity of supply will be higher for most goods in the long run than in the short run. In the short run, a manufacturer's inability to augment existing stocks of capital equipment and skilled labour may make it impossible to expand output beyond a certain limit. But if a shortage of managers is the bottleneck, new MBAs can be graduated in only two years if they already have bachelor's degrees. Or if a shortage of legal staff is the problem, new lawyers can be trained in three years. In the long run, firms can always buy new equipment, build new factories, and hire additional skilled workers.

If a product can be copied (in the sense that any company can acquire the design and other technological information required to produce it), and if the inputs needed for its production are used in roughly fixed proportions and are available at fixed market prices, then the long-run supply curve for that product will be horizontal. But as we will presently see, many products do not satisfy these conditions, and their supply curves remain steeply upward sloping, even in the long run.

**The Short Run and the Long Run** While at least one factor of production is fixed in the short run, for many goods all factors of production are variable in the long run. Therefore, an increase in price will cause a greater increase in quantity supplied in the long run than in it will in the short run. The same is true for decreases in price. In general, price elasticity of supply is greater in the long run than it is in the short run. Chapter 6 provides a detailed analysis of supply in the long run.

## UNIQUE AND ESSENTIAL INPUTS: THE ULTIMATE SUPPLY BOTTLENECK

Fertile agricultural land is a historically scarce resource. As the English economist David Ricardo noted over 175 years ago, one can increase agricultural output by adding more inputs, such as labour or fertilizer, to a given amount of land, or one can expand the area under cultivation. But since it makes sense to use the most fertile land first, as the amount of land under cultivation expands, eventually less fertile land will have to be used. When all the best land has been used, farmers can start using even more inputs to squeeze a higher yield from their acreage, or turn to land with inherently lower productivity; either way, the costs of production will increase. Thus, when an essential input into production is inherently limited in availability, the supply curve will be upward sloping, even in the long run.[6]

---

6  David Ricardo, *The Principles of Political Economy and Taxation*, (1817), introduction by Donald Winch, (London: Everyman's Library, Dent, 1973), pp. 33–47.

> **RECAP** ⤴
>
> **PRICE ELASTICITY OF SUPPLY**
>
> The price elasticity of supply of a good is the percentage change in the quantity supplied that results from a one percent change in its price. Mathematically, the elasticity of supply at a point on a supply curve is equal to $(P/Q)(1/slope)$, where $P$ and $Q$ represent price and quantity and $1/slope$ is the reciprocal of the slope of the supply curve at that point.
>
> Elasticity of supply for a good tends to be larger when the inputs required for its production are also widely used to produce other goods, when inputs are more mobile, when production is possible using substitutes for existing inputs, and when suppliers have more time to augment their productive capacities. If the inputs needed for a good's production are used in roughly fixed proportions and are available at fixed market prices, then the long-run supply curve will be horizontal. In the long run, the only goods that tend to have upward-sloping supply curves are those whose production requires essential inputs that cannot be duplicated.

## SUMMARY

- The supply curve for a good or service tells us the quantity sellers want to supply at a given price. The prices at which goods and services are offered for sale in the market depend, in turn, on the opportunity cost of the resources required to produce them. **LO1**

- The law of diminishing marginal returns says that when technology and at least one factor of production are held fixed, beyond some point the marginal product of the variable factor of production diminishes. **LO2**

- In markets where individual firms can supply whatever quantity they want at a constant price, firms are price takers. In such markets, the seller maximizes profit by selling that quantity of output for which price equals marginal cost (provided that price exceeds minimum average variable cost). The firm's supply curve thus coincides with its marginal cost curve above minimum average variable cost. The marginal cost curve measures the cost of producing additional units of output. This is why we sometimes say the supply curve represents the cost side of the market (in contrast to the demand curve, which represents the benefit side of the market). **LO4, LO8**

- The law of diminishing marginal returns directly affects short-run marginal cost. If marginal product is increasing, short-run marginal cost is decreasing; if marginal product is decreasing, short-run marginal cost is increasing. Also, marginal product intersects average product at maximum average product, and marginal cost intersects average variable cost at minimum average variable cost. Both intersections occur at the same quantity of output. Thus, short-run marginal cost is a mirror image of marginal product, and average variable cost is a mirror image of average product. **LO3, LO6, LO8**

- If a firm shuts down, it will make no sales, will receive no revenue, and its losses will be equal to its total fixed costs. But a firm's losses need never exceed its total fixed costs; if the price of its product falls below minimum average variable cost, a price-taking firm will minimize losses by shutting down. The price-taking firm's short-run supply curve, therefore, is positively sloped and coincides with a short-run marginal cost curve above minimum average variable cost. **LO5, LO7, LO8**

■ The law of diminishing marginal returns causes the price-taking firm's short run supply curve to slope upward. As output increases above the quantity that minimizes average variable cost, the law of diminishing marginal returns also causes average variable cost to increase. Increasing average variable cost causes cost per unit (i.e., average total cost) to increase. **LO6**

■ Average fixed cost always decreases as the quantity of output increases, because overhead is spread over more units of production. This tends to reduce average total cost. However, diminishing marginal returns cause average total cost to rise. As output increases beyond the quantity that minimizes average total cost, the effect of diminishing marginal returns dominates, and average total cost increases. **LO6**

■ An important terminological distinction from the demand side of the market also applies on the supply side of the market. *A change in supply* means a shift in the entire supply curve, whereas *a change in the quantity supplied* means a movement along the supply curve. The factors that cause supply curves to shift include technology, input prices, the number of sellers, expectations of future price changes, and the prices of other products that firms might produce. **LO1**

■ Price elasticity of supply is defined as the percentage change in quantity supplied that occurs in response to a 1 percent change in price. The mathematical formula for the price elasticity of supply at any point is $(\Delta Q/Q)/(\Delta P/P)$, where $P$ and $Q$ are the price and quantity at that point, $\Delta P$ is a small change in the initial price, and $\Delta Q$ is the resulting change in quantity. This formula can also be expressed as $(P/Q)(1/\text{slope})$, where 1/slope is the reciprocal of the slope of the supply curve. **LO8**

■ The price elasticity of supply of a good depends on how difficult or costly it is to acquire additional units of the inputs involved in producing that good. In general, the more easily additional units of these inputs can be acquired, the higher the price elasticity of supply will be. It is easier to expand production of a product if the inputs used to produce that product are similar to inputs used to produce other products, and if inputs are relatively mobile. And like the price elasticity of demand, the price elasticity of supply is greater in the long run than in the short run. Except for the existence of unique and essential inputs, all goods and services would have highly elastic supply curves in the long run. There are no fixed costs in the long run; thus, the long run affords more flexibility in adjusting costs than does the short run. **LO8**

## KEY TERMS

average fixed cost (146)
average total cost (146)
average variable cost (140)
average product (133)
capital (131)
elastic supply (150)
entrepreneur (131)
factor of production (130)
fixed cost (136)
fixed factor of production (132)
inelastic supply (150)
intermediate inputs (131)

labour (130)
land (130)
law of diminishing marginal returns (132)
long run (131)
marginal cost (137)
marginal product (131)
marginal revenue (137)
perfectly elastic supply curve (152)
perfectly inelastic supply curve (151)

price elasticity of supply (150)
price taker (130)
production function (131)
profit (130)
profit-maximizing firm (130)
short run (131)
short-run cost-minimizing quantity of output (147)
short-run shutdown point (148)
variable cost (136)
variable factor of production (131)

## REVIEW QUESTIONS

1. Explain why you would expect supply curves to slope upward based on the principle of increasing opportunity cost. **LO1**

2. Which do you think is more likely to be a fixed factor of production for an ice cream producer during the next two months, its factory building or its workers who operate the machines? Explain. **LO8**

3. Economists often stress that diminishing marginal returns result from increasingly more workers using the same workspace and tools. With this in mind, explain why it would be impossible to feed all the people on earth with food grown in a single flowerpot, even if unlimited water, labour, seed, fertilizer, sunlight, and other inputs were available. **LO2, LO3**

4. True or false: The price-taking firm will *always* produce the output level for which price equals marginal cost. **LO4**

5. What is the effect of diminishing marginal product on short-run marginal cost? Why is short-run marginal cost a mirror image of marginal product? Why is average variable cost a mirror image of average product? **LO6**

6. If average fixed cost always decreases as the quantity of output rises, why does it not follow that cost per unit of output always decreases as output rises? **LO6**

7. Why does minimum average variable cost occur at a smaller quantity of output than minimum average total cost? **LO5, LO6**

8. A firm's losses need never exceed its total fixed costs. Why? Why does this imply that a price-taking firm's short-run supply curve is given by its short-run marginal cost curve above minimum average variable cost? **LO5, LO6**

9. Does a firm maximize profits by minimizing cost per unit of output? Why or why not? **LO4, LO7**

10. Why is supply elasticity higher in the long run than in the short run? **LO8**

## PROBLEMS

1. Zoe is trying to decide how to divide her time between her job as a wedding photographer, which pays $27/hour for as many hours as she chooses to work, and as a fossil collector, in which her pay depends both on the price of fossils and the number of fossils she finds. Earnings aside, Zoe is indifferent between the two tasks, and the number of fossils she can find depends on the number of hours a day she searches, as shown in the following table. **LO1, LO8**

| Hours/day | Total fossils/day |
|---|---|
| 1 | 5 |
| 2 | 9 |
| 3 | 12 |
| 4 | 14 |
| 5 | 15 |

a. Derive a table with price in dollar increments from $0 to $30 in the first column and the quantity of fossils Zoe is willing to supply per day at that price in the second column.

b. Plot these points in a graph with price on the vertical axis and quantity per day on the horizontal axis. What is this curve called?

2. A price-taking firm makes air conditioners. The market price of one of their new air conditioners is $120. Its total cost information is given in the following table. **LO1, LO3, LO4**

| Air conditioners/ day | Total cost ($/day) | Marginal cost ($) |
|---|---|---|
| 1 | 100 | |
| 2 | 150 | |
| 3 | 220 | |
| 4 | 310 | |
| 5 | 405 | |
| 6 | 510 | |
| 7 | 650 | |
| 8 | 800 | |

a. Complete the column labelled "Marginal cost."

b. How many air conditioners will the firm produce per day if its goal is to maximize its profit?

c. Does your answer to (b) imply that the firm is setting marginal revenue equal to marginal cost? Why or why not?

3. The Paducah Slugger Company makes baseball bats out of lumber supplied to it by Acme Sporting Goods,

which pays Paducah $10 for each finished bat. Paducah's only factors of production are lathe operators and a small building with a lathe. The number of bats per day it produces depends on the number of employee-hours per day, as shown in the following table. LO1, LO4

| Number of bats/day | Number of employee-hours/day |
|---|---|
| 0 | 0 |
| 5 | 1 |
| 10 | 2 |
| 15 | 4 |
| 20 | 7 |
| 25 | 11 |
| 30 | 16 |
| 35 | 22 |

a. If the wage is $15/hour and Paducah's daily capital cost for the lathe and building is fixed at $60, what is the profit-maximizing quantity of bats?

b. What would be the profit-maximizing number of bats if the capital cost were not $60/day but only $30?

4. In problem 3, how would Paducah's profit-maximizing level of output be affected if the government imposed a tax of $10/day on the company? What would Paducah's profit-maximizing level of output be if the government imposed a tax of $2 per bat? LO4

5. Explain how the following would affect supply in the indicated market: LO8
   a. An increase in the world price of honey in the market for beeswax candles.
   b. An increase in the world price of cauliflower in the market for cabbage. (Assume the demand for cabbage does not shift.)
   c. An increase in the world price of ice cream in the market for ice cream.

6. How would each of the following affect the Canadian market supply curve for corn? LO8
   a. A new high-yielding strain of corn is discovered.
   b. The price of fertilizer falls.
   c. The government offers corn farmers a subsidy of $1/bushel.

7. Which of the following are true? Why? The price elasticity of supply for Basmati rice (an aromatic strain of rice) is likely to be LO8
   a. Higher in the long run than the short run, because farmers cannot easily change their decisions about how much Basmati rice to plant once the current crop has been planted.

b. High, because consumers have a lot of other kinds of rice and other staple foods to choose from.

c. Low in both the long run and short run, because rice farming requires only unskilled labour.

d. High in both the long run and the short run, because the inputs required to produce Basmati rice can easily be duplicated.

8. What are the respective values for price elasticity of supply at $A$ and $B$ on the supply curve shown in the following figure? LO8

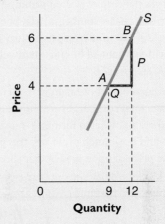

9. The supply curves for the only two firms in a competitive industry are given by $P = 2Q_1$ and $P = 2 + Q_2$, where $Q_1$ is the output of firm 1 and $Q_2$ is the output of firm 2. What is the market supply curve for this industry? (*Hint:* Graph the two curves side by side, and then add their respective quantities at a sample of different prices.) LO5, LO8

10. Consider two companies, Slap-Shot and Slapstick. Both companies make hockey sticks. Slap-Shot's contract with its employees says that if it lays off any of its workers, it must pay each of them severance pay. Slapstick's contract does not include a similar clause. LO1, LO5, LO6
    a. In which case does it make sense to say that labour represents a fixed cost? Why?
    b. Suppose the price of hockey sticks decreases so that both companies are making losses. If price continues to decrease, which company will shut down first? That is, which company will have the lower shutdown price? Why?
    c. If the price of hockey sticks drops low enough to cause both companies to shut down, which company will suffer the greater loss? Why?

11. A union is negotiating a new contract with its employer. The employer says that it cannot pay higher wages because it already is making losses. In fact, says the employer, it can make good case for reducing wages. LO5, LO7
    a. Why would an employer operate at a loss?

b. Suppose that the employer's annual losses are $1 million and its total fixed costs are $2 million per year. Does the union have any room to bargain for increased wages? Consider two different cases: (i) The union is convinced that over the next three years the employer will run the factory until it falls apart, then move its operations to Southeast Asia. The union believes this will happen regardless of any agreement between the employer and the union. (ii) The union believes the employer is considering moving its operations to Southeast Asia, but it will not move if it can modernize its factory and reach an agreement that will be consistent with a modest increase in wages.

12. For the pizza seller whose marginal, average variable, and average total cost curves are shown in the accompanying diagram, what is the profit-maximizing level of output and how much profit will this producer earn if the price of pizza is $2.50 per slice? **LO7**

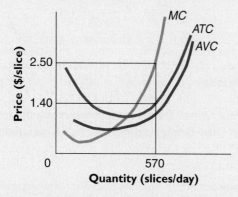

13. For the pizza seller whose marginal, average, and average total cost curves are shown in the accompanying diagram, what is the profit-maximizing level of output and how much profit will this producer earn if the price of pizza is $0.80 per slice? **LO7**

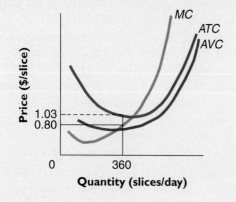

14. For the pizza seller whose marginal, average variable, and average total cost curves are shown in the accompanying diagram, what is the profit-maximizing level of output and how much profit will this producer earn if the price of pizza is $0.50 per slice? **LO7**

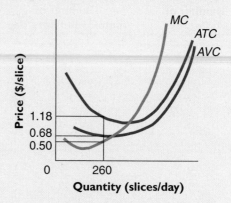

15. For the pizza seller whose marginal, average variable, and average total cost curves are shown in the accompanying diagram (who is the same seller as in problem 14), what is the profit-maximizing level of output and how much profit will this producer earn if the price of pizza is $1.18 per slice? **LO7**

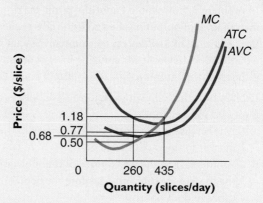

## ANSWERS TO IN-CHAPTER EXERCISES

**5.1** The profit figures corresponding to a price of $5/hundred are as shown in the last column of the following table, where we see that the profit-maximizing output (which here means the loss-minimizing output) is 0 bottles/day. Note that the company actually loses $40/day at that output level. But it would lose even more if it produced any other amount. If the company expects conditions to remain unchanged, it will want to go out of the bottle business as soon as its equipment lease expires. **LO4, LO5**

| Q (bottles/day) | Total revenue ($/day) | Total labour cost ($/day) | Total cost ($/day) | Profit ($/day) |
|---|---|---|---|---|
| 0 | 0 | 0 | 40 | −40 |
| 200 | 10 | 20 | 60 | −50 |
| 300 | 15 | 40 | 80 | −65 |
| 400 | 20 | 70 | 110 | −90 |
| 500 | 25 | 110 | 150 | −125 |
| 600 | 30 | 160 | 200 | −170 |
| 700 | 35 | 220 | 260 | −225 |

**5.2** The profit figures corresponding to a price of $25/hundred are as shown in the last column of the following table, where we see that the profit-maximizing output (which here means the loss-minimizing output) is 300 bottles/day. Note that the company actually loses $5/day at that output level. But as long as it remains committed to its daily lease payment of $40, it would lose even more if it produced any other amount. If the company expects conditions to remain unchanged, it will want to go out of the bottle business as soon as its equipment lease expires. **LO5, LO6**

| Q (bottles/day) | Total revenue ($/day) | Total labour cost ($/day) | Total cost ($/day) | Profit ($/day) |
|---|---|---|---|---|
| 0 | 0 | 0 | 40 | −40 |
| 200 | 50 | 20 | 60 | −10 |
| 300 | 75 | 40 | 80 | −5 |
| 400 | 100 | 70 | 110 | −10 |
| 500 | 125 | 110 | 150 | −25 |
| 600 | 150 | 160 | 200 | −50 |
| 700 | 175 | 220 | 260 | −85 |

# CHAPTER 6

# Production, Cost, and the Quest for Profit: The Supply Side in the Long Run

## LEARNING OBJECTIVES

When you have completed this chapter, you will be able to:

**LO1** Define and explain the differences between accounting profit and economic profit.

**LO2** Show how economic profit and economic loss can cause resources to enter or exit an industry.

**LO3** Explain the difference between the long run and the short run.

**LO4** Explain how economic profit and economic loss spur price takers to operate at minimum long run average cost.

**LO5** Distinguish among economies of scale, constant returns to scale, and diseconomies of scale.

**LO6** Explain the difference between economic profit and economic rent.

**LO7** Explain why technological innovations tend to be adopted by all firms in an industry.

Consider the choice of cuisine in any small Canadian city. Twenty-five years ago, the city might have offered a few Italian and Chinese restaurants and perhaps one or two Greek. Today, the same city with roughly the same population might have added Spanish, Indian, Thai, Japanese, Mexican, Vietnamese, and Ethiopian restaurants.

Rare indeed is the marketplace in which buyers and sellers remain static for extended periods. Our small city is likely to have more body-piercing studios and fewer gas stations than it did 25 years ago. In most cases, even within the same profession, the type of services provided has changed dramatically; one prime example is secretarial services. Fifty years ago, managers dictated letters to secretaries who transcribed them in shorthand and then typed paper copies from their notes. In the 1970s, typewriters were replaced by dedicated word-processing machines,[1] which were themselves replaced by personal computers in the 1980s. Today, the ability to take shorthand is obsolescent, and the IBM Selectric typewriter is a museum artifact.

What drives these changes? The business owner's quest for profit motivates firms to migrate to industries and locations in which profit opportunities abound and desert those whose prospects appear bleak. In perhaps the most widely quoted passage from his landmark treatise, *The Wealth of Nations*, Adam Smith wrote,

It is not from the benevolence of the butcher, the brewer, or the baker that we expect our dinner, but from their regard of their own interest. We address ourselves not to their humanity, but to their self-love, and never talk to them of our necessities, but of their advantage.[2]

Smith went on to argue that although the entrepreneur "intends only his own gain," he is "led by an invisible hand to promote an end which was no part of his intention." As Smith saw it, even though self-interest is the prime mover of economic activity, the end result is an allocation of goods and services that serves society's collective interests

1 Automated Electronic Systems (AES), a Canadian firm, introduced the world's first programmable word processor that came complete with a video screen in 1972.

2 Adam Smith, *An Inquiry into the Nature and Causes of the Wealth of Nations*, (1776). This edition includes introductions by Max Lerner and Edwin Cannan, edited by Edwin Cannan, (New York: Random House, 1965), Book I, Chapter II, p. 14.

remarkably well. If producers are offering "too much" of one product and "not enough" of another, profit opportunities alert entrepreneurs to that fact and provide incentives for them to take remedial action. All the while, the system exerts relentless pressure on producers to hold the price of each good close to its cost of production and, indeed, to reduce that cost in any way possible.

Our task in this chapter is to gain deeper insight into the nature of the forces that guide Adam Smith's "invisible hand." In Chapter 5, we looked at how a firm that maximizes profits will behave in the short run if it is a price taker; that is, it can sell as much or as little as it produces without having any noticeable impact on price. To understand how Smith's invisible hand might guide self-interested competition so that it serves society's collective interests, we need to understand the circumstances of market competition that cause firms to be price takers. We also need to carefully examine the behaviour of markets in the long run. Sections two and three of this chapter address these issues. First of all, however, we will state clearly what we mean by a "profit-maximizing firm," and we will explain how the long run differs from the short run. What exactly does "profit" mean? How is it measured, and how does the quest for profit serve society's ends?

Why do most Canadian cities now have more tattoo parlours and fewer watch repair shops than in 1972?

# 6.1 THE CENTRAL ROLE OF ECONOMIC PROFIT

In Chapter 5, we developed the theory of production and cost in the short run, and we defined the short run as the period of time in which technology and *at least one* factor of production are fixed. In this chapter, we develop the theory of production and cost in the long run. In the long run, no factors of production are fixed, so every firm can change any input, including the amount of capital it uses, its size, and the combination of labour, capital, and other factors of production it uses. In the long run, new firms may also enter a market or existing ones may leave it. Thus, not only are the factors of production for each firm variable in the long run, the number of firms in any industry is as well. Indeed, in the long run, entirely new industries (like social media) appear and old ones (like home floor polishers) disappear.

Why might any of this happen? The short answer is, because of the presence or absence of opportunities to make profits. But what, exactly, does profit mean?

### THREE MEANINGS OF PROFIT

The economist's definition of profit differs a bit from the accountant's. **Accounting profit** is the difference between the *revenue* a firm takes in over the year and its *explicit costs* for the same period. **Revenue** is the value of income received by a firm during a period of time in return for supplying goods and services. **Explicit costs** are the actual payments the firm makes during a period of time to its factors of production and other suppliers.[3] Accounting profit is the most familiar profit concept used. For example, it is the one that people think of when companies provide statements about their profits in press releases or annual reports.

accounting profit = total revenue − explicit costs

**accounting profit** the difference between a firm's total revenue and its explicit costs

**revenue** the value of income received by a firm during a period of time in return for supplying goods and services

**explicit costs** the actual payments a firm makes during a period of time to its factors of production and other suppliers

---

3 Sometimes the degree of match between the timing of payments and the actual use of resources creates accounting complications. For example, if a firm's financial year runs from January 1 to December 31, how should it account for the goods it ships to a customer toward the end of December, given that the cheque which pays for the goods may only actually be received in January or February of the next financial year? Typically, that income should be credited against December's shipments. As well, a capital good (e.g., a delivery truck) that is bought this year will normally produce output for several years in the future before wearing out. Although the truck could be bought new every January 1 and sold (used) at the end of the every year, it usually is not. Hence, if a firm wants to calculate the true cost of using the truck, it will not use the full purchase price in the year in which it was bought. Instead, the firm will calculate the explicit cost of the truck as the out-of-pocket costs of use (i.e., fuel and maintenance) plus any change in the truck's market value (i.e., depreciation). Accountants must develop and use accounting standards to allocate receipts and explicit costs to the correct financial year, but they define net income (or "accounting profit") for a financial year as revenue less all explicit costs that can properly be charged against goods sold in that year.

Particularly in the small business sector, however, the owners of a company may supply labour or other resources (e.g., land) to the firm without fully charging explicitly for the opportunity cost of the resources supplied by the owners; for example, a lawyer who could make $100 per hour doing other work but only charges $40 per hour for the time he spends in running his firm has an additional implicit cost of $60 per hour. Economists, therefore, define profit as the difference between the firm's total revenue and its explicit costs plus its **implicit costs**, which are the opportunity costs of all the resources supplied by the firm's owners. Profit thus defined can be called **economic profit**:

**implicit costs** all the firm's opportunity costs of the resources supplied by the firm's owners

$$\text{economic profit} = \text{total revenue} - \text{explicit costs} - \text{implicit costs.}$$

**economic profit** the difference between a firm's total revenue and the sum of its explicit and implicit costs

To illustrate the difference between accounting profit and economic profit, consider a firm with $400 000 in total annual revenue. The firm incurs explicit costs of $250 000/year to lease its building and pay its employees. The owners of this firm also have invested $1 million in the shares of the company to finance the firm's operations. This firm's accounting profit, then, is the difference between its total revenue of $400 000/year and its explicit costs of $250 000/year, or $150 000/year.

However, explicit costs often are only part of the opportunity costs a firm incurs. Some opportunity costs are implicit. To calculate a firm's economic profit, we must include both explicit and implicit opportunity costs. Suppose the current annual interest rate on savings accounts is 5 percent. Suppose, too, that this is the best alternate use of the funds the owners have invested. Had the owners not put their funds into the firm, they could have earned an additional $50 000/year interest by depositing their $1 million in a savings account. So the firm's economic profit is $400 000/year − $250 000/year − $50 000/year = $100 000/year.

Note that this economic profit is smaller than the accounting profit by exactly the amount of the firm's implicit costs: the $50 000/year opportunity cost of the resources supplied by the firm's owners. This difference between a business's accounting profit and its economic profit is called its *normal profit*. **Normal profit** *is simply the opportunity cost of the resources supplied to a business by its owners.* A normal profit is just sufficient to hold a firm in an industry, but it provides no incentive for new firms to enter the industry.

**normal profit** the opportunity cost of the resources supplied by the firm's owners; equal to accounting profit minus economic profit

Figure 6.1 illustrates the difference between accounting and economic profit. Panel (a) represents a firm's total revenues, while panels (b) and (c) show how these revenues are apportioned among the various cost and profit categories.

## FIGURE 6.1
**The Difference between Accounting Profit and Economic Profit**
Panel (a): a firm's total revenue. Panel (b): accounting profit is the difference between total revenue and explicit costs. Panel (c): normal profit is the opportunity cost of all resources supplied by firm's owners. Economic profit is the difference between total revenue and all costs, explicit and implicit. Economic profit is also sometimes called "excess profit," since it is equal to the difference between accounting profit and normal profit, and it is the amount of profit in excess of normal profit.

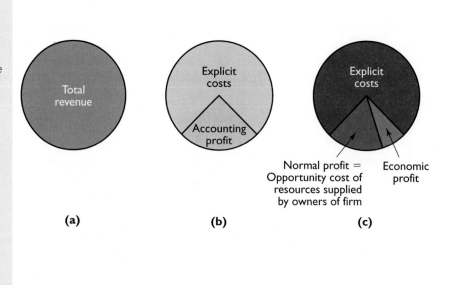

*"All I know, Harrison, is that I've been on the board forty years and have yet to see an excess profit."*

Examples 6.1 to 6.5 illustrate why the distinction between accounting and economic profit is so important.

## EXAMPLE 6.1

### Will Bernard Buffet stay in the farming business?

Bernard Buffet is a farmer who lives near Regina. His annual expenses are $6000 to lease the land he farms, plus $4000 for equipment rental and supplies. The only input he supplies is his own labour, and he considers farming just as attractive as his best other employment opportunity, which is managing a retail store at a salary of $11 000/year. Apart from the matter of pay, Bernard is indifferent between farming and being a manager. Wheat sells for a constant price per bushel, which is unaffected by any one farmer's wheat production. Bernard's revenue from wheat sales is $22 000/year. What is his accounting profit? economic profit? normal profit? Will he remain a wheat farmer?

As shown in Table 6.1, Bernard's accounting profit is $12 000/year, the difference between his $22 000 annual revenue and his $10 000 yearly payment for land, equipment, and supplies. His economic profit is that amount less the opportunity cost of his labour, which is the $11 000/year he could have earned as a store manager. Thus, he is making an economic profit of $1000/year. Finally, his normal profit is the $11 000 opportunity cost of the only resource he supplies; namely, his labour. Since Bernard likes the two jobs equally well, he will be better off by $1000/year if he remains in farming.

**TABLE 6.1**
**Revenue, Cost, and Profit Summary for Example 6.1**

| Total revenue ($/year) | Explicit costs ($/year) | Implicit costs ($/year) | Accounting profit (total revenue − explicit costs) ($/year) | Economic profit (total revenue − explicit costs − implicit costs) ($/year) | Normal profit (implicit costs) ($/year) |
|---|---|---|---|---|---|
| 22 000 | 10 000 | 11 000 | 12 000 | 1000 | 11 000 |

## EXAMPLE 6.2

### If Bernard's annual revenue falls by $2000, will he stay in farming?

Refer to Example 6.1. How will Bernard's economic profit change if his annual revenue from wheat production is not $22 000 but $20 000? Will he continue to farm?

As shown in Table 6.2, Bernard's accounting profit is now $10 000, the difference between his $20 000 annual revenue and his $10 000/year payment for land, equipment, and supplies. His economic profit is that amount minus the opportunity cost of his labour, again, the $11 000/year he could have earned as a store manager. So Bernard is now earning a negative economic profit, –$1000/year. As before, his normal profit is $11 000/year, the opportunity cost of his labour. Although an accountant would say Bernard is making an annual profit of $10 000, that amount is less than a normal profit for his activity. An economist would therefore say that Bernard is making an **economic loss**, or an economic profit that is less than zero, of $1000/year. Since Bernard likes the two jobs equally well, he will be better off by $1000/year if he leaves farming to become a manager.

**economic loss** an economic profit that is less than zero

**TABLE 6.2**
**Revenue, Cost, and Profit Summary for Example 6.2**

| Total revenue ($/year) | Explicit costs ($/year) | Implicit costs ($/year) | Accounting profit (total revenue – explicit costs) ($/year) | Economic profit (total revenue – explicit costs – implicit costs) ($/year) | Normal profit (implicit costs) ($/year) |
|---|---|---|---|---|---|
| 20 000 | 10 000 | 11 000 | 10 000 | –1000 | 11 000 |

If Bernard makes an economic profit in farming, he will prefer farming to his best alternative occupation. If he makes a negative economic profit as a farmer, he will prefer his best alternative occupation to farming. When he makes a normal profit (i.e., when his economic profit is zero), Bernard will be indifferent between farming and his best alternative occupation; he will have no reason to leave farming.

Recall that in Example 6.2, Bernard was making an economic loss of $1000 annually. His expenditures included $6000/year to lease land. You might think that if Bernard could save enough money to buy his land, his best option would be to remain a farmer. After all, he no longer would be spending $6000 to lease land. But, as Example 6.3 makes clear, that impression is based on a failure to perceive the difference between accounting profit and economic profit.

## EXAMPLE 6.3

### Does owning the land make a difference?

Continue with the previous example, but suppose Bernard's Uncle Warren, who owns the farmland Bernard has been renting, dies and leaves Bernard that parcel of land. If the land could be rented to some other farmer for $6000/year, is Bernard better off to remain in farming?

As shown in Table 6.3, if Bernard continues to farm his own land, his accounting profit will be $16 000/year, or $6000 more than before. But his economic profit will be the same as before (–$1000/year) because Bernard must deduct the $6000/year opportunity cost of farming his own land. The reduction of $6000 in explicit costs is exactly offset by an increase of $6000 in implicit costs. If others have preferences like Bernard's together with similar outside employment opportunities, then the normal profit from owning and operating a farm like his will be $17 000/year; that is, the opportunity cost of the land and labour provided. But, since Bernard earns an accounting profit of only $16 000, he will again be better off if he abandons farming for the managerial job.

**TABLE 6.3**
Revenue, Cost, and Profit Summary for Example 6.3

| Total revenue ($/year) | Explicit costs ($/year) | Implicit costs ($/year) | Accounting profit (total revenue − explicit costs) ($/year) | Economic profit (total revenue − explicit costs − implicit costs) ($/year) | Normal profit (implicit costs) ($/year) |
|---|---|---|---|---|---|
| 20 000 | 4000 | 17 000 | 16 000 | −1000 | 17 000 |

Needless to say, Bernard would be wealthier as an owner than he was as a renter. But the question of whether to remain a farmer is answered the same way whether Bernard rents his farmland or owns it.

## EXAMPLE 6.4

### What would happen to land values if *all* farmers around Regina earned less than normal profit?

Suppose the conditions confronting Bernard Buffet in Example 6.2 are essentially the same as those confronting all other farmers around Regina; that is, all earn less than a normal profit. What economic changes will result?

We have been assuming that if a farmer leaves farming, he can do something else. As an alternative to farming, Bernard can manage a store. Some farmland may not have alternative uses: either it is farmed or it is not used for anything. If all farmers around Regina are making economic losses, some farmers will switch to other activities. This will reduce the demand for farmland, and, especially if there are no competing uses for farmland, the market price of farmland will fall. As its market price falls, the opportunity cost of farmland to any individual farmer will fall. If Bernard owns his own land, the payment any other farmer is willing to make for use of that land will fall as the demand for farmland declines. The price of farmland will continue to fall until farmers around Regina can once again earn a normal profit. Specifically, the price of land will fall until the yearly rental for a farm like Bernard's is only $5000, because at that rent the accounting profit of those who farmed their own land would be $16 000/year, exactly the same as normal profit. Their economic profit would be zero.

## EXAMPLE 6.5

### What will happen to land values if all farmers earn *more* than a normal profit?

Suppose wheat growers farm 80 hectares of their own land, which sells for $1000/hectare. Each farm's revenue from wheat sales is $20 000/year. Equipment and other supplies cost $4000/year, and the current annual interest rate on savings accounts is 5 percent. Farmers can earn $11 000/year in alternative jobs that they like equally as well as farming. What is normal economic profit for these farmers? How much accounting profit will they earn? How much economic profit? Is their economic situation stable? If not, how is it likely to change?

As shown in Table 6.4, accounting profit, the difference between the $20 000 annual revenue and the $4000 annual expense for equipment and supplies, is $16 000/year, as in Example 6.3. Normal profit is the opportunity cost of the farmer's time and land—$11 000 for his time and $4000 for his land (since, had he sold the land for $80 000 and put the money in the bank at 5 percent interest, he would have earned $4000/year in interest)—for a total of $15 000. Accounting profit thus exceeds normal profit by $1000/year, which means that farmers are earning an economic profit of $1000/year.

**TABLE 6.4**
Revenue, Cost, and Profit Summary for Example 6.5

| Total revenue ($/year) | Explicit costs ($/year) | Implicit costs ($/year) | Accounting profit (total revenue − explicit costs) ($/year) | Economic profit (total revenue − explicit costs − implicit costs) ($/year) | Normal profit (implicit costs) ($/year) |
|---|---|---|---|---|---|
| 20 000 | 4000 | 15 000 | 16 000 | 1000 | 15 000 |

To see whether this situation is stable, we must ask whether individuals have an incentive to change their behaviour. Consider the situation from the perspective of a manager who is earning $11 000/year. To switch to farming, he would need to borrow $80 000 to buy land, which would mean interest payments of $4000/year. With $20 000/year in revenue from wheat sales and $4000/year in expenses for supplies and equipment, in addition to $4000/year in interest payments, the manager would earn an accounting profit of $12 000/year. And since that amount is $1000/year more than the opportunity cost of the manager's time, he will want to switch to farming. Indeed, *all* managers will want to switch to farming because at current land prices, a farmer can make an economic profit.

As we know from the equilibrium principle, however, such situations are not stable. There is only so much farmland to go around, so as demand for farmland increases, its price will begin to rise. The price will keep rising until there is no longer any incentive for managers to switch to farming.

How much must the price of land rise to eliminate the incentive to switch? If 80 hectares of land sold for $100 000 (that is, if land sold for $1250/hectare), the interest on the money borrowed to buy a farm would be $5000/year, an amount that would reduce economic profit to zero and make workers indifferent between farming or being a manager. But if land sells for anything less than $1250/hectare, there will be excess demand for farmland.

EQUILIBRIUM

**firm** an organization that combines factors of production to produce a good or service or some combination of goods and services

A farm is a type of *firm*. A **firm** is an organization that combines factors of production to produce a good or service or some combination of goods and services. In this chapter, we assume a firm that is a price taker produces one good of uniform quality. A wheat farm can be seen as a firm that combines factors of production to produce wheat.[4]

## WHAT HAPPENS IF ALL FARMERS MAKE AN ECONOMIC PROFIT?

**capital (or capital goods)** durable, long-lasting inputs produced by the economy and used as inputs to the production process

Consider panel (a) of Figure 6.2. Assume that technology and the stock of *capital* used on the farm are fixed. As was discussed in Chapter 2, durable, long-lasting inputs produced by the economy and used as inputs to the production process, such as tools, machinery, and buildings, constitute the stock of **capital** (or **capital goods**). The curve labelled $ATC_s$ is a graph of average total cost for different quantities of wheat produced by an 80-hectare farm. Because the size of the farm, capital, and technology cannot be changed quickly, they are fixed in the short run. Therefore, $ATC_s$ is a short-run cost curve. Given a farm of 80 hectares, $ATC_s$ represents the lowest cost per unit of wheat that can be achieved for any given quantity of wheat. For example, $ATC_s$ shows that if 12 000 bushels (bu) are produced, the cost per bushel will be $2.12. If 12 000 bushels are produced on an 80-hectare farm, it is not possible to reduce the cost per bushel below $2.12. Notice, too, that if the

4  Note that when we assumed that the wheat farm was a "price taker" we did not need to specify whether this was because a single agency (such as the Canadian Wheat Board) bought all the firm's output at a fixed price or because the firm was selling to a market with many competing buyers, all of whom were willing to pay the same price. The crucial issue is simple—can the firm sell as much or as little as it wants, without affecting the price it receives?

farm produces 10 000 bushels of wheat per year, the cost per bushel will be $2.10. Given that the size of Bernard's farm and its capital stock are fixed, this is the lowest cost per bushel that can be achieved.

The curve labelled $MC_s$ in panel (a) is the marginal cost curve for wheat. For example, if Bernard chooses to produce 12 000 bu/yr, marginal cost is $2.20: when 12 000 bu/yr are being produced, one more bushel can be produced for $2.20. Because the size of Bernard's farm and the amount of capital being used are fixed, $MC_s$ is a short-run marginal cost curve.

Up to this point, we have assumed that the firm is a price taker; that is, able to sell all the output that it wants to produce at a constant price. One way this can happen is when the output of each firm is small *in relation to the sales of the whole industry*. Each wheat farmer, for example, knows that the output of even a large-scale local farmer is a trivial percentage of the tonnage of wheat sold on world markets. Since supply and demand in the global market for wheat set the world price of wheat, each farmer can produce as much wheat as he wants to, knowing that his own output will be too small to affect global supply and demand, and therefore, too small to affect price.

But what happens when *everybody* increases (or decreases) production at the same time? To answer this, we look at panel (b) of Figure 6.2, which represents the market for wheat. To be consistent with panel (a), which gives a short-run picture for one farm, panel (b) gives a short-run picture of the market. In the short run, the number of farms serving the market, the size of each farm, and the amount of capital each farm uses are fixed. The wheat industry is the group of farms that supplies the market for wheat, and the number of firms in the wheat industry is fixed in the short run.

To keep things simple, we assume that, initially, 1000 identical farms supply wheat to the wheat market. When 1000 farms serve the market, the short-run supply curve *SRS* of panel (b) pertains. Suppose equilibrium price is $2.10/bu, as determined by *SRS* and the

**FIGURE 6.2**
**The Firm, the Market, and a Shift in Short-Run Supply: Responses of a Wheat Farm and the Wheat Market**
Panel (a) pertains to the firm in the short run and shows its marginal and average total cost curves for wheat. Panel (b) pertains to the market for wheat and shows the shift of the short-run supply curve in response to an increase in demand.

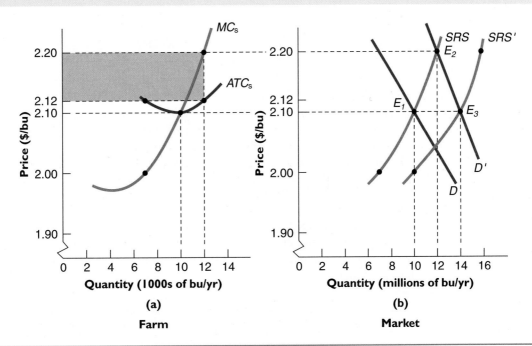

demand curve *D*. The market determines the price of wheat and every individual farmer takes it as given. Like all the other wheat farmers, Bernard is a price taker, and his marginal revenue equals market price. To maximize profit, Bernard produces the quantity of wheat that causes price to equal marginal cost. Thus, panel (a) shows that Bernard will produce 10 000 bu/yr of wheat. Panel (b) shows that when 1000 identical farmers make the same decision, 10 million bu/yr of wheat are supplied to the wheat market:

$$1000 \text{ farms} \times 10\ 000 \text{ bu/farm/yr} = 10\ 000\ 000 \text{ bu/yr}.$$

Further, because price per bushel equals cost per bushel, each farmer makes a normal profit by producing 10 000 bu/yr. Short-run equilibrium in the market is at $E_1$, the intersection of demand curve *D* and short-run supply curve *SRS*. Because each and every farmer is making a normal profit, $E_1$ also is a long-run equilibrium.

Now suppose that some outside shock disturbs that equilibrium. Suppose, for example, that because a virulent strain of potato bug appears, the world's supply of potatoes is greatly reduced and the price of potatoes rises dramatically. As a result, consumers reduce consumption of potatoes and increase consumption of bread and pasta. The demand for wheat increases to $D'$ [panel (b)], causing the price of wheat to rise to $2.20/bu. Following the rule for maximizing profits, Bernard increases the amount of wheat he produces to 12 000 bu/yr [panel (a)], as do every one of the 1000 wheat farmers. Thus, panel (b) shows the new equilibrium $E_2$, where demand curve $D'$ intersects supply curve *SRS*. At a price of $2.20, 12 million bu/yr are supplied to the wheat market.

Panel (a) shows that if price is $2.20/bu and 12 000 bushels/year are supplied, average total cost will be $2.12/bu. Therefore, a farmer makes an economic profit of $0.08/bu:

$$\$2.20/\text{bu} - \$2.12/\text{bu} = \$0.08/\text{bu}.$$

The area of the green rectangle in panel (a) represents Bernard's total economic profit per year:

$$\$0.08/\text{bu} \times 12\ 000 \text{ bu/yr} = \$960.00/\text{yr}.$$

This is an amount in excess of Bernard's normal profit. Each of the 1000 identical wheat farmers is earning the same annual economic profit. As long as price is $2.20/bu, and no new farmers enter the market to supply wheat, the farmers will continue to make this economic profit.

Now suppose that the new, more virulent potato bug is a permanent change, one that generates a long-run response in agricultural markets. What happens if new farmers can enter the wheat market? (One way this could happen is if farmers switch crops; e.g., farmers who are now producing canola or soybeans decide to grow wheat instead.) This would allow the number of wheat farms to increase, which would increase competition and the size of the wheat industry. Any change in the number of farms that supply wheat is a long-run adjustment.[5]

Can positive economic profit persist in the long run? Remember that economic profit is a return in excess of opportunity cost. If people who are not now wheat farmers perceive that by supplying wheat they can make an economic profit, they will enter the market and supply wheat. As they enter, short-run supply will increase, and competition in the wheat market will cause prices to fall. As long as new firms are entering the industry (because they can make positive economic profit), total supply will increase, which puts downward pressure on prices.

How long will this process continue? The short answer is, as long as the incentive of positive economic profit remains. When every firm's revenues are just sufficient to cover the opportunity cost of its factors of production and inputs, economic profit is zero and

5 The crucial parts of this example are the shift of the demand curve (from *D* to *D'*) and the response of price-taking firms supplying that demand. Initially, only existing firms respond, but in the long run, new firms enter. We do not really care either *why* the demand curve shifts or *why* supplier firms are price takers. We would get the same outcome if there was a single buyer for all wheat, and its demand curve shifted.

there is no incentive for new firms to enter. Thus, long-run equilibrium is reached when economic profit is zero and there is no incentive for any firm to change its production decisions. Farmers will enter the industry until the price of wheat falls low enough to reduce economic profit to zero; that is, until they are making normal profits, no more and no less. Panel (b) of Figure 6.2 shows a new long-run equilibrium at $E_3$, where price returns to \$2.10/bu when short-run supply has increased to $SRS'$ and the quantity of wheat supplied has risen to 14 million bu/yr. Because $SRS'$ intersects $D'$, $E_3$ also is a short-run equilibrium. At a price of \$2.10/bu, Bernard again produces 10 000 bu/yr, where cost per bushel is minimized. At the same time, 400 new wheat farmers have entered the market, increasing the total number of identical wheat farms to 1400. Each farm produces 10 000 bu/yr, each farmer makes a normal profit, cost per bushel is minimized, and the total quantity of wheat supplied is 140 million bu/yr:

$$1400 \text{ farms} \times 10\,000 \text{ bu/farm/yr} = 14\,000\,000 \text{ bu/yr.}$$

If firms are free to enter (or leave) the market, in the long run, economic profit will be competed away by new suppliers. This implies that the price paid by buyers is equal to minimum average total cost in long-run equilibrium.

EQUILIBRIUM

**RECAP**

**THE CENTRAL ROLE OF ECONOMIC PROFIT**

A firm's *accounting profit* is the difference between its revenue and the sum of all explicit costs it incurs. *Economic profit* is the difference between the firm's revenue and *all* costs it incurs: both explicit and implicit. *Normal profit* is the opportunity cost of the resources supplied by the owners of the firm.

## 6.2  HOW COMPETITION AFFECTS THE SIZE OF FIRMS

In the long run, a firm can choose the size of its operation; for example, a farmer can change the size of his farm. In principle, land could be bought and sold in any arbitrary amount. However, in much of the Canadian prairie, lots were initially surveyed in "quarter sections" of 160 acres, and farmers still often buy and sell in those units. Suppose that all wheat farmers could choose from among five different sizes of farms. Figure 6.3 graphs average total cost for each of the five sizes. If each size presents the same cost structure to every farmer, *ATC1* graphs average total cost for farms of the smallest size, *ATC2* graphs average total cost for the next largest size, and so on.

Now consider the intersection of *ATC1* and *ATC2*, which is marked "A" in Figure 6.3. The intersection designates an output of 4500 bushels per year. Curve *ATC2* shows that for crops of more than 4500 bushels per year, farms of the size represented by *ATC2* can produce wheat at a lower cost per bushel than can farms represented by *ACT1*. Similarly, the intersection of *ATC2* and *ATC3* indicates the size of harvest at which the cost advantage shifts to the next larger farm. **Long-run average cost** is the minimum cost per unit that can be achieved for a given level of output, assuming that technology is constant. Thus, the heavy blue curve of Figure 6.3, labelled *LRAC*, is the long-run average cost curve for wheat farmers, given that farms of five different sizes are possible.

Because all factors of production, all costs, and the size of a firm are variable in the long run, managers of a firm can plan the best way to combine factors of production, including the best size for the firm. Therefore, the long run can also be referred to as a firm's planning horizon. When Bernard considers the long run, he presumably will try to plan the most profitable combination of factors of production for his farm, including the

**long-run average cost** the lowest cost per unit that can be achieved for a given level of output when all factors of production, all costs, and the size of the firm are variable, but technology is constant

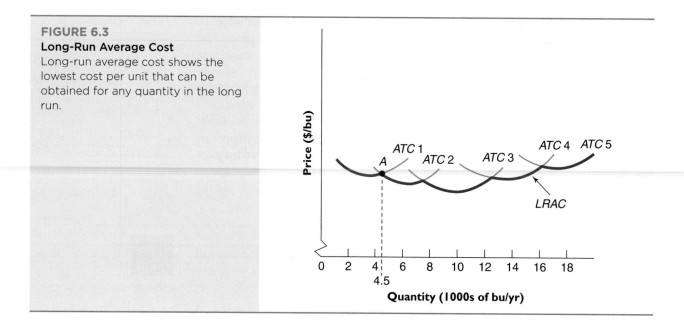

**FIGURE 6.3**
**Long-Run Average Cost**
Long-run average cost shows the lowest cost per unit that can be obtained for any quantity in the long run.

most profitable size of his farm. He can, in the long run, buy new machinery, change the amount of land allocated to different crops, or change the size of his farm; indeed, he can choose whether to continue farming. In the long run, existing farms can exit the industry and new ones can enter. Competition, together with exit and entry, will, in the long run, force farms to the size that minimizes long-run average cost. Thus, in long-run competitive equilibrium, minimum long-run average cost equals market price, and farms that are either too small or too large to produce at minimum long-run average cost will disappear.

Now, consider again the long-run average cost curve of Figure 6.3. It is scalloped because we assumed that a farm had to be of five distinct sizes. However, if it is possible to vary the size of a farm continuously, the long-run average cost curve takes the smooth, U-shape shown in panel (a) of Figure 6.4. But regardless of whether a long-run average cost curve is smooth or scalloped, it is a locus of points that plots the lowest cost per unit that can be achieved at each possible rate of output.[6] Moreover, the end result of competition together with exit and entry is the same. Farms are forced to operate at minimum long-run average cost.

## LONG-RUN MARKET SUPPLY

Long-run market supply can be developed from short-run market supply curves, such as those shown in Figure 6.2. The average total cost curve in panel (a) and the demand and short-run market supply curves in panel (b) of Figure 6.4 are the same as the cost, demand, and short-run supply curves shown in Figure 6.2, though a long-run average cost curve has been added to Figure 6.4. Notice, too, that $ATC_s$ is the short-run average cost curve that pertains to the size of farm that accomplishes the lowest cost per bushel. Minimum cost per bushel will be higher for any other size of farm. Also, in Figure 6.4, the equilibrium point of $D$ and $SRS$ is joined with the equilibrium point of $D'$ and $SRS'$ to form the long-run market supply curve, which is labelled $LRS$. Recall that in the long run, the number of farms that produce wheat can rise or fall. Panel (b) of Figure 6.4 shows that if demand rises from $D$ to $D'$, in the long run, the quantity of wheat exchanged in the wheat market rises from $Q1$ to $Q3$. However, when long-run adjustments are complete,

6  In mathematical terms, a long-run average cost curve is the envelope of a family of short-run average cost curves.

**FIGURE 6.4**

**Long-Run Supply (LRS) with Free Entry and Exit, Case I: Constant Opportunity Cost of Inputs and Factors of Production**

Panel (a) shows the firm's long-run average cost curve, while panel (b) shows the demand curve and the short-run and long-run market supply curves. Long-run market supply is horizontal and pertains to a constant cost industry.

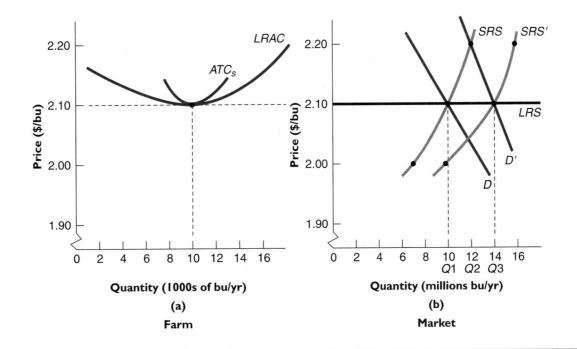

(a)

**Farm**

(b)

**Market**

the quantity of wheat produced by the farm represented in panel (a) is the same as it was before demand increased from $D$ to $D'$. In the long run, the entire increase from $Q1$ to $Q3$ is accomplished by the entry of new farms, each producing at its minimum long-run average cost. The number of farms has increased, but the quantity of wheat produced by each farm is unchanged and each farm earns zero economic profit (as it did initially). Further, because long-run market supply in Figure 6.4 is horizontal, market price returns to what it was before demand increased from $D$ to $D'$. Figure 6.4 portrays a constant cost industry.

Long-run market supply is horizontal because we assumed that the number of wheat farms rises, but the prices of the factors of production and intermediate inputs they use remain constant.

However, we can relax this assumption and consider what happens if prices paid for factors of production (such as labour) or intermediate inputs (such as fertilizer) used by farmers are bid up. This would cause the cost curves of individual farms to shift up, and long-run market supply would then have a positive slope. Figure 6.5 shows this case. As the number of farms increases in response to an increase in the demand for wheat, from the point of view of individual farmers, long-run average cost increases from $LRAC1$ to $LRAC2$, as shown in panel (a). As a result, even after long-run adjustments are complete, market price is higher. Thus, panel (b) shows long-run market supply with a positive slope.[7] Thus Figure 6.5 portrays an increasing cost industry. Again, profits are zero in long-run equilibrium.

EQUILIBRIUM

---

7  It is conceptually possible for long-run average cost to shift down as the number of firms serving a market increases; for example, if intermediate inputs become cheaper because of economies of scale in their production, long run average cost would shift down. In this case, long-run market supply would have a negative slope. Laptop computer manufacturers might be an example, because they buy crucial components from chip manufacturers with a very high set up cost and low marginal cost of production.

## FIGURE 6.5

### Long-Run Supply with Free Entry and Exit, Case II: Cost of Inputs and Factors of Production Rises as Short-Run Supply Increases

Panel (a): As the number of farms increases in response to an increase in the demand for wheat, long-run average cost increases from *LRAC1* to *LRAC2*. Panel (b): After long-run adjustments are complete, market price is higher, so long-run market supply has a positive slope. Thus Panel (b) shows an increasing-cost industry.

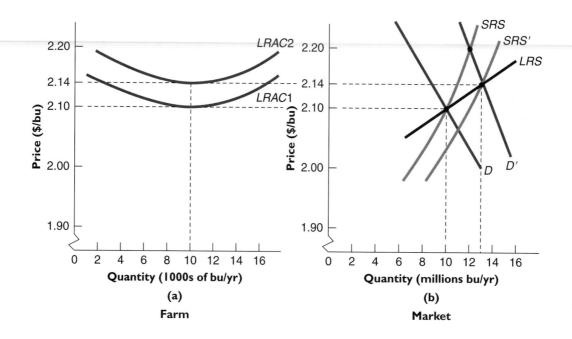

(a)
**Farm**

(b)
**Market**

### Why do supermarket checkout lines all tend to be roughly the same length?

Suppose you are approaching the checkout lanes in the supermarket and see one line that is significantly shorter than the others. Which line will you choose? You and the other shoppers will probably check the size of the load in each other's carts and the speed of the cashiers and select the line with lowest expected waiting time. But when everyone does this, any short lines will quickly lengthen. Generally, shoppers will change lines until expected waiting time is equalized. Thus the equilibrium principle can work not only in the face of opportunities to make an economic profit, but also in the face of other opportunities to achieve a more desirable outcome.

**RECAP**

### HOW COMPETITION AFFECTS THE SIZE OF FIRMS

When a firm's accounting profit is exactly equal to the opportunity cost of the inputs supplied by the firm's owners, the firm's economic profit is zero. When firms earn a positive economic profit (sometimes called excess profits), the industry will attract new firms. Firms leave industries in which they sustain an economic loss. In each case, the adjustments continue until economic (excess) profit equals zero.

If a market of price-taking firms initially is in equilibrium, but there is an increase in market demand and price, the number of firms serving a market does not change in the short run. Firms already in the market respond to the higher price by increasing their output, thus causing the quantity sold to increase. The higher market price lets existing firms earn an economic profit. That economic (excess) profit attracts new firms, which enter the market. Additional supply pushes down prices until economic profit is zero (i.e., firms are only earning a normal profit). When long-run adjustments are complete, more firms are supplying the market, and each firm is operating at minimum long-run average cost and earning a normal profit. If the prices of factors of production used by the firms are not bid up as new firms enter, market price will return to what it was before the increase in demand, and the long-run market supply curve will be horizontal. If prices of factors of production, or intermediate inputs, rise as new firms enter, long-run market supply will have a positive slope. If a decrease in demand causes economic losses in a perfectly competitive market, a similar set of adjustments occurs, though working in the opposite direction.

## 6.3  FIRM SIZE AND THE SHAPE OF THE LONG-RUN AVERAGE COST CURVE

Figure 6.4 shows minimum long-run average cost occurring at a single quantity of output. This implies that a farm of only one size can achieve minimum long-run average cost. If this is true, in the long run wheat farms will all be the same size. However, it is possible, perhaps even likely, that minimum long-run average cost can be achieved over a range of output, and by farms of a number of different sizes. This possibility is represented in Figure 6.6.

The long-run average cost curve, *LRAC*, of Figure 6.6 is divided into sections I, II, and III, which represent economies of scale, constant returns to scale, and diseconomies of scale, respectively. **Scale** refers to the size of a firm relative to other possible sizes of firms serving a particular market. Over section I, **economies of scale** are achieved as the size, or scale, of an operation increases and causes long-run average cost to decrease as output increases.

**scale** the size of a firm relative to other possible sizes of firms serving a particular market

**economies of scale** a situation in which long-run average cost decreases as a firm's output increases

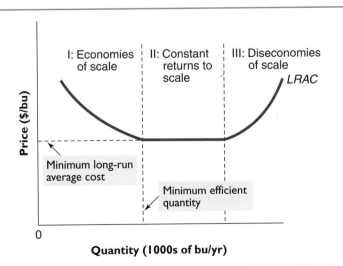

**FIGURE 6.6**
**Long-Run Average Cost and Returns to Scale**
The curve *LRAC* portrays economies of scale, constant returns to scale, and diseconomies of scale.

One reason for economies of scale is that specialization and the division of labour can be greater in a larger firm than in a smaller one. Adam Smith noted in 1776 that the manufacturing of pins was then divided into as many as 18 different tasks: one worker straightened the wire, another cut it, another fastened the head, and so on.[8] Workers are much more productive if they specialize, because they learn a limited set of tasks well, and they spend less time moving from one task to another.

In addition to the productivity gains from specialization and learning by doing, economies of scale may also occur because some factors of production and, therefore, some costs of setup are indivisible. Some minimal amount of an **indivisible factor of production** may be necessary if a productive activity, even of minimal size, is to occur at all. If, for example, a farm is to have a tractor capable of pulling machinery that will till the soil, it has to be a minimum size. Even if it is technically possible to manufacture very small tractors, beyond some point a small tractor is not useful. A very small one would just get lost in the weeds. The cost of an indivisible factor of production is an **indivisible cost**.

A third source of economies of scale is derived from geometry. A farmer who, for example, wants to build a round silo will find that the cost of materials and labour depends mainly on the height and circumference of the silo. Geometry tells us that circumference is equal to $2\pi r$ (where r is the radius of the silo), so if h is its height, total costs will be a function of $2\pi rh$; that is, costs will increase proportionately with increases in the radius $r$. However, the storage capacity of the silo depends on the volume of the silo (which is equal to $\pi r^2 h$). The silo's storage capacity thus increases more than proportionately (as the square of the radius) when the radius of the silo increases. Since the total cost is proportionate to the radius, the average cost per unit stored will fall as capacity rises. Similarly, constructing additional capacity for pipelines and oil refineries inherently increases capacity proportionately more than it increases cost.

Over section II of *LRAC* in Figure 6.6, *constant returns to scale* are in effect. If constant returns to scale are in effect, and everything that the firm needs for production is just "scaled up" (e.g., the firm uses 2/3 more capital, 2/3 more labour, 2/3 more raw material, etc.) then output goes up by exactly the same proportion (i.e., by 2/3). With **constant returns to scale**, long-run average cost is constant as output changes; that is, a change in the scale of an operation leaves long-run average cost unchanged. Notice that the boundary between section I and section II indicates a *minimum efficient quantity of output*. The **minimum efficient quantity** is the smallest quantity of output that will achieve minimum long-run average cost. The presence of constant returns to scale means that firms of a number of different sizes can simultaneously earn a normal profit. Thus, firms of different sizes can simultaneously serve a market, all of them making a normal profit. For example, with constant returns to scale, farms of different sizes could produce wheat while earning a normal profit.

Section III of *LRAC* portrays *diseconomies of scale*. With **diseconomies of scale**, long-run average cost increases as output increases. If output always increased in the same proportion as the scale of a firm increased, diseconomies would not exist. Do we want twice as much wheat? With constant returns to scale in wheat production, twice as much wheat could always be obtained by doubling the size of a farm without causing any increase in cost per unit of wheat. Do we again want twice as much wheat? Just double the size of the farm again, and so on. However, diseconomies of scale can appear as a firm becomes larger if the firm becomes increasingly difficult (i.e., costly) to organize and coordinate as it grows. If diseconomies of scale appear, output will increase less than in proportion to an increase in scale, causing long-run average cost to increase as output increases.

**indivisible factor of production** a factor of production that must be available in some minimum amount if a productive activity, even of minimal size, is to occur at all

**indivisible cost** the cost of an indivisible factor of production

**constant returns to scale** a situation in which long-run average cost does not change as scale changes

**minimum efficient quantity** the smallest quantity of output that will achieve minimum long-run average cost

**diseconomies of scale** a situation in which long-run average cost increases as a firm's output increases

8  Smith, *The Wealth of Nations* (1776) (New York, 1965), Book I, Chapter I, p. 4.

**FIRM SIZE AND THE SHAPE OF THE LONG-RUN AVERAGE COST CURVE**

If long-run average cost decreases as the relative size, or scale, of a firm increases, economies of scale are present. If long-run average cost remains constant as the scale of a firm increases, constant returns to scale are present. Diseconomies of scale are present when long-run average cost rises as the scale of a firm increases. If constant returns to scale are present, it is possible for firms of different sizes to be present in a market that has reached long-run competitive equilibrium.

# 6.4 ENTRY, EXIT, AND INNOVATION

Competition among price-taking firms will not lead to minimum long-run average cost unless firms can enter new markets and leave existing ones easily. If new firms could not enter a market in which existing firms were making a large economic profit, economic profit would not tend to fall to zero over time, and price would not tend to gravitate toward the minimum possible cost of production.

## THE IMPORTANCE OF FREE ENTRY

Forces that inhibit firms from entering new markets are sometimes called **barriers to entry**. In the economics textbook market, for example, the publisher of a text enjoys copyright protection granted by the government. Copyright law forbids other publishers from producing and selling their own editions of protected works. This barrier allows the price of a popular book to remain significantly above its cost of production for an extended period, all the while generating an economic profit for its publisher.[9]

Barriers to entry may result from practical constraints as well as legal ones. In the railway boom of the nineteenth century, for example, the first firm to build a rail line could often pre-empt the best route. Once one rail line to Vancouver was built down the Fraser River valley, there was only one remaining side of the river to build on. In today's Internet age, some economists have argued that the compelling advantages of product compatibility have created barriers to entry in the computer software market. Because more than 80 percent of new personal computers come with Microsoft's Windows software already installed, rival companies have difficulty selling other operating systems, the use of which would prevent most users from exchanging files with friends and colleagues. This fact, more than any other, explains Microsoft's spectacular profit history.

Microsoft does not possess a complete monopoly. Other, smaller firms also sell operating systems. However, if one firm can supply an entire market at a lower average cost than two or more firms can, economies of scale can lead to a complete monopoly. Water utilities provide an example, because it is much cheaper to connect additional customers to an existing water main than to have another firm build a second, competing water main parallel to the first one. The first water utility to serve a market has an enormous advantage, and it is generally not profitable for another to enter. Brand loyalty, geographical constraints, patents, licensing laws, franchises, control of essential materials, property rights, and a need to construct massive manufacturing facilities before entering an industry can all constitute barriers to entry, as we will discuss in more depth in Chapter 8.

**barrier to entry** any force that prevents firms from entering a new market

---

9 A copyright provides no *guarantee* of a profit. Publishers would like to print only books which sell well, but they cannot predict exactly which manuscript will be popular. They stay in business if the losses they experience on some (most?) of their new books are outweighed by the profits they make on their popular titles.

## ECONOMIC RENT VERSUS ECONOMIC PROFIT

Microsoft chairman Bill Gates is one of the two or three wealthiest people on the planet, largely because the problem of compatibility prevents rival suppliers from competing effectively in the many software markets dominated by his company. Yet numerous people have become fabulously rich even in markets with no conspicuous barriers to entry. If market forces push economic profit toward zero, how can that happen?

The answer to this question hinges on the distinction between economic profit and *economic rent*. Most people think of rent as the payment they make to a landlord, but the term economic rent has a different meaning. **Economic rent** is that portion of the payment for an input that is above the lowest price the supplier would accept for that input. Suppose, for example, that the lowest price a landowner would accept for a hectare of land is $100/year. That is, suppose he would be willing to lease it to a farmer as long as he receives an annual payment of at least $100, but for less than that amount he would rather leave it fallow. If the farmer pays him more than his minimum price ($100), the excess is economic rent. For example, if he is paid $1000, the landowner's economic rent from that payment will be $900/year.

Economic profit is like economic rent in that it, too, may be seen as the difference between what someone is paid (the business owner's total revenue) and the lowest amount she would accept for remaining in business (the sum of all her costs, explicit and implicit). But, whereas competition pushes economic profit toward zero, it has no such effect on the economic rent for inputs that cannot be replicated easily. For example, although the lease payments for land may remain substantially above the landowner's lowest acceptable price, year in and year out, new land cannot come onto the market to reduce or eliminate the economic rent through competition. There is, after all, only so much land to be had.

As Example 6.6 illustrates, economic rent can accrue to people as well as land.

**economic rent** that part of the payment for a factor of production that exceeds the owner's reservation price, the price below which the owner would not supply the factor

## EXAMPLE **6.6**

### How much economic rent will a talented chef get?

A community has 100 restaurants, 99 of which employ chefs of normal ability at a salary of $30 000/year, the same as the amount they could earn in other occupations that are equally attractive to them. But the 100th restaurant has an unusually talented chef. Because of her reputation, diners are willing to pay 50 percent more for the meals she cooks than for those prepared by ordinary chefs. Assume owners of the 99 restaurants with ordinary chefs each collect $300 000/year in revenue, which is just enough to pay all costs, ensuring that each restaurant owner earns exactly a normal profit. If the talented chef's opportunities outside the restaurant industry are the same as those of ordinary chefs, how much will she be paid by her employer at equilibrium? How much of her pay will be economic rent? How much economic profit will her employer earn?

Because diners are willing to pay 50 percent more for meals cooked by the talented chef, the owner who hires her will take in total receipts not of $300 000/year but of $450 000. In the long run, if it becomes known that the tastier meals at this restaurant are due to the talents of this particular chef, other restaurants can be expected to try to lure her away with promises of higher pay. If they compete among themselves, the talented chef's pay will be bid up. Restaurant owners can profit from increasing the chef's total pay each year until it is $180 000/year, the sum of the $30 000 that ordinary chefs get and the $150 000 in extra revenues for which she is solely responsible. Since the talented chef's lowest acceptable price is the amount she could earn outside the restaurant industry—by assumption, $30 000/year, the same as for ordinary chefs—her economic rent is $150 000/year. The economic profit of the owner who hires her will be zero in long-run equilibrium.

Since the talented chef's opportunities outside the restaurant industry are no better than an ordinary chef's, why is it necessary to pay the talented chef so much? Suppose her employer were to pay her only $60 000, which they both would consider a generous salary since it is twice what ordinary chefs earn. The employer would then earn an economic profit of $120 000/year, since his annual revenue would be $150 000 more than that of ordinary restaurants, but his costs would be only $30 000 more.

But this economic profit would create an opportunity for the owner of some other restaurant to bid the talented chef away. For example, if the owner of a competing restaurant were to hire the talented chef at a salary of $70 000, the chef would be $10 000/year better off, and the rival owner would earn an economic profit of $110 000/year rather than his current economic profit of zero. Furthermore, if the talented chef is the sole reason that a restaurant earns a positive economic profit, the bidding for that chef will continue as long as any economic profit remains. Some other owner will pay her $80 000, still another $90 000, and so on. Equilibrium will be reached only when the talented chef's salary has been bid up to the point that no further economic profit remains—in Example 6.6, at an annual paycheque of $180 000.

This bidding process assumes, of course, that the reason for the chef's superior performance is that she possesses some personal talent that cannot be copied. If instead it were the result of, say, training at a culinary institute in France, then her privileged position would erode over time as other chefs sought similar training.[10]

## TECHNOLOGICAL CHANGE AND COST-SAVING INNOVATIONS

Until now we have assumed that the production decisions of individual firms have no perceptible impact on the market price. While we analyzed the decisions of these firms, we assumed that technology was fixed. However, all profit-maximizing firms have powerful incentives to develop and introduce cost-saving innovations. If a firm can reduce its cost by $1, then in the short run it can increase its profit. Example 6.7 illustrates the incentive a price-taking firm has to research cost-saving innovations. It also illustrates why a cost-saving innovation is likely to spread to all firms that serve a market, eventually leading to a lower market price for buyers.

### EXAMPLE 6.7

#### How do cost-saving innovations affect economic profit?

Suppose that the total costs of an optimally sized farm, including a normal profit, are $500 000. Suppose further that one farmer realizes that instead of deep plowing every field before planting, he can leave the stubble in the field, till just a narrow furrow, and then save $20 000 in fuel and other costs by planting in the furrow. How will this innovation affect accounting and economic profits? Will these changes persist in the long run?

At first, the reduction in a single farm's costs will have no impact on the market price. The farm with the more efficient tillage practices will thus earn an economic profit of $20 000 (since its total revenue will be the same as before, while total costs are now $20 000 lower). If other farms learn about the new methods, however, they will begin to adopt it, causing their individual supply curves to shift downward (since costs at these farms will drop by $20 000). The shift in these individual supply curves will cause the market supply curve to shift, which in turn will result in a lower market price and a decline in economic profit at the farm where the innovation originated. When all farms have adopted the new, efficient tillage practices, the long-run supply

---

10 Whether the talented chef gets more pay depends entirely on the structure of information. If the chef is to get the economic rent, the chef must be known to be the reason for the restaurant's good meals. If the fame lies with the restaurant, the restaurant will capture the economic rent, as is discussed in Chapter 12.

*curve for the industry will have shifted downward, and each farm will again be earn-*
*ing only a normal profit. At that point, any farm that did not adopt the new methods*
*would suffer an economic loss of $20 000.*

The incentive to develop cost-saving innovations to reap economic profit is one of the most powerful forces on the economic landscape. Competition among price takers will cause the resulting cost savings to be passed along to consumers in the form of lower prices.

If we return to the example of agriculture and wheat farms, we can see that our analysis of competitive price takers explains how city dwellers have benefited from the downward trend in food prices of the last century. Competition causes farm owners to configure their operations to produce at minimum long-run average cost. Over time, technological change has consistently lowered minimum long-run average cost while at the same time causing the operations to become both fewer in number and larger in size. Technological change and long-run agricultural adjustment have given Canadians abundant, high-quality food at low cost. However, the process of adjustment is ongoing and difficult for those who work in the agricultural sector.

In Figure 6.7 we can see, graphically, the effects of long-run adjustment in a wheat market when technological improvement reduces production costs. We assume that the amount of fertile land available to grow wheat is limited, or at least that beyond a certain point any additional lands being used will be less fertile and less productive. As a result, the long-run supply curve for the wheat market is positively sloped; that is, if technology were to remain unchanged, wheat production would be an increasing-cost industry. The curve labelled $LRS_{1955}$ shows the long-run supply of wheat for 1955 using then-current technology. However, technology did change over the subsequent 50 years and resulted in a reduction in the cost of producing wheat and a shift in the long-run supply curve, to $LRS_{2005}$.

The equilibrium price in the market depends on what happens to both demand and supply in the long run, but if demand for wheat had not changed between 1955 and 2005, equilibrium price would have decreased from $P_{1955}$ to $P_{2005}$. This would have been the case because technological improvement increased the supply of wheat during that period. Other things remaining equal, an increase in supply reduces price. Consumers would have benefited from lower prices for bread, pasta, and any other products that use wheat as an intermediate input. Producers in those years had a strong incentive to implement new technology since, if they had tried to use old methods, their higher costs of production would have caused them to incur an economic loss.

---

**FIGURE 6.7**

**The Impact of Improvement in Technology on Long-Run Supply**
Technological improvement causes long-run supply to shift to the right. If demand remains constant in this graph, which represents the market for wheat, the price of wheat will be lower in 2005 than it was in 1955.

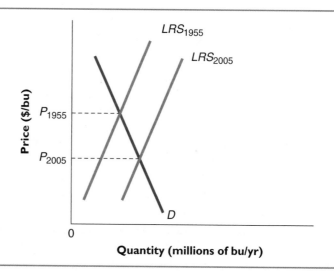

## PROBLEMS

1. Explain why the following statements are true or false. **LO1, LO3**
   a. The economic maxim that when in equilibrium a market provides no economic profits, means that there are never any unexploited opportunities to make economic profit.
   b. Firms in competitive environments make no accounting profit when the market is in long-run equilibrium.
   c. Firms that can introduce cost-saving innovations can make an economic profit in the short run.

2. Explain why new software firms that give away their software products at a short-run economic loss are nonetheless able to sell their stock at positive prices. **LO2**

3. John Jones owns and manages a café in Collegetown. His monthly revenue is $5000. Monthly expenses are shown in the following list: **LO1, LO2**

| Labour | $2000 |
|---|---|
| Food and drink | 500 |
| Electricity | 100 |
| Vehicle lease | 150 |
| Rent | 500 |
| Interest on loan for equipment | 1000 |

   a. Calculate John's monthly accounting profit.
   b. John could earn $1000/month as a recycler of aluminum cans. However, he prefers to run the café. In fact, he would be willing to pay up to $275/month to run the café rather than to recycle. Is the café making an economic profit? Will John stay in the café business? Explain.
   c. Suppose the café's revenues and expenses remain the same, but recyclers' earnings rise to $1100/month. Is the café still making an economic profit? Explain.
   d. Suppose that instead of borrowing $10 000 at a monthly interest rate of 10 percent to buy equipment, John had invested $10 000 of his own money in equipment. How would your answers to parts (a) and (b) change?
   e. If John can earn $1000/month as a recycler and he likes recycling just as well as running the café, how much additional revenue would the café have to collect each month to earn a normal profit?

4. Suppose the city of Vancouver has 200 advertising companies, 199 of which employ designers of normal ability at a salary of $100 000/year. Paying this salary, each of the 199 firms makes a normal profit on $500 000 in revenue. However, the 200th company employs Janus Jacobs, an unusually talented designer. This company collects $1 000 000 in revenues because of Jacobs's talent. **LO4, LO6**
   a. How much will Jacobs earn? What proportion of his annual salary will be economic rent?
   b. Why won't the advertising company for which Jacobs works be able to earn an economic profit?

5. Explain carefully why, in the absence of a patent, a technical innovation invented and pioneered in one tofu factory will cause the supply curve for the entire tofu industry to shift to the right. What will finally halt the rightward shift? **LO4, LO7**

6. The government of the Republic of Self-Reliance has decided to limit imports of machine tools to encourage development of locally made machine tools. To do so, the government offers to sell a small number of machine tool import licences. Operating a machine tool import business costs $30 000, excluding the cost of the import licence. An importer of machine tools can expect to collect total receipts of $50 000/year. If the annual interest rate is 10 percent, for how much will the government be able to auction the import licences? Will the owner of a licence earn an economic profit? **LO6**

7. Unskilled workers in a poor cotton-growing region must choose between working in a factory for $6000/year or being tenant cotton farmers. One farmer can work a 120-hectare farm, which rents for $10 000/year. Such farms yield $20 000 worth of cotton each year. The total nonlabour cost of producing and marketing the cotton is $4000/year. A local politician whose motto is "working people come first" has promised that if he is elected, his administration will fund fertilizer, irrigation, and marketing that will triple cotton yields on tenant farms at no charge to tenant farmers. **LO2, LO3, LO6**
   a. If the market price of cotton was unaffected by this policy and no new jobs were created in the cotton-growing industry, how would the project affect the incomes of tenant farmers in the short run? in the long run?
   b. Who would reap the benefit of the scheme in the long run? How much would they gain each year?

8. You have a friend who is a potter. He holds a permanent patent on an indestructible teacup whose sale generates $30 000/year more revenue than

production costs. If the annual interest rate is 20 percent, what is the market value of his patent? **LO4**

9.  You have an opportunity to buy an apple orchard that produces $125 000/year in accounting profit. To run the orchard, you would have to give up your current job, which pays $50 000/year. If both jobs are equally satisfying, and the annual interest rate is 10 percent, what is the highest price you would be willing to pay for the orchard? **LO1, LO6**

10. Louisa, a renowned chef, owns one of the 1000 spaghetti restaurants in Sicily. Each restaurant serves 100 plates of spaghetti a night at $5/plate. Louisa knows she can develop a new sauce at the same cost as the current sauce, which would be so tasty that all 100 000 spaghetti eaters would buy her spaghetti at $10/plate. There are two problems: developing the new sauce would require some experimental cost, and the other spaghetti producers could figure out the recipe after one day. **LO1, LO7**

   a.   What is the highest experimental cost Louisa would be willing to incur?

   b.   How would your answer change if Louisa could enforce a year-long patent on her new sauce? (Assume that the interest rate is zero.)

## ANSWERS TO IN-CHAPTER EXERCISES

6.1   If the increase in demand is small relative to the increase in supply, price will still fall, though not by as much. The effect on the wheat industry will be the same, though its severity will be reduced. If demand does not change and it is inelastic, total income of all wheat farmers as a group will decrease. Notice that if this case pertains, total income earned by the wheat industry is less in 2005 than in 1955 even though the wheat industry is producing more wheat. **LO2, LO4**

# CHAPTER 7
# Economic Surplus and Exchange

In Canada today, as we decide daily on what to buy and what to sell, we pay close attention to market prices. Markets for consumer goods, financial assets, and labour markets are fundamentally important to our consumption, savings, and employment decisions and, therefore, important for our economic well-being. But what is required for economic life to be organized by market processes? Is this the way economic life *should* be organized? What can we expect markets to do well? What can we expect markets to do poorly? Should some issues be addressed by government regulation? Which issues should be left to the market?

The role that markets can or should play in determining social and economic outcomes has been debated for generations. And although it may be easy to see why a billionaire might be happy with the outcomes that markets produce, it is less obvious why low-income families struggling to pay their bills should think that a market allocation of resources is desirable. Under what conditions might both the rich and the poor agree that market solutions are the best answers to society's problems?

Nobody would voluntarily buy a good or service if she did not think it would improve her well-being—and nobody would voluntarily sell that good or service if he thought the transaction would make him worse off. Hence, if a market transaction is voluntary, then one can at least say that both the buyer and the seller thought it would make them better off, compared to the alternative of not making the transaction. Both the billionaire who buys a new company and the minimum-wage worker who buys a loaf of bread do so for the same reason. Each thinks that the purchase improves his or her own well-being.

## LEARNING OBJECTIVES

When you have completed this chapter, you will be able to:

**LO1** Explain the circumstances under which markets can be expected to maximize total economic surplus.

**LO2** Explain why a market in disequilibrium can offer opportunities for mutually beneficial exchange.

**LO3** Use a graph to represent consumer surplus, producer surplus, and total economic surplus.

**LO4** Calculate consumer surplus, producer surplus, and total economic surplus.

**LO5** Demonstrate how price controls affect total economic surplus.

**LO6** Explain why distribution is important for maximization of economic surplus.

**LO7** Demonstrate the impact of price elasticity of demand and supply on total economic surplus.

**LO8** Explain the difference between maximum economic surplus and a social optimum.

**LO9** Analyze the effect of an excise tax on total economic surplus.

But will these expectations sometimes be disappointed? Under what conditions will individual, self-oriented decisions add up to a social optimum? Is there a cost to society of interfering in the market mechanism and, if so, what is it? Part of the art of economics is learning both the strengths and the limitations of markets. Markets cannot solve all problems, but it is a bad idea to prevent markets from performing those functions for which they are well suited. In this chapter, we will explore why some tasks are best left to the market. But in order to conclude that markets will function in an efficient way, we must first discuss the social conditions that enable economic markets to function at all, and we must discuss the assumptions about the structure of markets themselves. We define and carefully develop the term "economic surplus," and we explore the conditions under which unregulated markets generate the largest possible economic surplus. We will also discuss why attempts to interfere with market outcomes can lead to unintended and undesired consequences.

# 7.1 PRE-CONDITIONS FOR MARKETS

**invisible hand** *Adam Smith's metaphor for his theory stating* that under carefully specified circumstances, the actions of independent, self-interested buyers and sellers will result in the largest possible economic surplus

Adam Smith is justly famous for his book *The Wealth of Nations*, and for his celebrated metaphor of the **invisible hand**. Smith argued that under carefully specified circumstances, an "invisible hand" caused the market system to channel the interests of individual buyers and sellers so as to promote the greatest good for society. Smith's revolutionary idea was that under the correct circumstances, legitimate competition among buyers and sellers would cause self-interest to promote the common good. The carrot of economic profit and the stick of economic loss would cause the production of the largest possible *economic surplus* for the society, as if organized by an *invisible hand*.

But first, what do we mean by economic surplus? Suppose that you are willing to pay a maximum of $750 for a new laptop computer. You go shopping and discover a computer priced at $725 that meets your specifications. If you pay $725 for the computer, you will realize an economic surplus of $25. Why? Your willingness to pay $750 reveals that the value of the computer to you is $750; however, you need pay only $725. Now suppose further that the seller is willing to sell the computer for $690, but no less. If the seller receives $725 for the computer, the seller will realize an economic surplus of $35. Why? His willingness to accept $690 indicates that he regards the opportunity cost of the computer to be $690, which is $35 less than $725. The total economic surplus realized from the transaction will be $60—the sum of the purchaser's surplus plus the seller's surplus. Thus, we define an **economic surplus** as the benefit of an action minus its cost. The purchaser values the benefit of the computer at $750 because that is the maximum she is willing to pay. The seller values the opportunity cost of the computer at $690 because that is the minimum he will accept. The difference between the purchaser's maximum and the seller's minimum is the economic surplus that can be derived from the transaction. Notice, too, that this transaction is *mutually beneficial* because both the buyer and seller realize a surplus.

**economic surplus** the benefit of an action minus its cost

But why should we expect a market system to provide the largest possible economic surplus for society as a whole, as if led by an invisible hand? A skeptical student might well ask, what are the correct circumstances? What is legitimate competition? Modern scholars who study Smith's work are struck by the incisiveness and subtlety he brings to these questions, and a few lines (or pages) cannot do justice to his discussion. For Smith, the "right" circumstances include competition among a large number of small participants in markets, none of whom have any power to influence market price. But this is far from sufficient to harmonize unbridled pursuit of self-interest with the common good. In his earlier book, *The Theory of Moral Sentiments*, Smith discusses the origin of the social institutions that play a central role in aligning self-interest with the common good. In Smith's view, a commercial society cannot function well without institutions of justice that protect lives, provide security of person and property, and uphold the rights that arise from contracts freely made with others. "Justice," says Smith, "is the main pillar that upholds the whole edifice [of society]." Remove justice and "the immense fabric of human society . . . must in a moment crumble into atoms."[1]

Why did Smith think justice is so important? If firms compete with each other to supply better quality at lower prices, consumers benefit from the lower prices and higher

---

1　Adam Smith, *The Theory of Moral Sentiments*, (1759), in *The Glasgow Edition of the Works and Correspondence of Adam Smith Volume 1*, edited by D.D. Raphael and A.L. MacFie, (Oxford: Clarendon Press, 1976), pp. 84, 86.

quality. But there would be no benefit for consumers if an unscrupulous firm decided to firebomb their competitors' factories or assassinate their competitors' sales staff. These sorts of strategies would certainly eliminate the competition more quickly (and might require less work) than making a better product at a lower price but, says Smith, a society that permits this kind of competitive strategy cannot become a commercial state. To take a less extreme case, suppose contracts could be broken without consequence. Mutually beneficial exchange would not occur because no one could be confident that, once made, a bargain would be kept. If there is a danger that delivery of goods might be met with arbitrary withholding of payment, the incentive to produce goods to be offered in exchange disappears. Under such circumstances, it would be very difficult, if not impossible, for a society to produce an economic surplus. Societies, therefore, need laws (and courts to enforce them) to ensure competition takes legitimate forms. A society that cannot provide a regular administration of justice cannot become a successful commercial state.[2]

A well-designed framework of laws is, therefore, an essential pre-condition for a successful market economy, but a market economy could not work effectively if every firm had to go to court to enforce all its transactions. Successful market economies also depend on generalized norms of honest dealing to ensure that commercial disputes are the exception, rather than the rule. Those norms are really only possible if there is a widespread acceptance of a society's economic and social outcomes as being fair and equitable. Partly for this reason, economic analysis has always stressed both *equity* and the *size of total economic surplus* as crucial criteria when weighing policy choices, a theme we will return to later in this chapter.

Assuming that the necessary framework of laws and norms is in place, what type of market structure will allow it to function *efficiently* in the limited sense that it will produce the largest possible total surplus? Our analysis of production and cost in Chapter 5 assumed that a firm's primary goal is to maximize profits. In both Chapters 5 and 6, we just assumed that all firms are price takers; that is, they can sell whatever they decide to produce at a given or fixed price, and that this price will exactly equal marginal revenue. In those discussions, we made only the minimum assumptions necessary to build the case for the existence of short-run and long-run market equilibria. Now, however, we wish to justify the assumption of price taking behaviour.

The most important reason for price-taking behavior by firms is *perfect competition*. Modern economists define **perfectly competitive markets** as markets in which each individual firm has no influence over the market price of the products it sells. Any single firm, being just one of many sellers of the product, cannot hope to charge more than its rivals and has no motive to charge less. Because of their inability to influence market price, **perfectly competitive firms** are **price takers**.[3]

Four conditions are required to produce a perfectly competitive market:

1. All firms sell the same standardized product. This condition implies that buyers are willing to switch sellers if it allows them to buy at a better price.
2. The market has many buyers and sellers, and each buys or sells only a small fraction of the total quantity exchanged. This implies that individual buyers and sellers are price takers, regarding the market price of the product as fixed and beyond their control.
3. Productive resources are mobile; that is, both buyers and sellers are able to move their resources freely between markets in pursuit of business opportunities.
4. Buyers and sellers are well informed. They know the market price and quality of the standardized product.

**perfectly competitive market** a market in which no individual supplier has significant influence on the market price of the product

**price taker** a firm that has no influence over the price at which it sells its product

---

2  Smith, *The Wealth of Nations*, (1776) (New York, 1965), Book IV, Chapter IX; Book V, Chapter III, pp. 651, 862.
3  Perfectly competitive markets are the most important example of a situation in which all firms are price takers, but there are others. As we discussed in Chapter 6, if there is a sole buyer in the market, perhaps a marketing board, that sets the price and will buy everything that is produced at the stated price, each producer is a price taker even though the market as a whole is not perfectly competitive.

Economists know perfectly well that many real world markets do not fit this model. For example, because Microsoft's share of the market for operating systems for desktop computers exceeds 80 percent, the market is far from being perfectly competitive. Microsoft has significant control over the prices it charges. It is not a price taker. If Microsoft were to raise the price of the latest edition of its Windows operating system by, say, 20 percent, some consumers might switch to Macintosh or Linux, and others might postpone their next upgrade; but many, perhaps even most, would continue with their plans to buy.

By now you may be asking, why study perfect competition? Why not study markets in which buyers and sellers can influence the price of their product? Although many markets may not be perfectly competitive, there are three good reasons for studying perfect competition:

1. Some markets (e.g., foreign exchange, many agricultural products) are closer to perfect competition than to other market types.
2. It is easier to first analyze perfect competition and then proceed to other market types than it is to do the reverse.
3. When individuals make mutually beneficial transactions in a perfectly competitive market, their self-interested behaviour is harmonized with the common good. Therefore, perfect competition provides a benchmark against which the outcomes of other market types can be compared.

For an example that approximates perfect competition, consider how well the market faced by a wheat farmer in Manitoba meets the criteria:

1. The different grades of wheat are highly standardized with very specific criteria for each.
2. Each farmer's crop is only a fraction of Canadian and world wheat production. Even when the Canadian Wheat Board acted for many years as sole sales agent for Canadian wheat exports, it had no control of world wheat market prices.
3. Some farmers can choose to produce other crops even if they are unwilling to leave farming, which provides a degree of mobility of resources.
4. All buyers and sellers can be well informed because the Internet provides access to information about prices and grades of wheat as published by the Canadian Wheat Board and others.

www.cwb.ca
Canadian Wheat Board

Although the market faced by a wheat farmer in Manitoba does not match all four conditions to the letter, it comes close. The farmer in Manitoba, like other wheat farmers, cannot obtain a price for wheat that is higher than the going price, and has no reason to accept a lower price. All farmers are price takers and must take the price of wheat as given.

## THE DEMAND CURVE FACING A PERFECTLY COMPETITIVE FIRM

From the perspective of an individual firm in a perfectly competitive market, what does the demand curve for its product look like? When the firm produces only a very small part of industry output and can sell as much or as little as it wants at the prevailing market price, the demand curve facing the firm is perfectly elastic at the market price. Figure 7.1(a) shows the market demand and supply curves intersecting to determine a market price of $P_0$. Figure 7.1(b) shows that the product demand curve $D_i$ as faced by any individual firm in this market is a horizontal line at the market price level $P_0$.

Since a perfectly competitive firm has no control over the market price of its product, it must accept the price established in the industry by the intersection of the industry supply and demand curves. The perfectly competitive firm has only one choice to make—it chooses the output level that enables it to make as much profit as it can.

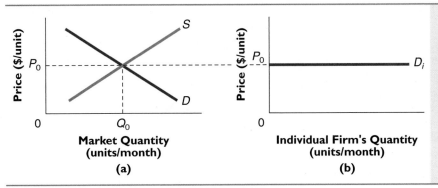

**FIGURE 7.1**

**The Demand Curve Facing a Perfectly Competitive Firm**

Panel (a): The market demand and supply curves intersect to determine the market price of the product. Panel (b): The individual firm's demand curve ($D_i$) is a horizontal line at the market price.

## 7.2 MARKET EQUILIBRIUM AND MUTUALLY BENEFICIAL EXCHANGE

In a perfectly competitive market, each seller is a price taker facing a horizontal demand curve at the existing equilibrium price, and each buyer is also a price taker facing a horizontal supply curve at the existing equilibrium price. We described in Chapter 3 how a market composed of price takers reaches equilibrium where both the quantity that buyers are willing and able to purchase and the quantity that sellers are willing and able to supply are equal at the existing market price. What happens if this is not the case? We will now see that if markets are perfectly competitive and price and quantity take anything other than their equilibrium values, it is always possible to identify an unrealized transaction that would make both buyer and seller better off.

### EXAMPLE 7.1

**How does holding the price of milk below its equilibrium level prevent mutually beneficial exchange?**

Suppose the supply and demand curves for milk are as shown in Figure 7.2, and the current price of milk is $1/litre. Describe an unrealized transaction that would benefit both buyer and seller.

At a price of $1, sellers offer only 2000 litres of milk per day. At that quantity, buyers value an extra litre of milk at $2 (the price on the demand curve that corresponds to 2000 litres/day, which represents what buyers are willing to pay for an additional litre). We also know that the cost of producing an extra litre of milk is only $1 (the price that corresponds to 2000 litres/day on the supply curve, which equals marginal cost).

Furthermore, a price of $1/litre leads to excess demand of 2000 litres/day, which means that many potential buyers cannot buy as much milk as they want at the going price. Now suppose a supplier sells an extra litre of milk to the most eager of these

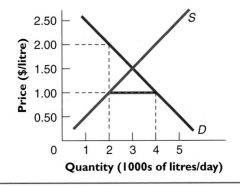

**FIGURE 7.2**

**A Market in Which Price is Below the Equilibrium Level**

In this market, milk is currently selling for $1/litre, $0.50 below the equilibrium price of $1.50/litre.

**FIGURE 7.3**

**How Excess Demand Creates an Opportunity for a Surplus-Enhancing Transaction**

At a market price of $1/litre, the most intense potential buyer is willing to pay $2 for an additional litre, which a seller can produce at a cost of only $1. If this buyer pays the seller $1.25 for the extra litre, the potential buyer gains an economic surplus of $0.75 and the seller gains an economic surplus of $0.25.

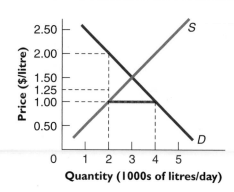

potential buyers for $1.25, as in Figure 7.3. Since the extra litre costs only $1 to produce, the seller is $0.25 better off than before. And since the most eager potential buyer values the extra litre at $2, that buyer is $0.75 better off than before. In sum, the transaction creates an extra $1 of economic surplus.

If the price of milk rises to $1.25/litre for all purchasers, those who previously purchased 2000 litres of milk for $1/litre will be worse off. However, the sellers of those 2000 litres will be better off by the same monetary amount by which the purchasers are worse off. Therefore, it is potentially possible for the sellers to exactly compensate the purchasers for their loss. In other words, if compensating payments can be made to those who lose when the price of milk rises, it is possible for additional buyers and additional sellers to be better off while no one is worse off. Thus, milk selling for only $1/litre does not provide the largest possible economic surplus because it prevents mutually beneficial exchange. Indeed, if milk sells for *any* price below $1.50/litre (the market equilibrium price), we can design a transaction in which each participant's benefit exceeds his or her cost, which means that selling milk for any price less than $1.50/litre cannot produce the largest possible economic surplus.

**EXERCISE 7.1**

**In Example 7.1, suppose that milk initially sells for $0.50/litre. Describe a transaction that will create additional economic surplus for both buyer and seller without causing harm to anyone else.**

What is more, it is also possible to describe a transaction that will create additional surplus for both buyer and seller whenever the price lies above the market equilibrium level. Suppose, for example, that the current price is $2/litre in the milk market shown in Figure 7.3. At that price, we have excess supply of 2000 litres per day (see Figure 7.4). Suppose the most dissatisfied producer sells a litre of milk for $1.75 to the buyer who values it most highly. This buyer, who would have been willing to pay $2, will be $0.25 better off than before. Likewise the producer, who would have been willing to sell milk for as little as $1/litre (the marginal cost of production at 2000 litres/day), will be $0.75 better off than before. As when the price was $1/litre, the new transaction creates $1 of additional economic surplus without harming any other buyer or seller. Since we could design a similar surplus-enhancing transaction at any price above the equilibrium level, selling milk for more than $1.50/litre cannot produce the largest possible total surplus.

If exchange is voluntary, neither the buyer nor the seller can be compelled to purchase or sell more than is optimal for them given the going price. When the market price is different from the equilibrium price, there is a state of disequilibrium, and typically "the short side of the market rules." That is, the quantity actually exchanged is less than the equilibrium quantity.

Prices read from the supply and demand curves thus make it clear why opportunities for additional mutually beneficial exchanges cease only if the equilibrium price pertains

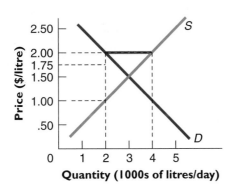

**FIGURE 7.4**

**How Excess Supply Creates an Opportunity for a Surplus-Enhancing Transaction**

At a market price of $2/litre, buyers are only willing to purchase 2,000 litres. At that quantity of total production, sellers can produce an additional litre of milk at a cost of only $1, which is $1 less than the marginal buyer would be willing to pay for it. If the buyer pays the seller $1.75 for that extra litre, the buyer gains an economic surplus of $0.25 and the seller gains an economic surplus of $0.75.

in a market. When the price is either higher or lower than the equilibrium price, the quantity exchanged in the market will always be lower than the equilibrium quantity. If the price is below equilibrium, the quantity sold will be the amount that sellers offer. If the price is above equilibrium, the quantity sold will be the amount that buyers wish to buy. In either case, the price on the demand curve at the quantity exchanged, which is the value of an extra unit to buyers, must be larger than the seller's reservation price on the supply curve, which is the marginal cost of producing that unit.

Indeed, the market equilibrium price is the *only* price at which buyers and sellers cannot design a new surplus-enhancing transaction. In this *specific, limited sense*, market transactions maximize total economic surplus and can be said to allocate goods and services efficiently.

Remember, however, that to get this result we assumed markets are perfectly competitive. In addition, the individual marginal cost curves that add up to the market supply curve must include all relevant costs of producing the product, and the individual demand curves that make up the market demand curve must capture all the relevant benefits of buying additional units of the product. In later chapters, we will take up the implications of relaxing these assumptions. For now, we will confine our attention to perfectly competitive markets whose demand and supply curves capture all relevant benefits and costs.

**RECAP**

**MARKET EQUILIBRIUM AND MUTUALLY BENEFICIAL EXCHANGE**

When a perfectly competitive market is not in equilibrium, an unrealized transaction can always be found from which both buyer and seller would benefit. A perfectly competitive market in equilibrium is efficient in the sense that total economic surplus is maximized.

# 7.3 ECONOMIC SURPLUS

Earlier in this chapter, we encountered the concept of economic surplus, which in a buyer's case is the difference between the most she would have been willing to pay for a product and the amount she actually pays for it. The same concept applies to sellers of goods and services, for whom economic surplus is the difference between what they are paid for the goods they sell and the smallest amount they would have been willing to

**total economic surplus** the sum of all the individual economic surpluses gained by buyers and sellers who participate in the market

accept. In any given market, **total economic surplus** is the sum of all economic surpluses attributable to participation in that market by buyers and sellers. Stated another way, it is a measure of the total amount by which buyers and sellers benefit from their participation in the market. A perfectly competitive market maximizes its economic surplus when it reaches equilibrium price and quantity, which is one reason for removing obstacles that could prevent a perfectly competitive market from reaching equilibrium.

## CALCULATING ECONOMIC SURPLUS

Consider a hypothetical market for a service with 11 potential buyers and 11 potential sellers. Suppose that the buyers and sellers live in a neighbourhood of 11 houses, each with a similar driveway. As morning dawns, the neighbourhood wakens to a common Canadian scene. During the night, a heavy blanket of snow has covered the ground. All the driveways are covered to the same depth. A teenager lives in each household and, for the right price, has the time to shovel one driveway; it does not matter which one. After considering her opportunity costs, Anna is willing to shovel a driveway for no less than $1; Beth, however, requires at least $2, Celine wants at least $3, and so on for all 11 teenagers. Each teenager wants $1 more than the previous one to shovel a driveway. When the 11 teenagers are arranged from the lowest to the highest minimum price each will accept for shovelling a driveway, supply forms the staircase-shaped supply curve shown in Figure 7.5. Each teenager's minimum price is a **supplier's reservation price**, or the lowest price a supplier will accept in return for providing a service.

**supplier's (or seller's) reservation price** the lowest price a supplier will accept in return for providing a good or service

All heads of household will pay to have their driveways shovelled, provided an acceptable price is charged for shovelling. Angela's reservation price (the maximum price she is willing to pay) for having her driveway cleared is $11, Bernard's reservation price is $10, Claude's is $9, and so on for all heads of households. Each head is willing to pay $1 less than the previous one. Each head's maximum price is a **demander's reservation price**. When the potential purchasers are arranged from highest to lowest reservation price, demand forms the staircase-shaped demand curve in Figure 7.5. The supply and demand curves of Figure 7.5 can be thought of as discrete counterparts of the traditional continuous supply and demand curves.

**demander's (or buyer's) reservation price** the highest price a demander will offer in order to obtain a good or service

Let us assume that everyone has full information about the price paid for shovelling a driveway and that, in the end, every homeowner pays the same price for having a driveway cleared. The equilibrium price in Figure 7.5 is $6/driveway, and the equilibrium quantity is six driveways. (This means that five driveways are not shovelled and five teenagers do not shovel.) Shovelling the sixth driveway produces no surplus for either the buyer or the seller because both have the same reservation price. But the first five driveways yielded surpluses for both buyers and sellers. Angela, the owner of the first driveway, for example, would have been willing to pay as much as $11 to have it shovelled, but since the market price was only $6, she realized a surplus of $5. Likewise, Anna, the teenager who shovelled the first driveway, would have been willing to clear it for as little as $1, so she also received a surplus of $5. Bernard, owner of the second driveway, would have been willing to pay as much as $10 to have it shovelled, and Beth, who cleared the driveway, was willing to shovel for $2. Thus, both Bernard and Beth received a surplus of $4. Similarly, the owners of the third, fourth, and fifth driveways receive surpluses of $3, $2, and $1, respectively, and so do the three teenagers who clear those driveways.

**consumer surplus** the total economic gain of the buyers of a product, as measured by the cumulative difference between their respective reservation prices and the price they actually paid

If we add all the buyers' surpluses, we get a total of $15 of buyers' surplus for each storm. The total economic gain of the buyers of a product as measured by the cumulative difference between their respective reservation prices and the price they actually paid is often referred to as **consumer surplus**. Similarly, the sum of the corresponding surpluses for sellers is also $15 per storm. The total economic gain of the sellers of a product as measured by the cumulative difference between the price received and their respective reservation prices is often referred to as **producer surplus**. Although both consumer surplus and producer surplus are $15 here, this is just an accident of this example. The surplus

**producer surplus** the total economic gain of the sellers of a product, as measured by the cumulative difference between the price received and their respective reservation prices

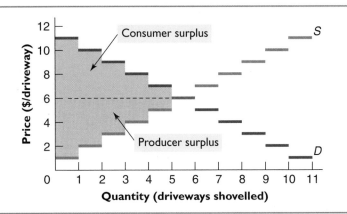

**FIGURE 7.5**
**Consumer and Producer Surplus**
Consumer surplus (blue area) is the cumulative difference between the most that buyers are willing to pay for each unit and the price they actually pay. Producer surplus (green area) is the cumulative difference between the price at which producers sell each unit and the smallest amounts they would be willing to accept.

received by buyers and sellers will generally not be the same dollar value. But it is always true that the total economic surplus for a market is the sum of consumer surplus and producer surplus, in this case $30 per storm, which corresponds to the combined blue and green areas in Figure 7.5.

Now suppose we want to measure total economic surplus in a market with conventional straight-line supply and demand curves. As Example 7.2 illustrates, this task is a simple extension of the method used for discrete supply and demand curves.

## EXAMPLE **7.2**

### How much do buyers and sellers benefit from their participation in the market for milk?

Consider the market for milk, whose demand and supply curves are shown in Figure 7.6, The equilibrium price is $2/litre and equilibrium quantity is 4000 litres/day. How much total economic surplus do the participants in this market reap?

In Figure 7.6, note first that, the last unit exchanged generates no surplus at all, either for buyers or sellers. Note also that for all milk sold up to 4000 litres/day, buyers receive consumer surplus and sellers receive producer surplus. For sellers, the surplus is the cumulative difference between market price and marginal cost. For buyers, the surplus is the cumulative difference between the most they would be willing to pay for milk (as measured on the demand curve) and the price they actually pay.

Because we have made the simplifying assumption of straight-line demand and supply curves, we can use geometry to calculate total consumer surplus received by buyers in the milk market, which is equal to the area of the blue triangle between the demand curve and the market price in Figure 7.6. This is a right triangle whose

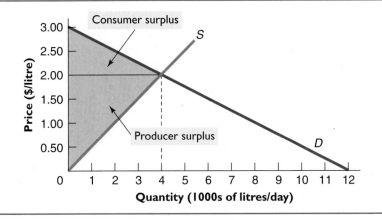

**FIGURE 7.6**
**Total Economic Surplus in the Market for Milk**
For the supply and demand curves shown, the equilibrium price of milk is $2/litre and the equilibrium quantity is 4000 litres/day. Consumer surplus is the area of the blue triangle ($2000/day). Producer surplus is the area of the green triangle ($4000/day). Total economic surplus is the sum of the two, or $6000/day.

vertical arm is $h$ = \$1/litre and whose horizontal arm is $b$ = 4000 litres/day. And since the area of any triangle is equal to $(\frac{1}{2})bh$, consumer surplus in this market is equal to

$$(\tfrac{1}{2})(4000 \text{ litres/day})(\$1/\text{litre}) = \$2000/\text{day}.$$

Likewise, total producer surplus is the area of the green triangle between the supply curve and the market price. The height of this triangle is $h$ = \$2/litre and the base is $b$ = 4000 litres/day, so producer surplus is equal to

$$(\tfrac{1}{2})(4000 \text{ litres/day})(\$2/\text{litre}) = \$4000/\text{day}.$$

The total economic surplus from this milk market is the sum of consumer and producer surplus, or \$6000/day.[4]

Another way of thinking about surplus is to ask, what is the highest amount consumers and producers would pay, in the aggregate, for the right to continue participating in the milk market? For buyers, the answer is \$2000/day, since that is the amount by which their combined benefits exceed their combined costs. Sellers would pay up to \$4000/day, since that is the amount by which their combined benefits exceed their combined reservation prices. Together, then, buyers and sellers would be willing to pay up to \$6000/day for the right to continue participating in this market.

---

At any price other than the equilibrium price, the total economic surplus produced by a perfectly competitive market will be less than it would be at the equilibrium price. Stated another way, the equilibrium price and quantity serve to maximize the total economic surplus created by a market.

This feature of market equilibrium is hugely important and attractive, but it is not the only thing we might care about. For example, the market for milk may be in equilibrium at a price of \$2/litre, yet this could be an equilibrium in which poor families are unable to afford milk for their children while rich families waste much of what they buy.

In our milk market example, we have assumed that the attributes of buyers and sellers are predetermined; that is, the tastes of buyers and the distribution of wealth among individuals have already been established. Supply and demand then generate a particular set of prices and quantities as outcomes in markets, and the specific market outcomes we observe depend on buyers' tastes and the underlying distribution of wealth. If either tastes or the distribution of wealth were to change, market outcomes typically would also change. Poor families may not be able to afford to buy milk at equilibrium prices, but it is because they are poor, not because milk is being sold in the market. The prices and quantities that we observe as equilibrium outcomes in markets are *conditional* on tastes and the distribution of wealth.

As Chapter 10 will discuss in more detail, we are also assuming that the producer pays all the costs of production (including any environmental impacts). Also, as will be discussed in Chapter 11, an important part of our assumption of "perfect competition" is the assumption of "perfect information." The conditions under which a market process can be expected to maximize total economic surplus are thus quite specific. But even if these conditions are satisfied and total surplus is maximized, each person's share of the surplus will depend on the initial distribution of wealth in the economy. If we are concerned about inequality in market outcomes, we should not blame the market process for inequalities in outcomes, which just reflect initial inequalities in the distribution of wealth or income.[5]

---

4  Some economists would argue that "producer surplus" can be defined as economic rent (any payment in excess of the owner's opportunity cost). An owner of a productive resource with a perfectly elastic supply curve cannot receive either economic rent or a producer's surplus.

5  This section has referred at various points to the pre-market distribution of assets, wealth, and income, because these are the terms used interchangeably in common parlance to capture the economic theorist's concept of pre-market "endowments." (Strictly speaking, a person's wealth is equal to their assets minus their liabilities, and a person's income from wealth depends on both the amount of wealth and its rate of return.) In the text, we neglect these finer distinctions, because the key idea is the distribution of whatever individuals own before they consider their options for market exchanges.

The claim that equilibrium in the market for milk maximizes total surplus means simply that, *taking people's wealth and tastes as given,* the resulting allocation of milk cannot be altered to help some people without at the same time harming others. Maximizing total surplus is important because it enhances our ability to achieve other goals. Whenever a perfectly competitive market is out of equilibrium, it is always possible to generate additional economic surplus. A larger economic surplus means that, at least potentially, it is possible to make at least some people better off without making anyone worse off.

---

**RECAP ↑**

### ECONOMIC SURPLUS

The economic surplus generated by a market is the total dollar amount by which buyers and sellers benefit from their participation in that market. It is the sum of consumer surplus and producer surplus. Consumer surplus is the cumulative difference between what buyers would have been willing to pay for the product and the price they actually do pay. Graphically, it is the area between the demand curve and the market price. Producer surplus is the cumulative difference between the market price and the reservation prices at which producers would have been willing to make their sales. Graphically, it is the area between market price and the supply curve.

Total economic surplus in a perfectly competitive market is maximized when exchange occurs at the equilibrium price. But this does not mean the same as "social optimum." All markets can be in equilibrium, yet some people may lack sufficient income to buy even basic goods and services. However, when economic surplus is maximized, it is possible to pursue other goals more fully.

---

## 7.4 THE COST OF PREVENTING PRICE ADJUSTMENTS

### PRICE CEILINGS

In 1998, the average price of crude petroleum was about US$12/bbl, but two years later the average had more than doubled ($27/bbl). For the next four years, the price was fairly stable, but it rose sharply to $60/bbl in 2006 and then soared to over $140/bbl at one point in 2008 before declining and fluctuating in the $70 to $80 range during 2009 and 2010, and then bumping back up to over $110 in 2011.[6]

In some respects, living through the oil price fluctuations of the first decade of the twenty-first century was like watching an old movie. In the mid-1970s, the price of oil quadrupled. A second shock occurred in the aftermath of the 1979 Iranian Revolution when the price of oil increased by more than 250 percent. With these two shocks, the price of oil rose from about US$2/bbl in mid-1973 to US$30/bbl in 1980.

But back then, the response of government was very different from today. Back then, the Canadian government responded by freezing the price of oil and then allowing it to rise toward the world price at a controlled rate. As a result, the price of oil in Canada in 1980 was about half the world price. Keeping the price of oil below the equilibrium price is an example of a **price ceiling**—a maximum allowable price, specified by law or regulation—which Example 7.3 considers.

**price ceiling** a maximum allowable price, specified by law or regulation

---

6  For current oil prices, see http://www.bloomberg.com/energy/.

## EXAMPLE **7.3**

### How much is an economic surplus reduced by price controls?

Suppose the demand and supply curves for oil are as shown in Figure 7.7, in which the equilibrium price is $14/bbl. These prices are close to those experienced after the oil shock of the mid-1970s. And suppose that legislators pass a law setting the maximum price at $10/bbl. How much lost economic surplus does this policy cost society?

First, let's calculate the surplus without price controls. If this market is not regulated, 3000 bbl/day will be sold at a price of $14/bbl. In Figure 7.7, the economic surplus received by buyers is the area of the blue triangle. Since the height of this triangle is $6/bbl and its base is 3000 bbl/day, its area is equal to (½)(3000 bbls/day) ($6/bbl) = $9000/day. The economic surplus received by producers is the area of the green triangle. Since this triangle also has an area of $9000/day, total economic surplus in this market will be $18 000/day.

**FIGURE 7.7**

**Economic Surplus in an Unregulated Market for Oil**

For the supply and demand curves shown, the equilibrium price of oil is $14/bbl, and the equilibrium quantity is 3000 bbl/day. Consumer surplus is the area of the blue triangle ($9000/day). Producer surplus is the area of the green triangle (also $9000/day).

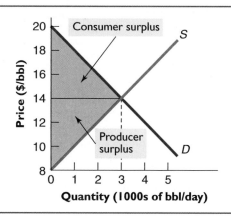

**FIGURE 7.8**

**The Economic Surplus Lost by Price Controls**

By limiting output in the oil market to 1000 bbl/day, price controls cause a loss in economic surplus of $8000/day (area of the lined triangle).

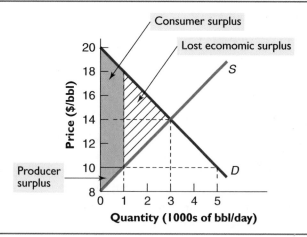

If the price of oil is kept at $10/bbl, only 1000 bbl/day will be sold, and the total economic surplus will be reduced by the area of the lined triangle in Figure 7.8. Since the height of this triangle is $8/bbl and its base is 2000 bbl/day, its area is (½) (2000 bbl/day)($8/bbl) = $8000/day. Producer surplus falls from $9000/day in the unregulated market to the area of the green triangle, or (½)(1000 bbl/day)($2/bbl) = $1000/day, which is a loss of $8000/day. Note that consumer surplus under controls is the area of the blue figure, which is again $9000/day. (*Hint:* To compute this area, first split the figure into a rectangle and a triangle.) By preventing the oil market from reaching equilibrium, price controls in this particular case reduce total surplus by $8000 per day.

Defenders of price controls might respond that those who managed to buy some oil at the lower price received welcome budget relief. While this is true, the same objective could be accomplished in a much less costly way. Income could be transferred to those who pay more for oil in order to compensate them for their loss. In principle, *if the alternative is to impose price controls that would be even more costly than the income transfers,* oil producers ought to be willing to pay some amount in additional taxes to escape the burden of controls. After all, the price ceiling as implemented ends up costing oil sellers $8000 each day in lost economic surplus.

If the price ceiling is removed, all those who previously purchased oil at $10/bbl will be worse off. But if producer surplus will rise by more than enough to offset any reduction in consumer surplus, then transferring some of the greater producer surplus to consumers can make some (or all) people better off without making anyone worse off.

This point is so important that we will state it another way. Think of economic surplus as a pie to be divided among the market participants. If the price of oil is limited to no more than $10/bbl, total economic surplus is $10 000/day. If the price of oil is allowed to rise to its equilibrium price, total economic surplus rises to $18 000/day. *In effect, removal of the price ceiling creates a larger pie. With a larger pie, it is possible for every participant to have a larger piece of pie.* Price controls in a perfectly competitive market prevent buyers and sellers from making mutually advantageous transactions by preventing transactions that pass the cost–benefit test.

THE COST-BENEFIT
OF CONTROLS

But this raises another interesting question: why would price ceilings ever be implemented? Everything we have said to this point about price controls has been known for many decades. Any program that can make some people better off without making anyone else worse off would be sure to get votes, so why would any political leader worth the name implement price controls? Nevertheless, the National Energy Program adopted by the Canadian government in 1980 provided for price controls for the next 10 years.

Why in 1980 did the Canadian government find price controls on oil to be politically viable? Removal of a price ceiling increases producer surplus and has the potential to make some people better off, while leaving nobody worse off. However, more than 75 percent of Canada's oil industry was then owned by foreign companies, most of them American. Some Canadians believed that an increased producer surplus just would have flowed out of the country into the hands of foreign owners. If this happened, the producer surplus generated by higher prices would have been unavailable to compensate Canadians who would have been paying higher energy prices. If Canadian consumers were worse off because of higher energy prices and the primary beneficiaries of the higher prices for our resources were foreign investors, many Canadians would object, and the transfers that might have compensated the losers from higher energy prices would have been impossible to make.

Because Alberta sells a large amount of oil to the U.S., it opposed any controls that held the price of oil below the world price, and a struggle between Ottawa and Edmonton over oil prices ensued. In an economic sense, the issue became moot when the price of oil on world markets declined dramatically in 1985. (In a political sense, the memory of the National Energy Program (NEP) of the 1980s remains important, to the present day, in Alberta.) But the basic issue remains important—only if compensating transfers are actually made will it be true that everyone is made equally well off or better off in market equilibrium. If compensating transfers are, for some reason, not feasible, the distribution of gains and losses becomes a crucial dimension of policy choices.

## WHY DISTRIBUTION IS IMPORTANT FOR SURPLUS MAXIMIZATION

Even if removal of price controls would increase total economic surplus, a majority of voters might not be in favour. If some people have reason to believe that economic surplus might increase but none of that increase will benefit them, they have good reason to prefer price controls. Even if the total pie is bigger without controls, if they believe that they will have an absolutely smaller piece of it, they have reason to vote for price controls. *The success of any policy designed to make a society's economic pie as large as possible depends on how the pie is distributed among members of the society.* If a policy makes the total pie larger but provides absolutely smaller pieces to some people, the policy will tend to attract opposition from those who lose out.

Furthermore, there is a world of difference between *actual* and *potential* compensation. For a policy to be efficient in the special sense that all members of society actually benefit from greater total surplus, it must include an appropriate system for distributing the economic surplus. It may be costly to design and administer a system that shares the benefits of greater economic surplus. Nevertheless, if such a system is not available, those who lose out personally have no reason to support surplus-maximizing policies. When incentives to help create a surplus are weak or absent, it is much more difficult for a society to create a surplus.

## ELASTICITY AND THE AMOUNT OF TOTAL ECONOMIC SURPLUS

Thus far, we have not considered the impact that the price elasticity of supply or demand can have on the size of total economic surplus. We have focused on the general theoretical principle that price controls will reduce economic surplus without discussing the empirical question, *how much* does economic surplus change? As we will see by comparing two rental markets, one of which has greater elasticity of supply than does the other, *elasticity of supply* can make a big difference to the impacts of price controls.

Consider a city like Winnipeg, where new apartments can be constructed either by making buildings taller or by extending new construction further out in the suburbs. Compare this to another city, like Vancouver, hemmed in on all sides by either mountains or the sea. With very few vacant lots, new apartments can be constructed only by making buildings taller. Given these different situations, the long-run supply of apartments will be more elastic in Winnipeg than in Vancouver. To keep things simple, we will assume that both cities have the same demand curve for apartments, and we will focus on the market for similar, one-bedroom apartments.

Suppose the supply and demand curves for rental housing in Winnipeg are as shown in panel (a) of Figure 7.9. Equilibrium rent in this market is $200/month, and the equilibrium quantity is 4000 apartments/month. The area of the blue triangle in panel (a) represents renters' consumer surplus:

$$\text{consumer surplus} = (\tfrac{1}{2})bh = (\tfrac{1}{2})(4000 \text{ apts/month})(\$800/\text{apt})$$

$$= \$1\,600\,000/\text{month}.$$

Landlords' producer surplus is represented by the green triangle in panel (a), Figure 7.9:

$$\text{producer surplus} = (\tfrac{1}{2})bh = (\tfrac{1}{2})(4000 \text{ apts/month})(\$200/\text{apt})$$

$$= \$400\,000/\text{month}.$$

Total economic surplus in the Winnipeg market is the sum of consumer and producer surpluses, which is $2 000 000/month.

Now consider panel (b) of Figure 7.9, which portrays the market in Vancouver. Suppose that the demand curve, equilibrium price, and equilibrium quantity of apartments are identical, as in panels (a) and (b). Therefore, consumer surplus in Vancouver is the same as in Winnipeg, $1 600 000/month. However, the supply curve for apartments in Vancouver is less elastic than in Winnipeg.[7] Producer surplus in Vancouver as shown by

---

7   To be precise, we should say that supply is less elastic in Vancouver than in Winnipeg, *over the relevant range of prices* ($100 to $200 in this example).

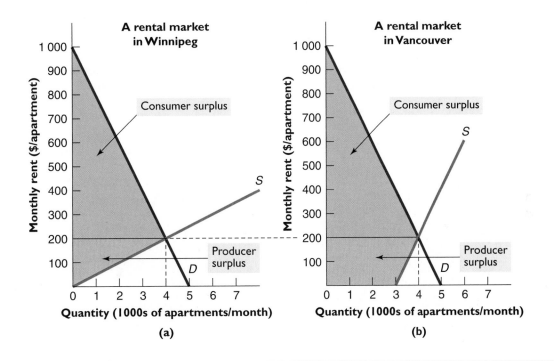

**FIGURE 7.9**
**Economic Surplus in Two Unregulated Housing Markets**
For the supply and demand curves shown in panel (a) (Winnipeg), consumer surplus is $1 600 000/month (blue triangle area) and producer surplus is $400 000/month (green triangle area). Total economic surplus in Winnipeg's rental market is $2 000 000/month. For panel (b) (Vancouver), consumer surplus also is $1 600 000/month, but producer surplus (green figure area) is $700 000/month. Total economic surplus in Vancouver's rental market is $2 300 000/month. Because the two markets are identical except for elasticity of supply, the difference arises solely because supply is less elastic in Vancouver than in Winnipeg.

the green area of panel (b) is calculated as the area of the rectangle with base zero to three, *plus* the area of the triangle with the base three to four. This is $700 000/month.

$$\text{total economic surplus} = \text{consumer surplus} + \text{producer surplus}$$

$$= \$2\ 300\ 000/\text{month}.$$

Thus, calculations confirm the visual impression given by Figure 7.9, and total economic surplus is $300 000/month larger in Vancouver than in Winnipeg. The difference arises solely because supply is less elastic in Vancouver than in Winnipeg, which causes producer surplus to be larger in Vancouver.

## ELASTICITY OF SUPPLY AND LOSS OF TOTAL ECONOMIC SURPLUS WITH RENT CONTROL

Historically, rent control has been introduced when a rapid increase in demand causes rents to rise dramatically. Resource booms and wartime mustering of troops at central points are examples. Landlords realize that they can charge more, and renters discover that apartments they have occupied for years quickly become more expensive.

Suppose that, for historical reasons, rents in Vancouver and Winnipeg have been capped at $100/month—at some point in the past, an identical price ceiling was imposed on both markets. With this rent cap, Figure 7.10 shows that 2000 apartments/month

**FIGURE 7.10**

**Lost Surplus and Redistribution of Surplus Arising from a Price Ceiling**

When rent is prevented from rising above $100/month in Winnipeg [panel (a)], the triangle containing the black lines represents the decrease in total economic surplus ($500 000/month). The rectangle outlined in black represents the amount transferred from landlords to renters by the rent control ($200 000/month). When the same ceiling is imposed on rental housing in Vancouver [panel (b)], the reduction in total economic surplus is represented by the triangle containing the black lines ($50 000/month). The area of the rectangle outlined in black represents the amount transferred from landlords to renters by the price ceiling on rental housing in Vancouver ($350 000/month). In Vancouver, the loss of economic surplus is much smaller and the redistributive effect much larger compared with Winnipeg. Because the two markets are identical except for supply, the difference arises entirely because supply is less elastic in Vancouver.

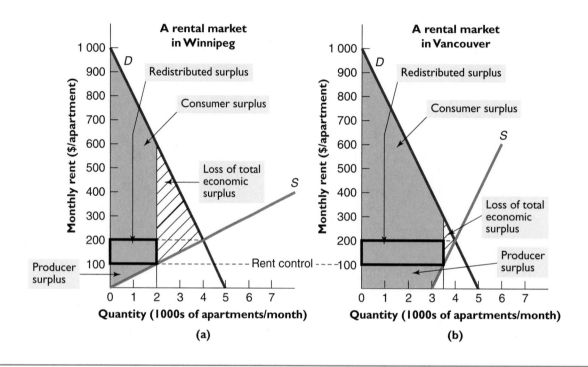

are supplied in the Winnipeg market and 3500 are supplied in the Vancouver market. Because the reduction in the number of apartments supplied is smaller in Vancouver, we might expect the reduction in total economic surplus from the price ceiling to be smaller in Vancouver than in Winnipeg. The reduction in total economic surplus in Winnipeg is equal to the area of the triangle that contains the black lines in panel (a) of Figure 7.10:

$$(\tfrac{1}{2})bh = (\tfrac{1}{2})(2000 \text{ apts/month})(\$500/\text{apt}) = \$500\ 000/\text{month}.$$

In comparison, the area of the triangle in panel (b) of Figure 7.10 containing the black lines gives the reduction in total economic surplus stemming from an identical price ceiling in Vancouver:

$$(\tfrac{1}{2})bh = (\tfrac{1}{2})(500 \text{ apts/month})(\$200/\text{apt}) = \$50\ 000/\text{month}.$$

Thus, calculations confirm the visual impression given by Figure 7.10. The loss of total economic surplus in Vancouver is one-tenth the size of the loss in the Winnipeg rental market. The difference arises entirely because suppliers in Vancouver make a much smaller response to a reduction in price than do suppliers in Winnipeg—supply is less elastic in Vancouver. The likely differences in the effect on landlords and renters are outlined in more detail below.

## ELASTICITY OF SUPPLY AND THE DISTRIBUTIVE EFFECTS OF RENT CONTROL

Suppose that, for whatever reasons, rent control has existed for some time in Winnipeg and Vancouver. If rent control in Winnipeg is removed, the number of apartments supplied will rise from 2000 to 4000 each month. Because of this, total economic surplus will rise by $500 000/month. Further, renters who choose to rent the 2000 new apartments and the landlords who choose to make them available will be better off. However, unless they are compensated, the renters who previously paid $100/month for each of 2000 apartments will be worse off after rent control is removed. They will be worse off by ($100/month) (2000 apartments) = $200 000/month. The same $200 000/month is transferred to landlords, making them better off. Landlords will favour removal of rent control. The rectangle that is outlined in black in panel (a) of Figure 7.10 represents the monthly amount transferred from renters to landlords when rent control in Winnipeg is removed. Because total economic surplus is larger by $500 000/month, it is possible to compensate those renters who pay more when rent control is removed. It is possible for renters of old apartments, renters of new apartments, and landlords all to be better off. However, unless there actually is compensation, the renters of the 2000 apartments will have good reason to oppose removal of rent control.

An identical price ceiling in the Vancouver rental market does not produce the same quantitative effects on consumer and producer surplus as in Winnipeg. Because the supply curve is less elastic in Vancouver, rent control produces a smaller reduction in the quantity of apartments supplied in Vancouver than in Winnipeg. Further, the consumer surplus under rent control in Vancouver is the area of the blue figure in panel (b) of Figure 7.10. The blue figure also can be divided into a rectangle and a triangle, and its area calculated as

$$(3500 \text{ apts/month})(\$200) + (\tfrac{1}{2})(3500 \text{ apts/month})(\$700/\text{apt})$$

$$= \$1\,925\,000/\text{month}.$$

In Vancouver, rent control actually increases consumer surplus from $1 600 000/month in the uncontrolled market to $1 925 000/month in the controlled market. At the same time, *total* economic surplus is $50 000/month more in the uncontrolled market because, with the removal of rent control, 500 more apartments become available.

By itself, though, removing rent control will not make some individuals better off while making no one worse off. Why? Landlords who collect $200/month for each of 3500 apartments where previously they collected $100 obviously will be better off by an amount equal to the area of the rectangle in panel (b) of Figure 7.10, outlined in black. Its area is

$$(\$100/\text{month})(3500 \text{ apartments}) = \$350\,000/\text{month}.$$

However, unless they receive compensation, the renters of those apartments will be worse off by the same amount and will have reason to oppose removal of rent control. The rectangle outlined in black represents a transfer from renters to landlords when rent control is removed.

Notice that in Vancouver, the transfer ($350 000/month) arising from removal of rent control is much larger than in Winnipeg ($200 000/month). In Vancouver, the transfer affects renters of more apartments (3500/month) than in Winnipeg (2000/month). Further, when rent control is removed, fewer new apartments become available in Vancouver (500/month) than in Winnipeg (2000/month). Therefore, the increase in total economic surplus is much smaller in Vancouver ($50 000/month) than it is in Winnipeg ($500 000/month). In Vancouver, the renters of 500 new apartments and the landlords who supply them will be better off. However, this will be a smaller group than in

Winnipeg, where 2000 new apartments become available. All of these differences between Vancouver and Winnipeg arise from one basic point: *Other things remaining equal, the less elastic supply is, the smaller is the loss of total economic surplus arising from price control and the larger is its redistributive impact.* A similar analysis could be made for price elasticity of demand.[8]

Rent controls are an example of a price ceiling. When implemented as a ceiling price, rent controls prevent landlords from charging more than a specified amount for rental housing. Tenants lucky enough to find a rent-controlled apartment often end up paying less than they would have in the absence of rent controls. Of course, when there is a gap between the controlled price and the price people are willing to pay, landlords may react by slipping in extra charges of dubious legality; for example, for delivery of keys or removal of trash. The greater the gap between the controlled price and the price that renters would be willing to pay, the more likely it is landlords will use such strategies. Notice, when you compare panels (a) and (b) of Figure 7.10, that given the difference in elasticity of supply in Vancouver and Winnipeg, rent controls a much bigger gap between quantity supplied and quantity demanded in Winnipeg than in Vancouver. Therefore, one can expect "black market" problems raised by rent controls to be much more common in Winnipeg.

The bottom line is that, in general, rent controls reduce total economic surplus, but the size of that loss in surplus and the size of other problems created by rent control depend on the elasticity of supply (and the elasticity of demand). Further, the size of the elasticities of supply and demand will affect the size of the distributive impact of a price ceiling. These distributive impacts are central to the political support for, and political opposition to, rent control.

**EXERCISE 7.2**    **How much total economic surplus would have been lost in Winnipeg if the rent ceiling had been set at $150 instead of $100?**

## PRICE FLOORS

**price floor** a minimum allowable price, specified by law or regulation.

A price ceiling prevents sellers from charging more than a specified amount. In contrast, a *price floor* guarantees that suppliers will receive at least a specified amount for their product. A **price floor** is a minimum allowable price established by law or regulation. A price ceiling attempts to hold price below its equilibrium level, while a price floor attempts to peg price above its equilibrium level. To implement a price ceiling, governments need only to impose penalties on sellers who charge too much. However, if a price floor is to be effective and price is pegged above the equilibrium level, excess supply develops, because firms want to supply more than consumers want to buy at the pegged price. The government must then either become an active buyer in the market or set a quota to regulate the total production of the industry, if the pegged price is to be enforced.

COST-
BENEFIT

Agricultural price supports are an example of a price floor. They represent another attempt by government to prevent markets from reaching equilibrium in order to provide benefits for some citizens. But as Example 7.4 demonstrates, price ceilings and price floors do have one fundamental characteristic in common: both stand in the way of actions that satisfy the cost-benefit test, and both therefore reduce total economic surplus.

8  Richard Arnott, ["Time for Revisionism on Rent Control?" *Journal of Economic Perspectives, 9* (Winter 1995), p. 99–120] reports that, where they are used in North America, rent controls have evolved into forms that govern relationships between landlords and tenants. The controls try to take into account market imperfections, incentives that operate on landlords and tenants, distributive effects, and the effect of controls on the availability of rental housing. New York City provides an important exception. There, rent control takes the form of a ceiling price, consequently raising the issue of housing shortages and lost economic surplus. Arnott also reports that New York's experience is similar to that of a number of European cities where rent control has had a major effect on housing markets.

## EXAMPLE **7.4**

### By how much do price supports for wheat reduce total economic surplus?

Suppose the supply and demand for wheat are as shown in Figure 7.11. The government offers to buy as much wheat as necessary to clear the market at a price of $40/ton. Assuming that the government then gives the wheat it buys to the consumers who value it most, by how much will price supports reduce the total economic surplus generated in the wheat market?

Without the price support, the equilibrium price in this market would be $30/ton. With the price support set at $40/ton, the public purchases 2 million tons/month and the government purchases the remaining 2 million tons/month offered by farmers at that price. If the government then gives the wheat to the consumers who value it most,[9] the total quantity consumed is 4 million tons/month. The first million tons that are given away effectively restore the economic surplus that would have been produced had the market been left unregulated (see Figure 7.11), since the cost of producing this wheat is the same as before and the same consumers end up getting it. But the second million tons the government gives away cost farmers more to produce (as measured by the supply curve) than what buyers were willing to pay for it (as measured by the demand curve). The resulting reduction in economic surplus is represented by the area of the blue triangle in Figure 7.11, which is $10 million per month.

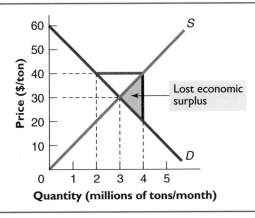

**FIGURE 7.11**
**Lost Surplus from Price Supports for Wheat**
A price support of $40/million tons results in 4 tons of wheat/month being produced, of which the government buys half and the public buys half. Lost economic surplus from the program is equal to $10 million/month.

**In Example 7.4, by how much would total economic surplus be reduced by the price support if none of the wheat purchased by the government was given to consumers?**          E X E R C I S E   7 . 3

## SUPPORT PRICES VERSUS QUOTAS

Instead of setting a support price of $40/ton as in Example 7.4, the government could have achieved the same result by imposing a quota. Limiting production to 2 million tons each month would also have brought sellers a price of $40/ton, which exceeds the equilibrium price. A quota would, like support prices, also reduce total economic surplus because both cause the buyers' reservation price to exceed the sellers' reservation price.

There are, however, two differences between a support price and a quota. First, with a support price, the government must purchase any wheat in excess of the amount buyers are willing to purchase at a price of $40/ton; 2 million tons per month in the case of Example 7.4. In the case of the quota example, the government does not have to purchase anything because buyers are willing to purchase all 2 million tons at a price of $40.

---

9  It is a strong assumption to imagine that government could costlessly identify those who would most value the extra wheat; the case against price supports is even stronger if it does not hold.

A second difference arises with respect to the transfer of income to farmers. In the case of a support price, the taxpayers provide the revenue that the government uses to purchase the excess quantity from farmers and the buyers transfer income by paying a higher price for the wheat, for a total of $40 million on 4 million tons per month in our example. In the case of a quota, farmers can receive $40/ton on only the 2 million tons that are produced. Thus, a support price provides a larger transfer to farmers. Quotas tend to be used in Canadian agricultural policy while the U.S. more often uses support prices.

**RECAP**

### THE COST OF BLOCKING PRICE ADJUSTMENTS IN PERFECTLY COMPETITIVE MARKETS

When price adjustments are blocked in perfectly competitive markets, total economic surplus is reduced. Loss of economic surplus is wasteful and to be avoided. If price controls have been implemented for historical reasons, removal of the controls will increase total economic surplus, making it possible for at least some individuals to better off without anyone becoming worse off. However, if no one is to be actually worse off, compensation must actually be paid to those who are worse off when price controls are removed. Unless they receive compensating payments, removing a price ceiling hurts anyone who previously could make purchases at the ceiling price, and removing a price floor hurts those who previously could sell at the floor price.

## 7.5    THE INVISIBLE HAND IN REGULATED MARKETS

The carrot of economic profit and the stick of economic loss guide resource movements in both regulated and unregulated markets. Consider the taxi industry, which many cities regulate by selling licences in the form of medallions. A medallion must be affixed to the hood of the cab where enforcement officials can easily see it. Cities that regulate cabs in this fashion typically issue fewer medallions than the equilibrium number of taxicabs that would appear in an unregulated market. If medallions can be bought and sold in the marketplace, the issuance of taxi medallions alters the equilibrium number of taxicabs but does not change the fundamental rule that resources flow in response to profit and loss signals.

### ECONOMIC NATURALIST  7.1

#### Why do some taxicab medallions sell for more than $250 000?

Because most cities with taxi regulation issue far fewer taxi medallions than would-be taxi owners could operate profitably, the equilibrium passenger fare is higher than the direct cost of operating a taxicab. Suppose the cost of operating a cab full-time—including car, fuel, maintenance, depreciation, and the opportunity cost of the driver's time, but excluding the purchase price of a medallion—is $40 000/year, and a cab in full-time operation will collect $60 000/year in fares. Since investing in the taxi industry has more risks and aggravations than just putting money into a savings account, we should make some allowance for these factors, but if a comparable investment in another industry could yield a return of 8 percent, how much will a medallion cost at equilibrium? Will the owner of a medallion earn an economic profit?

If the medallion was free and could not be sold to others, its owner would earn an economic profit of $20 000 per year, the difference between $60 000 in fares and $40 000 in operating cost. But the equilibrium principle tells us that the lure of this economic profit would induce outsiders to enter the taxi industry, which could be done by purchasing an owner's medallion.

How much would the entrant be willing to pay for a medallion? If one were available for, say, $100 000, would it be a good buy? Since $100 000 in a comparably risky investment would earn only $8000/year in interest, but would bring $20 000 in earnings if used to purchase a taxi medallion, the answer must be yes. In fact, when the interest rate is 8 percent, a rational buyer's lowest acceptable price for a stream of economic profits of $20 000 per year is the amount of money the buyer would have to put in that investment to earn $20 000 each year—namely, $250 000. At any amount less than that, medallions would be underpriced.

Clearly, the owner of a $250 000 medallion has a valuable asset. The opportunity cost of using it to operate a taxi is foregone interest of $20 000 per year. So the medallion owner who takes in $60 000 in fares actually covers only the cost of the resources invested in the operation. The owner's economic profit is zero. From the perspective of the medallion owner, the $20 000 difference between the owner's fares and explicit costs is an economic rent. With an equilibrium based on a restricted number of medallions, drivers earn only their opportunity costs. Any new driver who wants to enter the market must purchase a medallion from a driver who leaves the market, resulting in a windfall for those drivers who were given medallions when the system was first established. The initial generation of taxi medallion recipients may be able to sell their medallions to finance their retirement years when they leave the industry, but the new entrants get no such benefit. Thus, a system that designers probably thought would improve the incomes of all drivers actually only leads to a great gain for the initial recipients of medallions.

(A full consideration of the equity impacts of taxi regulation also would include the effect of higher taxi fares on consumers, some of whom take cabs because they cannot afford to own a car yet still occasionally need the use of one, for doctor's appointments or grocery shopping, for example.)

**How much would the medallion in the preceding example sell for if the annual interest rate were not 8 percent but 4 percent? (Assume the city's population is stable at the initial level.)**

EXERCISE 7.4

**RECAP**

**THE INVISIBLE HAND IN REGULATED MARKETS**

The quest for advantage guides resources not only in perfectly competitive markets but also in heavily regulated ones. Firms can almost always find ways to expand sales in markets in which the regulated price permits an economic profit or withdraw service from markets in which the regulated price results in an economic loss.

# 7.6 THE DISTINCTION BETWEEN AN EQUILIBRIUM AND A SOCIAL OPTIMUM

The example discussed in the preceding section illustrates the equilibrium principle, which tells us that when a market reaches equilibrium, no further opportunities for gain are available to individuals, because there is no incentive for those individuals to change their behaviour.

EQUILIBRIUM

The story is told of two economists on their way to lunch when they spot what appears to be a $100 bill lying on the sidewalk. When the younger economist stoops to pick up the bill, his older colleague restrains him, saying, "That can't be a $100-dollar bill." "Why not?" asks the younger colleague. "If it was, someone would have picked it up by now," the older economist replies.

Unfortunately, the older economist misunderstood the equilibrium principle to mean that there are *never* any valuable opportunities to exploit. But it only means that there are none when the market is *in equilibrium.* Occasionally a $100 bill does lie on the sidewalk, and the person who first spots it and picks it up gains a windfall. Likewise, when a company's earnings prospects improve significantly, *somebody* must be the first to recognize the opportunity, and that person can make a lot of money by purchasing the stock quickly.

Nevertheless, when a market is in equilibrium, no additional opportunities are available *to individuals for mutually beneficial exchange.* But this does not imply that the resulting market allocation of resources is necessarily best from the point of view of society as a whole.

We cannot, for example, make a mutually beneficial trade with people who do not yet exist. Some of the decisions we make today—for example, on $CO_2$ emissions and climate change—will have implications for centuries to come. Although we might think the interests of future generations (who cannot now affect the prices observed in today's markets) should count in today's economic decisions, we cannot rely on markets to reflect adequately those interests.

As well, we have emphasized that market outcomes depend on the distribution of initial wealth. One may think that it is not just the total size of the economic pie that matters, but also how it is divided. Deciding what a "fair" distribution is depends on values, and markets cannot tell us what our values should be.

Equilibrium is, therefore, an important and powerful concept in economics, but it should not be confused with "social optimum." Adam Smith's profound insight was that the individual pursuit of self-interest often promotes the broader interests of society. But Smith was under no illusion that this is *always* the case. Note, for example, Smith's elaboration on his description of the entrepreneur led by the invisible hand "to promote an end which was no part of his intention":

> Nor is it *always* the worse for society that it was no part of it.
> By pursuing his own interest he *frequently* promotes that of society more effectively than when he really intends to promote it.[10] [Italics added.]

As Smith was well aware, the pursuit of self-interest may not coincide with society's interest. Activities that generate environmental pollution are an example of conflicting economic interests, and we noted earlier that behaviour which may make sense at the individual level may, at the same time, be contrary to society's best interests.

In general, the efficacy of the invisible hand depends on the extent to which the individual costs and benefits of actions taken in the marketplace coincide with the respective costs and benefits of those actions to society. If the two diverge, the invisible hand cannot be expected to harmonize individual self-interest with the common good.

---

**RECAP**

### EQUILIBRIUM VERSUS SOCIAL OPTIMUM

A market in equilibrium is one in which no additional opportunities for gains remain available to individual buyers or sellers. The equilibrium principle describes powerful forces that help push markets toward equilibrium. But even if all markets are in equilibrium, the resulting allocation of resources need not be socially optimal. Defining the social optimum requires some statement of social values, and economists often emphasize the importance of both equity and sustainability, as well as the maximization of total surplus. Equilibrium will not be socially optimal when the costs or benefits to individual participants in the market differ from those experienced by society as a whole.

---

10 Smith, *The Wealth of Nations,* (1776) (New York, 1965), Book IV, Chapter II, p. 423.

# 7.7 TAXES AND ECONOMIC SURPLUS

## WHO PAYS A TAX IMPOSED ON SELLERS OF A GOOD?

We began this chapter noting that police services and courts are needed if contracts are to be enforced and a market system is to be viable. But judges and policemen have to be paid—and that means taxes. Some may argue that corporations can better afford to pay taxes than consumers, but suppose they pass the tax on to consumers? Who, in the end, actually bears the burden of taxation?

### EXAMPLE 7.5

**How will the imposition of a tax of $1/kilogram collected from potato farmers affect the equilibrium price and quantity of potatoes?**

Suppose the demand and supply curves for potatoes are shown by $D$ and $S$ in Figure 7.12, resulting in an initial equilibrium price and quantity of $3/kg and 3 million kg/month, respectively. From the farmers' perspective, the imposition of a tax of $1/kg is essentially the same as a $1 increase in the marginal cost of producing each kg of potatoes. Thus the tax can be seen as an upward shift in the supply curve by $1/kg.

As shown in Figure 7.12, the new equilibrium price (including the tax) will be $3.50, and the new equilibrium quantity will be 2.5 million kg/month. The net price per kilogram received by producers is $1 less than the price paid by the consumer, or $2.50. Note that though the tax was collected entirely from potato sellers, the burden of the tax fell on both buyers and sellers: on buyers, because they pay $0.50/kg more than before the tax, and on sellers because they receive $0.50/kg less than before the tax.

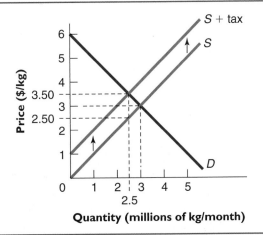

**FIGURE 7.12**

**The Effect of a Tax on the Equilibrium Quantity and Price of Potatoes**

With no tax, 3 million kg of potatoes are sold each month at a price of $3/kg. With a tax of $1/kg collected from sellers, consumers end up paying $3.50/kg (including tax), while sellers receive only $2.50/kg (net of tax). Equilibrium quantity falls from 3 million kg/month to 2.5 million.

The burden of the tax need not fall equally on buyers and sellers. Indeed, as the following Economic Naturalist case illustrates, a tax levied on sellers may end up being paid almost entirely by buyers.

Although the long-run supply curve shown in Figure 7.13 is in one sense an extreme case (since its price elasticity is infinite), it is by no means an unrepresentative one. As we discussed in Chapter 6, the long-run supply curve will tend to be horizontal when it is possible to acquire more of all the necessary inputs at constant prices. As a first approximation, this can be accomplished for many goods and services in a typical economy.

## ECONOMIC NATURALIST  7.2

### How will a tax on cars affect automobile prices in the long run?

Denmark is a country that does not manufacture any of its automobiles. All the cars sold in Denmark are imported. Honda, Volkswagen, Peugeot, and all the world's other car companies are quite willing to supply the Danish market, but they want to make as much profit per car from sales in Denmark as they make from sales anywhere else. If the inputs required to produce an entry-level, sub-compact car cost $10 000, how will the long-run equilibrium price of automobiles be affected if a tax of $100/car is levied on manufacturers?

The fact that the long-run marginal cost of making cars is constant means that the long-run supply curve of cars is horizontal at $10 000/car. A tax of $100/car effectively raises marginal cost by $100/car

and thus shifts the supply curve upward by exactly $100. If the demand curve for cars is as shown by curve D in Figure 7.13, the effect is to raise the equilibrium price of cars by exactly $100, to $10 100. The equilibrium quantity falls from 2 million cars per month to 1.9 million. (In fact, Denmark has much higher taxes on automobiles than this example would suggest; indeed, Danish prices for cars are nearly the highest in the world. Although the importer initially pays excise taxes, these are passed on to buyers in higher prices, and Danish consumers ultimately bear the *entire* burden of these taxes.)

### FIGURE 7.13
**The Effect of a Tax on Sellers of a Good with Infinite Price Elasticity of Supply**
When the supply curve for a good is perfectly elastic, the burden of a tax collected from sellers falls entirely on buyers.

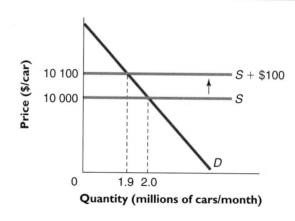

For goods with perfectly elastic supply curves, the entire burden of any tax is borne by the buyer.[11] That is, the increase in the equilibrium price is exactly equal to the tax. For this empirically relevant case, then, there is special irony in the common political practice of justifying taxes on business by saying that businesses have greater ability to pay than consumers.

## HOW A TAX COLLECTED FROM A SELLER AFFECTS ECONOMIC SURPLUS

We saw earlier that perfectly competitive markets distribute goods and services efficiently if demand curves reflect all relevant benefits and supply curves reflect all relevant costs. In Example 7.6, we will consider how the imposition of a tax on a product might affect the size and distribution of a market's total economic surplus.

---

11  In the example given, the tax was collected from sellers. If you go on to take intermediate microeconomics, you will see that the same conclusions apply when a tax is collected from buyers.

# EXAMPLE 7.6

## How does a tax on potatoes affect the size and distribution of total economic surplus?

An **excise tax** is a tax charged on each unit of a good or service. It can be distinguished from a sales tax, which is charged on all or most goods, whereas an excise tax is charge on one or a few goods. Suppose the supply and demand for potatoes are as shown by the curves *S* and *D* in Figure 7.14. How would the imposition of an excise tax of $1/kg, collected from potato sellers, affect total economic surplus in the potato market?

In the absence of a tax, 3 million kilograms of potatoes per month would be sold at a price of $3/kg, and the resulting total economic surplus would be $9 million each month (which is the area of the blue triangle plus the green quadrilateral in Figure 7.14).

With a tax of $1/kg collected from potato sellers, the new equilibrium price of potatoes would be $3.50/kg (of which sellers receive $2.50, net of tax), and only 2.5 million kilograms of potatoes would be sold each month (see Figure 7.14) The total economic surplus reaped by buyers and sellers in the potato market would be the area of the blue triangle shown in Figure 7.14, which is $6.25 million per month, or $2.75 million less than before.

**excise tax** a tax charged on each unit of a good or service

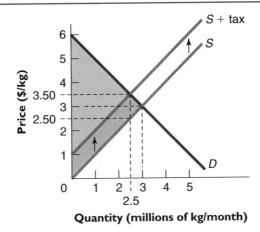

**FIGURE 7.14**
**The Effect of a $1/kg Tax on Potatoes**
A $1/kilogram tax on potatoes would cause an upward shift in the supply curve by $1. Total surplus would shrink to the area of the blue triangle, $6.25 million/month, which is a reduction of $2.75 million/month.

This drop in surplus may sound like an enormous loss. But it is a misleading figure, because it fails to take account of the value of the additional tax revenue collected, which is equal to $2.5 million—$1/kg on 2.5 million kilograms of potatoes. That revenue is available for transfer payments to households, to reduce other taxes, or to fund public services, all of which provide benefits to households. For example, potato tax revenue could fund total transfer payments to households of $2.5 million each month. So although buyers and sellers lose $2.75 million per month in economic surplus from their participation in the potato market, they also enjoy a $2.5 million in services or transfer payments. On balance, then, their net reduction in economic surplus is $0.25 million.

---

Graphically, the loss in economic surplus caused by the imposition of the tax can be shown as the area of the small blue triangle in Figure 7.15. This reduction in economic surplus is often described as the **deadweight loss** from the tax.

A tax typically reduces economic surplus because a tax drives a wedge between the price that consumers actually pay and the price that producers actually receive. That "tax wedge" distorts the basic cost–benefit criterion that would otherwise guide decisions about production and consumption. In Example 7.6, the cost–benefit test tells us to expand potato production up to the point at which the benefit of the last kilogram of

COST-
BENEFIT

**deadweight loss** the reduction in economic surplus that results from adoption of a policy

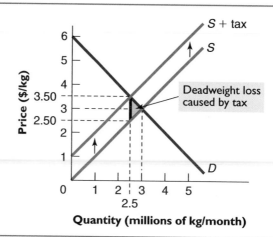

potatoes consumed (as measured by what buyers are willing to pay for it) equals the cost of producing it (as measured by the producer's marginal cost). That condition was satisfied in the potato market before the tax, but it is not satisfied once the tax is imposed. In Figure 7.15, for example, note that when potato consumption is 2.5 million kilograms per month, the value of an additional kilogram of potatoes to consumers is $3.50, whereas the cost to producers is only $2.50, not including the tax. (The cost to producers, including the tax, is $3.50/kg, but again we note that this tax is not a cost to society as a whole because it offsets other taxes that would otherwise have to be collected.)

Does a tax on potatoes necessarily lower total economic surplus? To answer this question, we must first identify the best realistic alternative to taxing potatoes. Those who say, "don't tax anything at all!" have to explain how they expect to pay for even minimal services, such as police and courts (and road maintenance, fire protection, and national defense) necessary to maintain a market system. (In Chapter 14, we will consider why we also often empower government to provide public goods.) On balance, if taxing potatoes were the best way to avoid doing without highly valued public services, then a small deadweight loss in the potato market would be worth it.

So the real question is, what is the least harmful tax? Can one find a more efficient tax that would be better than taxing potatoes? The problem with a tax on any activity is that if market incentives encourage people to pursue the surplus-maximizing amount of an activity, then a tax will encourage them to pursue too little of it. As economists have long recognized, this observation suggests that taxes will cause smaller deadweight losses if they are imposed on goods for which the equilibrium quantity is not highly sensitive to changes in prices.

## TAXES, ELASTICITY, AND ECONOMIC SURPLUS

Suppose the government put a tax of $0.50/kg on table salt. How would this affect the amount of salt you and others use? In Chapter 4, we saw that the demand for salt is highly inelastic with respect to price, because salt has few substitutes and occupies only a minuscule share in most family budgets. Because the imposition of a tax on table salt would not result in a significant reduction in the amount of it consumed, the deadweight loss from this tax would be relatively small. More generally, the smaller the price elasticity of demand for the good is, the smaller the deadweight loss from a per-unit tax imposed on the seller of a good also is.

Figure 7.16 illustrates how the deadweight loss from a tax declines as the demand for a good becomes less elastic with respect to price. In both parts, the original supply and demand curves yield an equilibrium price of $2/unit and an equilibrium quantity of 24 units per day. The deadweight loss from a tax of $1/unit imposed on the good shown

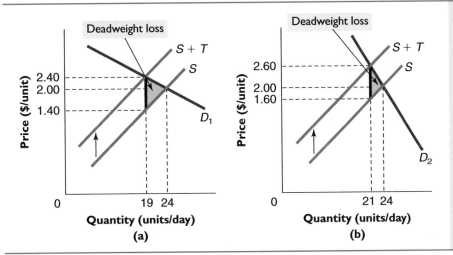

**FIGURE 7.16**

**Elasticity of Demand and the Deadweight Loss from a Tax**

At the equilibrium price and quantity, price elasticity of demand is smaller for the good shown in panel (b) than for the good shown in panel (a). The area of the deadweight loss triangle in panel (b), $1.50/day, is smaller than the area of the deadweight loss triangle in panel (a), $2.50/day.

in panel (a) is the area of the blue triangle in panel (a), which is $2.50/day. The demand curve $D_2$ in panel (b) is less elastic at the equilibrium price of $2 than the demand curve $D_1$ in panel (a), which follows from the fact that $P/Q$ is the same in both cases, while $1/slope$ is smaller in panel (b). The deadweight loss from the same $1/unit tax imposed on the good in panel (b) is the area of the blue triangle, which is only $1.50/day.

## ECONOMIC NATURALIST 7.3

### Why did 60 000 people risk imprisonment rather than pay a tax on salt?

Because salt has no real substitutes, it could be called a "necessity," and in very poor countries even a small tax on salt might be significant to some households. So when the British rulers of colonial India decided to institute a tax on salt, there were widespread protests. Those who felt the burden of the tax most keenly were the poorest of India's poor. In March 1930, Mahatma Gandhi led a massive march of protest to gather salt from the sea, rather than pay the tax. More than 60 000 people were imprisoned, but in the spring of 1931, the British permitted the making of salt for personal use. Although British colonial administrators may have known their economics, there is more to tax policy than the size of total economic surplus and amount of revenue collected by a tax. The people affected believed the tax was unjust. The march to the sea was one of Gandhi's most effective protests. Though its immediate purpose was to protest against the inequity of the tax, it also focused attention on the ethical question of whether India, or any country, should be a colony at all. India became an independent nation in 1947, thus beginning the dissolution of the British Empire.[12]

The smaller the elasticity of supply of the good is, the smaller the reduction in equilibrium quantity that results from a tax on a good will also be. In Figure 7.17, for example, the original supply and demand curves for the markets portrayed in panels (a) and (b) yield an equilibrium price of $2/unit and an equilibrium quantity of 72 units per day. The deadweight loss from a tax of $1/unit imposed on the good shown in panel (a) is the area of the blue triangle in panel (a), which is $7.50/day. The supply curve $S_2$ in panel (b) is less elastic at the equilibrium price than the supply curve $S_1$ in panel (a), again because $P/Q$ is the same in both cases, while $1/slope$ is smaller in panel (b). The deadweight loss from the same $1/unit tax imposed on the good in panel (b) is the area of the blue triangle in panel (b), which is only $4.50/day.

12 *Encylopædia Britannica,* 15th ed. (1986), vol. 5, p. 109; vol. 19, p. 652.

**FIGURE 7.17**
**Elasticity of Supply and the Deadweight Loss from a Tax**
At the equilibrium price and quantity, price elasticity of supply is smaller for the good shown in panel (b) than for the good shown in panel (a). The area of the deadweight loss triangle in panel (b), $4.50/day, is smaller than the area of the deadweight loss triangle in panel (a), $7.50/day.

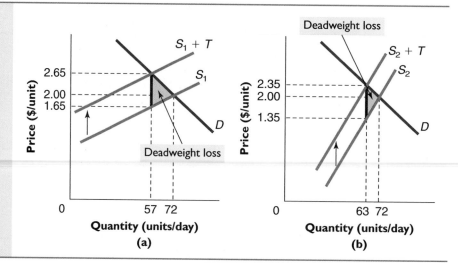

Similarly, the deadweight loss from a tax imposed on a good whose supply curve is perfectly inelastic will be zero. This explains why in the nineteenth century Henry George proposed that all taxes on labour and goods be abolished and replaced by a single tax on land. Such a tax, he argued, would cause no significant loss in economic surplus because the supply of land is almost perfectly inelastic. If either demand or supply is highly inelastic, then the equilibrium quantity changes little when a tax is imposed.

If demand for a good is highly inelastic, then much the same amount of the good is consumed, regardless of how much tax is added to consumer prices. If the supply of the good is highly inelastic, then producers will supply about the same amount of the good, whatever the producer price is. And if the equilibrium quantity produced and sold in the market changes little, the deadweight loss of taxation will be correspondingly small.

## TAXES, EXTERNAL COSTS, AND TOTAL SURPLUS

While there are attractive aspects to taxing goods with inelastic supply or demand, taxing activities that people tend to pursue to excess is even more attractive. We mentioned activities that generate environmental pollution as one example; in later chapters we will discuss others. Whereas a tax on land does not reduce economic surplus, a tax on pollution can actually increase total economic surplus. Taxes on activities that cause harm to others have a "double dividend": they generate revenue to pay for useful public services and at the same time discourage people from pursuing the harmful activities, as we will discuss in more detail in Chapters 10 and 14.

> ### RECAP
>
> **TAXES AND TOTAL SURPLUS**
>
> A tax levied on each unit of a seller's product has the same effect on equilibrium quantity and price as a rise in marginal cost equal to the amount of the tax. The burden of a tax imposed on sellers will generally be shared among both buyers and sellers. In the extreme case of a good whose elasticity of supply is infinite, the entire burden of the tax is borne by buyers.

A tax imposed on a product whose supply and demand curves embody all relevant costs and benefits associated with its production and use will result in a deadweight loss—a reduction in total economic surplus in the market for the taxed good. Such taxes may nonetheless be justified if the value of the public services financed by the tax outweighs this deadweight loss. In general, the deadweight loss from a tax on a good will be smaller, the smaller are the good's price elasticities of supply and demand. Taxes on activities that generate harm to others may produce a net gain in economic surplus, even apart from the value of the public services they finance.

## SUMMARY

- In a perfectly competitive market, when the supply and demand curves for a product capture all the relevant costs and benefits of producing and consuming that product, the market equilibrium for that product will maximize total surplus. In such a market, if price and quantity do not equal their equilibrium values, a transaction can be found that could make at least some people better off without harming others. **LO1, LO2**

- Total economic surplus is a measure of the amount by which participants in a market benefit by participating in it. It is the sum of total consumer surplus and total producer surplus in the market. For an individual buyer, the economic surplus from a transaction is the difference between the most the buyer would have been willing to pay and the amount actually paid. For an individual seller, the economic surplus from a transaction is the difference between the price received and the lowest amount at which the seller would have been willing to make the sale. Total economic surplus in a market is the sum of all producer and consumer surplus in that market. One of the attractive properties of market equilibrium under perfect competition is that it maximizes the value of total economic surplus. **LO3, LO4**

- Maximization of total economic surplus should not be equated with a social optimum. If we believe that the distribution of income among people is unjust, we will not like the results produced by the intersection of the supply and demand curves based on that income distribution, even if those results maximize total economic surplus. **LO8**

- Nevertheless, whenever a perfectly competitive market is out of equilibrium, the economic pie can be made larger. And with a larger pie, everyone can have a larger slice, provided a system is in place for distributing the larger pie so that at least some individuals are actually made better off and no one is actually made worse off. **LO2**

- Regulations or policies that prevent competitive markets from reaching equilibrium—such as rent controls, or price supports for agricultural products—are often defended on equity grounds. Such schemes reduce economic surplus, meaning that alternatives under which everyone is better off are conceivable, but the size of the reduction depends crucially on the elasticity of supply and the elasticity of demand for the good. **LO5, LO6, LO7**

- A tax will reduce economic surplus if the supply and demand curves in the market for the taxed good reflect all the relevant costs and benefits of its production and consumption. But this decline in surplus has to be compared with the increase in economic surplus (if any) made possible by public goods financed with the proceeds of the tax. Taxes imposed on activities that would otherwise be pursued to excess, such as activities that generate environmental pollution, do not reduce economic surplus; they can actually increase it. **LO9**

## KEY TERMS

consumer surplus (190)
deadweight loss (207)
demander's (or buyer's)
 reservation price (190)
economic surplus (184)
excise tax (207)

invisible hand (184)
perfectly competitive market (185)
price ceiling (193)
price floor (200)
price taker (185)
producer surplus (190)

supplier's (or seller's)
 reservation price (190)
total economic surplus (190)

## REVIEW QUESTIONS

1. Why do economists emphasize maximization of consumer and producer surplus as an important goal of public policy? **LO2**

2. You are an MP considering how to vote on a policy that would reduce the economic surplus of workers by $1 million/year but increase the economic surplus of retirees by $10 million/year. What additional measure might you combine with the policy to ensure that the overall result is a better outcome for everyone? **LO2, LO6**

3. How do elasticity of supply and elasticity of demand affect the size of the economic surplus that a perfectly competitive market can offer? **LO7**

4. How does elasticity of supply affect the loss of economic surplus caused by a price ceiling? **LO5, LO7**

5. How does elasticity of supply affect the distributive impact of a price ceiling? **LO7**

6. Why does the loss in total economic surplus directly experienced by participants in the market for a good that is taxed overstate the overall loss in economic surplus which results from the tax? **LO9**

7. Why do price supports reduce economic surplus? **LO9**

## PROBLEMS

1. Calculate the producer and consumer surplus for the market whose demand and supply curves are shown as follows. **LO4**

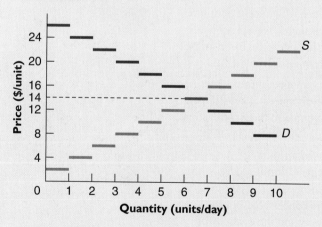

2. Suppose the weekly demand curve for wristwatches in Winnipeg is given by the equation $P = 12 - 0.25Q$, and the weekly supply of wristwatches is given by the equation $P = 6 + 0.75Q$, where $P$ is the dollar price of a wristwatch and $Q$ is the quantity of wristwatches measured in 100s. Sketch the weekly demand and supply curves in Winnipeg, and calculate
   a. the weekly consumer surplus.

   b. the weekly producer surplus.
   c. the maximum weekly amount that producers and consumers in Winnipeg would be willing to pay to be able to buy and sell wristwatches in any given week. **LO3, LO4**

3. Refer to problem 2. Suppose a coalition of high school students succeeds in persuading the local government to impose a price ceiling of $7.50 on wristwatches, on the grounds that local suppliers are taking advantage of teenagers by charging exorbitant prices. **LO2, LO5, LO6**
   a. Calculate the weekly shortage of wristwatches that will result from this policy.
   b. Calculate the total economic surplus lost every week as a result of the price ceiling.
   c. In the face of the price ceiling, describe a transaction that would benefit both a buyer and a seller of wristwatches.

4. The Kubak crystal caves are renowned for their stalactites and stalagmites. The warden of the caves offers a tour each afternoon at 2 P.M. sharp. Only four people per day can see the caves without disturbing their fragile ecology. Occasionally, however, more than four people want to see the caves on the same

day. The following table shows the list of people who wanted to see the caves on one such day together with their respective times of arrival and reservation prices for taking the tour that day. **LO2, LO4, LO6**

|         | Arrival time | Reservation price ($) |
|---------|--------------|-----------------------|
| Herman  | 1:48         | 20                    |
| Jon     | 1:50         | 14                    |
| Kate    | 1:53         | 30                    |
| Jack    | 1:56         | 15                    |
| Penny   | 1:57         | 40                    |
| Fran    | 1:59         | 12                    |
| Faith   | 2:00         | 17                    |

a.  If the tour is free and the warden operates it on a first-come, first-served basis, what will the total consumer surplus be for the four people who arrive on time to make the tour on that day?

b.  Suppose the warden solicits volunteers to postpone their tour by offering increasing amounts of cash compensation until only four people still want to see the caves that day. If he gives each volunteer the same compensation payment, how much money will he have to offer to generate the required number of volunteers? What is the total economic surplus under this policy?

c.  In what sense is the compensation policy more "efficient" than the first-come, first-served policy?

d.  Describe a way of financing the warden's compensation payments that will make everyone, including the warden, either better off or no worse off than under the first-come, first-served approach.

5.  Suppose the weekly demand for a certain good, in thousands of units, is given by the equation $P = 8 - Q$, and the weekly supply of the good by the equation $P = 2 + Q$, where $P$ is the price in dollars and $Q$ is quantity. **LO4, LO9**

a.  Calculate the total weekly economic surplus generated at the market equilibrium.

b.  Suppose a per-unit tax of $2, to be collected from sellers, is imposed in this market. Calculate the direct loss in economic surplus experienced by participants in this market as a result of the tax.

c.  How much government revenue will this tax generate each week? If the revenue is used to offset other taxes paid by participants in this market, what will be their net reduction in total economic surplus?

6.  a.  Graph the supply and demand equations given in problem 5. **LO3, LO4, LO7**

b.  Now suppose that weekly demand for a good is the same as in problem 5, but weekly supply is $P = (5/3)Q$. Graph supply and demand on a pair of axes separate from the axes you used for 6(a).

c.  Determine equilibrium price and quantity implied by the equations given in 6(a), and compare with equilibrium price and quantity implied by the equations given in problem 5.

d.  Calculate the total surplus implied by the equations given in 6(a). Compare this with your answer for problem 5(a). Explain any difference you find, using no more than four sentences.

7.  Refer to in-chapter Exercise 7.1. Suppose that a price ceiling of $0.50/litre is in effect for milk. Suppose the price ceiling is removed, and that equilibrium price and quantity are established, but nothing else happens. Who are the winners and losers when the price ceiling is removed? By how much do they win or lose? **LO4, LO9**

8.  A price support for milk will lead to a loss of economic surplus because (Choose one.) **LO5**

a.  it will raise the marginal cost of milk above the marginal benefit of milk to consumers.

b.  it will cause a reduction in economic surplus.

c.  it will lead consumers to buy less milk than they would otherwise have bought.

d.  all of the above.

9.  The government of Islandia, a small island nation, imports heating oil at a price of $2/litre and makes it available to citizens at a price of $1/litre. If Islandians' demand curve for heating oil is given by $P = 6 - Q$, where $P$ is the price per litre in dollars and $Q$ is the quantity in millions of litres per year, how much economic surplus is lost as a result of the government's policy? **LO4, LO5**

10. Refer to problem 9. Suppose each of the one million Islandian households has the same demand curve for heating oil. **LO4, LO5, LO9**

a.  Write an equation that gives an individual household's demand for oil.

b.  How much consumer surplus would each household lose if it had to pay $2/litre instead of $1/litre for heating oil, assuming there were no other changes in the household budget?

c.  With the money saved by not subsidizing oil, by how much could the Islandian government afford to cut each family's annual taxes?

d.  If the government abandoned its oil subsidy and implemented the tax cut, by how much would each family be better off?

e.  How does the resulting total gain for the one million families compare with your calculation of the lost surplus in problem 9?

11. Is a company's producer surplus the same as its profit? (*Hint:* A company's total cost is equal to the sum of all marginal costs incurred in producing its output, plus any fixed costs.) **LO3**

12. Suppose that you live in a small island state with a population of 100 000. The wealthiest 1000 people have annual incomes of $10 million each. The other

99 000 are poor, having annual incomes of $2500 each. **LO1, LO8**

a.  If all markets in which islanders buy their goods and services are perfectly competitive, will their economy achieve maximum total economic surplus? Why or why not?

b.  Suppose the island maximizes its total economic surplus. Will it also have achieved a social optimum? Do you think the wealthy people would answer this question differently from the poor people? Explain your answers.

## ANSWERS TO IN-CHAPTER EXERCISES

7.1    At a price of $0.50/litre, there is excess demand of 4000 litres/day. Suppose a seller produces an extra litre of milk (marginal cost = $0.50) and sells it to the buyer who would value it most (reservation price = $2.50) for $1.50. Both buyer and seller will gain an additional economic surplus of $1, and no other buyers or sellers will be hurt by the transaction. **LO2**

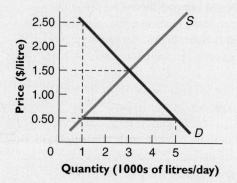

7.2    In Winnipeg, the new lost surplus is the area of the lined triangle in the following figure: (½)($250/month)(1000 apartments/month) = $125 000/month. **LO3, LO4, LO5**

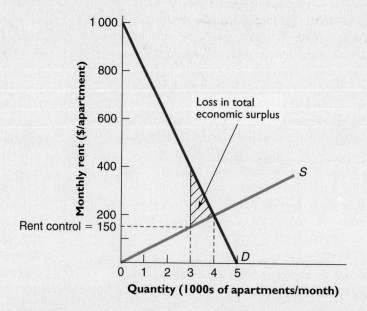

**7.3**   With the price support set at $40/ton, the public again purchases 2 million tons/month, and the government purchases the remaining 2 million tons farmers offer at that price. If none of the wheat purchased by the government goes to consumers, it will generate no benefit. So compared to the case without price supports, the lost benefit is equal to the area under the demand curve between 2 million and 3 million tons/month. The cost of producing the extra 1 million tons/month, which is the area under the supply curve between 3 million and 4 million tons/month, is also lost. The total loss in economic surplus caused by the price support is thus the area of the blue region shown in the following diagram, which is $70 million/month. **LO3, LO4, LO5**

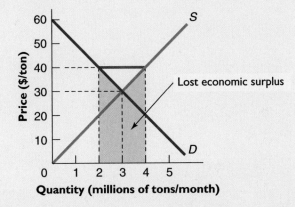

Notice that though the loss in total economic surplus is $70 million/month, the government actually pays $40 × 2 million tons = $80 million/month for the 2 million tons it purchases. You can unravel this paradox as follows. Producers receive a producer surplus of $20 million on the wheat the government buys [½($20 × 2 million tons) = $20 million]. In addition, when price is supported at $40/ton, consumers reduce their consumption from 3 to 2 million tons. Consumers thus lose a consumer surplus of ½($20 × 1 million tons) = $10 million. When the two effects are taken together, the net effect is an increase of $10 million in economic surplus: $20 million − $10 million = $10 million. Therefore, the monthly loss in total economic surplus is actually $10 million less than what the government pays for the wheat it buys: $80 million − $10 million = $70 million.

**7.4**   If the taxi medallion were available free, it would still command an economic profit of $20 000/year. So its value is still the answer to the question, how much would you need to put in the bank to generate interest earnings of $20 000/year? When the interest rate is 4 percent/year, the answer is $500 000, or twice what the medallion was worth at an interest rate of 8 percent. **LO5**

# PART 3

# THE REAL WORLD IS AN IMPERFECT PLACE

We now leave the frictionless world of perfect competition to investigate what happens in the real world when people and firms interact in markets with a variety of imperfections. Not surprisingly, the invisible hand that could serve society so well in the perfectly competitive world may go astray in this new environment.

Our focus in Chapter 8 will be on how markets served by only one or a small number of firms differ from those served by perfectly competitive firms. We will see that although monopolies often escape the pressures that constrain the profits of their perfectly competitive counterparts, the two types of firms also have many important similarities.

In Chapters 1 to 8, we discuss markets in which economic decision makers confront an environment that is essentially fixed. In Chapter 9, however, we will consider cases in which people can expect their actions to alter the behaviour of others, as when a firm's decision to advertise or launch a new product induces a rival to follow suit. Interdependent actions of this sort are very common, and we will explore how to take them into account, using simple game theory.

In Chapter 10, we will investigate how the allocation of resources is affected when activities generate costs or benefits that accrue to people not directly involved in those activities. We will see that if parties cannot easily negotiate with one another, the self-interested actions of individuals may not lead to efficient outcomes.

Although the invisible hand assumes that buyers and sellers are perfectly informed about all relevant options, this assumption is almost never completely satisfied. In Chapter 11, we will analyze how basic economic principles can still help imperfectly informed individuals and firms make the best use of the limited information they possess.

# CHAPTER 8
# Monopoly, Oligopoly, and Monopolistic Competition

In the late 1990s, there was a craze throughout North America for Pokémon cards. Unlike ordinary playing cards, which could be bought in most stores for only a dollar or two, a deck of Pokémon cards sold for as much as $15. And since Pokémon cards cost no more to manufacture than ordinary playing cards, their producer earned an enormous economic profit.

In a normal competitive market, entrepreneurs would see this economic profit as an incentive to produce Pokémon cards and sell them at slightly lower but still highly profitable prices. As more and more firms entered the market, the cards would eventually sell for roughly their cost of production, just as ordinary playing cards do. However, though Pokémon cards were on the market for several years, their price did not fall because the cards were copyrighted; that is, the firm owning the copyright had an exclusive licence to sell them.

A holder of a copyright is an example of an *imperfectly competitive firm,* or *price setter;* that is, a firm with at least some latitude to set its own price. The competitive firm, by contrast, is a price taker, a firm with no influence over the price of its product.

This chapter focuses on how markets served by imperfectly competitive firms differ from those served by perfectly competitive firms. The imperfectly competitive firm can, under certain circumstances, charge more than its cost of production without losing all its sales. But if so, why did the producer of Pokémon cards charge "only" $15 per deck? Why not charge $100, or even $1000? We will see that even if a company is the only seller of its product, its pricing decisions will still be influenced by the market. We will also see how some imperfectly competitive firms manage to earn an economic profit, even in the long run, and even without government protections like copyright. We will also explore why the ability of Adam Smith's invisible hand to maximize total economic surplus is compromised in a world served by imperfectly competitive firms.

# 8.1 IMPERFECT COMPETITION

The perfectly competitive market is an ideal type. We study perfect competition partly because by maximizing total economic surplus, perfect competition sets a benchmark against which the performance of other market types can be assessed. In the real world, we can distinguish among three broad types of imperfectly competitive markets: pure monopoly, oligopoly and monopolistic competition.

## DIFFERENT FORMS OF IMPERFECT COMPETITION

Furthest from the perfectly competitive ideal is the **pure monopoly**, which can be defined as a market in which a single firm is the lone seller of a unique product. For example, as long as the copyright is in force, the producer of Pokémon cards is a pure monopolist. Providers of natural gas or electric power are a different sort of example. If the residents of a particular neighborhood must either buy electricity from their local supplier or do without, the local supplier of electricity has a monopoly.

Somewhat closer to the perfectly competitive ideal is **oligopoly**, the market structure in which only a few rival firms sell a given product. Examples include the market for long-distance telephone service, in which firms like Rogers, Sprint, and MCI are the principal providers. Closer still to perfect competition is the market structure known as **monopolistic competition**, which typically consists of a relatively large number of firms selling slightly differentiated products that are reasonably close substitutes for one another. Examples include markets for wine and Scotch whisky, where brands differ not so much in alcohol content as in their subtle taste differences. Table 8.1 summarizes characteristics of different market types, ranging from monopoly to perfect competition.

**pure monopoly** a market in which there is only one supplier of a unique product with no close substitutes

**oligopoly** a market in which there are only a few rival sellers (each of which is called an oligopolist)

**monopolistic competition** a market structure in which a large number of firms sell slightly differentiated products that are reasonably close substitutes for one another

**TABLE 8.1**
**The Spectrum of Market Structures**

| | Monopoly | Oligopoly | | Monopolistic Competition | Perfect Competition |
|---|---|---|---|---|---|
| | | **Undifferentiated Oligopoly** | **Differentiated Oligopoly** | | |
| **Number of suppliers** | single producer | small number of producers | small number of producers | many producers | many producers |
| **Degree of product differentiation** | product is without close substitutes | little or no difference in product | some differentiation of products | many real or perceived differences in product | identical: the product is undifferentiated, homogeneous |
| **Examples** | electricity, water distribution, liquor distribution in most Canadian provinces | cigarettes, gasoline, tires, batteries, cell phone services | computers, breakfast cereal, soft drinks | restaurants, barber shops, beauty salons | some agricultural products |
| **Degree of firm's ability to control price** | considerable, however often restrained by regulation | often significant but usually less than monopoly | | limited | none |
| **Methods of marketing** | promotion of services, advertising | advertising, promotion of new products, promotion of bundled services, promotion of either real or perceived differences in quality, brand loyalty | | advertising, real or perceived differences in products | market exchange |

Because pure monopoly, oligopoly, and monopolistic competition represent three different types of *imperfectly* competitive markets, the firms that participate in any of these three market types can be called *imperfectly competitive* firms.

## THE ESSENTIAL DIFFERENCE BETWEEN PERFECTLY AND IMPERFECTLY COMPETITIVE FIRMS

A perfectly competitive firm can no more change the market price than a child with a bucket can change the level of the sea. In a perfectly competitive market, each individual firm produces a standardized commodity and provides such a small share of the total quantity supplied to the market that no individual firm can influence the market price. Since the market price is fixed by supply and demand for the industry as a whole, each and every firm in a perfectly competitive industry decides how much to produce *given* the market price; thus, a perfectly competitive firm is **a price taker**. This is not the case in an imperfectly competitive market, where the market share of an imperfectly competitive firm is large enough for the firm's decisions to influence the market price. This implies that an imperfectly competitive firm makes its decisions about how much to produce *knowing that the quantity it produces will affect the market price*. An imperfectly competitive firm, therefore, is a **price setter**; it can, at least within some range, set its own price knowing that sales will probably be affected, but it will still be able to sell *some* output.

A single, common feature differentiates all imperfectly competitive firms from their perfectly competitive counterparts: *whereas the perfectly competitive firm faces a perfectly elastic demand curve for its product, the imperfectly competitive firm faces a downward-sloping demand curve.*

In the perfectly competitive industry, supply and demand curves intersect to determine an equilibrium market price. At that price, the individual perfectly competitive firm can sell as many units as it wants. It cannot charge more than the market price. If it tries to do so, it will sell nothing because a multitude of competitors stand ready to sell at the market price. Nor does it have any incentive to charge less than the market price, because it can sell as many units as it wants to at the market price. The perfectly competitive firm's demand curve is thus a horizontal line at the market price, as we saw in Chapter 7. The equilibrium principle states that total economic surplus is maximized when a perfectly competitive market is in equilibrium. Thus, as an ideal case, perfect competition establishes a benchmark against which the performance of imperfectly competitive markets can be measured.

By contrast, if a brand of whisky increases its price a bit above its rivals', some customers may desert it. But others will remain, perhaps because they are willing to pay a little extra to continue enjoying their favourite taste. An imperfectly competitive firm thus faces a negatively sloped demand curve. Figure 8.1 summarizes this contrast between the demand curves facing perfectly competitive and imperfectly competitive firms.

**price taker** a firm that has no influence over the price at which it sells its product

**price setter** a firm that can set its own price, recognizing that the price it sets will affect the quantity it can sell.

**FIGURE 8.1**
**The Demand Curves Facing Perfectly and Imperfectly Competitive Firms**
Panel (a): The demand curve confronting a perfectly competitive firm is perfectly elastic at the market price.
Panel (b): The demand curve confronting an imperfectly competitive firm is downward sloping.

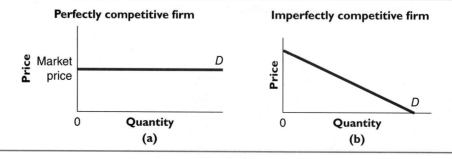

### IMPERFECT COMPETITION

Perfect competition is an ideal case, at best only approximated in actual industries. It provides a benchmark against which the performance of all other market types can be compared. Economists study three other types of market structure that differ in varying degrees from perfect competition: monopoly, a market with only one seller of a unique product; oligopoly, a market served by only a few rival sellers; and monopolistic competition, a market in which many firms sell products that are close, but imperfect, substitutes for one another. The demand curve confronting a perfectly competitive firm is perfectly elastic at the market price, while the demand curve confronting an imperfectly competitive firm is downward sloping.

## 8.2 SOURCES OF MARKET POWER

Firms that confront downward-sloping demand curves enjoy **market power**—they can raise the prices of their products without losing all their sales. A perfectly competitive firm has no market power. If it attempts to charge a price higher than the market price, it will lose all of its sales to other firms. When a firm has market power, it can increase the price of its product and lose only part of its sales (at least for small increases in the price). The greater the market power of firms in an industry, the less competitive is that industry. However, even a firm with market power cannot sell *any* quantity at *any* price it wants. All it can do is pick a price-quantity combination along the demand curve for its product. If the firm chooses to raise its price, it is choosing a different point on its demand curve. A higher price means a smaller quantity demanded by consumers, which means the quantity sold by the firm is smaller. If price is increased too much (to the price represented by the vertical intercept of the demand curve or higher), quantity demanded falls to zero and the firm sells nothing.

Why do some firms have market power while others do not? Market power enables some firms to charge a price above the cost of production, and arises from factors that limit competition, such as exclusive control over inputs, economies of scale, patents, licences or franchises, and network economies.

**market power** a firm's ability to raise the price of a good without losing all its sales

If the Petro Canada station on Quinpool Road raised its gasoline prices by 1 cent/litre, would all its customers buy their gas elsewhere?

### EXCLUSIVE CONTROL OVER IMPORTANT INPUTS

Location is a key determinant of the sales of many retail operations, such as gasoline stations for which the best located land on which to build is an important input. To the extent that potential tenants are willing to pay a premium for corner locations with good traffic counts, the owner of that land has market power because he has exclusive control over an important input.

### ECONOMIES OF SCALE (NATURAL MONOPOLIES)

Figure 6.6 in Chapter 6 shows that economies of scale occur if long-run average cost decreases when a firm increases its scale of operation. If economies of scale are still present when the quantity supplied by a single seller is large enough to serve an entire market, a single seller will monopolize the market, because the largest firm has the lowest costs and can drive competitors out of business by undercutting any price a competitor can afford to charge. A monopoly that results from economies of scale is called a **natural monopoly**. For example, once an electric utility has built transmission lines and transformer stations

**natural monopoly** a monopoly that results from economies of scale

to link up a neighbourhood, it can connect additional customers at relatively low marginal cost. When economies of scale are significant, but somewhat smaller, a market tends to be served by only a few sellers.

## NETWORK ECONOMIES

Most commodities are consumed by individuals without affecting the usefulness of the product to other individuals (do any of us, for example, know or care what brand of dental floss others use?). However, some products become much more valuable to us as the number of other users increases. There would be, for example, no point at all in owning a telephone if you were the *only* person who had one; your telephone becomes more valuable to you as the number of people whom you can call increases. Hence, a telephone network becomes more useful as more people join the network, which creates a network economy.

A *network economy* occurs when a product's value increases as more people join the network of users. The increased value of an expanded network is equivalent to an improvement in the product's quality, or one could also say that any given quality level can be produced at lower cost as sales volume increases. Thus, a **network economy** is a reduction in the cost of providing a given quality of a product that occurs if the value of the product to individual users increases as more people join the network of users. Network economies may thus be viewed as another form of economies of scale in production, and that is how we will treat them here.

Network economies help to account for the dominant position of Microsoft's Windows operating system, which, as noted in Chapter 6, is currently installed in more than 80 percent of all personal computers. Because Microsoft's initial sales advantage gave software developers a strong incentive to write for the Windows format, the inventory of available software in the Windows format is now vastly larger than that for any competing operating system. And although general-purpose software like word processors and spreadsheets continues to be available for multiple operating systems, specialized professional software and games usually appear first—and often only—in the Windows format. This software gap and the desire to achieve compatibility for file sharing gave people a good reason for choosing Windows, even if, as in the case of many Apple Macintosh users, they believed a competing system was otherwise superior.

## PATENTS, COPYRIGHTS, LICENCES, AND FRANCHISES

Patents, copyrights, licences, and franchises are all legally enforceable restrictions on free competition. For example, patents give the inventors or developers of patented new products the exclusive, legally enforceable right to sell those products for a specified time. Patent legislation enables firms that believe their patents have been infringed to sue for redress, and the courts will enforce any award of damages. In Canada, for example, a patent insulates a new drug from competition for 20 years from the date an application for a patent is filed. For the life of the patent, only the patent holder may legally sell the drug.

Patent legislation is clearly a restriction on free competition. Its justification is that by insulating sellers from competition for some period of time, patents enable innovators to charge higher prices to recoup their product's development costs. Pharmaceutical companies, for example, spend millions of dollars on research in the hope of discovering new drug therapies for illnesses. Patent protection enables the patent holder to set a price above the marginal cost of production to recoup the cost of the research on the drug. In the same way, copyrights protect the authors of published works (such as this textbook). Nevertheless, holders of patents and copyrights may face competition from products that serve the same purpose but that are sufficiently differentiated to avoid violation of patents or copyrights. There is more than one type of patented medication for managing pain and

---

**network economy** a reduction in the cost of providing a given quality of a product that occurs if the value of the product to individual users increases as more people join the network of users

more than one economics textbook. Patents and copyrights do insulate their owners from competition, but economies of scale are a far more enduring source of market power.

Historically, in order to obtain outcomes that might not be available if the market were left to itself, governments have sometimes granted licences that give one firm the exclusive right (i.e., a monopoly right) to provide a specific service. Canada's oldest firm (Hudson's Bay Company) was initially founded in 1670 on that basis; the British gave the company an exclusive licence to conduct the fur trade from posts on Hudson's Bay, an arrangement that served to divert furs from the French trading network, which operated through Montreal. At that time, France was the only superpower that could challenge the British. The British believed their geo-political interests in North American would be best served if they issued an exclusive licence for the fur trade in order to divert the fur trade from Montreal.

In many industries, franchising and private sector licensing are common today. A company with a unique product or service (e.g., McDonald's hamburgers, Molly Maid cleaners) will sell to another firm the right to use their technology, and sometimes their brand name, in a specific local market. A licence to use a specific technology will usually include a prohibition against resale of the licence to a third party. The franchise usually includes a guarantee that the franchisor will not sell any other franchises in the same market area. Thus the purchaser of a franchise or licence obtains a local monopoly of the production of that specific good or service. However, a franchised firm may face competition from firms that offer a slightly different product and that might or might not be franchised under a different brand. For example, four different coffee shops might serve the same university campus, one selling Tim Hortons coffee, one selling Starbucks coffee, one selling Second Cup coffee, and one independent shop selling coffee without a franchise.

> **RECAP**
>
> **THREE SOURCES OF MARKET POWER**
>
> A firm's power to raise its prices without losing its entire market stems from (1) exclusive control of important inputs, (2) legally enforceable restrictions on competition (patents, copyrights, licences and franchises) and (3) economies of scale, or network economies. By far the most important and enduring of these are economies of scale and network economies.

## 8.3 ECONOMIES OF SCALE AND THE IMPORTANCE OF FIXED COSTS

As we saw in Chapter 5, variable costs are defined as those costs that vary with the level of output produced, while fixed costs are costs whose amount does not depend on output. There are no fixed costs in the long run, because in the long run all inputs can be varied. Nevertheless, as indicated in Chapter 6, economies of scale can arise from indivisible costs, which are the costs of indivisible factors of production. For some products, a minimum amount of an indivisible factor of production is necessary before even the smallest quantity of the product can be produced. However, once a sufficient amount of the indivisible factor has been acquired, marginal cost may be quite low.

Software development is an example of this. Consumers want to buy software that works effectively, so a software firm has to write and debug the whole computer program before making a single sale. Hence, indivisible costs are a fixed cost, at least in the short run.

We stated in Chapter 6 that, because all factors of production are variable in the long run, managers of a firm can in the long run (sometimes referred to as the "planning horizon") plan the best way to combine factors of production and the most profitable size for their firm. Suppose a firm is considering whether or not to produce new software. The managers know that large costs will be incurred for a considerable period of time before a single copy is produced. They also know that if the new software is successful, the marginal cost of making and selling each additional copy will be very low. The only alternative to incurring very large, one-time costs is to incur no costs, which also means no software. Until they make their choice, they are operating in the long run. Once they sign contracts that commit them to startup costs, they are operating in the short run.

Equation 8.1 describes the cost structure the managers commit to if they decide to produce new software:

$$TC = TFC + MQ. \tag{8.1}$$

Total fixed cost is $TFC$, $M$ is marginal cost (assumed constant, which is critical in this illustration), and $Q$ is the total quantity of output produced. Because marginal cost is constant, it also is equal to average variable cost ($AVC$). For a production process with this simple total cost function, total variable cost ($TVC$) is simply $MQ$, the multiplicative product of marginal cost and quantity. Panel (a) of Figure 8.2 graphs total cost ($TC$) for a firm whose total cost is given by Equation 8.1. Notice that the vertical intercept ($TFC$) in panel (a) of Figure 8.2 gives the firm's total fixed cost. (In this discussion, definitions of different categories of cost are the same as those used in Chapters 1 and 5.)

To find average total cost ($ATC$), divide Equation 8.1 by $Q$:

$$ATC = TC/Q = TFC/Q + M. \tag{8.2}$$

Notice that as quantity ($Q$) increases, average fixed cost ($TFC/Q$) must decrease and average total cost ($TC/Q$) also must decrease. As the quantity of output rises, cost per unit decreases because total fixed cost is spread over more and more units of output.

Equation 8.2 can also be written as

$$ATC = AFC + AVC = AFC + M, \tag{8.3}$$

where $ATC$ is average total cost, $AVC$ is average variable cost, $ATC = TC/Q$, and $AVC = TVC/Q = M$. Panel (b) of Figure 8.2 shows an average total cost curve ($ATC$) that corresponds to Equations 8.2 and 8.3. Panel (b) also shows the constant marginal cost,

**FIGURE 8.2**
**Total and Average Costs for a Production Process with Constant Marginal Cost**
For a firm whose total cost curve of producing Q units of output per year is $TC = TFC + MQ$, total cost in panel (a) rises at a constant rate as output grows, while average total cost in panel (b) declines. Average total cost is always higher than marginal cost for this firm, but the difference becomes less and less significant as output increases to higher and higher levels.

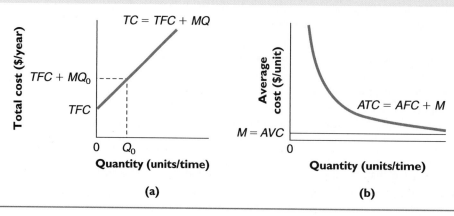

*M*, which is equal to constant average variable cost (*AVC*). The average total cost curve in panel (b) shows that cost per unit (i.e., average total cost) always decreases as output increases. And, though average total cost is always higher than marginal cost for this firm, the difference between the two diminishes as output grows. At extremely high levels of output, average cost is very close to marginal cost *(M)*. When the firm is spreading its fixed cost over an extremely large volume of output, average fixed cost becomes almost insignificant.

When we developed the model of production costs in Chapter 5, we used the example of a small bottle manufacturer to support the idea of diminishing returns and rising short-run marginal cost.[1] Software production is very different. It can take thousands of programming hours and millions of dollars to prepare a complex game or design package, but, once it is finished, the marginal cost of production is very small. Burning and packaging one more CD costs very little, and is a cost that remains nearly constant from small to very large quantities of output. Indeed, many software firms now sell their products as downloads from an Internet site and therefore have a marginal cost of production that is constant at zero. In Figure 8.2, short-run marginal cost and average variable cost remain constant at *M*. Therefore, in Figure 8.2, the spreading of total fixed cost over an increasingly large quantity of output must always cause average total cost to decrease. Software managers facing long-run decisions recognize that if they choose to produce software, they commit themselves to a cost structure in which spreading total fixed cost over ever larger quantities of output is the only relevant factor in determining cost per unit. The examples of video game production in Equation 8.1 and software in Figure 8.2 illustrate the fact that the law of diminishing marginal returns has important practical exceptions.

## EXAMPLE **8.1**

Two manufacturers of video game consoles, Sony and Microsoft, each have fixed costs of $200 000 and marginal costs of $0.80/ game. Sony makes PlayStation and Microsoft makes Xbox. Suppose each holds a large share of the market they serve. If Microsoft produces 1 million units/year and Sony produces 1.2 million units/ year, how much lower will Sony's average production cost be?

Table 8.2 summarizes the relevant cost categories for the two firms. Note in the bottom row that Sony enjoys only a $0.03 average cost advantage over Microsoft. Even though Microsoft produces 20 percent fewer copies of its video game than Sony, it does not suffer a significant cost disadvantage because fixed cost is a relatively small part of total production cost.

**TABLE 8.2**
**Costs for Two Video Game Producers (1)**

|  | Microsoft | Sony |
| --- | --- | --- |
| Annual production | 1 000 000 | 1 200 000 |
| Fixed cost | $200 000 | $200 000 |
| Variable cost | $800 000 | $960 000 |
| Total cost | $1 000 000 | $1 160 000 |
| Average cost per game | $1.00 | $0.97 |

1   If you compare the average total cost curve in Figure 5.6 of Chapter 5 with average total cost in Figure 8.2, you will notice that in Figure 8.2 average total cost always decreases as output increases, but in Figure 5.6, average total cost reaches a minimum and thereafter increases as quantity of output increases. The difference between the two diagrams occurs because each diagram is based on different underlying assumptions. In Figure 5.6, beyond a certain point, the law of diminishing marginal returns causes short-run marginal cost and average variable cost to increase. However, we assumed marginal cost to be constant in Figure 8.2.

The next example shows how the picture changes when fixed cost looms large relative to marginal cost.

## EXAMPLE 8.2

Now suppose Microsoft and Sony each have fixed costs of $10 000 000 and marginal costs of $0.20/video game. Again, Microsoft and Sony each hold a large share of the market they serve. If Microsoft produces 1 million units per year and Sony produces 1.2 million units per year, how much lower will Sony's average production cost be?

The relevant cost categories for the two firms are now summarized in Table 8.3. The bottom row shows that Sony enjoys a $1.67 average cost advantage over Microsoft, substantially larger than in Example 8.1.

**TABLE 8.3**
**Costs for Two Video Game Producers (2)**

|  | Microsoft | Sony |
|---|---|---|
| Annual production | 1 000 000 | 1 200 000 |
| Fixed cost | $10 000 000 | $10 000 000 |
| Variable cost | $200 000 | $240 000 |
| Total cost | $10 200 000 | $10 240 000 |
| Average cost per game | $10.20 | $8.53 |

If the video games the two firms produce are essentially similar, the fact that Sony can charge significantly lower prices and still cover its costs should enable it to attract customers away from Microsoft. As more and more of the market goes to Sony, its cost advantage will become self-reinforcing. Table 8.4 shows how a shift of 500 000 units from Microsoft to Sony would cause Microsoft's average cost to rise to $20.20/unit, while Sony's average cost would fall to $6.08/unit.

Table 8.4 shows that by spreading a much larger output over the same total fixed cost Sony accomplishes a large cost advantage over Microsoft. The fact that a firm cannot long survive at a severe cost disadvantage helps to explain why the video game market is served by only a small number of firms at any given time. Consider the case of Sony, Microsoft, Nintendo, and SEGA. Sony launched PlayStation 2 in 2000. In 2001, Microsoft launched Xbox, and Nintendo launched GameCube. By mid-2004, Sony had sold nearly 71 million game consoles, Microsoft had sold fewer than 15 million, and Nintendo fewer than 14 million. SEGA, a company that once led the industry with its SEGA Genesis is no longer on the radar. Fast forward to 2011, and industry giants Google and Apple have come out of nowhere to take a third of total market revenue as new tablet computers and

**TABLE 8.4**
**Costs for Two Video Game Producers (3)**

|  | Microsoft | Sony |
|---|---|---|
| Annual production | 500 000 | 1 700 000 |
| Fixed cost | $10 000 000 | $10 000 000 |
| Variable cost | $100 000 | $340 000 |
| Total cost | $10 100 000 | $10 340 000 |
| Average cost per game | $20.20 | $6.08 |

smart phones pushed the industry into selling apps for other devices instead of stand-alone hardware like game consoles.[2]

**Use the costs given in Example 8.2. How large will Sony's unit cost advantage be if it sells 2 000 000 units/year, while Microsoft sells only 200 000?**

During recent decades, an increasing share of the value embodied in the goods and services we buy stems from fixed investment in research and development. For example, in 1984 some 80 percent of the cost of a computer was in its hardware (which has relatively high marginal cost); the remaining 20 percent was in its software. But as early as 1990, those proportions were reversed. Software now accounts for about 85 percent of total costs in the computer industry, whose products are included in a growing share of ordinary manufactured goods.

## ECONOMIC NATURALIST 8.1

### Why does Intel sell the majority of microprocessors used in personal computers?

The fixed investment required to produce computer chips is enormous; Intel's Fab 42 chip factory in Arizona is forecast to cost more than $5 billion by the time it opens in 2013. But once a chip has been designed and the manufacturing facility built, the marginal cost of producing each chip is only pennies.

This cost pattern explains why Intel currently sells roughly 80 percent of all microprocessors. Of course, new generations of chips will continue to be developed, and the fixed costs of developing them will be high.

Economies of scale can be the result of large fixed costs. If economies of scale occur over quantities of output that are a large share of the market being served, the perfectly competitive pattern of many small firms, each producing only a small share of its

---

2 Notice that in the case of video games, network economies can play an important role in establishing a cost advantage. If it appeared that one system would dominate the market, software developers would have a strong incentive to tailor their software to that system. Selling to the dominant firm means the fixed costs of developing and writing software can be spread over a larger quantity of output.

industry's total output, cannot survive. Because economies of scale can be important, we must develop a clear sense of how the behaviour of a firm with market power differs from that of the perfectly competitive firm.

---

**RECAP**

### ECONOMIES OF SCALE AND THE IMPORTANCE OF FIXED COSTS

Research, design, engineering, and other fixed costs account for an increasingly large share of all costs required to bring products successfully to market. Managers often must choose between using a large scale of operation to manufacture a product or using no operation at all. In choosing to manufacture the product, they will incur large fixed costs, often with relatively low marginal cost. In such a situation, average total cost declines, often sharply, as output grows. This cost pattern explains why many industries are dominated by either a single firm or a small number of firms.

---

## 8.4 PROFIT MAXIMIZATION FOR THE MONOPOLIST

We can assume that firms want to maximize profit. Regardless of whether a firm is a price taker or a price setter, it will choose the quantity of output that maximizes the difference between total revenue and total cost. The constraints faced by a price taker are different from the constraints faced by a price setter. As a result, there are important differences in how the two types of firm choose the quantity of output that maximizes profit. To help focus attention on these differences, we begin with a brief review of how the perfectly competitive firm chooses its level of output.

### THE PERFECTLY COMPETITIVE FIRM'S DECISION RULE: A REVIEW

Recall from Chapter 7 that a perfectly competitive firm is one firm among many, all of which are producing the same product. As the following example reminds us, the competitive firm maximizes profit by selling that quantity of output at which marginal cost equals the market price.

### EXAMPLE 8.3

#### How many watermelons will a farmer produce?

Consider a perfectly competitive watermelon farmer whose marginal cost is shown in Figure 8.3. If this grower can sell as many tons of melons as he chooses at a price of \$200/ton, how many tons will he sell to maximize his profit?

Any producer, whether it is perfectly competitive or a monopolist or something in between, will expand output if and only if the benefit of doing so exceeds the cost. If the farmer in this example were producing only 12 tons/year, his marginal cost would be \$160/ton, while his benefit from expanding production would be the market price at which he can sell the melons, \$200/ton. So this farmer will expand his production of melons until he reaches 18 tons/year, the quantity at which marginal cost exactly equals the market price.

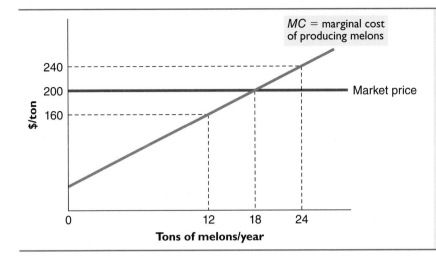

**FIGURE 8.3**
**The Profit-Maximizing Output Level for a Perfectly Competitive Watermelon Farmer**
At a market price of $200/ton, the perfectly competitive farmer maximizes profit by selling 18 tons of watermelon a year, the quantity for which price equals marginal cost.

For both the perfectly competitive firm and the monopolist, the marginal benefit of increasing output by one unit is the additional revenue the firm will receive if it sells one additional unit of output. In both cases, this marginal benefit is called the firm's **marginal revenue**. For the perfectly competitive firm, because selling one more unit does not affect the price of previous units sold and generates additional revenue equal to the price, marginal revenue is exactly equal to the market price of the product.

**marginal revenue** the increase in total revenue obtained by producing and selling one more unit of output

## MARGINAL REVENUE FOR THE MONOPOLIST

The logic of profit maximization is precisely the same for the monopolist as for the perfectly competitive firm. In both cases, the firm increases output as long as the benefit of doing so exceeds the cost. The calculation of marginal cost is also precisely the same for the monopolist as for the perfectly competitive firm. *The only significant difference between the two cases concerns the calculation of marginal revenue.*

As we saw in Chapter 5, marginal revenue for a perfectly competitive firm is simply the market price. If that price is $6, then the marginal benefit of selling an extra unit is exactly $6. However, a monopolist's demand curve is not perfectly elastic—it slopes downward. Therefore, if a monopolist is to sell an additional unit, it must reduce price on *all* units. *In contrast to a perfect competitor, the marginal benefit to a monopolist of selling an additional unit is always less than the market price.* Examples 8.4 to 8.6 make it clear that, because the monopolist faces a downward-sloping demand curve, it can sell an additional unit only if it reduces the price on all units. And when the monopolist reduces the price, it affects the revenue received from each unit it is currently offering for sale.

### EXAMPLE 8.4

**How much extra revenue would a monopolist get by increasing its output?**

A monopolist with the demand curve shown in Figure 8.4 is currently selling two units of output at a price of $6/unit. What would be its marginal benefit from selling an additional unit, if all units must sell at the same price?

This monopolist's total revenue from the sale of two units/week is ($6/unit) × (2 units/week) = $12/week. Its total revenue from the sale of three units/week would be $15/week (= 3 × 5). The difference, $3/week, is the marginal revenue from the sale of the third unit each week. Note that this amount is not only smaller than the original price ($6) but smaller than the new price ($5) as well. Marginal revenue is $2 less than the new price because the two units that previously sold for $6 each now sell for $5 each, a decrease of $1 per unit or $2 in total.

**FIGURE 8.4**
**The Monopolist's Benefit from Selling an Additional Unit**
The monopolist shown receives $12/week in total revenue by selling 2 units/week at a price of $6 each. This monopolist could earn $15/week by selling 3 units/week at a price of $5 each. Thus the benefit from selling the third unit would be $15 − $12 = $3, which is $2 less than its selling price of $5, because the firm has to accept $1 less for each of the two units it sells if price is $6.

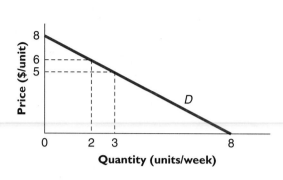

EXERCISE 8.2 **Calculate marginal revenue for the monopolist in Example 8.4 as it increases output from 3 to 4 units/week, and then from 4 to 5 units/week.**

Consider again the monopolist whose demand curve is shown in Figure 8.4. In Example 8.4 and Exercise 8.2, a sequence of increases in output—from two to three, from three to four, and from four to five—yield marginal revenue of $3, $1, and -$1, respectively. The first two columns of Table 8.5 just report in tabular form the same information that is in Figure 8.4. They display the demand relationship—the relationship between the price the firm charges and the quantity the firm will be able to sell. Column three reports total revenue, which is equal to price times quantity (i.e., the product of the first two columns). When the firm considers increasing production by one unit, it will want to ask, how much does total revenue increase when production is increased by one unit? Marginal revenue is reported in column four.

Note that in Table 8.5, the marginal revenue values are displayed between the two quantity figures to which they correspond. For example, when the firm increased its output from 2 units/week to three, its marginal revenue was $3. Strictly speaking, this marginal revenue corresponds to neither quantity but to the movement between the two quantities; hence, its placement in the table. Likewise, in moving from 3 to 4 units/week, the firm earned marginal revenue of $1. Therefore, the figure is placed midway between the quantities of three and four, and so on.

To graph marginal revenue as a function of quantity, we plot marginal revenue for the movement from two to three units of output per week ($3) at a quantity of 2.5, because 2.5 lies midway between two and three. Similarly, we plot the marginal revenue for the movement from 3 to 4 units/week ($1) at a quantity of 3.5 units/week, and the marginal

**TABLE 8.5**
**Marginal Revenue for a Monopolist**

| Price | Quantity Sold | Total Revenue | Marginal Revenue |
|---|---|---|---|
| 6 | 2 | 12 | |
| | | | +3 |
| 5 | 3 | 15 | |
| | | | +1 |
| 4 | 4 | 16 | |
| | | | −1 |
| 3 | 5 | 15 | |

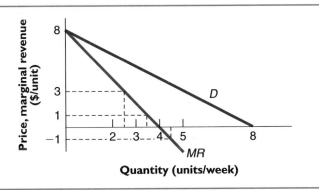

**FIGURE 8.5**
**Marginal Revenue in Graphical Form**
Because a monopolist must reduce price to sell an extra unit not only for the extra unit sold but also for all units that it sells, marginal revenue from the sale of the extra unit is less than its selling price.

revenue for the movement from 4 to 5 units/week ( −$1) at a quantity of 4.5. The resulting marginal revenue curve, *MR*, is shown in Figure 8.5.[3]

We also can show that the monopolist's demand curve is its average revenue curve. A firm's total revenue for any quantity it sells is given by the equation

$$Total\ revenue = price \times quantity.$$

Dividing both sides of the equation by quantity gives

$$Total\ revenue/quantity = average\ revenue = price.$$

It follows that the *demand curve is the firm's average revenue curve* because each price on the demand curve is paired with a unique quantity. Each point on a firm's demand curve plots the average revenue the firm will obtain from that quantity of sales. Notice, too, that price equals average revenue. These two results pertain for all imperfectly competitive firms.

## THE MONOPOLIST'S PROFIT-MAXIMIZING DECISION RULE

Having derived the monopolist's marginal revenue curve, we are now in a position to describe how the monopolist chooses the quantity of output that maximizes profit. As for the perfectly competitive firm, the cost–benefit principle says that the monopolist will continue to increase output as long as the gain from doing so exceeds the cost. At any given level of output, the benefit from increasing output is the marginal revenue that corresponds to that quantity of output. The cost of an increase in output is the marginal cost for that additional quantity of output. Whenever marginal revenue exceeds marginal cost, the firm will increase its output. Conversely, whenever marginal revenue is less than marginal cost, the firm will reduce its output. We can say then that the **rule for profit maximization** for monopolistic firms is that profits are maximized at the quantity of output where marginal revenue equals marginal cost.

When the monopolist's profit-maximizing rule is stated in this way, we can see that the perfectly competitive firm's rule is the same as the monopolist's rule. When the

**COST-BENEFIT**

**rule for profit maximization** profits are maximized by producing the quantity of output at which marginal revenue equals marginal cost

---

3  More generally, a monopolist with a straight-line demand curve whose vertical intercept is $a$ and whose horizontal intercept is $Q_0$, will have a marginal revenue curve that has vertical intercept of $a$ and a slope that is twice as steep as the demand curve's slope. Thus, its horizontal intercept will not be $Q_0$, but $Q_0/2$; marginal revenue has twice the slope because marginal revenue is the new, reduced price charged in order to sell an extra unit *less* the reduction in revenue caused when *all* units are sold at the new, lower price. Marginal revenue curves can also be expressed algebraically. Let P = price and Q = quantity. If the equation for the monopolist's demand curve is $P = a − bQ$, then the equation for its marginal revenue curve will be $MR = a − 2bQ$. Using the terminology of calculus, marginal revenue is the derivative (or rate of change) of total revenue with respect to output. If $P = a − bQ$, then total revenue will be given by $TR = PQ = aQ − bQ^2$, which means that $MR = dTR/dQ = a − 2bQ$.

perfectly competitive firm expands output by one unit, its marginal revenue exactly equals the product's market price (because the perfectly competitive firm can increase sales by a unit without having to decrease the price of existing units). So when the perfectly competitive firm equates price with marginal cost, it is also equating marginal revenue with marginal cost. The rule for maximizing profits is the same for all firms.

### EXAMPLE 8.5

#### What is the monopolist's profit-maximizing quantity of output?

Consider a monopolist with the demand and marginal cost curves shown in panel (a) of Figure 8.6. If this firm is currently producing 12 units/week, will it increase or decrease production? What is the profit-maximizing quantity of output?

In panel (b) of Figure 8.6, we begin by constructing the marginal revenue curve that corresponds to the monopolist's demand curve. It has the same vertical intercept as the demand curve, and its horizontal intercept is half as large. Note that the monopolist's marginal revenue at 12 units/week is zero, which is clearly less than its marginal cost of $3/unit. Therefore, this monopolist will earn a higher profit by reducing production until marginal revenue equals marginal cost, which occurs at an output of 8 units/week. At the profit-maximizing quantity of output, the firm will charge $4/unit, the price that corresponds to 8 units/week on the demand curve.

---

**FIGURE 8.6**
**The Demand, Marginal Revenue, and Marginal Cost Curves for a Monopolist**
Panel (a) shows that price equals marginal cost at the midpoint of the demand curve when price is $3 and output is 12 units/week, but this would not maximize profits for a monopoly firm. Panel (b) shows that marginal revenue is zero at a price of $3/unit and an output of 12 units. This output level cannot maximize profits. Panel (b) shows that the monopolist will maximize its profit when price is $4/unit and output is 8 units/week.

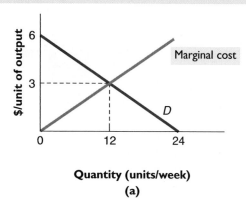

(a)

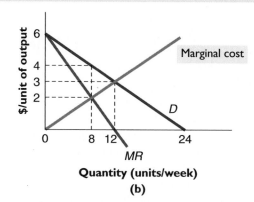

(b)

---

A profit maximizing monopolist will set price so that demand for its product is elastic. Appendix 4A, Chapter 4 shows that demand is elastic above the midpoint of the demand curve. To achieve positive marginal revenue, the profit maximizing monopolist will set price above the midpoint of the demand curve, where cost and marginal revenue are both positive. In this range of the demand curve, demand for the product is price elastic.

---

**EXERCISE 8.3**   **Find the profit-maximizing price and quantity of output for a monopolist with the demand curve $P = 12 - Q$ and the marginal cost curve $MC = 2Q$, where $P$ is the price of the product in dollars per unit and $Q$ is output in units per week.**

## MONOPOLY: A GRAPHICAL SUMMARY

The downward-sloping demand curve faced by individual firms is the key characteristic of imperfect competition in general and monopoly in particular. On the supply side, a number of cost situations are possible. In Section 8.3 of this chapter we outlined the cost situation of a software firm. The software producer's technology is likely to be quite different from the technology used by a firm that enjoys a monopoly conferred by an exclusive licence, patent, or franchise. If a monopoly exists because a firm holds a licence, patent, or franchise for a unique product, it is quite possible that the firm has a U-shaped cost curve similar to those we developed in Chapters 5 and 6. Panel (a) of Figure 8.7 portrays such a monopolist, operating in the long run. The monopolist's demand curve is labelled $D$, $MR$ is marginal revenue, $AC$ is average total cost, and $MC$ is marginal cost. The monopolist maximizes profit when it produces the quantity $Q_M$, where marginal revenue equals marginal cost. By selecting the price $P_M$, the monopolist determines that the quantity sold will be $Q_M$. By choosing a price, the monopolist also implicitly chooses the quantity it can sell at that price—the monopolist chooses a point on its demand curve. Point $B$ in panel (a) of Figure 8.7 is the point on the monopolist's demand curve that it chooses when it chooses the quantity of output that maximizes profit.

When the quantity of output is $Q_M$, average total cost is $AC_M$, which is read from curve $AC$. Profit per unit of output is the difference between price and average total cost:

$$\textit{Profit per unit} = P_M - AC_M.$$

Total profit is obtained by multiplying profit per unit by the quantity of units produced:

$$\textit{Total profit} = (P_M - AC_M) \times Q_M.$$

---

**FIGURE 8.7**

**Monopoly: A Graphical Summary**

The monopolist portrayed in panel (a) maximizes profit by choosing price $P_M$ and quantity $Q_M$ as defined by point $B$ on the demand curve. At quantity $Q_M$, average cost is $AC_M$; therefore, total profit is represented by the green rectangle. The same monopolist is portrayed in panel (b), and the same demand curve is shown in both panels. When marginal cost decreases from $MC$ to $MC'$, the monopolist moves from point $B$ to point $C$ on its demand curve; it reduces price to $P_M'$ and increases quantity to $Q_M'$. The monopolist's profits are higher with the cost reduction and the new price-quantity combination.

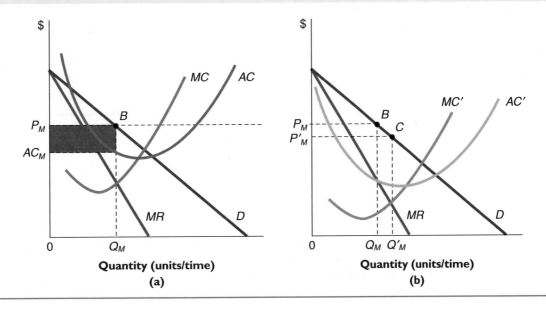

The monopolist's profit is represented by the green rectangular area in panel (a) of Figure 8.7. It is the area obtained by multiplying profit per unit times the quantity of units.

Suppose a technological improvement reduces the monopolist's costs. This is shown in panel (b) of Figure 8.7 by the shift to the lower curves, $AC'$ and $MC'$. Nothing has changed for consumers, so the monopolist's demand curve is unchanged from panel (a). However, with the new marginal cost curve, it will be profitable for the monopolist to increase quantity to $Q_M'$ and reduce price to $P_M'$. Notice that in choosing the new profit maximizing price and quantity, the monopolist has moved from point $B$ on its demand curve to point $C$; it has chosen a new point on its demand curve and passed on part of the cost reduction. The monopolist did not move from one point to another on a supply curve. Given its cost structure, a monopolist chooses the point on its demand curve that maximizes profit.

> **RECAP**
>
> **PROFIT MAXIMIZATION FOR THE MONOPOLIST**
>
> Both the perfectly competitive firm and the monopolist maximize profit by choosing the quantity of output at which marginal revenue equals marginal cost. But whereas marginal revenue equals market price for the perfectly competitive firm, marginal revenue is always less than market price for the monopolist. A monopolist chooses the point on its demand curve that maximizes profit.

# 8.5 WHY THE INVISIBLE HAND FAILS UNDER MONOPOLY

Equilibrium in perfectly competitive markets has important implications, as we discussed in Chapter 7. Under these assumptions, the self-serving pursuits of consumers and firms are consistent with the broader interests of society as a whole, in the sense that total economic surplus is maximized. Does the same conclusion hold true for the case of imperfectly competitive firms?

Consider the monopolist in Example 8.5. Does this firm's profit-maximizing output maximize total economic surplus? For any given level of output, the corresponding price on the demand curve indicates the amount buyers would be willing to pay for an additional unit of output. When the monopolist is producing 8 units/week, the marginal benefit to society of an additional unit of output is thus $4 [see panel (b) of Figure 8.6]. And since the marginal cost of an additional unit at that output level is only $2 (again, see Figure 8.6), there would be a net social benefit of $2/unit if the monopolist were to expand production by one unit above the monopolist's profit-maximizing level. As long as marginal cost is less than marginal benefit to society, total economic surplus will increase if output increases by another unit. Both panels of Figure 8.6 show that as long as output is less than 12 units, total economic surplus will increase if output is increased by one more unit.

Because monopoly causes total economic surplus to be smaller than the maximum possible, the profit-maximizing monopolist's production is socially inefficient, in the sense that the economic pie is smaller than it could be. If so, why does the monopolist not simply increase production? The answer is that the monopolist would gladly do so, if there were some way to maintain the price of existing units and reduce the price of only the extra units. As a practical matter, however, that is not always possible.

Consider again the monopolist in Example 8.5, whose demand, marginal revenue, and marginal cost curves are taken from panel (b) of Figure 8.6 and reproduced in Figure 8.8. For the market served by this monopolist, what is the quantity of output that maximizes total economic surplus?

At any output level, the cost to society of an additional unit of output is the value of the resources used in production, which is the amount shown on the monopolist's

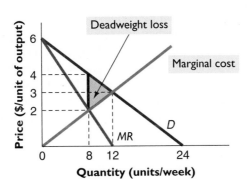

**FIGURE 8.8**
**The Deadweight Loss from Monopoly**
A loss in economic surplus results because the profit-maximizing quantity of output (8 units/week) is less than the quantity of output that maximizes total economic surplus (12 units/week). The deadweight loss arising from the profit-maximizing quantity of output is the area of the pale blue triangle, $4/week.

marginal cost curve. The marginal benefit *to society* of an extra unit of output is simply the amount people are willing to pay for it, which is the amount shown on the monopolist's demand curve. To maximize total economic surplus, the monopolist needs to increase production until the marginal benefit to society equals the marginal cost, which in this case occurs at a level of 12 units/week, the output level at which the market demand curve intersects the monopolist's marginal cost curve.

The fact that marginal revenue is less than price for the monopolist results in a deadweight loss. For the monopolist just discussed, the size of this deadweight loss is equal to the area of the blue triangle in Figure 8.8, which is (½)($2/unit) (4 units/week) = $4/week. That is the amount by which total economic surplus is reduced because the monopolist produces too little.[4]

For a monopolist, profit maximization occurs when marginal cost equals marginal revenue. Since the monopolist's marginal revenue is always less than price, the monopolist's profit-maximizing output level is always below the surplus maximizing level. Under perfect competition, by contrast, price is equal to marginal revenue. Therefore, profit maximization occurs when marginal cost equals the market price—the same criterion that must be satisfied for surplus maximization. Although the invisible hand of self-interest may serve the common good under perfectly competitive conditions, it will not do so under monopoly.

If perfect competition would maximize total surplus and monopoly does not, what should be done? One policy option is to have Parliament limit the extent of monopoly through antitrust laws, at the same time recognizing that the alternatives to monopoly often entail problems of their own.

For example, would society be better off without patents? Monopoly is the result of patent protections preventing all but one firm from manufacturing some highly valued product, and if patents were eliminated, anyone would be free to copy a new product as soon as it appeared. Patent protection, and the monopoly profits it enables, gives firms a chance to recover research and development costs. For public policy, the question is, what is the appropriate length of patent protection? There is a trade-off; if patent protection lasts too long, the cost in the form of monopoly's reduced output will outweigh the benefits of innovation. If it is too short, the costs arising from loss of innovation will outweigh the benefits of the greater output that occurs when monopoly is reduced.

---

4  As well, firms with market power may employ lobbyists, lawyers, and other scarce talent to convince regulators and legislators to enact rules that protect market power. This is known as rent-seeking behaviour, since it does not produce additional output but just seeks to reallocate existing output. In addition, rent seeking is costly over and above the cost represented by the deadweight loss, because valuable resources are absorbed in lobbying for favourable rules.

As well, patent protection may motivate competitors to engage in the socially wasteful strategy of developing alternative duplicate technologies that achieve the same function. Firms may respond by taking out pre-emptive patents, which they do not use, in order to maintain their market leadership. The problems created by patents are part of the reason why, in all technologically sophisticated societies, research is not conducted only by firms in the private sector, but also by universities, government laboratories, and foundations. The results of their research are placed in the public domain.

Although, for example, the pharmaceutical industry develops and patents many drugs, some of the most important drugs, such as penicillin and the polio vaccine, were discovered and developed by research conducted in the public sector.[5] If such publicly available research is to happen, of course, citizens have to be willing to pay the higher taxes necessary to fund more drug research in universities or other public research institutes. If those public institutions then made their research results freely available, successful drugs could be rapidly copied and produced by many firms. A competitive market for drugs in which drug producers would only have to cover their direct costs of production (which are typically rather small) would be the result. Prices would be much lower, since monopoly profits would be competed away and since drug companies would not have to recover their development and testing costs (which are often huge—particularly since drug companies also have to cover the costs of their unsuccessful research). If the public sector paid for drug research, citizens would pay more in taxes, but less in drug prices.

Which is the better solution? The answer depends, in part, on one's perspective. Humanity as a whole receives the benefits of more public knowledge about effective drug treatments—if it is not subject to patent protection, the drug research that is published by Canadian scientists will benefit people around the world.[6] If this research is done in Canada by the public sector, Canadian taxpayers will finance *all* the costs but would receive only *part* of the benefits. The alternative is to do drug research in the private sector and to enforce the patent laws that prevent competition in drug production—in which case, taxes will be lower, and drug prices will be higher.

One argument for private sector pharmaceutical research is the fact that multinational drug firms can use their worldwide sales revenue to finance research. If taxpayers in each country consider only the potential benefits of improved drugs to themselves, they may not be as willing to pay for "enough" research. However, when drug prices are higher, people who cannot afford to pay for drugs have to do without—at the cost of preventable suffering and, sometimes, premature death. Since Canadians are, on average, relatively prosperous and can (usually) afford to purchase drugs, relatively few Canadians may be in this position. However, in the poor countries of this world, there are many millions of people who cannot afford to pay.[7] In recent years, the prices charged by multinational drug companies for the retroviral drugs needed to combat HIV/AIDS have been a particularly important issue in sub-Saharan Africa, where the AIDS epidemic has affected large sectors of the population.

As well, when research is driven by the profit motive, ability and willingness to pay for drugs are what determines the direction of research. Viagra, for example, is a hugely profitable pharmaceutical product, demand for which increases with affluence and with age. Getting a share of these profits has been the motivation for research on competitive substitutes, even if none of this expenditure will save any lives. Because

5    For a discussion of private and public sector research and development of therapeutic drugs, see Dean Baker, "Patent Medicine," *American Prospect, 12*(2), January 29, 2001.

6    Advances in medical knowledge can be seen as a "public good," a concept we will discuss in more detail in Chapter 14. A pure public good is both "non-rival" and "non-excludable." A private good is both "rival" and "excludable." These terms are all defined in Chapter 14.

7    In 2006, annual per capita total health spending in Tanzania was $72, compared to $6719 in the U.S. and $3673 in Canada. See World Health Statistics 2009 at www.who.int/whosis/whostat/EN_WHS09_Table7.pdf.

there is less money to be made in finding cures for illnesses (such as malaria or bilhar-zia) which kill mainly poor people in poor countries who cannot afford expensive drug treatments, these ailments get much less research effort. We live in an imperfect world. *Monopoly is socially inefficient in the sense that it fails to maximize economic surplus, but the alternatives to monopoly are not perfect, either.* To determine whether one arrangement would be better for society than another requires that the costs and benefits of each be compared. Accurate measurement of costs and benefits may be very difficult to achieve. By itself, however, this is not a sufficient reason to avoid attempts to measure costs and benefits.

## THE DISTRIBUTIVE EFFECT OF MONOPOLY

As we have already shown, monopoly reduces total economic surplus by the amount of the deadweight loss. In the case of Figure 8.8, the deadweight loss was calculated as $4/week. However, a monopoly also redistributes the remaining economic surplus in favour of the monopolist. When compared to the surplus maximizing outcome, the monopolist's surplus is larger because the consumers' surplus is smaller.

Consider Figure 8.9, where demand, marginal revenue, and marginal cost are the same as in Figure 8.8. Figure 8.9 contrasts the price and quantity that are obtained under perfect competition, with the price and quantity that a monopolist would select. At the surplus maximizing price, the area of the blue triangle represents the consumer surplus. Therefore,

$$Consumer\ surplus = (\tfrac{1}{2})(\$3)(12\ units/week) = \$18/week.$$

The area of the green triangle represents the producer surplus. As a result,

$$Producer\ surplus = (\tfrac{1}{2})(\$3)(12\ units/week) = \$18/week.$$

(In this example, the producer surplus equals the consumer surplus, but this is just coincidental to the way the supply and demand curves are drawn.) Total economic surplus with the socially efficient price and quantity is the sum of consumer and producer surplus, $36.

As shown in the previous section, the monopoly price and quantity are $4 and 8 units/week, respectively. Further, the monopoly causes a deadweight loss of $4/week. Thus, total economic surplus decreases by $4/week. Therefore,

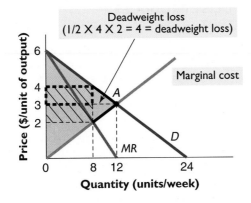

**FIGURE 8.9**
**The Distributive Effect of Monopoly**
When contrasted with perfect competition, monopoly not only reduces total economic surplus by the amount of the deadweight loss, it redistributes the remaining surplus in favour of the monopolist. With the monopoly price, the area containing the diagonal black lines represents the producer's surplus. The producer's (monopolist's) surplus is made larger by making the consumers' surplus smaller.

*Total economic surplus under monopoly = $36/week − $4/week*

*= $32/week.*

However, this is only part of the story, because the monopoly also redistributes the smaller economic surplus. At the monopoly price, the area of the blue triangle above the figure containing the black lines represents consumer surplus:

*Consumer surplus under monopoly = (½)($2)(8 units/week) = $8/week.*

In addition, the figure containing the black lines represents the monopolist's producer surplus. The figure can be divided into a rectangle and a triangle, which permits the following calculation:

*Producer surplus under monopoly = (½)($2)(8 units/week) + ($2)(8 units/week)*

*= $8/week + $16/week = $24/week.*

Notice that at $24/week, the monopolist's producer surplus is $6 more than it would be at the price and quantity that maximize total economic surplus. The consumer surplus at $8/week is $10 less. Taken together, the two effects cause total economic surplus to decrease by $4/week, which is consistent with what was calculated earlier. Even though total economic surplus is smaller, the monopolist's producer surplus is larger because that part of the smaller total economic surplus represented by the rectangle with heavy, dark, broken borders has been redistributed from consumers to the monopolist. The monopolist's producer surplus can also be interpreted as profit.

Notice that we have not said anything at all about whether it is a "good thing" to redistribute from consumers to the monopoly producer. Is the monopoly firm owned by a rapacious capitalist who spends the profits on outrageously wasteful personal consumption? Or is the firm owned by a charitable foundation that spends the monopoly profits on projects which save the environment and reduce disease and poverty? Nothing in the discussion thus far enables us to guess.

Notice also that the amount of deadweight loss and redistribution caused by monopoly depends on the elasticity of the demand and supply curves in this particular market. If, for example, a demand curve steeper than demand curve *D* in Figure 8.9 intersected marginal cost at point *A,* total economic surplus at the socially efficient price and quantity would be larger, and so would the deadweight loss and redistribution caused by monopoly.

**RECAP**

**WHY THE MONOPOLIST PRODUCES "TOO LITTLE" OUTPUT**

The monopolist maximizes profit at the output level for which marginal revenue equals marginal cost. Because its profit-maximizing price exceeds marginal revenue, and hence also marginal cost, the benefit to society of the last unit produced (the market price) must be greater than the cost of the last unit produced (the marginal cost). So the output level for an industry served by a profit-maximizing monopolist is smaller than the surplus-maximizing level of output. Monopoly also distributes the smaller surplus in favour of the monopolist, causing the absolute size of the monopolist's surplus to be larger and the absolute size of the consumer surplus to be smaller than a perfectly competitive equilibrium.

## 8.6   USING DISCOUNTS TO EXPAND THE MARKET

Monopoly is inefficient because the monopolist's benefit from expanding output is less than society's. Return to Figure 8.9, which shows that if the monopolist charges $4, it will sell 8 units per week. Suppose the monopolist reduces price to $3. What benefit will the monopolist receive? The monopolist's additional benefit is the additional revenue it receives when it reduces its price. Thus, the answer can be divided into two parts.

First, at $3 the monopolist will sell 4 more units, for a total of 12 units per week. Because it sells 4 more units, the monopolist's weekly revenue will increase by $12: $3 × 4 units/week = $12/week. Second, all 8 units/week the monopolist sold when price was $4, now sell for $3 each—$1 less each than it did previously. Because it has reduced price by $1/unit on each of 8 units, the monopolist's weekly revenue decreases by $8: −$1 × 8 units/week = −$8/week. Taken together, these two effects show that if the monopolist reduces price from $4 to $3, its weekly revenue will increase by only $4: $12/week − $8/week = $4/week. Figure 8.9 shows that the monopolist will not reduce price to $3/unit, because if it does, its increase in costs will exceed its increase in revenue.

At the same time, the demand curve of Figure 8.9 shows that if price were reduced from $4 to $3, buyers would increase their purchases from 8 to 12 units per week. Buyers are willing to pay $3 for each of those 4 additional units. Therefore, we can infer that buyers attach a value of at least $12 to the 4 additional units. These buyers would be better off if they could buy at a $3 price.

Clearly, the monopolist would like to have the added revenue ($12) from selling more output, but it would like to avoid the loss in revenue (−$8) from charging a lower price and having to sell all its output at that same lower price. Would the monopolist not be better off if it could somehow charge a different price to each of its different consumers? Would society also be better off? Why, for example, does the monopolist of Figure 8.9 not charge two prices? Why not sell the first 8 units/week at a price of $4, and then reduce the price for more price-sensitive buyers? Would this not increase the size of the economic pie?

### PRICE DISCRIMINATION DEFINED

Sometimes, when it is possible, the monopolist does precisely that. Charging different buyers different prices not based on differences in cost for essentially the same good or service is known as **price discrimination**. Examples of price discrimination include senior citizens' and children's discounts on movie tickets, supersaver discounts on air travel, and rebate coupons on retail merchandise.

**price discrimination** the practice of charging different buyers different prices, not based on differences in cost of production, for essentially the same good or service

Attempts at price discrimination seem to work effectively in some markets, but not in others. Buyers are not stupid, after all; if the monopolist periodically offered a 50 percent discount on the $8 list price, those who were paying $8 might anticipate the next price cut and postpone their purchases to take advantage of it. In some markets, however, buyers may not know how the price they pay compares to the prices paid by other buyers (or simply may not take the trouble to find out). Alternatively, the monopolist may be in a position to prevent some groups from buying at the discount prices made available to others. In such cases, a monopolist must be able to do two things: (1) separate its market into submarkets, each with a different demand curve, and charge a different price in each submarket; (2) prevent buyers from buying at a low price in one submarket and reselling at a higher price in another submarket. If the monopolist can do both, it can practise price discrimination.

**Why do some movie theatres offer discount tickets to students and senior citizens?**

Whenever a firm offers a discount, it wants to target buyers who would not purchase the product without the discount. People with low incomes generally have lower reservation prices for movie tickets than people with high incomes. Because students and pensioners generally have lower disposable incomes than working adults, theatre owners can increase ticket sales by offering discounts to them. Offering them discounts also entails no risk of some people buying the product at a low price and then reselling it to others at a higher price.

## HOW PRICE DISCRIMINATION AFFECTS OUTPUT

Examples 8.6 to 8.7 show how the ability to price discriminate affects the monopolist's profit-maximizing level of output. First we will consider a baseline case in which the monopolist must charge the same price to every buyer.

### EXAMPLE 8.6

**How many manuscripts will Carla edit?**

Carla supplements her income as a teaching assistant by editing term papers for undergraduates. There are 8 students/week for whom she might do this. Each student must submit one paper. Each student's reservation price for having Carla edit his or her paper appears in the second column of Table 8.6.

Carla is a profit maximizer. If each paper takes her two hours to edit, and she could work elsewhere for $14.50 per hour, the opportunity cost of her time to edit each paper is $29. If she must charge the same price to each student, how many papers will she edit? How much profit will she make?

Table 8.6 summarizes Carla's total and marginal revenue at various output levels. To generate the amounts in the total revenue column, we simply multiplied the corresponding reservation price by the number of students whose reservation prices were at least that high. For example, to edit 4 papers/week (for students *A*, *B*, *C*, and *D*),

**TABLE 8.6**
**Total and Marginal Revenue from Editing**

| Student | Reservation price ($/paper) | Total revenue ($/week) | Marginal revenue ($/paper) |
|---------|----------------------------|------------------------|----------------------------|
|         |                            |                        | 40                         |
| *A*     | 40                         | 40                     |                            |
|         |                            |                        | 36                         |
| *B*     | 38                         | 76                     |                            |
|         |                            |                        | 32                         |
| *C*     | 36                         | 108                    |                            |
|         |                            |                        | 28                         |
| *D*     | 34                         | 136                    |                            |
|         |                            |                        | 24                         |
| *E*     | 32                         | 160                    |                            |
|         |                            |                        | 20                         |
| *F*     | 30                         | 180                    |                            |
|         |                            |                        | 16                         |
| *G*     | 28                         | 196                    |                            |
|         |                            |                        | 12                         |
| *H*     | 26                         | 208                    |                            |

Carla must charge a price no higher than *D*'s reservation price ($34). So her total revenue when she edits 4 papers/week is (4)($34) = $136/week. Carla will increase the number of students she serves as long as her marginal revenue exceeds the opportunity cost of her time. Marginal revenue, or the difference in total revenue that results from adding another student, is shown in the last column of Table 8.6.

Note that if Carla were editing 2 papers/week, her marginal revenue from editing a third paper would be $32. Since that amount exceeds her $29 opportunity cost, she will edit the third paper. But since the marginal revenue of editing a fourth paper would be only $28, Carla will not edit a fourth paper. She will edit 3 papers/week. The total opportunity cost of the time required to edit the 3 papers is (3)($29) = $87, so Carla's profit is $108 − $87 = $21/week.

## EXAMPLE **8.7**

### What is the surplus maximizing number of papers Carla can edit?

Again, suppose that Carla's opportunity cost of editing is $29/paper and that she could edit as many as 8 papers/week for students whose reservation prices remain as given in Table 8.6. What is the surplus maximizing number of papers Carla can edit? If she must charge the same price to each student, what will her profit be if she edits the socially efficient number of papers?

Refer to Table 8.6. Students *A* to *F* are willing to pay more than Carla's opportunity cost, so serving these students is socially efficient. But students *G* and *H* are unwilling to pay at least $29 for Carla's services. The surplus maximizing outcome, therefore, is for Carla to edit 6 papers/week. To attract that number, she must charge a price no higher than $30/paper. Her total revenue will be (6)($30) = $180/week, slightly more than her total opportunity cost of (6)($29) = $174/week. Her profit will thus be only $6/week.

## EXAMPLE **8.8**

### If Carla can price discriminate, how many papers will she edit?

Suppose Carla realizes that students with more expensive clothes are willing to pay more. Suppose she finds out, with experience, that she can accurately predict each student's reservation price. The reservation prices of her potential customers remain as given in Table 8.6. If Carla can charge students the maximum price each is willing to pay (i.e. their respective reservation prices), how many papers will she edit, and how much profit will she make?

Refer again to Table 8.6. Carla will edit papers for students *A* to *F* and charge each exactly his or her reservation price. Because students *G* and *H* have reservation prices below $29, Carla will not edit their papers. Carla's total revenue will be $40 + $38 + $36 + $34 + $32 + $30 = $210/week. Her total opportunity cost of editing 6 papers is (6)($29) = $174/week, so her profit will be $210 − $174 = $36/week, or $15/week more than when she was constrained to charge each customer the same price.

A monopolist who can charge each buyer exactly his or her reservation price is called a **perfectly discriminating monopolist.** Notice that when Carla was discriminating among customers in this way, her profit-maximizing level of output was exactly the same as the surplus maximizing level of output: 6 papers/week. With a perfectly discriminating monopoly, there is no loss of total surplus and all buyers who are willing to pay a price high enough to cover marginal cost will be served.

Notice, too, that although total economic surplus is maximized by a perfectly discriminating monopolist, consumers would have little reason to celebrate if they found themselves dealing with such a firm. A monopolist that practices perfect price discrimination captures the entire economic surplus. Total economic surplus and producer surplus are the same. Therefore, when price discrimination is perfect, consumer surplus is zero. If we think of "efficiency" as maximizing total surplus, perfect competition and perfect price discrimination produce the same "efficiency." The difference between them lies entirely in the *distribution* of the surplus arising from market transactions.

**perfectly discriminating monopolist** a firm that charges each buyer exactly his or her reservation price

## PRICE DISCRIMINATION: A GRAPHICAL SUMMARY

The situation for Carla and her clients can also be portrayed graphically. The data from Table 8.6 are graphed in Figure 8.10. Because Carla cannot sell partially edited papers, continuous lines cannot represent her demand and marginal revenue schedules. Therefore, demand is graphed in panels (a) and (b) as a series of points are connected by a straight line labelled *D* to show how Carla's demand curve would appear if she had the option of editing term papers in whatever fractions she wanted. Likewise, marginal revenue is graphed in panel (a) as a series of points that are connected by a straight line labelled *MR*. The opportunity cost of the time Carla spends to edit each paper is $29. Therefore, her marginal cost is constant at $29. It is graphed as a series of points in both panels (a) and (b). The points are connected by a horizontal line with a vertical intercept at $29 to show how Carla's marginal cost curve would appear if she had any reason to edit fractions of term papers. Because marginal cost is constant, it is equal to average cost; therefore, the graph of the marginal cost data is labelled *MC = AC*.

Panel (a) shows that if Carla must charge the same price to each of her clients, she will choose a price of $36 and edit three papers, because the third paper is the last paper for which marginal revenue exceeds marginal cost. Carla's total opportunity cost is $87. Carla's profit/paper is $36 − $29 = $7. Therefore, her total profit is ($7/paper) × 3 papers = $21. The total profit can also be regarded as Carla's producer surplus. Carla's total revenue for editing the three papers is ($36)3 = $108, which equals the sum of total cost and total

### FIGURE 8.10
**Two Monopoly Pricing Strategies**

In both panels, the demand for Carla's editing services is graphed as a series of discrete points. In panel (a) she is portrayed as a monopolist who charges the same price to all her clients; therefore, she sets her price at $36 and edits 3 papers. In panel (b) she practices perfect price discrimination, charging each client his or her reservation price. She edits 6 papers, the quantity that maximizes total economic surplus. She also captures the entire economic surplus.

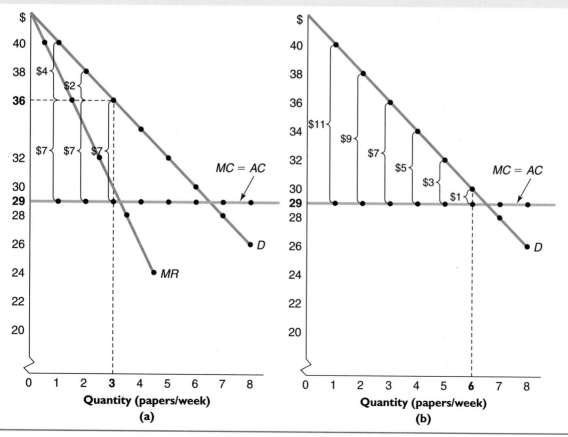

profit. Notice, too, that each of Carla's three clients receives a consumer surplus equal to the difference between the student's reservation price and the price Carla charges. Thus student A's consumer surplus is $40 − $36 = $4. In the same way, students B and C each have a consumer surplus of $2 and $0, respectively; therefore, total consumer surplus is $6.

When Carla practices perfect price discrimination, a different picture emerges. As panel (b) shows, she charges each student his reservation price and edits six papers. Her opportunity cost is $29 for each paper she edits. Her profit on each paper is the difference between the client's reservation price and $29. Thus her profit on the first paper is $40 − $29 = $11; on the second, it is $38 − $29 = $9; and so on through the sixth paper, which gives her a total profit of $36. Again, her profit can also be interpreted as her producer's surplus.

Notice two results that emerge from panel (b). First, with perfect price discrimination, Carla maximizes total economic surplus—in this specific sense, she produces the socially efficient quantity. Second, Carla captures the entire total economic surplus—there is no consumer surplus.

Because no seller knows each and every buyer's precise reservation price, perfect price discrimination is no more attainable in practice than perfect competition. But even if some sellers did know their customers' reservation prices, practical difficulties may stand in the way of their charging a separate price to each buyer. In many markets, the seller would be unable to prevent buyers who bought at low prices from reselling to other buyers at higher prices, capturing some of the seller's business in the process.[8] Despite these difficulties, price discrimination is widespread. But it is generally *imperfect price discrimination;* that is, price discrimination in which at least some buyers are charged less than their reservation prices.

## PERFECT PRICE DISCRIMINATION: THE ESSENTIAL ISSUE

Firms with some market power, not only monopolists, always have an incentive to price discriminate. When such firms develop new, improved mechanisms for price discrimination, two things happen: (1) their total output increases and gets closer to the socially efficient level of production, and (2) their share of the total economic surplus increases. If a monopolistic firm could *perfectly* price discriminate, it would produce exactly the surplus maximizing amount, but it would also capture the entire consumer surplus, as well as the entire producer surplus. In this case, equity is the key issue, not the maximization of total economic surplus. In the case of perfect price discrimination, the key issue is the *distribution* of economic surplus, not its *size*. Is it fair for a monopolist to capture an industry's entire economic surplus? What would your answer be if the monopolist is (a) a multinational corporation owned entirely by wealthy foreigners, (b) a charitable foundation that uses all its profits to combat world hunger, or (c) owned equally by all Canadian citizens? Typically, students' assessments of the desirability of a perfectly discriminatory monopolist depend somewhat on how they think its profits will be distributed, but economic theory cannot tell us the answer.

## THE HURDLE METHOD OF PRICE DISCRIMINATION

The profit-maximizing seller's goal is to charge each buyer the highest price that buyer is willing to pay. Two primary obstacles prevent sellers from achieving this goal. First, sellers do not know exactly how much each buyer is willing to pay. And second, they need some means of preventing those who are willing to pay a high price from buying at a low price. These are formidable problems, which no seller can hope to solve completely.

One common method by which sellers achieve a crude solution to both problems is the **hurdle method of price discrimination**, which requires buyers to overcome some obstacle

**hurdle method of price discrimination** the practice by which a seller offers a discount to all buyers who overcome some obstacle

---

8 The market for airline tickets is, however, an exception, since security procedures enable airlines to enforce a no-resale policy by matching the identity of travellers to that of ticket purchasers.

to be eligible for a discount price.[9] For example, the seller might sell a product at a standard list price and offer a rebate to any buyer who takes the trouble to mail in a rebate coupon.

The hurdle method therefore solves both of the seller's problems, *provided* that buyers with low reservation prices are more willing than others to jump the hurdle (i.e., mail in the coupon for the rebate). Because the decision to jump the hurdle is subject to the cost–benefit test, buyers with low incomes are more likely than others to have low reservation prices (at least in the case of normal goods). Because of the low opportunity cost of their time, they are more likely than others to take the trouble to send in rebate coupons. Rebate coupons thus target a discount toward those buyers whose reservation prices are low and who might not buy the product otherwise.

COST–
BENEFIT

**perfect hurdle** one that completely segregates buyers whose reservation prices lie above some threshold from others whose reservation prices lie below it, imposing no cost on those who jump the hurdle

A **perfect hurdle** is one that separates buyers precisely according to their reservation prices, and in the process imposes no cost on those who jump the hurdle. With a perfect hurdle, the highest reservation price among buyers who jump the hurdle will be lower than the lowest reservation price among buyers who choose not to jump the hurdle. In practice, perfect hurdles do not exist. Some buyers will always jump the hurdle, even though their reservation prices are high. And hurdles will always exclude at least some buyers with low reservation prices. Even so, many commonly used hurdles do a remarkably good job of targeting discounts to buyers with low reservation prices.

Once you understand the hurdle method of price discrimination, you will begin to see many examples of it. Monopolistic competitors, oligopolists, and monopolists all have incentives to practice price discrimination. The following are some examples:

- Cash rebates or temporary special pricing for consumers who take the time to find out when the sales are happening.
- Cheaper paperback editions of books for those willing to wait one year from the time the hardcover edition is first released.
- Less-expensive models of similarly valued cars for those who don't need the "name" or fancy trim package.
- Successively cheaper ways of watching major films for those who are willing to wait longer and accept a lower quality of product.
- Supersaver or last minute airline deals for those who are willing to buy tickets at the last minute.

Recall that single-price monopoly reduces total economic surplus because, to the monopolist, the benefit of expanding output is smaller than the benefit to society as a whole. The hurdle method of price discrimination reduces this loss by giving the monopolist a practical means of cutting prices for price-sensitive buyers only. In general, the more finely the monopolist can partition a market by using the hurdle method, the

## ECONOMIC NATURALIST 8.3

**Why were U.S. drug companies concerned about U.S. citizens shopping for prescription drugs in Canada? Will they be concerned again?**

High though the prices of prescription drugs may seem to Canadians, for many years they were significantly lower in Canada (and in Mexico) than in the U.S. Bus loads of American senior citizens from border states, therefore, came into Canada to fill their prescriptions. Seniors tend to have lower incomes and a greater need for drugs than younger people. Although these people were purchasing the same drugs, made by the same companies, and at lower prices in Canada than they would have had to pay in the States, the U.S. drug companies did not attempt to interfere. The time necessary to make the trip to Canada meant that only low-income people who had lots of time available would make the effort necessary to purchase drugs in Canada,

---

9   The hurdle method often is referred to as third-degree price discrimination. The cost of administering the hurdle (i.e., the postage and time to mail in the coupon, the clerical labour to process the rebate, etc.) is a loss in productive efficiency.

and they might not have had the income necessary to purchase as many drugs at the higher prices charged in the States. Cross-border shopping for prescription drugs could therefore be seen as an example of the hurdle method of price discrimination—a way that U.S. drug companies could charge higher prices to the large majority of their customers who do not have the time to travel to Canada, while also profiting from the additional sales made at lower Canadian prices to cross-border shoppers.

However, the hurdle method of price discrimination relies on the cost of the hurdle to potential consumers. In a social sense, it is inefficient to make people travel to another country to buy something that they could get from their corner drugstore. As Internet use spread in the population, Internet-based pharmacies in Canada, which deliver by courier or parcel post, started to target a broader U.S. market. It was no longer necessary to travel to Canada to obtain prescriptions at the lower Canadian price, because the Internet removed the hurdle. U.S. drug companies became seriously concerned. However, by 2007 the high value of the Canadian dollar against the U.S. dollar had removed much of the advantage of purchasing drugs in Canada and allayed the concern of the drug companies. The drug companies will become concerned again only if the value of the Canadian dollar declines substantially.

smaller the loss of surplus and the greater the share of total economic surplus captured by the monopolist. Hurdles are not perfect, however, and some amount of surplus will inevitably be lost.

> **RECAP**
>
> ### USING DISCOUNTS TO EXPAND THE MARKET
>
> A price-discriminating seller is one who charges different prices to different buyers for essentially the same good or service. A common method of price discrimination is the hurdle method, which involves granting a discount to buyers who jump over a hurdle, such as mailing in a rebate coupon. An effective hurdle is one that is more easily cleared by buyers with low reservation prices than by buyers with high reservation prices. In many cases, such a hurdle enables the seller to expand output and thereby reduce the deadweight loss from monopoly pricing. The amount of increase in output and the magnitude of the distributional implications of price discrimination will depend on characteristics such as the elasticity of the demand curves in submarkets.

# 8.7 PUBLIC POLICY TOWARD MONOPOLY

Monopoly is problematic not only because of the lost total economic surplus associated with restricted output, but also because the monopolist earns an economic profit at the buyer's expense. For these reasons, voters in many societies have empowered governments to adopt policies aimed at controlling natural monopolists (defined on page 222).

There are several ways to achieve this aim. A government may *assume ownership and control* of a natural monopoly, or it may merely attempt to *regulate* the *prices* it charges. In some cases, government *solicits competitive bids* from private firms to produce natural monopoly services. In still other cases, governments attempt to *dissolve natural monopolies into smaller entities* that compete with one another. But many of these policies create economic problems of their own. In each case, the practical challenge is to choose the solution that yields the greatest surplus of benefits over costs. Natural monopoly may be inefficient and unfair, but the alternatives to natural monopoly are far from perfect.

## STATE OWNERSHIP AND MANAGEMENT

Figure 8.11 portrays a natural monopoly, where the monopolist has substantial fixed costs and constant marginal cost per unit of output. The firm's long-run decision requires it to either choose a scale of operation characterized by the cost structure portrayed in Figure 8.11 or to not serve the market.

**FIGURE 8.11**

**Demand, Costs, and Revenues for a Natural Monopolist**

If a natural monopolist maximizes its profit, total economic surplus is reduced below its potential value. If price is set equal to marginal cost in order to maximize total economic surplus, the natural monopolist incurs a loss.

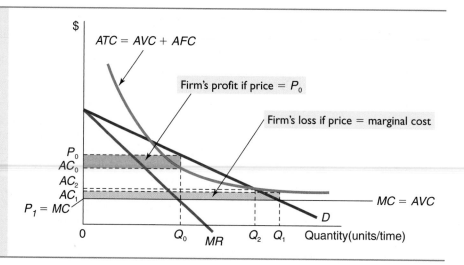

Left to itself, a profit-maximizing monopolist will set marginal revenue equal to marginal cost. In Figure 8.11, this gives price $P_0$, quantity $Q_0$, and average cost $AC_0$. Total economic profit will be $Q_0 (P_0 - AC_0)$, represented by the grey rectangle in Figure 8.11. In contrast, total economic surplus is maximized when price is set equal to marginal cost, which occurs at $Q_1$. However, if output is set at $Q_1$, price will be less than average cost and the firm will suffer a total loss of $Q_1 (P_1 - AC_1)$, represented by the pink rectangle in Figure 8.11. It appears either that the firm will earn a profit and total economic surplus will be below its potential or, if total economic surplus is maximized, the firm will suffer a loss. What is to be done?

As we have seen, in the long run any privately owned firm will stop serving an industry that fails to provide at least a normal profit. A natural monopolist is no different in this regard. Hence, one possible policy is for the government to own the industry and then maximize total economic surplus by setting output at $Q_1$ while paying a subsidy out of general tax revenue to offset the resulting losses.

In Chapter 7 we discussed the deadweight loss that is produced by taxation, so a choice to cover the financial losses of the firm would have to be made with the knowledge that there would be some deadweight loss as a result of the taxes that pay for this subsidy. Hence, the policy question is whether a subsidy has greater or fewer costs than the alternatives. If a government-owned firm was instructed to cover its costs, but no more, it would set price equal to average cost and produce at $Q_2$, the "break even" level of production in Figure 8.11. Producing at $Q_2$, rather than at $Q_1$, would imply foregoing the consumer surplus on the difference $(Q_2 - Q_1)$ in output levels. Therefore, two questions concerning public policy arise. First, is the subsidy consistent with the cost–benefit principle? To answer this question, we must ask how much revenue the tax must collect in order to provide the subsidy. Then we need to know how large the deadweight loss of the tax is compared to the loss in consumer surplus if the firm is not subsidized. The second question concerns a distributional matter: are the people who pay the tax the same people who receive the additional consumer surplus that becomes available if the monopoly is subsidized? In other words, will the additional consumer surplus be distributed fairly?

Critics of publicly owned firms often argue that such firms are technically inefficient, even if they set price equal to marginal cost. They contend that a firm owned by government does not have the same interest in cost minimization that a privately owned firm has. Therefore, according to this argument, costs for a publicly owned firm tend to be higher than costs for a privately owned firm, causing the publicly owned firm's marginal costs to be higher than necessary. Of course, because a privately owned monopoly does not face competitive pressure to keep its costs low, its marginal cost might well be inflated, too. Either way, if costs are higher than the minimum necessary for a given level of production, the firm is not achieving *technical efficiency in production*. **Technical efficiency in production** occurs when the least possible amounts of inputs are used to produce a given level of output.

An economist would predict that the decisions of managers will reflect the incentives they face. If a manager's salary and prospects for promotion are based on her effectiveness in cutting production costs, then we would expect the manager to act in accordance with their personal self-interest, and cut costs. If both privately owned and publicly owned firms make cost cutting an objective, the decisions emerging from either type of firm are likely to be similar—both are likely to accomplish technical efficiency in production.[10]

If managers are asked to achieve other social objectives, comparisons of relative performance necessarily become more complicated. In their public relations statements, both publicly and privately owned firms often express support for social goals such as protection of the environment, job creation, or the integration of disadvantaged groups into their labour force, but how much emphasis, in practice, do they really place on objectives other than profit maximization? If publicly owned firms are in fact more likely to assign their managers multiple objectives, the evaluation and reward of managerial performance will be more difficult than when multiple objectives are not being pursued.

## STATE REGULATION OF PRIVATE MONOPOLIES

In Canada, government regulation, not ownership, of a natural monopoly is probably the most common method of curbing monopoly profits. Most provinces, for example, take this approach with electric utilities and natural gas providers. The standard procedure in these cases is called **cost-plus regulation**—government regulators gather data on the monopolist's explicit costs of production and then permit the monopolist to set prices that cover those costs, plus a markup to ensure a normal return on the firm's investment. In terms of Figure 8.11, price is set equal to average total cost and output is $Q_2$. This is less than the socially optimal output level $Q_1$, but it represents an improvement on the monopoly output level $Q_0$ (and there is no need to find a way to cover the firm's financial losses from taxes, unlike the situation at $Q_1$).

Cost-plus regulation is not a panacea. It requires costly administrative proceedings in which regulators and firms quarrel over which of the firm's expenditures can properly be included in the costs it is allowed to recover, and the more rapid the rate of technological change, the harder is the problem of optimal regulation.

For example, in Europe and Australia, the historic public policy choice was to provide telephone service through the public sector, typically by expanding the post office into a publicly owned post and telecommunications company. In Canada, telephone service was usually provided by privately owned monopolies, subject to government regulation. In the era when telephones were all always connected to landlines, the sector was seen as the classic natural monopoly, since the cost of connecting one more person to a telephone line that is already serving the neighbours is much less than the average cost of putting up the telephone pole and lines in the first place. Furthermore, the benefits of having a telephone increase with the number of other people whom each person can call; each subscriber is better off when other people also decide to have telephone service. For decades, charges on long distance calls were set much higher than cost in order to cross-subsidize residential telephone service, a practice encouraged by regulators who wanted to ensure that access to local telephone service was within everyone's financial reach.

**technical efficiency in production** occurs when the least possible amounts of inputs are used to produce a given level of output

**cost-plus regulation** a method of regulation under which the regulated firm is permitted to charge a price equal to its explicit costs of production plus a markup to cover the opportunity cost of resources provided by the firm's owners

10 Caves and Christensen, for example, compared and found essentially no difference in the operating efficiencies of Canada's two national railway systems (CN and CP) at a time when one was publicly owned and the other was not. See Douglas W. Caves and Laurits R. Christensen, "The Relative Efficiency of Public and Private Firms in a Competitive Environment: The Case of Canadian Railroads," *The Journal of Political Economy*, Vol. 88, No. 5, Oct. 1980, pp. 958–976.

In the last forty years, however, technical change in telecommunications has been dramatic. In the 1980s and 1990s it became technically possible to have many long-distance service providers, some of whom could provide much lower-cost service, using fibre optics or satellite transmission. Telephone companies also developed technology to provide new types of services (such as burglar alarms and call forwarding) through the telephone line. More recently, the Internet and vast increases in bandwidth and data transmission capability have blurred old distinctions between computing, broadcasting, and telephony. Cell phones have become ubiquitous and whole new capabilities for service delivery have been created. There is no sign that innovation in the sector is slowing. Can regulators continue to ensure that basic telephone service is provided at a reasonable cost? This question is difficult to answer even in theory. If local telephone service is subject to cost-plus regulation but other products and services provided by the same company are unregulated, many employees, from the president on down, are involved in both regulated and unregulated activities. How should their salaries be allocated between the two? The company has a strong incentive to argue for greater allocation to the regulated activities where it will be part of the cost of service that regulators consider when rates are set, thus allowing the company to capture more revenue from captive customers in the local telephone market.

A second problem with cost-plus regulation is that it blunts the firm's incentive to adopt cost-saving innovations. If it does cut costs, regulators may require the firm to cut its rates. Furthermore, in cases in which regulators set rates by allowing the monopolist to add a fixed-percentage markup to costs incurred, the regulated monopolist may actually have an incentive to *increase* costs rather than reduce them. Under cost-plus regulation, the price will be marked up by the same percentage over costs regardless of whether or not costs are inflated. Finally, cost-plus regulation does not solve the natural monopolist's basic problem—the inability to set price equal to marginal cost without losing money. Although these are all serious problems, governments seem to be in no hurry to abandon cost-plus regulation.

## EXCLUSIVE CONTRACTING FOR NATURAL MONOPOLY

Another possibility for dealing with natural monopoly is for the government to invite private firms to bid for the natural monopolist's market. The government could specify in detail the service it wants—cable television, fire protection, garbage collection—and have firms submit bids describing how much they will charge for the service. The low bidder wins the contract.

The firm's incentive to cut costs under such an arrangement is every bit as powerful as that facing ordinary competitive firms, and if the government is willing to provide a cash subsidy to the winning bidder, exclusive contracting could even allow the monopolist to set price equal to marginal cost. However, the success of this strategy does depend on there being effective competition among bidders, and there may only be a few credible ones.

Contracting out has been employed with good results for some services (e.g., garbage collection). Despite its attractive features, however, exclusive contracting has problems, especially when the service to be provided is complex or requires a large fixed investment in capital equipment. In such cases, contract specifications may be so detailed and complicated that they become tantamount to regulating the firm directly and in detail. And in cases involving a large fixed investment—electric power generation and distribution or service centre franchises on a freeway, for example—officials face the question of how to transfer the assets if a new firm later wins the contract at renewal time. The winning firm naturally wants to acquire the assets as cheaply as possible, but the retiring firm is entitled to a reasonable price for them. What, in such cases, is the optimal price?

Garbage collection is a simple enough service that the costs of contracting out this function are not prohibitive. But in other cases, experience has shown that such costs can sometimes outweigh any savings made possible by exclusive contracting.

## VIGOROUS ENFORCEMENT OF COMPETITION LEGISLATION

When the Soviet Union disintegrated in the early 1990s, there was great optimism among many economists that a competitive market economy would replace central planning and foster a new spirit of enterprise. Many predicted that, with its well educated populace and large capital stock, the countries of the former Soviet Bloc would experience a surge of economic growth. Instead, national income in the countries of the old Soviet Union shrank continuously for 6½ years to half of what it had been in 1989. Eleven years later, total output was still 37 percent below what it had been in 1989.[11] The collapse occurred partly because the capital stock proved to be of poor quality and design, but it also became apparent that these countries lacked the social and legal institutions that are necessary for a productive market system.

The importance of the social and legal framework can be illustrated by posing a hypothetical question. If you are running a factory that produces shoes and you discover that you are losing sales to a competitor, will you make the effort to improve designs, streamline the production process, cut costs, and deliver a better product at a lower price to win back market share? Or is it easier and quicker to hire an arsonist to destroy your competitor's factory?

In the absence of a generally accepted and enforced system of law—particularly competition law—gangster capitalism became entrenched in much of the former Soviet Union, an important illustration of the fact that when laws and social norms do not constrain some types of firm behaviour, competition may become socially destructive. A well-designed legal framework will channel competitive behaviour into patterns that are economically productive. Society as a whole has an interest in setting up a system of law to ensure that firms compete by innovating and cutting costs, and not by hiring better arsonists.

Destroying your competitor's factory is an extreme example of an obviously illegal (but very effective) anticompetitive strategy. Competition law in Canada revolves around much more subtle issues.

For example, during 2000, the long competitive struggle between Canadian Airlines (initially owned by Canadian Pacific) and Air Canada (initially a Crown corporation, but privatized in the 1990s) was resolved with the absorption of Canadian by Air Canada. The domestic air travel market in Canada then became dominated by a single carrier, and a large airline has significant advantages over its competitors (e.g., the ability to schedule frequent connecting flights).

www.aircanada.ca
Air Canada

Once it was established as the dominant carrier, Air Canada's shares initially rose rapidly in value, as the stock market anticipated healthy dividends for Air Canada stockholders resulting from the carrier's ability to charge high fares (particularly for business travellers). However, those high prices also presented opportunities for new firms to enter the market. In Eastern Canada, a new airline (CanJet) soon opened, offering low fares and friendly service.

Where natural monopoly is not present, the prospect of monopoly profits can lead firms to undertake actions that limit competition. Under Canadian competition law, *predatory pricing* is illegal, but competitive pricing is perfectly legitimate. Dominant firms are not allowed to artificially set prices below their cost of production for the express purpose of squeezing competitors out of the market. Laws against predatory pricing are necessary to maintain competition; otherwise, a dominant firm could scare off rivals by threatening potential competitors with a devastating price war should they challenge its position. A dominant firm that is willing to take temporary losses in a price war can, in the long run, continue to charge excessively high prices by deterring potential competitors.

11 The World Bank Group, *Transition—The First Ten Years: Analysis and Lessons for Eastern Europe and the Former Soviet Union*, Washington, D.C.: The International Bank for Reconstruction and Development/The World Bank, 2002. See Part 1, Table 1.1 p. 5.

However, firms are allowed, encouraged even, to match the market and to pass on cost savings. If a large carrier can offer lower fares because it has lower costs, the public interest demands that it be allowed to do so. When Air Canada cut its prices drastically on those routes and times that CanJet serviced at the same time as CanJet opened for business, CanJet protested that this was predatory pricing (Air Canada argued that it was just being competitive).

Determining whether activities restrain competition or encourage it is a never ending and subtle endeavour. Air Canada lost this particular case, and discount carriers dramatically increased their share of the Canadian air travel market. By 2003, Air Canada shares had collapsed as it filed for bankruptcy protection. Air Canada laid off thousands of employees and contracted out services to match the prices of its discount competitors, and emerged from bankruptcy in 2004. The airline industry continues to be a turbulent environment. CanJet ceased scheduled service in 2006, West Jet expanded to provide coast to coast services, and Porter emerged as a new industry player. Nevertheless, the general problem, ensuring that the competitive process is healthy and is channelled in socially constructive directions, remains.

**RECAP**

### PUBLIC POLICY TOWARD MONOPOLY

The unregulated natural monopolist sets price above marginal cost, resulting in too little output from society's point of view. The unregulated natural monopolist may also earn an economic profit at the buyers' expense (the fairness problem). Policies for improving the performance and fairness of natural monopolies include government ownership and management, government regulation, and exclusive contracting. Vigorous enforcement of competition laws can thwart anticompetitive practices. Each of these remedies entails problems of its own.

## 8.8 OLIGOPOLY

An oligopoly is just a market dominated by a few sellers. When there are only a few firms in a given market, the decisions of each firm will have an impact on the sales and profits of each of its competitors– and each competitor will probably react. So in deciding what price to charge, what ads to buy, how to develop their product, and much else, each firm has to think through how its competitors will respond. Many markets are characterized by a few, mutually interdependent firms. Economists have found game theory to be very helpful in understanding these markets. We will develop game theory in more detail in the next chapter.

In some oligopolistic markets, firms sell much the same products. In the market for wireless phone service, for example, the offerings of Rogers, Bell, and Virgin are essentially identical; that is, undifferentiated. The cement industry is another example of an oligopoly selling an undifferentiated product. In this type of oligopoly market, pricing and advertising are important strategic decisions. However, in other oligopoly markets, differences in perceived product features have significant effects on consumer demand. Some long-time Pepsi buyers, for example, would not even consider buying a Coke. When the product is differentiated, there is an additional margin of strategic decision making. Firms must decide which specific product features to develop, knowing that other firms will respond.

Why would a market only have a few firms? Cost advantages associated with large size are usually an important reason, but this implies there is no presumption that entry and exit will push economic profit to zero. If, for example, minimum long-run average cost is attained at a production level of 3 million units and consumer demand at that price level is about 8 million units, the market will certainly support two firms, each of which would earn an economic profit. Will a new firm be profitable if it enters this market? Possibly, but it also might be that a third firm large enough to achieve the cost advantages of the two incumbents would effectively flood the market, driving price so low that all three firms would suffer economic losses. Knowing this, a third firm would not enter the market. However, there also is no guarantee that an oligopolist will realize an economic profit, just as there is no guarantee that a monopolist will realize an economic profit.

If there are only a few firms in an industry, and they can cooperate among themselves and refrain from price competition, market performance would be similar to what we have discovered for monopoly. Such an oligopoly would tend to keep quantity too low to minimize average cost, which means that price would be above the perfectly competitive benchmark. As we have already discussed, one public policy alternative to deal with this situation is to bring in legislation to regulate competition; in Canada, as in other advanced market economies, oligopoly price fixing is illegal (but because it is profitable, it does sometimes happen).[12]

---

**RECAP**

### OLIGOPOLY

Oligopoly is a market structure in which a small number of mutually interdependent firms sell either a homogeneous or a differentiated product. An oligopolist must consider the possible reactions and countermoves of its competitors when it develops pricing and marketing strategies. An oligopoly will tend to keep quantity below the amount that minimizes average cost and prices above the perfectly competitive benchmark. Oligopolists will tend to realize an economic profit, though there is no guarantee that they will.

---

## 8.9 MONOPOLISTIC COMPETITION: A BLEND OF COMPETITION AND LIMITED MARKET POWER

How should we think of firms like hair salons, restaurants, clothing stores, and gas stations, which operate in industries where a number of rival firms offer close, but not perfect, substitutes? How should we analyze markets for scotch whisky or economics textbooks, in which each producer has the monopoly of supply for a unique product, but that product has numerous close substitutes? A hair salon in a small city or the producer of a specific brand of single malt scotch may have a *monopoly* based on its specific characteristics, but it will face *competition* from a large number of competitors. Monopolistic competition is a market structure characterized by three features: first, many firms serve the market; second, the firms sell *differentiated* products that nevertheless are reasonably close substitutes for each other; third, there are no barriers to entry. Thus, product differentiation is the *sole* feature that distinguishes monopolistic competition from perfect competition.

### PRODUCT DIFFERENTIATION AND MARKET POWER

A monopolistically competitive firm differentiates its product from competing products by advertising, or by some functional feature. When we look at markets for many consumer goods and services—for example, florists, barbershops, restaurants, automobile repair shops, roofers, or gardening services—we see many varieties of essentially the same

---

12 Adam Smith recognized price fixing as a distinct possibility: "People of the same trade seldom meet together, even for merriment and diversion, but the conversation ends in a conspiracy against the public, or in some contrivance to raise prices." Smith, *The Wealth of Nations* (1776) (New York, 1965), Book I, Chapter X, Part II, p. 128.

product competing for our dollars. In some cases, the differentiation is largely artificial, and advertising is used to create product differentiation in the consumer's mind. In other cases (e.g., restaurants or automobiles or economics texts) there are real differences in the characteristics even though they perform the same function. Whether real or artificial, it is this product differentiation that provides the monopolistic competitor with a limited degree of market power. The monopolistic competitor faces a downward-sloping demand curve. However, if barriers to entry are absent (nearly anybody can, for example, open a pizza parlour), a monopolistic competitor in long-run equilibrium earns a normal rate of return.[13]

Consider Figure 8.12, which represents a monopolistically competitive firm in short-run equilibrium. The firm has used advertising to differentiate its product; therefore, its demand curve, represented by $D$, is downward sloping. Also, because the firm incurs expenses by advertising, its long-run average cost curve, represented by $LRAC$, is higher than it would be for a comparable perfectly competitive firm. (Recall that the perfect competitor does no advertising.) The monopolistic competitor represented in Figure 8.12 maximizes profit by selecting price $P$ and output $Q$ because this is where marginal revenue equals marginal cost (represented by $MR$ and $MC$). Average cost is $C$; therefore, the monopolistic competitor realizes an economic profit, represented by the green rectangle.

However, if there are no barriers to entry in monopolistic competition, this economic profit cannot persist in the long run. New firms will be attracted by the promise of economic profit to enter the market. Each new firm will supply a somewhat different but competing product. New firms will continue to enter the market as long as the "typical" firm is making economic profits (i.e., more than is necessary to pay the opportunity cost of capital, labour, and entrepreneurship). Eventually, when enough new firms have entered the market, long-run equilibrium will occur with the typical firm making zero economic profit. This situation is represented in Figure 8.13. The cost curves in Figure 8.13 are identical to those in Figure 8.12. And, just as before, the firm chooses the price and quantity that cause marginal revenue to equal marginal cost. However, compared with Figure 8.12, the firm's demand curve has shifted to the left. As Figure 8.13 shows, the monopolistic competitor in long-run equilibrium earns only a normal profit. Because the firm's demand curve slopes downward, demand is tangent to the firm's long-run average cost curve at quantity $Q_1$ and price $P_1$. Both $Q_1$ and $P_1$ are smaller than $P$ and $Q$, respectively, of Figure 8.12.

**FIGURE 8.12**
**A Monopolistically Competitive Firm in Short-Run Equilibrium**
In the short run, a monopolistically competitive firm earns an economic profit by differentiating its product. However, profits cannot persist in the long run because entry will squeeze them out.

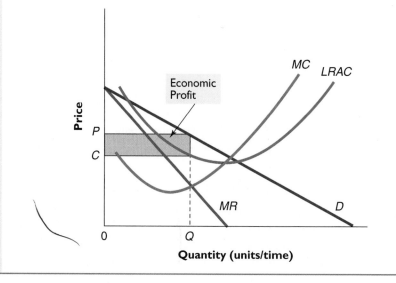

13 Edward Chamberlin developed the theory of monopolistic competition in order to analyze markets that combined a high degree of competition with product differentiation. See Edward Chamberlin, *The Theory of Monopolistic Competition* (Cambridge: Harvard University Press, 1938).

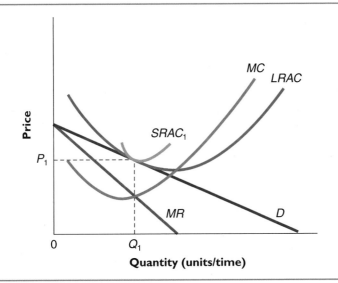

**FIGURE 8.13**
**A Monopolistically Competitive Firm in Long-Run Equilibrium**
In the long run, competition causes a monopolistically competitive firm to earn a normal profit.

In long-run equilibrium, even though the firm is earning a normal profit, *price exceeds marginal cost*. Furthermore, quantity $Q_1$ is too small to achieve minimum long-run average cost. As Figure 8.13 shows, the firm chooses the scale of operation that is represented by the short-run average cost curve which is labelled $SRAC_1$. This scale is too small to fully realize economies of scale. Even having chosen $SRAC_1$, the firm produces quantity $Q_1$, which is too small to reach the lowest short-run average cost that can be accomplished, given $SRAC_1$. Because quantity is too small to minimize short-run average cost, a monopolistically competitive firm in long-run equilibrium operates with excess capacity. As well, the monopolistically competitive firm has advertising costs, which perfectly competitive firms do not. All these features cause a monopolistically competitive market to produce a smaller total economic surplus than its perfectly competitive

---

**ECONOMIC NATURALIST   8.4**

### Why is there such a wide range of prices for whisky?

A typical liquor store will feature several varieties of generic, blended Scotch whisky, a selection of single-malt Scotches (some of which retail for four or five times the price of the most inexpensive blended Scotch whisky), plus many varieties of rye and bourbon, also at considerably varying prices. However, they all have approximately the same alcohol content, and all are produced using much the same technology. Why do some brands of whisky sell for so much more than others?

Each producer of single malt Scotch has a monopoly—the production of a particular distillery. If consumers can be convinced that there is something unique, and extra desirable, about "the peaty aroma" or "the purity of rainfall" of that particular distillery, then "monopoly" or market power can be created. Success in differentiating a product means that consumers will pay a higher price for the product because they like the qualities it offers. At the same

time, the theory of monopolistic competition hypothesizes that economic profit cannot persist in the long run. If Figure 8.12 represented the situation of a "typical" distillery of specialty Scotch, the existence of economic profit would provide an incentive for new producers to invest in building distilleries. When economic profits are present, the producers of "no name" whiskies also have an incentive to invest in an advertising campaign extolling the virtues of their products and helping them to sell more. Entry of a new producer and its advertising would steal some customers from the firm represented in Figure 8.12, which would experience a decrease of demand. But, even though large differences in prices persist, a monopolistic competitor in long-run equilibrium earns only a normal profit, as shown in Figure 8.13.

counterpart, thus making monopolistic competition inefficient. However, as Economist Naturalist 8.4 shows, monopolistic competition does offer variety, and monopolistically competitive firms use advertising to keep their customers informed.

---

**RECAP**↑

### MONOPOLISTIC COMPETITION

Monopolistic competition is a market structure in which a large number of firms sell differentiated products that compete with each other. Product differentiation is the sole feature that distinguishes monopolistic competition from perfect competition. Monopolistic competition is inefficient because advertising makes costs higher than they need to be, monopolistic competitors chose inefficiently small scales of operation, and they operate their plants with excess capacity. The theory of monopolistic competition can be used to analyze markets that combine a high degree of competition with product differentiation.

---

## SUMMARY

- Our concern in this chapter was the conduct and performance of the imperfectly competitive firm, a firm that has at least some latitude to set its own price without losing all its sales. Economists often distinguish among three different types of imperfectly competitive firms: the pure monopolist, the lone seller of a product in a given market; the oligopolist, one of only a few rival sellers of a given product; and the monopolistic competitor, one of a relatively large number of firms that sell similar though slightly differentiated products. **LO1**

- Although advanced courses in economics devote much attention to differences in behaviour among these three types of firms, our focus was on the common feature that differentiates them from perfectly competitive firms. Whereas the perfectly competitive firm faces a perfectly elastic demand curve for its product, the imperfectly competitive firm faces a downward-sloping demand curve. **LO1**

- Firms with market power have some ability to increase the price of their product without losing all their sales. Market power stems from exclusive control over important inputs, from economies of scale, patents, licences or franchises, and network economies. The most important and enduring of these sources of market power is economies of scale. **LO2**

- Large fixed cost may cause marginal cost to be less than average total cost. Such a situation can be an important factor in economies of scale. **LO3**

- For the perfectly competitive firm, marginal revenue exactly equals market price. For the imperfectly competitive firm, marginal revenue is always less than the price, because to sell more output, the firm must reduce the price not only to additional buyers but to existing buyers as well. **LO4**

- Whereas the perfectly competitive firm maximizes profit by producing at the level at which marginal cost equals the market price, the imperfectly competitive firm maximizes profit by equating marginal cost with marginal revenue, which is significantly lower than the market price. The resulting output level maximizes profit for the imperfectly competitive firm but is less than the level that maximizes total economic surplus for society as a whole. Total economic surplus is smaller, and a smaller share of it goes to consumers. At the profit-maximizing level of output, the benefit of an extra unit of output (the market price) is greater than its cost (the marginal cost). At the surplus-maximizing level of output, where the marginal cost curve intersects the market demand curve, the benefit and cost of an extra unit are the same. **LO5, LO6**

- If the firm can grant discounts to price-sensitive buyers, it can increase profits. The extreme example is the perfectly discriminating monopolist, who charges each buyer exactly his or her reservation price. Such producers maximize total surplus, because they sell to every buyer whose reservation price is at least as high as the marginal cost. However, a monopolist that practices perfect price discrimination will capture the entire economic surplus. Under perfect price discrimination, consumer surplus will be zero. **LO7**

- The hurdle method of price discrimination, in which the buyer becomes eligible for a discount only after overcoming some obstacle such as mailing in a rebate coupon, is a mechanism for targeting discounts toward price-sensitive buyers. This technique works because those buyers who care most about price are more likely than others to jump the hurdle. Although the hurdle method reduces the loss in economic surplus associated with single-price monopoly, it does not completely eliminate it. **LO7**

- Natural monopolies occur in industries where a single firm experiences economies of scale sufficient to serve an entire market. Left to itself, a profit-maximizing natural monopolist will charge a monopoly price, which implies output will be below the surplus maximizing level. Governments' policies to improve the performance and fairness of natural monopolies include government ownership and management of natural monopolies, government regulation, private contracting, and vigorous enforcement of antitrust laws. Each of these options entails costs as well as benefits. **LO8**

- An oligopoly is a market characterized by a few rival sellers. When an oligopolist considers pricing and marketing strategies, it must consider the possible countermoves of its competitors. Oligopolists may sell either a homogenous or a differentiated product, depending on the market they are serving, and they have a mutual interest in avoiding direct price competition. The economic performance of an oligopoly raises issues similar to those of a monopoly. **LO1, LO5, LO6**

- Monopolistic competition is a market structure in which many firms sell differentiated products that compete with each other. It reduces total economic surplus relative to perfect competition because advertising increases costs unnecessarily, firms choose inefficiently small scales of operation and operate their plants with excess capacity, and price is greater than marginal cost. The theory of monopolistic competition can be used to analyze markets characterized by differentiated products and substantial competition. However, monopolistic competition does offer variety, and consumers may prefer variety, even at some cost in the form of reduced total economic surplus. **LO2, LO4**

## KEY TERMS

cost-plus regulation (247)
hurdle method of price
   discrimination (244)
marginal revenue (229)
market power (220)
monopolistic competition (219)
natural monopoly (222)

network economy (222)
oligopoly (219)
perfect hurdle (244)
perfectly discriminating
   monopolist (241)
price discrimination (239)
price setter (220)

price taker (220)
pure monopoly (219)
rule for profit maximization (231)
technical efficiency in
   production (247)

## REVIEW QUESTIONS

1. What important characteristic do all three types of imperfectly competitive firms share? **LO1**

2. True or false: A firm with market power can sell whatever quantity it wants at whatever price it chooses. **LO2**

3. Why do most successful industrial societies offer patents and copyright protection, even though these protections enable sellers to charge higher prices? **LO2**

4. Why is marginal revenue always less than the price for a monopolist but equal to the price for a perfectly competitive firm? **LO4**

5. Explain how a monopoly that charges a single price transfers part of a smaller total economic surplus from consumers to itself. **LO5, LO6**

6. Explain how a monopolist can use price discrimination to transfer part or all of total economic surplus to itself. **LO7**

7. Explain how a monopolist that practices price discrimination can produce a larger economic surplus than a monopolist that charges one price to all buyers. **LO7**

8. True or false: Because a natural monopolist charges a price greater than marginal cost, it necessarily earns a positive economic profit. **LO3, LO8**

9. Explain why monopolistic competition produces a smaller economic surplus than perfect competition. Is your answer affected when you consider the variety of products offered by monopolistic competitors? Why? **LO1**

## PROBLEMS

1. Two car manufacturers, Saab and Volvo, have fixed costs of $1 billion and marginal costs of $10 000/car. If Saab produces 50 000 cars/year and Volvo produces 200 000, calculate the average production cost for each company. Based on these costs, which company's market share do you think will grow in relative terms? **LO3**

2. State whether the following statements are true or false, and explain why. **LO1, LO2, LO3**
   a. In a perfectly competitive industry, the industry demand curve is horizontal, whereas for a monopoly it is downward sloping.
   b. Perfectly competitive firms have no control over the price they charge for their product.
   c. For a natural monopoly, average cost declines as the number of units produced increases over the relevant output range.

3. State whether the following statements are true, false, or uncertain, and explain why. A single-price profit-maximizing monopolist **LO4**
   a. causes excess demand, or shortages, by selling too few units of a good or service.
   b. chooses the output level at which marginal revenue begins to increase.
   c. always charges a price above the marginal cost of production.
   d. maximizes marginal revenue.
   e. none of the above statements are true.

4. State whether the following statements are true, false, or uncertain, and explain why. If a monopolist could perfectly price discriminate, **LO7**
   a. the marginal revenue curve and the demand curve would coincide.
   b. the marginal revenue curve and the marginal cost curve would coincide.
   c. every consumer would pay a different price.
   d. marginal revenue would become negative at some output level.
   e. the resulting quantity of output would still not maximize total economic surplus.

5. What is the socially desirable price for a natural monopoly to charge? Why will a natural monopoly that attempts to charge the socially desirable price invariably suffer an economic loss? **LO8**

6. Tots Poses Inc., a profit-maximizing business, is the only photography business in town that specializes in portraits of small children. Sven, who owns and runs Tots Poses, expects to encounter an average of eight customers per day, each with a reservation price shown in the following table. **LO4, LO5, LO6**

| Customer | Reservation price ($/photo) |
|---|---|
| A | 50 |
| B | 46 |
| C | 42 |
| D | 38 |
| E | 34 |
| F | 30 |
| G | 26 |
| H | 22 |

   a. If the marginal cost of each photo is $12, how much will Sven charge if he must charge a single price to all customers and still maximize profits? At this price, how many portraits will Sven produce each day? What will be his economic profit?
   b. How much consumer surplus is generated each day at this price?
   c. What is the number of portraits that maximizes total economic surplus?

d. Sven is very experienced in the business and knows the reservation price of each of his customers. If he is allowed to charge any price he likes to any consumer, how many portraits will he produce each day, and what will his economic profit be?

e. In this case, how much consumer surplus is generated each day?

f. Suppose Sven is permitted to charge two prices. He knows that customers with a reservation price above $30 never bother with coupons, whereas those with a reservation price of $30 or less always use them. At what level will Sven set the list price of a portrait? At what level will he set the discount price? How many photos will he sell at each price?

g. In this case, what is Sven's economic profit, and how much consumer surplus is generated each day?

7. Suppose that the Charlottetown Cinema is a local monopoly whose demand curve for adult tickets on Saturday night is $P = 12 - 2Q$, where $P$ is the price of a ticket in dollars and $Q$ is the number of tickets sold in hundreds. The demand for children's tickets on Sunday afternoon is $P = 8 - 3Q$, and for adult tickets on Sunday afternoon, $P = 10 - 4Q$. On both Saturday night and Sunday afternoon, the marginal cost of an additional patron, child or adult, is $2. **LO4**

a. What is the marginal revenue curve in each of the three submarkets?

b. What price will the cinema charge in each of the three markets if its goal is to maximize profit?

8. Suppose you are a monopolist in the market for a specific video game. Your demand curve is given by $P = 80 - Q/2$, and your marginal cost curve is $MC = 10$. Your fixed costs equal $400. **LO4, LO5**

a. Graph the demand and marginal cost curve.

b. Derive and graph the marginal revenue curve.

c. Calculate and indicate on the graph the monopoly price and quantity.

d. What is your profit?

e. What is the level of consumer surplus?

9. Indira is a second grader who sells lemonade on a street corner in your neighbourhood. She is the only seller in the neighbourhood. Each cup of lemonade costs Indira $0.20 to produce; she has no fixed costs. The reservation prices for the 10 people who walk by Indira's lemonade stand each day are listed in the following table. (Notice that the table continues in the right hand column.)

| Person | A | B | C | D | E |
|---|---|---|---|---|---|
| Reservation Price | $1.00 | $0.90 | $0.80 | $0.70 | $0.60 |

| Person | F | G | H | I | J |
|---|---|---|---|---|---|
| Reservation Price | $0.50 | $0.40 | $0.30 | $0.20 | $0.10 |

Indira knows the distribution of reservation prices (that is, she knows that one person is willing to pay $1, another $0.90, and so on), but she does not know any specific individual's reservation price. **LO4, LO5, LO6, LO7**

a. Calculate the marginal revenue of selling an additional cup of lemonade. (Start by figuring out the price Indira would charge if she produced only one cup of lemonade and calculate the total revenue; then find the price Indira would charge if she sold two cups of lemonade; and so on.)

b. What is Indira's profit-maximizing price?

c. At that price, what are Indira's economic profit and total consumer surplus?

d. What price will Indira charge if she wants to maximize total economic surplus?

e. Now suppose Indira can tell the reservation price of each person. What price would she charge each person if she wanted to maximize profit? Compare her profit to the total surplus calculated in part (d).

10. Refer to problem 9 and its table. This time, suppose that a number of other children are selling lemonade in Indira's neighbourhood. However, Indira's family owns a greenhouse in which a few lemon and lime trees are growing (along with many other plants). They are the only lemon and lime trees anywhere near Indira's town. On the advice of an older sister, Indira blends juice from freshly picked lemons and limes into her lemonade. She posts paper signs at her corner advertising that her lemonade uses juice from the freshest lemons and limes that can be found anywhere. Her signs also state that her lemonade has a wonderful, unique flavour because she uses a special blend of lemon and lime juices. Suppose that Indira's variable cost remains at $0.20 per cup. However, her signs cost $1.00 to make. Indira knows the distribution of reservation prices (that is, she knows one person is willing to pay $1.00 and so on), but she does not know any specific individual's reservation price. **LO1, LO4**

a. Given the assumptions for this problem, is Indira selling in a perfectly competitive market or a monopolistically competitive market? Why?

b. What price will Indira charge? How many cups of lemonade will she sell? Explain.

c. Suppose Indira operates her stand five days per week. Because of wear and tear, she must replace her signs once per week. Also, her sister has advised her that she can keep the attention of her customers if she changes the colour and design of the signs each week. What are Indira's total *weekly* costs? Would her costs be higher or lower if she were selling in a perfectly competitive market? How much higher or lower? Explain.

d. Calculate Indira's *weekly* economic profit. When making your calculations, include the data given in (c). Also, assume that the variable cost of lemonade includes the opportunity cost of Indira's time.

e. If Indira is a monopolistic competitor, will her profits persist in the long run? Why or why not?

11. Consider the market for taxicab drivers in a city. Assume that each driver owns and drives her own cab—she is the owner-operator of a small business. Each driver also pays for the services of a dispatcher. **LO1, LO4**

a. Assume the market for taxi services is perfectly competitive. Use a graph to show the price a driver will charge and the number of kilometres she will drive in long-run equilibrium. Explain.

b. Now assume that the market for taxi services is monopolistically competitive and answer (a). Explain your answer.

c. Suppose a driver's shift is 10 hours long. Will a driver do more driving per shift if the market is perfectly competitive or monopolistically competitive? Why? In which case will a passenger pay a higher price for a trip? Why?

d. Suppose the opportunity cost of a driver's time is $10/hour. How much will a driver earn when the market for taxi services is in long-run equilibrium and the market is perfectly competitive? What if the market is monopolistically competitive? If your answers are the same, explain why. If they are not the same, explain why not.

e. Your answer to (c) should reveal that a driver will drive fewer kilometres during a 10-hour shift if the market is monopolistically competitive. Your answer to (d) should reveal that in long-run equilibrium, a driver will earn $10/hour for each hour of a 10-hour shift, regardless of whether the market is perfectly or monopolistically competitive. How is it possible for a driver to drive less in a monopolistically competitive market yet earn the opportunity cost of her time?

## ANSWERS TO IN-CHAPTER EXERCISES

8.1    The relevant cost figures are as shown in the following table, which shows that Sony's unit cost advantage is now $50.20 − $5.20 = $45.00. **LO3**

|  | Microsoft | Sony |
| --- | --- | --- |
| Annual production | 200 000 | 2 000 000 |
| Fixed cost | $10 000 000 | $10 000 000 |
| Variable cost | $40 000 | $400 000 |
| Total cost | $10 040 000 | $10 400 000 |
| Average cost per game | $50.20 | $5.20 |

8.2    When the monopolist expands from 3 to 4 units/week, total revenue rises from $15 to $16/week, which means that the marginal revenue from the sale of the fourth unit is only $1/week. When the monopolist expands from 4 to 5 units/week, total revenue drops from $16 to 15/week, which means that the marginal revenue from the sale of the fifth unit is actually negative, or −$1/week. **LO4**

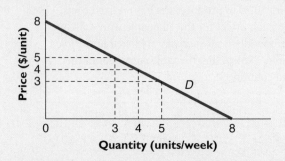

8.3     For the demand curve $P = 12 - Q$, the corresponding marginal revenue curve is MR = $12 - 2Q$. Equating *MR* and *MC*, we solve the equation $12 - 2Q = 2Q$ to obtain $Q = 3$. Substituting $Q = 3$ into the demand equation, we solve for the profit-maximizing price, $P = 12 - 3 = 9$. **LO4**

# CHAPTER 9
# Thinking Strategically

## LEARNING OBJECTIVES

When you complete this chapter, you will be able to:

**LO1** Describe the basic elements of a game.

**LO2** Identify dominant strategies.

**LO3** Find an equilibrium for a game.

**LO4** Analyze the effects of dominant strategies.

**LO5** Identify games in which the equilibrium is a prisoner's dilemma.

**LO6** Explain why a prisoner's dilemma produces an equilibrium that is not optimal for a group as a whole.

**LO7** Demonstrate how games in which timing matters differ from games in which it does not.

**LO8** Identify commitment problems and explain how norms, morals, and preferences can resolve them.

At a dinner party in 1997, actor Robert DeNiro pulled singer Tony Bennett aside for a moment. "Hey, Tony—there's a film I want you in," DeNiro said. He was referring to the project that became the 1999 Warner Brothers hit comedy *Analyze This,* in which the troubled head of a crime family, played by DeNiro, seeks the counsel of a psychotherapist, played by Billy Crystal. In the script, both the mob boss and his therapist are big fans of Bennett's music.

Bennett heard nothing further about the project for almost a year. Then his son and financial manager, Danny Bennett, got a phone call from Warner Brothers in which the studio offered Tony $15 000 to sing "Got the World on a String" in the movie's final scene. As Danny described the conversation, ". . . they made a fatal mistake. They told me they had already shot the film. So I'm like, 'Hey, they shot the whole film around Tony being the end gag and they're offering me $15 000?'"[1] Warner Brothers paid $200 000 for Bennett's performance.

In business negotiations, as in life, timing can be everything. If executives at Warner Brothers had thought the problem through carefully, they would have negotiated with Bennett *before* shooting the movie. At that point, Bennett would have realized that the script could be rewritten if he asked too high a fee. By waiting, studio executives left themselves with no other option than to pay Bennett's price.

The payoff of many actions depends not only on the actions themselves but also on when they are taken and how they relate to actions taken by others. In previous chapters, economic decision makers confronted an environment that was essentially fixed. A firm in a perfectly competitive market has no control over price—it is fixed by supply and demand in the market. Each firm can only decide the quantity of output that will maximize profit at that market price. A monopolistic firm, on the other hand, faces a fixed demand curve. It too decides on the quantity of output that will maximize profit, knowing its own costs *and* how much it can sell at any specific price.

---

1 As quoted by Geraldine Fabrikant, "Talking Money with Tony Bennett," *The New York Times*, May 2, 1999, Money & Business, p. 1.

In both pure monopoly and perfect competition, the firm does not need a business strategy that takes into account possible countermoves by rival firms. Most real-world firms, however, are neither perfect competitors nor pure monopolists. As a result, when considering an action, they have to think about the possible actions competitors might make in response. For example, when a monopolistic competitor differentiates its product, it knows that its actions are likely to trigger reactions from similar firms. When BMW offers instant links to roadside repair and rescue services in their new models, General Motors is likely to respond by offering customers competing services for their Cadillacs and other high-end cars. Since most markets are neither perfectly competitive nor purely monopolistic, the firms that operate in these markets understand that anticipating the likely responses of their competitors is crucial to business success—*thinking strategically* matters.

Game theory has therefore played an important role in analyzing oligopoly. Recall that oligopoly is characterized by mutual interdependence. If an oligopolist considers a new advertising campaign, a change in the design of one of its products, or the development of a new product, it can expect its rivals to respond. Strategic thinking can also apply to the behaviour of individuals. If the owner of a business considers hiring a manager to manage in new office in another town, can she count on the new manager to be honest and conscientious? An analysis of strategic thinking can help answer this question as well. We can make better sense of the world we live in if firms and people anticipate the effect of their behaviour on others.

# 9.1 THE THEORY OF GAMES

In chess, tennis, or any other game, your payoff from a given move depends on what your opponent does in response. In choosing your move, therefore, you will try to anticipate your opponent's responses, how you might respond, and what further moves your own response might elicit. When the payoffs to different actors depend on the actions their opponents take, the theory of games, developed by mathematicians, economists, and other behavioural scientists, uses logical deduction to explore the consequences. It can be used to study warfare, crime, and many topics that some might not regard as subjects of conventional economics. Indeed, "games" can be very serious—game theory has been used to study strategies with momentous outcomes, like the possibility of nuclear war.

## THE THREE ELEMENTS OF A GAME

Any game has three **basic elements**: the players, the list of possible actions (or strategies) each player can choose from, and the payoffs the players receive for each combination of strategies. These elements combine to form an analysis of the outcomes of each actor's choices.

**basic elements of a game**
the players, the strategies available to each player, and the payoffs each player receives for each possible combination of strategies

### EXAMPLE 9.1

**Will Pepsi spend more money on advertising?**

Imagine that Pepsi and Coca-Cola are the only makers of cola drinks. Both are earning economic profits of $6000 per day and both want to increase their profits. Assume that if Pepsi increases its advertising expenditures by $1000 per day and Coca-Cola spends no more on advertising than it does now, Pepsi's profit will increase to $8000 each day and Coca-Cola's will decrease to $2000. If both spend $1000 on advertising, each will earn an economic profit of $5500 per day. These payoffs are symmetric, so if Pepsi stands pat while Coca-Cola increases its spending by $1000, Pepsi's economic profit will fall to $2000 per day, and Coca-Cola's will increase to $8000. If each must decide independently whether to increase spending on advertising, what will Pepsi do?

Think of this situation as a game. What are its three elements? The players are the two soft drink companies, each of which must choose one of two strategies: raise

**payoff matrix** a table that describes the payoffs in a game for each possible combination of strategies

spending by $1000 or leave it the same. The payoffs are the economic profits that correspond to the four possible scenarios resulting from their choices. One way to summarize the relevant information about this game is to display the players, strategies, and payoffs in a simple table called a **payoff matrix** (see Table 9.1).

**TABLE 9.1**
**The Payoff Matrix for an Advertising Game**

|  |  | Coca-Cola | |
|---|---|---|---|
|  |  | Raise spending on advertisements | Leave spending on advertisements the same |
| **Pepsi** | Raise spending on advertisements | $5500 for Pepsi $5500 for Coca-Cola | $8000 for Pepsi $2000 for Coca-Cola |
|  | Leave spending on advertisements the same | $2000 for Pepsi $8000 for Coca-Cola | $6000 for Pepsi $6000 for Coca-Cola |

Confronted with the payoff matrix in Table 9.1, what will Coca-Cola do?

The essence of strategic thinking is to begin by looking at the situation from the other party's point of view. Suppose Pepsi raises its spending on advertising (the top row in Table 9.1). In that case, Coca-Cola's best option would be to also raise ad spending (the left column in Table 9.1). The left column is Coca-Cola's best response when Pepsi chooses the top row because Coca-Cola's economic profits (see the upper left cell of Table 9.1) will be $5500 as compared with only $2000 if it keeps spending constant (see the upper right cell).

Alternatively, suppose that Pepsi does not change its expenditures on advertising (that is, Pepsi chooses the bottom row in Table 9.1). Coca-Cola would still do better to increase spending, because it would earn $8000 (the lower left cell) as compared with only $6000 if it keeps spending constant (lower right cell).

In this particular game, no matter which strategy Pepsi chooses, Coca-Cola will earn a higher economic profit by increasing its spending on advertising. And since this game is perfectly symmetric, a similar conclusion holds for Pepsi: no matter which strategy, Coca-Cola chooses, Pepsi will do better by increasing its spending on advertisements.

**dominant strategy** one that yields a higher payoff no matter what the other players in a game choose

**dominated strategy** any other strategy available to a player who has a dominant strategy

When one player has a strategy that yields a higher payoff no matter which choice the other player makes, that player is said to have a **dominant strategy**. Not all games involve dominant strategies, but both players in this game have one, and that is to increase spending on advertisements. For both players, to leave ad spending the same is a **dominated strategy**—one that leads to a lower payoff than an alternative choice, regardless of the other player's choice.

Notice, however, that when each player chooses the dominant strategy, the resulting payoffs are smaller than if each had left spending unchanged. When Pepsi and Coca-Cola increase their spending on advertisements, each earns only $5500 in economic profits as compared to the $6000 each would have earned without the increase. (We will say more below about this apparent paradox.)

**Nash equilibrium** any combination of strategies in which each player's strategy is his or her best choice, given the other players' strategies

## NASH EQUILIBRIUM

A game is said to be in equilibrium if each player's strategy is the best he or she can choose, given the other players' strategies. This definition of equilibrium is called **Nash equilibrium** after the Nobel laureate John Nash who developed the concept in the early 1950s. When a game is in equilibrium, no player has any incentive to deviate from his or her current strategy.

If each player in a game has a dominant strategy, as in Example 9.1, equilibrium occurs when each player follows that strategy. But even in games in which not every player has a dominant strategy, we can often identify an equilibrium outcome. Consider, for instance, the following variation on the advertising game of Example 9.1.

## EXAMPLE 9.2

### Will Coca-Cola spend more money on advertising?

Suppose we change the payoff matrix for advertising decisions to that shown in Table 9.2. Does Pepsi now have a dominant strategy? Does Coca-Cola? If each firm does the best it can, given the incentives facing the other, what will be the outcome of this game?

**TABLE 9.2**
**Equilibrium When One Player Lacks a Dominant Strategy**

|  |  | Coca-Cola | |
|---|---|---|---|
|  |  | Raise spending on advertisements | Leave spending on advertisements the same |
| **Pepsi** | Raise spending on advertisements | $3000 for Pepsi<br>$8000 for Coca-Cola | $8000 for Pepsi<br>$4000 for Coca-Cola |
|  | Leave spending on advertisements the same | $4000 for Pepsi<br>$4000 for Coca-Cola | $5000 for Pepsi<br>$2000 for Coca-Cola |

In this game, no matter what Pepsi does, Coca-Cola will do better to increase its advertising, so raising the advertising budget is a dominant strategy for Coca-Cola. Pepsi, however, does not have a dominant strategy. If Coca-Cola raises its spending, Pepsi will do better to stand pat; if Coca-Cola stands pat, however, Pepsi will do better to spend more. But even though Pepsi does not have a dominant strategy, we can still predict what is likely to happen in this game. After all, if Pepsi's managers know what the payoff matrix is, they can predict that Coca-Cola will spend more on advertisements (since that is Coca-Cola's dominant strategy). And if Pepsi believes that Coca-Cola will spend more on advertisements, Pepsi's best strategy is to keep its own spending constant. When both players take account of the incentives each faces, and each chooses its best strategy, this game will end in the lower left cell of the payoff matrix: Coca-Cola will raise its spending on advertisements and Pepsi will not. The lower left cell represents a Nash equilibrium because when both players are positioned in the lower left cell, neither has any incentive to change its strategy.

A few large firms dominate the soft drink industry, which is a characteristic of oligopoly, as we saw in Chapter 8. We also saw that oligopolists prefer to avoid direct price competition, preferring instead to compete by differentiating their products. Advertising can be used to differentiate products, and game theory provides an explanation of how oligopolists might make decisions concerning advertising.

**EXERCISE 9.1**    **What will Pepsi and Coca-Cola do if their payoff matrix is modified as follows?**

|  |  | Coca-Cola | |
|---|---|---|---|
|  |  | Raise spending on advertisements | Leave spending on advertisements the same |
| Pepsi | Raise spending on advertisements | $3000 for Pepsi<br>$8000 for Coca-Cola | $4000 for Pepsi<br>$5000 for Coca-Cola |
|  | Leave spending on advertisements the same | $8000 for Pepsi<br>$4000 for Coca-Cola | $5000 for Pepsi<br>$2000 for Coca-Cola |

> **RECAP**
>
> **THE THEORY OF GAMES**
>
> The three elements of any game are the players, the list of strategies from which they can choose, and the payoffs to each combination of strategies. Players in some games have a dominant strategy, one that yields a higher payoff regardless of the strategies chosen by other players.
>
> Equilibrium in a game occurs when each player chooses the strategy that yields the highest payoff available, given the strategies chosen by other players. Such a combination of strategies is called a Nash equilibrium.

## 9.2   THE PRISONER'S DILEMMA

**prisoner's dilemma** a game in which each player has a dominant strategy, and when each plays it, the resulting payoffs are smaller than if each had played a dominated strategy

The game in Example 9.1 belongs to an important class of games called the **prisoner's dilemma**. In the prisoner's dilemma, when each player chooses his dominant strategy, the result is unattractive to the group of players as a whole.

### THE ORIGINAL PRISONER'S DILEMMA

Example 9.3 recounts the original scenario from which the prisoner's dilemma drew its name.

### EXAMPLE **9.3**

**Will the prisoners confess?**

Two prisoners, Horace and Jasper, are being held in separate cells for a serious crime that they did, in fact, commit. The prosecutor, however, has only enough hard evidence to convict them of a minor offence, for which the penalty is a year in jail. Each prisoner is told that if one confesses while the other remains silent, the one who confesses will go free and the other will spend 20 years in prison. (A confession by one prisoner implicates the other.) If both confess, each will receive an intermediate sentence of five years. These payoffs are summarized in Table 9.3. The two prisoners cannot communicate with one another. Do they have a dominant strategy? If so, what is it?

In this game, the dominant strategy for each prisoner is to confess. No matter what Jasper does, Horace will get a lighter sentence by confessing. If Jasper

www.uvic.ca/econ
University of Victoria,
search for prisoner's dilemma

**TABLE 9.3**
**The Payoff Matrix for a Prisoner's Dilemma**

| | | Jasper | |
|---|---|---|---|
| | | Confess | Remain silent |
| **Horace** | Confess | 5 years for each | 0 years for Horace<br>20 years for Jasper |
| | Remain silent | 20 years for Horace<br>0 years for Jasper | 1 year for each |

confesses, Horace will get five years (upper left cell) instead of 20 (lower left cell). If Jasper remains silent, Horace will go free (upper right cell) instead of spending a year in jail (lower right cell). Because the payoffs are perfectly symmetric, Jasper will also do better to confess, no matter what Horace does. When each follows his dominant strategy and confesses, both will do worse than if each had shown restraint. When both confess, they each get five years (upper left cell) instead of the one year they would have gotten by remaining silent (lower right cell). Hence, the name of this game is the prisoner's dilemma.

**GM and Ford must both decide whether to invest in developing a new engine. Games 1 and 2 below show how their profits depend on the decisions they make. Which of these games is a prisoner's dilemma?**

EXERCISE 9.2

| | | Game 1<br>Ford | | | | Game 2<br>Ford | |
|---|---|---|---|---|---|---|---|
| | | Not invest | Invest | | | Not invest | Invest |
| **GM** | Not invest | 10 for each | 4 for GM<br>12 for Ford | **GM** | Not invest | 4 for GM<br>12 for Ford | 5 for each |
| | Invest | 12 for GM<br>4 for Ford | 5 for each | | Invest | 10 for each | 12 for GM<br>4 for Ford |

During the 1950s and 1960s, when a few large North American firms dominated the automotive industry, it made sense to regard the industry as an oligopoly. Today, many firms from around the world produce automobiles, and it is difficult to say that the industry is dominated by a few large firms. A large number of firms selling a differentiated product is characteristic of monopolistic competition. Nevertheless, firms that once dominated the industry (Chrysler, Ford, General Motors) have experienced extended periods during which they generated large losses without leaving the industry. This contrasts with the easy exit and entry characteristic of monopolistic competition. Why? Easy entry and exit would quickly bring a monopolistic competitor to a normal rate of return. The automotive industry also retains other characteristics of oligopoly. Large, sophisticated factories, a large, technically competent labour force, and a well-developed network of dealers are necessary (though not sufficient) for an automobile manufacturer to be successful. These requirements constitute barriers to entry, a characteristic of oligopoly. In any case, once you solve Exercise 9.2 you should be able to see that a prisoner's dilemma provides an explanation for how excessive product development can occur. For instance, in one of the two games, a prisoner's dilemma leads both Ford and General Motors to invest in a new engine. Presumably Ford's new engine will be different from General Motor's engine. Yet the total payoff when both invest in new engines is half of what it would be if neither invested. Recently, some older firms, such as General Motors, have reduced their number of models and product lines as they attempt to reverse large losses—did they invest in too many different models in the first place?

The prisoner's dilemma is one of the most powerful metaphors in all of human behavioural science. Countless social and economic interactions have payoff structures analogous to the one confronted by the two prisoners. Some of those interactions occur between only two players, as in the examples just discussed; many others involve larger groups. But regardless of the number of players involved, the common thread is one of conflict between the narrow, immediate self-interest of individuals and the broader interests of larger communities. The core issue is whether individuals can coordinate their actions, and all end up better off, by *not* acting in their immediate, narrow self-interest.

## PRISONER'S DILEMMAS CONFRONTING IMPERFECTLY COMPETITIVE FIRMS

**cartel** a coalition of firms that agree to restrict output for the purpose of earning an economic profit

A **cartel** is any coalition of firms that conspire to restrict production for the purpose of earning an economic profit. As we will see in the next example, the problem confronting oligopolists who are trying to form a cartel is a classic illustration of the prisoner's dilemma.

---

### ECONOMIC NATURALIST 9.1

#### Why might cartel agreements be unstable?

Consider a market for bottled water served by only two firms, Aquapure and Mountain Spring. Each firm can draw water free from a mineral spring located on its own land. Customers supply their own bottles. Rather than compete with one another, the two firms decide to collude by selling water at the price a profit-maximizing pure monopolist would charge. Under their agreement (which constitutes a cartel), each firm would produce and sell half the quantity of water demanded by the market at the monopoly price (see Figure 9.1). The agreement is not legally enforceable, however, which means that each firm has the option of charging less than the agreed price. If one firm sells water for less than the other firm, it will capture the entire quantity demanded by the market at the lower price.

Why might this agreement collapse?

Since the marginal cost of mineral water is zero, the profit-maximizing quantity for a monopolist with the demand curve shown in Figure 9.1 is 1000 bottles/day,

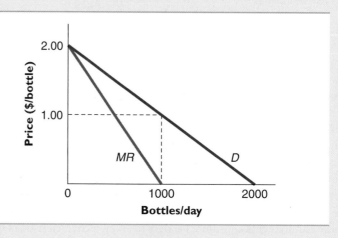

**FIGURE 9.1**
**The Market Demand for Mineral Water**
Faced with the demand curve shown, a monopolist with zero marginal cost would produce 1000 bottles/day (the quantity at which marginal revenue equals zero) and sell them at a price of $1/bottle.

## FIGURE 9.2
### The Temptation to Violate a Cartel Agreement
By cutting its price from $1/bottle to $0.90/bottle, Aquapure can sell the entire market quantity demanded, 1100 bottles/day, rather than half the monopoly quantity of 1000 bottles/day.

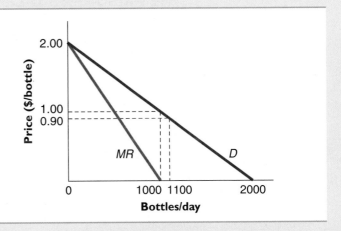

the quantity for which marginal revenue equals marginal cost. At that quantity, the monopoly price is $1/bottle. If the firms abide by their agreement to hold the price at $1, each will sell half the market total, or 500 bottles/day at a price of $1/bottle, for an economic profit of $500/day.

But suppose Aquapure reduced its price to $0.90/bottle. By underselling Mountain Spring, Aquapure would capture the entire quantity demanded by the market, which, as shown in Figure 9.2, is 1100 bottles/day. Aquapure's economic profit would rise from $500/day to ($0.90/bottle) (1100 bottles/day) = $990/day, almost twice as much as before. In the process, Mountain Spring's economic profit would fall from $500/day to zero. Rather than see its economic profit disappear, Mountain Spring could match Aquapure's price cut, recapturing its original 50 percent share of the market. But when each firm charges $0.90/ bottle and sells 550 bottles/day, each earns an economic profit of ($0.90/bottle)(550 bottles/day) = $495/day, or $5/day less than before.

Suppose we view the cartel agreement as an economic game in which the two available strategies are to sell for $1/bottle or to sell for $0.90/bottle. The payoffs are the economic profits that result from these strategies. Table 9.4 shows the payoff matrix

for this game. Each firm's dominant strategy is to sell at the lower price, yet in following that strategy, each earns a lower profit than if each had sold at the higher price.

The game does not end with both firms charging $0.90/bottle. Each firm knows that if it cuts the price a little further, it can recapture the entire market, and in the process earn a substantially higher economic profit. At every step the rival firm will match any price cut, until the price falls to the marginal cost, zero in this example.

Cartel agreements confront participants with the economic incentives inherent in the prisoner's dilemma, which explains why such agreements have historically been so unstable. Usually a cartel involves not just two firms, but several—a situation that can make retaliation against price cutters extremely difficult. In many cases, discovering which parties have broken the agreement is difficult. For example, the Organization of Petroleum Exporting Countries (OPEC) is a cartel of oil producers that was formed in 1960. The cartel came to prominence in the 1970s when it restricted oil production. However, it has no practical way to prevent member countries from increasing their sales by secretly offering to sell oil below the cartel price.

## TABLE 9.4
### The Payoff Matrix for a Cartel Agreement

| | | Mountain Spring | |
|---|---|---|---|
| | | Charge $1/bottle | Charge $0.90/bottle |
| **Aquapure** | Charge $1/bottle | $500/day for each | 0 for Aquapure<br>$990/day for Mt. Spring |
| | Charge $0.90/bottle | $990/day for Aquapure<br>0 for Mt. Spring | $495/day for each |

# THE PRISONER'S DILEMMA IN EVERYDAY LIFE

As the following example makes clear, the prisoner's dilemma helps the economic naturalist to make sense of human behaviour, not only in the world of business, but in other domains of life as well.

---

**ECONOMIC NATURALIST 9.2**

## Why do people often stand at concerts, even though they can see just as well when everyone sits?

A few years ago, an economic naturalist went with friends to a rock concert. They bought good seats, some 20 rows from the stage. But before the end of the first song, several people in front of them rose to their feet, presumably to get a better view. In doing so, they blocked the line of sight for others behind them, forcing those people to stand to have a better view. Before long, the entire crowd was standing. Then a few people in the front rows climbed atop their seats, blocking the views of those behind them and forcing them to stand on their seats too. The seats had fold-up bottoms, so from time to time someone who stood too close to the pivot point would tumble as the seat popped into its vertical position. All things considered, the outcome was far less satisfactory than if everyone had remained seated. Why this pattern of self-defeating behaviour?

To understand what happened at the concert, note that standing is self-defeating only when viewed from the group's perspective. From the individual's perspective standing passes the cost–benefit test. No matter what others do, an individual sees better by standing than by sitting. Suppose, for the sake of discussion, that you and other members of the audience would be willing to pay $2 to avoid standing and $3 to get a better view (or avoid having a worse one). In this multiperson prisoner's dilemma, you are one player and the rest of the audience is the other. The two strategies are to stand or to sit. Suppose everyone is seated to begin with. The payoffs you and others face will depend on the combination of strategies that you and others choose, as shown in Table 9.5.

COST-BENEFIT

Since standing is tiring and the view is no better when everyone stands than when everyone sits, why do people often stand at concerts?

The payoff of 0 in the lower right cell of the payoff matrix reflects the fact that when everyone remains seated, everyone is just as well off as before. Your payoff of −$3 in the lower left cell reflects the fact that if you sit while others stand, you will have a worse view. Your payoff of −$2 in the upper left cell reflects the fact that when you and others stand, you must endure the $2 cost of standing, even though you don't get a better view. Finally, your $1 payoff in the upper right cell represents the difference between your $3 benefit and your $2 cost of standing when you stand while others sit.

---

**TABLE 9.5**
**Standing versus Sitting at a Concert as a Prisoner's Dilemma**

|  |  | Others | |
|---|---|---|---|
|  |  | Stand | Sit |
| **You** | Stand | −$2 for each | $1 for you<br>−$3 for others |
|  | Sit | −$3 for you<br>$1 for others | 0 for each |

These payoffs mean that your dominant strategy is to stand. If others stand, you will get −$2 by standing, which is better than the −$3 you will get by sitting. If others sit, you will get $1 by standing, which is better than the $0 you will get by sitting. Since this game is symmetric, the dominant strategy for others is also to stand. Yet when everyone stands, everyone gets a payoff of −$2, which is $2 worse than if everyone had remained seated. As in all prisoner's dilemmas, the choice that is more attractive from the perspective of the individual turns out to be less attractive from the perspective of the group.

Notice, too, that the prisoner's dilemma and the fallacy of composition, which we saw in Chapter 1, are related—while an outcome may be optimal for each actor individually, it is a mistake to conclude that the combined total of the individual outcomes is optimal for the group. Though each individual prisoner, firm, or concert goer in the group may find it in his narrow self-interest to take an action, the combined total of those actions may be contrary to the best interests of the group.

## TIT-FOR-TAT AND THE REPEATED PRISONER'S DILEMMA

When all players cooperate in a prisoner's dilemma, each gets a higher payoff than when all defect. So people who confront prisoner's dilemmas repeatedly have an incentive to create mechanisms that encourage mutual cooperation, and which penalize players who defect from co-operation. When players interact with one another only once, this turns out to be difficult. But when they expect to interact repeatedly, new possibilities emerge.

A **repeated prisoner's dilemma** is a standard prisoner's dilemma that confronts the same players not just once but many times. Experimental research on repeated prisoner's dilemmas in the 1960s identified a simple strategy that proves remarkably effective at limiting defection. The strategy is called **tit-for-tat**, and here is how it works. The first time you interact with someone, you cooperate. In each subsequent interaction, you simply do what that person did in the previous interaction. Thus, if your partner defected on your first interaction, you would then defect on your next interaction with her. If she then cooperates, your move next time will be to cooperate as well.

Computer simulations have shown that tit-for-tat is a remarkably effective strategy, even when pitted against a host of ingenious counterstrategies designed for the explicit purpose of trying to exploit it. The success of tit-for-tat requires a reasonably stable set of players, each of whom can remember what other players have done in previous interactions. It also requires that players have a significant stake in what happens in the future, for it is the fear of retaliation that deters people from defecting.

Since rival firms in the same industry interact with one another repeatedly, it might seem that the tit-for-tat strategy would assure widespread collusion to raise prices. And yet, as noted earlier, cartel agreements are notoriously unsuccessful. One difficulty is that tit-for-tat's effectiveness depends on there being only two players in the game. In monopolistically competitive industries, there are generally many firms, and even in oligopolies there are often several. When there are more than two firms, and one defects now, how do the cooperators selectively punish the defector later? By cutting price? That will penalize everyone, not just the defector. Even if there are only two firms in an industry, these firms realize that other firms may enter their industry. So the would-be cartel members have to worry not only about each other, but also about the entire list of firms that might decide to compete with them. Each firm may see this as a hopeless task and decide to defect now, hoping to reap at least some economic profit in the short run. What seems clear, in any event, is that the practical problems involved in implementing tit-for-tat have often made it difficult to hold cartel agreements together for long.

**repeated prisoner's dilemma** a standard dilemma that confronts the same players repeatedly

**tit-for-tat** a strategy for the repeated prisoner's dilemma in which players cooperate on the first move, then mimic their partner's last move on each successive move

> **RECAP**
>
> **THE PRISONER'S DILEMMA**
>
> The prisoner's dilemma is a game in which each player has a dominant strategy and, when each chooses that strategy, the payoff to each player is smaller than if each had chosen a dominated strategy. Incentives analogous to those found in the prisoner's dilemma help to explain a broad range of behaviour in business and everyday life—among them, excessive spending on advertising, cartel instability, standing at concerts, and shouting at parties.

## 9.3  GAMES IN WHICH TIMING MATTERS

In the games discussed so far, players were assumed to choose their strategies simultaneously, and which player moved first didn't particularly matter. For example, in the prisoner's dilemma, players would follow their dominant strategies even if they knew in advance what strategies their opponents had chosen. But in other situations, such as the negotiations between Warner Brothers and Tony Bennett described at the beginning of this chapter, timing is of the essence.

As you work through the examples that follow, remember that they represent the logical implications of assuming that each participant in the game is *only* interested in maximizing his or her personal money income. *Behavioural economics* is a relatively new area of research within economics in which controlled experiments are used to test the realism of basic assumptions; for example, the "ultimatum game" has been used to test the realism of the assumption that people typically maximize their individual income and do not care about the distribution of income.

### THE ULTIMATUM BARGAINING GAME

#### EXAMPLE 9.4

> **Will Torben accept Kamal's offer?**

Kamal and Torben are subjects in an experiment. The experimenter begins by giving $100 to Kamal, who must then propose a division of the money between himself and Torben. Kamal can propose any division he chooses, provided the proposed amounts are whole dollars and he offers Torben at least $1. If Kamal proposes $X for himself and $(100 − X) for Torben, Torben must then say whether he accepts the proposal. If he does, each will get the proposed amount. But if Torben rejects the proposal, each player will get zero, and the $100 will revert to the experimenter. If Kamal and Torben know they will play this game only once, and each wants to make as much money for himself as possible, what will Kamal propose?

A payoff matrix is not a useful way to summarize the information in this game, because it says nothing about the timing of each player's move. For games in which timing matters, a **decision tree**, or **game tree**, is more useful. This type of diagram describes the possible moves in the sequence in which they may occur and lists the final payoffs for each possible combination of moves.

The decision tree for the game in Example 9.4 is shown in Figure 9.3. At *A*, Kamal begins the game by making his proposal. At *B*, Torben responds to Kamal's proposal. If he accepts (the top branch of the tree), Kamal will get $X and Torben will get $(100 − X). If he refuses (the bottom branch of the tree), both will get nothing.

In thinking strategically about this game, the key for Kamal is to put himself in Torben's shoes and imagine how he might react to various proposals. If Torben's goal is only to make as much money as possible, Kamal can predict that Torben will accept

**decision tree (or game tree)** a diagram that describes the possible moves in a game, in sequence, and lists the payoffs that correspond to each possible combination of moves

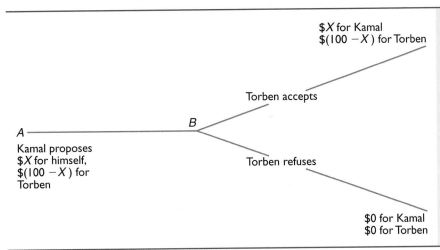

**FIGURE 9.3**

**Decision Tree for Example 9.4**
This decision tree shows the possible moves and payoffs for the game in Example 9.4 in the sequence in which they may occur.

his offer, no matter how small, because the alternative is to reject it and get nothing. For instance, suppose Kamal proposes $99 for himself and only $1 for Torben (see Figure 9.4). At *B*, Torben's best option is to accept the offer; $1 is not much, but it is more than zero (the payoff from rejecting). This is a Nash equilibrium, because neither player has any incentive to deviate from the strategy he chose.

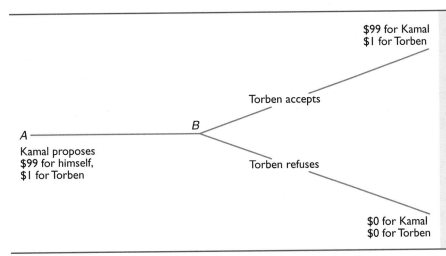

**FIGURE 9.4**

**Kamal's Best Strategy in an Ultimatum Bargaining Game**
If Kamal can predict that Torben will accept any positive offer, Kamal's income-maximizing strategy at *A* is to offer Torben the smallest positive amount possible, $1.

This type of game has been called the **ultimatum bargaining game**, because of the power of the first player to confront the second player with a take-it-or-leave-it offer. Torben could refuse a one-sided offer from Kamal, but doing so would leave him with less money than if he accepted it.

**ultimatum bargaining game** one in which the first player has the power to confront the second player with a take-it-or-leave-it offer

Example 9.5 illustrates the importance of the timing of moves in determining the outcome of the ultimatum bargaining game.

# EXAMPLE 9.5

## If Torben can specify his acceptance threshold, what will it be?

Suppose we change the rules of the ultimatum bargaining game so that Torben has the right to specify *in advance* the smallest offer he will accept. If Kamal's task is again to propose a division of the $100, what amount will maximize Torben's gains?

This seemingly minor change in the rules completely alters the game, because Torben now has the first move. Once Torben announces that $Y is the smallest offer he will accept, his active role in the game is over. If $Y$ is $60 and Kamal proposes anything less for Torben, his offer will be rejected automatically. The decision tree for this game is shown in Figure 9.5.

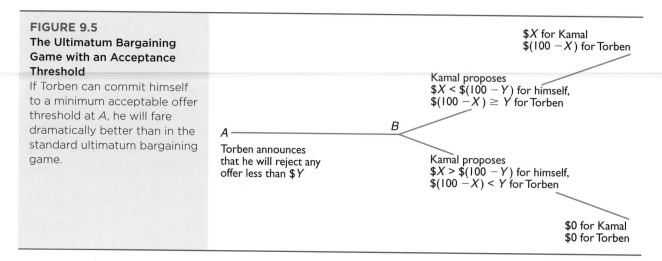

**FIGURE 9.5**
**The Ultimatum Bargaining Game with an Acceptance Threshold**
If Torben can commit himself to a minimum acceptable offer threshold at *A*, he will fare dramatically better than in the standard ultimatum bargaining game.

$X for Kamal
$(100 − X) for Torben

Kamal proposes
$X < $(100 − Y) for himself,
$(100 − X) ≥ Y for Torben

*A* ———————————— *B*

Torben announces that he will reject any offer less than $Y

Kamal proposes
$X > $(100 − Y) for himself,
$(100 − X) < Y for Torben

$0 for Kamal
$0 for Torben

When Torben announces that $Y is the smallest offer he will accept, the best Kamal can do is to propose $(100 − Y) for himself and $Y for Torben. If he proposes any amount less than $Y for Torben, both will get nothing at all. Since this reasoning holds for any value of *Y* less than $100, Torben's best strategy is to announce an acceptance threshold of $99, the largest whole number that is less than $100. The equilibrium outcome of the game will then be $99 for Torben and only $1 for Kamal, exactly the opposite of the outcome when Kamal had the first move.

## CREDIBLE THREATS AND PROMISES

**credible threat** a threat to take an action that is in the threatener's interest to carry out

Why couldn't Torben have threatened to refuse a one-sided offer in the original version of the game? In the language of game theory, a **credible threat** is one that is in the threatener's interest to carry out when the time comes to act. The problem in the original version of the game is that Torben would have no reason to carry out his threat to reject a one-sided offer in the event he actually received one. Once Kamal announced such an offer, refusing it would not pass the cost–benefit test.

The concept of a credible threat figured prominently in the negotiations between Warner Brothers managers and Tony Bennett over the matter of Mr. Bennett's fee for performing in *Analyze This*. Once most of the film had been shot, managers knew they couldn't credibly threaten to refuse Mr. Bennett's salary demand, because at that point the cost to adapt the film to another singer would have been prohibitive. In contrast, a similar threat made before production of the movie had begun would have been credible.

COST-BENEFIT

Here is another example in which one person suffers as a result of the inability to make a credible threat.

## EXAMPLE 9.6

### Is it safe to steal Veronica's briefcase?

When Veronica travels out of town on business, she usually brings along an expensive briefcase. A stranger sees her waiting for a plane at the airport, takes a liking to her briefcase, and assumes that because Veronica is an economist, she must be a self-interested, rational person. The stranger considers whether to walk off with Veronica's briefcase, knowing that she is watching and can call the police immediately.

If the cost to Veronica of pressing charges in the event her briefcase is stolen exceeds the value of the briefcase, can the stranger safely steal it?

Provided the thief's assumptions about Veronica are correct, he can get away with his crime. To press charges once her briefcase has been stolen, Veronica must call the police and will probably miss her flight home. Months later, she will have to return to testify at the thief's trial, and she may have to endure hostile cross-examination by the thief's lawyer. Since these costs clearly exceed the value of the briefcase, a rational, self-interested person would simply write off the briefcase. If Veronica could somehow make a credible threat to press charges in the event her briefcase was stolen, she could deter the thief. However, if the thief knows the cost of retaliation will exceed the benefit, the threat is not credible.

Just as in some games credible threats are impossible to make, in others **credible promises** are impossible. A credible promise is one that is in the interests of the promiser to keep when the time comes to act. In Examples 9.7 and 9.8, both players suffer because of their inability to make a credible promise.

**credible promise** a promise to take an action that is in the promiser's interest to keep

## EXAMPLE 9.7

### Will the business owner open a remote office?

The owner of a thriving business wants to start up an office in a distant city. If she hires someone to manage the new office, she can afford to pay a weekly salary of $1000—a premium of $500 over what the manager would otherwise be able to earn—and still earn a weekly economic profit of $1000 for herself. But can the owner monitor the manager's behaviour? She knows that the manager can boost his take-home pay to $1500 by managing the remote office dishonestly while causing the owner an economic loss of $500 per week. If the owner believes that all managers are selfish income maximizers, will she open the new office?

The decision tree for the remote office game is shown in Figure 9.6. At A, the managerial candidate promises to manage honestly, which brings the owner to B, where she must decide whether to open the new office. If she opens it, they reach C, where the manager must decide whether to manage honestly. If the manager's only goal is to make as much money as he can, he will manage dishonestly (bottom branch at C), since that way he will earn $500 more than by managing honestly (top branch at C).

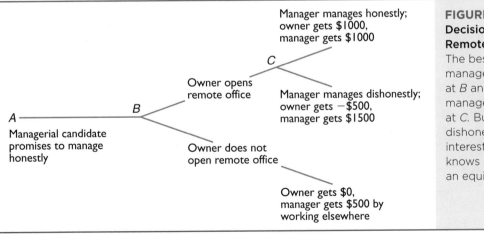

Manager manages honestly; owner gets $1000, manager gets $1000

C

Owner opens remote office

Manager manages dishonestly; owner gets −$500, manager gets $1500

B

A

Managerial candidate promises to manage honestly

Owner does not open remote office

Owner gets $0, manager gets $500 by working elsewhere

**FIGURE 9.6**
**Decision Tree for the Remote Office Game**
The best outcome is for the manager to open the office at B and for the manager to manage the office honestly at C. But if the manager is dishonest and purely self-interested and the owner knows it, this path will not be an equilibrium outcome.

So if the owner opens the new office and the manager is dishonest, she will end up with an economic loss of $500. If she had not opened the office (bottom branch at B), she would have realized an economic profit of zero. Since zero is better than −$500, the owner will choose not to open the remote office. In the end, the opportunity cost of the manager's inability to make a credible promise is $1500: the manager's foregone $500 salary premium and the owner's foregone $1000 return.

## EXAMPLE **9.8**

### Will the kidnapper release his victim?

A kidnapper who has seized a hostage for ransom suddenly changes his mind. He wants to set his victim free but is afraid that the victim will go to the police. Although the victim promises not to do so, both realize that the victim will have no incentive to keep his promise once he is free. The victim also realizes that the kidnapper would still pose a threat to him, out of fear that the victim may change his mind and go to the police. So if only to protect himself from the possibility of further harm, the victim has a powerful incentive to go to the police once he is free. Finally, if the victim goes to the police, the kidnapper will be caught and sentenced to life imprisonment. The kidnapper desperately wants to set his victim free, but he also fears what will happen to him in prison. He strongly believes that life imprisonment would be a fate worse than death. What will the kidnapper do?

The decision tree for the situation in Example 9.8 is shown in Figure 9.7. At *A*, the victim promises not to go to the police. He knows his life depends on the credibility of his promise, and at the moment he makes it, he sincerely means to keep it.

**FIGURE 9.7**
**Decision Tree for the Kidnapper and the Victim**
Both the kidnapper and the victim want to see the victim freed, but because the victim's promise to remain silent is not credible, the kidnapper kills him.

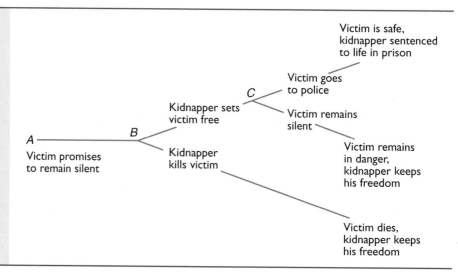

At *B* the kidnapper must decide what to do. If he sets his victim free (top branch at *B*), they reach *C*, where the victim must decide whether to go to the police. If the victim keeps his promise to remain silent (bottom branch at *C*), the kidnapper keeps his freedom and is a continuing threat to the victim. But if the victim goes to the police (top branch at *C*), the kidnapper will be caught and sent to prison, and the victim will be safe. Since the victim prefers the second outcome, he will go to the police if freed. *And since the kidnapper can anticipate what will happen if the game reaches C, he cannot let the game reach that point.* His only hope of keeping his freedom and avoiding a fate worse than death is to choose the bottom branch at *B*. The tragedy is that both he and the victim strongly prefer the alternative in which he sets the victim free and the victim remains silent. Having set the strategy in motion, the kidnapper finds that it has become his master.[2]

Here is another instance in which both parties suffer because of the inability to make a credible promise.

---

2  This example also illustrates how difficult it is to devise legal codes. In the example, the legal system presents the kidnapper with an incentive to compound his offence by committing murder. If the objective were to deter crime, an effective law would present the kidnapper with incentives that encourage release of the victim. Similarly, the example about the briefcase recalls Adam Smith's statement that a successful commercial state requires an effective system of justice. If a valuable briefcase always will be stolen, there will be no reason to acquire one in the first place, and nobody will produce them because a market for valuable briefcases will not develop. The design of legal codes and the incentives they present are taken up in the study of law and economics.

**Smith and Jones are playing a game in which Smith has the first move at *A* in the following decision tree. Once Smith has chosen either the top or bottom branch at *A*, Jones, who can see what Smith has chosen, must choose the top or bottom branch at *B* or *C*. If the payoffs at the end of each branch are as shown, what is the equilibrium outcome of this game? If before Smith chose, Jones could make a credible commitment to choose either the top or bottom branch when his turn came, what would he do?**

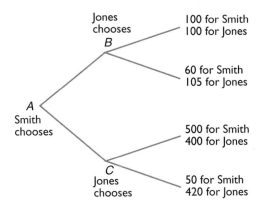

Jones chooses B — 100 for Smith / 100 for Jones; 60 for Smith / 105 for Jones. A Smith chooses. Jones chooses C — 500 for Smith / 400 for Jones; 50 for Smith / 420 for Jones.

## COMMITMENT PROBLEMS

Games like the one in Exercise 9.3, as well as the prisoner's dilemma, the cartel game, the ultimatum bargaining game, and the remote office game, confront players with a **commitment problem**, a situation in which they have difficulty achieving the desired outcome when they cannot make credible threats or promises. If both players in the prisoner's dilemma (Example 9.3) could make a binding promise to remain silent, both would be assured of a shorter sentence. Hence the logic of the underworld code of *omerta*, under which the family of anyone who provides evidence against a fellow mob member is killed.

A **commitment device** is a way of solving the commitment problem by ensuring that a particular strategy will not be chosen, either because the individual cannot now make that choice or will no longer find it in his or her interest to do so. For example, one way of reducing robberies from gas stations and convenience stores is to have all the cash placed in a safe that the clerk cannot open. The locked cashbox strategy makes it impossible for the clerk to choose the option of giving the thief the money when confronted with a holdup. It is thus pointless to threaten the clerk and try to hold up such a store.

The commitment devices just discussed and the underworld code of *omerta* work because they change the material incentives facing the decision makers. But as Example 9.9 illustrates, changing incentives in precisely the desired way is not always practical.

**commitment problem** a situation in which people cannot achieve their goals because of an inability to make credible threats or promises

**commitment device** a way of changing incentives so as to make otherwise empty threats or promises credible

## EXAMPLE 9.9

### Will Angelo leave a tip when dining on the road?

Angelo has just finished a $100 steak dinner at a restaurant on the Trans-Canada Highway, some 500 km from home. The waiter provided good service. If Angelo cares only about himself, will he leave a tip?

Once the waiter has provided good service, there is no way for him to take it back if the diner fails to leave a tip. In restaurants patronized by local diners, failure to tip is not a problem because the waiter can simply provide poor service the next time a non-tipper comes in. Repeated interaction makes it easier to develop credible commitments and threats. But the waiter lacks that leverage with out-of-town diners. Having already received good service, Angelo must choose between paying $100 or $115 for his meal. If he is an essentially selfish person, the former choice may be an appealing one. But are most people essentially selfish? As we will see shortly, most out-of-town diners actually do leave tips.

RECAP

**GAMES IN WHICH TIMING MATTERS**

The outcomes of many games depend on the timing of each player's moves. For such games, the payoffs are best summarized by a decision tree rather than a payoff matrix.

The inability to make credible threats and promises can prevent people from achieving desired outcomes in many games. Games with this property are said to confront players with commitment problems. Such problems can sometimes be solved by employing commitment devices—ways of changing incentives to facilitate making credible threats or promises.

## 9.4  THE STRATEGIC IMPORTANCE OF PREFERENCES

In thinking about the games we have discussed so far, you may have been a bit uncomfortable. In the discussion thus far, players were assumed to care only about themselves. No reference was made to any concept of morality or any norm of behaviour. Thus, each player's goal was just to get the highest monetary payoff, the shortest jail sentence, the best chance of survival, and so on. Yet the conclusion that managers of distant offices will be dishonest or that kidnappers will kill their hostages or that the owner of an expensive purse will not protest when it is stolen contradicts both our norms of how people *should* behave and our observations about how they very often *do* behave. And the irony, in most of these games, is that players who behave without regard to morality or norms do not even get the highest individual material rewards.

In his book *The Theory of Moral Sentiments,* Adam Smith said, "The regard to those general rules of conduct, is what is properly called a sense of duty, a principle of the greatest consequence in human life. . . ." Further, ". . .upon the tolerable observance of these duties depends the very existence of human society, which would crumble into nothing if mankind were not generally impressed with a reverence for these important rules of conduct."[3]

As Example 9.10 illustrates, in a society in which people are strongly conditioned to develop moral sentiments—feelings of guilt when they harm others, feelings of sympathy for their trading partners, feelings of outrage when they are treated unjustly—commitment problems arise less often than in more narrowly self-interested societies.

### EXAMPLE 9.10

**In a moral society, will the business owner open a remote office?**

Consider again the owner of the thriving business who is trying to decide whether to open an office in a distant city (Example 9.7). Suppose all citizens in this city have been strongly conditioned to behave honestly. Will she open the remote office? Suppose, for instance, that the managerial candidate would suffer terrible guilt pangs or believe that he would burn in hell forever if he embezzled money from the owner. Most people would be reluctant to assign a monetary value to such feelings.

But imagine instead, for a moment, finding an envelope full of money on the sidewalk. You might know you should find the owner of it, but you also know that you could keep it for yourself at no risk of detection. At what point would you be really tempted to keep the envelope—if there were $100, $10 000 or $100 000 in it? Would you perhaps start to think about all the good works and charitable giving that would

---

3  Adam Smith, *The Theory of Moral Sentiments* (1759) Part III, Ch. V, 6th ed., abridged and reprinted in Robert L. Heilbroner, ed., with the assistance of Laurence J. Malone, *The Essential Adam Smith,* (New York: W.W. Norton & Company, 1986), pp. 110, 112.

be possible with the money? How about if it was $200 000 000? How much money would it take to outweigh the immorality of keeping somebody else's property? What is the price of your honesty?

For the sake of discussion, let's suppose that the remote-office manager in this example would, if he were dishonest, have guilt feelings so unpleasant that he would be willing to pay at least $10 000 to avoid them. On this assumption, the manager's payoff, if he manages dishonestly, will not be $1500 as in Example 9.7, but ($1500 − $10 000) = −$8500. The new decision tree is shown in Figure 9.8.

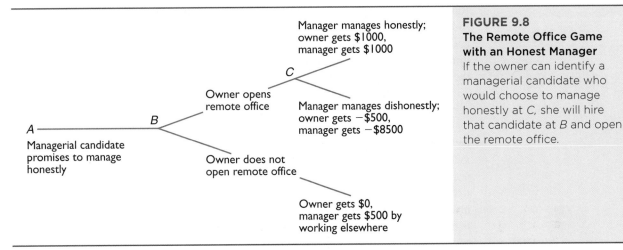

**FIGURE 9.8**
**The Remote Office Game with an Honest Manager**
If the owner can identify a managerial candidate who would choose to manage honestly at C, she will hire that candidate at B and open the remote office.

In this case, the owner's best choice at B is to open the remote office, because she knows that at C the manager's best choice will be to manage honestly. The irony, of course, is that the honest manager in this example ends up richer than the dishonest manager in Example 9.7 who earned only a normal salary. And notice that the stronger moral sentiments of honesty are, the more likely it is that the manager and owner are able to end up in the mutually advantageous position where the new office is actually opened.

## ARE PEOPLE FUNDAMENTALLY SELFISH?

As Example 9.10 suggests, the assumption that people are self-interested in the narrow sense of the term does not always capture the full range of motives that govern choice in strategic settings. Think, for example, about the last time you had a meal at an out-of-town restaurant. Did you leave a tip? If so, your behaviour was quite normal. Researchers have found that tipping rates in restaurants patronized mostly by out-of-town diners are essentially the same as in restaurants patronized mostly by local diners.

Reflect also on how you would behave in some of the other games we have discussed. In the ultimatum game, what would you do if the other player proposed $99 for himself and only $1 for you? Would you reject the offer? If so, you are perfectly normal. The ultimatum game provides a very clean test of the hypothesis of selfish behaviour and lack of concern with the fairness of outcomes. Economists have therefore studied it extensively and have discovered similar results in many contexts, in numerous countries. The most common proposal by the first player in this game is not a 99:1 split, but approximately a 50:50 split. And, on the few occasions when the first player does propose a highly one-sided split, the second player almost always rejects it. Subjects who reject the offer often mention the satisfaction they experienced at having penalized the first player for an "unfair" offer.

Indeed, the assumption that people are self-interested in the most narrow sense of the term often does not predict behaviour very well. People who have been treated unjustly often seek revenge even at ruinous cost to themselves. Every day, people walk away from profitable transactions whose terms they believe to be unfair. In countless ways, people do not seem to be pursuing self-interest as narrowly defined. And if motives beyond narrow self-interest are significant, we must take them into account when we attempt to predict and explain human behaviour.

## PREFERENCES AS SOLUTIONS TO COMMITMENT PROBLEMS

It is often useful to think carefully about what people motivated entirely by self-interest will do. What can we expect from a person who is motivated only by self-interested consumption and who is completely unconcerned about fairness, guilt, honour, sympathy, and the like? Some people are indeed a bit like that, and if their amoral behaviour undermines the norms of honesty or empathy that others have, it can be socially costly. However, the ubiquity of repeated strategic interactions among individuals, and the importance of norms and morals for that interaction, means that pure, narrow self-interest provides a very incomplete picture of economic life.

Preferences clearly affect the choices people make in strategic interactions. Sympathy for one's trading partner can make a business person trustworthy even when immediate material incentives favour cheating, and a reputation for honesty can enable better long-term economic outcomes. A sense of justice can prompt a person to incur the costs of retaliation, even when incurring those costs will not undo the original injury—which makes it less likely that others will think it worthwhile to behave injuriously. A sense of fairness can also induce people to reject one-sided offers, even when their wealth would be increased by accepting them. And when the people that make offers know this, they have an incentive to make their offers more even-handed. As Adam Smith noted, these moral sentiments are crucial to the efficient and equitable operation of society.

Note, however, that although preferences can clearly shape behaviour in these ways, preferences alone do not solve commitment problems. It is important not only that a person *have* certain preferences, but also that others have some way of *discerning* them. Unless the business owner can identify the trustworthy employee, that employee cannot land a job whose pay is predicated on trust. If the predator can identify a person whose character will motivate retaliation, that person is not likely to become a victim. And unless a person's potential trading partners can identify him as someone predisposed to reject one-sided offers, he will not be able to deter such offers. In societies with a very strong moral code of behaviour, it becomes a pretty safe prediction that almost any randomly selected other person will have those character traits, but in more diverse societies people may need to find some explicit way of signalling these traits.

In ventures requiring trust, can we identify reliable partners from among those whom we might engage? If people could make *perfectly* accurate character judgments, they could always steer clear of dishonest persons. That people continue to be victimized, at least occasionally, by dishonest persons suggests that perfectly reliable character judgments are either impossible to make or prohibitively expensive.

Vigilance in the choice of trading partners is an essential element in solving (or avoiding) commitment problems, for if there is an advantage in being honest and being perceived as such, there is an even greater financial advantage (for a thief) in only *appearing* to be honest.

Would you report the theft of your briefcase at an airport, even if it meant missing your flight? Do you know someone who would return an envelope containing $1000 in cash to you if you lost it at a crowded concert? If so, then you accept the claim that personal character helps people to solve commitment problems. As long as honest individuals can identify at least some others who are honest, and can interact selectively with them, then honest individuals can prosper in a competitive environment. And, as Adam Smith observed over 250 years ago, prosperity depends crucially on the "moral sentiments" of society.

> **RECAP** ↑
>
> ## THE STRATEGIC ROLE OF PREFERENCES
>
> Most applications of the theory of games assume that players are self-interested in the narrow sense of the term. In practice, however, many choices appear inconsistent with this assumption.
>
> The fact that people seem driven by a more complex range of motives makes behaviour more difficult to predict but also creates new ways of solving commitment problems. Psychological incentives can often serve as commitment devices when changing players' material incentives is impractical. For example, people who are able to identify honest trading partners and interact selectively with them are able to solve commitment problems that arise from lack of trust.

## SUMMARY

- Economists use the theory of games to analyze situations in which the payoffs of one agent's actions depend on the actions taken by others. Games have three basic elements: the players; the list of possible actions, or strategies, from which each player can choose; and the payoffs that the players receive for those strategies. For games in which the timing of the players' moves is not decisive, the payoff matrix is the most useful way to summarize this information. In games in which the timing of moves does matter, a decision tree provides a much more useful summary of the information. **LO1, LO7**

- A dominant strategy is one that yields a higher payoff regardless of which strategy is chosen by the other player. In some games, such as the prisoner's dilemma, each player has a dominant strategy. The equilibrium in such games occurs when each player chooses his or her dominant strategy. In other games, not all players have a dominant strategy. **LO2, LO3**

- Although the equilibrium outcome of any game is any combination of choices in which each player does the best he can, given the choices made by others, the result can be unattractive from the perspective of players as a group. The "prisoner's dilemma" is a type of game that has this feature. The incentive structure of this game has been used to explain such disparate social dilemmas as excessive advertising, the underworld code of *omerta*, and failure to reap the potential benefits of interactions requiring trust. **LO4, LO5, LO6**

- Individuals can often resolve these dilemmas if they can make binding commitments to behave in certain ways. Some commitments are achieved by restricting one player's available choices (e.g., the locked cash box) and thereby altering the material incentives confronting other players. **LO8**

- Commitments can also be achieved by relying on psychological incentives to counteract material payoffs. Moral sentiments like guilt, sympathy, and a sense of justice often foster better outcomes than can be achieved by narrowly self-interested players. For this type of commitment to work most effectively, the relevant moral sentiments must be discernible to one's potential trading partners. **LO8**

## KEY TERMS

basic elements of a game (261)
cartel (268)
commitment device (275)
commitment problem (275)
credible promise (273)

credible threat (272)
decision tree (or game tree) (270)
dominant strategy (262)
dominated strategy (262)
Nash equilibrium (262)

payoff matrix (262)
prisoner's dilemma (264)
repeated prisoner's dilemma (269)
tit-for-tat (269)
ultimatum bargaining game (271)

## REVIEW QUESTIONS

1. Explain why a military arms race is an example of a prisoner's dilemma. **LO5, LO6**

2. Why was it a mistake for Warner Brothers to wait until the filming of *Analyze This* was almost finished before negotiating with Tony Bennett to perform in the final scene? **LO7**

3. Suppose General Motors is trying to hire a small firm to manufacture the door handles for a new car model. The task requires an investment in expensive capital equipment that cannot be used for any other purpose. Why might the president of the small firm refuse to undertake this venture without a long-term contract

for supply that includes fixing the price of the door handles? **LO8**

4. Would you be irrational to refuse a one-sided offer in an ultimatum bargaining game if you knew that you would be playing that game many times with the same partner? **LO5, LO6**

5. Describe the commitment problem that narrowly self-interested diners and waiters would confront at restaurants located on the Trans-Canada Highway. Given that in such restaurants tipping does seem to assure reasonably good service, do you think people are always selfish in the narrowest sense? **LO8**

## PROBLEMS

1. In studying for his economics final, Sam is concerned about only two things: his grade and the amount of time he spends studying. A good grade will give him a benefit of 20; an average grade, a benefit of 5; and a poor grade, a benefit of 0. By studying a lot, Sam will incur a cost of 10; by studying a little, a cost of 6. Moreover, if Sam studies a lot and all other students study a little, he will get a good grade and they will get poor ones. But if they study a lot and he studies a little, they will get good grades and he will get a poor one. Finally, if he and all other students study the same amount of time, everyone will get average grades. Other students share Sam's preferences regarding grades and study time. **LO1, LO3, LO5, LO6**

   a. Model this situation as a two-person prisoner's dilemma in which the strategies are to study a little and to study a lot, and the players are Sam and all other students. Include the payoffs in the matrix.

   b. What is the equilibrium outcome in this game? From the students' perspective, is it the best outcome?

2. Consider the following "dating game," which has two players, *A* and *B*, and two strategies: to buy a movie ticket or a baseball ticket. The payoffs, given in points, are as shown in the following matrix. Note that the highest payoffs occur when both *A* and *B* attend the same event.

|  | | **B** | |
| --- | --- | --- | --- |
|  | | Buy movie ticket | Buy baseball ticket |
| **A** | Buy movie ticket | 2 for *A*<br>3 for *B* | 0 for *A*<br>0 for *B* |
|  | Buy baseball ticket | 1 for *A*<br>1 for *B* | 3 for *A*<br>2 for *B* |

Assume that players *A* and *B* buy their tickets separately and simultaneously. Each must decide what to do knowing the available choices and payoffs, but not what the other has actually chosen. Each player believes the other to be rational and self-interested. **LO2, LO3, LO4, LO5, LO6, LO7**

   a. Does either player have a dominant strategy?

b. How many potential equilibria are there? (*Hint:* To see whether a given combination of strategies is an equilibrium, ask whether either player could get a higher payoff by changing his or her strategy.)

c. Is this game a prisoner's dilemma? Explain.

d. Suppose player *A* gets to buy his or her ticket first. Player *B* does not observe *A*'s choice but knows that *A* chose first. Player *A* knows that player *B* knows he or she chose first. What is the equilibrium outcome?

e. Suppose the situation is similar to (d), except that player *B* chooses first. What is the equilibrium outcome?

3. Blackadder and Baldrick are rational, self-interested criminals imprisoned in separate cells in a dark medieval dungeon. They face the prisoner's dilemma displayed in the following matrix.

|  |  | **Blackadder** | |
|---|---|---|---|
|  |  | Confess | Deny |
| **Baldrick** | Confess | 5 years for each | 0 years for Baldrick<br><br>20 years for Blackadder |
|  | Deny | 0 years for Blackadder<br><br>20 years for Baldrick | 1 year for each |

Assume that Blackadder is willing to pay $1000 for each year by which he can reduce his sentence below 20 years. A corrupt jailer tells Blackadder that before he decides whether to confess or deny the crime, she can tell him Baldrick's decision. How much is this information worth to Blackadder? **LO5, LO6, LO7**

4. The owner of a thriving business wants to open a new office in a distant city. If he can hire someone who will manage the new office honestly, he can afford to pay that person a weekly salary of $2000 ($1000 more than the manager would be able to earn elsewhere) and still earn an economic profit of $800. The owner's concern is that he will not be able to monitor the manager's behaviour and that the manager would therefore be in a position to embezzle money from the business. The owner knows that if the remote office is managed dishonestly, the manager can earn $3100 while causing the owner an economic loss of $600/week. **LO2, LO8**

a. If the owner believes that all managers are narrowly self-interested income maximizers, will he open the new office?

b. Suppose the owner knows that a managerial candidate is a devoutly religious person who condemns dishonest behaviour and who would be willing to pay up to $15 000 to avoid the guilt she would feel if she were dishonest. Will the owner open the remote office?

5. Imagine yourself sitting in your car in a campus parking lot that is currently full, waiting for someone to pull out so that you can park your car. Somebody pulls out, but at the same moment a driver who has just arrived overtakes you in an obvious attempt to park in the vacated spot before you can. Suppose this driver was willing to pay up to $10 to park in that spot and up to $30 to avoid getting into an argument with you. (That is, the benefit of parking is $10, and the cost of an argument is $30.) At the same time, the other driver guesses, accurately, that you too would be willing to pay up to $30 to avoid a confrontation and up to $10 to park in the vacant spot. **LO3, LO7, LO8**

a. Model this situation as a two-stage decision tree in which the other driver's bid to take the space is the opening move and your strategies are (1) to protest and (2) not to protest. If you protest (initiate an argument), the rules of the game specify that the other driver has to let you take the space. Show the payoffs at the end of each branch of the tree.

b. What is the equilibrium outcome?

c. What would be the advantage of being able to be able to communicate credibly to the other driver that your failure to protest would be a significant psychological cost to you?

6. Newfoundland's fishing industry declined sharply in the early 1990s due to overfishing, even though fishing companies were supposedly bound by a quota agreement. If all fishing companies had abided by the agreement, yields could have been maintained at high levels. **LO5, LO6, LO8**

a. Model this situation as a prisoner's dilemma in which the players are Company *A* and Company *B* and the strategies are to keep the quota and break the quota. Include appropriate payoffs in the matrix. Explain why overfishing is inevitable in the absence of effective enforcement of the quota agreement.

b. Provide another environmental example of a prisoner's dilemma.

c. In many potential prisoner's dilemmas, a way out of the dilemma for a would-be cooperator is to make reliable character judgments about the trustworthiness of potential partners. Explain why this solution is not available in many situations involving degradation of the environment.

7. Consider the following game, called matching pennies, which you are playing with a friend. Each of you has a penny hidden in your hand, facing either heads up or tails up (you know which way the one in your hand is facing). On the count of "three" you simultaneously show your pennies to each other. If the face-up side of your coin matches the face-up side of your friend's coin, you get to keep the two pennies. If the faces do not match, your friend gets to keep the pennies. **LO1, LO2, LO3**

   a. Who are the players in this game? What are each player's strategies? Construct a payoff matrix for the game.

   b. Is there a dominant strategy? If so, what?

   c. Is there an equilibrium? If so, what?

8. Consider the following game. Harry has four quarters. He can offer Sally from one to four of them. If she accepts his offer, she keeps the quarters Harry offered her and Harry keeps the others. If Sally declines Harry's offer, they both get nothing ($0). They play the game only once, and each cares only about the amount of money he or she ends up with. **LO1, LO3, LO7**

   a. Who are the players? What are each player's strategies? Construct a decision tree for this ultimatum bargaining game.

   b. Given their goal, what is the optimal choice for each player?

9. Two airplane manufacturers are considering the production of a new product, a 150-passenger jet. Both are deciding whether to enter the market and produce the new plane. The payoff matrix is as shown (payoff values are in millions of dollars).

   The implication of these payoffs is that the market demand is large enough to support only one manufacturer. If both firms enter, both will sustain a loss. **LO3**

   a. Identify two possible equilibrium outcomes in this game.

|  |  | Airbus | |
|---|---|---|---|
|  |  | Produce | Do not produce |
| **Boeing** | Produce | −5 for each | 100 for Boeing<br>0 for Airbus |
|  | Do not produce | 0 for Boeing<br>100 for Airbus | 0 for each |

   b. Consider the effect of a subsidy. Suppose the European Union decides to subsidize the European producer, Airbus, with a cheque for $25 million if it enters the market. Revise the payoff matrix to account for this subsidy. What is the new equilibrium outcome?

   c. Compare the two outcomes (pre and postsubsidy). What qualitative effect does the subsidy have?

10. Jill and Jack both have two pails that can be used to carry water down a hill. Each makes only one trip down the hill, and each pail of water can be sold for $5. Carrying the pails of water down the hill requires considerable effort. Both Jill and Jack would be willing to pay $2 each to avoid carrying one bucket down the hill and an additional $3 to avoid carrying a second bucket down the hill. **LO3**

   a. Given market prices, how many pails of water will each fetch from the top of the hill?

   b. Jill and Jack's parents are worried that the two children don't cooperate enough with one another. Suppose they make Jill and Jack share their revenues from selling the water equally. Given that both are self-interested, construct the payoff matrix for the decisions Jill and Jack face regarding the number of pails of water each should carry. What is the equilibrium outcome?

## ANSWERS TO IN-CHAPTER EXERCISES

9.1   No matter what Coca-Cola does, Pepsi will do better to leave ad spending the same. No matter what Pepsi does, Coca-Cola will do better to raise ad spending. So each player will play its dominant strategy: Coca-Cola will raise its ad spending, and Pepsi will leave its ad spending the same. **LO2, LO3**

| Pepsi \ Coca-Cola | Raise spending on advertisements | Leave spending on advertisements the same |
|---|---|---|
| Raise spending on advertisements | $3000 for Pepsi<br>$8000 for Coca-Cola | $4000 for Pepsi<br>$4000 for Coca-Cola |
| Leave spending on advertisements the same | $8000 for Pepsi<br>$4000 for Coca-Cola | $5000 for Pepsi<br>$5000 for Coca-Cola |

**9.2** In game 1, no matter what Ford does, GM will do better to invest, and no matter what GM does, Ford will do better to invest. Each has a dominant strategy, but in following it, each does worse than if it had not invested. So game 1 is a prisoner's dilemma. In game 2, no matter what Ford does, GM again will do better to invest; but no matter what GM does, Ford will do better *not* to invest. Each has a dominant strategy, and in following it, each gets a payoff of 10—which is 5 more than if each had played its dominated strategy. So game 2 is not a prisoner's dilemma. **LO2, LO3, LO4, LO5, LO6**

**Game 1**

| GM \ Ford | Not invest | Invest |
|---|---|---|
| Not invest | 10 for each | 4 for GM<br>12 for Ford |
| Invest | 12 for GM<br>4 for Ford | 5 for each |

**Game 2**

| GM \ Ford | Not invest | Invest |
|---|---|---|
| Not invest | 4 for GM<br>12 for Ford | 5 for each |
| Invest | 10 for each | 12 for GM<br>4 for Ford |

**9.3** Smith assumes that Jones will choose the branch that maximizes his payoff, which is the bottom branch at either *B* or *C*. So Jones will choose the bottom branch when his turn comes, no matter what Smith chooses. Since Smith will do better on the bottom branch at *B* (60) than on the bottom branch at *C* (50), Smith will choose the top branch at *A*. So the equilibrium in this game is for Smith to choose the top branch at *A* and Jones to choose the bottom branch at *B*. Smith gets 60, and Jones gets 105. If Jones could make a credible commitment to choose the top branch no matter what, both would do better. Smith would choose the bottom branch at *A* and Jones would choose the top branch at *C*, giving Smith 500 and Jones 400. **LO3, LO7, LO8**

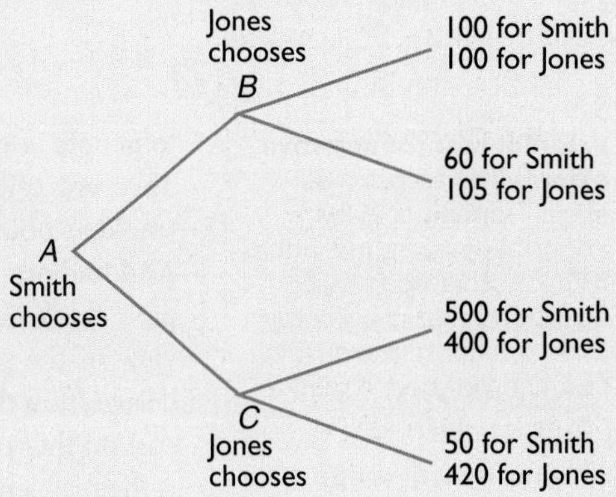


Mc Graw Hill connect™ Practise and learn online with Connect.

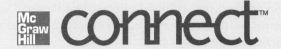

# CHAPTER 10
# Externalities and Property Rights

**external cost (or negative externality)** a cost that arises from an activity undertaken by an individual, firm, or other economic agent and that is borne by others because the cost is not incorporated in market prices the agent pays

**external benefit (or positive externality)** a benefit received by others that arises from an activity undertaken by an individual, firm, or other economic agent for which the agent is not compensated in the market price paid for the good or service involved

**externality** an external cost or benefit of an activity

A droll television ad for a British brand of pipe tobacco opens with a distinguished-looking gentleman sitting quietly on a park bench, smoking his pipe and reading a book of poetry. Before him lies a pond, unrippled except for a mother duck swimming peacefully with her ducklings. Suddenly a raucous group of teenage boys bursts onto the scene with a remote-controlled toy warship. Yelling and chortling, they launch their boat and manoeuvre it in aggressive pursuit of the terrified ducks.

Interrupted from his reverie, the gentleman looks up from his book and draws calmly on his pipe as he surveys the scene before him. He then reaches into his bag, pulls out a remote control of his own, and begins manipulating the joystick. The scene shifts underwater, where a miniature submarine rises from the depths of the pond. Once the boys' boat is in the sub's sights, the gentleman pushes a button on his remote control. Seconds later, the boat is blown to smithereens by a torpedo. The scene fades to a close-up of the tobacco company's label.

Many transactions generate costs or benefits that accrue to people not directly involved in those transactions. These effects are often unintended. They are called **external costs** and **benefits—externalities**, for short. From the pipe smoker's point of view, the noise generated by the marauding boys was an external cost. And had others been disturbed by the boys' rowdiness, they may well have regarded the pipe smoker's retaliatory gesture as an external benefit. The boys will have a different view of the situation. If the smoker has his tranquility, they cannot have the fun they derive from their toy warship. The boys can argue that the smoker's tranquility imposes a cost on them for which they are not compensated. Thus, the problem is reciprocal, and it is the problem of scarcity. If the smoker has his tranquility, the boys are deprived of their recreation. If the boys have their recreation, the smoker is deprived of his tranquility. The pond cannot simultaneously provide recreation for the boys and tranquility for the smoker and others.

How is the pond to be allocated between its competing uses? There is no established market through which an answer can be provided. Which of the two parties would have the right to demand and receive payment for use of the pond? But even if it makes for a good TV ad, we must question the smoker's method of determining how the pond will be used. Can a society function well if decisions about resource allocation are resolved by blowing up property or by relying on other forms of violent conflict?

This chapter focuses on how externalities affect the allocation of resources and on methods of resolving the problems caused by externalities. Adam Smith's theory of the invisible hand applies to an ideal marketplace in which externalities do not exist. Smith's structure included a system of justice that secured everyone's right to pursue his or her self-interest on equal footing with everyone else. In such situations, Smith argued, the self-interested actions of individuals would be harmonized with the interests of society as a whole. We will see that when the parties affected by externalities can easily negotiate with one another, the invisible hand can still produce an efficient outcome.

But in many cases negotiation is impractical. In those cases, we cannot expect the self-interested actions of individuals to be consistent with the interests of society as a whole. Because externalities are widespread, the attempt to forge solutions to the problems they cause is one of the most important rationales not only for the existence of government, but also for a variety of other forms of collective action, including compliance with norms of behaviour.

## 10.1 HOW EXTERNAL COSTS AND BENEFITS AFFECT RESOURCE ALLOCATION

The way that externalities distort the allocation of resources can be seen clearly in the next two examples.

### EXAMPLE 10.1

**Does the honeybee keeper face the right incentives? (Part 1)**

Phoebe earns her living as a keeper of honeybees. Her neighbours on all sides grow apples. Because bees pollinate apple trees as they forage for nectar, the more hives Phoebe keeps, the larger the harvests will be in the surrounding orchards. However, apple blossoms produce little nectar, so bees produce little honey when they forage on apple blossoms. Suppose (for now) that orchard owners do not compensate Phoebe for pollination. If she takes only her own costs and benefits into account in deciding how many hives to keep, will she keep the socially optimal number of hives?

For the orchard owners, Phoebe's hives constitute an external benefit. If she takes only her own personal costs and benefits from honey production into account, she will add hives until the added revenue she gets from the last hive just equals the cost of adding it. But since the orchard owners also benefit from additional hives, the total benefit of adding another hive at that point will be greater than its cost. Phoebe, then, will keep too few hives.

### EXAMPLE 10.2

**Does the honeybee keeper face the right incentives? (Part 2)**

As in Example 10.1, Phoebe earns her living as a keeper of honeybees, but an elementary school and a nursing home are now her neighbours. The more hives Phoebe keeps, the more students and nursing home residents will be stung by bees. If Phoebe takes only her own costs and benefits into account in deciding how many hives to keep, will she keep the socially optimal number of hives?

For the students and nursing home residents, Phoebe's hives constitute an external cost. If she considers only her own costs and benefits in deciding how many hives to keep, she will continue to add hives until the added revenue from the last hive is just enough to cover its cost. But since Phoebe's neighbours also incur costs when she adds a hive, the benefit of the last hive at that point will be smaller than its cost. Phoebe, in other words, will keep too many hives.

Every activity involves costs and benefits. When all the costs and benefits of an activity accrue directly to the person who makes the decision to carry it out—that is, when the activity generates no externalities—the level of the activity that is best for the individual will be best for society as a whole. But when an activity generates externalities, individual self-interest does not produce the best allocation of resources. Individuals who consider only their own costs and benefits will tend to engage in excessive levels of activities that generate external costs and insufficient levels of activities that generate external benefits. When an activity generates both external benefits and external costs, private and social interests will coincide only in the unlikely event that the opposing effects exactly offset one another.

## THE GRAPHICAL PORTRAYAL OF EXTERNALITIES

The effects of externalities on resource allocation can be portrayed graphically, as in Figure 10.1. In panel (a), the red line labelled Private *MC* (for marginal cost) plots the amount that firms would supply if they considered only their private costs. If production is accompanied by an external cost of *XC* per unit, the true social marginal cost is the sum of private *MC* and *XC*. When only private costs are considered, the market equilibrium level of output is $Q_{pvt}$, the output level at which the demand curve *D* intersects Private *MC*. Note that $Q_{pvt}$ is larger than the socially optimal level of output, $Q_{soc}$, the output level at which the demand curve intersects Social *MC*. Social *MC*, the socially optimal supply curve of the product, is the result of adding the external cost *XC* to every value along Private *MC*.

In Figure 10.1(b), the line labelled "Private demand" plots the amounts of output that private individuals would buy if they considered only their own benefits from consumption. But this is the demand curve for a product whose production generates an external benefit of *XB* per unit. The market equilibrium quantity of this good, $Q_{pvt}$, is the output level at which private demand intersects the supply curve of the product (*MC*). This time, $Q_{pvt}$ is smaller than the socially optimal level of output, $Q_{soc}$. The output level at which *MC* intersects the socially optimal demand curve (Social demand) is $Q_{soc}$. The socially optimal demand curve is the result of adding the external benefit *XB* to every value along private demand.

When externalities are present, the pursuit of individual self-interest will not result in the largest possible economic surplus; that is, the result is socially inefficient.

**FIGURE 10.1**

**How External Costs and Benefits Affect Resource Allocation**

The market equilibrium level of output ($Q_{pvt}$) is larger than the socially optimal level ($Q_{soc}$) for products accompanied by external costs [panel (a)], but smaller than the socially optimal level for products accompanied by external benefits [panel (b)].

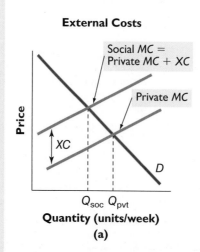

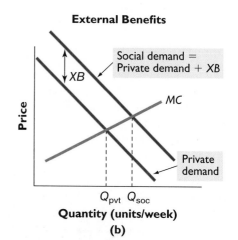

## THE COASE THEOREM

To say that total surplus is not maximized means that affairs could, in principle, be rearranged in a way that would make at least some people better off without harming others. Such situations, we have seen, can be a source of creative tension. When orchard owners want more pollination than beekeepers will provide on their own accord, orchard owners have an incentive to pay beekeepers to locate hives near their orchards. If beekeepers want access to crops that do not require pollination by honeybees but that produce abundant nectar, they have an incentive to pay crop owners for access to the crops. Beekeepers and orchard owners, in fact, frequently pay each other for provision of pollination and access to crops. Such **side payments** from farmers to bee keepers constitute a market mechanism that helps remedy any under-supply of hives.[1] (In the urban areas in which bee hives might have negative externalities for their neighbours, zoning laws typically prohibit their establishment.)

**side payment** a payment made by one party to another as compensation for an external cost or benefit

www.hmco.com/hmco/
college/economics/taylor/
micro/student/exercise/
mitaylor/coase.htm
**Coase Theorem**

## EXAMPLE 10.3

### Will Chabar dump toxins in the river? (Part 1)

Chabar's factory produces toxic waste. If Chabar dumps the waste in the river, he causes damage to Fitch, a fisherman located downstream. When the toxins are exposed to sunlight, they quickly chemically degrade into harmlessness and cause no damage to anyone other than Fitch. However, at a cost, Chabar can filter out the toxins, in which case Fitch will suffer no damage at all. The relevant gains and losses for the two individuals are listed in Table 10.1.

**TABLE 10.1**
**Costs and Benefits of Eliminating Toxic Waste (Part 1)**

|                  | With filter | Without filter |
|------------------|-------------|----------------|
| Gains to Chabar  | $100/day    | $130/day       |
| Gains to Fitch   | $100/day    | $50/day        |

If the law does not penalize Chabar for dumping toxins in the river, and if Chabar and Fitch cannot communicate with one another, will Chabar operate with or without a filter? Does Chabar's decision maximize total surplus?

Since Chabar earns $30 per day more without a filter than with one, his natural incentive is to operate without one. But if he does, the outcome does not maximize total economic surplus. Thus, when Chabar operates without a filter, the total daily gain to both parties is only $130 + $50 = $180, compared to $100 + $100 = $200 if Chabar had operated with a filter. The daily cost of the filter to Chabar is only $130 − $100 = $30, which is smaller than its daily benefit to Fitch of $100 − $50 = $50. The fact that Chabar does not install the filter implies a lost daily surplus of $20.

## EXAMPLE 10.4

### Will Chabar dump toxins in the river? (Part 2)

Suppose the costs and benefits of using the filter are as in Example 10.3 except that Chabar and Fitch can now communicate with one another at no cost. Even though the law does not require him to do so, might Chabar use a filter?

Recall the observation from Chapter 2 that when the economic pie grows larger, everyone can have a larger slice. Because use of a filter would result in the largest

---

1   For example, in Canada, 92 661 hives were rented in 1998 at prices that ranged from $40 to $108, varying by location and season. See http://www.seeds.ca/proj/poll/index.php?n=Honeybees, and Agriculture and Agri-Food Canada Market and Industry Services Branch, Horticulture and Special Crops Division, "The Value of Honey Bee Pollination in Canada," *Hivelights*, vol. 14, 15–21, November 2001. If a market is established so that side payments are consistently possible, the externality is internalized. It is no longer an externality. Stephen N.S. Cheung, "The Fable of the Bees: An Economic Investigation," *The Journal of Law & Economics*, v. 16, April 1973, pp. 11–33.

possible economic surplus, it would enable both Chabar and Fitch to have a larger net gain than before. Fitch thus has an incentive to *pay* Chabar to use a filter. For example, suppose Fitch offers Chabar $40/day to compensate him for operating with a filter. Both Chabar and Fitch will then be exactly $10/day better off than before, for a total daily net gain of $20. Their combined increase is exactly the increase in total daily economic surplus that results from using the filter.

**EXERCISE 10.1**

**In Example 10.4, what is the largest whole-dollar amount by which Fitch could compensate Chabar for operating with a filter and still be better off than before?**

Ronald Coase, a professor at the University of Chicago Law School, was the first to see clearly that if people can negotiate with one another, at no cost, over the right to perform activities that cause externalities, they have the incentive to arrive at a surplus-maximizing solution. This insight, which is often called the **Coase theorem**, is a profoundly important idea, for which Coase (rhymes with "dose") was awarded the 1991 Nobel Prize in Economics.[2]

**Coase theorem** if, at no cost, people can negotiate the purchase and sale of the right to perform activities that cause externalities, they can arrive at surplus-maximizing solutions to the problems caused by externalities

Why, you might ask, should Fitch pay Chabar to filter out toxins that would not be there in the first place if not for Chabar's factory? The rhetorical force of this question is undeniable. Yet Coase points out that externalities are reciprocal in nature. The toxins harm Fitch, to be sure, but preventing Chabar from emitting them would penalize Chabar, by exactly $30 per day. Why should Fitch necessarily have the right to harm Chabar by preventing Chabar from releasing toxins? Indeed, as Example 10.5 illustrates, even if Fitch has the right to prevent Chabar from releasing toxins, he will exercise that right only if filtering the toxins proves to increase total economic surplus.

## EXAMPLE 10.5

### Will Chabar dump toxins in the river? (Part 3)

Suppose the law says that Chabar may *not* dump toxins in the river unless he has Fitch's permission. If the relevant costs and benefits of filtering the toxins are as shown in Table 10.2, and if Chabar and Fitch can negotiate with one another at no cost, what are Chabar's incentives to filter the toxins?

Note that this time the most efficient outcome is for Chabar to operate without a filter, because the total daily surplus in that case will be $220 as compared to only $200 with a filter. Under the law, however, Fitch has the right to insist that Chabar use a filter. We might expect Fitch to exercise that right, since his own gain would increase from $70 to $100 per day if he did so. But because this outcome yields a smaller surplus, we know that each party can do better.

**TABLE 10.2**
**Costs and Benefits of Eliminating Toxic Waste (Part 3)**

|  | With filter | Without filter |
|---|---|---|
| **Gains to Chabar** | $100/day | $150/day |
| **Gains to Fitch** | $100/day | $70/day |

Suppose, for example, that Chabar pays Fitch $40 each day in return for Fitch's permission to operate without a filter. Each would then have a net daily gain of $110, which is $10 more for each of them than if Fitch had insisted that Chabar use a filter. To be sure, Chabar's pollution harms Fitch, but failure to allow the pollution would have caused even greater harm to Chabar.

2  Ronald Coase, "The Problem of Social Cost," *Journal of Law & Economics*, v. 3, October 1960, pp. 1–44.

These examples illustrate how, when externalities reduce surpluses below what is possible, the affected parties have the incentive to search for the outcome with the highest total economic surplus. Externalities are hardly rare and isolated occurrences. And our example of Chabar and Fitch relied heavily on assuming that there was no cost to negotiation, and that they are the only two parties to the transaction. In more complex cases, the Coase theorem may be hard to implement. Consider the following example of an externality that arises among six neighbours.

## EXAMPLE 10.6

### Will Bob practise his drum solo?

Bob is a drummer in a heavy metal rock band in Saskatoon who normally gets home from his gigs about 3 AM. When he has had a bad night (which is fairly often) he needs to practise his drum solo before he goes to sleep, so that he can keep his job in the band (which pays $100 more than pumping gas, his best available alternative).

Bob has five neighbours within earshot, all who have to go to work as restaurant waiters and waitresses the next morning. If he wakes them up with his drumming, they will be grouchy and irritable to their customers all day, and will lose tips of $80 each.

Table 10.3 shows the benefit that Bob will realize if he decides to practise his drum solo and the external cost that his decision will impose on his neighbours. If Bob has the legal right to make whatever noise he wants, and if he exercises that right, Table 10.3 shows that there will be a net loss to Saskatoon society (+$100 − $400 = −$300). However, this potential loss can also be seen as the incentive Bob's neighbours have to get him to *not* exercise his right. If each of his five neighbours were to contribute $21, they could pay him $105 to not practise. Each could pay $21 to avoid a loss of $80 and therefore be better off, while Bob would be better off by $5 if he accepted their side payment and did not practise.

**TABLE 10.3**
**The Effects of practising drum solos**

|  | Bob's Gains | Losses for Bob's Neighbours | Net Gain/Loss |
| --- | --- | --- | --- |
| **Bob practices drums** | +$100 | (−$80 each) × 5 = −400 | −300 |

We obtain the same outcome if we reverse the legal onus. If Bob does *not* have the right to make noise, and if he has to obtain the permission of his neighbours to do so, his potential gain of $100 is not enough to compensate his neighbours for their losses, so he cannot afford to buy them off. Therefore, regardless of whether Bob has the legal right to do what he wants, or his neighbours have the right to prevent him from making noise without their permission, he will not practise. The direction of payment between Bob and his neighbours is of no consequence to his decision: it is the same whether he has to pay his neighbours for the external costs they bear if he practises or they have to pay him to not practise.

Notice that, in this example, the legal system defines rights; it establishes who must pay whom, but regardless of how those rights are assigned, the response to the problem of scarcity is the same. As Table 10.3 shows, Bob makes the same decision regardless of who pays whom, *provided that negotiations between him and his neighbours are costless and perfectly informed.* Either way, it is socially inefficient for Bob to practise drum rolls, and he therefore does not practise them. However, the assumption that negotiations are costless and perfectly informed is crucial.

Bob's information about his neighbours' incentives might be incomplete. Suppose that one of Bob's neighbours (let's call him Dan) observes that Bob is receiving $105 in side payments for *not* doing something. If Dan decides that he, too, would like to be paid for *not* banging on drums, he can *threaten* to play drums too, and demand a side payment. In fact, Dan is not the only one who is *potentially* eligible for side payments; any of Bob's neighbours can also state that they are about to make a lot of noise at 3 AM. Who, then, will pay the side payments and who will receive them?

The assumption of "perfect information" underlying the Coase argument is really quite a strong assumption, since it rules out the possibility of posturing, bluffing, and other strategic behaviour. Such game playing is more likely if the legal system is one where Bob (or Dan or anybody else) has to be paid *not* to exercise a legal right that he could easily exercise. In general, imperfect information and transaction costs often mean that it may not be possible for a system of side payments to function effectively. However, we still get the socially efficient outcome if the legal system requires Bob to compensate his neighbours for their losses, because his gain from keeping his job as drummer is not enough (+$100) to pay them the full value of their $400 loss ($5 \times -\$80 = -\$400$).

## LEGAL REMEDIES FOR EXTERNALITIES

We have seen that surplus-maximizing solutions to externalities can be found whenever the affected parties can negotiate with one another at no cost, or at least at a cost that is less than the surplus that could be gained by negotiating. In the real world, beekeepers and orchard owners do negotiate over what otherwise would be external benefits. But negotiation is not always practical. A motorist with a noisy muffler, for example, imposes costs on others, yet they cannot flag him down and offer him a payment to fix his muffler. If they could, we would then have to worry that some people might drive around with noisy mufflers just to attract payments from those who are bothered by the noise. In recognition of this difficulty, most governments simply require that cars have working mufflers. Indeed, the explicit or implicit purpose of a large share of laws is to solve problems caused by externalities; that is, to help people achieve the solutions they might have reached had they been able to negotiate with one another.

When negotiation is costly, the task of adjustment generally falls on the party who can accomplish it at the lowest cost. For example, many municipal noise ordinances have restrictions on loud party music, which may take effect at a later hour on weekends than on weekdays. This pattern reflects costs and benefits because the gains from loud music tend to be larger on weekends while such music is more likely to disturb people on weekdays. If the noise curfew is set at different hours on different days of the week, the law can even place the burden on partygoers during the week and on sleepers during the weekend! Thus, laws and regulations are often used to control external costs. And we should never forget that laws and regulations function within a framework of social norms of reasonable behaviour. It is the fact that most people obey laws voluntarily that enables the police to concentrate their attention on the minority who do break laws; for example, most people would think it inconsiderate and boorish to practise drum solos at 3AM and wake up all the neighbours, and would never do it in the first place.

## THE OPTIMAL AMOUNT OF EXTERNAL COSTS IS NOT ZERO

Because people think of pollution as bad, many cringe when they hear the phrase "socially optimal level of pollution." How can any positive level of pollution be socially optimal? But to speak of a socially optimal level of pollution is not the same as saying that pollution is good. It merely recognizes that though society has an interest in cleaning up the environment, the cleanup incurs costs. The underlying idea is no different from the idea of an optimal level of dirt in an apartment. After all, even if you spent the whole day, every day, vacuuming your apartment, there would be *some* dirt left in it. And because you have better things to do than vacuum all day, you probably tolerate substantially more than the minimum possible amount of dirt. A dirty apartment is not good, nor is pollution in the air you breathe. But in both cases, the cost–benefit principle states that the cleanup effort is to be increased only until the marginal benefit equals the marginal cost.

COST-
BENEFIT

**RECAP**

### EXTERNAL COSTS AND BENEFITS

Externalities occur when the costs or benefits of an activity accrue to people other than those directly involved in the activity. The Coase theorem says that when affected parties can negotiate with one another without cost, activities will be pursued at levels that maximize total economic surplus, even in the presence of external costs or benefits. But when negotiation is prohibitively costly, total economic surplus is not maximized. Activities that generate external costs are pursued to excess, while those that generate external benefits are pursued too little. Laws, regulations, taxes, and subsidies are often adopted in an effort to alter inefficient behaviour that results from externalities. The effectiveness of laws and regulations will be related to social norms of behaviour.

## 10.2 PROPERTY RIGHTS AND THE TRAGEDY OF THE COMMONS

Once we start to recognize the importance of externalities, and the regulations they produce, we have to begin thinking about what we mean by the institution of private property. Although our intuitive sense may be that people have the right to own any property they acquire by lawful means and to do with that property whatever they see fit, these rights are abridged when the use of property is restricted. For example, Chabar faces a restriction on the use of his factory if he is prohibited from discharging pollution into the river. Bob bought his drums legally, but he cannot use them legally at 3 AM if an anti-noise bylaw is in force. Zoning ordinances, speed limits, rules of liability, and many other regulations restrict how property may be used, with the intention of reducing the loss of economic surplus caused by externalities.

When we are very young, our idea of property is pretty simple: there is a direct relationship between a person and a physical object (as in "that's *my* toy"). However, as we age, we begin to realize that property rights are much more complex than simple possession (consider, for example, a recording company's property right to receive royalty payments when music is digitally reproduced). Our attitudes to property are also sometimes complex, and may depend on what type of property is under consideration. In recent years, for example, many people who would never even consider walking off with somebody else's shirt have downloaded songs for free from the Internet.

The extent of property rights has, moreover, changed substantially over time in advanced industrial countries. In the nineteenth century in Britain, for example, it was taken for granted that in buying a country estate, a new owner also purchased the right to renovate the local castle however he pleased, no matter how ugly the changes or how old the castle. Today, because the U.K. electorate wants to preserve its inheritance of historic architecture (which is highly important for the tourism industry), heritage preservation laws restrict what owners can do to "listed" buildings. Because these conservation laws have wide public support, they are generally observed.

Economic analysis can help to design laws that will produce socially efficient outcomes, but one must also realize that the observance of those laws depends, crucially, on whether people think they are fair or reasonable. For instance, the Internet has made it easy to copy music without paying for it, even though the law states that musical artists are entitled to royalties when their music is copied. If millions of people continue to copy music files, it will not be practical to enforce the law on file sharing and it will fall into disuse. If musicians cannot collect royalties because laws on file sharing are unenforceable, then the right to collect royalties is, in effect, meaningless.[3]

## THE PROBLEM OF UNPRICED RESOURCES

To understand the laws that govern the use of property, we must begin by asking why societies created the institution of property in the first place. The following examples, which show what happens to a valuable resource that nobody owns, suggest why property rights may sometimes help to maximize total surplus.

### EXAMPLE 10.7

#### How many steers will villagers send onto the commons?

A village has five residents, each of whom has accumulated savings of $100. Suppose that they each have two options for investing that money: buy bonds or buy cattle. Each villager can either pay $100 for a bond that pays 13 percent interest per year or buy a one-year-old steer for $100 and send it onto the piece of land set aside for village use, the village commons, to let it graze for one year before selling it. The price the villager will get for the two-year-old steer depends on the amount of weight it gains while grazing on the commons, which in turn depends on the number of one-year-old steers sent onto the commons, as shown in Table 10.4.

**TABLE 10.4**
**The Relationship between Herd Size and Steer Price**

| Number of steers on the commons | Price per two-year-old steer ($) | Income per steer ($/year) |
|:---:|:---:|:---:|
| 1 | 126 | 26 |
| 2 | 119 | 19 |
| 3 | 116 | 16 |
| 4 | 113 | 13 |
| 5 | 111 | 11 |

Note: The value of a yearling is $100 when it begins grazing. Income per steer is derived by subtracting $100 from the selling price of a two-year-old steer.

The price of a two-year-old steer declines with an increase in the total number of steers grazing on the commons, because less grass is available to each. The villagers make their investment decisions one at a time, and the results are public. If each villager decides how to invest individually, how many one-year-old steers will be sent onto the commons, and what will be the village's total income?

If a villager buys a $100 government bond, he will earn $13 of interest income at the end of one year. Thus, he will send a one-year-old steer onto the commons if and only if that steer will command a price of at least $113 when it is two years old. When each villager chooses in this self-interested way, we can expect four villagers to send a steer onto the commons. (Actually, the fourth villager would be indifferent between investing in a one-year-old steer or buying a bond, since he would earn $13 either way. For the sake of discussion, we will assume that in the case of a tie, people choose to raise cattle.) The fifth villager, seeing that he would earn only $11 by sending a fifth

---

3 *Property rights* can be defined as the "...sanctioned behavioral relations among [individuals] that arise from the existence of things and pertain to their use." A society's system of property rights is "...the set of social and economic relations [that defines] the position of each individual with respect to the use of scarce resources." Any individual who does not observe the norms specified by the system of property rights bears the consequences for nonobservance. Eirik G. Furubotn and Svetozar Pejovich, "Property Rights and Economic Theory: A Survey of Recent Literature," *Journal of Economic Literature, 10,* December 1972, p. 1139. Furubotn and Pejovich (p. 1139, n. 3) state that the definition is consistent with Roman Law, Common Law, Marx and Engels, and modern legal usage.

steer onto the commons, will choose instead to buy a bond. As a result of these decisions, the total village income will be $65 each year: $13 for the one bondholder and 4($13) = $52 for the four cattle ranchers.

Has Adam Smith's invisible hand produced the most the largest possible economic surplus when these villagers individually allocate their resources? We can tell at a glance that it has not, since their total village income is only $65, precisely the same as it would have been had the possibility of cattle raising not existed. The source of the difficulty will become evident in Example 10.8.

# EXAMPLE 10.8

## What is the socially optimal number of steers to send onto the commons?

Suppose the five villagers in Example 10.7 confront the same investment opportunities as before, except that this time they can make their decisions as a group rather than individually. How many one-year-old steers will they send onto the commons, and what will be their total village income?

This time the villagers' goal is to maximize the income received by the group as a whole. When decisions are made from this perspective, a one-year-old steer will be sent onto the commons only if its marginal contribution to village income is positive. As the entries in the last column of Table 10.5 indicate, the first steer clearly meets this criterion, since it increases total village income by $13. How? We see that when the first yearling is purchased and put onto the commons, total income from steers increases from zero to $26. Because the price of a yearling steer is $100, the villager who purchases a yearling must forego the purchase of a bond for $100. At an annual return of 13 percent on the $100, $13 is sacrificed to obtain $26. Marginal village income from the first steer is $13 ($26 − $13 = $13).

A second steer causes total income from steers to increase by $12. However, if a second yearling is purchased instead of a bond, $13 is again sacrificed. Marginal village income is −$1, or a decrease of one dollar. Table 10.5 shows that as more yearlings are added after the first, ever larger reductions in total village income occur.

**TABLE 10.5**
**Marginal Income and the Socially Optimal Herd Size**

| (a) Number of steers | (b) Number of bonds | (c) Price per two-year-old steer ($) | (d) Income per steer (c) − $100 ($) | (e) Total income from steers, (d) × (a) ($) | (f) Total income from bonds, 13 × (b) ($) | (g) Total income, (e) + (f) ($) | (h) Marginal income derived from a steer ($) |
|---|---|---|---|---|---|---|---|
| 0 | 5 | — | — | 0 | 65 | 65 | |
| | | | | | | | 13 |
| 1 | 4 | 126 | 26 | 26 | 52 | 78 | |
| | | | | | | | −1 |
| 2 | 3 | 119 | 19 | 38 | 39 | 77 | |
| | | | | | | | −3 |
| 3 | 2 | 116 | 16 | 48 | 26 | 74 | |
| | | | | | | | −9 |
| 4 | 1 | 113 | 13 | 52 | 13 | 65 | |
| | | | | | | | −10 |
| 5 | 0 | 111 | 11 | 55 | 0 | 55 | |

In sum, when investment decisions are made with the goal of maximizing total village income, the best choice is to buy four bonds and send only a single one-year-old steer onto the commons. The resulting village income will be $78: $26 from sending the single steer and $52 from the four bonds. That amount is $13 more than the total income that resulted when villagers made their investment decisions individually. Once again, moving from an inefficient allocation to an efficient one causes the economic pie to grow larger. And when the pie grows larger, everyone can have a larger slice. For instance, if the villagers agree to pool their income and share it equally, each will get $15.60, or $2.60 more than before.

**EXERCISE 10.2**    **How would your answers to Examples 10.7 and 10.8 differ if the interest rate were not 13 percent but 11 percent per year?**

EQUILIBRIUM

Why do the villagers in Examples 10.7 and 10.8 earn a higher total income when they make their investment decisions collectively? When individuals make decisions in isolation, they ignore the external cost that their decisions will impose on others. In this example, one more steer grazing on the commons pasture land means that all other steers will gain less weight. The individual villagers' failure to consider this externality makes the return from sending another steer seem misleadingly high to each of them individually.

The grazing land is a valuable economic resource. When no one in particular owns it, no one has any incentive to take the opportunity cost of using it into account. As a result, when each villager decides in isolation, the village as a whole uses the common until its marginal benefit is zero. This problem and others similar to it are known as the **tragedy of the commons**. The tragedy of the commons occurs because one person's use of commonly held property imposes an external cost on others. The tragedy of the commons also provides a vivid illustration of the equilibrium principle (see Chapter 3). Each individual villager behaves rationally by sending an additional steer onto the commons, yet the overall outcome falls far short of the attainable ideal.

**tragedy of the commons** the tendency for a resource that has no price to be used until its marginal benefit falls to zero

## THE EFFECT OF PRIVATE OWNERSHIP

As Example 10.9 illustrates, private ownership of the village's grazing land offers one possible solution to the tragedy of the commons.

### EXAMPLE 10.9

**How much will a buyer pay for the right to control the village commons?**

Suppose the five villagers face the same investment opportunities as before, except that this time they decide to auction off the right to use the commons to the highest bidder. Assuming that villagers can borrow as well as lend at an annual interest rate of 13 percent, what price will the right to use the commons fetch? How will the owner of that property right use it, and what will be the resulting village income?

To answer these questions, simply ask yourself what you would do if you had complete control over how the grazing land would be used. As we saw in Example 10.8, the most profitable way to use this land is to send only a single steer to graze on it. If you do so, you will earn $26 per year. Since the opportunity cost of the $100 you spent on the single yearling steer is the $13 in interest you could have earned from a bond, your economic profit from sending a single steer onto the commons will be $13 per year, provided you can use the land for free. But you cannot; to finance your purchase of the property right, you must borrow money (since you used your $100 savings to buy a one-year-old steer).

What is the most you will pay for the right to use the commons? Since its use generates an income of $26 per year, or $13 more than the opportunity cost of your investment in the steer, the most you will pay is $100 (because that amount used to purchase a bond that pays 13 percent interest would also generate income of $13 each year). If the land were sold at auction, $100 is precisely the amount you would have to pay. Your annual earnings from the land would be exactly enough to pay the

$13 interest on your loan and cover the opportunity cost of not having put your savings into a bond.

Note that when the right to use the land is auctioned to the highest bidder, the village obtains a larger total surplus from its resources, because the owner has a strong incentive to take the opportunity cost of more intensive grazing fully into account. Total village income in this case will again be $78. If the annual interest on the $100 acquired from selling the land rights is shared equally among the five villagers, each will again have an annual investment income of $15.60.

---

The logic of maximizing economic surplus helps to explain why the most commercial nations have well-developed private property laws. It also reminds us of the importance of compliance with laws and regulations. Economic anthropologists have noticed that some traditional societies have developed implicit rules for their commonly owned resources that also restrict their use; for example, taboos on fishing on certain days, or in certain places.[4] These taboos can be explained as the eventual result of trial and error adaptations that move societies over many generations to more efficient solutions. However, larger, more complex commercial societies find such arrangements difficult to maintain, particularly when technological progress is rapid. In societies such as ours, property that belongs to everyone belongs, in effect, to no one. Not only is its potential economic value never fully realized, it usually ends up being of no value at all. Likewise, property rights that are not enforced by a legal system or that people completely ignore are tantamount to no property rights at all.

Bear in mind, however, that in most countries the owners of private property are not free to do *precisely* as they want with it. For example, local zoning laws may give the owner of a lot in a residential area the right to build a three-storey house but not a six-storey house. Here, too, the logic of maximizing economic surplus applies, for a fully informed and rational legislature would define property rights so as to create the largest possible total economic surplus. In practice, of course, such ideal legislatures never really exist. Yet the essence of politics is the cutting of deals that make people better off. If a legislator could propose a change in the property laws that would enlarge the total economic surplus, she could also propose a scheme that would give each of her constituents a larger slice, thus enhancing her chances for re-election.

As an economic naturalist, challenge yourself to use this framework when thinking about the various restrictions imposed on private property laws: zoning laws that constrain what you can build and what types of activities you can conduct on your land; traffic laws that constrain what you can do with your car; employment and environmental laws that constrain how you can operate your business. Your understanding of these and countless other laws will be enhanced by the insight that everyone can gain when property laws are defined so as to create the largest total economic surplus.

## WHEN PRIVATE OWNERSHIP IS IMPRACTICAL

Do not be misled into thinking that the law provides an *ideal* resolution of all problems associated with externalities and the tragedy of the commons. Defining and enforcing effective property rights entails costs, after all, and sometimes the costs outweigh the gains. For example, no single government (or even a small group of governments) has the authority to enforce property rights in the atmosphere and the oceans. So far, it has proven exceedingly difficult to form agreements that would control the release of pollutants into the atmosphere and the sea. But consider the system of tolls the city of London has devised in order to control congestion in its central core. The system is described in Economic Naturalist 10.1. Notice, too, that the municipal government of London had the authority to implement the tolls.

---

4  See Johan Colding and Carl Folke, "Social Taboos: 'Invisible' Systems of Local Resource Management and Biological Conservation," *Ecological Applications*, Vol. 11, No. 2 (Apr. 2001), pp. 584–600.

**ECONOMIC NATURALIST** 10.1

### Why does London, England, impose a tax on every vehicle that enters the central business district during business hours?

By 2001, traffic congestion in London was spiralling out of control, and each additional driver imposed an external cost in the form of additional congestion on other drivers. Motorists in central London spent 50 percent of their time in traffic jams. An estimated £2 to £4 million worth of time was being wasted every week. Everyone knew it was a problem, but drivers kept crowding onto the roads. Each person thought of roads as "common property" and considered only their own costs of travel time, ignoring the greater congestion and the increase in travel time that their presence on the roads caused. London mayor Ken Livingstone (a well-known left-wing politician) ran for election pledging to tackle

traffic congestion. He did it by using the market mechanism, and charging a price for using the central city roads during the day!

Since February 2002, motorists entering designated central zones between 7:00 AM and 6:30 PM have had to pay a tax, originally £5 but now £8 per day.[5] Around 230 cameras match car licence plates against a database of vehicles whose drivers have paid the charge, with a fine of £80 levied on any motorist who fails to pay before midnight. The revenues have been used to subsidize more frequent bus service. When the charge came into operation, traffic levels instantly fell by 20 percent.

---

**RECAP**

### PROPERTY RIGHTS AND THE TRAGEDY OF THE COMMONS

When a valuable resource has a price of zero, people will continue to exploit it as long as its marginal benefit remains positive. The tragedy of the commons describes situations in which valuable resources are squandered because users do not bear the opportunity cost of using them. In many cases, an efficient remedy for such waste is to define and enforce rights to use the valuable property. But this solution is difficult to implement for resources such as the oceans and the atmosphere, because no single government has the authority to enforce property rights for these resources.

---

## 10.3  CLIMATE CHANGE AND GREENHOUSE GASES

Negotiation between affected parties can potentially restrict activities with external costs to levels consistent with maximum economic surplus, but when direct negotiation between the private parties affected is costly or infeasible, goods with external costs tend to be overproduced. A hugely important example of the tragedy of the commons is no farther away than the air we breathe. As a very large volume of scientific research has stressed, the atmospheric concentration of "greenhouse gases" (primarily carbon dioxide, but also methane and others) has increased substantially in recent decades. A major cause is the burning of fossil fuels, particularly coal and petroleum products. An important consequence is climate change, and there are significant human costs to the warming of surface temperature, the increasing frequency of extreme weather events, and the rising sea levels that will accompany it.

Figure 10.2 below is taken from the Fourth Assessment Report: Climate Change 2007 of the United Nations Intergovernmental Panel on Climate Change. It shows the implications for surface temperatures given different scenarios for greenhouse gas (GHG) emissions. The panel shared the Nobel Peace Price in 2007.

---

5  For up-to-date details, see http://www.tfl.gov.uk/roadusers/congestioncharging/default.aspx.

## FIGURE 10.2

### Scenarios for GHG emissions from 2000 to 2100 (in the absence of additional climate policies) and projections of surface temperatures

Figure 10.2 is from the *Fourth Assessment Report: Climate Change 2007* of the United Nations Intergovernmental Panel on Climate Change with the 2007 Nobel Peace Prize. It shows the implications for surface temperatures of a number of the possible scenarios for control of Green House Gas emissions. Each of the six coloured lines in the left hand panel shows a different scenario for emissions of greenhouse gases (GHGs). $CO_2$ is not the only GHG, hence the vertical scale measures emissions in gigaton (Gt) equivalents of $CO_2$. (1 gigaton = 1 billion tons.) All six coloured lines fall within the dashed lines, which indicate the upper and lower limits of scenarios published after SRES. The grey area represents the 80th percentile range of scenarios published since SRES.

Now consider the right hand panel, which provides different projections about increases in surface temperatures. Three of the four lines show different scenarios for warming of Earth's surface. Each of the three lines represents an average of projections provided by several models. The fourth line (purple) is derived from Atmosphere-Ocean General Circulation simulations that assume atmospheric concentrations of GHGs remain at values for year 2000. Notice that the low projection is an increase of about 0.5°C, while the high projection is an increase of about 3.5°C. Six bars at the far right represent different scenarios for increases in temperature likely to be reached during the last decade of the 21st century. The solid section of each bar represents a best estimate of surface warming, while the bar itself indicates the likely range. All increases are relative to temperatures during 1980–1999. (See www.ipcc.ch/publications_and_data/ar4/syr/en/contents.html.)

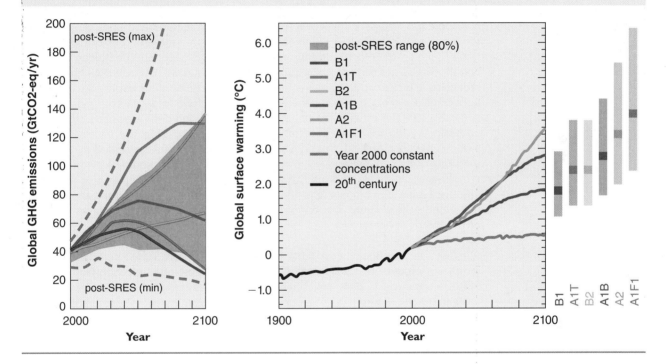

Suppose that a decision has been made to reduce emissions of GHG by some given amount. Economic analysis can help design climate change policy by identifying how to accomplish the reduction at least cost, whatever that reduction might be. The least-cost solution requires the cuts in GHG emissions to be distributed so that the **marginal abatement cost**—that is, the cost of reducing GHG by one unit—is the *same for all emitters*. If this condition is not met, then the cost of removing a ton of GHG from the air is larger for one firm than it is for another firm. As a result, one could achieve the same total reduction in GHG at lower cost by reallocating abatement; the first firm would implement a smaller quantity of abatement while the second firm would implement a larger quantity. The smaller amount of abatement achieved by the first firm would be exactly offset by the increase in abatement achieved by the second firm. GHG would be reduced by the same amount, but at a lower cost.

If government regulators were all seeing and all knowing, they could perhaps just order individual firms to cut back their $CO_2$ emissions by the optimal amounts. Unfortunately, limited knowledge is a fact of life, and regulators rarely have detailed information on how the cost of reducing GHG varies from firm to firm. The regulatory approach, therefore, requires all polluters simply either to cut back their emissions by the same proportion or meet the same absolute emissions standards. However, if different polluters have different marginal costs of GHG abatement, those approaches will not be efficient—they will not minimize the cost of achieving a given target.

**marginal abatement cost**
the cost to a polluter of reducing GHG by one unit

## TAXING POLLUTION

Can a mechanism be designed to distribute the cleanup efficiently, recognizing that the government does not know firms' detailed costs? One method is to implement a carbon tax, and allow firms to decide for themselves how much GHG to emit. The logic of this approach is illustrated in Example 10.10.

### EXAMPLE 10.10

#### What is the least costly way to cut GHG emissions by half?

Two firms, Sludge Oil and Northwest Lumber, have access to five production processes, each of which has a different cost and produces a different amount of GHG. For this example, assume that changes in their costs of production and prices are sufficiently small that they can stay in business for all the GHG control options under consideration. The daily costs of the processes and the number of tons of GHG emitted are shown in Table 10.6. (Emissions of GHG are measured in tons of $CO_2$ equivalent.) Emission of GHG is currently unregulated, and negotiation between the firms and those who are harmed by GHG is impossible. Each firm can see that, because no reduction in emission of GHG is required, process A is the cheapest to use. Therefore, both firms use process A, each one emitting 4 tons for a total of 8 tons per day.

Table 10.6 illustrates a key idea: the cost of reducing GHG emissions often varies according to the source of pollution. In general, it is possible, but usually costly, to reduce emissions of GHG by choosing a cleaner production process. If all firms had the same costs of reducing GHG, the government's decision would be simple: impose the same regulation on all firms. But when the costs of reducing GHG vary, there is an efficiency issue. If, in our example, the government wants to reduce total emissions by half, what is the efficient distribution of GHG abatement between the firms? A graph of the marginal abatement cost for Sludge Oil and Northwest Lumber can help us solve this problem.

Consider the first row of Table 10.6. It tells us that if Sludge selects process *B* instead of process *A*, it will increase its total daily cost of production from $100 to $200 and reduce its daily emissions by one ton; its marginal cost of abatement is $100, point *b* in Figure 10.3. If Sludge selects process *C* instead of process *B*, its total daily cost of production will increase from $200 to $600 and its daily emissions decrease by another ton. This time, Sludge's marginal abatement cost is $400, point *c* in Figure 10.3. Sludge can determine its schedule of marginal abatement cost by considering what happens to its total daily cost of production as it moves from the dirtiest to the cleanest production process. Sludge's marginal abatement cost is graphed as $MAC_S$, the blue line *bcde* in Figure 10.3.

**TABLE 10.6**
**Costs and GHG Emissions for Different Production Processes**

| Process (tons of $CO_2$ emitted) | A (4 tons/day) | B (3 tons/day) | C (2 tons/day) | D (1 ton/day) | E (0 ton/day) |
|---|---|---|---|---|---|
| Total Cost to Sludge Oil ($/day) | 100 | 200 | 600 | 1300 | 2300 |
| Total Cost to Northwest Lumber ($/day) | 300 | 320 | 380 | 480 | 700 |

The same process of plotting the increase in cost of production caused by reducing GHG by one more ton will result in Northwest's marginal abatement cost, $MAC_{NW}$, the red line *BCDE* in Figure 10.3.[6] If each firm is required to cut GHG by half, each must switch from process *A* to process *C*. The result will be that each firm emits 2 tons/day of GHG. The increase in cost due to the switch for Sludge Oil will be $600/day —

6  To keep things simple, in Table 10.6 we measured GHG in one-ton increments of $CO_2$, so the points in Figure 10.3 are labelled to correspond. In many real-world situations, it is feasible to vary emissions by much smaller changes; if so, a firm's marginal abatement cost can be represented by a continuous line.

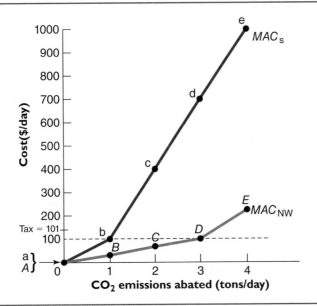

**FIGURE 10.3**
**Marginal Abatement Cost for Sludge Oil and Northwest Lumber**
The line labelled $MAC_S$ represents Sludge Oil's marginal abatement cost (which some might also call its cost of producing "clean" air). Curve $MAC_{NW}$ shows Northwest Lumber's marginal abatement cost. The labelled points on the curves represent the production processes listed in Table 10.6. The curves pertain if marginal abatement costs are continuous.

$100/day = $500/day. The increase in cost to Northwest Lumber will be $380/day − $300/day = $80/day. Requiring both firms to cut GHG by the same amount therefore has a total cost of $580/day.

Consider now how each firm would react to a carbon tax that converts to a charge of $40/ton of $CO_2$ emitted. If a firm can cut $CO_2$ by 1 ton/day, it will save $40/day in tax payments. Each firm has an incentive to switch to a cleaner process whenever a emissions of $CO_2$ can be reduced by one ton at a cost less than $40. Thus, Sludge Oil would continue to use process $A$, because switching to process $B$ would cost an additional $100/day but would save only $40/day in taxes. Northwest Lumber, however, would switch to process $B$, because the $40 saving in taxes would be more than enough to cover the $20 cost of switching.

Unfortunately, a tax of $40 reduces emissions by only 1 ton/day, 3 tons short of the 4-ton target. Suppose instead that the government imposed a tax of $101/ton. Sludge Oil would then adopt process $B$, because the $100 daily cost of doing so would be less than the $101 saved in taxes. Northwest Lumber would adopt process $D$, because for every process up to and including $D$, the cost of switching to the next process would be less than the resulting tax saving.

Overall, then, a tax of $101/ton would reduce emissions of $CO_2$ by 4 tons per day. The total cost of the reduction would be only $280/day ($100/day for Sludge Oil and $180/day for Northwest Lumber), or $300/day less than when each firm was required to cut its emissions of GHG by half. Notice that, in this example, once there is a carbon tax, the firm benefits from reducing $CO_2$ by avoiding a tax of $101 per ton. In fact, the firm's marginal benefit from any activity that reduces its $CO_2$ by one more ton is exactly the amount of the tax. Hence, the decisions of both Sludge and Northwest include the same type of cost–benefit comparison that is a part of their other production decisions: reduce $CO_2$ (produce clean air) up to the point where the marginal benefit is equal to the marginal cost. In Figure 10.3, the intersection of the horizontal Tax line with the $MAC$ line of each firm therefore indicates the profit-maximizing level of GHG for both of the firms.

COST-
BENEFIT

When Sludge reduced its $CO_2$ from 4 to 3 tons/day by switching from process $A$ to $B$, its total daily cost of production increased from $100 to $200. When Northwest Lumber reduced its GHG from 2 tons to 1 ton/day by switching from process $C$ to $D$, its total daily cost of production increased from $380 to $480. Marginal abatement cost was therefore $100 for both firms. When marginal abatement cost is equal for the two firms, the total cost of reaching a given target for reducing emissions is minimized. In this way a "clever" tax can achieve the social goal of cutting GHG by 50 percent at the lowest possible total cost.

Notice, too, that with the carbon tax of $101/ton of emissions, the government collects $404/day in taxes. These taxes are a financial cost to firms but, because they produce government revenue that can be used to reduce other taxes or fund other government services, they do not represent a *social* cost of production.

The tax approach has the advantage of concentrating GHG reduction in the hands of the firms that can accomplish it at the least cost while raising revenue that enables governments to cut other taxes but maintain the same level of public services. It is, in general, likely to be more efficient than a blanket regulation; for example, requiring each firm to cut emissions by the same proportion, ignoring the fact that some firms can reduce GHG much more cheaply than others.

The key problem is how high to set the carbon tax. A tax that is too low will result in too little GHG reduction, while a tax that is too high will result in too many resources being devoted to GHG reduction. Of course, the government could start by first setting a low tax rate, but announcing that the tax rate will gradually increase until GHG emissions are reduced to the target level. A slow phase-in of carbon taxes has often been advocated to minimize the immediate dislocations facing firms with energy-inefficient capital stock, while ensuring that there is a strong financial incentive for new investments to be energy efficient.

## CAP AND TRADE: GHG EMISSION PERMITS

An alternative is to cap or limit pollution to some predetermined level and then issue tradable permits allowing emissions to that level of pollution.

### EXAMPLE **10.11**

#### What will be the price of pollution permits?

The government's objective of reducing total pollution produced by the two firms from 8 to 4 tons/day can be accomplished by issuing four permits, each permit entitling the owner to emit one ton of pollution per day. This establishes a pollution cap of 4 tons/day. If the government wants to raise revenue to finance tax cuts, subsidies for energy efficiency, transfers to low income people, or for any other purpose, it could auction off the permits.

Alternatively, the government could give two permits free of charge to each firm and allow them to sell or purchase permits at whatever price they establish between themselves—with the proviso that no pollution may be emitted without a permit. (This is the trade part of a cap-and-trade system.) With this plan, the government can enforce limits on pollution without knowing the marginal abatement costs of individual firms. Each firm's marginal abatement cost is a commercial secret and neither firm knows the other's schedule.

Sludge Oil's two free permits allow it to emit 2 tons/day, so it can produce at point c in Figure 10.3. But each additional pollution permit will entitle it to increase its daily emissions by another ton while avoiding the cost of abating that ton. Sludge's *MAC* line in Figure 10.3 indicates that reducing its daily abatement from two tons to one ton of $CO_2$/day will cause its daily abatement cost to fall by $400/day. Sludge realizes that buying a pollution permit for any price less than $400 and using process *B* will be more profitable than not buying the permit and using process *C*. Sludge does not know Northwest's marginal abatement costs. However, suppose Sludge decides to test the water by offering $300 to purchase a permit. If that offer is accepted, Sludge will be better off by $100.

On the other hand, Northwest similarly starts with two free pollution permits and with the option of being at point *C* in Figure 10.3. But its *MAC* line in Figure 10.3 shows that it will be better off if it can sell one permit for any price greater than its own marginal abatement cost. Hence, because Northwest can increase its daily abatement from two to three tons of $CO_2$ at a marginal cost of $100, the sale of one permit at a

COST-
BENEFIT

price of $300 will result in a net gain of $200. The cost–benefit principle tells both firms that they will be better off if they make the transaction, and one permit is sold by Northwest to Sludge for $300. This authorizes Sludge to increase its daily emissions by one ton of $CO_2$, but requires Northwest to exactly offset the increase by reducing its daily emissions by one ton of $CO_2$ so that total daily emissions remain unchanged.

Will another permit change hands? As its marginal abatement cost schedule shows, Sludge knows that if it acquires a fourth permit, it can switch from process B to A and increase its daily emissions from three to four tons, which means that it can reduce its daily abatement to zero and avoid a marginal abatement cost of $100. The most Sludge will pay for another permit is $100. Northwest's marginal abatement cost schedule indicates that if it sells its last permit, it must increase its daily abatement from three to four tons at a marginal abatement cost of $220. So Northwest will not accept any price less than $220 for its last permit, a price that exceeds what Sludge will offer. Thus, in equilibrium, Northwest keeps one permit and sells one, operating at point D on its marginal abatement cost schedule, while Sludge buys an additional permit and operates at point B on its marginal abatement cost schedule.

EQUILIBRIUM

---

Carbon taxes and "cap and trade" permit systems are abatement mechanisms designed by economists as efficient solutions to the problem of excessive GHG emissions. A carbon tax, or any other tax on pollution, makes polluters aware of the cost of using the atmosphere for waste disposal, and the tax revenues constitute a valuable stream of income that governments can use for other purposes. If a cap-and-trade permit system is introduced, the right to pollute becomes a valuable asset. When the permits are auctioned off, the government gets the revenue; but if they are granted to polluters free of charge, there is a windfall gain for those who receive them and the elimination of a potential revenue source for the government. The foregone revenue is likely to be substantial: in the U.S., the Congressional Budget Office estimated that the total could be between $50 and $300 billion annually by 2020.[7]

Why might a government decide to give away such a valuable asset and grant permits free of charge? Proposals for a carbon tax or auctioned permits are likely to incite resistance from companies and individuals who would have to pay the full price of their impact on the environment. These political pressures may cause the government to give away permits or sell them for less than market value in order to make a cap-and-trade program more palatable.

**RECAP**

## ENVIRONMENTAL POLICY AND EXTERNALITIES

An efficient program for reducing GHG emissions, or other forms of pollution, is one for which the marginal cost of abatement is the same for all polluters. Taxing emissions has this desirable property, as does a system of pollution permits. A system of permits has the advantage that regulators can achieve a desired abatement target without having detailed knowledge of the abatement technologies available to polluters. A carbon tax gives the government a stream of revenue that will not be available from permits unless the government sells them at full market value. An ideal policy, be it a tax or a system of permits, will put a price on pollution and give individuals and firms an incentive to recognize the full cost of their economic decisions, including environmental costs.

---

7  Congressional Budget Office, "Issues in Climate Change: Statement of Peter R. Orszag, Director, Presentation for the CBO Director's Conference on Climate Change," November 16, 2007, p. 10. For a brief summary of the issues, see http://www.cbo.gov/ftpdocs/87xx/doc8769/11-01-CO2Emissions.pdf and http://www.cbo.gov/ftpdocs/80xx/doc8027/04-25-Cap_Trade.pdf.

# 10.4  POSITIONAL EXTERNALITIES

In professional sports, legal battles, and a host of other competitive situations, the rewards people receive depend not on how they perform in absolute terms but on how they perform relative to their closest rivals. In these situations, all competitors have an incentive to take actions that will increase their odds of winning, but not all can win. Someone, for example, who consistently wins major tennis tournaments will claim big prizes and be presented with lucrative opportunities to endorse products, but even if the second- and third-place finishers are *almost* as good as the winner, they will claim much smaller prizes and will receive fewer and less valuable opportunities to make endorsements. All contestants, therefore, have big incentives to do whatever it takes to get the maximum chance of winning.

## PAYOFFS THAT DEPEND ON RELATIVE PERFORMANCE

Suppose an individual tennis player can increase her chances of winning by hiring a personal fitness trainer and a sports psychologist, provided no other player does so. If she does not hire a trainer and a psychologist and her competitors do, her chances of winning will be greatly reduced. If every player knows this situation to be the case, they all will hire personal fitness trainers and sports psychologists, because anyone who fails to do so will have greatly diminished chances of winning tournaments.

Now suppose that spectators and those who pay athletes to endorse products will pay exactly the same amount regardless of whether the players hire personal trainers and sports psychologists—to the fans and sponsors, tournaments are of the same value either way. If additional resources are employed to obtain what spectators and sponsors regard as the same output, there can be no gain for spectators, sponsors, and athletes as a group. Indeed, when more resources are employed to obtain the same thing, total economic surplus must be smaller. To the extent that each contestant's payoff depends on his or her relative performance, the incentive to undertake such investments will be excessive from a collective point of view.

Consider the example presented below in Economic Naturalist 10.2.

**www.cfl.ca**
**Canadian Football League**
**www.nfl.com**
**National Football League**

**ECONOMIC NATURALIST 10.2**

### Why do some football players take anabolic steroids?

The offensive linemen of many National Football League teams currently average more than 330 pounds. In the 1970s, by contrast, offensive linemen in the league averaged barely 280 pounds, and the all-decade linemen of the 1940s averaged only 229 pounds. Size and strength are the two cardinal virtues of an offensive lineman, and other things being equal, the job will go to the larger and stronger of two rivals.

Size and strength, in turn, can be enhanced by the consumption of anabolic steroids. But if all players consume these substances, the rank ordering of players by size and strength, and hence the question of who lands the jobs, will be largely unaffected. And since the consumption of anabolic steroids entails potentially serious long-term health consequences, as a group, football players are clearly worse off if they consume these drugs. So why do some football players take steroids?

The problem here is that contestants for starting berths on the offensive line confront a prisoner's dilemma like the one analyzed in Chapter 9. Consider two closely matched rivals, Smith and Jones, who are competing for a single position. If neither takes steroids, each has a 50 percent chance of winning the job and a starting salary of $1 million/year. If both take steroids, each again has a 50 percent chance of winning the job. But if one takes steroids and the other does not, the first is sure to win the job. Notice we are assuming that even if steroids did not exist and linemen averaged 229 pounds, the starting salary would be $1 million/year. And, if steroids are used and the average lineman weighs 330 pounds, the starting salary is still $1 million/year. In either case, the loser ends up selling insurance for $30 000/year. Neither likes the fact that the drugs may have adverse health consequences, but each would be willing to take that risk in return for a shot at the big salary. Given that steroids do exist, the two competitors face the payoff matrix shown in Table 10.7.

Clearly, the dominant strategy for both Smith and Jones is to take steroids. Yet when they do so, each gets only the third-best outcome, whereas they could have gotten the second-best outcome by not taking the drugs. Hence the attraction of rules that forbid the consumption of anabolic steroids. Of course, the issue of compliance and enforcement is again present.

**TABLE 10.7**
**Payoff Matrix for Steroid Consumption**

| | | Jones | |
|---|---|---|---|
| | | Do not take steroids | Take steroids |
| **Smith** | Do not take steroids | Second best for each | Best for Jones Worst for Smith |
| | Take steroids | Best for Smith Worst for Jones | Third best for each |

## POSITIONAL ARMS RACES

When used to maintain relative position, the use of steroids is an example of a **positional externality**, a situation in which reward depends on relative performance so that an increase in one person's performance reduces another's expected reward. Whenever the payoffs to one contestant depend at least in part on how he or she performs relative to a rival, any step that improves one contestant's relative position must necessarily worsen than of the others. The example of standing at concerts discussed in Chapter 9 (Economic Naturalist 9.2) is another instance of a positional externality. Just as the invisible hand of the market is weakened by the presence of conventional externalities, it is also weakened by positional externalities. Why? Because positional externalities often lead contestants to engage in **positional arms races**, an escalating series of mutually offsetting investments in performance enhancement.

**positional externality** occurs when an increase in one person or firm's performance reduces the expected reward of another's in situations in which reward depends on relative performance

**positional arms race** a series of mutually offsetting investments in performance enhancement that is stimulated by a positional externality

## POSITIONAL ARMS CONTROL AGREEMENTS

As examples in Chapter 9 indicated, the prisoner's dilemma causes outcomes in which all parties are worse off. Likewise, positional arms races also produce outcomes in which all parties are worse off. Hence, there are gains to be had if participants can avoid outcomes produced by the prisoner's dilemma, an objective that can be accomplished with *positional arms control agreements*. **Positional arms control agreements** include any agreement contestants use to limit mutually offsetting investments in performance enhancement. (The practical problem is, as we saw in Chapter 9, how over time to enforce such agreements, if they can be negotiated initially.)

Once you become aware of positional arms races, you will begin to see examples of them almost everywhere. You can hone your skills as an economic naturalist by asking these questions about every competitive situation you observe: What form do the investments in performance enhancement take? What steps have contestants taken to limit these investments? Sometimes positional arms control agreements are achieved by the imposition of formal rules or by the signing of legal contracts. Some examples of this type of agreement follow.

**positional arms control agreement** an agreement in which contestants attempt to limit mutually offsetting investments in performance enhancement

### Roster Limits

Major League Baseball permits teams to have only 25 players on the roster during the regular season. The Canadian Football League sets its roster limit at 39, the National Basketball Association at 12. Why these limits? In their absence, any team could increase its chance of winning by simply adding players. Inevitably, other teams would follow suit. However, it is plausible to assume that, beyond some point, larger rosters do not add much to the entertainment value for fans. Roster limits are thus a sensible way to deliver sports entertainment at a more reasonable cost.

### Equipment Rules

In Formula 1 auto racing, detailed rules govern car design. A racing car might be able to go a bit faster if its designers saved car weight by skimping a bit on the roll bars and other design features that save drivers' lives in crashes, but other designers could then also skimp on crash worthiness. No racing team would end up with a lasting advantage and more drivers would die. Formula 1 auto racing thus distinguishes carefully between technical innovations that are permitted and those that are not.

### Arbitration Agreements

In the business world, contracting parties often sign a binding agreement that commits them to arbitration in the event of a dispute. By doing so, they sacrifice the option of pursuing their interests as fully as they might want to later, but they also insulate themselves from costly legal battles. Binding arbitration can also be used to limit the costs that might arise from strikes and lockouts.

### Mandatory Starting Dates

A child who is a year or so older than most of her kindergarten classmates is likely to perform better, in relative terms, than if she had entered school with children her own age. And since most parents are aware that admission to prestigious universities and eligibility for top jobs on graduation depend largely on *relative* academic performance, many are tempted to keep their children out of kindergarten a year longer than necessary. Yet there is no social advantage in holding *all* children back an extra year, since their relative performance would essentially be unaffected. In many jurisdictions, therefore, the law requires children who reach their fifth birthday before December 1 of a given year to start kindergarten the same year.

## SOCIAL NORMS AS POSITIONAL ARMS CONTROL AGREEMENTS

In some cases, social norms may take the place of formal agreements to curtail positional arms races. Some familiar examples follow.

### Work Effort Norms

In many workplaces, there is competition for promotions, and employers can use the probability of promotion as an incentive to increase the work effort of their labour force. Firms can let it be known (formally or informally) that working late without overtime, coming in on weekends, and taking work home are all activities that increase a worker's chances of getting promoted. Obviously, the owners of the firm will benefit, because if many of their workers provide extra labour for no extra pay, costs will fall and profits will increase. However, only one worker will actually be promoted. When each worker decides individually to increase her effort, she only takes into account the (positive) impact which the extra hours of work have on her own chances of promotion. But she does not consider the fact that an increase in the probability of her own promotion necessarily decreases the probability of promotion for each of her co-workers and that, as a result, she decreases their well-being. In the end, when each worker decides individually, each supplies offsetting amounts of overtime, so everyone's chance of promotion is unchanged.

In such a labour market, it is the *relatively* hardest working person who gets the prize (this has often been called the "tournament" or "rat race" model). Each worker's decision to increase voluntary unpaid overtime creates an externality for other workers by reducing their probability of promotion. As workers compete against each other for relative position, workers as a group get less leisure. All workers would be better off if they could sign an enforceable agreement that nobody works overtime for free, as a collective bargain can require if the workplace is unionized.

In nonunion workplaces, workers often realize that, as a group, they will be better off if there is an informal agreement among them to *not* compete in some ways, and, although traditions at each workplace do differ, strong workplace norms about *nobody* doing extra work at particular times (e.g., Christmas day) or about seniority requirements for promotion are often the result.

### Fashion Norms

Social norms regarding dress and fashion often change quickly because of positional competitions. Consider, for instance, the person who wants to be on the cutting edge of fashion. In some North American social circles during the 1950s, that goal could be accomplished by having pierced ears. But as more and more people adopted the practice, it ceased to communicate avant-garde status. At the same time, those who wanted to make a conservative fashion statement gradually became freer to have their ears pierced.

During the 1960s and 1970s, a person could be on fashion's cutting edge by wearing two earrings in one earlobe. But by the 1990s, multiple ear piercings had lost much of their social significance, the threshold of cutting-edge status having been raised to upward of a dozen piercings of each ear, or a smaller number of piercings of the nose, eyebrows, or other body parts. A similar escalation has taken place in the number, size, and placement of tattoos.

Is being on fashion's cutting edge more valuable now than in the 1950s?

The increase in the required number of tattoos or body piercings has not changed the value of avant-garde fashion status to those who desire it. Being on the outer limits of fashion has much the same meaning now as it once did. So to the extent that there are costs associated with body piercings, tattoos, and other steps required to achieve avant-garde status, the current fashions are wasteful compared to earlier ones. In this sense, the erosion of social norms against tattoos and body piercings has produced a social loss. Of course, the costs associated with this loss are small in most cases. Yet since each body piercing entails a small risk of infection, the costs will continue to rise with the number of piercings.

### Norms of Taste

Similar cycles occur with respect to behaviours considered to be in bad taste. In the 1950s, for example, prevailing norms prevented major national magazines from accepting ads that featured photographs of nude figures. Naturally, advertisers had a powerful incentive to chip away at such norms in an effort to capture the reader's limited attention. And indeed, taboos against nudes in photographs have eroded in the same way as taboos against tattoos and body piercings.

Consider, for instance, the evolution of perfume ads. First came the nude silhouette; then, increasingly well-lighted and detailed nude figures; and more recently, photographs of what appear to be group sex acts. Each innovation achieved just the desired effect—capture of the reader's instant and rapt attention. Inevitably, however, other advertisers followed suit, causing a shift in our sense of what is considered attention grabbing. Photographs that once would have shocked readers now often draw little more than a bored glance.

Opinions differ, of course, about whether this change is an improvement. Many believe that the earlier, stricter norms were ill-advised—the legacy of a more prudish and repressive era. Yet even people who take that view are likely to believe that *some* kinds of

*"We're looking for the kind of bad taste that will grab–but not appall."*

photographic material ought not to be used in magazine advertisements. Obviously, what is acceptable will differ from person to person, and each person's threshold of discomfort will depend in part on current standards. But as advertisers continue to break new ground in their struggle to capture attention, the point may come when people begin to mobilize in favour of stricter standards of "public decency." Such a campaign would provide yet another example of a positional arms control agreement.

## SUMMARY

- Externalities are the costs and benefits of activities that accrue to people who are not directly involved in the decisions to undertake those activities. When all parties affected by externalities can negotiate with one another and enforce any resulting agreement with no cost, the invisible hand of the market may produce an efficient allocation of resources. According to the Coase theorem, the allocation of resources maximizes total surplus in such cases because the parties affected by externalities can compensate others for taking remedial action. **LO1, LO2**

- Negotiation over externalities is often impractical, however. In these cases, the self-serving actions of individuals typically will not maximize total surplus. The attempt to forge solutions to the problems caused by externalities is one of the most important rationales for collective action. Sometimes collective action takes the form of laws and government regulations that alter the incentives facing those who generate, or are affected by, externalities. Such remedies work best when they place the burden of accommodation on the parties who can accomplish it at the lowest cost. Traffic laws, zoning laws, and environmental protection laws are examples. Social norms can help to make such rules more effective. **LO2**

- Curbing greenhouse gas emissions (GHG), pollution, and other external costs entails costs as well as benefits. The optimal amount of reduction is the amount for which the marginal benefit of further reduction just equals the marginal cost. In general, this formula implies that the socially optimal level of pollution, or of any other external cost, is greater than zero. **LO3**

■   When grazing land and other valuable resources are owned in common, no one has an incentive to take the opportunity cost of using those resources into account. This problem is known as the tragedy of the commons. Defining and enforcing private rights that govern the use of valuable resources can be an effective solution to the tragedy of the commons. Most economically successful nations have well-developed institutions of private property. Some traditional societies deal with the problem by developing implicit rules of use concerning commonly owned resources that have the effect of considering opportunity costs. This approach is difficult for large commercial societies to use. In such societies, property that belongs to everyone belongs, in effect, to no one. Not only is its potential economic value never fully realized; it usually ends up having no value at all. **LO4**

■   The difficulty of enforcing property rights in certain situations explains a variety of inefficient outcomes, such as pollution of the oceans or atmosphere. Since it is impossible to define or enforce property rights over the atmosphere, the global problem of climate change due to increasing GHG concentration in the atmosphere cannot be resolved by private side payments. **LO4**

■   An efficient program for reducing GHG emissions (or other forms of pollution) requires that marginal abatement cost be the same for all polluters. Either a properly designed carbon tax on pollution or a system of cap-and-trade permits will have this property. With a system of permits, regulators can achieve an abatement target without knowing the polluters' marginal abatement costs. A carbon tax could generate a revenue stream for the government, which would finance government spending or the reduction of other taxes. **LO2**

■   Situations in which rewards depend on performance relative to that of rivals can give rise to positional externalities. In these situations, any step that improves one side's relative position necessarily worsens that of the others. Positional externalities tend to spawn positional arms races—escalating patterns of mutually offsetting investments in performance enhancement. Collective measures to curb positional arms races are known as positional arms control agreements. These collective actions may take the form of formal regulations or rules, such as rules against anabolic steroids in sports, workplace norms, and binding arbitration agreements. Informal social norms can also curtail positional arms races. **LO5**

## KEY TERMS

Coase theorem (288)
external benefit
  (or positive externality) (284)
external cost
  (or negative externality) (284)

externality (284)
marginal abatement cost (297)
positional arms control
  agreement (303)
positional arms race (303)

positional externality (303)
side payment (287)
tragedy of the commons (294)

## REVIEW QUESTIONS

1.  What incentive problem explains why the freeways in cities like Vancouver suffer from excessive congestion? **LO1**

2.  How would you explain to a friend why the optimal amount of freeway congestion is not zero? **LO3**

3.  If Parliament could declare any activity that imposes external costs on others to be illegal, would such legislation be advisable? **LO2, LO3**

4.  Why does the Great Salt Lake, which is located wholly within the state of Utah, have lower levels of

pollution than Lake Erie, which is bordered by several states on the American side and by Ontario on the Canadian side? **LO2, LO4**

5. Explain why the wearing of high-heeled shoes might be viewed as the result of a positional externality. Further, how could high-heeled shoes create external costs? **LO5**

## PROBLEMS

1. Determine whether the following statements are true or false, and briefly explain why: **LO1, LO2, LO3**

   a. A given reduction of total emissions by a polluting industry will be achieved at the lowest possible total cost when the cost of the last unit of pollution curbed is equal for each firm in the industry.

   b. In an attempt to lower their costs of production, firms sometimes succeed merely in shifting costs to outsiders.

2. Phoebe keeps a bee farm next door to an apple orchard. She chooses her optimal number of beehives by selecting the honey output level at which her private marginal benefit from beekeeping equals her private marginal cost. **LO1, LO2**

   a. Assume that Phoebe's private marginal benefit and marginal cost curves from beekeeping are normally shaped. Draw a diagram of them.

   b. Phoebe's bees help to pollinate the blossoms in the apple orchard, increasing the fruit yield. Show the social marginal benefit from Phoebe's beekeeping in your diagram.

   c. Phoebe's bees are Africanized killer bees that aggressively sting anyone who steps into their flight path. Phoebe, fortunately, is naturally immune to the bees' venom. Show the social marginal cost curve from Phoebe's beekeeping in your diagram.

   d. Indicate the socially optimal quantity of beehives on your diagram. Is it higher or lower than the privately optimal quantity? Explain.

   e. Should Phoebe be banned from keeping Africanized killer bees?

3. Suppose the supply curve of boom box rentals in Stanley Park is given by $P = 5 + 0.1Q$, where $P$ is the daily rent per unit in dollars and $Q$ is the quantity of units rented in hundreds per day. The demand curve for boom boxes is $20 - 0.2Q$. If each boom box imposes $3/day in noise costs on others, by how much will the equilibrium number of boom boxes rented exceed the socially optimal number? **LO1**

4. Refer to problem 3. How would the imposition of a tax of $3/unit on each daily boom box rental affect efficiency in this market? **LO2**

5. Suppose the law says that Jones may *not* emit smoke from his factory unless he gets permission from Smith, who lives downwind. If the relevant costs and benefits of filtering the smoke from Jones's production process are as shown in the following table, and if Jones and Smith can negotiate with one another at no cost, will Jones emit smoke? **LO1**

|  | Jones emits smoke | Jones does not emit smoke |
| --- | --- | --- |
| Surplus for Jones | $200 | $160 |
| Surplus for Smith | 400 | 420 |

6. Barton and Statler are neighbours in an apartment complex in downtown Saskatoon. Barton is a concert pianist, and Statler is a poet working on an epic poem. Barton rehearses his concert pieces on the baby grand piano in his front room, which is directly below Statler's study. The following matrix shows the monthly payoffs to Barton and Statler when Barton's front room is and is not soundproofed. The soundproofing will be effective only if it is installed in Barton's apartment. **LO2, LO3**

|  | Sound proofed | Not sound proofed |
| --- | --- | --- |
| Gains to Barton | $100/month | $150/month |
| Gains to Statler | $120/month | $80/month |

   a. If Barton has the legal right to make any amount of noise he wants and he and Statler can negotiate with one another at no cost, will Barton install and maintain soundproofing? Explain. Is his choice socially efficient?

   b. If Statler has the legal right to peace and quiet and can negotiate with Barton at no cost, will Barton install and maintain soundproofing? Explain. Is his choice socially efficient?

   c. Does the attainment of an efficient outcome depend on whether Barton has the legal right to make noise or Statler the legal right to peace and quiet?

7. Refer to problem 6. Barton decides to buy a full-sized grand piano. The new payoff matrix is as follows: **LO2, LO3**

|  | Sound proofed | Not sound proofed |
| --- | --- | --- |
| Gains to Barton | $100/month | $150/month |
| Gains to Statler | $120/month | $60/month |

a. If Statler has the legal right to peace and quiet and Barton and Statler can negotiate at no cost, will Barton install and maintain soundproofing? Explain. Is this outcome socially efficient?

b. Suppose that Barton has the legal right to make as much noise as he likes and that negotiating an agreement with Statler costs $15/month. Will Barton install and maintain soundproofing? Explain. Is this outcome socially efficient?

c. Suppose Statler has the legal right to peace and quiet, and it costs $15/month for Statler and Barton to negotiate any agreement. (Compensation for noise damage can be paid without incurring negotiation cost.) Will Barton install and maintain soundproofing? Is this outcome socially efficient?

d. Why does the attainment of a socially efficient outcome now depend on whether Barton has the legal right to make noise?

8. A village has six residents, each of whom has accumulated savings of $100. Each villager can use this money either to buy a government bond that pays 15 percent interest per year or to buy a one-year-old llama, send it onto the commons to graze, and sell it after one year. The price the villager gets for the two-year-old llama depends on the quality of the fleece it grows while grazing on the commons. That in turn depends on the animal's access to grazing, which depends on the number of llamas sent to the commons, as shown in the following table: **LO4**

| Number of llamas on the commons | Price per two-year-old llama ($) |
|---|---|
| 1 | 122 |
| 2 | 118 |
| 3 | 116 |
| 4 | 114 |
| 5 | 112 |
| 6 | 109 |

The villagers make their investment decisions one after another, and their decisions are public.

a. If each villager decides individually how to invest, how many llamas will be sent onto the commons, and what will be the resulting net village income?

b. What is the socially optimal number of llamas for this village? Why is that different from the actual number? What would net village income be if the socially optimal number of llamas were sent onto the commons?

c. The village committee votes to auction the right to graze llamas on the commons to the highest bidder. Assuming villagers can both borrow and lend at 15 percent annual interest, what price will the right fetch at auction? How will the new owner use the right, and what will be the resulting village income?

## ANSWERS TO IN-CHAPTER EXERCISES

**10.1** Since Fitch gains $50/day when Chabar operates with a filter, he could pay Chabar as much as $49/day and still come out ahead. **LO2**

**10.2** The income figures from the different levels of investment in cattle would remain as before, as shown in the table. What is different is the opportunity cost of investing in each steer, which is now $11 per year instead of $13. The last column of the table shows that the socially optimal number of steers is now two instead of one. And if individuals still favour holding cattle and if each decides as an individual, all other things being equal, they will now send five steers onto the commons instead of four, as shown in the third column. **LO4**

| Number of steers on the commons | Price per two-year-old steer ($) | Income per steer ($/year) | Total income from steers ($/year) | Total village income ($/year) | Marginal village income ($/year) |
|---|---|---|---|---|---|
| 0 | — | — | 0 | 55 | — |
| 1 | 126 | 26 | 26 | 70 | 15 |
| 2 | 119 | 19 | 38 | 71 | 1 |
| 3 | 116 | 16 | 48 | 70 | −1 |
| 4 | 113 | 13 | 52 | 63 | −7 |
| 5 | 111 | 11 | 55 | 55 | −12 |

**Practise and learn online with Connect.**

# CHAPTER 11
# The Economics of Information

## LEARNING OBJECTIVES

When you have completed this chapter, you will be able to:

**LO1** Explain how middlemen increase total economic surplus.

**LO2** Use the concept of rational search to determine a market participant's optimal level of information.

**LO3** Define asymmetric information and explain how it leads to the "lemons" problem.

**LO4** Explain how statistical discrimination, warranties, and other instruments are used to address problems of asymmetric information.

Years ago, a naive young economist bought his first car. It had a famous brand name and a sunroof and a great stereo and no rust despite 150 000 kilometres on the odometer. It looked like a good deal at the time, and his younger brother (who said he knew a lot about cars) told him it was a bargain. So he drove the car around the block, paid the lawyer who had owned it the equivalent of $3000 (at today's prices) and then drove it away.

The proud owner had his first bad surprise when he paid $800 to have the car safety checked. His second bad surprise occurred 900 kilometres later when the transmission lost reverse, first, and fourth gears while he attempted to accelerate after going through a toll booth. With the remaining gears, the car limped home and sat forlornly in its parking spot for several months, dripping oil from a leaking engine seal, before being towed away (because the brakes had seized) and sold to the local scrap yard for $50.

Adam Smith's invisible hand presumes that buyers are fully informed about the myriad ways in which they might spend their money—what goods and services are available, what all their prices are, how long they last, how frequently they break down, and so on. Up to now, we have assumed that all buyers and sellers in a market possess "perfect information." They all have the same complete, accurate information on the good being traded, and about all the good's potential substitutes. Perfect information means that there is no uncertainty about the quality or any other characteristic of the good being traded, that all potential buyers and sellers know the prices that are being charged, and that they obtain all this information at no cost. Of course no one is ever really *perfectly* informed about anything. Still, life goes on, and most people muddle through somehow.

In the months after his car became immobile, the young economist pondered the economics of information. Maybe, before buying, he should have invested a bit more in acquiring better information about this vehicle. Maybe he should have hired a mechanic to check the car, rather than relying on the unpaid services of his brother. Maybe he should have taken more time to test drive the vehicle and to read its service history.

Consumers employ a variety of strategies for gathering information, some of which are better than others. They search the Internet for product reviews, talk to family and friends, visit stores, and so on. All these activities have a cost, but they increase a potential buyer's knowledge of which seller offers the best price, and they reduce the uncertainty that consumers would otherwise have about the quality of a commodity.

When he was in graduate school, the young economist studied "the economics of information." Although it was pretty obvious to him (in retrospect, after 900 kilometres) that he had made a bad deal, based on bad information, he also noticed that there were two themes in the "economics of information" that could help explain *why* this had happened. With the wisdom of hindsight, he saw that he should certainly have invested more time, money, and effort in acquiring more data. The first theme of "information economics" emphasizes that the process of acquiring information is a process of *investment*. Like all processes of investment, acquiring information necessitates the use of scarce resources.

Our young economist's investment in information had clearly been suboptimal. Nevertheless, the second theme in the economics of information emphasizes that in some circumstances, there is an *asymmetry of information* between the buyer and seller that no amount of investment in information can fully offset. Even if he had researched the vehicle more carefully, our young economist could never know its full history. The previous owner would still have had an advantage—the seller knew a lot about the car that he was unlikely ever to reveal. He knew the history of the vehicle, the conditions under which it had been driven, and the problems that had already emerged. This asymmetry of information alters fundamentally the way in which many markets work, in practice. The lawyer who sold the car had a strong incentive not to disclose any information that would hinder the sale (and when the young economist recalled the exact words which the lawyer had used in describing the car, he realized, far too late, how carefully chosen and how ambiguous they actually were).

This chapter will begin by considering how our conclusions about markets are affected by the problem of optimal investment in information. It will then consider the implications of asymmetric information. Of course, when there is little uncertainty about price or quality and when both parties have the same information, the assumption of perfect information can be a reasonable one. For example, when you purchase $2 \times 4$ lumber from your local building supply dealer, it is fairly easy to compare prices on such a standardized product, and you can easily check for obvious flaws. However, the art of practising good economics depends on recognizing when we need to make a different assumption—imperfect information is sometimes crucially important for market processes.

The economics of information is a relatively new subject. In 2001, George Akerlof, Michael Spence, and Joseph Stiglitz shared the Nobel Prize in Economics for their work in developing this field. Their work on asymmetric information has been fundamental to the analysis of many markets (e.g., insurance, health care services). Peter Diamond, Dale Mortensen and Christopher Pissarides shared the 2010 Nobel Prize for their work on labour market matching under imperfect information and the impact of imperfect information on the efficiency of recruitment and wage formation.

http://nobelprize.org/
nobel_prizes/economics/
laureates/2001/
Nobel Laureates Akerlof,
Spence, and Stiglitz

## 11.1 INVESTMENT IN INFORMATION: HOW AN INTERMEDIARY ADDS VALUE

One of the most common problems consumers confront is the need to choose among different versions of a product whose many complex features they do not fully understand. As Example 11.1 illustrates, in such cases, consumers can sometimes rely on the knowledge of others.

### EXAMPLE 11.1

**How can a consumer acquire information before deciding which pair of skis to buy?**

You need a new pair of skis, but the technology has changed considerably since you bought your last pair, and you do not know which of the current brands and models would be best for you. Skis R Us has the largest selection, so you go there and ask for advice. The salesperson appears to be well informed, and after asking about your experience level and how aggressively you ski, he recommends the Salomon X-Scream 9. You buy a pair for $600, then head back to your apartment and show them to your roommate, who says that you could have bought them on the Internet for only $400. How do you feel about your purchase? Are the different prices charged by the two suppliers related to the services they offer? Were the extra services you got by shopping at Skis R Us worth the extra $200?

Internet retailers can sell for less because their costs are so much lower than those of full-service retail stores. Those stores, after all, must hire knowledgeable sales people, put their merchandise on display, rent space in shopping malls, and so on. Internet retailers and mail-order houses, by contrast, typically employ unskilled telephone clerks, and they store their merchandise in cheap warehouses. But if you are a consumer who does not know which is the right product for you, the extra expense of shopping at a specialty retailer may be a good investment. Spending $600 on the right skis is smarter than spending $400 on the wrong ones.

---

Many people believe that wholesalers, retailers, and other agents who assist manufacturers in the sale of their products play a fundamentally different economic role from the one played by those who actually make the products. In this view, the production worker is the ultimate source of economic value added. Sales agents are often disparaged as mere intermediaries, parasites on the efforts of others who do the real work.

*"On the one hand, eliminating the middleman would result in lower costs, increased sales, and greater consumer satisfaction; on the other hand, we're the middleman."*

On a superficial level, this view might seem to be supported by the fact that many people will go to great lengths to avoid paying for the services of sales agents. Many manufacturers cater to them by offering consumers a chance to "buy direct" and sidestep the intermediary's commission. But on closer examination, we can see that the economic role of sales agents is essentially the same as that of production workers. Consider Example 11.2.

# EXAMPLE 11.2

## How does better information affect economic surplus?

Ellis has just inherited a rare Babe Ruth baseball card issued during the great slugger's rookie year. He would like to keep the card but has reluctantly decided to sell it to pay some overdue bills. His reservation price for the card is $300, but he is hoping to get significantly more for it. He has two ways of selling it: place a classified ad in the local newspaper for $5, or list the card on eBay, the Internet auction service. If he sells the card on eBay, the fee will be 5 percent of the winning bid.

Because Ellis lives in a small town with few potential buyers of rare baseball cards, the local buyer with the highest reservation price is willing to pay $400 at most. If Ellis lists the card on eBay, however, a much larger number of potential buyers will see it. If the two eBay shoppers who are willing to pay the most for Ellis's card have reservation prices of $900 and $800, respectively, how much larger will the total economic surplus be if Ellis sells his card on eBay? (For the sake of simplicity, assume that the eBay commission and the classified ad fee equal the respective costs of providing those services.)

In an eBay auction, each bidder reports his or her reservation price for an item. When the auction closes, the bidder with the highest reservation price wins, and the price he or she pays is the reservation price of the second highest bidder. So in this example, the Babe Ruth baseball card will sell for $800 if Ellis lists it on eBay. Net of the $40 eBay commission, Ellis will receive a payment of $760, or $460 more than his reservation price for the card. Ellis's economic surplus will thus be $460. The winning bidder's surplus will be $900 − $800 = $100, so the total surplus from selling the card on eBay will be $560.

If Ellis, instead, advertises the card in the local newspaper and sells it to the local buyer whose reservation price is $400, then Ellis's surplus (net of the newspaper's $5 fee) will be only $95, and the buyer's surplus will be $0. Thus, total economic surplus will be $560 − $95 = $465 larger if Ellis sells the card on eBay than if he lists it in the local newspaper.

Making information available to people who can make good use of it is a service eBay provides. A real increase in economic surplus results when an item ends up in the hands of someone who values it more highly than the person who otherwise would have bought it. That increase is just as valuable as the increase in surplus that results from manufacturing cars, growing corn, or any other productive activity.

---

**RECAP**

### HOW THE INTERMEDIARY ADDS VALUE

In a world of incomplete information, sales agents and other intermediaries add genuine economic value by increasing the extent to which goods and services are allocated to the consumers who value them most. When a sales agent causes a good to be purchased by a person who values it by $20 000 more than the person who would have bought it in the absence of a sales agent, that agent augments total economic surplus by $20 000, an achievement on a par with the production of a $20 000 car.

## 11.2 OPTIMAL INVESTMENT IN INFORMATION

Having more information is better than having less. But information is often costly to acquire, and it makes sense for people to use first their most effective information sources before turning to more costly sources (the principle of increasing opportunity cost). In most situations, the value of additional information, given that one already has acquired some information, will decline beyond some point. Typically, then, the marginal benefit of information will decline and its marginal cost will rise as the amount of information gathered increases.

INCREASING
OPPORTUNITY
COST

### THE COST-BENEFIT TEST

Information gathering is in one important respect an activity like any other. The cost–benefit principle tells us that a rational consumer will continue to gather information as

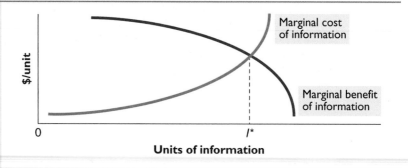

**FIGURE 11.1**
**The Optimal Amount of Information**
Beyond *I\**, additional information costs more to acquire than it is worth.

COST-
BENEFIT

long as its marginal benefit exceeds its marginal cost. Figure 11.1 illustrates that when the marginal cost of information increases and its marginal benefit decreases, a rational consumer will stop at the point where he has acquired I\* units of information, because I\* designates the amount of information for which the marginal benefit equals marginal cost.

In Figure 11.1, we have not specified the units of measurement, but one can also say that it shows the optimal level of ignorance. When the marginal cost of acquiring information exceeds its marginal benefit, acquiring additional information simply does not pay. If information could be acquired for free, decision makers would, of course, be glad to have it. But when the cost of acquiring the information exceeds the gain in value from the decision it will facilitate, there is no point to investing in excess information.

## TWO GUIDELINES FOR RATIONAL SEARCH

In practice, of course, the exact value of additional information is difficult to know, so the optimum amount of time and effort to invest in acquiring it is not always obvious. But as Examples 11.3 and 11.4 suggest, the cost–benefit principle provides a strong conceptual framework for thinking about this problem.

### EXAMPLE 11.3

**Will a person living in Paris, Ontario, be better off if she spends more or less time searching for an apartment than someone living in Paris, France?**

Suppose that rents for one-bedroom apartments in Paris, Ontario, vary between $300 and $500/month, with an average rent of $400/month. Rents for similar one-bedroom apartments in Paris, France, vary between $2000 and $3000/month, with an average rent of $2500. In which city will a rational person expect to spend a longer time searching for an apartment?

In both cities, for simplicity, let us assume that the time and expense of visiting one more apartment is the marginal cost of searching, and that it is the same in both places. In both cities, the more apartments one visits, the more likely it is that he or she will find one near the lower end of the rent distribution. However, rents are higher and are spread over a broader range in Paris, France. Therefore, the expected saving from further time spent searching will be greater in Paris, France, than in Paris, Ontario, which makes it rational to spend more time searching in Paris, France.

COST-
BENEFIT

Example 11.3 illustrates the principle that spending additional search time is more likely to be worthwhile for expensive items than for cheap ones. For example, if we apply the cost–benefit principle, we will spend more time searching for a good price on a diamond engagement ring than for a good price on a stone made of cubic zirconium; more time searching for a low fare from a city within Canada to Sydney, Australia, than for a low fare to Sydney, Nova Scotia; and more time searching for a car than for a bicycle. By extension, hiring an agent, someone who can assist with a search, is more likely to be a good investment in searching for something expensive than for something cheap. For example, people typically engage real estate agents to help them find a house, but they seldom hire agents to help them buy a litre of milk.

## EXAMPLE 11.4

### Who can expect to search longer for a job?

Both Tom and Tim are looking for a job. They both have the same qualifications, and they both figure that in today's labour market each will have to visit forty potential employers, in person, in order to get a job offer. Tom has a car, but Tim does not. Who is likely to spend the least amount of time unemployed?

In both cases, the benefits of job search are the same, but the costs are different. If Tim has to walk or take public transit to apply for a job, his job search time is less effective than Tom's, and he is likely to remain jobless for longer.

Example 11.4 makes the point that when searching becomes more costly, we will tend to do less of it. As a result, the outcomes we can expect in the market will tend to be poorer.

## THE GAMBLE INHERENT IN SEARCH

Suppose you are in the market for a one-bedroom apartment and have found one that rents for $400 per month. Will you be better off if you rent it or if you search further in hopes of finding a cheaper apartment? Even in a large market with many vacant apartments, there is no guarantee that searching further will turn up a cheaper or better apartment. Searching further entails a cost, which might outweigh the gain. In general, someone who engages in further search must accept known costs in return for unknown benefits. Thus, further search invariably carries an element of risk.

In thinking about whether to take any gamble, a helpful first step is to compute its **expected value**—the average amount you would win (or lose) if you played that gamble many times. To calculate the expected value of a gamble with more than one outcome, we first multiply each outcome by its corresponding probability of occurring, and then sum the resulting values.

For example, suppose you win $1 if a coin flip comes up heads and lose $1 if it comes up tails. Since the probability of heads is ½ (and ½ is also the probability of tails), the expected value of this gamble is $(½)($1) + (½)(-$1) = 0$. A gamble with an expected value of zero is called a **fair gamble**. If you played this gamble a large number of times, you would not expect to make money, but you also would not expect to lose money.

A **better-than-fair gamble** is one with a positive expected value. For example, a coin flip in which you win $2 for heads and lose $1 for tails is a better-than-fair gamble. A **risk-neutral person** is someone who would accept any gamble that is fair or better than fair. A **risk-averse person** is someone who would refuse to take any fair gamble.

**Consider a gamble in which you win $4 if you flip a coin and it comes up heads and lose $2 if it comes up tails. What is the expected value of this gamble? Would a risk-neutral person accept it?**

In Example 11.5 we apply these concepts to the decision of whether to search further for an apartment.

**expected value of a gamble** the sum of the possible outcomes multiplied by their respective probabilities

**fair gamble** a gamble whose expected value is zero

**better-than-fair gamble** a gamble whose expected value is positive

**risk-neutral person** someone who would accept any gamble that is fair or better than fair

**risk-averse person** someone who would refuse any fair gamble

EXERCISE 11.1

### EXAMPLE **11.5**

**Are you better off if you search further for an apartment?**

You have arrived in Montreal for a one-month summer visit and are searching for a one-bedroom sublet for the month. Vacant one-bedroom apartments in the neighbourhood in which you want to live are identical in every respect. Nevertheless, you know that 80 percent of them rent for $400 and 20 percent for $360. To discover the rent for a vacant apartment, you must visit it in person. The first apartment you visit rents for $400. If you are risk-neutral and your cost of visiting an additional apartment is $6, is it worthwhile to visit another apartment or will you rent the one you have found?

If you visit one more apartment, you have a 20 percent chance of finding one that rents for $360, thereby saving $40 in rent. You have an 80 percent chance of finding one that rents for $400 (same rent as before). Since the cost of a visit is $6, visiting another apartment is a gamble with a 20 percent chance to win $40 − $6 = $34 and an 80 percent chance of losing $6 (which means "winning" −$6). The expected value of this gamble is thus (0.20)($34) + (0.80)(−$6) = $2. Visiting another apartment is a better-than-fair gamble, and since you are risk neutral, you are better off if you take it.

**EXERCISE 11.2**    **Refer to Example 11.5. Suppose you visit another apartment and discover it rents for $400. If you are risk neutral, will you visit a third apartment?**

## THE COMMITMENT PROBLEM WHEN SEARCH IS COSTLY

If every seller of a commodity charged exactly the same price and if each unit of the commodity had exactly the same quality, there would be no benefit to getting more information about the market and no point in ever changing suppliers. If every consumer knew without any cost which supplier firm was the "best buy," everyone would buy from that firm, and all the other firms would go out of business. It is the imperfection of information in markets that enables firms which differ in either price or quality or both to survive in the same marketplace. Because the market contains a range of prices and qualities, there is also an incentive to consumers to search for the best buy. However, this creates a further problem, because nobody can ever be absolutely sure that she has gotten the best possible deal.

Many of our most important search problems concern long-term matches. When most people search for an apartment or for a job or a spouse, they want a match not for just a month but for a much longer time. Most landlords, for example, are looking for long-term tenants, because it is costly to renovate and re-advertise an apartment every time a tenant leaves. Similarly, few people accept a full-time job in their chosen field unless they expect to hold the job for several years. Firms, too, generally prefer employees who will stay for extended periods. And although dating many people yields valuable information, when most people search for mates, they are looking for someone with whom to stay for a while.

In all these cases, search is costly. Part of the cost may be direct out-of-pocket costs (e.g., the cost of gas needed to visit potential apartments) and sometimes there is an opportunity cost of foregoing available options (e.g., holding out for a really nice apartment and sleeping in your car until you find it). Because of these costs, examining every possible option will never make sense. Apartment hunters do not visit every vacant apartment, nor do landlords interview every possible tenant. Job seekers do not visit every employer, nor do employers interview every job seeker. And not even the most determined "searcher for love" can manage to date every potential mate. In these and other cases, people are rational to end their searches even though they know a more attractive option is out there somewhere.

But herein lies a difficulty. What happens when, by chance, a more attractive option comes along after the search has ceased? Few people would rent an apartment if they thought the landlord would kick them out the moment another tenant came along who was willing to pay a few dollars more rent. Few landlords would be willing to rent to a tenant if they expected her to move out the moment she discovers a cheaper apartment. Employers, job seekers, and people who are looking for mates would have similar reservations about entering relationships that could be terminated the instant a better option happened to come along.

This potential difficulty in maintaining stable matches between partners in ongoing relationships would never arise in a world of perfect information. In such a world, everyone would find the best possible relationship immediately, so no one would be tempted to renege. But when information is costly and the search must be limited, there will always be the potential for existing relationships to dissolve because a better partner fortuitously appears.

In most contexts, people solve this problem not by conducting a completely exhaustive search (which is usually impossible, in any event) but by committing themselves to remain in a relationship once a mutual agreement has been reached to terminate the search. Thus, landlords and tenants sign a lease that binds them to one another for a specified period, usually one year. Employees and firms enter into employment contracts, either formal or informal, under which each promises to honour his or her obligations to the other, except under extreme circumstances. And in most countries, a marriage contract penalizes those who abandon their spouses. Entering into such commitments limits the freedom to pursue one's own interests at a later date. Yet most people freely accept such restrictions, because they know the alternative is failure to solve the search problem.

---

**RECAP**

**THE OPTIMAL AMOUNT OF INFORMATION**

Additional information creates value, but it is also costly to acquire. A rational consumer will continue to acquire information until its marginal benefit equals its marginal cost. Beyond that point, it is rational to remain uninformed.

Search inevitably entails an element of risk, because costs must be incurred without any certainty that the search will prove fruitful. A rational consumer can reduce this risk by concentrating search efforts on goods for which the variation in price or quality is relatively high and on those for which the cost of the search is relatively low.

---

## 11.3 ASYMMETRIC INFORMATION

In Examples 11.1 to 11.5, the problem of incomplete information could be at least somewhat reduced by investing more effort in the search for information. However, the problem of incomplete information takes on a fundamentally different dimension if buyers and sellers have different bases of information. When, for example, our naïve young economist bought his first car, he did not fully appreciate how much more the owner of a used car typically knows about it. The potential buyers of used cars cannot fully verify the car's condition merely by inspecting it or taking it for a test drive. In the used car market, and in many other markets, sellers inevitably know more about true product quality than potential buyers. Economists use the term **asymmetric information** to describe situations in which buyers and sellers are not equally well informed about the characteristics of products or services.

In some markets, information is necessarily asymmetric because information is the commodity that is being sold. For example, when you go to the doctor, it is typically because you know you are sick but you do not know the exact nature of your illness. You know the

**asymmetric information**
situations in which buyers and sellers are not equally well informed about the characteristics of goods and services for sale in the marketplace

symptoms because you have them, but you want your physician to provide the diagnosis. The whole point of going to the doctor is that you believe she knows more about medicine than you do and you want to obtain information that you do not have. Information is necessarily asymmetric in such markets, because the transaction is based on the fact that the supplier of a service based on specialized information knows more than the buyer.

In many other cases, information may be asymmetric because of the incentives that market participants have to provide less than full disclosure. Because everyone who sells a good has an incentive to *say* that it is of high quality, potential buyers may be unable to distinguish between those sellers whose claims are true and those whose claims are false. (Remember the lawyer who sold our young economist his first car? He never did explicitly lie about the car's condition; he just said very little, using terms that were, in retrospect, quite ambiguous.) When buyers know that sellers have no incentive to tell them the true quality of a good, buyers will only be willing to pay a price that reflects the *chance* of getting a bad-quality product. As Example 11.6 illustrates, the problem of asymmetric information can easily prevent exchanges that would benefit both parties.

## EXAMPLE **11.6**

### Will Jane sell her car to Tom?

Jane's Miata is four years old and has 70 000 kilometres on the odometer, most of which are highway kilometres driven during weekend trips to see her boyfriend in Edmonton. (Highway driving causes less wear and tear on a car than city driving.) Moreover, Jane has maintained the car precisely according to the manufacturer's specifications and knows it to be in excellent condition. Because she is about to start graduate school in Halifax, however, Jane wants to sell the car. Today, four-year-old Miatas sell for an average price of $8000, but Jane's reservation price for her car is $10 000, because of its excellent condition.

Tom wants to buy a used Miata. He would be willing to pay $13 000 for one that is in excellent condition but only $9000 for one that needs work. Tom has no way of telling whether Jane's Miata is in excellent condition. (He could hire a mechanic to examine the car, but many problems cannot be detected even by a mechanic.) Will Tom buy Jane's car? Will the outcome maximize total surplus?

Because Tom cannot verify that Jane's car is in excellent condition, he will not pay $10 000 for it. After all, for only $8000, he can buy some other four-year-old Miata that is in just as good condition, as far as he can tell. Tom therefore will buy someone else's Miata, and Jane's will go unsold. This outcome does not maximize economic surplus. If Tom had bought Jane's Miata for, say, $11 000, his surplus would have been $2000 and Jane's another $1000. Instead, Tom ends up buying a Miata that is in average condition (or worse), and his surplus is only $1000. Jane gets no economic surplus at all.

## THE LEMONS MODEL

We cannot be sure, of course, that the car Tom ends up buying will be in worse condition than Jane's, since *someone* might have a car in perfect condition that must be sold even if the owner cannot get what it is really worth. Even so, the economic incentives created by asymmetric information suggest that most used cars that are put up for sale will be of lower-than-average quality, partly because people who mistreat their cars, or whose cars were never very good to begin with, are more likely than others to want to sell them. Buyers know from experience that cars for sale on the used-car market are more likely to be "lemons" than cars that are not for sale. This realization causes them to lower their reservation prices for a used car.

But that's not the end of the story. Once used car prices have fallen, the owners of cars that are in good condition have an even stronger incentive to hold onto them, because the price they would get is less than the value to owners of keeping a good used car. That causes the average quality of the cars offered for sale on the used car market to decline still further. Berkeley economist George Akerlof was the first to explain the logic behind this downward spiral.[1] Economists use the term **lemons model** to describe Akerlof's explanation of how asymmetric information affects the average quality of the used goods offered for sale.

Examples 11.7 and 11.8 illustrate the conditions under which asymmetric information about product quality results in a market in which *only* lemons are offered for sale.

**lemons model** George Akerlof's explanation of how asymmetric information tends to reduce the average quality of goods offered for sale

### EXAMPLE **11.7**

#### What price will a used car fetch?

Consider a world with only two kinds of cars, good ones and lemons. An owner knows with certainty which type of car she has, but potential buyers cannot distinguish between the two types. Ten percent of all new cars produced are lemons. Good used cars are worth $10 000 to their owners, but lemons are worth only $6000. Consider a naive consumer who believes that the used cars currently for sale have the same quality distribution as new cars (i.e., 90 percent good, 10 percent lemons). If this consumer is risk neutral, how much would he be willing to pay for a used car?

Buying a car of unknown quality is a gamble, but a risk-neutral buyer would be willing to take the gamble provided it was fair. If the buyer cannot tell the difference between a good car and a lemon, the probability that he will end up with a lemon is simply the proportion of lemons among the cars from which he chooses. The buyer believes he has a 90 percent chance of getting a good car and a 10 percent chance of getting a lemon. Given the prices he is willing to pay for the two types of car, his expected value of the car he buys will thus be 0.90($10 000) + 0.10($6000) = $9600. And since he is risk neutral, that is his reservation price for a used car.

**How would your answer to the question posed in Example 11.7 differ if the proportion of new cars that are lemons had been not 10 percent but 20 percent?**

**EXERCISE 11.3**

### EXAMPLE **11.8**

#### Who will sell a used car for what the naive buyer is willing to pay?

Refer to Example 11.7. If you were the owner of a good used car, what would it be worth to you? Would you sell it to a naive buyer? What if you owned a lemon?

Since you know your car is good, it is worth $10 000 to you, by assumption. But since a naive buyer would be willing to pay only $9600, neither you nor any other owner of a good car would be willing to sell to that buyer. If you had a lemon, of course, you would be happy to sell it to a naive buyer, since the $9600 the buyer is willing to pay is $3600 more than the lemon would be worth to you. So the only used cars for sale will be lemons. In time, buyers will revise their naively optimistic beliefs about the quality of the cars for sale on the used car market. In the end, all used cars will sell for a price of $6000, and all will be lemons.

In practice, of course, the mere fact that a car is for sale does not guarantee that it is a lemon, because the owner of a good car will sometimes be forced to sell it, even at a price that does not reflect its condition. The logic of the lemons model explains this owner's frustration. The first thing sellers in this situation want a prospective buyer to know is the reason they are selling their cars. For example, classified ads often announce, "Just had a baby, must sell my 2011 Corvette" or "Transferred to Germany, must sell my 2012 Toyota Camry." Any time you pay the red book price for a used car that is for sale for some reason unrelated to its condition, you are beating the market.

---

1  George Akerlof, "The Market for Lemons," *Quarterly Journal of Economics, 84,* 1970, pp. 488–500.

Why do new cars lose a significant fraction of their value as soon as they are driven from the showroom?

## THE CREDIBILITY PROBLEM IN TRADING

Why can someone selling a high-quality used car not simply *tell* the buyer about the car's condition? The difficulty is that buyers' and sellers' incentives tend to conflict. Sellers of used cars, for example, have an economic incentive to overstate the quality of their products. Buyers, for their part, have an incentive to understate the amount they are willing to pay for used cars (and other products). Potential employees may be tempted to overstate their qualifications for a job. And people searching for mates have been known to engage in deception.

Many people may not *consciously* misrepresent the truth in communicating with their potential trading partners. But people do tend to interpret ambiguous information in ways that promote their own interests.

Notwithstanding the natural tendency to exaggerate, the parties to a potential exchange can often gain if they can find some means to communicate their knowledge truthfully. In general, however, personal statements of relevant information will not be enough. People have long since learned to discount the used car salesman's inflated claims about the cars he is trying to unload. But as the next example illustrates, though communication between potential adversaries may be difficult, it may not be impossible.

### EXAMPLE 11.9

#### How can a used car seller signal high quality credibly?

Let's go back to Tom (who wants to buy a Miata) and Jane (who wants to sell one). If Tom cannot verify that Jane's car is in excellent condition, he will not pay $10 000 for it. After all, for only $8000, he can buy some other four-year-old Miata that is in just as good condition, as far as he can tell. Tom therefore will buy someone else's Miata, and Jane's will go unsold. This outcome does not maximize total surplus. If Tom had bought Jane's Miata for, say, $11 000, his surplus would have been $2000 and Jane's another $1000. Instead, Tom ends up buying a Miata that is in average condition (or worse), and his surplus is only $1000. Jane gets no economic surplus at all.

But if Jane knows her Miata is in excellent condition, and also knows that Tom would be willing to pay considerably more than her reservation price if he could be confident of getting such a car, what kind of signal about the car's quality would Tom find credible?

Mere statements about the car's quality are not likely to be persuasive. But suppose Jane agrees to remedy any defects the car develops over the next year; that is, she offers a warranty. Suppose she is willing to leave a signed credit card chit for such repairs at the local Mazda dealer, which the dealer agrees to rip up if no repairs are needed. Jane can afford to extend such an offer because she knows her car is unlikely to need expensive repairs. In contrast, the person who knows his car has a cracked engine block would never extend such an offer. The warranty is a credible signal that the car is in good condition. It enables Tom to buy the car with confidence, to both his and Jane's benefit.

## THE COSTLY-TO-FAKE PRINCIPLE

**costly-to-fake principle**
to communicate information credibly to a potential rival, a signal must be costly or difficult to fake

The preceding examples illustrate the **costly-to-fake principle**, which holds that if parties whose interests potentially conflict are to communicate credibly with one another, the signals they send must be costly or difficult to fake. If the seller of a defective car could offer an extensive warranty just as easily as the seller of a good car, a warranty offer would communicate nothing about the car's quality. But warranties entail costs that are significantly higher for defective cars than for good cars, hence their credibility as a signal of product quality.

## STATISTICAL DISCRIMINATION

In a competitive market with perfect information, the buyer of a service would pay the seller's cost of providing the service. In many markets, however, the seller does not know the exact cost of serving each individual buyer, but if the seller can come up with even a rough estimate of the missing information, she can improve her position. Firms often do so by imputing characteristics to individuals based on the groups to which they belong.

## ECONOMIC NATURALIST 11.1

### Why do males under 25 years of age often pay more than other drivers for auto insurance?

Gerald is 23 years old and is an extremely careful and competent driver. He has never had an accident or even a moving traffic violation. His twin sister Geraldine calls him a wuss; she has had several speeding tickets and a couple of near-miss accidents. Why does he pay more than she pays for auto insurance?

The expected cost to an insurance company of insuring any given driver depends on the probability that the driver will be involved in an accident. No one knows exactly what the actual probability is for any given driver in a specific year, but insurance companies can estimate rather precisely the proportion of drivers in specific groups who will be involved in an accident. Because males under 25 are much more likely than older males and females of any age to become involved in auto accidents, Gerald pays more than his sister. Even if, for example, it is true that Gerald never speeds, the insurance company is unlikely to believe him if he says so. The company knows that all young drivers have an incentive to say they never speed. Moreover, young male drivers tend, on average, to drive significantly faster than older drivers or young female drivers. Data gathered and analyzed over many years tell the insurance industry that even accident-free males under 25 are more likely to have an accident than females the same age who have had several speeding tickets. Gerald's true assertion that he is a safer driver than average cannot be distinguished from the bogus claims of other similar young male drivers, so he will be lumped in with all the other insurance purchasers who resemble him in their measurable characteristics—who are, in the jargon, "observationally equivalent." Gerald will pay more for his insurance than his twin sister pays.

Of course, females who have accumulated several tickets in the past three years are, like Geraldine, more likely to have an accident than a female with a spotless driving record. The insurance company knows that and has increased Geraldine's premium accordingly. Yet it may still be less than her brother's premium. If insurance companies had perfect information and knew how cautious Gerald really is, they might be able to predict (accurately) that Gerald is less likely to have an accident than Geraldine. But in the real world of imperfect information, they have to set rates according to the information they do possess.

To remain in business, an insurance company must collect enough premiums to cover administrative expenses plus the cost of the claims it pays out. Consider an insurance company that charges the same rates for young male and female drivers. If, statistically, males are more likely to have accidents than the females, a company that charges both the same will make money on the female drivers it covers and lose money on the males. But if it does so, rival insurance companies can offer females slightly lower rates without incurring losses, luring them away from the first company. In addition, more young males will be attracted to the first company by its lower rates. The first company will end up insuring mainly young male policyholders, and, because they have poorer accident records, it will suffer an economic loss at the low rates it charges. That is why, in market equilibrium, young males with clean driving records pay higher insurance rates than young females.[2]

Gerald has no choice about buying insurance. If he wants to drive, the law requires him to purchase liability insurance, regardless of the price he must pay. This law is, in fact, a practical example of how a law can deal with an external cost, as discussed in Chapter 10. A driver who causes an accident involving someone else imposes a cost on that person. When the law requires liability insurance, it is providing a way of dealing with an external cost by requiring a driver to have the means of compensating other persons for any injury he may cause them.

---

2 In *Ontario Human Rights Commission v. Zurich Insurance Co.,* the Supreme Court of Canada stated, "The determination of insurance rates and benefits does not fit easily within traditional human rights concepts. The underlying philosophy of human rights legislation is that an individual has a right to be dealt with on his or her own merits and not on the basis of group characteristics. Exceptions to this legislation should be narrowly construed. Insurance rates, however, are based on statistics relating to the degree of risk associated with a class or group of persons. Although not all persons in the class share the same risk characteristics, it is wholly impractical that each insured be assessed individually." Hence, because no practicable alternative was available, the court permitted age- and gender-based premiums as reasonable. See http://csc.lexum.umontreal.ca/en/1992/1992rcs2-321/1992rcs2-321.html. However, in Newfoundland such differentiation was prohibited by regulation in 2005. See "Nfld. bans insurance rates based on age, gender," available at http://www.cbc.ca (November 2008).

**statistical discrimination**
the practice of making judgments about the quality of people, goods, or services based on the characteristics of the groups to which they belong

The insurance industry's policy of charging high rates to young male drivers is an example of **statistical discrimination**. Statistical discrimination occurs whenever people or products are judged based on the groups to which they belong. Notice that if all car insurance companies are forbidden by law from using gender to differentiate insurance premiums, no company can get a competitive advantage by quoting lower rates for women, so there is no danger of competition between firms driving gender-blind insurers out of the market.

Even though insurance companies know perfectly well that *some* young males are careful and competent drivers, unless they can identify *which* males are the better drivers, competitive pressure forces them to act on the knowledge that, as a group, young males are more likely than others to generate insurance claims.[3] Statistical discrimination is the *result* of observable differences in group characteristics, not the cause of those differences.

On average, young males do generate more accident claims. On average, the group's rates will be appropriate to the claims its members generate. Still, none of us are exactly average, and these observations do little to ease the frustration of the young male who knows himself to be a careful and competent driver. Although firms have an incentive to identify such individuals and give them a better deal on premiums, they know that if they do so, unsafe drivers will have an incentive to mimic the safe drivers in order to get that premium break. The costly-to-fake principle tells us that insurance firms have to look for information (e.g., higher grades in school or graduation from a recognized driver's education program) that unsafe drivers cannot easily imitate.

## ADVERSE SELECTION AND MORAL HAZARD

Although insurance companies routinely practise statistical discrimination, each individual within a group pays the same rate, even though individuals within the group can differ sharply in terms of their likelihood of filing claims. Within each group, buying insurance is thus most attractive to those individuals with the highest likelihood of filing claims. As a result, if purchasing insurance is voluntary, high-risk individuals are more likely to buy insurance than low-risk individuals, a pattern known as **adverse selection**.

**adverse selection** the increase in average risk of the insured population that occurs when, at any given cost of insurance, people with a greater expectation of loss buy insurance while people with a lower expected value of claims choose not to buy insurance

Insurance companies use the information that they have about their policy holders to charge a premium that is expected to cover, on average, the losses experienced by the insured population, plus enough to pay administration costs and have some profit. However, people who voluntarily buy health insurance or life insurance may have more information about their risk of loss than the insurance company does. *Adverse selection* occurs when the average risk of the insured population increases because people decide whether or not to buy insurance based on information about their risk of loss that is not available to the insurer.[4] Thus, at a given cost in premiums, individuals who know they are at high risk of loss are more likely to choose to insure, while individuals who know they are at low risk are less likely to insure. Adverse selection forces insurance companies to raise their premiums, which makes buying insurance even less attractive to low-risk individuals and further increases adverse selection. This raises still further the average risk level of those who remain insured. In some cases, only those individuals faced with extreme risks may continue to find insurance an attractive purchase.

---

3   There are many examples of statistical discrimination in the labour market; for example, employers know that some people with only a high-school diploma are more productive than the average university graduate, but they cannot tell in advance who those people are. Hence, competitive pressure leads them to offer higher wages to university graduates, who are more productive, on average, than high-school graduates.

4   Adverse selection can be seen as an example of the lemons model in action. In the used car market that we discussed earlier, the seller of the car had more knowledge than the buyer, while in the individual health insurance market it is the buyer of insurance who knows more (e.g., about his heart condition). But fundamental to both markets is asymmetry of information; so the lemons model applies in both cases. In the used car market, the probability of buying a car that is a lemon drives down the market price of used cars, until in equilibrium there may only be lemons on the market. In the individual health insurance market, adverse selection means the prevalence of poor health risks (who could be called "lemon" policyholders) drives up insurance premiums. In equilibrium, the price may be so high that few or none will buy.

Individuals often can influence the probability that they will experience a loss, at some cost to themselves. Building owners, for example, can decrease their risk of loss due to fire if they incur the cost of sprinklers and alarms. The cost–benefit principle predicts that people will compare the cost of reducing their loss with the potential benefits of loss reduction, which implies that insurance against loss can affect the cost–benefit calculation. If someone is completely insured against the cost of any loss, there is no benefit to reducing risk. For example, a building owner who has 100 percent insurance against any loss due to fire has no incentive to spend a lot of money on sprinklers and fire alarms, particularly if fire insurance premiums won't be reduced anyway. The tendency to exert less care or allocate fewer resources in preventing potential losses that are insured is referred to as **moral hazard**.

Insurance companies are well aware of moral hazard and, consequently, they rarely insure 100 percent of a given loss. For example, car insurance policies typically have a deductible clause so that the first few hundred dollars of a loss is paid by the client, and companies insuring against fire risk may quote lower premium rates for clients who make verifiable efforts to avoid risk, for example, by installing a sprinkler system.

In the next section we discuss how adverse selection can affect health insurance, since private health care insurers must recognize that the people with the greatest incentive to purchase insurance, at any given premium rate, are the relatively unhealthy (those who have the greatest likelihood of making claims). Joseph Stiglitz's insights about insurance markets and about adverse selection and moral hazard are among the contributions that caused him to be selected as a Nobel Laureate in 2001.

COST-
BENEFIT

**moral hazard** the tendency of people to exert less care or allocate fewer resources to prevent losses that are insured

---

**RECAP**

### ASYMMETRIC INFORMATION

*Asymmetric information* describes situations in which not all parties to a potential exchange are equally well informed. In the typical case, the seller of a product will know more about its quality than do the potential buyers. Such asymmetries often stand in the way of mutually beneficial exchange in the markets for high-quality goods, because buyers' inability to identify high quality makes them unwilling to pay a commensurate price.

Information asymmetries and other communication problems between potential exchange partners can sometimes be solved through the use of signals that are *costly or difficult to fake*. Product warranties are such a signal, because the seller of a low-quality product would find them too costly to offer.

Buyers and sellers also respond to asymmetric information by attempting to judge the qualities of products and people on the basis of the groups to which they belong, a process which can be called *statistical discrimination*. A young male may know he is a good driver, but auto insurance companies must nonetheless charge him high rates because they know only that he is a member of a group that is frequently involved in accidents.

In voluntary insurance markets, *adverse selection* is the increase in average risk of the insured population that occurs when, at any given cost of insurance, people with a greater expectation of loss buy insurance, while people with a lower expected value of claims choose not to buy insurance. *Moral hazard* is the tendency of people to exert less care or allocate fewer resources to prevent losses that are insured.

---

## 11.4 IMPERFECT INFORMATION AND HEALTH CARE

In Canada, as in other developed countries, the government is heavily involved in the health care system. (Even prior to the Obama health care reforms, the United States was only a partial exception, since their Medicaid and Medicare programs provided health care insurance for many senior citizens and social assistance recipients.)

Why is the health care sector organized differently from the construction industry? We let market forces organize most industries, including construction, because in many sectors of the economy consumers are well informed, and competition between alternative suppliers creates continual pressure for decreased costs and improved quality. When buying or selling a commodity of known characteristics, such as lumber of a particular quality grade, both buyer and seller can make their decisions based solely on price, and can shop around for the best price. As we have argued in Chapter 6, a decentralized market process will, in these circumstances, usually converge to an equilibrium in which production costs are minimized. Total output will then be determined by the relative utility that consumers derive from one commodity compared to others.

The health care sector, however, is different. People buy lumber to build things they enjoy and they go to cinemas and restaurants because they derive utility from those activities. But people typically do not go to doctors because they enjoy it. Rather, patients consult physicians because something unpleasant has happened to their health, and they want a diagnosis of the cause and some guidance as to the cure. Health care is dominated by informational asymmetry between consumer and producer. It is inherent in the doctor-patient relationship that the patient needs the physician because the doctor has knowledge that the patient lacks. Although the patient experiences the symptoms, the physician provides the diagnosis and suggests the remedy. If the patient knew enough to assess accurately the validity of the doctor's diagnosis and proposed remedy, the patient could self-medicate, and the physician's services would be unnecessary. Unlike markets for commodities whose characteristics are known by both buyer and seller, in the market for health services, the purchaser of health care does not have the same level of knowledge as the seller. As we will also discuss, asymmetry of information is also the reason why third parties (either public or private insurers) typically pay the bills for health care, even if it is individual patients who get the benefits.

## HOW INFORMATION AFFECTS THE PROVISION OF HEALTH CARE

As we have just discussed, markets work very differently when information is asymmetric. In the health care sector, the supplier of health care services (the physician) diagnoses the problem and prescribes the remedy, while health care insurers pay most of the bills. The health economics literature has therefore long recognized the potential importance of the problem of supplier-induced demand and adverse selection in this sector of the economy.

The term "supplier-induced demand" refers to the ability of health care service providers to influence the level of demand for their services. When a doctor tells a patient that their ailment might be serious and to come back again next week for another examination, most people comply. As a result, *unlike other markets, in health care supply and demand are not independent.* Supplier-induced demand is only partly due to the economic motivation physicians have to recommend an operation for which they will be paid. As well, as the adage says, "If the only tool you have is a hammer, pretty soon every problem starts looking like a nail." Physicians and surgeons diagnose the types of problems they were trained to solve in medical school, which is part of the reason why surgeons tend to recommend surgical procedures more often than do general practice physicians.

In the Canadian health care system, physicians are the gatekeepers to specialists, prescription drugs, and hospital services, all of which can only be obtained on the recommendation of a doctor. As a result, physicians initiate more than 90 percent of the costs of the health care sector, leaving relatively little room for consumer choice by patients, which makes the market for health care different from most other markets. However, in markets for consumer goods like automobiles or electronic appliances, our society relies on consumer choice and price competition to allocate resources. Why not do the same in health care?

The TV series, "The Simpsons," offers a caricature of what might happen. In one episode, Homer is convinced by a TV commercial that he has a heart problem. When he sees a "Special Sale Price" of $179.95 being advertised for heart transplants, he signs up for this bargain. (On the day of the operation, the masked surgeon looks suspiciously like the owner of the corner grocery. Fortunately for Homer, Lisa is able to read up on what should be done and finishes the job.)

In health care, the "quality" of service is crucial. But how can a consumer judge this? Good bedside manners may be a very poor predictor of clinical outcomes, and even after a patient is treated, it is hard to know what would have happened with a different treatment. Because the information available in the health care sector is so different from the information available in markets for standardized commodities, these markets function differently.

In, for example, the lumber industry, grading standards ensure that everyone knows the quality of each piece of, for example, two-by-four fir. The price charged then serves as a rationing device to allocate that lumber to its most productive use. In the market for physicians' services, the price signal cannot play the same role. The price charged by individual health care providers serves both as a signal of their relative quality *and* as a mechanism for rationing access to their services. Thus, even when consumers know what medical procedure they want, those who want "the best" will often choose the highest-priced physician because they take high price to be an indicator of high quality. As a result, consumer choice cannot possibly produce the same pressures for cost minimization as in normal commodity markets.

Because of the informational structure inherent in the health care sector, the rational pursuit of perceived self-interest by individuals would generate a very different market equilibrium than it does in the market for lumber. But health care is also expensive. Given the potential cost of medical services, rational individuals will generally want to insure themselves against the risk of catastrophic health expenses, but the private market for individual health insurance faces the informational problem of adverse selection. In the health care insurance industry, insurance companies make money on their healthy policyholders and lose money on the policyholders who get sick. Hence, their profitability depends on whether enough healthy people (who do not make many insurance claims) will pay the insurance premium.

We saw earlier that car insurance companies have to charge the same premium to both careful and reckless drivers when they are "observationally equivalent"; that is, when the insurance firm cannot tell them apart. The health sector is bedeviled by the same problem of asymmetric information. Individuals may not know exactly what is wrong with them (they need the physician for that), but they often have some idea of their general state of health. However, they have no incentive to reveal all that they know to insurers, so the insurance company must charge the same premium to all observationally equivalent people in the pooled population.

At any given level of premiums for individual health care insurance, the relatively healthy will therefore have less incentive to purchase insurance. Although better information about their own health may mean that people are less vulnerable to "supplier-induced demand," better informed consumers are also better able to calculate their expected costs and benefits of private purchase of health care insurance—so adverse selection increases in importance. Those who expect to have large medical bills have an incentive to buy insurance, so the relatively ill will find it more worthwhile to purchase a health care insurance policy. This self-selection of insurance purchasers means that if people buy individual policies, the purchasers of health insurance will tend to be a high-risk group. However, insurance companies that raise their premiums to cover their losses will simply drive away their lower-risk clients (i.e., the profitable ones).

Private markets for health care insurance can work effectively only if low-risk and high-risk individuals are pooled together by some criterion unrelated to health, such as the fact that they all work for the same employer. Because of the problem of adverse selection for individual insurance, and because there are administrative savings involved in group health plans, it is cheaper for firms than for individuals to buy health care insurance. (As well, in both Canada and the United States, health insurance premiums are tax deductible.) As a result, employers have an incentive to pay part of their employees' wages as an untaxed in-kind benefit, in the form of prepaid health insurance. Unlike normal commodities, whose purchase is decided on and paid for by the consumer, in both public and private health care, the service provider usually decides the level of services and a third party usually pays the bills.

## COST SAVINGS

Insurance companies are, of course, vitally interested in whether their company, or some other one, has to pay a particular bill. Even if the employer provides health insurance to new employees, if their ailments already existed at the time that they were hired (a so-called pre-existing condition), the costs of treatment might not be covered. Private insurance companies are also vitally concerned with underwriting—assessing the risks of illness or injury of each particular group of employees and the costs associated with those risks. Consequently, a multi-payer market-driven health care system contains significant incentives for firms to do a lot of detailed financial analysis and record keeping. For example, a skilled underwriter with sophisticated records might be able to argue that her company is not liable for a claim because the injury in question pre-existed.

If health care is viewed as a basic right of citizenship and is financed from tax revenue, the system is a single-payer, public health care system. In such a system, there is little point in detailed underwriting analysis. As a result, a fundamental difference between the Canadian and American health care systems is that in Canada the health care sector employs a much smaller ratio of clerical and financial workers to health care providers, with a substantial savings in administrative and record-keeping costs.[5]

These differences in administrative overhead are easily explicable by economic theory. The self-interest of each insurance corporation causes it to maximize the difference between its premium income and its claims expense. Multiple-payer systems are therefore dominated by the attempts of individual insurers to offload health care risk, either to other firms or to individuals. Such strategies as denying coverage for pre-existing ailments, screening of new clients, and experience rating of individual firms are privately profitable for insurance companies. However, these efforts to shuffle costs to another payer in a multi-payer system absorb administrative resources and do not effectively control aggregate expenditures.

On average, Canadians have had better health outcomes than Americans. In 2009, life expectancy at birth was 79.1 for males in Canada compared to 76.2 in the U.S. and 83.5 for women in Canada, compared to 81.2 in the U.S. However, the more interesting statistic may be the probability of a 15-year-old dying before reaching age 60. A much higher fraction of male youth will not make it to old age in the U.S. (14.1 percent) than in Canada (9.2 percent). (The adult female mortality rate was 8.1 percent in the U.S., compared to 5.6 percent in Canada.)

In Canada, total health care expenditure (public plus private) was about 10.4 percent of GDP in 2008, well below the 16.0 percent of GDP spent in the United States. Since the United States is spending a greater percentage of a higher average income on health care, the cost ratio in absolute dollars is even higher. The United States spent US$7538 per person, which was about 1.8 times per person spending in Canada (US$4079). Even when only the elderly and the very poor got public health care in the U.S. (that is, before the reforms instituted by the Obama administration), the burden on United States taxpayers of their fragmented system was in fact quite comparable to the costs paid by Canadian taxpayers. In the United States, public health expenditures by all levels of government were about 7.14 percent of GDP in 2007, almost exactly the same as in Canada (7.08

---

5  In 1999, health administration costs in the U.S. totalled $1059 per capita, compared with US$307 per capita in Canada. This gap of $752 per person would add up to about US$23.3 billion for Canada as a whole. Moreover, these numbers do not include any allowance for patients' "compliance costs"—the time and hassle involved in completing forms to claim reimbursement for medical expenses and to negotiate disputes over claims. See S. Woolhandler, T. Campbell, and D. Himmelstein, "Costs of Health Care Administration in the United States and Canada," *New England Journal of Medicine*, Vol. 349, Aug. 21, 2003, pp. 768–776.

percent).[6] The major objective of the Obama reforms was to extend some coverage to the 13.5 percent of the American population—roughly 40 million people—who had no health insurance coverage. However, it remains to be seen how effective the Obama changes will be at containing aggregate costs. With continued fragmentation among private-sector insurers, there is, for example, little reason to anticipate lower administrative costs.

Furthermore, in a fragmented private market, there is no incentive for individual insurers to ask, in general, what is making people sick? Insurers *are* interested in improving the claims history of their own policyholders, but there is no profit incentive to pay for something that improves the overall health of the general public. A private company has little incentive to incur significant expenses in promoting a general public health measure. Where, for example, seat belt laws exist, all health care insurance companies will spend less on claims from car accidents, but there is no way that an individual company could institute such a law. General improvements in the health of the population as a whole will reduce the claims cost of the industry as a whole, but will not give any particular company a competitive advantage.

Some of the biggest gains in public health can come from improvements in such things as early childhood care and nutrition, but the returns from such programs are far in the future and are too diffused in the general population to help the bottom line of any particular private insurance company. Since no individual private insurer can expect to see the benefits in higher profits of a higher *general* level of health, a health care system dominated by private insurers has a systematic tendency to under-invest in preventative public health. By contrast, a public system has the incentive to recognize interdependencies among the determinants of health, and to invest in the general health of the population.

---

> **RECAP**
>
> **IMPERFECT INFORMATION AND HEALTH CARE**
>
> The health care sector is characterized by asymmetric information. Physicians have information that patients do not have about diagnoses and treatments. As a result, the supply and demand of health care are not independent. Moreover, individuals want insurance against health care costs, but health insurance companies are unable to predict the health of their clients; hence, markets for individual health insurance are influenced by adverse selection and moral hazard. Risk pooling through universal health insurance can reduce the potential inefficiency arising from asymmetric information in the health care sector.

---

6   Data are drawn from "World Development Indicators" and "OECD Health Data 2010: Frequently Requested Data," at http://data.worldbank.org/data-catalog.

## SUMMARY

- Incomplete information is of two types: (1) uncertainty that can be reduced if more effort or resources are *invested* in acquiring information; (2) *asymmetry* of information between buyers and sellers that cannot be eliminated, because of the nature of the market or the inherent incentives that some agents have not to disclose true and complete information. **LO2, LO3**

- More information is beneficial both to buyers and to sellers, but information is often costly to acquire. The rational individual therefore acquires information only up to the point at which its marginal benefit equals its marginal cost. Beyond that point it is rational to remain ignorant. **LO2**

- Retailers and other sales agents are important sources of information. To the extent that they enable consumers to find the right products and services, they add economic value. In that sense they are no less productive than the workers who manufacture goods or perform services directly. **LO1**

- Searching more intensively makes sense when the cost of a search is low, when quality is highly variable, or when prices vary widely. Search is always a gamble. A risk-neutral person will search whenever the expected gains outweigh the expected costs. Because rational search will terminate before all possible options have been investigated, in a search for a partner in an ongoing bilateral relationship, there is always the possibility that a better partner will turn up after the search is over. In most contexts, people deal with this problem by entering into contracts that commit them to their partners. **LO2**

- Many potentially beneficial transactions do not occur because of asymmetric information—the fact that one party lacks information that the other has. For example, the owner of a used car may know if it is in good condition, but potential buyers do not. Even though a buyer may be willing to pay more for a good car than the owner of such a car would require, the fact that the buyer cannot be sure he is getting a good car often discourages the sale. More generally, asymmetric information often prevents sellers from supplying the same quality level that consumers would be willing to pay for. **LO3**

- Both buyers and sellers can often gain by finding ways of communicating what they know to one another. But because of the potential conflict between the interests of buyers and sellers, mere statements about the relevant information may not be credible. For a signal between potential trading partners to be credible, it must be costly to fake. For instance, the owner of a high-quality used car can credibly signal the car's quality by offering a warranty—an offer that the seller of a low-quality car could not afford to make. **LO4**

- Firms and consumers often try to estimate missing information by making use of what they know about the groups to which people or things belong. For example, insurance firms estimate the risk of insuring individual young male drivers based on the accident rates for young males as a group. This practice is known as statistical discrimination. **LO4**

- Adverse selection is the increase in average risk of the insured population that occurs when, at any given cost of insurance, people with a greater expectation of loss buy insurance, while people with a lower expected value of claims choose not to buy insurance. Moral hazard refers to the tendency of people to exert less care or allocate fewer resources to prevent losses that are insured. **LO3**

- Economic principles can also help to show how different methods of paying for health care affect the efficiency with which medical services are delivered. In the case of health care, the basic asymmetries of information in health care and insurance make a private multi-payer system more expensive than a single payer public system. **LO4**

## KEY TERMS

adverse selection (322)
asymmetric information (317)
better-than-fair gamble (315)
costly-to-fake principle (320)

expected value of a gamble (315)
fair gamble (315)
lemons model (319)
moral hazard (323)

risk-averse person (315)
risk-neutral person (315)
statistical discrimination (322)

## REVIEW QUESTIONS

1. Can it be rational for a consumer to buy a Chevrolet without having first taken test drives in competing models built by Ford, Chrysler, Honda, Toyota, and others? **LO2**

2. Explain why a gallery owner who sells a painting might actually create more economic surplus than the artist who painted it. **LO1**

3. Explain why used cars offered for sale are different, on average, from used cars not offered for sale. **LO3**

4. Explain why the used-car market would be likely to function more efficiently in a community in which

moral norms of honesty are strong than in a community in which such norms are weak. **LO4**

5. Angelo smoked heavily from the time he was 14 years old until he died at the age of 92. He was rarely ill. Insurance companies always quoted Angelo much higher premiums for life insurance than they did for his nonsmoking, male friends who where the same age as he was. Angelo outlived all those friends. Why was Angelo always confronted with higher premiums for life insurance? **LO4**

## PROBLEMS

1. State whether the following are true or false, and briefly explain why: **LO3, LO4**
   a. Depreciation is the sole factor that causes the market value of a two-year-old car to be much lower than it was when the car was in the showroom.
   b. You may not get the optimal level of advice from a retail shop when you go in to buy a lamp for your bike because of the free-rider problem.
   c. If you need a lawyer, and all your legal expenses are covered by insurance, you should *always* choose the best-dressed lawyer with the most expensive car and the most ostentatiously furnished office.
   d. The benefit of searching for a spouse is affected by the size of the community you live in.

2. Consumers know that some fraction $x$ of all new cars produced and sold in the market are defective. The defective ones cannot be identified except by those who own them. Cars do not depreciate with use. Consumers are risk neutral and value non-defective cars at $10 000 each. New cars sell for $5000 and used ones for $2500. What is the fraction $x$? **LO3**

3. Carlos is risk neutral and has an ancient farmhouse with great character for sale near Kingston. His reservation price for the house is $130 000. The only possible local buyer is Whitney, whose reservation price for the house is $150 000. The only other houses on the market are modern ranch houses that sell for $125 000, which is exactly equal to each potential buyer's reservation price for such a house. Suppose that if Carlos does not hire a realtor, Whitney will learn from her neighbour that Carlos's house is for sale, and will buy it for $140 000. However, if Carlos

hires a realtor, he knows that the realtor will put him in touch with an enthusiast for old farmhouses who is willing to pay up to $300 000 for the house. Carlos also knows that if he and this person negotiate, they will agree on a price of $250 000. If realtors charge a commission of 5 percent of the selling price, and all realtors have opportunity costs of $2000 for negotiating a sale, will Carlos hire a realtor? If so, how will total economic surplus be affected? **LO1**

4. Ann and Barbara are computer programmers in Winnipeg who are planning to move to Ottawa. Each owns a house that has just been appraised for $100 000. But whereas Ann's house is one of hundreds of highly similar houses in a large, well-known suburban development, Barbara's is the only one that was built from her architect's design. Who will benefit more by hiring a realtor to assist in selling her house, Ann or Barbara? **LO1**

5. Brokers who sell stocks over the Internet can serve many more customers than those who transact business by mail or over the phone. How will the expansion of Internet access affect the average incomes of stockbrokers who continue to do business in the traditional way? **LO1**

6. Whose income do you predict will be more affected by the expansion of Internet access? **LO1**
   a. stockbrokers or lawyers
   b. doctors or pharmacists
   c. bookstore owners or the owners of galleries that sell original oil paintings

7. How will growing Internet access affect the number of film actors and musicians with active fan clubs? **LO2**

8. Suppose that all four-year-old Miatas available in the used-car market are in either excellent or average condition. Tom is willing to pay $13 000 for one that is in excellent condition, but only $9000 for one that is in average condition. The going price for a four-year-old Miata is $8000. Tom has no way of determining which ones are in excellent condition. He is risk neutral. **LO3, LO4**

a. Suppose 10 percent of all Miatas available for sale are in excellent condition; the rest are in average condition. If Tom purchases a Miata for $8000, what will his economic surplus be? Why?

b. If Tom buys a four-year-old Miata in the used-car market, what is his probability of acquiring one that is in excellent condition? Explain.

c. Suppose that Tom knows his aunt has kept her four-year-old Miata in excellent condition. If she is willing to sell it to Tom at the market price ($8000), what will Tom's economic surplus be? Explain.

d. Suppose a dealership can guarantee that any Miata it sells will be in excellent condition. What is the maximum price that it could charge for a warranty and still sell a four-year-old Miata to Tom? (Assume that his aunt's car is not available.) Explain.

e. If Tom is risk averse, will the maximum price a dealer is able to charge him for a warranty be higher or lower than the price you calculated in your answer for (d)? Why?

## ANSWERS TO IN-CHAPTER EXERCISES

11.1    The probability of getting heads is 0.5, the same as the probability of getting tails. Thus, the expected value of this gamble is $(0.5)(\$4) + (0.5)(-\$2) = \$1$. Since the gamble is better than fair, a risk-neutral person would accept it. **LO3**

11.2    Since you still have a 20 percent chance of finding a cheaper apartment if you make another visit, the expected outcome of the gamble is again $2, and, being risk neutral, you will search again. The bad outcome of any previous search is a sunk cost, and therefore it is irrelevant to your decision about whether to search again. **LO2, LO3**

11.3    The expected value of a new car will now be $0.8(\$10\ 000) + 0.2(\$6000) = \$9200$. Any risk-neutral consumer who believed that the quality distribution of used cars for sale was the same as the quality distribution of new cars off the assembly line would be willing to pay $9200 for a used car. **LO3**

# PART 4

# LABOUR MARKETS
# AND THE PUBLIC SECTOR

The market imperfections discussed in Part 3 help to explain why no country leaves all important economic decisions entirely in the hands of market forces. Recognizing, also, that the real world is a mixed economy, we have to analyze how government decisions affect both the equity and efficiency of economic outcomes. In Chapter 12 we will, therefore, examine the labour market and discuss the human capital model, which emphasizes the importance of investment in education and other skills. We will also discuss discrimination and other reasons why people with similar personal characteristics can earn sharply different incomes. This discussion leads naturally into Chapter 13, Income Distribution, which discusses how to measure the extent of poverty and inequality, recent trends in Canada, and the why and how of what might be done about these. In Chapter 14, we examine government's role more directly: how large government should be, what sorts of goods and services it should provide, and how it should raise the revenue to pay for public expenditure.

# CHAPTER 12
# Labour Markets

In 2010, *Forbes* magazine estimated Lady Gaga's income to be $62 million, placing her fourth in their rankings of the pay of 100 celebrities.[1] Meanwhile, in thousands of bars and night clubs across Canada, aspiring entertainers with only slightly less natural talent (or, some would say, more talent) earned barely enough to cover their expenses. In the 2006 Census, Canadians with a university certificate, diploma, or degree above bachelor level earned an average $69 230—more than twice as much as the average earnings ($30 116) of those with a certificate or diploma below bachelor level, and about three times as much as the average earnings ($22 700) of Canadian artists.[2]

Why do some people earn so much more than others? Why do the more highly educated usually (but not always) earn more than those with less education? Our aim in this chapter is to employ simple economic principles in an attempt to explain why different people earn different salaries. We'll discuss the human capital model, which emphasizes the importance of differences in education and other personal skills. But our focus will be on why people with similar personal characteristics often earn sharply different incomes. Among the factors that we will consider are labour unions, winner-take-all labour markets, discrimination, and the effect of non-wage conditions of employment.

## 12.1 WAGE DETERMINATION IN COMPETITIVE LABOUR MARKETS

In some respects, the sale of human labour is profoundly different from the sale of other goods and services. For example, although someone may legally relinquish all future rights to the use of her television set by selling it, the law does not permit people to sell themselves into slavery. Legally, we can only "rent out" our services to employers.

However, in some key ways, the rental market for labour services functions much like the market for most other goods and services. Supply and demand are crucial concepts that help us understand both the equilibrium wage and the equilibrium quantity of employment for each category of labour. Just as shifts in the demand and supply for other

EQUILIBRIUM

---

1   http://www.limelife.com/blog-entry/Lady-Gaga-Debuts-On-Forbes-Celebrity-Power-List/51729.html.

2   See http://www40.statcan.gc.ca/l01/cst01/labor50a-eng.htm; http://www.hillstrategies.com/docs/Artists_Canada2006.pdf

goods and services help us analyze changes in their prices and quantities, so also shifts in demand and supply of labour can explain changes in both the equilibrium wage and the equilibrium level of employment.

As in our discussions of other markets, we will investigate the labour market using a series of examples. We begin with an example that illustrates the basic benefit-cost calculation which determines the wage an employer will be willing to pay.

## EXAMPLE 12.1

### How much will the potters earn?

Mackintosh Pottery Works is one of numerous identical companies that hire potters who mould clay into pots. These companies sell the pots for $1.10 each to a finishing company that glazes and fires them and then sells them in the retail marketplace. Rennie and Laura are currently the only two potters who work for Mackintosh, whose costs, other than potters' salaries, are 10 cents for clay and all other inputs for each pot it delivers to the finisher. If we assume that this 10 cents completely accounts for the firm's costs of operation (including a "normal profit" sufficient to cover the opportunity cost of the owner's time), then $1.00 is the "net price" the firm gets from each pot produced. If all workers in this industry have the same productivity (e.g., 100 pots per week), competition among firms will produce an equilibrium wage of $100 per week for all workers. If Mackintosh were paying less than this amount, it could expect to lose Rennie and Laura to the competition, since a competing firm could make extra profits by hiring more workers, as long as the wage paid is anything less than $100 weekly. The competition of firms for workers in the labour market would bid up wages until the firm earned only a normal rate of profit, in equilibrium.

In Example 12.1, the number of pots each potter delivered each week is that potter's *marginal physical product,* or *marginal product, MP* for short. A worker's **marginal product** is the extra output the firm gets as a result of hiring that worker. Let us assume that the firm sells in a perfectly competitive product market, so the price that it gets for its output does not change regardless of how much it decides to produce. When we multiply a worker's marginal product by the net price for which each unit of the product sells, we get that worker's **value of marginal product**, or **VMP**. (In Example 12.1, the net price of each pot is $1.00, the difference between the $1.10 sale price and the $0.10 in non-labour costs.) In competitive labour markets where individual output is observable, *competition among employers ensures that a worker's pay in long-run equilibrium will be equal to his or her VMP—the net contribution he or she makes to the employer's revenue.* Employers would be delighted to pay workers less than their respective VMPs, to be sure. But if labour markets are truly competitive and fully informed, firms cannot do so for long, because those that pay less than VMP will find that their workers are hired away by competitors.

Labour markets sometimes function in this manner, but often there are important differences. Because people differ in their skills and abilities, and because those skills and abilities change over time, an individual worker's *quality* often cannot be graded in the same easy, unambiguous way that commodities (such as coal or apples or lumber) can be graded. Information about a worker's output is crucial, but the output of individuals is often difficult to observe directly, particularly if, as is common, they work as part of a team. Furthermore, firms and workers have incentives of their own to not reveal true information. (Everybody, for example, would like to be regarded as "highly productive.").

Imperfect information about a worker's true output and the incentives that firms and workers have to misrepresent that output are two pervasive problems in the labour market. In some cases (e.g., the scoring statistics of NHL hockey players or the batting averages of professional baseball players), it is possible for all potential employers to observe a

**marginal (physical) product of labour (MP)** the additional output a firm gets by employing one additional unit of labour

**value of marginal product of labour (VMP)** the dollar value of the additional output a firm gets by employing one additional unit of labour

worker's production. However, this situation is relatively rare. Usually, it is only a worker's current employer who directly observes her output. Other firms cannot directly know and workers cannot credibly signal exactly how much they personally add to total output.

As a result, firms end up paying a wage that reflects what they *expect* a typical worker's level of output to be, *given* the worker's observable characteristics. In some respects, labour markets function much like the insurance example that we considered in Chapter 11. Recall that insurance companies charge the same premium to all young male drivers with the same observable characteristics. Because no company can directly observe which drivers are reckless and which are careful, insurers have to estimate what the average person of a particular type will do. Similarly, firms have to estimate what workers will produce, based on what they know about them.

Although the firm where a worker is now employed may know quite a bit more about that person than is provided on his resume, that extra information is specific to the firm. Other firms, who might consider hiring that worker away, have much less information and they know that references are often unreliable (it could be in a competitor's interest to give good reference letters to their bad employees in order to export their personnel problems to the competition). Imperfect information thus constrains competitive pressures. Nevertheless, if one firm systematically underpays workers with observable characteristics that accurately predict good productivity, that firm faces the threat that other firms may hire them away.

In Example 12.1, each worker's VMP is independent of the number of other workers employed by the firm. In such cases, we cannot predict how many workers a firm will hire. Mackintosh could make a normal profit with two potters, with 10, or even with 1000 or more. In many other situations, however, we can predict how many workers a firm will want to hire. Consider Example 12.2.

## EXAMPLE 12.2

### How many workers will Abitibi want to hire? (Part 1)

The Abitibi Woodworking Company hires workers to make kitchen cutting boards. Because it uses scrap material from the local sawmill, the cost of its materials is zero. Suppose that Abitibi can hire as many workers as it decides is profitable at the going wage (currently $350/week). If the boards sell for $20 each and if the company's weekly output varies with the number of workers hired as shown in Table 12.1, how many workers will Abitibi want to hire?

**TABLE 12.1**

**Employment and Productivity in a Woodworking Company (when cutting boards sell for $20 each)**

| Number of workers | Total number of cutting boards/week | MP (extra cutting boards/week) | VMP ($/week) |
|---|---|---|---|
| 0 | 0 | | |
| | | 30 | 600 |
| 1 | 30 | | |
| | | 25 | 500 |
| 2 | 55 | | |
| | | 20 | 400 |
| 3 | 75 | | |
| | | 15 | 300 |
| 4 | 90 | | |
| | | 10 | 200 |
| 5 | 100 | | |

We assume here that all workers are of the same type; that is, they are **observationally equivalent**. Although workers may actually differ in productive ability, there is no feasible way for this firm or its competitors to tell those workers apart, so they all get the same wage in the labour market. Hence, the firm faces a fixed market wage for each worker. The fact that the marginal product of labour declines with the number of workers hired is a consequence of diminishing returns. (As discussed in Chapter 5, the law of diminishing marginal returns says that when technology, a firm's capital, and other productive inputs are held fixed in the short run, adding workers beyond some point results in ever smaller increases in output.)

The third column of Table 12.1 reports the Marginal Product (MP) for each additional worker; that is, the benefit to the firm of one more hire (measured in units of output). The far right-hand column reports the Value of Marginal Product (VMP), or each successive worker's addition to total revenue, which is calculated as the added number of cutting boards times the selling price of $20. The VMP is the financial benefit to the firm of one more hire; that is, the benefit measured in dollars rather than in units of output. The cost–benefit principle states that a profit-maximizing firm will increase employment as long as the extra benefit is greater than the extra cost. Hence, if the market wage is $350, Abitibi will hire an additional worker as long as the additional worker's expected benefit (their VMP) is at least equal to the cost of hiring the additional worker. The first three workers have VMPs larger than $350, so Abitibi will hire three employees, but no more. Why? Hiring the fourth worker would add only $300 to weekly revenue, while costing $350 in additional wages. Therefore, Abitibi will not hire the fourth worker.

**observationally equivalent workers** workers of the same type; that is, with the same generally known personal characteristics (age, education, gender, work experience, race, ethnicity, etc.)

Note the similarity between the firm's decision about how many workers to hire and the firm's output decision, which we considered in Chapter 5. When labour is the only variable factor of production, the two decisions are essentially the same. Deciding how many workers to hire implies deciding how much output to supply. In general, a firm's demand for labour is a *derived demand,* which depends on how much the firm decides to produce. If we consider the economy as a whole, the total demand for labour depends on the output decisions of many firms, which, in turn, depend on the sales they expect to make. Thus, the demand for labour is an important topic in both macro and microeconomics. Example 12.3 shows how the level of employment depends on the wage. Example 12.4 illustrates that the benefit to the employer of hiring workers depends not only on how many cutting boards each employee produces but also on the price of cutting boards.

# EXAMPLE **12.3**

### How many workers will Abitibi want to hire? (Part 2)

Now suppose that the cost–benefit calculation of the employer changes on the cost side. Suppose that cutting boards again sell for their original price of $20, but the wage rate of workers is not $350/week but $410/week. If the company's weekly output of cutting boards again varies with the number of workers as shown in Table 12.1, how many workers will it want to hire?

This time, note that although the third worker was an attractive hire at a wage of $350/week, she will not cover her costs at a wage of $410. Her VMP is now smaller than her wage, so the company will hire only two workers. In fact, when the cost of labour changes but the financial benefit to the firm of hiring workers is unchanged, we can use the benefit-cost principle and the VMP calculations in Table 12.1 to trace out the labour demand curve of the firm. Remember that the demand curve for labour represents the amount of labour which a firm would be just willing to hire at each given price for labour. At a wage of $599, Abitibi will find it just worthwhile to hire one worker, since the wage cost ($599) would be just a bit less than the financial benefit (VMP = $600). Similarly, if the wage were $499, Abitibi would just be willing to hire two workers. At a wage of $299, hiring three workers would pass the benefit-cost

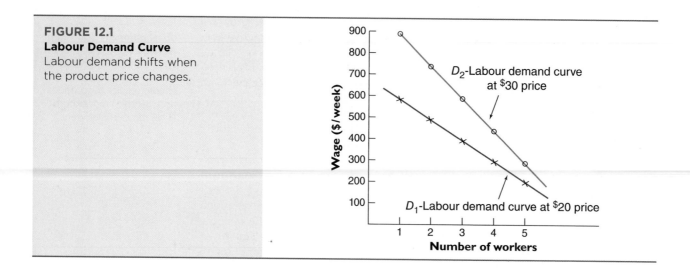

**FIGURE 12.1**
**Labour Demand Curve**
Labour demand shifts when
the product price changes.

test, since the third worker hired would produce additional output that would sell for $300, but the third worker's addition to the firm's costs would be $299. We can plot those points with *xs* in Figure 12.1.

Although the numeric example of Table 12.1 looks just at unit numbers of workers, firms often have a bit more flexibility; for example, sometimes labour can be hired on an hourly basis or for fractions of a workweek. If so, we can trace out the demand curve for labour when the price of cutting boards is $20 to obtain $D_1$ in Figure 12.1. We could equally well have labelled it $VMP_1$, since a competitive firm's demand curve for labour is the same as the firm's value of marginal product of labour. If, for some reason, the wage that Abitibi has to pay for labour changes but the price it receives for its cutting boards is unchanged, then the firm moves *along* its demand curve for labour.

## EXAMPLE 12.4

### How many workers will Abitibi hire? (Part 3)

Refer back to Example 12.2. Suppose that the demand curve for cutting boards shifts up. (Perhaps a celebrity chef endorses stir-fry on TV, and finely chopped vegetables suddenly become fashionable.) This increase in demand means that the selling price of cutting boards suddenly rises from $20 to $30. If the wage rate and marginal product are as before, how many workers will Abitibi now hire?

As shown in the last column of Table 12.2, the 15 cutting boards produced by the fourth worker now add (15)($30) = $450 to weekly revenue. If her wage is only $350, the company will make money by hiring her.

Because the price of a cutting board has increased from $20 to $30, the benefit of hiring labour has changed. Therefore, we must recalculate the numbers that are the basis for the demand curve for labour. To see this, refer to the VMP column in Table 12.2. At a wage of $899, Abitibi would now find it just worthwhile to hire one worker, since the wage cost ($899) would be just a bit less than the financial benefit (VMP = $900). Similarly, if the wage were $749, Abitibi would just be willing to hire two workers. At a wage of $599, hiring three workers would just pass the benefit-cost test. As before, we can plot those points in Figure 12.1—this time with *os*. If, again, labour can be hired for fractions of a workweek, with a cutting board price of $30 we could trace out the firm's demand curve for labour (i.e. the competitive firm's VMP) and plot it as $D_2$ in Figure 12.1. If, for some reason, the price that Abitibi receives for its cutting boards changes, its demand curve for labour *shifts*; in this case, from $D_1$ to $D_2$.

**TABLE 12.2**
**The Effect of an Increase in the Price of Cutting Boards on Employment**

| Number of workers | Total number of cutting boards/week | MP (extra cutting boards/week) | VMP ($/week) |
|---|---|---|---|
| 0 | 0 | | |
| | | 30 | 900 |
| 1 | 30 | | |
| | | 25 | 750 |
| 2 | 55 | | |
| | | 20 | 600 |
| 3 | 75 | | |
| | | 15 | 450 |
| 4 | 90 | | |
| | | 10 | 300 |
| 5 | 100 | | |

**In Example 12.4, what is the lowest cutting board price at which Abitibi will hire two workers?**

EXERCISE 12.1

**In Example 12.4, how many workers would Abitibi hire if the wage rate were $275/week?**

EXERCISE 12.2

**RECAP**

**WAGE AND SALARY DETERMINATION IN COMPETITIVE LABOUR MARKETS**

In competitive labour markets, employers face pressure to pay the typical worker the expected value of his or her marginal product. When a firm can hire as many workers as it wants at a given market wage, it will increase employment as long as the value of marginal product of labour exceeds the market wage. In a competitive labour market in which the firm can hire all the labour it needs at a constant wage, the firm's demand curve for labour is the firm's marginal value product of labour.

# 12.2   MONOPSONY AND IMPERFECT COMPETITION IN LABOUR MARKETS

In perfectly competitive product markets, sellers have no control over product prices. Market supply and demand curves intersect, and firms take the resulting prices as given. Similarly, in perfectly competitive labour markets, firms have no control over wage rates. The wage in each market is completely determined by supply and demand. In Examples 12.2 to 12.4, Abitibi Woodworking was a buyer in a perfectly competitive labour market. The supply curve of labour facing such an employer is perfectly elastic—a horizontal line at the market wage.

**monopsony** a market
with only a single buyer

Let's now go to the other extreme and examine a firm (Bluenose Woodworking) that is just like Abitibi, except that it is a **monopsony**; that is, the only buyer of labour services in its local labour market. The labour supply curve facing the company is now the labour supply curve for the market as a whole. There is no market wage per se. Workers are paid whatever Bluenose chooses to offer. But Bluenose also knows that if its offer is extremely low, workers may decide to relocate, or they may stop working. Even so, Bluenose has some discretion about the wage it pays. In general, the more workers the company wants to hire, the more it will have to pay each worker. How much will it pay its workers and how many will it hire?

In many ways, the problem facing the monopsonist (the only buyer) is similar to that facing a monopolist (the only seller). When a monopoly firm is the only seller in a product market, its demand curve for the product is the same as the demand curve for the market as a whole, so the only way the monopolist can increase its sales is by reducing its price. Similarly, when a monopsony firm is the only buyer of labour in a labour market, the supply curve of labour confronting the monopsonist is the supply curve for the local labour market as a whole, so the only way the monopsonist can hire additional workers is by offering higher wages. But raising the wage for an additional worker generally means also having to raise the wage for the workers hired earlier. And as Example 12.5 illustrates, this implies that the monopsonist has an incentive to limit employment, much as the monopolist has an incentive to limit output.

## EXAMPLE **12.5**

### How many workers will Bluenose hire? (Part 4)

The Bluenose Woodworking Company is the only employer in a small town in rural Nova Scotia. It sells kitchen cutting boards for $30 each, and its weekly output again varies with the number of workers in exactly the same way as for Abitibi, as shown in Example 12.3. If there are five workers that Bluenose might hire within commuting range, if the smallest payment each would accept for the job (each one's "reservation wage") is as shown in Table 12.3, and if Bluenose must pay each worker the same wage, how many workers will it hire?

**TABLE 12.3**
**Reservation Wages for the Monopsonist's Potential Employees**

| Worker | Reservation wage ($/week) |
|---|---|
| Alisha | 100 |
| Bertram | 300 |
| Carrie | 500 |
| Donna | 700 |
| Ernesto | 900 |

**marginal labour cost** the
amount by which a firm's
total wage bill goes up if it
hires an extra worker

For the monopolist in the product market, recall that the decision rule is to sell another unit if marginal revenue (the amount by which its total revenue increases when it sells an extra unit) exceeds marginal cost. For the monopsonist in the labour market, the corresponding rule is to hire another worker if that worker's VMP exceeds **marginal labour cost**—the amount by which the total wage bill of the monopsony firm would increase if it hired the extra worker. Marginal labour cost in this example is shown in the second last column of Table 12.4. (Again, we assume that the monopsonist does not know each worker's reservation wage and must, therefore, pay each worker the same wage.)

**TABLE 12.4**
Calculating Marginal Labour Cost for the Monopsonist

| Worker | Reservation wage ($/week) | Total labour cost ($/week) | Marginal labour cost ($/week) | VMP ($/week) |
|---|---|---|---|---|
| None | — | 0 | | |
| | | | 100 | 900 |
| Alisha | 100 | 100 | | |
| | | | 500 | 750 |
| Bertram | 300 | 600 | | |
| | | | 900 | 600 |
| Carrie | 500 | 1500 | | |
| | | | 1300 | 450 |
| Donna | 700 | 2800 | | |
| | | | 1700 | 300 |
| Ernesto | 900 | 4500 | | |

Figure 12.2 graphs the numbers we have presented in Tables 12.2, 12.3, and 12.4. The figure's blue line, labelled VMP, plots the last column of Tables 12.2 and 12.4 (the value of marginal product) and illustrates that, as more workers are added to the production line at Bluenose, the increase in output resulting from each additional worker declines.

The red line labelled $SS_L$ plots the supply curve of labour; that is, the number of workers who would be willing to supply their labour at a given wage. Point A shows that Alisha is willing to work at a wage of $100, while both Alisha and Bertram are willing to work at point B, at a wage of $300. At point C, with a wage of $500, Alisha, Bertram, and Carrie will want to work.

Because it is a monopsonistic employer, Bluenose knows that if it offers a wage of $100, the only worker it will attract is Alisha. If the company also wants to hire a second worker (who will be Bertram, the only additional person willing to work for

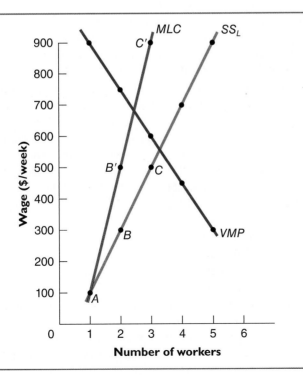

**FIGURE 12.2**
**Labour Supply and Marginal Labour Cost for a Monopsonist**
The line labelled $SS_L$ plots the number of workers willing to supply labour at a given wage, while line MLC indicates the increase in total labour cost associated with hiring each additional employee. The line labelled VMP illustrates that as more workers are added, the increase in total value of output from hiring each additional worker declines.

$300), it must not only pay him $200/week more than it is currently paying Alisha, but it must also raise Alisha's pay to $300/week. (Note again the importance of information. Each person knows his or her own reservation wage, but the firm does not. Obviously, individual workers like Alisha have no incentive to tell firms the minimum wage they would accept.) Thus, as Table 12.4 shows, the company's total labour cost will go from $100 to $600/week if it hires Bertram. Therefore, the marginal labour cost of hiring Bertram is $500/week. We can plot this as point *B'* in Figure 12.2.

The third employee (who would be Carrie) will cost Bluenose $500 in personal wages. However, if the firm cannot be sure that Alisha and Bertram would work for less than Carrie, it must pay all three the same wage of $900, so total pay rises to $1500. The increase in total labour cost caused by going from two to three workers is $600, which we can plot as point *C'* in Figure 12.2. The grey line labelled *MLC* (marginal labour cost) corresponds to the marginal labour cost associated with hiring one, two, or three workers.

How many workers will Bluenose hire? Since Bertram's *VMP* is $750/week, and hiring him increases labour costs by less than that ($500), hiring him is clearly in Bluenose's interest. Carrie is not a worthwhile hire because her marginal labour cost is $900/week, which exceeds her *VMP* of $600. So even though Carrie's reservation wage of $500 is less than her *VMP*, the cost–benefit principle tells us that Bluenose will do better by not hiring her. Thus, the company will hire only two workers, Alisha and Bertram, and pay each a wage of $300/week.

COST-
BENEFIT

**EXERCISE 12.3**    **In Example 12.5, how many workers will Bluenose hire if cutting boards sell for $50?**

In Chapter 8, we saw that a monopolist produces too little output (compared to the output level that would maximize total surplus) because price exceeds marginal revenue. A similar result occurs with a monopsonist in the labour market. In Example 12.5, note that Bluenose, the monopsony firm, has the same *VMP* schedule as its perfectly competitive counterpart, Abitibi, in Example 12.4 (Table 12.2). In the situation outlined in Figure 12.2, both companies *could* hire three workers at a wage of $500/week. Yet the monopsonist hires one less worker than its perfectly competitive counterpart. With only two workers on the monopsonist's payroll, the *social* cost of adding another worker is just the third worker's reservation wage, namely, $500. Because the third worker would add 20 cutting boards at $30 each to the weekly production total, the gain in total revenue is $600. Therefore, society would gain output worth $100 more than the social cost of hiring the third worker. Yet the monopsonist does not hire a third worker, because the private cost (marginal labour cost) of doing so is $900.

For the monopsonist, the private cost of an additional hire is greater than the social cost of that hire, so the monopsonist hires too few workers and produces too little. The discrepancy occurs because each new hire necessitates paying existing workers more. Although the monopsonist understandably views the increase in the total wage bill as a real cost, from society's perspective a higher wage bill for the firm is merely a transfer from the monopsonist to the existing workforce (who would see it as a benefit).

Both monopolists (in product markets) and monopsonists (in labour markets) have some *market power*; that is, some latitude in naming the price charged for output, or paid for inputs. The monopolist chooses the profit-maximizing point on its product demand curve, and the monopsonist chooses the profit maximizing point on its input supply curve. In both cases, the result is a level of output and employment that is less than socially optimal.

As we saw in Chapter 8, pure monopoly in product markets—only one seller, with no substitutes—is the extreme case. Imperfect competition among only a few sellers is more common. Similarly, imperfect competition among employers is much more common in practice than pure monopsony. The classic examples of monopsony in labour markets—for example, the pulp mill or mine or fish plant that is the only employer in an isolated community—are not as common now as they were in the past. A greater proportion of workers now live in cities, giving them more choice of employers within commuting distance of their homes. Nevertheless, few firms would lose *all* their workers if their wages were a bit lower; that is, few firms face a *perfectly* elastic supply curve of labour. Within specific geographical markets for specific types of labour, imperfect competition on the input side in labour markets is often a question of degree, and each firm typically has to make decisions on what wage to offer, knowing that this decision will affect the number and quality of job applicants it can attract.

---

**RECAP**

**MONOPSONY**

Unlike the perfectly competitive employer, which can hire as much labour as it wants at the market wage, the monopsonist can expand employment only by offering higher wages. And unlike the perfectly competitive employer, which continues hiring only until *VMP* equals the market wage, the monopsonist continues hiring until *VMP* equals marginal labour cost, which exceeds the market wage. The profit-maximizing employment level for the monopsonist is lower than the level that would maximize total economic surplus.

---

## 12.3 DEMAND AND SUPPLY IN COMPETITIVE LABOUR MARKETS

An employer's reservation price for a worker in a perfectly competitive labour market is simply *VMP*, the value of the worker's marginal product. Because of diminishing marginal returns, the marginal product of labour, and hence *VMP*, declines in the short run as the quantity of labour employed rises. The individual employer's demand curve for labour in any particular occupation may thus be shown, as in Figure 12.3(a), as a downward-sloping function of the wage rate. When several firms are in the same labour market, we can add up the number of workers each would like to hire at any given wage to get the total demand for labour. For example, if firm 1 [panel (a)] and firm 2 [panel (b)] are two firms that employ computer programmers in a given community, the demand for programmers in that community will then be the horizontal sum of the individual firms' demands [panel (c)].

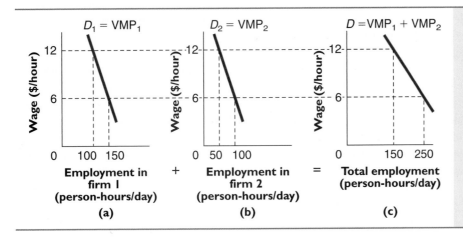

**FIGURE 12.3**

**The Occupational Demand for Labour**

If firm 1 and firm 2 are firms that employ labour in a given occupation, we generate the demand curve for labour in that occupation by adding the individual demand curves horizontally.

So far, we have only looked at the demand side of labour markets—how many workers each firm would like to employ, at any given wage. But whenever we observe somebody working, we necessarily observe the joint outcome of *two* decisions: (1) a firm's decision to offer a job and (2) a person's decision to accept the job. If we want to understand labour market outcomes, we always have to look at both decisions and examine *both* the demand for labour by firms and the supply of labour by individuals.

For the labour market as a whole, the "supply curve" of labour is the total number of hours that workers want to work, at any given wage. One can think of this at various levels of aggregation; for example, the total number of hours that workers would like to work, for a particular wage, in a given country **or** in a specific city **or** at a particular firm **or** in a particular occupation. We also need to specify the unit of time over which work hours are supplied; for example, hours per week, hours per year, or lifetime hours of work.

The big, long-term trends for Canadian males have been a tendency to stay in school longer and retire earlier.[3] Added together, the result is a decrease in their lifetime supply of paid labour. Canadian women now supply many more hours to the paid labour market over their lifetimes than previously. Until the 1950s, most women withdrew from paid employment after marriage. Today, this is rare. Women's participation in the labour market rose dramatically between the 1960s and 1990s in Canada and is increasingly similar to the labour force participation of men.

Overall, the increase in female labour supply has been greater than the decline in male labour supply, so the aggregate labour force participation rate in Canada has increased. Furthermore, the decline in male labour supply has been concentrated in the under-25 and over-54 age groups. From a family perspective, that implies that middle-aged Canadian families, many of whom have young children, are now generally supplying the labour of two people to the paid labour market while still having to do the unpaid household tasks that have always been there. This combination of greater paid labour supply by families and continuing unpaid household chores generates the time crunch that so many families feel.

## 12.4  EQUILIBRIUM—SUPPLY AND DEMAND

If we examine the labour market for a particular occupation, such as computer programming, the supply of labour is almost always upward sloping because wage differences among occupations influence occupational choice. If we assume that wages in other potential occupations are fixed, then higher wages can be expected to induce more people in other occupations to shift to work in programming. Thus, the supply curve will slope up. Curve $S$ in Figure 12.4 represents the supply curve of computer programmers.

However, the actual wage at any point in time will depend on the intersection of demand and supply. Suppose, for example, that as more tasks become computerized, the demand for programmers grows, as shown by the shift from $D_1$ to $D_2$ in Figure 12.4. Equilibrium in the market for computer programmers occurs at the intersection of the relevant supply and demand curves. A shift in demand from $D_1$ to $D_2$ leads to an increase in the equilibrium level of employment from $L_1$ to $L_2$ and an increase in the equilibrium wage from $W_1$ to $W_2$.

As discussed in Chapter 7, markets differ in the time it takes to reach equilibrium in the wake of shifts in the underlying supply and demand curves. Labour markets are often very slow to adjust. It takes quite a while to learn the skills required to be a good cabinet-maker or computer programmer or geologist. When the demand for workers in a given profession increases, shortages may remain for months or years, depending on how long it takes people to recognize the change and then to acquire the skills and training needed to enter the profession. (And some labour markets are highly regulated: e.g., physicians.)

---

3  The average retirement age for Canadian men was 65.3 in 1976, declining to 61.6 in 1998, but increasing slightly to 62.8 in 2010. See *CANSIM* series V2342638.

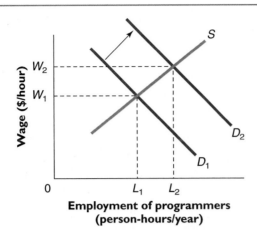

**FIGURE 12.4**
**The Effect of a Shift in the Demand for Computer Programmers**
An increase in the demand for programmers that shifts the demand curve from $D_1$ to $D_2$ results in an increase in the equilibrium level of employment (from $L_1$ to $L_2$) and an increase in the equilibrium wage (from $W_1$ to $W_2$).

By contrast, it does not take very long to train people how to operate the cash register in a grocery store or how to flip hamburgers. Low-skill labour markets, therefore, tend to adjust more quickly than specialized labour markets. As our economy shifts toward more specialized and more highly skilled occupations, the problem of adjustment time increases in importance.

**RECAP**↑

### EQUILIBRIUM IN THE LABOUR MARKET

The demand for labour in a perfectly competitive labour market is the horizontal sum of each employer's *VMP* curve. The supply curve of labour for an individual labour market is typically upward sloping. In each labour market, demand and supply both influence the observed wage rate and level of employment.

## 12.5 EQUILIBRIUM AND UNEMPLOYMENT

The interplay of the demand for labour by firms and the supply of labour by individuals may determine the equilibrium level of wages and employment, but that does not mean that there is no *unemployment*.

Statistics Canada uses what is known as the "search activity" criterion for counting unemployment. Every month, Statistics Canada's *Labour Force Survey* asks a representative sample of Canadians if they have a job. If they do not have a job, the interviewer asks whether they have looked for work in the last month. Jobless individuals who have actively looked for work are classified as *unemployed*, but people who did not look for work and those who have given up looking for work are both labelled *not in the labour force*.

COST-
BENEFIT

In real-world labour markets, there is continual change and turnover. When, for example, a new business opens, job vacancies are created. When existing firms cease operations, the laid-off workers have to look for new jobs. When students leave school, they become job seekers, and when experienced workers retire, vacancies are created. If we all had perfect information, job seekers might all be able to instantaneously match themselves up with the most appropriate job vacancies, but as we saw in Chapter 11, imperfect information is a fact of life.

As we noted in Chapter 11, Peter Diamond, Dale Mortensen, and Christopher Pissarides shared the 2010 Nobel Prize in Economics for their work on labour market matching under imperfect information. Typically, firms do not just fill every vacancy with the first person who applies, and job seekers may not necessarily accept the first offer of employment they get. For both firms and workers, a cost–benefit calculation will determine a reasonable amount of effort and time to invest in search. But job search does take time, and during that time a jobless individual who is looking for work is classified as *unemployed.*

Because there is, even in long-run equilibrium, continual turnover of job vacancies and job holders, and because job search takes time, labour market statistics distinguish between the *employed* (those who have jobs) and the *labour force (*those who have jobs *plus* those who are looking for jobs—the unemployed).[4] Strictly speaking, we probably should think of the supply curve of labour in terms of the labour force; that is, the number of people who want employment at a given wage (which is equal to the number of unemployed plus the number of employed).

In order to get aggregate national numbers on employment and unemployment, Statistics Canada has to add up the statistics from local labour markets in different parts of the country—some of which may reflect unique local realities. If a car assembly plant closes in Ontario at the same time as a mine opens in Labrador, the location and the skills of the job vacancies and the job seekers do not match up—in this example, the laid-off auto workers are said to be *structurally unemployed.* Seasonal jobs in tourism, agriculture or retail sales (e.g., ski lift attendants in Banff, or grape pickers in the Okanogan) come with the implication that the people hired have to look for other work in the off season. If this work is not available, *seasonal* unemployment is the result.

Understanding unemployment is a key issue in economics. The level of *frictional (search) unemployment* is determined by the time it takes workers to locate vacancies in their local labour market, while *structural unemployment* increases if more rapid technical or market changes increase the mismatch between the skills and location of available workers and existing job vacancies. At different times of the year, predictable short-term changes can affect both labour supply and demand (e.g., retail stores often hire staff to help with the Christmas-sales rush, and lay them off after January sales), giving rise to *seasonal unemployment.* When a recession hits—for example, following the financial crisis of 2008—the fact that some firms are laying off workers and few firms are hiring creates *cyclical unemployment,* which declines as the economy recovers from the recession. These issues are dealt with in more detail in the study of macroeconomics, a good reason to take "Principles of Macroeconomics," the companion to this course!

## 12.6  EXPLAINING DIFFERENCES IN EARNINGS

We often see large salary differences even between people who appear equally talented and hard-working. Why, for example, do lawyers earn so much more than plumbers who are just as smart and work just as hard? And why do surgeons earn so much more than general practitioners?

---

4  The *unemployment rate* is the number of unemployed as a percentage of the labour force.

## HUMAN CAPITAL THEORY

One explanation is suggested by the **human capital theory**, which holds that an individual's *VMP* is proportional to his or her stock of **human capital**—the skills produced by education, experience, and training that affect a worker's marginal product. According to this theory, some occupations pay better than others because they require larger stocks of human capital. For example, a general practitioner could become a surgeon, but only by extending her formal education by several years, so surgeons are paid more than GPs. Similarly, more years of education are required to become a lawyer than to become a secretary.

In general, a decision to invest in human capital, like decisions to invest in other assets, requires comparing costs incurred in the present with benefits received in the future. As Example 12.6 illustrates, intelligent decisions of this sort require us to determine the present value of any payments received or expenditures made in the future.

**human capital theory**
a theory of pay determination stating that a worker's wage will be proportional to his or her stock of human capital

**human capital** the skills produced by education, training, and experience that affect a worker's marginal product

### EXAMPLE **12.6**

#### Will Mary be better off if she gets an MA?

Mary is 22 years old and has just graduated with a BA in economics. She now has a job as a local manager for a major corporation. However, she knows that her opportunities for promotion are limited and if she were to go back to school and get an MA in economics, she would be eligible for a better paying job as a financial analyst. She is certain she can pass all her MA courses and that after she graduates, she would get the same level of job satisfaction from her new job as from her current job.

If Mary goes back to school, she will have to pay $8000 per year for tuition and books. She will also have to pay rent for an apartment and buy groceries, but she would have to do this whether she goes back to school or not. Because these costs are the same regardless of her decision, they cannot be counted as a cost of the MA. Out-of-pocket costs of the MA are therefore $8000 per year for two years. In addition, she would have to forego her current earnings while in school.[5] Foregone earnings are a classic example of *opportunity cost*, since Mary cannot both go back to school full-time and continue to receive her current pay cheque.

Since she has to pay the costs of tuition and books right away and has to forego salary, Mary faces an expensive decision. She knows that it will take a while for her earnings as a financial analyst to recoup her investment in a Master's degree. The question is, do the future benefits repay the early costs? Is the investment in an MA worth it?

## DISCOUNTING AND PRESENT VALUE

Because Mary wants to compare the value of receipts and payments that are received or paid at different times in the future, she needs to make these money values comparable. Having $100 today is not the same as having $100 one year from now, because if you have $100 today you could always invest it and earn a rate of interest for the next year. To compare payments at different points in time, Mary has to calculate the value of those payments at a single point in time.

Suppose that, like most people, Mary is impatient. Suppose, to be specific, that a dollar she receives a year from now is worth about the same to her as 90 cents available right now. In economics jargon, we say she has a "discount rate" of about 11 percent[6] on the

---

5  To keep this example simple, we assume Mary is not eligible for any scholarships, nor does she get any assistance from her family. In reality, both are important, since most universities offer scholarships to some of their MA students and parents often provide financial assistance for their children's education. (If parental transfers are really contingent on school attendance, they are, like scholarships, a reduction in the cost to the student of school attendance, but only if parents would not have given their children the same money regardless of whether they are students.)

6  10/90 = 11 percent.

value of income one year in the future. And this discount rate compounds in impact: a dollar received two years from now is only worth about 81 cents [(0.9)(0.9) = 0.81] to Mary today, because it involves a wait of a year followed by another wait of a year. A dollar received three years from now is worth even less [(0.9)(0.9)(0.9) = 0.729] to Mary since she has to wait three years to use that dollar. Since the return from an MA is spread over many years, Mary wants to know how much each future payment or receipt would be worth today (after discounting for the delay in receiving it). To get the total value of her investment in an MA, Mary has to add up all her costs and benefits over the near future to get a total *net present value*. If she does not calculate net present value, she cannot know the value of her investment.

Mary can make this calculation a little easier by constructing a table such as Table 12.5. To keep things simple, this table only goes up to age 30. A more realistic version of Table 12.5 would profile earnings through Mary's entire working life. However, with a discount rate as high as Mary's, earnings differences later in life will make little difference to the calculation.

**TABLE 12.5**
**Mary's Choice: MA or Not?**

| | Cash Flow | | | | |
|---|---|---|---|---|---|
| | As local manager ($) | As financial analyst ($) | Net difference ($) | Discount factor ($) | Present value ($) |
| Age | (a) | (b) | (c)= (b) − (a) | (d) | (e) = (c) × (d) |
| 22 | 35 000 | −8000 | −43 000 | 1 | −43 000 |
| 23 | 35 000 | −8000 | −43 000 | 0.9 | −38 700 |
| 24 | 40 000 | 40 000 | 0 | 0.81 | 0 |
| 25 | 40 000 | 50 000 | 10 000 | 0.73 | 7300 |
| 26 | 45 000 | 60 000 | 15 000 | 0.66 | 9900 |
| 27 | 45 000 | 70 000 | 25 000 | 0.59 | 14 750 |
| 28 | 45 000 | 80 000 | 35 000 | 0.53 | 18 550 |
| 29 | 45 000 | 90 000 | 45 000 | 0.48 | 21 600 |
| 30 | 45 000 | 100 000 | 55 000 | 0.43 | 23 650 |
| | | | | Total | 14 050 |

In Table 12.5, column (a) reports the after-tax earnings Mary expects if she sticks with her current job. She can expect her salary to go up a little, but then stall at $45 000. Column (b) is her after-tax cash flow if she chooses the MA option; note that it involves two years of cash deficit (−$8000) followed by rapid increases. The next column reports (b) − (a) or the *net* cost or benefit, in that year, of choosing the MA option. For the first two years, the net cost of an MA is the cost of tuition and books, *plus* the opportunity cost of her time—the earnings Mary will forego if she returns to school. In year three, earnings are the same in either option, so the net gain is zero. After that, her earnings as a financial analyst rise much more rapidly than if she had not chosen to do an MA in economics, so the net benefit of choosing the MA option increases over time. (The *net* advantages of choosing the MA option are the earnings Mary gets as a financial analyst *minus the opportunity cost of her time*.)

Figures 12.5(a) and (b) present graphs that make the same points visually by plotting the first three columns of Table 12.5. In panel (a), Mary's cash flow as a BA graduate is the blue line and her cash flow from the MA option (the out-of-pocket costs of returning to school and subsequent earnings as a financial analyst) is the red line. Since the first two

## ECONOMIC NATURALIST 12.1

### What is the present value of *your* financial return from attending university?

Table 12.5 presents a hypothetical example of a fictitious choice by an imaginary person, but you could use the same format to analyze the real choice (to attend university) of a real person (you). If you fill in column (a) with your best estimate of the after-tax earnings that you could have expected if you had not gone to university, and fill in column (b) with your best estimate of your earnings after university, it is straightforward to calculate the net difference in cash flow, as in column (c). To help with the calculation of present value, use a spreadsheet program like Excel, and notice that using a spreadsheet makes it very easy to change your assumptions and to see how much any such changes in assumptions actually matter. (Spreadsheet programs like Excel also contain pre-written functions to calculate present value at whatever rate of interest you think is appropriate. If you experiment with different rates of discount, you can also see how sensitive your conclusion about the net present value of university education is to the choice of discount rate.) Why not give it a try?

years of her MA involve a cash deficit, the red line is in negative territory until Mary is 23, but, as panel (a) indicates, it is important to focus on the *difference* between earnings streams. Panel (b), therefore, plots the third column from Table 12.5 to show how a period of initial costs is followed by long-term benefits. But the question still remains: is the investment in education worth it? Are the benefits greater than the costs?

To keep things simple, we'll assume that all receipts and payments in a year are made at the start of the year. Nevertheless, Mary still incurs the costs now and receives the benefits later. As already noted, Mary considers a dollar received one year from now to be worth about 90 cents today. From her perspective, a payment made or received two years in the future is worth about 90 percent of the 90 percent that remains after one year. Column (d) of Table 12.5 calculates the implications of Mary's approximately 11 percent discount rate for payments made two, three, four, and more years into the future.

Column (e) of Table 12.5 pulls things together. It multiplies the current dollar cost or benefit of choosing the MA option in each future year, column (c), by the discount factor, column (d), to get the *present value* of the costs or benefits of the MA option in that particular year. Because Mary values a dollar received in the present at more than a dollar received in the future, as far as she is concerned, the **present value** of one dollar either received or paid in the future is less than one dollar. When Mary says that $1 received a year from now is, in her view, worth 90 cents received today (i.e., she is indifferent between $1 in one year and 90 cents now), the discount (10 cents), as a fraction of today's value (90 cents), is approximately 11 percent $= 10/90$.[7] Economists call this Mary's discount rate (i.e., the annual rate at which Mary discounts the future).

If she gets an MA, Mary can make over twice as much at age 30 as a senior analyst than as a local manager ($100,000 compared with $45 000). However, she also recognizes that she has to wait quite a while for that payoff, and that she should only count the *net* benefits of her choice. How much are the added earnings of $55 000 at age 30 worth to her today? If her discount rate on the future is 11 percent per year and she has to wait eight years, the additional earnings she will get at age 30 have a present value to Mary of $23,650 at age 22.

Of course, earnings at age 30 are only part of the story. Mary also has to consider the net costs and net benefits of choosing the MA option in each intervening year. She has to add up the present value of all future years, column (e), to find out whether her

**present value** the current value of an amount paid or received in the future; preferring current consumption to future consumption means a payment or receipt that occurs in the future will be discounted to a present value

---

7  If we know the discount rate, call it "r," we can compute the *discount factor*, call it "D." The discount factor is a coefficient necessary to calculate the present value of a payment at some particular number of years, called *t*, in the future. The discount factors given in Table 12.5 are approximations. See Appendix 12A for the exact formula for calculating a discount factor (*D*).

**FIGURE 12.5**
**The Returns of an MA in Economics**
Costs are incurred during the period an MA is being acquired. Once acquired, the MA provides benefits.

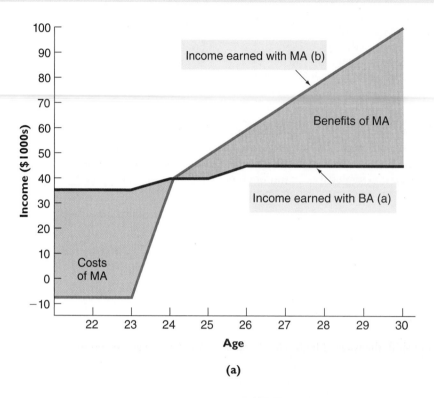

(a)

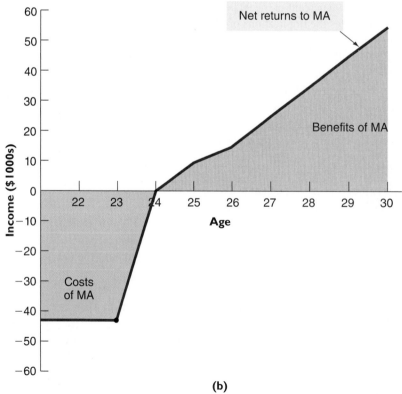

(b)

investment in a MA is worthwhile financially. The total is called the *net present value* of her investment, which in this case is +$14 050. Since a positive net present value means that the benefits of the investment outweigh the costs, Mary concludes that it is financially worthwhile to get an MA, recognizing that three variables drive her calculations:

1. Costs = opportunity cost (foregone earnings) + out-of-pocket cost (how much she gives up by choosing to invest in education),
2. Benefits = the additional salary Mary forecasts that she will earn if she chooses to invest in an MA (these benefits have to be discounted to reflect the time she has to wait before she receives the additional salary), and
3. Discount rate = how impatient she is in waiting for future returns.

In the human capital perspective, a society`s supply of skills is, in the long run, driven by many millions of people making calculations such as Mary's. If there is a substantial net return to more education (in the sense of a positive net present value, obtained by adding up appropriately discounted earnings over all future years), the human capital approach forecasts that the supply of more highly educated labour will increase. It will increase because high school graduates will decide to go to university, and university graduates will decide to go to graduate school, and so on.

If the supply of post-secondary graduates increases because high school graduates enroll in post-secondary schools, there will be fewer people who only have a high school education. Hence, the supply of high school graduates to the labour market will fall. As more people decide to continue in school, the supply curve of post-secondary graduates to the labour market shifts to the right and the supply curve of high school graduates shifts to the left. Figure 12.6 illustrates the process. Assuming the demand curves for both types of labour do not shift, the wage of high school graduates will tend to go up and the wage of post-secondary graduates will tend to go down. Both tendencies will narrow the differential between post-secondary and high school wages, and the differential will continue to narrow as increasingly more people go on to higher education. These narrowing differentials will decrease the incentive for people to continue their educations, but as long as there is a positive net present value from the decision, people will invest in more education. The final equilibrium occurs where the wage advantage of university graduates is just sufficient to repay the total costs of their investment in skills.

In this final equilibrium, the average level of earnings is higher because more people now earn the higher wages associated with post-secondary education. There still is a difference in pay between post-secondary and high school graduates, but the inequality of annual earnings is now less than previously because that differential is smaller.

The policy implication is that if governments can increase the supply of skills, Canadians will have both higher average income and less inequality. Because individuals will respond to changes in the costs as well as in the benefits of further education or training, governments can influence this calculation by providing low-interest student

www.statcan.gc.ca
Statistics Canada

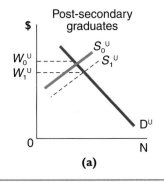

(a)

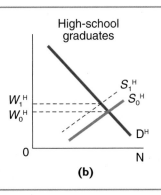

(b)

**FIGURE 12.6**

**Wage Effects of an Increase in Post-Secondary Enrollment**

An increase in the supply of post-secondary graduates reduces the wage gap between high-school and post-secondary graduates.

loans or scholarships or by reducing the out-of-pocket cost of post-secondary education (like tuition). In most European countries, for example, university tuition is either free or a nominal amount.[8]

EXERCISE 12.4

**Refer to Example 12.6. If Mary had been indifferent between getting an MA or not at a discount rate of 11 percent, which option will she choose if the discount rate is 12 percent?**

## LABOUR UNIONS

**labour union** a group of workers who bargain collectively with employers for better wages and working conditions

Two workers with the same amount of human capital may earn different wages if one of them belongs to a *labour union* and the other does not. A **labour union** is an organization through which workers attempt to bargain collectively with employers for better wages and working conditions.

The impact of a union on wages can be analyzed by using the simple model of monopoly developed in Chapter 8. However, the simple monopoly model of unionization focuses solely on the reduced quantity of labour and higher wage rate that unionization would imply. This leaves unexplained the fact that although unionized firms pay their employees more, unionized and non-unionized firms often manage to compete directly for extended periods of time. If their total costs were significantly higher, how could the unionized firms manage to survive?

Wages paid to workers in a unionized firm are sometimes 50 percent or more above the wages paid to their non-unionized counterparts. But this difference overstates the difference between the labour costs of the two types of firms. Because the higher union wage attracts an excess supply of workers, unionized employers can adopt more stringent hiring requirements than their non-unionized counterparts. As a result, unionized workers tend to be more experienced and skilled than non-unionized workers. Studies estimate that the union wage premium for workers with the same amount of human capital is considerably less than the apparent average wage differential—perhaps only about 10 percent.

Unions also have a number of other implications that may lessen their overall impact on labour costs. Labour turnover is significantly lower in unionized firms, which reduces hiring and training costs. If the implementation of formal grievance procedures in combination with higher pay boosts morale among unionized workers, and if that leads to higher productivity, these productivity gains may also offset some of the premium in union wages.[9] In Canada, the unionization rate has decreased slightly over time, falling from 33.7 percent in 1997 to 31.4 percent in 2009, but it remains quite different from the US rate of 11.9 percent.[10]

## WINNER-TAKE-ALL MARKETS

Differences in human capital do much to explain observed differences in earnings. Yet earnings differentials have also grown sharply in many occupations within which the distribution of human capital among workers seems essentially unchanged. Consider the example provided in Economic Naturalist 12.2.

**winner-take-all labour market** a market in which small differences in human capital translate into large differences in pay

The market for singers is an example of a **winner-take-all labour market**, one in which small differences in ability or other dimensions of human capital translate into large differences in pay. Long familiar in entertainment and professional sports, this reward pattern may be becoming more common in other professions, as technology enables the most talented individuals to serve broader markets. A winner-take-all market does not

---

8  See "Tuition Fees in Europe 2010/2011," at www.cesifo-group.de/DocDL/dicereport111-db6.pdf.

9  A classic study is R. Freeman and J. Medoff, *What do Unions Do?* (New York: Basic Books, 1984).

10 See http://www4.hrsdc.gc.ca/.3ndic.1t.4r@-eng.jsp?iid=17 and http://www.bls.gov/news.release/pdf/union2.pdf.

### Why does Lady Gaga earn millions more than singers of only slightly lesser ability?

Although the best singers have always earned more than others with slightly lesser talents, the earnings gap is sharply larger now than it was at the beginning of the last century. Today, Lady Gaga earns thousands of times what singers only marginally less talented earn. Given that listeners in blind hearings often have difficulty identifying the most highly paid singers, why is this earnings differential so large?

The answer lies in a fundamental change in the way we consume most of our music. In the 19th century, virtually all professional musicians delivered their services in concert halls in front of live audiences. Audiences of that day would have been delighted to listen to the world's best singers, but no one singer could hope to perform in more than a tiny fraction of the world's concert halls. Today, in contrast, most of the music we hear comes in recorded form, which enables the best singer to be literally everywhere at once. As soon as the master recording has been made, Lady Gaga's performance can be burned onto CDs at the same low cost as for a slightly less-talented singer's performance.

Tens of millions of buyers worldwide are willing to pay a few dollars extra to hear the most talented performers. Recording companies would be delighted to hire those singers at modest salaries, for by so doing they would earn an enormous economic profit. But that would unleash bidding by rival recording companies for the best singers. Such bidding ensures that the top singers will earn multi-million-dollar annual salaries (most of which constitute economic rents, as discussed in Chapter 7). Slightly less-talented singers earn much less, because the recording industry simply does not need those singers.

mean a market with literally only one winner. Indeed, hundreds of professional musicians earn multi-million-dollar annual salaries. Yet tens of thousands of others, many of them nearly as good, struggle to pay their bills.

## COMPENSATING WAGE DIFFERENTIALS

Why do garbage collectors earn more than daycare workers? Picking up the trash is important, to be sure, but is it more valuable than caring for young children? What accounts for the difference in rates of pay?

Other things being equal, jobs with attractive working conditions will pay less than jobs with less-attractive conditions. Wage differences associated with differences in working conditions are known as **compensating wage differentials**. Economists have identified compensating differentials for a host of different specific working conditions; for example, safe jobs tend to pay less than otherwise similar jobs that entail greater risks to health and safety.[11] Wages also vary in accordance with the attractiveness of the work schedule.

**compensating wage differential** a difference in the wage rate, negative or positive, that reflects the attractiveness of a job's working conditions

We also see compensating wage differentials even for such hard-to-measure characteristics as the autonomy associated with different jobs, and for an example, you may not have to look further than your economics professor. Almost all professors, it is safe to say, could have gone into an MBA program and then become a business executive rather than an academic. The marks required for entry into MBA programs have always been somewhat lower than the marks required for entry into Ph.D. programs of comparable status, and MBA programs (two years) are typically shorter than Ph.D. programs (four years or more). As Chapter 13 will discuss, the salaries of top business executives have grown quickly in the past 20 years; however, even before then it was always clear that salaries in business are significantly higher than in universities.

11  W. Kip Viscusi, "The Value of Risks to Life and Health," *Journal of Economic Literature,* v. 31 (December 1993), pp. 1912–1946.

So why did your professor not make the same calculation for an MBA as Mary did for an MA? If a higher salary is obtained after an MBA, and an MBA requires less investment, isn't this an easy choice? The short answer is that there is much more to life than money. We made a crucial assumption when we assumed that Mary would get the same job satisfaction from either career path. If the *only* way in which two jobs differ is in terms of the salary, it makes sense to use income as the basis for choice. However, jobs typically differ in many more ways, too, and life as a business executive is quite different from life as a professor.

One of the key ways in which a professor's job differs from that of a business executive is in personal autonomy. To see this in a superficial way, consider how some of your professors dress. Ask yourself honestly, could they get away with dressing like that in the head office of a major corporation? The phrase "get away with" is revealing, because it indicates the social pressures to adhere to a dress code that are part of the business world. On a more substantive level, Canadian professors, to a remarkable extent, make their own decisions about how they do their jobs: professors determine their own research priorities, decide what issues to emphasize in class, and so on. The job descriptions of "professor" and "business executive" differ in other ways as well, but the bottom line is that, despite lower salaries in academia, people continue to enroll in Ph.D. programs because they prefer the lifestyle and the type of work. Of course, the presence of compensating differentials does not eliminate the importance of wages. If academic salaries go too low, fewer people will be willing to pay the price in lower salaries for the difference in job satisfaction they experience. Canadian universities can expect a wave of retirements in the next few years as professors who were hired in the 1970s reach age 65. If not enough graduate students are trained to replace them, salaries will have to rise to entice more people to go to graduate school and fill these vacancies.

Not everybody likes the academic lifestyle to the same degree. Because tastes as to job attributes differ, *the size and the sign* of the compensating differential depend on relative supply *and* demand. For example, some people clearly prize personal autonomy more strongly, while others prefer to be team players. Indeed, tastes differ for many other job characteristics. Some people like to be sociable, but others find crowds stressful. Some people like to work outdoors, while others prefer to be indoors, and so on.

When tastes differ, the crucial issue is how many jobs there are that have a particular characteristic *relative to* the number of people who like it. For example, if there are many outdoor jobs and only a few people who prefer being outdoors, then firms will have to pay higher wages for outdoor jobs to lure some indoor enthusiasts outside. On the other hand, if the number of people who prefer being outdoors is greater than the number of outdoor jobs, then outdoor jobs will pay less than indoor jobs. Economic theory provides no way of determining how many people will have particular tastes, so it is often hard to predict if compensating differentials will produce higher or lower wages in a particular occupation.

## RECAP↑

### EXPLAINING DIFFERENCES IN EARNINGS

Earnings differ among people in part because of differences in their *human capital*. Two people with the same amount of human capital may earn different wages if one belongs to a *labour union* and the other does not. Their earnings may also differ because a given amount of human capital has greater leverage in some contexts than others. The world's most talented singer is far more valuable, for example, if people can listen to her music not just in live performances but on CDs as well. Earnings may also differ between equally productive individuals because of *compensating wage differentials*—the positive or negative wage differentials attributable to differences in working conditions.

# 12.7 DISCRIMINATION IN THE LABOUR MARKET

Women and some minorities continue to receive lower wage rates, on average, than white males with similar education and years of experience. This pattern poses a profound challenge to standard theories of competitive labour markets, which hold that competitive pressures will eliminate wage differentials not based on differences in productivity. Defenders of standard theories sometimes attribute the wage gap to unmeasured differences in human capital. Critics of these theories, who reject the idea that labour markets are effectively competitive, often attribute a significant portion of the gap to various forms of discrimination.

## DISCRIMINATION BY EMPLOYERS

**Employer discrimination** is the term used to describe wage differentials that arise from an arbitrary preference by the employer for one group of workers over another. Suppose, for example, that two groups, such as males and females, are known to be equally productive, on average. If we think back to the example of Mackintosh Pottery Works at the start of the chapter, some employers ("discriminators") in the industry may prefer to hire males and may be willing to pay higher wages to do so.

**employer discrimination**
an arbitrary preference by the employer for one group of workers over another

However, the continuation of employer discrimination is subject to competitive pressures. If most consumers are not willing to pay more for good pots produced by males than for identical ones produced by females (if indeed they even *know* which type of worker produced the pot), then the product price is unaffected by the composition of the workforce that produces the product. If so, a discriminating firm's profit will be smaller the more males it employs, because males cost more yet are no more productive. Thus, the most profitable firms will be ones that employ only females.

EQUILIBRIUM

An arbitrary initial wage differential would provide an opportunity for employers who hire mostly females to grow at the expense of their rivals. Because such firms make an economic profit on the sale of each clay pot, they have an incentive is to expand as rapidly as possible. And to do that, they would naturally want to continue hiring only the less-expensive female workers.

But as profit-seeking firms continue to pursue this strategy, the supply of females at the lower wage rate will run out. The short-run solution is to offer females a slightly higher wage. But if other firms also start offering a higher wage, females' wages will be bid up. The upward pressure on female wages will only stop when the wage of females reaches parity with the wage of males. Thus in long-run equilibrium, the wage for both males and females will settle at the common value of their *VMP*.

Any employer who wants to voice a preference for hiring males must now do so by paying males a wage in excess of their *VMP*. Employers can discriminate against females if they wish, but only if they are willing to pay premium wages to males out of their own profits.

Why then has study after study found an unexplained gap in the pay of men and women, even after accounting for the influence of all the measurable characteristics (such as education, experience, or industry of employment) that economists can think of? Why did this gap not disappear long ago? Why have similar "unexplained" wage gaps also been found for different minority groups (such as aboriginal Canadians)?

To understand this, we have to remember that the above example is limited, because it is based on a firm that manufactures pottery. It assumes that (1) the consumers did not know or care who actually produced the good they purchased; (2) although employers knew that men and women were of equal inherent productivity, they still preferred males; and (3) nondiscriminatory firms could easily obtain access to the capital and distribution networks necessary to expand production.

The assumption that consumers do not know or care who produced the product is only reasonable in part of the economy. More than 75 percent of the Canadian workforce is in the service sector. Far more Canadians work in offices, restaurants, and department stores than in pottery works or car factories, and the same is true in all the other developed countries. Although it is reasonable to assume that the purchasers of clay pots or automobiles have no real way of knowing whether assembly line workers in the plant were male or female, the diners in a restaurant are certainly aware of whether a waiter or a waitress served them.

Much of the service sector is characterized by personal contact of the service provider and the service consumer. Furthermore, in the service sector, the *quality* of the product is often hard to define precisely; indeed, it is often said that good quality is whatever the customer thinks it is. This means that customer attitudes can matter a great deal. If, for example, some investors have the idea that men are wise, dispassionate, and good with numbers while women are not, such investors may prefer to purchase the services of male investment brokers and financial analysts, rather than trust their money with female advisers. If such consumers are numerous enough, it will not be worthwhile for financial services firms to hire women, or to pay them the same amount of money. And since financial analysts signal their success in delivering financial advice by their own prosperity, it will not do female financial analysts much good to try to compete by offering to accept lower pay. Saying "I'll advise you financially for less pay" is likely to be interpreted as "my advice is worth less."

The structural problem is that if women are faced with barriers to advancement in some areas, such as the financial services sector, then it is reasonable for them to look elsewhere for a career. The combination of barriers to advancement and the supply response to those barriers then produces occupational segregation, which remains important. As Statistics Canada has noted, "In 2009, 67.0% of employed women worked in teaching, nursing and related health occupations, clerical or other administrative positions, or sales and service occupations. In contrast, 31.0% of employed men worked in these fields."[12]

Occupational segregation interacts with the second assumption—that employer discrimination occurs when employers know men and women to be of equal productivity yet prefer to hire men anyway. It is rare for people in Canada today to express such openly discriminatory attitudes, even to themselves, but it not quite so rare to find stereotyped thinking about the capabilities of different types of employees. Stereotyped thinking then produces the type of discrimination that comes from the assumption that a particular type of person "just couldn't do the job."

Stereotyped thinking about job performance may not be universally negative. Women, for example, may be assigned the stereotyped virtue of compassionate empathy even as they are denied the stereotyped capability for tough decision making. Stereotypes may also be particularly strong where they reinforce traditional roles in family life. However, whatever the origins of stereotypes, the result is that people are assumed to have only the ability for some of the jobs in the labour market.

**statistical discrimination**
the practice of making judgments about the quality of people, goods, or services based on the characteristics of the groups to which they belong

Recall again our discussion of **statistical discrimination** in Chapter 11. When potential employers cannot directly observe what an individual at another firm is actually producing or capable of producing, competition among firms will force them to pay the same wage to particular "types" of observationally equivalent workers. The only way that incorrect assumptions about productivity are then weeded out is with experience. However, an employer who acts on a prejudiced assumption and never hires a member of the stereotyped group is never proven wrong, because he or she cannot observe whether that person could have done the job.

Incorrect stereotypes, like any misconception about quality, are a cost to the economy. If, for example, the Canadian building industry believed pine to be a better wood than spruce for $2 \times 4$ lumber, house prices in Canada would be higher than they need to be. If contractors were not using an equally good type of lumber and were bidding up the price of pine unnecessarily, the output of the industry would be unnecessarily expensive.

12 Women in Canada: Paid Work, in The Daily, Thursday, December 9, 2010, at http://www.statcan.gc.ca/daily-quotidien/101209/tdq101209-eng.htm.

Similarly, prejudice and misinformation are the sources of inequity for the people who are denied access to employment and inefficiency for the economy as a whole.

The public policy issue at the root of this discussion is how to eliminate prejudice in a reasonably short time. It may well be that the market will, itself, eventually weed out misconceptions. However, if the market is thought to be taking too much time, it may be reasonable for public policy to aim at speeding the process along a little. In particular, two major emphases of Canadian public policy have been antidiscrimination legislation and employment equity programs. By helping women and minorities get into nontraditional jobs, it speeds up the process of showing how incorrect traditional misconceptions actually are.

---

**RECAP**

### DISCRIMINATION IN THE LABOUR MARKET

Women and some minorities continue to receive lower wages than would be predicted by the standard human capital model. The theory of *employer discrimination* holds that part of the observed wage gaps are the result of employer preferences, while theories of *statistical discrimination* (defined in Chapter 11) emphasize the role of continued stereotypes of employee productivity on the part of employers.

---

## SUMMARY

- Value of marginal product (*VMP*) is the market value of whatever goods and services an additional worker of a given type, on average, produces for an employer. Diminishing marginal returns implies that when a firm's capital and other productive inputs are held fixed in the short run, adding workers beyond some point results in ever-smaller increases in output. If firms can hire more labour at a constant wage, they will maximize profits by hiring labour up to the point at which *VMP* equals the market wage. In imperfectly competitive labour markets, in which more labour can only be hired if the firm increases the wages it pays, the profit maximizing firm will hire labour up to the point at which *VMP* equals marginal labour cost. **LO1, LO2**

- Because some occupations require large amounts of human capital, labour markets may respond slowly to changes in demand for labour that will fill those occupations. **LO3**

- Structural unemployment occurs when there is a poor match between the skills required by the labour market and skills that workers possess. Frictional unemployment occurs because workers and vacant jobs cannot be matched instantly. Search time is required if the match is to be made. Seasonal unemployment occurs because demand for some types of labour fluctuates during the year. Cyclical unemployment occurs when the economy goes through booms and recessions. **LO4**

- Human capital theory says that a worker's *VMP* is proportional to that worker's stock of human capital—education, experience, training, and other factors that influence productivity. According to this theory, some occupations pay better than others because they require larger stocks of human capital. **LO5**

- Wages often differ between individuals whose stocks of human capital appear nearly the same, as when one belongs to a labour union and the other does not. Technologies that allow the most productive individuals to serve broader markets can also sometimes translate even small differences in performance into enormous differences in pay. Such technologies give rise to winner-take-all labour markets. **LO5**

- Compensating wage differentials are those wage differences associated with differences in working conditions. They predict that individuals with a given stock of human capital will tend to earn more in jobs that have working conditions that are less attractive to most people. However, because the tastes of individuals differ, compensating differentials for many job characteristics could be either positive or negative. **LO5**

- Many firms pay members of certain groups, notably some ethnic-minority groups and females, less than they pay white males with similar personal characteristics. Wage gaps that are the result of employer discrimination create profit opportunities for firms that do not discriminate. The prevalence of stereotypes and discrimination by customers may also explain at least part of observed wage gaps. **LO6**

## KEY TERMS

compensating wage differential (351)
employer discrimination (353)
human capital (345)
human capital theory (345)
labour union (350)

marginal labour cost (338)
marginal (physical) product of labour (*MP*) (333)
monopsony (338)
observationally equivalent workers (335)

present value (348)
value of marginal product of labour (*VMP*) (333)
winner-take-all labour market (350)
statistical discrimination (354)

## REVIEW QUESTIONS

1. Why is the supply curve of labour for any specific occupation likely to be upward sloping even if, for the economy as a whole, people work fewer hours when wage rates increase? **LO3**

2. True or false: If the human capital possessed by two workers is nearly the same, their wage rates will be nearly the same. Explain. **LO5**

3. True or false: Economic surplus would be larger if a profit-maximizing monopsonist in the labour market were required to hire one more worker than it otherwise would have chosen to. Explain. **LO2**

## PROBLEMS

1. Kevin Capitalist is thinking of going into hydroponics. He knows that he can get $20 per gram for high-value herbs and that any legal problems that he might personally have in connection with herb production can be solved with a payoff of $5 per gram to the appropriate legal authorities. The cost of electricity, fertilizer, rental space, and other inputs is $3 per gram. Each plant he grows produces 10 grams of herbs and takes 60 days to grow to maturity. Sasha and Bobbi are willing to work for him, but Kevin knows that Sasha can tend 25 plants while Bobbi can only take care of 20 plants. What is the maximum amount that Kevin can pay each worker per day and still make a profit? **LO1**

2. Stone Inc. owns a clothing factory and hires workers in a competitive labour market to cut and sew denim fabric into jeans. The fabric required to make each pair of jeans costs $5. The company's weekly output of finished jeans varies with the number of workers hired, as shown in the following table: **LO1**

| Number of workers | Jeans (pairs/week) |
| --- | --- |
| 0 | 0 |
| 1 | 25 |
| 2 | 45 |
| 3 | 60 |
| 4 | 72 |
| 5 | 80 |
| 6 | 85 |

a. If the jeans sell for $35/pair, and the wage that other firms are offering workers is $250/week, how many workers will Stone hire if he wants to maximize his profit? How many pairs of jeans will the company produce each week?

b. Suppose the market wage other firms are willing to pay changes to $230/week. How does that change in the wages that other firms are willing to pay affect Stone's decision about how many workers to hire?

c. If the market wage had changed to $400/week, how would this affect Stone's decision about how many workers to hire?

d. If Stone again faces a market wage of $250/week, but the price of jeans rises to $45/week, how many workers will the company now hire?

e. If the reason why Stone Inc. has to change its wage rate were different (e.g., if the wage rate changed because of union action or government regulation), would that change your answer to parts (b) and (c) above?

3. The Jiffy-Fast Stone Carving Company is the only employer in a small town on Baffin Island. After paying transportation and materials costs, its net receipts per carving are $5, and its weekly output of carvings varies with the number of workers, as shown in the following table: **LO2**

| Number of workers | Carvings/week |
|---|---|
| 0 | 0 |
| 1 | 50 |
| 2 | 90 |
| 3 | 120 |
| 4 | 140 |
| 5 | 150 |
| 6 | 155 |

There are six people in town potentially available to work at Jiffy-Fast. The six people, together with their reservation wages, are shown in the following table:

| Worker | Reservation wage ($/week) |
|---|---|
| Jon | 75 |
| Joe | 80 |
| Jenny | 85 |
| Jeff | 90 |
| Jessica | 100 |
| Luke | 150 |

a. If Jiffy-Fast must pay the same wage to all workers, how many workers will the firm hire? What wage will it pay?

b. What is the socially optimal number of workers to hire?

c. If Jiffy-Fast could pay each worker exactly his or her reservation wage, how many workers would the company hire?

4. Acme Inc. supplies rocket ships to the retail market and hires workers to assemble the components. A rocket ship sells for $30 000, and Acme can buy the components for each rocket ship for $25 000. Wiley and Sam are two workers for Acme. Sam can

assemble one-fifth of a rocket ship per month, and Wiley can assemble one-tenth. If the labour market is perfectly competitive, every other firm knows that Sam is twice as productive as Wiley, and rocket components are Acme's only other cost, how much will Sam and Wiley be paid? **LO5**

5. Carolyn owns a soda factory and hires workers in a perfectly competitive labour market to bottle the soda. Her company's weekly output of bottled soda varies with the number of workers hired, as shown in the following table: **LO1, LO3, LO5**

| Number of workers | Cases/week |
|---|---|
| 0 | 0 |
| 1 | 200 |
| 2 | 360 |
| 3 | 480 |
| 4 | 560 |
| 5 | 600 |

a. If each case sells for $10 more than the cost of the materials used in producing it and the perfectly competitive market wage is $1000/week, how many workers will Carolyn hire? How many cases will be produced per week?

b. Suppose the Soda Bottlers Union now sets a weekly minimum acceptable wage of $1500/week. All the workers Carolyn hires belong to the union. How does the minimum wage affect Carolyn's decision about how many workers to hire?

c. If the wage is again $1000/week but the price of soda rises to $15 more than the cost of materials per case, how many workers will Carolyn now hire?

d. Suppose that a big automobile assembly plant opens up in town and, because of the general increase in local demand for labour, the going wage rises from $1000 to $1500 per week. Suppose further that workers at the soda factory are not in a union and that soda sells for $10 more than the cost of the materials used in producing it. How many workers will Carolyn hire?

6. Laura has a nursing degree and 2 years of experience working at Women's College Hospital. If she continues along her present career path, the present value of her lifetime earnings will be $200 000. If she takes 2 years off and completes a midwifery degree, the present value of her lifetime earnings will be $221 000. She has a scholarship that will cover the cost of books and incidental expenses. However, she must make two tuition payments for the midwifery course, one now and one a year from now, both of $10 500. Apart from her salary, Laura is indifferent between nursing

and midwifery. If the interest rate is 5 percent, is Laura better off if she goes to midwifery college? Explain. **LO5**

7. Stefano is thinking about getting a law degree. If he continues along his present career path, the present value of his lifetime earnings will be $500 000. If instead he takes 3 years off and gets the law degree, the present value of his lifetime earnings will be $550 000. He has a scholarship that will cover the costs of books and incidental expenses. However, he must make annual tuition payments of $20 000 at the beginning of each academic year. If the interest rate is 20 percent, will Stefano be better off financially if he goes to law school? Explain. If we observe Stefano going to law school, even after making all these calculations, what does that say about his preferences for his current occupation, compared to being a lawyer? **LO5**

8. A simple economy has two labour markets for carpenters: one for residential houses, the other for commercial buildings. The demand for residential carpenters is given by $W_R = 40 - 10L_R$, where $W_R$ is the wage of residential carpenters in dollars per hour and $L_R$ is the number of residential carpenters

in hundreds per day. The demand for commercial carpenters is given by $W_C = 40 - 5L_C$, where $W_C$ is the wage of commercial carpenters in dollars per hour and $L_C$ is the number of commercial carpenters in hundreds per day. The economy has 300 carpenters, each of whom has the skills required to be either a residential or a commercial carpenter, and each of whom wants to work full-time in whichever type of carpentry pays best. What will be the equilibrium wage and employment level for each type? (*Hint:* To find the total demand curve for carpenters, first graph the two demand curves side by side and then add them horizontally.) **LO3**

9. In Problem 8, suppose commercial carpenters form a union and announce that they will not work for less than $30/hour. Any union member who cannot find work in the commercial market will work in the residential market. How many carpenters work in each market, and what is the wage in the residential market? Are carpenters as a group better off or worse off? **LO5**

10. Refer to Problem 9. By how much does the formation of the commercial carpenters' union reduce the total value of carpenters' services provided each hour? **LO5**

## ANSWERS TO IN-CHAPTER EXERCISES

**12.1**   Abitibi will hire a second worker only if the *VMP* with two workers is at least $350. Since $VMP = (P)(MP)$, and since the marginal product of the second worker is 25 cutting boards, the lowest $P$ for which the company will hire two workers is found by solving $(P)(25) = \$350$ to obtain $P = \$14$. **LO1**

**12.2**   Since the *VMP* of each worker exceeds $275, Abitibi will now hire five workers. **LO1**

**12.3**   As shown in the following table, *VMP* for each of the first three workers now exceeds marginal labour cost when cutting boards sell for $50, so Bluenose will now hire three workers. **LO2**

| Number of Workers | Total number of cutting boards/week | MP (extra cutting boards/week) | VMP ($/week) | Marginal labour cost |
|---|---|---|---|---|
| 0 | 0 | | | |
| | | 30 | 1500 | 100 |
| 1 | 30 | | | |
| | | 25 | 1250 | 500 |
| 2 | 55 | | | |
| | | 20 | 1000 | 900 |
| 3 | 75 | | | |
| | | 15 | 750 | 1300 |
| 4 | 90 | | | |
| | | 10 | 500 | 1700 |
| 5 | 100 | | | |

**12.4**   A higher interest rate reduces the present value of both the cost of an MA degree and the resulting higher earnings. But the cost of getting an MA occurs during the next two years, while the salary increase is spread out over many years. The higher interest rate will therefore reduce the present value of the benefit of the degree by more than it will reduce the present value of its cost. Since Mary was indifferent at an interest rate of 10 percent, she will choose not to get the degree if the interest rate is 12 percent. **LO5**

# Calculating the Present Value of Future Costs and Benefits

In Chapter 12, calculations of present value are made in the context of human capital theory. However, the calculation of present values is a general problem that occurs in many contexts. For example, someone who is trying to estimate how much a business is worth must take into account that earnings received in the future are less valuable than earnings received today. Consider a company whose only profit, $14 400, will occur exactly two years from now. At all other times its profit will be exactly zero. How much is ownership of this company worth today?

Our goal is to calculate what economists call the present value of $14 400 to be received two years in the future. To make this calculation, we must employ the concept of the *time value of money*. The time value of money is closely related to the growth of an initial amount at compound interest.

To start, suppose we deposit $10 000 in a bank account. Let the annual interest rate be 20 percent. At the end of one year, the value of the deposit will grow to the principal amount ($10 000) plus interest earned. If $M_1$ represents the value reached at the end of year one, we can write

$$M_1 = \$10\ 000 + 0.2(\$10\ 000) = \$10\ 000 + \$2000 = \$12\ 000.$$

If $12 000 remains in the bank account for another year, its value will grow to $12 000 plus interest earned. If $M_2$ is the value reached at the end of year two, we can write

$$M_2 = \$12\ 000 + 0.2(\$12\ 000) = \$12\ 000 + \$2400 = \$14\ 400.$$

At the end of two years, $10 000 deposited at an interest rate of 20 percent per year grows to $14 400—growth has been compounded over two years at an annual rate of 20 percent. The implication is that if interest rates are 20 percent per year, a payment of $10 000 now and a payment of $14 400 in two years have equal value.

The calculation of $M_1$ can be written in more general notation,

$$M_1 = PV + r(PV) = PV\,(1 + r) \tag{12A.1}$$

where $PV$ is the amount deposited now, $r$ is the annual interest rate expressed as a decimal fraction, and $M_1$ is as defined previously. Similarly, the expression for $M_2$ is

$$M_2 = M_1 + r(M_1) = M_1(1 + r). \tag{12A.2}$$

If Equation 12A.1 is substituted into 12A.2, then

$$M_2 = PV(1 + r)(1 + r)$$
$$M_2 = PV(1 + r)^2. \tag{12A.3}$$

Equation 12A.3 can be generalized to

$$M_T = PV(1 + r)^T, \tag{12A.4}$$

where $T$ is the number of years over which an initial amount $PV$ grows, $M_T$ is the value reached after $T$ years, and other terms remain as defined previously. For example, if $PV$ is \$10 000, the annual interest rate is 20 percent, and $T$ is 2 years, Equation 12A.4 can be used to calculate $M_T$:

$$M_T = PV(1 + r)^T = \$10\,000(1 + 0.2)^2 = \$10\,000(1.44) = \$14\,400.$$

Notice that the higher is the interest rate or the longer the time over which the initial amount remains on deposit, the greater is the value of $M_T$.

Equation 12A.4 gives the value that an initial deposit reaches over a given period of time. However, suppose we do not know the initial amount, but we do know the amount that will be reached after a specified interval of time has elapsed—we know the future value, but we do not know the present value. For example, suppose we know that two years in the future, we will have \$14 400. What is the present value of \$14 400?

To answer this question, divide Equation 12A.4 by $(1 + r)^T$ to solve for $PV$, which represents present value:

$$PV = \frac{M_T}{(1 + r)^T} = \frac{1}{(1 + r)^T} M_T = DM_T. \tag{12A.5}$$

Notice that the term $\frac{1}{(1 + r)^T}$ has been factored out in Equation 12A.5. This term is

**discount factor** a coefficient, $D$, used to discount a payment or receipt that occurs in the future to a present value; can be defined algebraically as

$$D = \frac{1}{(1 + r)^T}$$

where $r$ = annual interest rate and $T$ = number of years that will elapse before the payment is received

known as the **discount factor**. It is a coefficient used to discount a payment or receipt that occurs in the future to a present value. In Equation 12A.5, $D$ represents the discount factor.

We know $M_T$ is \$14 400 and that $T$ is 2. Again, we will let the annual interest rate be 20 percent. When these values are placed in Equation 12A.5, the result is

$$PV = \frac{\$14\,400}{(1 + 0.2)^2} = \frac{\$14\,400}{1.44} = \frac{1}{(1 + 0.2)^2} \$14\,400 = \frac{1}{1.44} (\$14\,400) = 10\,000.$$

**present value (PV)** the amount that would have to be deposited today at an annual interest rate $r$ to generate a balance of $M$ after $T$ years:

$$PV = \frac{M_T}{(1 + r)^T} = DM_T$$

Given an annual interest rate of 20 percent, the present value of \$14 400 received two years from now is to \$10 000. More generally, given an annual interest rate $r$, the **present value (PV)** of a payment $M$ received $T$ years in the future is the amount that must be deposited today if a balance $M$ is to be reached after $T$ years. Equation 12A.5 provides a convenient shorthand statement of this definition.

Notice two things about the calculation of present value. First, it is the algebraic reciprocal of calculating the value reached by an initial amount deposited at compound interest. The calculation of present value is mathematically consistent with the calculation of values reached at compound interest. Second, as Equation 12A.4 shows, the higher the rate of interest or the longer the interval of time that elapses, the greater will be the value reached by an amount deposited at compound interest. Therefore, as Equation 12A.5 shows, the reciprocal must follow: the higher is the rate of interest or the longer is the interval of time that elapses, the lower will be the present value of a given amount received in the future.

Up to this point, we have calculated the present value of a single amount that will be received at a point in the future. However, it is easy to modify Equation 12A.5 to calculate the present value of a stream of payments. Suppose we receive payment $M_1$ one year in the future, $M_2$ two years in the future, and $M_3$ three years in the future. The present value of this stream of payments is calculated as

$$PV = \frac{1}{(1 + r)^1} M_1 + \frac{1}{(1 + r)^2} M_2 + \frac{1}{(1 + r)^3} M_3, \qquad (12A.6)$$

where the exponents indicate the number of years in the future each payment will be received and all other terms are as previously defined. Equation 12A.6 can be rewritten as

$$PV = \sum_{t=1}^{3} \frac{1}{(1 + r)^t} M_t = \sum_{t=1}^{3} D_t M_t, \qquad (12A.7)$$

where $\Sigma$ is a summation operator and $t$ is an index that states the point in time at which a payment is received. Equation 12A.7 can be generalized to

$$PV = \sum_{t=1}^{T} \frac{1}{(1 + r)^T} M_T = \sum_{t=1}^{T} D_T M_T, \qquad (12A.8)$$

where $T$ indicates the point in time at which the last payment is received, and all other terms remain as previously defined.

**What is the present value of a payment of $1728 to be received 3 years from now if the annual interest rate is 20 percent?**

EXERCISE 12A.1

## KEY TERMS

discount factor (360)                    present value (360)

## PROBLEMS

1. Suppose you are the winner of a lottery. As your prize, you will receive a payment of $10 000 today, when you present your winning ticket to the Lottery Commission. You will also receive $10 000 one year from now, $10 000 two years from now, and a final payment of $20 000 three years from now. LO12A.2, LO12A.3

   a. The Lottery Commission wants to encourage people to buy lottery tickets, so it advertises that you, the lucky winner, have won a prize worth $50 000. Do you agree with this statement? Why or why not?

   b. Suppose the prevailing interest rate is 5 percent. Calculate the present value of your prize.

   c. Suppose the prevailing interest rate is 2.5 percent. Calculate the present value of your prize.

   d. Suppose your prize can be sold to anyone who is willing to buy it. If the prevailing interest rate is 2.5 percent, what is the maximum price someone would be willing to pay for your prize today? Why?

2. You are shopping for a car. You have found a dealer who will sell you a car for $12 000. If you purchase from him, you must make a down payment of $2000. The dealer will arrange for you to borrow the remaining $10 000 at an annual interest rate of 1 percent, and the loan will be payable in full one year from now. LO12A.1, LO12A.2, LO12A.3

a.  If you take the loan the dealer is offering to arrange, what is the amount you must pay at the end of one year? What is the present value of this payment given an interest rate of 1 percent per year?

b.  Suppose you have sufficient cash to purchase the car outright for $12 000. You also have an opportunity to deposit this cash at an interest rate of 6 percent per year. What is the opportunity cost of using your cash to pay for the car instead of depositing it with interest? (For simplicity, ignore depreciation of the car and income tax.) What is the present value of your opportunity cost, given an interest rate of 6 percent?

c.  If you borrow $10 000 under the terms offered by the dealer, and deposit $10 000 of cash at 6 percent per year, what is the net amount of interest you will earn? From your point of view, what is the size of the discount from a price of $12 000 that the dealer is offering to you when he offers the $10 000 loan at an annual interest rate of 1 percent?

d.  Suppose the dealer can also deposit any cash he has at 6 percent per year. Given the terms of the loan he has offered, do you think the dealer would be interested if you offered to buy the car for less than $12 000, provided you offer to pay cash? How much less? Why?

3.  You deposit $1000 today at an annual interest rate of 10 percent. Is it logical to state that $1100 received one year from today has the same value as $1000 received today? Why or why not? **LO12A.4**

## ANSWER TO IN-APPENDIX EXERCISE

**12A.1**   Present value $= \$1728/(1.2)^3 = \$1000$. **LO12A.2, LO12A.3**

# CHAPTER 13
# Income Distribution

Some Canadians wake up in the morning and enjoy a quick dip in their indoor pool before a leisurely breakfast in the cathedral-ceilinged dining room. Every day they make economic decisions; for example, investment decisions about the allocation of their stock portfolio or consumption decisions such as choosing whether to go to Florida or Jamaica for their winter vacation. On the same morning, other Canadians wake up on the sidewalk, trying to find a bit of privacy amid the street cleaners and pedestrians. The homeless also start their day looking for breakfast, but their first economic problem is whether they can get enough change together for a coffee and a doughnut. The vast majority of Canadians are somewhere in between. Some wake up in cramped apartments, some in small row houses, and some in single-family dwellings. Wherever they sit in the hierarchy of incomes, they all face the economic problem of allocating their income among competing, possible expenditures. But the affluent have many choices, while the poor have very few.

Some degree of economic inequality is present in all societies, but the extent of inequality varies considerably between nations, and it has differed over time within Canada and in other countries as well. All the economic policy issues that we have discussed in this text affect both total output and the distribution of income within society. Hence, both *efficiency and equity matter,* because good economic policy helps enable society both to maximize the economic surplus that individuals can obtain from the production and consumption of scarce commodities and to ensure the fair distribution of that surplus. As we have also discussed, the efficient functioning of a market system depends on widespread observance of the framework of laws surrounding economic transactions—a framework that is unlikely to survive long if it is generally believed that economic outcomes are unjust.

But how "fair" is the distribution of income in Canada? What (if anything) should we do about it? If we are to answer these questions in a reasonable way, we need to know (1) how much inequality and poverty exists in Canada now, (2) what criteria might help us to judge how much inequality would be "fair," and (3) what the costs and benefits of specific policies to reduce inequality and poverty might be. This chapter will introduce some of the essential conceptual tools and basic data on trends and quantities needed for analysis.

## LEARNING OBJECTIVES

When you have completed this chapter, you will be able to:

**LO1** Describe trends in the Canadian distribution of income during recent decades.

**LO2** Compare changes in the Canadian distribution of income with changes in those of other developed nations.

**LO3** Use a Lorenz curve and a Gini coefficient to portray inequality.

**LO4** Describe trends in the distribution of wealth in Canada during recent decades.

**LO5** Use the "veil of ignorance," utilitarian analysis, and human rights arguments to evaluate the distribution of income and wealth.

**LO6** Explain how taxes, social assistance, and a negative income tax can be used to influence the distribution of wealth.

**LO7** Analyze concerns that policies designed to influence the distribution of income and wealth will erode incentives to work.

# 13.1 RECENT TRENDS IN INCOME INEQUALITY

In 2009, the top 20 percent of Canadian family units received an average of $168 400 in total income, while the bottom 20 percent received an average total income of $15 100.[1] Those in the top end of the income distribution have a huge range of affluence, from salaried professionals to the billionaires who control much of Canadian media and industry. At the bottom, there is less room for differences among people who share a common reality of inadequacy of income. The inequality in economic rewards that is at the heart of a capitalist system raises fundamental questions of equity and social policy—but is it true that the rich get richer while the poor get poorer?

**www.statcan.gc.ca**
**Statistics Canada**

In some countries, the answer has clearly been "yes." Since the early 1980s, some countries, particularly the United Kingdom and the United States, have seen a strong trend toward increased inequality in the distribution of income. In the United States, the bottom 20 percent of households had an average income of $11 552 in 2009, which, if incomes are measured in comparable 2009 dollars, was not a big change (about 5 percent) from the average income of the bottom fifth in 1979 ($11 031). By contrast, over the same thirty-year period, the average income of the top 20 percent rose by more than 43 percent (to $170 844), while the average income of the top 5 percent jumped by 62.5 percent (to $295 388 in 2009).[2]

The United Kingdom has witnessed similar trends. However, different countries make different choices in economic and social policy, and some countries, such as France, saw a trend to greater equality in the late 1990s.[3]

**quintile** each fifth of a group of individuals who are arranged in order of income, beginning with the lowest ranking fifth

Table 13.1 summarizes the long-term picture of income distribution in Canada. If we lined up all the families and unattached individuals in Canada in order of their total household income, and divided the line into five equal parts, or **quintiles**, we could ask, what is the share of total money income (before tax) received by the poorest fifth of households? How much does the next 20 percent get? What share do the middle 20 percent get? the 20 percent who are second from the top? the top 20 percent? Table 13.1 presents the answers.

## THE LORENZ CURVE

The problem with Table 13.1 is that it contains a lot of numbers—too many, sometimes, to provide a clear answer to the question of whether inequality has decreased or increased. Fortunately, we can use the table to construct a measure of overall inequality in any given year.

**TABLE 13.1**
**Share of Aggregate Pre-Tax Incomes Received by each Quintile of Families and Unattached Individuals (percent)**

|  | 1951 | 1961 | 1971 | 1981 | 1991 | 1996 | 2001 | 2006 | 2009 |
|---|---|---|---|---|---|---|---|---|---|
| Bottom 20% (poorest) | 4.4 | 4.2 | 3.6 | 4.6 | 4.5 | 4.2 | 4.1 | 4.1 | 4.2 |
| Second 20% | 11.2 | 11.9 | 10.6 | 11 | 10 | 9.6 | 9.7 | 9.7 | 9.6 |
| Middle 20% | 18.3 | 18.3 | 17.6 | 17.7 | 16.4 | 16 | 15.6 | 15.6 | 15.4 |
| Fourth 20% | 23.3 | 24.5 | 24.9 | 25.1 | 24.7 | 24.6 | 23.7 | 23.7 | 23.6 |
| Top 20% (richest) | 42.8 | 41.1 | 43.3 | 41.6 | 44.4 | 45.6 | 46.9 | 46.8 | 47.2 |

SOURCES: Statistics Canada, *Income Distribution by Size in Canada,* (1998), Catalogue No. 13-207; J.R. Podoluk, *Incomes of Canadians*, Dominion Bureau of Statistics, (1968). Adapted from Statistics Canada, CANSIM, CANSIM Table 202-0701 and from the Statistics Canada website, http://www40.statcan.gc.ca/l01/cst01/ECON04-eng.htm. Extraction date, June 20, 2011.

1  CANSIM Table 202-0703.

2  See http://www.census.gov/hhes/www/income/data/historical/household/index.html.

3  For a recent survey see L. Osberg, *A Quarter Century of Economic Inequality in Canada 1981–2006*, Canadian Centre for Policy Alternatives, April 2009, http://www.policyalternatives.ca/documents/ National_Office_Pubs/2008/Quarter_Century_of_Inequality.pdf.

If all Canadian households were lined up in order of income, from poorest to richest, and if we went down this line asking people their incomes, at each point in the line we could calculate how much of national income is, in total, received by all the people[4] up to that point in the income distribution.

If we have data on each individual family's income, we can get the answer exactly, but even if we do not have complete data, we can get a close approximation if we have a table like Table 13.1, which reports the income received by each 20 percent of the income distribution. We can also use a graph to present the answer visually. Using Table 13.1, we can easily plot the percentage of income received by the bottom 20 percent (4.2 percent in 2009) as point A in Figure 13.1. If we go a little further up the income distribution and ask how much of the nation's total income was received by the poorest 40 percent, we can find the answer by adding the top two entries from the last column of Table 13.1 (4.2 percent + 9.6 percent = 13.8 percent) and plot it as point B. The total share of the poorest 60 percent can be calculated in the same way (4.2 percent + 9.6 percent + 15.4 percent = 29.2 percent) and plotted as point C. To get the share of the poorest 80 percent of families, we just add 23.6 percent from Table 13.1 and plot the answer as point D. Connecting points A, B, C, and D, we get the red line in Figure 13.1, which graphs the relationship between the cumulative percentage of income received on the horizontal axis and the cumulative percentage of population on the vertical axis. This line is called a **Lorenz curve**, in honour of the first person to draw the relationship in this way.

We can use Figure 13.1 to compare the degree of inequality in different societies or at different points in time. To see this, suppose that everyone in society had the same income (perfect equality). In this case, each 20 percent of families would get 20 percent of income. Since the bottom 20 percent would get 20 percent of income while the bottom

**Lorenz curve** a graph that orders the members of a population from poorest to richest; on the horizontal axis is the percentage of the population below a given income, and on the vertical axis is the cumulative percentage of total income received by them

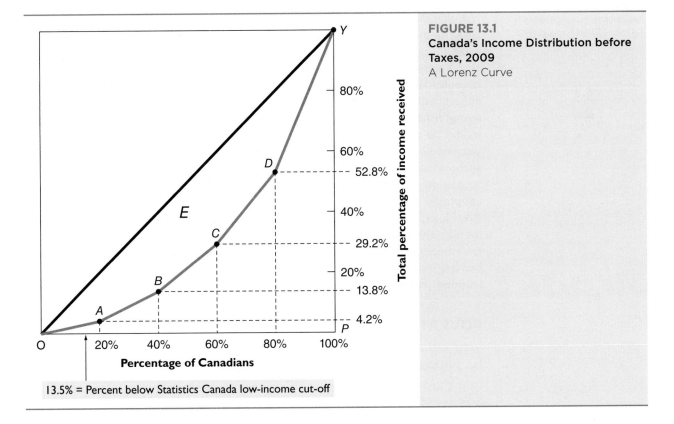

**FIGURE 13.1**

**Canada's Income Distribution before Taxes, 2009**

A Lorenz Curve

13.5% = Percent below Statistics Canada low-income cut-off

4 In most data sets it is not possible to measure inequality within families, so economists typically have to make the assumption that everyone in the same family has the same income; see Shelley A. Phipps and Peter S. Burton, "Sharing within Families: Implications for the Measurement of Poverty among Individuals in Canada," *The Canadian Journal of Economics*, Vol. 28, No. 1 (Feb., 1995),

40 percent would get 40 percent, and the bottom 60 percent would get 60 percent, and so on, the Lorenz curve would be the straight black line *OY* of Figure 13.1. Alternately, if one person in society had all the income and the rest had nothing (perfect inequality), then the income share of the bottom 99.99 percent of the population would be zero. In this case, the Lorenz curve would lie along the horizontal axis for almost all its length, line *OPY*.

## THE GINI INDEX OF INEQUALITY

To summarize the extent of inequality, an Italian economist of the late nineteenth century, Corrado Gini, proposed a measure of inequality that has become known as the Gini index. He realized that the area between the Lorenz curve and the line of perfect equality (area *E* in Figure 13.1) is zero if everyone has the same income (perfect equality). He also saw that if there is perfect inequality (one person has all the income), the area between the Lorenz curve and the line of perfect equality (area *E* in Figure 13.1) and the triangle *OPY* are the same, so their ratio will be one.

Since actual societies are somewhere between perfect equality and perfect inequality, Gini proposed that the *degree* of inequality in a society can be summarized by calculating the *ratio* of the area between the Lorenz curve and the line of perfect equality (area *E* in Figure 13.1) to the area of the triangle *OPY*. This is known as the **Gini coefficient**. When the Lorenz curve for one country lies entirely above the Lorenz curve for another, inequality comparisons are unambiguous. The country with the higher Lorenz curve is, at every point, closer to the line of perfect equality (OY) and thus has a lower degree of inequality. In this case, whether we want to look at the poorest 20 percent, the poorest 40 percent, or some other point in the income distribution, a larger share of total income is going to the less well off and it is straightforward to say that there is less inequality. (Notice that Table 13.1 can be used to compare the income shares of each quintile of households in 1996 and 2009. The income shares of the poorest quintiles of the population were the same or lower in 2009 than in 1996, so the trend to greater inequality in Canada is unambiguous.)

One can calculate the Gini coefficient in a number of slightly different ways. If, for example, one measures inequality of *total income across families*, one gets a somewhat different estimate of the level of the Gini coefficient than if inequality of *after-tax income among individuals* is examined. The main trends are, however, clear. Because of the income tax system, inequality in after-tax income in Canada is lower than inequality in income before tax, and it changed only a little during the 1980s and early 1990s. However, after-tax income inequality increased substantially during the late 1990s in Canada, both because pre-tax market income inequality increased and because the tax system became less progressive. Comparing 1980 and 2009, the Gini index for after-tax income among individuals in Canada increased substantially, from 0.286 to 0.320.[5] By comparison, in the mid-2000s the Gini index was higher in the United States (0.38), but lower in northern European countries like Norway (0.28) and Finland (0.27). In short, Canada in 2009 had less income inequality than the United States, but more inequality than northern European nations, and noticeably more inequality than Canada used to have.[6]

## POVERTY

So far, we have considered the extent of income *inequality* among all families in Canada, but *poverty* is a somewhat different issue. Figure 13.1 also marks, on the horizontal

**Gini coefficient** an index, ranging between zero and one, of the amount of inequality in a population; when all persons have the same income (perfect equality), it equals zero; when only one person has all the income (perfect inequality), it equals one; graphically, it can be represented as the ratio of the area between the Lorenz curve and the line of perfect equality to the area of the triangle below the line of perfect equality

5  See CANSIM series v46442331 and OECD Factbook 2010.

6  For more international comparisons, see key figures at http://www.lisdatacenter.org/. Note that the LIS data report income distribution statistics that make adjustment for differences in size of household. In early calculations of income shares such as those reported for Canada in 1951 in Table 13.1, it was not possible to do this. To get a long span of data, Table 13.1 reports comparably calculated data on quintile shares among all households; for the period 1976–2009, Canadian quintile-share data, which adjusts for household size, is available at CANSIM Table 202-0707.

axis, the proportion of the Canadian population that have incomes less than the before-tax "low-income cut-off" (LICO) of Statistics Canada (in 2009, some 13.5 percent of Canadians). As can be seen from the vertical axis, in aggregate, the people whose incomes were below the LICO received well under 4 percent of the total income of Canadian households.

Statistics Canada publications always refer to the LICO as "the low-income cut-off," but many people outside the agency call it "the poverty line." The LICO is not the only criterion of poverty in Canada, and debate exists about exactly where the poverty line should be drawn.[7] However, most poverty lines are not very different, and all poverty lines imply that only a small minority of the population are poor. (In fact, using the before-tax LICO, one could equally well say that 13.5 percent of the population is poor or that 86.5 percent is not poor.) Since most members of the population are not poor, inequality among the middle class, and inequality between the middle class and the very affluent, necessarily dominates inequality in the income distribution as a whole. As Figure 13.1 illustrates, most of the Lorenz curve is drawn for the 86.5 percent of the population whose incomes are above the LICO.

In describing trends in poverty, the most common statistic used is the *poverty rate*—the percentage of the population whose incomes fall below the poverty line. However, the number of people who are poor is only one dimension of the problem. The seriousness of poverty also depends on whether poor people are mildly deprived, with incomes just below the poverty line, or very deprived, with incomes far below the poverty line. If we look just at the poverty rate, we will have no way of knowing how far below the poverty line the poor are, on average. Many analysts, therefore, also emphasize the *average poverty gap* (i.e., the average shortfall between the actual incomes of poor people and the poverty line, expressed as a percentage of the poverty line). Putting these two elements together provides a good index of poverty called *poverty intensity*, which is the product of both terms:

$$\text{poverty intensity} = (\text{poverty rate}) \times (\text{average poverty gap}).$$

Poverty intensity is an indicator of poverty that can pick up shifts in the economy that the poverty rate would miss. If, for example, the government were to cut social assistance payments, this would decrease the incomes of Canada's most deprived. However, *when people who are already poor get poorer, the poverty rate does not change*. Since people on social assistance are already well below the poverty line, a cut to social assistance payments would not show up in the poverty rate. However, poverty is worse, since the average poverty gap has increased. Hence, a measure like poverty intensity is preferred, since it will increase when the average depth of poverty increases.

If we use the before-tax low-income cut-off (LICO) from Statistics Canada (adjusted for inflation) as our definition of the poverty line, we can see in Figure 13.2 the trend in the poverty rate in Canada over the period 1976–2009. In the periods 1980–82 and 1990–93, unemployment levels in Canada rose significantly as the economy went into recession. As Figure 13.2 illustrates, the poverty rate also rose strongly during these recessions and then fell during the subsequent recoveries. As more data become available from the "great recession" following the financial crisis of late 2008, one can expect to see its impacts on both the poverty rate and the unemployment rate.

However, what Figure 13.2 does not show is the average depth of poverty. There has been a long-term upward trend in the per person poverty gap. Measured in 2009 dollars, the average poverty gap has increased by one-fifth, moving from $3335 to $4026 per poor person.

www.worldbank.org
**World Bank**
Type "poverty rate" into the search engine to find sources of information about poverty.

---

7  In 2009, a family of four living in a city with a population of 100 000 to 499 999 was counted as "low income" if the total before tax income for all family members was below $35 573. The "after-tax LICO" was lower: $29 455. The LICO is revised each year to reflect any increase in consumer prices. See CANSIM, v25745096 and Tables 2020801 and 2020802.

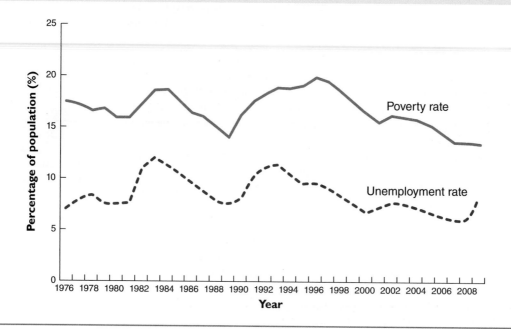

**FIGURE 13.2**
**Poverty Rate and Unemployment Rate, Canada, 1976–2009**
Unemployment in Canada rose significantly when the economy went into the 1980–1982 and 1990–1993 recessions. One implication, as this graph shows, was an increase in the poverty rate, which rises strongly during recessions and then falls during the subsequent recoveries.
SOURCE: Adapted from Statistics Canada, CANSIM Tables 202-0802 and 282-0086, and from the Statistics Canada website, http://www40.statcan.gc.ca/l01/cst01/ECON04-eng.htm. Extraction date June 20, 2011.

## INEQUALITY AT THE TOP

Since the early 1980s, there has been a trend toward increased inequality of market income in Canada, but until 1994–95, this was largely offset by redistribution through taxes and transfers. Since then, inequality in after-tax, after-transfer income has increased sharply. In the United States, trends to greater inequality have been going on longer.

Executives' total annual pay packets in the United States have inflated more than in most other countries, setting a standard that corporate leaders in other countries envy. But top Canadian CEOs have not exactly been suffering. For example, Aaron Regent of Barrick Gold topped Canada's executive compensation rankings in 2009 with a pay package of $24.2 million, although he dropped to 22nd in the rankings with $9.6 million in 2010.[8] As income tax data from a wide range of countries have revealed, the trend in income distribution in the U.S., U.K., and Canada has seen a rapidly increasing share of earnings going to the top 1 percent of earners and a relative stagnation in the income distribution among the rest of the population. (Interestingly, this has not been the case in continental Europe.[9])

As Figure 13.3a illustrates, there is a big contrast between the income gains of the top 1 percent of Canadian families, whose average income rose from $380 000 to $684 000 (in 2004 dollars), and the income gains of everyone else. Relative stagnation for the middle classes and rapid gains at the top indicate that the income share of the top-earning 1 percent rose from 7.4 percent of taxable income in 1982 to 11.2 percent in 2004.

---

8  See Janet McFarland, "Executive compensation rankings for Canada's 100 biggest companies," *The Globe and Mail* Update, May 29, 2011.

9  See A.B. Atkinson and T. Piketty, *Top Incomes Over the 20th Century: A Contrast Between Continental European and English-Speaking Countries,* (Oxford University Press, 2007).

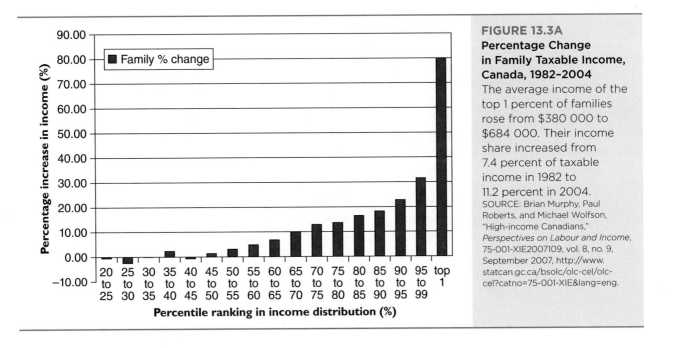

**FIGURE 13.3A**
**Percentage Change in Family Taxable Income, Canada, 1982–2004**
The average income of the top 1 percent of families rose from $380 000 to $684 000. Their income share increased from 7.4 percent of taxable income in 1982 to 11.2 percent in 2004.
SOURCE: Brian Murphy, Paul Roberts, and Michael Wolfson, "High-income Canadians," *Perspectives on Labour and Income*, 75-001-XIE2007109, vol. 8, no. 9, September 2007, http://www.statcan.gc.ca/bsolc/olc-cel/olc-cel?catno=75-001-XIE&lang=eng.

Figure 13.3b is taken from the work of Mike Veall of McMaster University.[10] Using income tax data, it shows how the share of the top 1 percent fell precipitously during the wage and price controls of World War II, and, because income growth for the bottom 99 percent was robust until the late 1970s, the *share* of the top 1 percent continued to decline until about 1980. The rapid growth of the incomes of this group since then, combined with the relative stagnation of other incomes, has produced a dramatic rise in their income share—to 13.8 percent in 2007.

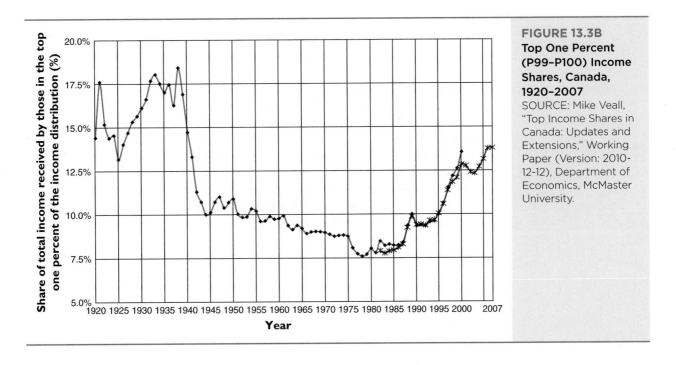

**FIGURE 13.3B**
**Top One Percent (P99–P100) Income Shares, Canada, 1920–2007**
SOURCE: Mike Veall, "Top Income Shares in Canada: Updates and Extensions," Working Paper (Version: 2010-12-12), Department of Economics, McMaster University.

10 Mike Veall, "Top Income Shares in Canada: Updates and Extensions," Working Paper (Version: 2010-12-12), Department of Economics, McMaster University. In 2007, the top 1 percent of individual tax payers had market income (other than capital gains) in excess of $169 231.

# 13.2 WEALTH INEQUALITY

Strictly speaking, when we say that somebody is "rich," we mean that they have a lot of *wealth*. To calculate a person's wealth, we add up the value of all their assets (real estate, bank balances, stock holdings, automobiles, etc.) and subtract the total amount of their liabilities (mortgages, personal debts).

Wealth, of course, is a *stock* while income is a *flow*. Although the two are linked, they are not the same. To see the difference, think of your bathtub. The level of water in the bathtub is the *stock* of water you have available to bathe in at any given point in time, much like your *stock* of assets is the amount you could potentially consume at any given point in time. The *flow* of water over a period of time into the tub from the tap is, like your income, the rate at which the stock tends to increase. But the more water you splash out of the tub (or the more you spend), the slower is the rate at which the stock increases. Thus, income and wealth are not the same, but they are always related by the following identity:

$$\text{income} - \text{consumption} = \text{change in wealth.}$$

For some people, the distinction between income and wealth is very important. Some senior citizens, for example, may have significant assets (e.g., a house or farm), but their current income from pensions and interest payments may be quite modest. Alternatively, someone with a high current income (such as a hockey player who has just made it into the NHL) may not have had much time to accumulate many assets. Nonetheless, wealth does produce income. People from a rich family who will inherit assets from their parents may never earn a particularly high income on their own, but they receive interest and dividend payments from their assets.

Because large, unearned incomes strike many people as being unfair and because many believe in the social value of "equality of opportunity," most countries collect taxes on large inheritances to limit the concentration of wealth across generations. Canada is one of the few developed countries that now has no estate or inheritance tax.

Because surveys of wealth are only periodically conducted by Statistics Canada, data on the distribution of wealth in Canada are currently available only for the years 1984, 1999, and 2005. Furthermore, since the billionaires of this world are so few in number and so likely to refuse to answer surveys, much of the wealth of the very rich is missed in these surveys. Nevertheless, these data do unambiguously indicate an increase in wealth inequality in Canada. The Gini index of inequality in wealth increased from 0.691 in 1984 to 0.727 in 1999 and reached 0.746 in 2005.[11] Figure 13.4 indicates that the poorest 40 percent of Canadian families had very little wealth in 1984, and that this did not change by 2005. Meanwhile, the wealth of the top 40 percent rose substantially, with the largest increases at the very top. For example, in constant 2005 dollars, the net worth of the family at the 95th percentile was $534 980 in 1984, $723 590 in 1999, and $1 194 000 in 2005, which represents an increase of 65 percent in 2005 over 1999, and an increase of 35 percent in 1999 over 1984. There was no gain at all in the bottom half of the distribution.

In general, there is more inequality in the wealth distribution than in the distribution of annual income. And although Figure 13.4 presents a snapshot of wealth inequality at a point in time, we would really need a moving picture to follow the fortunes of families over time. At the extremes of the distribution, there may be little change. In 2005, as in previous years, the assets and the debts of the poorest 30 percent of the population roughly balanced, leaving little or no net worth. But for the next 60 percent, the middle class, the key asset is the family home. People who can buy a house will, by paying off the mortgage over time, work their way up the distribution of wealth as their debt declines and their net worth increases. As they age, they may move up the wealth deciles as they acquire more consumer durables and financial assets such as RRSPs. But some will also

11  René Morissette and Xuelin Zhang, "Revisiting Wealth Inequality," *Perspectives on Labour and Income*, December 2006, Statistics Canada Catalogue no. 75-001-XIE.

**FIGURE 13.4**
**Wealth Distribution of Canadian Families: 1984, 1999, 2005**
The average net worth of the top 40 percent of Canadian families was 65 percent higher in 2005 than in 1999, and 35 percent higher in 1999 than in 1984. The wealth of the poorest 40 percent of families was negligible in all years.
SOURCE: René Morissette and Xuelin Zhang, "Revisiting wealth inequality," *Perspectives on Labour and Income,* December 2006, Statistics Canada, Catalogue no. 75-001-XIE.

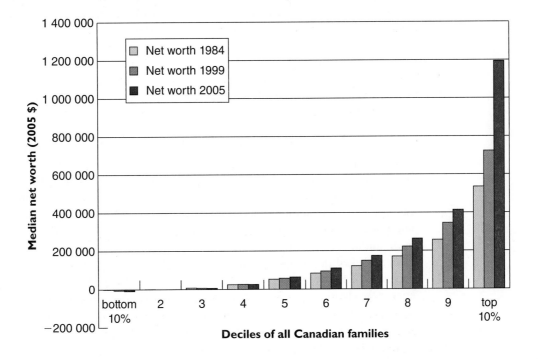

find that life events such as divorce or unemployment or major illness may deplete their wealth. At the very top, one finds both inherited wealth (e.g., the Thomson, Weston and Irving families with $23.4, $8.5 and $7.5 billion, respectively) and new money.[12]

Most financial assets are held by the top 10 percent of households who, in total, owned 58.2 percent of total net worth in 2005, a significant increase from 55.7 percent in 1999 and 51.8 percent in 1984. The 6.4 percentage point increase in the wealth share of the top 10 percent of families happens to be twice as large as the total wealth share, 3.2 percent, of the poorest *half* of Canadian families. Increasing wealth inequality is a concern for Canada because it means that many Canadians will have little or no accumulated savings to support themselves in their retirement years. This, along with declining coverage of registered pension plans, will leave many Canadians depending entirely on the public pension system in their old age.

The United States has better data on wealth distribution, and those data indicate an even bigger increase in wealth inequality. Wealth holdings for the richest 1 percent of Americans have, roughly, doubled since 1980. The combined wealth of the richest 1 percent of Americans now exceeds the combined wealth of the bottom 95 percent of Americans.

To say that recent changes in the distributions of income and wealth have produced a fundamental shift in the North American economic landscape is hardly an exaggeration. Because those near the top of the income ladder are prospering as never before, while those farther down the ladder have seen their living standards grow much more slowly, or even decline, an increasingly large gulf separates the top from the middle of the income distribution.

www.forbes.com/
Forbes 400

12 See http://list.canadianbusiness.com/rankings/rich100/2010.

**RECENT TRENDS IN INEQUALITY**

Over the past 25 years, some countries, particularly the United States and the United Kingdom, have seen very significant increases in economic inequality. In Canada, increases in the inequality of market income were largely offset by the tax and transfer systems until the mid-1990s, but inequality surged in the latter part of the decade. The top 1 percent of the income distribution has received most of the gains in wealth of the past quarter century.

# 13.3   HOW MUCH INEQUALITY WOULD BE "FAIR"?

Thus far, we have described the inequality of outcomes, but we have not discussed why income and wealth are unequally distributed. To some extent, inequality of opportunity shapes the actual degree of inequality we observe. On entering the world, some people are born into penniless families, while others can expect to inherit millions of dollars; some face discrimination, while others do not; and some are born with disabilities, while others are naturally talented. These differences in initial conditions may be accentuated, or diminished, over time by chance events (e.g., there is some chance that even the most naturally gifted person can get hit by a bus and be unable to work afterwards) and by personal and family choices (such as the decision to continue in school). As well, all societies make choices that affect economic inequality, such as whether or not to pass anti-discrimination legislation, to provide remedial education for the disabled, or how much to give in transfers or take in taxes from households at the top or bottom of the income distribution.

The degree of inequality of outcomes that we observe in any society, therefore, depends on both the inequality in initial conditions and the extent to which inequalities of opportunity are accentuated or diminished over time by chance events and by personal and social choices. Since all societies have to make some set of decisions on taxes, transfers, and the distribution of government services (like education), it is inescapable that government decisions in all societies will affect, to some degree, the distribution of income. But what criteria should guide these social decisions? What degree of redistribution of income is appropriate? Does redistribution blunt incentives to work and exercise initiative, and, if so, is the effect large or small? To what extent should taxes or transfers depend on the process that generates income (e.g., is redistribution to the poor equally appropriate for both those able to work and for the disabled?) To answer questions such as these, we need to be explicit about our values. The three perspectives that follow have been particularly influential in economics.

## "JUSTICE AS FAIRNESS"

What would a just distribution of income look like? John Rawls was a moral philosopher at Harvard University who suggested we should imagine ourselves meeting to choose the rules for distributing income.[13] He argued that a "fair" set of rules is the set of rules which we would choose if the meeting took place behind a "veil of ignorance," which concealed from participants any knowledge of what talents and abilities each has. If no individual knew whether he or she is smart or stupid, beautiful or ugly, male or female, no one would know which rules of distribution would work to his or her own advantage. One way to understand the thought experiment that Rawls proposes is to ask yourself the following questions:

13 John Rawls, *A Theory of Justice,* (Cambridge, Mass.: Harvard University Press, 1971).

- If you did not know whether you would be born male or female, black or white, aboriginal or non-aboriginal, would you think it fair that women or black people or aboriginals receive lower incomes than others? If so, how much lower?
- If you did not forecast that the person you chose to marry after graduation would turn out to be abusive, and that eventually your marriage would break up and you would become a single parent, or if you got pregnant in high school and became a single parent, would you think it fair that single parent families have a high probability of poverty? If so, how high?
- If you did not know whether you would dive off a wharf just before graduation from university and be paralyzed for the rest of your life, would you think it fair that paraplegics receive lower incomes than others? If so, how much lower?
- If you did not know whether, in the end, all your investments for your retirement would turn out badly and you would end up penniless in your old age, would you think it fair that society should expect seniors to entirely finance their own retirement years? If not, would you suggest there be any assistance for penniless senior citizens, and if there were assistance, how much?

Rawls argued that we think of a game as fair if its rules do not confer an advantage on any particular participant. In reality, we all actually know whether we were born black or white, rich or poor, with or without a disability. However, if we try to think of what the rules of society *should* be like, we would think of life as fair if those rules were not tilted in favour of particular people (including ourselves). The idea of asking what we would freely and rationally agree on as the rules of the game *if we had to choose those rules from behind "the veil of ignorance"* asks us to accept the chance that we might personally have the characteristics that would put us at the bottom of the socioeconomic heap, and to think about how badly off we might be, in that event.

Rawls' concept of "the rules of the game" is very broad and encompasses both the mechanisms by which life's rewards are allocated and the size of those rewards. He argues that even if we all chose from behind the veil of ignorance, free and rational individuals would probably not choose to equalize incomes entirely—some inequalities are likely to be necessary to provide incentives for labour supply, savings, and effort. However, if there were a chance that we personally would get the lowest prize in life's lottery, it would be rational for us to want that prize to be as high as possible. Rawls, therefore, argues that the fairness of social arrangements depends on how they affect the least well-off members of society. Economists often refer to this as the idea of "maxi-min," since it means that a society should try to *maxi*mize the *min*imum income in that society.

Rawls argues that the rules people would choose in such a state of ignorance would necessarily be fair, and if the rules are fair, the income distribution to which they give rise will also be fair. Rawls also argues that people would be willing to accept a certain degree of inequality as long as these rewards produced a sufficiently large increase in the total amount of output available for distribution.

But how much inequality would people accept? Much less than the amount produced by purely competitive markets, Rawls argues. The idea is that behind the veil of ignorance, each person would fear being put in a disadvantaged position, so each would choose rules that would produce a more equal distribution of income than now exists. And since such choices *define* the just distribution of income, he argues, fairness requires at least some attempt to reduce the inequality produced by the market system.

## THE UTILITARIAN ARGUMENT

The branch of moral philosophy called **utilitarianism** holds that the right course of action is the one that results in the highest total level of utility. Utilitarians argue against income inequality on the grounds that the marginal utility of income is typically smaller for a wealthy person than for a poor person. In their view, transferring $1000 of income

**utilitarianism** a moral theory in which the right course of action is the one that results in the highest total utility

from a rich person to a poor person is justified because the extra happiness experienced when the poor person receives the money outweighs the decline in happiness when the rich person gives it up.

The argument for this is based on the concept of diminishing marginal utility presented in Chapter 4. To understand it, it is useful to review the example presented in Table 4.2. That example referred to the utility Lamar gained from eating four ice cream cones. The utility derived from eating the first ice cream cone is 100, while the second cone eaten yields additional utility of 50, the third cone consumed provides 25 additional utils, and the fourth cone has a benefit of 12 utils. This example captures the idea of diminishing marginal utility, because Lamar gets more utility from consuming more ice cream but the first cones eaten are more enjoyable than the last few consumed.

Now let us extend the example and suppose there are two people with identical tastes, Lamar and Angelo. If there are four ice cream cones and Lamar eats them all, his utility is 187 (= 100 + 50 + 25 + 12). Angelo then consumes nothing, so his utility is zero. Total utility is 187.

The transfer of one ice cream cone from Lamar to Angelo would give Angelo 100 utils while Lamar now has 175 utils, producing total utility of 275 for a net gain in total utility of 88 (Lamar loses 12 utils while Angelo gets 100 utils). If we were to go further and transfer another ice cream cone to Angelo so they now have two each, then total utility rises to 300 ( = 150 + 150). Total utility is maximized when consumption is equalized, if both individuals have identical tastes.

This argument for greater equality based on diminishing marginal utility has been an influential one, but notice that the example of Lamar and Angelo illustrates two levels of equalizing transfers: moving from a (4:0) division of extreme inequality to a (3:1) division of moderate inequality, and then moving from moderate inequality to total equality (2:2). Notice also that the move from high to moderate inequality produces a large gain (88) in total utility, while the move from moderate inequality to total equality produces a much smaller gain in total utility (25). The principle of diminishing marginal utility implies that total utility increases in both cases; it also implies that the closer a society is to absolute equality, the smaller is the size of the gains in total utility of *further* reductions in inequality.

The principle of diminishing marginal utility applies both to incomes in general and to ice cream cones in particular. However, in real life we cannot measure utility and we know that different people have different tastes. People may also differ in their general ability to derive pleasure from their incomes. Unfortunately, we have no way of knowing how much utility different people get from the same bundle of goods. Hence, we cannot actually add the utility of different people and use the criterion of maximizing total utility as a guide to public policy. Furthermore, the issue of how to divide a given amount of goods (as in the example of four ice cream cones and two people) ignores the problem of how to establish incentives for people to produce goods. Hence, although most people accept the claim that an extra dollar generally meets more pressing demands for a poor person than for a rich person, even utilitarians do not argue for complete equalization on these grounds.

## POVERTY AND HUMAN RIGHTS

As Adam Smith recognized over two centuries ago, local consumption standards influence the goods and services that people consider essential for life, or "necessaries," as Smith called them:

> By necessaries I understand not only the commodities which are indispensably necessary for the support of life, but whatever the custom of the country renders it indecent for creditable people, even of the lowest order, to be without. A linen shirt, for example, is, strictly speaking, not a necessary of life. The Greeks and Romans lived, I suppose, very comfortably, though they had no linen. But in the present

times, through the greater part of Europe, a creditable day-labourer would be ashamed to appear in public without a linen shirt, the want of which would be supposed to denote that disgraceful degree of poverty which, it is presumed, no body can well fall into without extreme bad conduct. Custom, in the same manner, has rendered leather shoes a necessary of life in England. The poorest creditable person of either sex would be ashamed to appear in public without them.[14]

The absolute standard of living in Canada today is vastly higher than it was in Adam Smith's 18th-century Scotland. Yet Smith's observations apply with equal force to contemporary industrial societies. The general level of income crucially affects contemporary standards as to what is "decent" or "acceptable" in every aspect of life. A century ago it was, for example, considered entirely normal for most families in Canada to use an outdoor toilet. Today, a home without indoor plumbing would be considered substandard and probably would be demolished. Rising living standards have thus altered both the availability of commodities and the frame of reference that defines an acceptable standard of living.

Nobel Prize winner Amartya Sen has also argued that "poverty must be seen as the deprivation of basic capabilities rather than merely as lowness of income."[15] His focus is on the "substantive freedoms—the capabilities—to choose a life one has reason to value" that individuals actually possess, and he argues that individuals are not really "free" unless they possess "capabilities." For example, one capability Sen considers to be basic is the capability to appear in public without shame. As Adam Smith remarked more than two hundred years ago, this requires "decent" clothing, by the standards of the society in which a person lives. A second basic capability is the ability to visit friends or go to work, which requires a means of transportation.[16] Another example is the capability to understand the world around us, which requires some level of literacy and education. A fourth is the ability to function without pain (health is a very general capability, which requires some level of medical care). Sen's point is that it is substantive freedoms, not formal legal guarantees, that actually matter in people's lives, and people who do not have basic capabilities do not actually have much freedom.

Sen's work is also a reminder that public services in health care, education, and the urban environment (e.g., mass transit) are even more important to the poor than to the affluent, since the poor do not have the money to purchase private market substitutes. In Europe, these services are often referred to as the "social wage," since they are available to all citizens. The point is, that whether individuals get public services or pay privately, if individuals are to have substantive freedoms, they need access to economic resources.

In drawing the link among poverty, capabilities, and freedom, Sen is echoing a long tradition in the human rights literature. The actual exercise of human rights typically requires a basic level of economic resources. For example, Article 12 of the UN's *Universal Declaration of Human Rights* asserts a right to privacy, and so does the Canadian *Charter of Rights and Freedoms*. However, privacy requires control over a definable personal space, which, in a market economy, generally requires the ownership of property or the income with which to rent property. The lack of income to rent housing (or the lack of public housing for those who have no income) means that people have no choice but to live on the street. For the homeless, privacy rights are nothing but hollow words. The lack of income, or compensating public services, can therefore be seen as a human rights issue.

14 Smith, *The Wealth of Nations,* (1776) (New York, 1965), Book V, Chapter II, Article 4th, pp. 821–822.

15 A.K. Sen, *Development as Freedom,* (New York: A.A. Knopf Publishers, 1999).

16 Transportation is actually a good example of why social context matters for individual capabilities. Although having enough money to pay for bus fare may enable individuals to get around in Canadian cities, in rural areas and in most small towns there typically is no bus service available.

> **RECAP**
>
> **HOW MUCH INEQUALITY WOULD BE "FAIR"?**
>
> High levels of income inequality have drawn moral objections on several grounds. John Rawls argued that the degree of inequality typical of unregulated market systems is unfair because people would favour substantially less inequality if they chose distributional rules from behind a veil of ignorance. Utilitarians favour reducing inequality because the marginal utility of income is smaller for wealthy persons than for poor persons. Poverty can also be seen as a human rights issue, since the actual attainment of effective functioning, or of the actual exercise of freedoms, requires access to goods and services.

# 13.4 METHODS OF INCOME REDISTRIBUTION

Even if one decides that something should be done about poverty and inequality, the next question is, what is the best way to do it? There are costs and benefits to each possible public policy to alter the distribution of income, so economic analysis can be useful in deciding both *whether* and *how* we might want to change inequality and poverty.

## SOCIAL ASSISTANCE

If Canadians have no other way to get income, they must turn to their provincial government for social assistance. Since social assistance regulations are set by the provinces, they differ across the country. However, in all provinces, to receive social assistance, individuals have to pass a needs test—that is, they must have no source of income and typically they must have spent down their assets. In 2009, for example, a single parent with one child in Ontario would not qualify for benefits if she had more than $1550 in liquid assets (including any RRSP savings), but the same person in Alberta could not retain assets worth more than $1062.[17]

Social assistance payments vary by family status and family size but in all provinces are well below the low-income cut-off. For example, even when we add together all federal tax credits and the maximum provincial social assistance, in 2009 a single employable person in Ontario received $7501 yearly, only about 41 percent of the after-tax low-income cut-off (LICO); a single parent with one child got $17 732, about 77 percent of the after-tax LICO; and a couple with two children got $22 695, about 65 percent of LICO. Social assistance payments are much lower in some of the poorer provinces; for example, single employable individuals in New Brunswick received only $3773 per year in 2009, which was about 24 percent of the after-tax LICO.

Many economists have also noted that people on social assistance face a very high tax rate on any earnings. Although the details differ by province, social assistance recipients typically face a high penalty in reduced benefits if they start to earn income. Typically, they are allowed to keep only a small amount, if anything, before benefits are reduced. In 2009, for example, Quebec allowed a single employable individual or a single parent to keep the first $200 of a month's earnings, but Ontario allowed no exemption for the first three months of a claim, and after that benefits are reduced by 50 percent of any further earnings. In Nova Scotia and Manitoba, benefits are cut by 70 percent of any earnings. In effect, this means that social assistance clients face a marginal tax rate that is well above the rate facing any other segment of society. Since social assistance clients may also lose

---

17 Data in this section are taken from: *Welfare Incomes: 2009,* National Council of Welfare, see http://www.ncw.gc.ca/h.4m.2@-eng.jsp

some other benefits (such as access to public housing) if their incomes rise, some analysts have labelled these very high tax rates "the welfare trap."

Measured in constant dollars, the incomes of Canada's neediest citizens have declined over the last twenty years. Although the federal government has increased child support somewhat, the provinces have all let inflation erode the real value of social assistance payments and some provinces have cut them dramatically. For example, despite booming oil revenues, Alberta's 2009 provincial social assistance payments of $10 668 for a single parent with one child were about 23 percent less in real value than the $13 770 in provincial benefits that the same person would have received in 1989. Cuts for other types of social assistance clients in other provinces have varied in magnitude, but there is a common denominator of increasing deprivation for Canada's least fortunate citizens.

## THE NEGATIVE INCOME TAX

Nobel Laureate Milton Friedman and Conservative Senator Hugh Segal have proposed that current welfare programs be replaced by a **negative income tax (NIT)**.[18] Under the NIT, every man, woman, and child, rich or poor, receives an income tax credit. A person who earns no income would receive the credit in cash. People who earn income would be taxed at some rate less than 100 percent. By lowering the effective tax rate facing the poor, a NIT is intended to increase their incentive to earn income.

Under a negative income tax, the initial credit and the tax rate would combine to determine a **breakeven income level** at which a person's tax liability exactly offsets the initial tax credit. People earning below that level would receive a net benefit payment from the government; people earning above it would make a net tax payment. Example 13.1 illustrates how the breakeven income level would be calculated.

**negative income tax (NIT)** a system under which the government would grant every citizen a cash payment each year, financed by an additional tax on earned income

**breakeven income level** under a negative income tax, the level of before-tax income at which a family's tax liability exactly offsets its initial tax credit

## EXAMPLE **13.1**

### What is the breakeven level of earned income in an NIT program?

Consider a negative income tax program with a tax credit of $16 000/year and a tax rate of 50 percent. At what income level would an individual in this program neither pay a tax nor receive a benefit? How large a net benefit would a person earning $16 000/year receive? How large a net tax payment would a person earning $38 000/year owe?

The horizontal axis of Figure 13.6 shows an individual's before-tax income, while the vertical axis measures after-tax income. With the credit payment set at $16 000/year, someone with a before-tax income of $0 would end up with an after-tax income of $16 000/year. From that point, net income would rise by 50 cents for each dollar

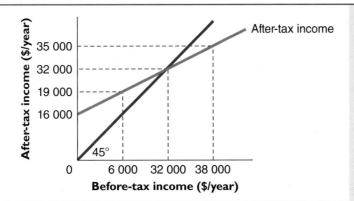

**FIGURE 13.5**

**A Hypothetical Negative Income Tax Program**

Under this negative income tax program, each person starts with a cash grant of $16 000/year, which is reduced at the rate of 50 cents for each dollar of income earned during the year. The breakeven income level is $32 000/year.

18 See: Why Corporate Canada Should Support a Negative Income Tax May 6, 2008 Hon. Hugh D. Segal, C.M., Senator (Kingston-Frontenac-Leeds)

earned, as shown by the red line labelled "After-tax income," until at some point it equaled his before-tax income. The 45° line shows all the points at which after-tax income equals before-tax income. In this program, the breakeven level of income is the before-tax income level at which the two lines intersect, which is $32 000/year. A person who earned $6000/year would receive an after-tax income of $19000—that is, earnings of $6000 plus a negative income tax cheque for $13 000. A person who earned $38 000/year would, on the other hand, pay $3000 in taxes and have an after-tax income of $35 000.

**EXERCISE 13.1**    **In Example 13.1, what would the breakeven income level be if the tax credit were $18 000/year?**

The negative income tax would help maintain work incentives, because it would ensure that someone who earned an extra dollar would keep more of it. However, the negative income tax is by no means a perfect solution to the income-transfer problem. The core problem is maintaining adequacy of benefits for those who cannot work, while preserving incentives to work for those who can. As a practical matter, the negative income tax idea has only actually been enacted for a group who are not really expected to work—Canada's senior citizens. Transfer payments under the OAS/GIS system (Old Age Security/Guaranteed Income Supplement) are available to all senior citizens. The GIS is reduced by 50 cents for every dollar in other income received. In 2010, the maximum annual income from the GIS was $15,888.

## ECONOMIC NATURALIST  13.1

### The Peanut Lady, whom one does not see in Canada

Recently, an economic naturalist spent a year working in Dar es Salaam, Tanzania. On his way home from work every day, he would stop to purchase two small bags of peanuts, for about 8 cents (Cdn) each, from an old lady who sat all day, every day, by the side of the road. Since her total inventory was no more than 30 bags, and she had to pay for the peanuts and their packaging, she could not possibly have made more than $2.00 per day. But Tanzania is a very poor country, and less than 5 percent of elderly Tanzanians receive a pension of any kind, so there is no expectation of "retirement"—people just work as long as they possibly can, at whatever will bring in a bit of income.

Sometimes, economic naturalism is about what one does not see in one place but does see elsewhere. In Canada, one does not observe old women selling peanuts by the roadside, because here they do not have to do so to survive. Many elderly women in Canada do not have pension income of their own, both because many have been "housewives" for much of their lives and because only a minority of Canadian jobs have pension coverage.

However, in Canada (as in other affluent countries), a universal, basic public pension system provides a minimum income for everyone in old age. If Canada's old age security system did not exist, the elderly would have to do whatever they could to survive, as they now have to do in Tanzania. Although the cost of providing a basic pension in Tanzania would be surprisingly small, about 1.3 percent of GDP,[19] the governments of poor countries do not have the tax revenue to pay for many of the expenditures that Canadians take for granted.

In the Tanzanian case, part of the reason for low tax revenue is that the government has committed itself to low tax rates in order to attract foreign investment. For example, Barrick Gold Corporation (a Canadian company) has four gold mines in Tanzania, which in 2010 produced 716 000 ounces of gold. In 2010, a world price of over US$1400 and average production costs of $725 per ounce (including amortization and royalties of $37 per ounce),

---

19 See Thadeus Mboghoina and Lars Osberg (2011), *Social Protection of the Elderly in Tanzania: Current Status and Future Possibilities*, Research on Poverty Alleviation (REPOA), Special Paper 10/5 PO Box 33223, Dar es Salaam, Tanzania.

Lars Osberg

meant that Barrick Gold had operating profits on its Tanzanian operations of approximately US$514 million.[20] No corporate income tax was paid to Tanzania. In 2010, the U.S. corporate income tax rate was 35 percent, a bit higher than the 30 percent tax rate in Canada (federal plus provincial). If taxed at either rate, the revenue from Barrick's gold profits could have funded a universal pension for all Tanzanians over 65 at the food poverty line. The more general point is that the tax rate on resource rents, and how that tax revenue is spent, could have big impacts on the distribution of income, at both the very top and the very bottom.

Of course, the elderly who have been able to save enough from their working years to finance their retirement, or who have an adequate pension, do not need to worry about poverty in their old age. But, as we have already seen in this chapter, most Canadian families are not able to accumulate much wealth, and private pension plan coverage has been declining in Canada: less than half the labour force is covered by a private pension plan, people with pension coverage tend to have higher-income jobs, workers often lose coverage when they change jobs, and the proportion of workers covered by private pensions has been shrinking over time. Therefore, as a practical matter, transfer payments from governments are crucial, and poverty reduction among senior citizens has been a Canadian success story. In 1961, before the introduction of the Canada/Quebec Pension Plan (CPP/QPP) and the OAS/GIS system, almost half of families with a head of household over 65 and over two-thirds of single senior citizens fell below the low-income cut-off. In 2009, the elderly poverty rate was 6.5 percent.[21]

In Canada today, "retirement" is a generally expected stage of life—people over 65 are not expected to be in the workforce. Perhaps for that reason, policy-makers have not been particularly worried about undermining the work ethic among seniors; transfer payments have been made available to deal with the poverty problem among senior citizens. For people under 65, however, there has always been a concern among policy-makers that transfer payments might be "too generous," and the work ethic might be undermined.

However, whether or not people *want* to work, are they *able* to work? In 2006, about 2.5 million Canadians between the ages of 15 and 64 (a prevalence rate of 11.5 percent[22]) reported that they have a long-term disability. Although many of them can and do hold down jobs, there are also many others for whom this is not feasible.

Remember, also, that throughout this text we have emphasized supply and demand—that both sides of the labour market matter. As Figure 13.2 shows, labour demand is a crucial determinant of the poverty rate. When the economy moves into recession, firms stop hiring and start firing. When there are few jobs of any kind to be had, employers tend to demand better credentials, even for entry-level jobs. The people who then find

20  All financial and production data on Barrick are taken from http://www.barrick.com/Theme/Barrick/files/docs_annualquarterly/2010/Q4-Year-End-Mine-Stats.pdf.

21  See L. Osberg, "Poverty Among Senior Citizens—a Canadian Success Story," *The State of Economics in Canada: Festschrift in Honour of David Slater*, Patrick Grady and Andrew Sharpe (ed.), John Deutsch Institute for the Study of Economic Policy, Queen's University, Kingston, 2001, pp. 151–182; CANSIM V1564236.

22  See the 2006 Participation and Activity Limitation Survey: Disability in Canada Catalogue no. 89-628-XWE Statistics Canada (2010), http://www.statcan.gc.ca/bsolc/olc-cel/olc-cel?catno=89-628-X&lang=eng.

themselves at the back end of the job queue may look in vain for work, and in some parts of the country there is a chronic shortage of paid employment at any time. Whether or not individuals have enough incentives to accept job offers is always only part of the story; incentives are only relevant if job offers actually exist, which depends on an individual's ability to work and the availability of work. Unfortunately, however, debate on the design and level of social assistance support has often tended to focus just on the "supply side" of labour markets.

---

**RECAP**

### METHODS OF INCOME REDISTRIBUTION

For those aged 65 and over, OAS, the GIS, and CPP/QPP have succeeded in pulling the incomes of many seniors above the LICO. For those under 65 years of age, social assistance payments are the major instrument in the battle against poverty. Because benefits under this program are means tested, beneficiaries often experience only a small increase in net income when they accept paid employment while receiving assistance.

The negative income tax (NIT), if enacted, would apply universally—a NIT would pay a basic, guaranteed income to all people. Payments are reduced in proportion to other income, so that above a *breakeven income* people pay net taxes; below it, they receive benefits. The Guaranteed Income Supplement in Canada is essentially a negative income tax for seniors.

---

## 13.5   PAYING FOR INCOME-SUPPORT PROGRAMS

Policy-makers must choose not only which policies to employ in the effort to reduce poverty and income inequality, but also how to pay for them. A common proposal is to make the federal income tax more progressive. Proponents contend that such a change would not only finance additional transfers to low-income families, but would also reduce the gap between the after-tax incomes of wealthy and middle-class families. Opponents of this proposal worry about the unintended side effects of increasing the top tax rates.

### ADVERSE EFFECTS ON INCENTIVES

Most liberals, and even many conservatives, have always considered a more progressive tax structure to be desirable on the grounds of equity. But would more steeply progressive taxes kill the proverbial goose that lays the golden egg? Would high tax rates on top earners weaken their incentive to work hard and take risks?

At the very top of the income pyramid, where the CEOs of major corporations receive multi-million dollar compensation packages, one encounters the "problem" of how to spend it all. How exactly could one spend four or five or twenty million dollars, without being ostentatious? Or is it possible that ostentatious consumption is the whole point? If one takes "monster" homes, which are becoming ever bigger and more grandiose, as an example, the grand halls and big rooms primarily serve to impress guests, even if their owners find that they actually make little personal use of most of their space. As Thorstein Veblen noted over a century ago, the whole point of ostentatious consumption is to display one's ability to consume, thereby deriving *relative* status, compared with those who cannot afford to consume as much. At the very top of the income pyramid, income may be the competitive scorecard, and ostentatious consumption may be the way one shows who is "winning," but the underlying issue is comparison: am I a bigger success than everybody else?

As an article in *The Globe and Mail* commented,

What does a successful financier do when Porsches become passé, and the bank account has more zeroes than ever seemed possible way back when studying for that MBA, three decades ago? How does one stay motivated when bank buyouts, tech scores and leveraged co-investment wins have given a small-town kid the ability to buy a small town?

Simple. It's time to move the goalposts farther down the field. Got to get "the jet."[23]

The crucial part of competitive consumption is relative rank—having more and bigger goodies *compared with* others, however much everyone else actually has. But a person's *relative rank* in the pecking order is not affected if everyone at the top pays the same tax rate. When, for example, the average income tax rate is 50 percent, a CEO who makes $5 million before tax will have $2.5 million after tax, and the vice-president with $2 million before tax will have $1 million after tax. If the tax rate changes to 20 percent, the CEO's after-tax income will rise to $4 million and the VP's after-tax income increases to $1.6 million—but the CEO still has two and half times as much disposable income.

Hence, *the pecking order of relative consumption status is unaffected by changes in the tax rate.* Because the post-tax income ratio does not change, a decrease or increase in tax rates that applies to everybody leaves status rankings unchanged. If relative status is what people want, the president still has the same incentive to want to be "top dog." Since higher tax rates for *everyone* do not affect the *relative* ranking of individuals, they do not affect the incentive that each senior executive has to try to get ahead. The international evidence indicates that although there are large differences across countries in the tax rates that people at the top end of the income distribution pay, top executives work hard everywhere. There are relatively small international differences in the weekly hours of work that top income earners supply.[24]

---

**RECAP**

### PAYING FOR INCOME-SUPPORT PROGRAMS

Although some fear that the higher taxes on top earners needed to pay for income transfers will reduce effort and investment, an increase in current top tax rates would not change *relative* income rankings or the incentive to achieve relative status, at the very top end.

---

23 In 2004, the up-front cost of a 1/16th share in a basic Learjet 40 was $515 000, with annual operating costs estimated at $145 000. Andrew Willis, "Getting the jet's the big dream on Bay St." *The Globe and Mail*, June 16, 2004. Reprinted with permission.

24 L. Osberg "Understanding Growth and Inequality Trends: The Role of Labour Supply in the U.S.A. and Germany," *Canadian Public Policy,* Vol. XXIX, Supplement January 2003, pp. S163–S184.

---

## SUMMARY

- The Lorenz curve and Gini coefficient can be used to portray the degree of inequality in the distribution of income and wealth. **LO3**

- Income growth since the mid-1970s has been concentrated among top earners. **LO2, LO3**

- The distribution of income and wealth in Canada has become more unequal in recent decades with the changes favouring those at the top of both distributions. Inequality also has increased in the United States and the United Kingdom. In some countries, France, for example, inequality has been reduced. **LO1, LO2, LO4**

- John Rawls argued that if the distribution of income were chosen in a meeting held behind a "veil of ignorance," the result would be a distribution closer to equality than what is produced by a competitive economy. Utilitarians argue that diminishing marginal utility of income indicates that it is appropriate to reduce inequality in the distribution of income. Poverty deprives people of basic capabilities such as the ability to work or to have privacy; therefore, poverty can be seen as a denial of human rights. **LO5**

- Social assistance is one method of reducing poverty. Social assistance payments vary with family size and characteristics, but in Canada they are set well below the poverty line. Because social assistance payments are cut drastically when recipients earn income, many analysts worry that it creates insufficient incentives to accept employment. **LO6, LO7**

- A negative income tax is a universal program that pays a basic, guaranteed income to all people. Payments are reduced in proportion to other income, so that above a *breakeven income* people pay net taxes. In Canada, the Guaranteed Income Supplement is essentially a negative income tax for the elderly. **LO6, LO7**

- If relative status depends on relative consumption, higher tax rates that apply to all incomes would not change post-tax income ratios and would not reduce the incentive to achieve higher relative status. **LO7**

## KEY TERMS

breakeven income level (377)
Gini coefficient (366)

Lorenz curve (365)
negative income tax (NIT) (377)

quintile (364)
utilitarianism (373)

## REVIEW QUESTIONS

1. What costs does greater concentration of income among top earners impose on middle-class families? **LO1, LO2**

2. Why does John Rawls believe that policies to redistribute income would command support behind a veil of ignorance? **LO5**

3. Name two self-interested reasons that a top earner might favour policies to redistribute income. **LO6**

4. Why is exclusive reliance on the negative income tax unlikely to provide a complete solution to the poverty problem? **LO5, LO6, LO7**

## PROBLEMS

1. What is the breakeven level of before-tax earned income in a negative income tax program with a tax credit of $5000/year and a tax rate of 40 percent? How large a net benefit would be received by a person earning $6000/year? How large a net tax would be paid by someone earning $15 000/year? **LO6**

2. Enfield is a small economy consisting of five identical people who can earn a living in either of two ways: by acting or by growing corn. A corn farmer can earn $10 000 (corn farmers can earn more, but this suits our example), and the best actor in Enfield will be chosen for a film contract that pays in accordance with the performer's acting ability. The only audition requirement is to be filmed working as an unpaid actor in a theatre in Montreal, which means being unable to work as a farmer. From among the filmed performances, a winner is chosen and paid. All contestants perceive the same likelihood of being chosen, and the payment to the winner increases with the number of contestants in the manner shown in the following table. **LO6, LO7**

| Number of contestants | Expected payment to the winner ($1000s) | Expected payoff per contestant ($1000s) |
|---|---|---|
| 1 | 21.0 | 21.0 |
| 2 | 34.0 | 17.0 |
| 3 | 45.0 | 15.0 |
| 4 | 50.0 | 12.5 |
| 5 | 55.0 | 11.0 |

a. If all villagers have the same tastes and are risk-neutral, how many will compete to become an actor? What will be the total income of the residents of Enfield?

b. What is the socially optimal number of villagers to enter the competition? How much would village income be if only the optimal number entered?

3. Refer to Problem 2. What is the smallest lump-sum tax on the winner's earnings that would ensure that the optimal number of villagers entered the competition? **LO6, LO7**

## ANSWERS TO IN-CHAPTER EXERCISES

**13.1**  The breakeven level increases from $32 000/year to $36 000. **LO6**

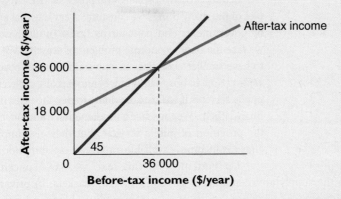

 **Practise and learn online with Connect.**

# CHAPTER 14
# Public Goods

## LEARNING OBJECTIVES

When you have completed the material in this chapter, you will be able to:

**LO1** Distinguish among private goods, public goods, collective goods, and commons goods by using the concepts of rivalry and excludability.

**LO2** Explain how government provides and pays for goods and services.

**LO3** Determine the optimal quantity of a public good.

**LO4** Explain how rent-seeking activity can reduce total economic surplus.

**LO5** Explain the roles of municipal, provincial, and national governments in a federal system.

Canadian university students attend institutions that receive substantial funding from the government. To get to class, they travel on roads paid for by governments, sometimes in buses whose costs are subsidized by governments. If they have an accident and are injured en route, they expect to be taken to a hospital where government will pay the nurses and doctors. However, they also hope that this event is unlikely—in part because they know that police, who are paid by the government, are directing traffic and keeping dangerous drivers off the road.

Schools, roads, hospitals, and police services are some examples of the many things we consume every day that are provided by governments and paid for by taxes. In all these instances, we face the basic economic problem of scarcity. We would like to have smaller class sizes in universities, better roads, and less waiting time in hospitals, but we cannot really expect to get these public services if we are not willing to pay the taxes necessary to finance them. We thus face a fundamental trade-off: taxes enable the provision of public services, but they also imply that less after-tax income is available for private consumption.

Up until now in this text, we have concentrated our attention on the supply and demand for goods in private markets. In private markets, individual consumers decide how much of each commodity to buy and personally pay for, while profit-maximizing firms decide how much to supply. However, when governments decide how much of a good or service is to be produced, and when the cost of these goods and services is paid from taxes, a model intended to explain private sector economics clearly does not apply.

Although there may be a broad consensus in contemporary politics that some government is necessary (and a general realization that this necessarily implies that some taxes are also required), debate rages over the appropriate size and functions of government.

How big, exactly, should government be? What goods and services should it provide? How should it raise the revenue to pay for them? What other powers (if any) should it have to constrain the behaviour of its citizens? And how should the various powers we assign to government be apportioned among local, provincial, and federal levels? Our goal in this chapter is to employ the principles of microeconomics in an attempt to answer these pragmatic questions.

## 14.1 GOVERNMENT PROVISION OF PUBLIC GOODS

The theory of perfectly competitive supply developed in Chapters 5 and 6 applies to private goods, of which basic agricultural products are good examples. However, although governments do produce and pay for some private goods, one of the primary tasks of government is to provide what economists call *public goods,* such as national defence and the criminal justice system.

## PUBLIC GOODS VERSUS PRIVATE GOODS

**Public goods** are those goods or services that are, in varying degrees, *nonrival* and *nonexcludable.* A **nonrival good** is one whose consumption by one person does not diminish its availability for others. For example, if the military prevents a hostile nation from invading your city, your enjoyment of that protection does not diminish its value to your neighbours. A good is **nonexcludable** if it is difficult to prevent nonpayers from consuming it. For instance, even if your neighbours do not pay their share of the cost of maintaining an army, they will still enjoy its protection.

When the City of Toronto puts on a fireworks display to celebrate Canada Day, it is difficult to charge admission, because the display can be viewed from many different locations in the city. And the fact that so many people view the display does not in any way diminish its value to other potential viewers. In contrast, a price can be charged fairly easily for the typical **private good**, and it is diminished one-for-one by any individual's consumption of it. For instance, when you buy and eat a cheeseburger, it is no longer available for anyone else. Moreover, people can be easily prevented from consuming cheeseburgers they don't pay for.

**Which of the following, if any, is nonrival?**
**a. The Web site of Statistics Canada at 3 A.M.**
**b. The World Cup soccer championship game watched in person.**
**c. The World Cup soccer championship game watched on television.**

There are two big reasons for government provision of public goods. First, because a public good is nonexcludable, no firm can charge a price for using it. Any private sector firm would have obvious difficulty in recovering the cost of producing a public good. Thus a private company would make a loss by producing public goods. Therefore, we cannot expect the private sector to produce public goods, at least in most cases. Economists often call this the "free-rider problem," using the example of how, if bus operators could not charge fares, many people would ride for free. The bus company would probably go bankrupt, even if the benefits to travellers of having bus service are more than sufficient to cover the cost of producing it.

Second, because a public good is nonrival, the marginal cost of serving additional users is zero once the good has been produced. In this case, charging for the good would not maximize total surplus (even if it was possible), because consumption can be increased at zero cost. However, *any* price will prevent some consumption. This loss of potential consumer surplus characterizes the provision of **collective goods**—nonrival goods for which it is possible to exclude nonpayers. Pay-per-view cable television is an example. People who do not pay cannot watch, a restriction that excludes many viewers who would have benefited from watching. Since the marginal cost to society of their tuning in is literally zero, excluding these viewers is wasteful. The waste is increased if it takes real resources to administer the pricing system, such as technicians to connect and disconnect subscribers.

A different kind of problem is posed by **commons goods**—goods which are rival but also nonexcludable, a combination of characteristics that almost always results in a tragedy of the commons (see Chapter 10). Fish in ocean waters are an example.

The classification scheme defined by the nonrival and nonexcludable properties is summarized in Table 14.1. The columns of the table indicate the extent to which one person's consumption of a good fails to diminish its availability for others. Goods in the right column are nonrival, while those in the left column are rival. The rows of the table

**private good** a good for which nonpayers can easily be excluded and for which each unit consumed by one person means one fewer unit is available for others

**public good** a good or service that, to at least some degree, is both nonrival and nonexcludable

**nonrival good** a good whose consumption by one person does not diminish its availability for others

**nonexcludable good** a good that is difficult, or costly, to prevent nonpayers from consuming

E X E R C I S E 1 4 . 1

**collective good** a good or service that, to at least some degree, is nonrival but excludable

**commons good** a good for which nonpayers cannot easily be excluded and for which each unit consumed by one person means one fewer unit is available for others

**TABLE 14.1**
**Private, Public, and Hybrid Goods**

|  | Rival | Nonrival |
|---|---|---|
| **Nonexcludable** | Commons good (fish in the ocean) | Public good (national defence) |
| **Excludable** | Private good (hamburgers) | Collective good (pay-per-view TV) |

indicate the difficulty of excluding nonpayers from consuming the good. Goods in the top row are nonexcludable, those in the bottom row, excludable. Private goods (lower left cell) are rival and excludable. Public goods (upper right cell) are nonrival and nonexcludable. The two hybrid categories are commons goods (upper left cell), which are rival but nonexcludable, and collective goods (lower right cell), which are excludable but nonrival.

Economists' definitions of the "public" or "private" nature of a good do not, in the real world, align neatly with which type of organization provides specific goods. Collective goods are sometimes provided by government, sometimes by private companies. Most public goods are provided by government, but even private companies can sometimes find profitable ways of producing goods that are both nonrival *and* nonexcludable. An example is broadcast radio and television, which covers its costs by selling airtime to advertisers.

Furthermore, we should always remember our basic "benefit-cost" approach. The only public goods the government should even *consider* providing are those whose benefits exceed their costs. The cost of a public good is simply the sum of all explicit and implicit costs incurred to provide it. The benefit of a public good is measured by how much people would be willing to pay for it. Although that sounds similar to the way we measure the benefit of a private good, an important distinction exists. The benefit of an additional unit of a private good, such as a cheeseburger, is the highest sum that any individual buyer would be willing to pay for it. In contrast, the benefit of an additional unit of a public good, such as an additional broadcast episode of "Dragon's Den," is the sum of the reservation prices of all people who would like to watch that episode.

www.cbc.ca
CBC

Even if the amount that all beneficiaries of a public good would be willing to pay exceeds its cost, that only implies that government should *provide* the public good in question. One must distinguish between *provision* (who pays for a good or service) and *production* (who actually makes the good or provides the service).

Typically, the services provided by the public sector are actually produced by a mix of civil servants and private sector employees. For example, when city governments put on fireworks displays, they almost invariably hire private companies to do the job. At the national level, having an adequate defense is a public good provided by the state, from which all citizens benefit, but the military often subcontracts aircraft or building maintenance to private firms, so defense uses a mix of public and private sector employees. Another example comes from the public and private employees who operate the criminal justice system. It is often efficient to subcontract some functions (e.g., courthouse cleaning) to private firms. As long as the job is openly tendered and the lowest bidder gets the work, this subcontracting is not controversial. But the *quality* of justice is hard to measure, so we do not use the same tendering process to allocate the jobs of judges.

The issue of maintaining the quality of public services lies behind much of the controversy surrounding subcontracting. Proponents argue that the public sector can use competition among private sector firms to restrain costs. Opponents typically question the size of financial savings and point to other social costs. If, for example, competitive bidding determines which private firms will operate prisons, bidders who want to maximize profits will have an incentive to skimp on costs, such as rehabilitation programs. From society's point of view, ex-cons who commit crimes and are returned to prison represent a social cost, but prison firms may see them as repeat business. Nevertheless, governments often use the threat of subcontracting as a way of limiting wage demands by public setor unions.

It is important to distinguish between *provision* and *production* by the public sector because even if we agree that the public sector should be responsible for the *provision* of a service, the optimal method of *production* of that service may include private firms. This section focuses on the issue of whether the public sector should *provide* a service. The basic rule is that if the benefit of a public good exceeds its cost, we are better off if we have it.

COST-
BENEFIT

## PAYING FOR PUBLIC GOODS

Not everyone benefits equally from the provision of a given public good. For example, some people find fireworks displays highly entertaining, but others simply don't care about them, and still others actively dislike them. Ideally, it might seem that the most equitable method of financing a given public good would be to tax people in proportion to their willingness to pay for the good. To illustrate this approach, suppose Chen values a public good at $100, Smith values the same good at $200, and the cost of the good is $240. Chen would then be taxed $80, and Smith would be taxed $160. The good would be provided, and each taxpayer in this example would reap a surplus equal to 25 percent of his tax payment: $20 for Chen, $40 for Smith.

However, we saw in Chapter 11 (The Economics of Information) that sometimes it is not in peoples' interest to reveal true information. In particular, if citizens know they will be taxed in proportion to the amount they state they are willing to pay, they have an incentive to understate their willingness to pay in order to get low taxes. Examples 14.1 to 14.3 illustrate some of the problems that arise in financing public goods and suggest possible solutions to these problems.

### EXAMPLE 14.1

#### Will Prentice and Wilson buy a water filter?

Prentice and Wilson own adjacent summer cottages along an isolated stretch of shoreline on Lake Huron. Because of a recent invasion of zebra mussels, each must add chlorine to his water intake valve each week to prevent it from becoming clogged by the tiny mollusks. A manufacturer has introduced a new filtration device that eliminates the nuisance of weekly chlorination. The cost of the device, which has the capacity to serve both houses, is $1000. Both owners feel equally strongly about having the filter. But because Wilson earns twice as much as Prentice, Wilson is willing to pay up to $800 to have the filter, whereas its value to Prentice, a retired schoolteacher, is only $400. Would either person be willing to purchase the device individually? Is it efficient for them to share its purchase?

Neither will purchase the filter individually because each has a reservation price that is below its selling price. But because the two together value the filter at $1200, sharing its use would maximize total economic surplus, which would be $200 higher than if they did not buy the filter.

Since sharing the filter maximizes total surplus, we might expect that Prentice and Wilson would quickly reach an agreement to purchase it. However, if Wilson proposes that they just split the cost of the filter equally, it will yield a net benefit to him of $300 (= $800 benefit − $500 cost) but Prentice will turn the idea down because he would incur a net cost of $100 (= $400 benefit − $500 cost). Without some agreement on the sharing of costs, the joint purchase and sharing of facilities is often more easily proposed than accomplished. An additional hurdle is that people must incur costs merely to get together to discuss joint purchases. With only two people involved, those costs might not be significant. But if hundreds or thousands of people are involved, communication could be prohibitively costly.

With large numbers of people, the free-rider problem emerges. If there are thousands of people involved, the contribution of any one person is only a tiny percentage of the cost, and everyone knows the project can go ahead without any one person's contribution. Everyone, thus, has a personal incentive to withhold contributions; that is, get a free ride in the hope that others will pay.

Even when only a few people are involved, reaching agreement on a fair sharing of the total expense may be difficult. For example, Prentice and Wilson might be reluctant to disclose their true reservation prices to one another. Suppose Prentice can keep his own reservation price secret while getting Wilson to reveal that he would be willing to pay up to $800 for the filter. Prentice could then announce that he is willing to pay $205. He knows that the filter will be installed because Wilson will be better off paying $795 than with no deal at all. If Prentice can follow this strategy successfully, he will be better off by $195, and Wilson will be better off by $5, compared to the "no deal" option. In total, the consumer surplus of installing the filter is $200, and since Prentice pays much less than he would really have been willing to pay, he gets almost all of it. Of course, as soon as Wilson figures this out, he will understate his true willingness to pay. Since both Prentice and Wilson have an incentive to play games with each other by understating their personal benefits, the filter may never be installed.

These practical concerns may lead us to empower government to buy public goods on our behalf. But as Example 14.2 makes clear, this does not eliminate the need to agree on how public purchases are to be financed.

### EXAMPLE 14.2

**Will the government buy the water filter if there is an "equal tax" rule?**

Suppose Prentice and Wilson from Example 14.1 could ask the government to help broker the water filter purchase. Suppose too, that the government's tax policy must follow a "nondiscrimination" or "equal charging" rule and that public goods can be provided only if a majority of citizens approve of them. Will a government bound by these rules provide the filter that Prentice and Wilson want?

A tax that collects the same amount from every citizen is called a **head tax**. If the government must rely on a head tax, it must raise $500 from Prentice and $500 from Wilson. But since the device is worth only $400 to Prentice, he will vote against the project, thus denying it a majority. So a democratic government would not provide the water filter if it must rely on a head tax.

**head tax** a tax that collects the same amount from every taxpayer

A head tax is an example of a **regressive tax** on income, one for which the proportion of a taxpayer's income that is paid in taxes declines as the taxpayer's income rises.

The point illustrated by Example 14.2 is not confined to the specific public good considered. It applies whenever taxpayers place significantly different valuations on public goods, as will almost always happen whenever people earn significantly different incomes. An equal tax rule under these circumstances will almost invariably rule out the provision of many public goods whose provision could benefit everyone.

As Example 14.3 suggests, one solution to this problem is to allow taxes to vary by income.

**regressive tax** a tax under which the proportion of income paid in taxes declines as income rises

## EXAMPLE 14.3

### Will the government buy the filter if there is a proportional tax on income?

Suppose that Prentice proposes that the government raise revenue by imposing a proportional tax on income to finance the provision of the water filter described in Example 14.1. Will Wilson, who earns twice as much as Prentice, support this proposal?

A **proportional income tax** is one under which all taxpayers pay the same percentage of their incomes in taxes. Under such a tax, Wilson would support Prentice's proposal, because if he didn't, each would fail to enjoy a public good whose benefit exceeds his share of its cost. Under the proportional tax on income, Prentice would contribute $333 toward the $1000 purchase price of the filter and Wilson would contribute $667. The government would buy the filter, resulting in additional surpluses of $67 for Prentice and $133 for Wilson.

**proportional income tax** a tax under which all taxpayers pay the same proportion of their incomes in taxes

The water filter in the previous example is not a pure public good. In this case, excludability is not a problem, since either Prentice or Wilson could buy the filter and not share its use. However, since the capacity of the filter is more than enough for both of them, not using it would be inefficient because their consumption is nonrivalrous. The water filter is thus best seen as a collective good, at the level of Prentice and Wilson.

Often, whether a good is "public" can partially depend on the level of analysis. For example, when a group of students decide to rent an apartment together, their choice of apartment is both rival and excludable, and, therefore, a private good for them as a household. However, although it is normal for bedrooms to be private, other rooms typically are common space. Furthermore, each apartment has some common attributes; for example, its location determines the travel times of all inhabitants and (unless each room has a separate thermostat) all the inhabitants enjoy (or tolerate) the same temperature, whatever that is. Thus, the common space, heating, location, and some other aspects of the apartment, like the general level of noise or cleanliness, can be seen as a "local public good" *for household members*. Students who share an apartment are familiar with the problem of deciding on how often to clean the toilet and how much to pay for common services such as telephone or internet connections, which can be seen as an experience at the household level of some of the problems that occur when providing public goods at the societal level. In practice, students typically select as potential roommates other students who have roughly similar budgets, so equal contributions may work as a way to pay for public goods. However, equal payments can often be a poor way to share expenses within the household or a society when incomes are unequal. Consider Economic Naturalist 14.1.

**ECONOMIC NATURALIST 14.1**

### Why do spouses not contribute equally to joint purchases?

Suppose Roberto met Gina when she worked at her father's pizza parlour, but Roberto has just signed a 12-year, $64 million NHL deal while Gina still makes only $20 000 selling pizzas. Given that level of income, Roberto as an individual would want to spend much more than Gina would on housing, travel, entertainment, education for their two children, and the many other items they consume jointly. What will happen if the couple adopts a rule that each must contribute an equal amount toward the purchase of such items?

This rule would constrain the couple to live in a small house, take only inexpensive vacations, and skimp on entertainment, dining out, and their children's education. It is, therefore, easy to see why Roberto might find it attractive to pay considerably more than 50 percent for jointly consumed goods, because doing so would enable *both* of them to consume in the manner their combined income permits.

Public goods and jointly consumed private goods are different from individually consumed private goods in the following important way: *Different individuals are free to consume whatever quantity and quality of most private goods they choose to buy, but jointly consumed goods must be provided in the same quantity and quality for all persons.*

As in the case of private goods, people's willingness to pay for public goods normally increases with income. Wealthy individuals tend to assign greater value to public goods than low-income people do, not necessarily because the wealthy have different tastes but because they have more money. A head tax would result in high-income persons getting smaller amounts of public goods than they want. By increasing the total economic surplus available for all to share, a tax system that assigns a larger share of the tax burden to people with higher incomes makes possible a better outcome for both rich and poor alike. Indeed, virtually all industrialized nations have tax systems that are at least mildly **progressive**, which means that the proportion of income that is taxed actually rises with a family's income.

**progressive tax** a tax in which the proportion of income paid in taxes rises as income rises

Progressive taxation and even proportional taxation of income have often been criticized as being unfair to the wealthy who are forced to pay more than others for public goods that all consume in common. The irony in this charge, however, is that exclusive reliance on head taxes, or even proportional taxes, would curtail the provision of public goods and services that are of greatest value to high-income families. Studies have shown, for example, that the income elasticity of demand for public goods such as parks and recreation facilities, clean air and water, public safety, uncongested roads, and aesthetically pleasing public spaces is substantially greater than one. Failure to rely on progressive taxation would result in gross underprovision of such public goods and services.

**TABLE 14.2**

**A Summary of Different Types of Income Taxes**

| | |
|---|---|
| Head Tax | Same dollar amount paid by all taxpayers, regardless of income |
| Regressive Tax | Low-income taxpayers pay a higher percentage of their income in tax than high-income taxpayers |
| Proportional Tax | Same percentage of income paid by all taxpayers, regardless of income |
| Progressive Tax | Low-income taxpayers pay a lower percentage of income in tax than high-income taxpayers |

# 14.2 THE OPTIMAL QUANTITY OF A PUBLIC GOOD

In the examples considered thus far, the question was whether to provide a particular public good and, if so, how to pay for it. In addition, we often have to decide what level and quantity of a public good to provide.

## THE DEMAND CURVE FOR A PUBLIC GOOD

The process for calculating the socially optimal quantity of a public good differs in an important way from how we determine the optimum quantity of a private good.

For a private good, all buyers face the same price and each chooses the quantity they want to purchase at that price. Recall that to construct the demand curve for a private good from the demand curves for individual consumers, we place the individual demand curves side by side and add them horizontally. That is, for each of a series of fixed prices on the individual demand curves, we ask, how much would each individual want? and then we add the resulting quantities demanded. In Figure 14.1, for example, we add the individual demand curves for a private good, $D_1$ and $D_2$ [panels (a) and (b)], horizontally, to obtain the market demand curve for the good $D$ [panel (c)].

COST-
BENEFIT

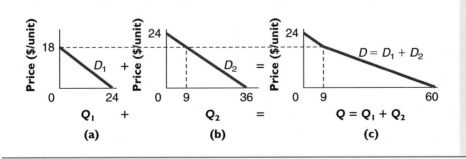

**FIGURE 14.1**

**Generating the Market Demand Curve for a Private Good**

To construct the market demand curve for a private good [panel (c)], we add the individual demand curves [panels (a) and (b)] *horizontally*.

For a public good, all buyers necessarily consume the same quantity, although each may differ in terms of willingness to pay for additional units of the good. Constructing the demand curve for a public good thus entails not horizontal summation of the individual demand curves, but vertical summation. That is, for each of a series of quantity values, we ask, what is the total amount of money which people would be willing to pay for this unit of the good? That is, we add up the prices that individuals are willing to pay for an additional unit of the good. The curves $D_1$ and $D_2$ in Figure 14.2, panels (a) and (b), show

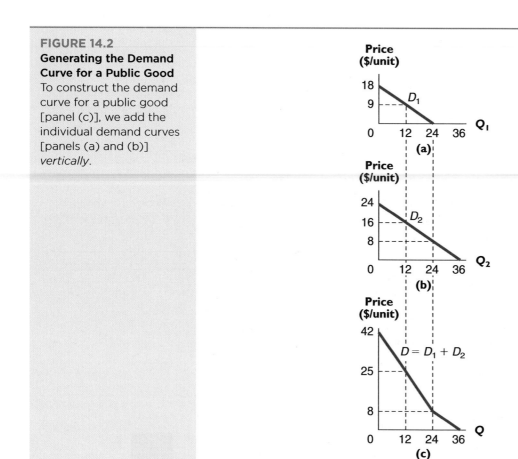

**FIGURE 14.2**
**Generating the Demand Curve for a Public Good**
To construct the demand curve for a public good [panel (c)], we add the individual demand curves [panels (a) and (b)] *vertically*.

individual demand curves for a public good by two different people. At each quantity, these curves tell how much each individual would be willing to pay for an additional unit of the public good. If we add $D_1$ and $D_2$ vertically, we obtain the total demand curve $D$ for the public good [panel (c)].

**EXERCISE 14.2**

**Bill and Tom are the only demanders of a public good. If Bill's demand curve is $P_B = 6 - 0.5\ Q$ and Tom's is $P_T = 12 - Q$, construct the demand curve for this public good.**

In Example 14.4, we see how the demand curve for a public good might be used in conjunction with information about costs to determine the optimal level of parkland in a city.

## EXAMPLE **14.4**

### What is the optimal quantity of urban parkland?

The city government of a new planned community must decide how much parkland to provide. The marginal cost curve and the public demand curve for urban parkland are as shown in Figure 14.3. Why is the marginal cost curve upward sloping and the demand curve downward sloping? Given these curves, what is the optimal quantity of parkland?

The marginal cost schedule for urban parkland will be upward sloping if the city acquires the cheapest parcels of land first, and only then turns to more expensive parcels. Likewise, the marginal willingness-to-pay curve will be downward sloping

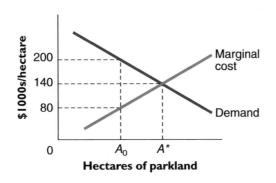

**FIGURE 14.3**
**The Optimal Quantity of Parkland**
The optimal number of hectares of urban parkland is $A^*$, the quantity at which the public's willingness to pay for additional parkland is equal to the marginal cost of parkland.

if the law of diminishing marginal utility applies. Just as people are generally willing to pay less for their fifth hot dog than for their first, they are usually also willing to pay less for the 101st hectare of parkland than for the 100th hectare. Given these curves, $A^*$ is the optimal quantity of parkland. For any quantity less than $A^*$, the benefit of additional parkland exceeds its cost, which means that total economic surplus can be made larger by expanding the amount of parkland. For example, at $A_0$, the community would be willing to pay \$200 000 for an additional hectare of urban parkland, but its cost is only \$80 000. Similarly, for any quantity of parkland in excess of $A^*$, the community would gain more than it would lose by selling off some parkland.

## PRIVATE PROVISION OF PUBLIC GOODS

Government has several advantages in providing public goods. First, once a tax collection agency has been established to finance a single public good, it can be expanded at relatively low cost to generate revenue for additional public goods. Second, because government has the power to tax, it can summarily assign responsibility for the cost of a public good without endless haggling over who bears what share of the burden. And in the case of goods for which nonpayers cannot be excluded, the government may be the only feasible provider.

INCREASING
OPPORTUNITY COST

However, governments are not the exclusive providers of public goods in any society. Indeed, many public goods are routinely provided through private channels. The challenge, in each case, is to devise a scheme for raising the required revenues.

COST-
BENEFIT

### Funding by Donation

Approximately one quarter of Canadian taxpayers report making a charitable donation each year. In 2009, Canadians gave \$7.8 billion to private charities,[1] many of which provide public goods to their communities. Furthermore, many Canadians voluntarily donate their time to activities that benefit their community rather than themselves personally. In everything from coaching youth soccer to providing meals to housebound seniors, Canadians depend heavily on the voluntary motivation of concerned citizens.

Why do people voluntarily provide their time and money to worthy causes? If we think of individuals as utility maximizers, the answer will be that the individuals who coach soccer or provide meals get some satisfaction from the idea that these social needs are being met. The problem, however, with relying entirely on the warm glow that volunteers get from their voluntary efforts is that the warm glow is much less than total

---

1   The median donation was about 0.5 percent of median income. See http://www40.statcan.gc.ca/l01/cst01/famil90-eng.htm.

benefits. For example, when volunteers coach youth soccer, the players benefit and so do the other parents who know their children enjoy soccer but who are too busy to coach. Volunteers who maximize only their own utility will not take into account these benefits to other people. In consequence, purely voluntary provision will cause these services to be undersupplied.

Undersupply is a general problem that arises from relying on private donations to provide public goods. For example, if road maintenance were to depend on voluntary effort to fill potholes, we can be sure that some people would voluntarily contribute their own time and resources to help solve the pothole problem. However, others would reason that, given the deterioration of the road system, they might as well just buy sport utility vehicles with stronger suspensions and higher road clearance. Similarly, some people now devote their own time and resources to community recreation projects that divert youth from crime while others just try to protect themselves from robbery. As well, when hard times come (as in the recession of 2008), charitable donations tend to decline—just when needs are greatest.

### Development of New Technology

Excludability is a criterion used to determine if something is a public good; however, the difficulty of excluding those who have not paid for a service depends on the available technology. As a consequence, the boundary line between public and private goods can depend on the available technology.

For example, lighthouses have been used for decades as a classic example of a public good. Once a lighthouse is built, all boaters in the area can use its signal to avoid dangerous rocks (nonrivalrous consumption), and no vessel can be prevented from seeing the lighthouse's signal (nonexcludability). For centuries, lighthouses were the most practical way of warning ships about hazards to navigation, and since the time of the Egyptian pharaohs, governments have generally paid for their construction.

In the 1990s, with the advent of global positioning satellite systems (GPS), a new technology became available to tell navigators how close they are to hazards. The launching of satellites is expensive, but once they are in place and broadcasting signals, the information they provide is still nonrivalrous in consumption. However, in principle, the signal could be scrambled, and a charge made for the sale of each receiver equipped with a decoder (i.e., location information would no longer be nonexcludable). This has not happened, and GPS signals are presently provided free to the world (courtesy of the U.S. military), but in principle, a charge could be made.

Similarly, TV and radio broadcast signals were classic public goods during the era when broadcasting was the only way that such signals could be sent and received. However, broadcast television stations now have the ability to scramble their signals, making them available only to those consumers who purchase or rent descrambling devices.

### Sale of By-Products

Some public goods are financed by the sale of rights or services that are generated as by-products of the public goods. For instance, as noted earlier, radio and television programming is a public good that is paid for in many cases by the sale of advertising messages. Internet services are also underwritten in part by commercial messages that appear in the headers or margins of Web pages.

One way to reduce the inefficiency that arises when advertisers choose programming is to employ pay-per-view methods of paying for television programming. These methods allow viewers to register not just which programs they prefer but also the strength of their preferences, as measured by how much they are willing to pay. This implies that pay-per-view TV is more likely to select the programs the public most values. However, it is also less efficient than broadcast TV in one important respect. As noted earlier, charging each household a fee for viewing discourages some households from tuning in at all. And since the marginal social cost of serving an additional household is exactly zero, limiting the audience in this way means total surplus is not maximized. Which of the two inefficiencies is more important—free-TV's inefficiency in choosing among programs, or pay-TV's inefficiency in excluding potential beneficiaries—is an empirical question.

In any event, the mix between private and public provision of public goods and services differs substantially from society to society and from arena to arena within any given society. These differences depend on the nature of available technologies for delivering and paying for public goods, and also on people's preferences.

## EXAMPLE 14.5

### By how much is economic surplus reduced by a pay-per-view charge?

Suppose World Wrestling Entertainment (WWE) is shown on pay-per-view television, and the demand curve for each event is given by $P = 20 - Q$, where $P$ is the price per household in dollars and $Q$ is the number of households who choose to watch the program (in millions). If the regulated pay-per-view charge is $10 per household, by how much would economic surplus rise if the same event were shown instead on "free" broadcast public TV?

With a fee of $10 per event 10 million households will watch (see Figure 14.4). But if the same event was instead broadcast on public TV, 20 million households would watch. The additional economic surplus reaped by the extra 10 million households is the area of the blue triangle, $50 million. The marginal cost of permitting these additional households to watch the event is zero, so the total gain in surplus is $50 million.

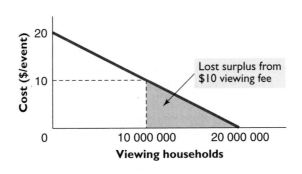

**FIGURE 14.4**
**The Loss in Surplus from a Pay-per-View Fee**
Twice as many households would watch the program if its price were zero instead of $10. The additional economic surplus is the area of the blue triangle, or $50 million.

A similar situation arises when government departments charge fees for services that do not cost any extra resources to provide. For example, Statistics Canada, unlike its U.S. counterpart, charges user fees for access to its data—fees that are well in excess of the cost of storing that data on its computers. As a result, Canadian citizens who cannot afford to pay user fees are prevented from getting information. Regardless of whether those data might have helped them to make better private economic decisions or to represent themselves more effectively in public policy debates, a loss in economic surplus results because of less-informed decision making. And, as this example illustrates, the loss in economic surplus from charging a price in excess of marginal cost is *not* an issue that depends on whether the provider of the service in question is a private firm or a government department. There is a loss in consumer surplus whenever a price is charged but consumption is nonrivalrous. If letting one more person consume a service has zero real resource cost, charging a price just prevents potential consumers from deriving a real benefit while transferring revenue to the agency or firm.

In general, charging a positive price for a good whose marginal cost is zero will result in a loss in surplus. As we saw in Chapter 7, the size of the loss that results when price is set above marginal cost depends on the price elasticity of demand. When demand is more elastic, the loss in surplus is greater. Exercise 14.3 provides an opportunity to see that principle at work.

**EXERCISE 14.3**   **How would your answer to Example 14.5 have been different if the demand curve had been given instead by P = 15 − 0.5Q?**

## HUMAN RIGHTS AS PUBLIC GOODS

Public spending on healthcare (at 8.0 percent of GDP in 2009) and education (6.3 percent of GDP) are the two biggest uses of resources by government in Canada.[2] However, neither is a pure public good from the point of view of the individual consumer. In both healthcare and education, it is easy to exclude people from consumption who have not paid. In both, consumption is rival as well as excludable, since the space used for one patient or student is not available for another. Both these goods are, therefore, better analyzed as "publicly provided private goods," rather than "public goods" in the sense in which economists use the two terms. Indeed, during the nineteenth century and before, in Canada (as in many poor countries today), to the extent that healthcare and education were provided at all, they were provided mostly by private suppliers. Why is government the provider now?

In part, greater economic efficiency explains why Canadian governments are now involved in education and health. Chapter 11 has already discussed the efficiency arguments for public health insurance. Similarly, the public sector provides schooling because it is inefficient for a society not to make use of the potential abilities of all its citizens. If parents have to pay for all the education that their children get, some parents will not be able to pay and some will not want to pay, even if they can. But why should the education of children depend on who had the good or bad luck to be born to which set of parents? Equality of opportunity for all citizens has historically been a major argument for a system of high-quality public education, but this has always been only part of the story. Support for public schooling also has always been partly based on a pragmatic concern that talent not be wasted.

However, education and healthcare can also be seen as human rights issues. Canadians like to feel that their society is a fair one in which basic human rights are observed. And to a greater or lesser degree, Canadians, like other nationalities, take pride in the accomplishments of their country and feel shame at its failures. Not only is there a vicarious enjoyment of the moments of triumph when Canadian athletes win medals or Canadian scientists win international prizes, but Canadians also care about Canada's human rights reputation. Since the human rights record and fairness of Canadian society is a source of utility that is freely available to all Canadians (i.e., nonrivalrous and nonexcludable in consumption), it can be seen as a public good.

Human rights are partly an economic issue, because making sure that rights are provided is often expensive. Guaranteeing the legal rights of the accused in the criminal justice system is, for example, costly. It is more expensive for governments to pay for judges and legal aid lawyers than it would be to assume that the police never make mistakes. Trials cost money, so why do we not just lock up whomever the police decide to arrest? It is rational for Canadians to spend money on maintaining human rights—both because individuals know that someday they personally may benefit from the protection of their rights and because of the utility that they get from knowing they live in a fair society.

2 See CANSIM Table 385-0001.

Furthermore, when it comes to education and healthcare, a perception of fairness is important in part because it enables the affluent to conclude that their own advantages in life were justly acquired. *Equality of opportunity* is an important component of most conceptions of a fair society (indeed, it is explicitly recognized as an objective of Canadian governments in Article 36 [1] of the Constitution Act of 1982), but it is hard to see how a society where poor children were condemned to illiteracy and poor health could claim to offer meaningful equality of opportunity. For this reason, the Universal Declaration of Human Rights of 1948 clearly identified healthcare and education as basic human rights:

> Article 25. Everyone has the right to a standard of living adequate for the health and well-being of himself and of his family, including food, clothing, housing, and medical care and necessary social services, and the right to security in the event of unemployment, sickness, disability, widowhood, old age or other lack of livelihood in circumstances beyond his control.

> Article 26. Everyone has the right to education. Education shall be free, at least in the elementary and fundamental stages. Elementary education shall be compulsory. Technical and professional education shall be made generally available and higher education shall be equally accessible to all on the basis of merit.

Since somewhat similar wording is contained in the International Covenant on Economic, Social and Cultural Rights (1966) and other human rights treaties ratified by Canada, spending on healthcare and education can be seen as necessary to abide by Canada's international obligations to protect basic human rights. In economic terms, this produces the pure public good that arises from Canada's record of observing human rights. Like any other pure public good, this record may be valued to different degrees by different people, Nevertheless, the total utility generated by it is the social benefit that arises from Canada's record of observing human rights.

## ENVIRONMENTAL PUBLIC GOODS

Canadians also value the quality of the natural environment in which they live. Since no one has figured out how to charge for the consumption of clean air, and since each of us breathes an infinitesimal fraction of the air available, clean air is both nonrivalrous and nonexcludable. It is a classic public good. Consequently, regulation of pollution is another function of government. In Chapter 10 we discussed how economic principles can be used to control pollution in the most efficient manner possible. However, atmospheric pollution illustrates the limitations of governments, as well as those of markets.

Often, the various sources of atmospheric pollution are not subject to regulatory control by a single government. Much of the acid rain that falls in Canada, for example, is the result of sulphur dioxide emissions from industrial sources in the upper mid-west of the United States. These emissions are beyond the reach of Canadian environmental regulations. Many years of negotiations did eventually produce cross-border agreements on sulphur dioxide emissions, but this was a relatively simple case where only two national governments were involved. Negotiations to limit the discharge of greenhouse gases are far more complex. Carbon dioxide emitted anywhere on the planet disperses to uniform concentrations around the globe in a matter of months. Moreover, climate change is a global problem that no one government can solve, and negotiations have not yet been successful in producing cooperative action.

The choice between different levels of government, then, often confronts us with difficult trade-offs. Ceding the power of taxation to a federal government often entails painful compromises for voters in individual provinces. But the loss of political autonomy is an even less attractive option. Similarly, nations are understandably reluctant to cede any of their sovereign powers to a higher authority, but failure to take such steps may entail unacceptable environmental costs in the long run.

**THE OPTIMAL QUANTITY OF A PUBLIC GOOD**

A *public good* is *nonrival* and *nonexcludable*. Therefore, the quantity of a public good must be the same for every consumer and the total demand curve for a public good is constructed by adding individual demand curves vertically. Optimal production of a public good occurs at the quantity for which the demand curve intersects the marginal cost curve of the public good.

## 14.3   EXTERNALITIES AND GOVERNMENT

The provision of public goods is not the only rationale for the existence of government. Government also creates and enforces the rules without which the efficient production of private goods would not be possible.

As we saw in Chapter 10, for example, externalities often stand in the way of socially optimal resource allocation. We saw, too, that optimal allocations are unlikely to result whenever property rights are poorly defined (for example, the tragedy of the commons). Many laws, in fact, can be interpreted either as attempts to define property rights or to control externalities. The law requiring motorists to drive on the right, for example, attempts to prevent the activities of one motorist from causing harm to others, which could be analyzed either as conferring a temporary property right to your side of the road or as preventing the externality which occurs when oncoming cars drive there. Some issues (for example, excess emission of $CO_2$ and other greenhouse gases) can be analyzed either as a problem caused by an inadequate definition of property rights (since nobody owns the right to clean air) or as a problem of externalities (since emissions are generated as a by-product of other activities) or as the problem of producing an environmental public good. Economists use these different theoretical approaches because each perspective offers slightly different, but complementary, insights. The bottom line, however, is that regulation of activities that generate externalities and the definition and enforcement of property rights are important roles for government. This is why most governments regulate activities that generate pollution, control access to fishing waters and public timber lands, and enforce zoning laws. However, the mere existence of an externality does not necessarily mean that the best outcome will be achieved by governmental regulation. As we will see, regulation entails costs of its own. The ultimate question is, therefore, a practical one: Will government regulation of the externality in question do more good than harm?

**EXTERNALITIES AND GOVERNMENT**

Government creates economic surplus not only by providing public goods but also by regulating activities that generate externalities and by defining and enforcing property rights. These rationales explain why governments regulate pollution, control access to fishing waters and public timber lands, and enforce zoning laws.

## 14.4   RENT-SEEKING

Inefficiency in the public sphere can occur when the gains from a government decision are concentrated in the hands of a few beneficiaries while the costs are spread among many. Beneficiaries then have a powerful incentive to organize and lobby in their own favour. Individual taxpayers, by contrast, may have little at stake and, therefore, have little incentive to incur the cost of mobilizing themselves in opposition.

The Canadian pharmaceutical industry is one example. In the 1980s, local firms in Canada began manufacturing generic drugs under licence. These drugs did the same thing as the drugs made by multinational drug companies, but retailed at far lower prices. When the federal government extended Canada's patent laws to restrict the manufacture of generic drugs, critics charged that the result was a net loss to Canada since all Canadians paid higher drug prices while the profits flowed out of the country. However, since the industry promised to locate high-profile research facilities in Montreal, members of parliament from that area lobbied strongly for the change.

Still other sources of inefficiency arise in the case of projects whose benefits exceed their costs. Government contracts for major defence projects (such as building naval frigates) often ignite intense competition among different constituencies, each one vying through its representatives to win the contract. Millions of dollars can be spent on preparing proposals, consultants' fees, and various other lobbying activities. When such investments are mutually offsetting, they are known as **rent-seeking**, and they tend to be inefficient for the same reason that investments by contestants in other positional arms races are inefficient (see Chapter 10).

**rent-seeking** the socially unproductive efforts of people or firms to win a prize

> ### RECAP
>
> **RENT-SEEKING**
>
> Government does much to help the economy function more efficiently, but it can also be a source of waste. Rent-seeking occurs when individuals or firms use real resources in an effort to win favours from the regulator.

## 14.5 MUNICIPAL, PROVINCIAL, OR FEDERAL?

Thus far in this chapter we have discussed government in the abstract, without being at all specific about which level of government is being considered. However, as a practical matter, in all countries, public services are delivered by a variety of government agencies operating at several levels: national, regional, and local. In some countries, such as Sweden, the United Kingdom, and France, all these levels of government are created by acts of the national legislature. This type of government is called a *unitary* system, since the legislation that establishes regional and local government authorities can be amended by the national legislature at its discretion, and the national government can, therefore, decide how much power it wants to delegate to local authorities.

The Canadian system is different. Like many other countries (such as the United States, Australia, India, and Germany), Canada has a federal system of government and a constitution that establishes the jurisdiction and the powers of both the federal and provincial levels of government. Consequently, changes in the jurisdiction of the provinces and the federal government can only come about by mutual agreement or amendment of the constitution. (There is no similar constitutional protection of municipal governments, whose powers and responsibilities can be altered by provincial legislation.) But since neither the federal nor the provincial levels of government can unilaterally alter their responsibilities, they must constantly negotiate how to avoid duplication or conflict in overlapping areas of tax and program jurisdiction. When there are multiple levels of government, politicians at each level can be tempted to claim credit for all successes and to blame other levels of government for all failures. Local politicians can also divert discontent by protesting that their jurisdiction has somehow been unfairly treated in taxes or services or both. As the daily news attests, many provincial and federal politicians in Canada are unable to resist these temptations.

Given the stresses and strains of federalism, why do we bother? Why not do away with continual negotiation and posturing for political advantage? Why not just have a single government that provides all public services?

The primary reason for having multiple levels of government is to better enable government to differentiate its delivery of services to meet the differing preferences and needs of local communities. For example, Canada has always recognized that the majority of the residents of Quebec want to be educated in French, while in other provinces the majority prefers to be educated in English. As long as Quebec was a separate colony, its francophone majority could protect their desires for French-language education, but if a wider union, in which francophones would be a minority, was to be established, the Quebecois required some guarantee that education in French would not be at risk. The British North America Act of 1867, therefore, assigned to the provinces exclusive control over education (and other social services). Ever since, the Government of Quebec has insisted on protecting the constitutional right to provincial jurisdiction over education, because it sees provincial control as essential to the continued existence of a distinct francophone culture in North America.

Language preference is just one aspect of the ways in which local communities may differ. Some communities may prefer to have soccer fields for youth sports, while baseball may be more popular elsewhere. In some places, the preservation of historic buildings may be considered more important than speeding up traffic flow by widening roads, but other places may prefer to avoid traffic jams. The devolution of decision making on these and many other practical matters to the local level enables government to have a better chance of matching local decisions to local preferences.

Even though many useful activities of government are best designed at the local level, others are most efficiently done at regional or national levels. It is, for example, extremely useful for businesses to have reliable and timely statistics to assist their planning and investment decisions, so Statistics Canada collects them. It would be very inefficient for each municipality in Canada to design and administer its own survey of local business conditions, both because of the waste of duplicated design effort and because it would be impossible for survey results to be added up or compared if each local jurisdiction asked slightly different questions in a different way.

There are, therefore, efficiency advantages to devolving some public activities to local or provincial levels while centralizing others. Although, in every federal country, the constitution establishes an initial division of jurisdiction and powers, the divisions are not carved in stone. The courts can interpret the constitution to favour one level of government or the other, and governments can agree to transfer power and responsibility (as, for example, in the 1990s when the federal government offered the provinces control and funding of labour market training programs). In Canada, the balance between provincial and federal governments has changed over time, as economic conditions and policies have changed.

However, in all federations, the central government has more sources of tax revenue available to it than the provinces do, and some of its revenue is transferred to the provinces for their use. In Canada, federal-provincial transfer payments were once a much larger fraction of provincial revenues than they are today. At the time of Confederation, import tariffs and duties were the major revenue source for governments. However, if the separate colonies were to realize the economic benefits of free trade in a wider economic union, it was essential for them to surrender their power to levy import taxes to the new Dominion of Canada—but for that to happen, the federal government had to agree to replace their lost revenues.

Over time, the provincial governments developed new sources of taxation to meet the needs of a growing population for schools, roads, wharves, and other public works. However, during the Great Depression of the 1930s, the provinces (particularly Alberta and Saskatchewan) found that although the need for relief payments grew dramatically, their capacity to raise revenue fell with depressed business conditions. In April 1936 Alberta defaulted on payment of its provincial debt. In response to the crisis in provincial public finances, the Rowell-Sirois Commission was appointed. Before it could deliver its report (which recommended a major expansion of the federal government's role in maintaining national standards in education, healthcare, and public assistance), World War II created a massive increase of defence expenditure by the federal government. A massive expansion of heavy industry ensued, and the size and authority of the federal government relative to the provinces increased greatly.

Since that surge, the dominant long-run trend has been the declining relative role of the federal government. For about 50 years after World War II, total federal program spending was typically around 15 percent to 16 percent of GDP. Since 1994, this has decreased significantly. Federal spending on programs was 13 percent of GDP every year from 2006 to 2009.[3] However, because that figure includes transfers to the provinces equal to approximately 2.9 percent of GDP, federal expenditures on goods, services, and direct transfers to individuals amounted was 10.1 percent of GDP—less than the 10.3 percent of GDP that the federal government spent in 1949–50.[4]

By contrast, in the past 60 years, provincial government expenditures have grown significantly. In 1949–1950, direct federal spending dwarfed provincial government spending (10.3 percent of GDP federal compared to 5.8 percent provincial). Twenty years later, in 1969–1970, expenditures by the provinces and the federal government were close to being equal. Since then, the federal government has been, in expenditure terms, the "junior order of government." During 2006–2009, local, provincial and territorial governments in Canada spent an average of 25.2 percent of GDP, or about 2.5 times the amount of federal spending.

This growth in provincial spending arose because the constitution assigned to the provinces jurisdiction over healthcare, education, and social spending, and these public services have grown in importance over time. The three main budget items of provincial governments are healthcare, education, and social services. Between 2006 and 2009, they averaged 74 percent of total provincial spending. In addition, provincial governments are locked into the financing costs of past debt—on average about 7 percent of spending. Added together, this leaves just 19 percent of spending to pay for all other services (roads, police and courts, parks, agricultural services, environmental regulation, etc.).[5]

3  All figures from *Fiscal Reference Tables*, available online at www.fin.gc.ca/pub/frt-trf/index-eng.asp.

4  Federal spending rose in 2009–2010 by three percentage points of GDP, but the Minister of Finance stated clearly that this was a temporary increase in response to the recession, and would be reversed in future.

5  See CANSIM series V645186, V645194, V645198, V645203, V645210.

## SUMMARY

- A good is nonrival if one person's consumption does not diminish the amount available for others. A good is nonexcludable if nonpayers cannot be prevented from consuming the good. Goods that are both highly nonexcludable and nonrival are called public goods. One of government's principal tasks is to provide public goods, such as national defence and the criminal justice system. **LO1**

- A collective good, such as pay-per-view cable television, is nonrival but excludable. Commons goods are goods that are rival but nonexcludable. **LO1**

- Because not everyone benefits equally from the provision of any given public good, charging all taxpayers equal amounts for the provision of public goods will generally not be either feasible or desirable. As in the case of private goods, people's willingness and ability to pay for public goods generally increases with income, and most governments therefore levy higher taxes on the rich than on the poor. Tax systems with this property have been criticized on the grounds that they are unfair to the wealthy, but this criticism ignores the fact that alternative tax schemes generally lead to worse outcomes for both rich and poor. **LO2**

- The economic criterion for providing the optimal quantity or quality of a public good is to increase quantity or quality only as long as the marginal benefit of doing so exceeds the marginal cost. One advantage of using the government to provide public goods is that once a tax collection agency has been established to finance a single public good, the agency can be expanded at relatively low cost to generate revenue to finance additional public goods. A second advantage is that because government has the power to tax, it can easily assign responsibility for the cost of a public good. And in the case of goods for which nonpayers simply cannot be excluded, the government may be the only feasible provider. **LO2, LO3**

■ Some public goods are provided through private channels with the necessary funding provided by donations, sale of by-products, by development of new means to exclude nonpayers, and, in many cases, by private contract. A loss in economic surplus results, however, whenever monetary charges are levied for the consumption of a nonrival good. Reliance on purely voluntary private provision will usually result in the undersupply of public goods. **LO2, LO3**

■ In addition to providing public goods, government regulates activities that generate externalities, and it defines and enforces property rights. **LO2**

■ Rent-seeking occurs when individuals or firms seek favours from legislators. It can reduce total economic surplus by using real resources in mutually offsetting efforts to influence governments. **LO4**

■ Canada has a federal system of government in which the constitution assigns specific functions to the federal and provincial levels of government. The provinces have responsibility for the two biggest areas of public expenditure, healthcare and education, as well as social assistance, policing, and construction and maintenance of most infrastructure. Because the federal government has access to more sources of revenue than the provinces do, federal-provincial revenue transfers are a significant part of intergovernmental relations in Canada. Unlike the federal and provincial governments, municipal governments do not have constitutional protection. Provincial legislation can alter the powers and responsibilities of municipal governments. **LO5**

## KEY TERMS

| | | |
|---|---|---|
| collective good (385) | nonrival good (385) | public good (385) |
| commons good (385) | progressive tax (390) | regressive tax (389) |
| head tax (389) | proportional income tax (389) | rent-seeking (399) |
| nonexcludable good (385) | private good (385) | |

## REVIEW QUESTIONS

1. a. Which of the following goods are nonrival? **LO1**
   (i) Apples
   (ii) Stephen King novels
   (iii) Street lighting on campus
   (iv) CBC radio broadcasts
   b. Which of the above goods are nonexcludable?

2. Give examples of goods that are, for the most part **LO1**
   a. Rival but nonexcludable
   b. Nonrival but excludable
   c. Both nonrival and nonexcludable

3. Why might even a wealthy person prefer a proportional income tax to a head tax? **LO2**

4. True or false: A tax on an activity that generates external costs will improve resource allocation in the private sector and also generate revenue that could be used to pay for useful public goods. Explain. **LO2**

5. Consider a good that would be provided optimally by private market forces. Why is the direct loss in surplus that would result from a tax on this good an overstatement of the loss in surplus caused by the tax? **LO2**

## PROBLEMS

1. Jack and Jill are the only two residents in a neighbourhood, and they would like to hire a security guard. The value of a security guard is $50/day to Jack and $150/day to Jill. Irrespective of who pays the guard, the guard will protect the entire neighbourhood. **LO2**

**14.2** To construct the demand curve [panel (c)], we first graph Bill's demand curve [panel (a)] and Tom's demand curve [panel (b)] and then add the two individual demand curves vertically. The equation for the demand curve is $P = 18 - 1.5Q$. **LO2**

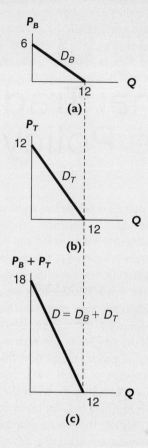

(a)

(b)

(c)

**14.3** Whereas elasticity of demand was 1 at a price of $10 on the original demand curve, it is 2 on the new demand curve. As a result, the $10 fee now excludes 20 million viewers, and the resulting loss in surplus (again the area of the blue triangle) is now $100 million. **LO2**

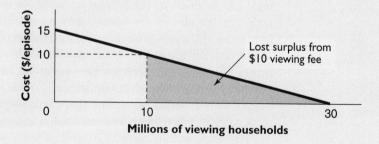

a. What is the most a guard can charge per day and still be assured of being hired by at least one of them?

b. Suppose the competitive wage for a security guard is $120/day. The local government proposes a plan whereby Jack and Jill each pay 50 percent of this daily fee, and asks them to vote on this plan. Will the plan be voted in? Would economic surplus be higher if the neighbourhood had a guard?

2. Refer to Problem 1. Suppose Jack earns $10 000/month and Jill earns $110 000/month. **LO2**

a. Suggest a proportional tax on income that would be accepted by majority vote and would pay for the security guard.

b. Suppose instead that Jack proposes a tax scheme under which Jack and Jill would each receive the same net benefit from hiring the guard. How much would Jack and Jill pay now? Would Jill agree to this scheme?

c. What is the practical problem that prevents ideas like the one in part (b) from working in real-life situations?

3. The following table shows all the marginal benefits for each voter in a small town whose town council is considering a new swimming pool with capacity for at least three citizens. The cost of the pool would be $18 per week and would not depend on the number of people who actually used it. The interest rate is 1 percent per week. **LO2, LO3**

| Voter | Marginal benefit ($/week) |
| --- | --- |
| A | 12 |
| B | 5 |
| C | 2 |

a. If the pool must be financed by a weekly head tax levied on all voters, will the pool be approved by majority vote? Does this outcome maximize total economic surplus? Explain.

b. The town council instead decides to auction a franchise off to a private monopoly to build and maintain the pool. If it cannot find such a firm willing to operate the pool, then the pool project will be scrapped. If all such monopolies are constrained by law to charge a single price to users, will the franchise be sold, and if so, how much will it sell for? Does this outcome maximize total economic surplus? Explain.

4. Refer to Problem 3. Suppose now that all such monopolies can perfectly price discriminate. **LO2, LO3, LO4**

a. Will the franchise be sold, and if so, how much will it sell for? Does this outcome maximize total economic surplus? Explain.

b. The town council decides that, rather than auction off the franchise, it will give it away to the firm that spends the most money lobbying council members. If there are four identical firms in the bidding and they cannot collude, what will happen?

5. Two consumers, Smith and Jones, have the following demand curves for Podunk Public Radio broadcasts of recorded opera on Saturdays: **LO3**

Smith: $P_S = 12 - Q$
Jones: $P_J = 12 - 2Q$

where $P_S$ and $P_J$ represent marginal willingness to pay values for Smith and Jones, respectively, and $Q$ represents the number of hours of opera broadcast each Saturday.

a. If Smith and Jones are the only public radio listeners in Podunk, construct the demand curve for opera broadcasts.

b. If the marginal cost of opera broadcasts is $15 per hour, what is the socially optimal number of hours of broadcast opera?

6. Suppose the demand curves for hour-long episodes of the "Jerry Springer Show" and "Masterpiece Theater" are as shown in the following diagram. A television network is considering whether to add one or both programs to its upcoming fall lineup. The only two time slots remaining are purchased by Colgate, which is under contract to pay the network 10 cents for each viewer who watches the program, out of which the network will have to cover its production costs of $400 000 per episode. (The number of viewers can be estimated accurately with telephone surveys.) Any time slot the network does not fill with "Springer" or "Masterpiece Theater" will be filled by infomercials for a weight-loss program, for which the network incurs no production costs and for which it receives a fee of $500 000. Viewers will receive $5 million in economic surplus from watching each installment of the infomercial. **LO2, LO3**

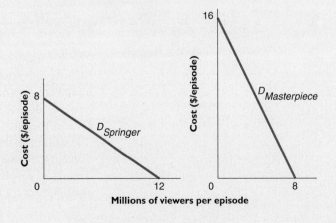

Millions of viewers per episode

a. How will the network fill the two remaining slots in its fall lineup?

b. Does this outcome maximize total economic surplus?

7. Refer to Problem 6. How much larger would total economic surplus be if each episode of "Masterpiece Theater" were shown on Ontario's TVO free of charge than if it were shown by a profit-maximizing pay-per-view network? **LO2**, **LO3**

8. When a TV company chooses a pay-per-view scheme to pay for programming, which of the following statements is true? Explain. **LO1**, **LO3**

a. This outcome maximizes total economic surplus.

b. The programs selected will maximize advertising revenue.

c. The marginal cost to an additional viewer of watching the programs is lower than when advertising is used to finance programming.

d. This outcome maximizes total economic surplus more often than when advertising is used to finance programming.

e. The variety of programs provided is likely to rise.

9. Answer each of the following statements as true or false and explain why. When a group of people must decide whether to buy a shared public good or service, the free-rider problem frequently occurs because **LO1**

a. People have an incentive to understate how much the facility is really worth to them if they have to pay taxes to finance it.

b. Each individual's needed contribution is an insignificant amount of the total required.

c. People have an incentive to overstate how much the facility is worth to them if they don't have to pay taxes to finance it.

d. People hope that others will value the facility enough to pay for it entirely.

e. Only one of the above statements is [...] for the existence of the free-rider pr[...]

10. The town of Smallsville is considering bu[...] museum. The interest on the money Sma[...] have to borrow to build the museum will [...] year. Each citizen's marginal benefit from [...] is shown in the following table, and this [...] benefit schedule is public information. **L[...]**

| Citizen | Marginal bene[...] museum ($/[...] |
|---|---|
| Anita | 340 |
| Brandon | 290 |
| Carlena | 240 |
| Dallas | 190 |
| Emiko | 140 |

a. Assuming each citizen voted accord[...] her private interests, would a referen[...] build the museum and raise each cit[...] taxes by $200?

b. A citizen proposes that the city let a [...] pany build the museum and charge t[...] a lump-sum fee each year to view it a[...] they like. Only citizens who paid the [...] be allowed to view the museum. If th[...] company were allowed to set a single [...] any company offer to build the muse[...]

c. A second citizen proposes allowing t[...] company to charge different prices to[...] citizens and auctioning the right to b[...] museum to the highest bidding comp[...] only the citizens who pay the fee may [...] the museum. What is the highest bid[...] company would make to supply the r[...] Smallsville?

14.1    a. The Statistics Canada Web site at 3 in the morning is nonriva[...] capacity to serve far more users than it attracts, so an additional [...] up the site does not prevent some other user from doing so. Othe[...] however, do not show the nonrival property, at least during ce[...] because they attract more users than their servers can accommo[...]

b. The stadium at the championship game is always full, so anyone v[...] watches the game in person prevents someone else from doing so[...]

c. Additional people can watch the game on television without dimi[...] availability of the telecast for others, making it nonrival.

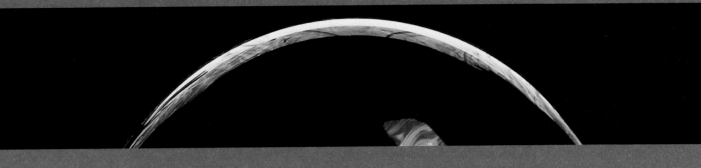

# CHAPTER 15
# International Trade and Trade Policy

## LEARNING OBJECTIVES

When you have completed the material in this chapter, you will be able to:

**LO1** Demonstrate by using a production possibilities curve that the opportunity cost of a good increases as more of that good is produced.

**LO2** Demonstrate graphically how international trade increases consumption possibilities.

**LO3** Demonstrate by using supply and demand how prices, quantities produced, imports, and exports are affected if an economy is opened to trade.

**LO4** Demonstrate graphically how total economic surplus changes if an economy is opened to international trade.

**LO5** Discuss why international trade agreements often are controversial.

**LO6** Identify, by using a graph, who wins and who loses when an economy is opened to international trade.

**LO7** Explain the impact of tariffs and quotas on domestic prices and quantities, imports, exports, and total economic surplus.

**LO8** Demonstrate, by using supply and demand, how a foreign exchange rate is determined.

Chapter 2 developed an argument that is as old as economics: specialization enhances productivity, and market exchange enables the cooperation and coordination that allow people to take advantage of the greater productivity offered by specialization. For a specific example, think of air travel, something that is possible only because highly specialized people such as pilots, jet engine mechanics, and air traffic controllers cooperate to provide their specific skills. None of these people is a jack of all trades, so each must rely on trading with others for the goods and services that make modern life possible. Moreover, as Adam Smith insisted, the greater is the degree of specialization, the wider the extent of the market must be.

In Chapter 2, the example of Rikke and Beth was used to illustrate the general proposition that the gains from trade depend on *comparative* advantage, not on absolute advantage. David Ricardo was the first to show, almost 200 years ago, that specialization according to comparative advantage enables all partners in trade to be better off, even those who are absolutely more efficient in everything they are able to produce. This chapter, therefore, addresses international trade and its effects on the broader economy. We begin by reviewing the idea of *comparative advantage*, which was introduced in Chapter 2. We show that total output of goods and services will increase if nations specialize in those products in which they have a comparative advantage, and then trade freely among themselves. Furthermore, if trade is unrestricted, market forces will ensure that countries produce those goods in which they have a comparative advantage.

Having shown the *potential* benefits of trade, we turn next to the reasons for opposition to it. Although opening an economy to trade can increase economic welfare overall, trade may make some groups, such as workers in industries that face competition from foreign producers, may be made worse off. The fact that open trade may hurt some groups creates political pressure to enact measures restricting trade, such as taxes on imported goods (*tariffs*) and limits on imports (*quotas*). We will analyze the effects of these trade restrictions, along with other ways of responding to concerns about affected industries and workers. Throughout Chapter 15, we use a simple analytical framework in which two goods are produced and traded.

# 15.1 COMPARATIVE ADVANTAGE AS A BASIS FOR TRADE

The old English expression "jack of all trades, master of none" captures succinctly the core idea that a person who tries to do everything will never have the time to practice any single activity enough to get really good at anything. Birkhaman, the Nepalese cook of Chapter 2, was a remarkable jack of all trades, capable of many tasks from butchering a goat to repairing an alarm clock. But precisely because he did so many things, Birkhaman could not hope to become as productive in each separate activity as someone who specialized. Furthermore, although Birkhaman was very skilled, he was uneducated. Chapter 2 went on to show that individuals can benefit from specializing according to their comparative advantages and then trading, but Birkhaman would have been even better off if he could have gone to school. We developed in Chapter 12 the human capital model of investment in education and training, by which individuals can change their comparative advantage in particular types of skills.

The insights of Chapter 2 also apply to nations. Factors such as climate, natural resources, technology, workers' skills and education, and culture provide countries with initial comparative advantages in the production of different goods and services. For example, France's climate and topography provided that country an initial comparative advantage in producing wine, but it is the accumulated knowledge of generations of vintners that make it possible for France to produce really good wine and sell it at the high prices that good wines can command.

The *principle of comparative advantage* tells us that we can all enjoy more goods and services when each country produces according to its comparative advantage and then trades with other countries. Comparative advantage is not, however, static, and it changes as countries invest in skills and fixed capital. In the next section we explore this fundamental idea in greater detail.

# 15.2 PRODUCTION AND CONSUMPTION POSSIBILITIES AND THE BENEFITS OF TRADE

In this section we will consider how international trade affects an individual country. To do so, we will contrast the production and consumption opportunities in a **closed economy**—one that does not trade with the rest of the world—with the opportunities in an **open economy**—one that does trade with other economies.

Recall from Chapter 2 that the production possibilities curve (PPC) for a two-good economy is a graph that shows the maximum amount of one good that can be produced for every possible level of production of the other good. For purposes of illustration, we consider an economy that produces only two goods, coffee and computers. In such an economy, the point *C* on the PPC shown in Figure 15.1 tells us that the maximum production of coffee is 100 000 kilograms per year when the economy is producing 1000 computers per year.

In Chapter 2 we noted that the smoothly bowed shape of a PPC such as the one in Figure 15.1 is typical for an economy that has a large number of firms and workers. The slope of the PPC at each point reflects the opportunity cost of producing an additional computer. (For example, the opportunity cost, in terms of coffee, of producing an extra computer at point *C* is given by the slope of the line tangent to the PPC at that point.) If computers are produced first by firms and workers with the greatest comparative advantage in computers (the lowest opportunity cost in terms of coffee), the slope of the PPC becomes steeper (more sharply negative) as we move from left to right along the curve. Thus, at point *D*, where the economy is producing 40 000 kilograms per year of coffee and 2000 computers per year, the slope of the PPC is steeper

**closed economy** an economy that does not trade with the rest of the world

**open economy** an economy that trades with other countries

**FIGURE 15.1**
**Production Possibilities Curve for a Many-Worker Economy**
The PPC for a many-worker economy has a smooth, outwardly bowed shape. At each point on the PPC, the slope of the curve reflects the opportunity cost, in terms of coffee foregone, of producing an additional computer. For example, the opportunity cost of a computer at point *C* equals the slope of the line tangent to the PPC at that point, and the opportunity cost of a computer at point *D* equals the slope of the line tangent to the PPC there. Because the opportunity cost of producing another computer increases as more computers are produced, the slope of the PPC becomes steeper (more sharply negative) as we read from left to right on the graph.

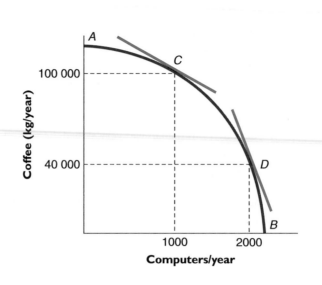

than at *C*. This means that the opportunity cost of an additional computer (the number of kilograms of coffee that must be foregone to produce an additional computer) is greater at *D* than at *C*.

## CONSUMPTION POSSIBILITIES WITH AND WITHOUT INTERNATIONAL TRADE

A country's production possibilities curve shows the quantities of different goods that its economy can produce. However, economic welfare depends most directly not on what a country can *produce,* but on what its citizens can *consume.* The combinations of goods and services that a country's citizens might feasibly consume are called the country's **consumption possibilities.**

**consumption possibilities** the combinations of goods and services that a country's citizens might feasibly consume

The relationship between a country's consumption possibilities and its production possibilities depends on whether or not the country is open to international trade. In a closed economy with no trade, people can consume only the goods and services produced within their own country. *In a closed economy, then, society's consumption possibilities are identical to its production possibilities.* A situation in which a country does not trade with other nations, instead producing everything its citizens consume, is called **autarky.**

**autarky** a situation in which a country does not trade with other nations

The case of an open economy, which trades with the rest of the world, is quite different. In an open economy, people are not restricted to consuming what is produced in their own country, because part of what they produce can be sent abroad in exchange for other goods and services. Thus, *in an open economy, a society's consumption possibilities are typically greater than (and will never be less than) its production possibilities.* Very large countries, such as the U.S. or China, can sometimes influence world prices by their decisions. However, for most countries and for most commodities, each individual country's trade will be a small fraction of global trade, so world prices will be unaffected by how much they buy or sell on international markets. Hence, in this chapter, we assume that each country is a "price taker" in international markets.

We will begin with the example of "Costa Rica" at a particular point in time, which, for simplicity, is assumed to produce and consume only two goods—coffee and computers. In this initial example, we *hold constant* the skills of Costa Rican workers and the capital stock of its firms; we assume, in short, that comparative advantage does not change. Consider then the PPC shown as curve *ACDB* in Figure 15.2. Point *A,* where the PPC intercepts the vertical axis, indicates the maximum amount of coffee that Costa Rica can produce, and point *B,* the horizontal intercept of the PPC, shows the maximum number of computers it can produce. As before, the intermediate points on the PPC represent alternative combinations of coffee and computers that can be produced.

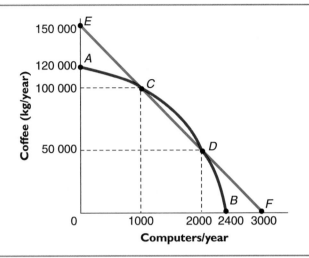

**FIGURE 15.2**

**Buying and Selling in World Markets**

If Costa Rica produces at point *D* and can buy or sell computers and coffee in world markets at prices of $500 per computer and $10 per kilogram of coffee, respectively, it can consume at any point along the line *EF*.

Now suppose that the Costa Rican economy, which was operating at point *D* as a closed economy (meaning that it both produced and consumed 2000 computers per year and 50 000 kg per year of coffee), gains the opportunity to buy or sell either good in the world market at prices of $10 per kilogram for coffee and $500 per computer. Without changing its production at all, we see that it immediately enjoys a new range of consumption possibilities. For example, if it sold its entire production of 2000 computers in the world market at $500 apiece, the $1 000 000 it would earn would enable it to purchase an additional 100 000 kg of coffee each year. Thus, the point *E* in Figure 15.2, which was not available to Costa Ricans in the absence of international trade, is now attainable.

Alternatively, suppose that Costa Ricans again start at *D* and now sell their annual production of 50 000 kg of coffee in the world market. The $500 000 they receive from this sale will enable them to buy an additional 1000 computers each year. Thus, the point *F* in Figure 15.2, which was also not a consumption option in the absence of international trade, now becomes available. And as you can easily verify, any other point along the line *EF* also becomes available to Costa Ricans if they produce at *D* and can exchange their goods in world markets at the stated prices.

**Suppose prices in world markets are again $500 per computer and $10 per kilogram for coffee. Show that if Costa Rica starts by producing at point *C* in Figure 15.2, it can consume 500 computers per year and 125 000 kilograms per year of coffee. To do so, how many units of each good will it buy or sell in world markets?**

EXERCISE 15.1

**If prices remain as before and if Costa Rica again starts by producing at point *C* in Figure 15.2 and can trade in world markets, it can consume 2500 computers per year and 25 000 kilograms per year of coffee. To do so, how many units of each good will it buy or sell in world markets?**

EXERCISE 15.2

If Costa Rica could buy or sell in world markets at $500 per computer and $10 per kilogram for coffee, would its best option be to produce at point *C* in Figure 15.2? No, because it could do better by producing at point *G* in Figure 15.3.

**FIGURE 15.3**
**Production Possibilities, Consumption Possibilities, and the Optimal Production Mix for an Open Economy**
If Costa Rica can buy or sell computers and coffee in world markets at prices of $500 per computer and $10 per kilogram, the line *LM* maximizes the country's consumption possibilities. The slope of this line is the rate at which coffee can be traded for computers at the stated world prices—namely, 50 kg of coffee per computer. The line *LM* is tangent to the production possibilities curve at *G*. Costa Rica's best option is to produce at point *G* and then trade in world markets (either sell computers and buy coffee or vice versa) so as to reach its most desired point on the line *LM*.

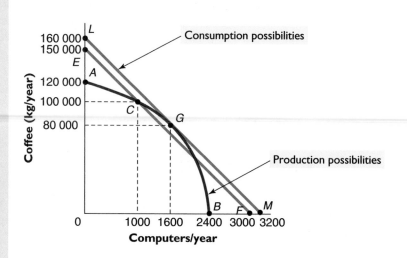

If Costa Rica produces at point *G* in Figure 15.3 and can buy or sell computers and coffee in world markets at prices of $500 per computer and $10 per kilogram, the country's consumption possibilities will now lie along the line *LM*. This line has two key features. First, it is drawn so that it is tangent to the PPC at point *G* in Figure 15.3. Second, the slope of line *LM* is determined by the relative prices of coffee and computers on the world market. Specifically, the absolute value of the slope of line *LM*, which is

(160 000 kg of coffee/year)/(3200 computers/year) = 50 kg of coffee per computer,

tells us how much coffee must be exchanged on world markets to obtain an additional computer.

With access to international trade, Costa Rica can consume the greatest amount of both coffee and computers by producing at point *G* on the PPC and trading on the international market to obtain the desired combination of coffee and computers on line *LM*. (The exact combination of coffee and computers Costa Ricans will choose depends on the preferences of its population.)

What benefit do Costa Ricans obtain by producing at point *G*? At point *G*, and only at that point, the slope of the PPC equals the slope of the consumption possibilities line, *LM*. Hence, only at point *G* is the opportunity cost of increasing domestic computer production equal to the opportunity cost of purchasing an extra computer on the world market. If the opportunity cost of producing a computer domestically exceeded the opportunity cost of purchasing a computer on the world market, Costa Rica would gain by reducing its computer production and importing more computers. Likewise, if the opportunity cost of producing a computer domestically were less than the opportunity cost of purchasing a computer abroad, Costa Rica would gain by increasing computer production and reducing computer imports. Costa Rica therefore maximizes the value of total consumption at point *G*, where the domestic and international opportunity costs of acquiring an extra computer, measured in terms of coffee foregone, are equal. The combination of goods at point *G* is also the one whose sale at world prices produces the largest possible total revenue.

We have already stated the general conclusion that trade enables a country to consume more of *every* good than if it relied solely on its own production (*autarky*). Graphically,

INCREASING
OPPORTUNITY COST

the consumption possibilities line in Figure 15.3 lies above the production possibilities curve, showing that, through trade, Costa Rica can consume combinations of computers and coffee that would not be attainable if its economy were closed to trade.[1] Thus, we have an application of the principle of increasing opportunity cost on a global scale.

---

**RECAP**

### CONSUMPTION POSSIBILITIES AND PRODUCTION POSSIBILITIES

- The *production possibilities curve* (PPC) for a two-good economy is a graph that shows the maximum amount of one good that can be produced at each possible level of production of the other good.

- The slope of a PPC at any point indicates the opportunity cost, in terms of foregone production of the good on the vertical axis, of increasing production of the good on the horizontal axis by one unit.

- As production of a good that is already being produced is increased, the opportunity cost of an additional unit of that good increases still further. Thus, the slope of the PPC becomes steeper (more sharply negative) as we move from left to right, imparting the characteristic outwardly bowed shape of the curve.

- A country's *consumption possibilities* are the combinations of goods and services that its citizens might feasibly consume.

- In an economy that is closed to trade, residents can consume only what is produced domestically (*autarky*). Hence, in a closed economy, consumption possibilities equal production possibilities.

- The residents of an open economy can trade part of what they produce on international markets, which makes it possible for the population to consume more than they could otherwise. Thus, in an open economy, consumption possibilities are typically greater than, and will never be less than, production possibilities.

- Graphically, consumption possibilities in an open economy are described by a downward-sloping straight line whose slope equals the amount of the good on the vertical axis that must be traded on the international market to obtain one unit of the good on the horizontal axis. Each country maximizes its consumption possibilities by producing at the point where the consumption possibilities line is tangent to the PPC, and then trading so as to reach its most preferred point on the consumption possibilities line.

---

## 15.3  A SUPPLY-AND-DEMAND PERSPECTIVE ON TRADE

Although a country can improve its overall consumption possibilities by trading with other countries, we also need to look carefully at how international trade affects supply and demand in the markets for specific goods. We will see that, when it is costly for workers and firms to change industries, opening up trade with other countries may create groups of winners and losers among producers, even as it helps consumers of imported goods.

---

1  The single point at which consumption possibilities do *not* lie above production possibilities in Figure 15.3 is at point *G*, where production possibilities and consumption possibilities are the same. If Costa Rican residents happen to prefer the combination of computers and coffee at point *G* to any other point on *LM*, then they realize no benefit from trade.

Figure 15.4 shows the supply and demand for computers in Costa Rica. As usual, the price is shown on the vertical axis and the quantity on the horizontal axis. We assume that computers sell in the world market for a price of $1000 each. The upward-sloping curve in Figure 15.4 is the supply curve of computers, in this case for computers produced in Costa Rica, and the downward-sloping curve is the demand curve for computers by Costa Rican residents.

If the Costa Rican economy is closed to imports, then market equilibrium occurs where the domestic supply and demand curves intersect, at point E in Figure 15.4(a). The equilibrium price will be $1400 per computer and the equilibrium quantity, 2000 computers per year. Domestic computer buyers enjoy a consumer surplus of $1 million per year, and domestic computer producers enjoy a producer surplus of $1 million per year.

**world price** the price at which a good or service is traded on international markets

If Costa Rica opens its market to trade, however, the relevant price for computers becomes the **world price** of computers, the price at which computers are traded internationally. The world price for computers is determined by the worldwide supply and demand for computers. Assuming that Costa Rica's computer market is too small to have a perceptible effect on the world price for computers, the world price can be treated as fixed, and represented by a horizontal line in the figure. Figure 15.4(b) shows the world price of $1000 per computer as being lower than Costa Rica's closed-economy price of $1400.

If Costa Ricans can buy computers on the international market for $1000, computers made in Costa Rica will have to meet that price. Figure 15.4(b) shows that at the world price of $1000, Costa Rican consumers and firms demand 2800 computers each year, but Costa Rican computer producers supply only 1200. The difference between total sales and

---

**FIGURE 15.4**

**The Market for Computers in Costa Rica**

If Costa Rica is closed to imports, panel (a), the equilibrium price and quantity of computers are determined by the intersection of the domestic supply and demand curves at point E. But if Costa Rica is open to trade, panel (b), the domestic price of computers must equal the world price of $1000. At that price, Costa Ricans will demand 2800 computers each year, but domestic producers will supply only 1200. The difference between total sales and local production (2800 − 1200 = 1600) is imported each year from abroad. Compared to the closed-economy outcome, computer buyers gain $960 000 per year of additional consumer surplus with trade, and domestic computer sellers lose $640 000 per year of producer surplus. For Costa Rican computer buyers and sellers as a whole, total economic surplus is thus $320 000 per year larger with trade.

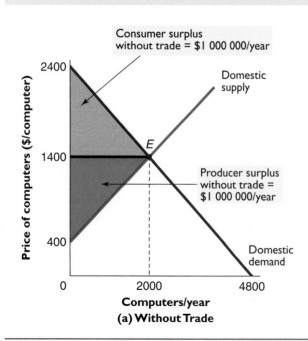

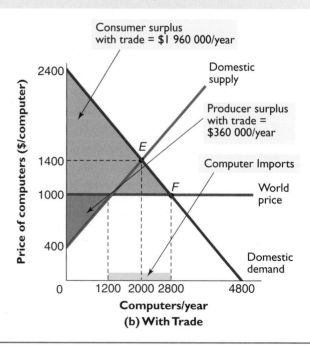

(a) Without Trade

(b) With Trade

local production (2800 − 1200 = 1600) is the number of computers that Costa Rica must import from abroad each year. Figure 15.4(b) illustrates a general conclusion: *If the price of a good or service in a closed economy is greater than the world price, and that economy opens itself to trade, the economy will tend to become a net importer of that good or service.*

Note that in Figure 15.4(b), domestic computer buyers now enjoy $1 960 000 per year of consumer surplus, or $960 000 per year more than before trade. Domestic computer producers, for their part, now receive only $360 000 per year of producer surplus, or $640 000 less than before trade. Adding together the gains of consumers and the losses of producers in the Costa Rican computer market, there is a net increase of $320 000 per year in total economic surplus.

A different outcome occurs in Costa Rica's coffee market, shown in Figure 15.5. The price of coffee is shown on the vertical axis and the quantity of coffee on the horizontal axis. The downward-sloping demand curve in the figure shows how much coffee Costa Rican consumers want to buy at each price, and the upward-sloping supply curve shows how much coffee Costa Rican producers are willing to supply at each price. If Costa Rica's economy is closed to trade with the rest of the world, then equilibrium in the market for coffee will occur at point *E*, where the domestic demand and supply curves intersect. The quantity produced will be 100 000 kilograms of coffee each year and the price will be $7 per kilogram of coffee, as shown in Figure 15.7(a). Domestic coffee buyers enjoy a consumer surplus of $250 000 per year and domestic coffee producers enjoy a producer surplus of $150 000 per year.

**FIGURE 15.5**

**The Market for Coffee in Costa Rica**

With no international trade, panel (a), the equilibrium price and quantity of coffee in Costa Rica are determined by the intersection of the domestic supply and demand curves (point *E*). But if the country opens to trade, panel (b), the domestic price of coffee must rise to equal the world price. At the higher world price, Costa Ricans will demand only 40 000 kg of coffee each year, which is less than the 200 000 kg Costa Rican producers supply at that price. The difference, 160 000 kg, is exported each year. Compared to the closed-economy outcome, domestic coffee buyers suffer a loss of $210 000 per year of consumer surplus from trade, and domestic coffee sellers gain $450 000 per year of producer surplus from trade. When the losses of Costa Rican coffee buyers and the gains of sellers are summed, total economic surplus is $240 000 per year larger with trade, but, just as was the case in the computer market, some individuals win and some lose when trade increases.

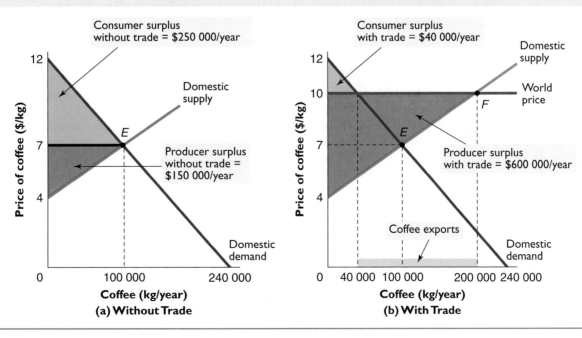

(a) Without Trade

(b) With Trade

If Costa Rica opens its coffee market to international trade, the prevailing price for coffee in Costa Rica must be the same as the world price. However, the world price of coffee as shown in Figure 15.5(b) is *higher* than the domestic equilibrium price. We know that the world price of coffee will be higher than the domestic price because, in an example with only two goods, if non-Costa Rican producers have a comparative advantage in computers, as reflected in the fact that computers exchange for coffee at a lower price in the world market than in the domestic Costa Rican market, then Costa Rican producers must have a comparative advantage in coffee. And that means that the domestic price of coffee in Costa Rica without trade will be lower than the world price.

Figure 15.5(b) shows that at the world price for coffee, Costa Rican producers are willing to supply 200 000 kilograms of coffee each year, while Costa Rican consumers want to purchase a much smaller amount, only 40 000 kilograms. The difference between domestic production and domestic consumption (200 000 − 40 000 = 160 000 kg/year) is exported to the world market. Note in Figure 15.5(b) that domestic coffee buyers now enjoy a consumer surplus of $40 000 per year, a reduction of $210 000 per year in comparison with the surplus they enjoyed without trade. But domestic coffee producers now receive $600 000 per year of producer surplus, or $450 000 per year more than before trade. As in the case of the domestic computer market, the gain in total economic surplus of $240 000 per year as a result of opening the market to trade is the sum of gains to some and losses to others. Note, finally, that we have set up this example to illustrate the equilibrium case where proceeds from the export of coffee ($1 600 000/year) are exactly enough to enable the Costa Ricans to pay for the 1600 computers per year they import (see Figure 15.4(b)).

The general conclusion is, *if the price of a good or service in a closed economy is lower than the world price, and that economy opens itself to trade, the economy will tend to become a net exporter of that good or service.* And again, the result will be a net increase in the total economic surplus experienced by domestic buyers and sellers.

These examples illustrate how the market translates comparative advantage into mutually beneficial gains from trade. If trade is unrestricted, then countries with a comparative advantage in a particular good will profit by supplying that good to the world market and using the revenue earned to import goods in which they do not have a comparative advantage.

## IF INTERNATIONAL TRADE IS BENEFICIAL, WHY ARE FREE-TRADE AGREEMENTS SO CONTROVERSIAL?

The North American Free Trade Agreement (NAFTA) has, since 1994, greatly reduced trade barriers between Canada, the United States, and Mexico. But NAFTA remains a contentious political issue, and discussions among world leaders about global trading arrangements are often controversial. If international specialization and trade are so beneficial, why are trade agreements controversial?

Although international trade can increase the total value of goods and services produced, it does not guarantee that everyone will participate in those benefits. As we have already noted, when trade replaces autarky, some people win and some people lose in both exporting and importing sectors of the economy. Although the net sum of gains and losses may be positive, those who lose are not likely to be consoled simply by knowing that their losses are exceeded by someone else's gains. If and when there is compensation of those who lose from more open trade, then everyone will end up at least as well off as they were originally. However, there may be a reasonable fear that there will be no compensation.

As well, in Chapter 10, we discussed externalities and pollution. Governments that want to reduce environmental damage can, within their own borders, charge pollution taxes or impose environmental regulations. But if firms could evade those policies by just hopping across the border and then exporting their output back, the environmental policy would be completely undermined. Similarly, labour standards (e.g., on child labour or unsafe workplaces) could be undermined if firms could easily move their production to low-standard jurisdictions and still service the same markets. But without a common legislature to decide environmental or labour standards, how should they be set? In the end, the NAFTA compromise was to sign two supplementary agreements, the North American Agreement on Environmental Cooperation (NAAEC) and the North American Agreement on Labor Cooperation (NAALC).

In the NAFTA case, both Canada and Mexico have also always been very conscious that they are trading with a superpower. Nationalists in both countries have long been concerned that the U.S. would use trade as an instrument of foreign policy, thereby reducing the sovereignty of its smaller partners. The issue of sovereignty may be closely linked to the distribution of trade benefits. If foreigners own a large part of the small country's industry, much of the benefit of trade might flow to foreigners, not to the domestic population.

Opponents of trade agreements also fear that such agreements will lock existing patterns of comparative advantage into place, making it difficult to develop new industries. Economic Naturalist 15.1 recounts the development of Canada's pulp and paper industry during the early 20th century. The American pulp and paper industry would have preferred that Canada use its comparative advantage to supply pulpwood as raw material to the American industry. Canadian provincial governments opted instead to change Canada's comparative advantage by using barriers to trade to support the development of a Canadian pulp and paper industry.

## ECONOMIC NATURALIST   15.1

### How does comparative advantage arise? Canadian Pulp and Paper

In 1890, the Canadian pulp and paper industry was small and insignificant, with only very limited access to the American market. Forty years later, Canada was the world's largest papermaker and exported much of its product to the United States. Today, pulp and paper remains one of Canada's most important industries. How did Canada "create" a pulp and paper industry? Is this case relevant to today's trade?

In the mid-19th century, paper was produced in costly, small-scale operations. Rags, grasses, and straw provided the raw material. Beginning in 1851, a series of technological advances allowed cellulose to be isolated from wood and used as the raw material for paper. The new processes operated on a much larger scale and required large amounts of electricity. The new technology gave Canada, with its vast forests and large potential to produce hydroelectricity, a potential comparative advantage in the manufacture of paper.

By 1900, there was growing demand for newsprint in the United States, but the U.S. protected its pulp and paper industry from Canadian competition by imposing high tariffs on imported pulp and paper and no duties on imported raw pulpwood. This enabled the American pulp and paper industry to obtain inexpensive pulpwood from Canada and then

to manufacture it into pulp and paper sold in the United States.

Under Canadian federalism, the provinces have the right to manage their natural resources. In 1902, Ontario placed an embargo on the export of pulpwood harvested from Crown lands, to prevent pulpwood from being exported to the United States. No restrictions were imposed on the export of pulp and paper. The purpose was to encourage export of pulp and paper manufactured in Ontario to the United States. By 1915, all other provinces had taken similar measures.

The United States responded to pressure from its own pulp and paper industry by increasing its tariffs on Canadian pulp and paper, which made the Canadian product more expensive, thereby also raising the costs of American newspapers. In 1913, the interests of the American newspaper industry prevailed over the interests of the American pulp and paper industry, and Congress removed the tariffs against Canadian pulp and newsprint. By 1929, Canada was producing more than twice as much newsprint as the United States and was the world's largest papermaker.

"Natural" advantages obviously facilitated the creation of a Canadian pulp and paper industry, but political economy also played a crucial role in converting a potential comparative advantage into an actual comparative advantage. The American newspaper industry's desire for access to inexpensive Canadian newsprint aligned with the interests of Canadian pulp and paper, whose influence with provincial governments produced Canadian trade policies that offset the impact of U.S. trade policies. Eventually, the United States removed its trade barriers to Canadian pulp and paper, and the Canadian industry was able to actually develop a comparative advantage that had previously been latent; but politics mattered, at every step.[2]

For many years, Canada and the United States have engaged in a series of trade disputes over another forest product, softwood lumber. The Softwood Lumber Agreement of 2006 ended the most recent dispute when it came into effect on October 12, 2006. Canada provides the United States with about 35 percent of its softwood lumber.

Restrictions on the importation of Canadian lumber serve the interests of the American lumber industry, but they can cost the American construction industry billions of dollars annually, because they increase U.S. lumber prices. The interests of Canadian lumber and American construction converge in ways that can prove useful to Canadian negotiators. However, for 20 years prior to the new agreement, the political influence of U.S. lumber producers was sufficient to cause the U.S. to take repeated trade actions against Canadian softwood lumber. The dispute provides an example of a failure to take advantage of comparative advantage due to protectionism. U.S. lumber producers lose from greater trade, even if the potential gains from greater trade (in this case, for the U.S. construction industry) are larger than the total losses. If the losers from greater trade are not compensated for their losses, they have a self-interested reason to propose restraints on trade, and they sometimes can do so successfully. The dispute over softwood lumber, though dormant now, could flare again.[3]

In the 21st century, globalized supply chains and international trade provide nearly instant access to worldwide markets. Every day, each of us relies on human beings living around the world to provide the goods and services we consume. As an example, consider where the clothing that you are now wearing came from, and where the raw materials that went into that clothing came from. International trade has already reshaped much of the world we live in and continues to do so, every day.

**EXERCISE 15.3**  **If the domestic supply and demand curves for computers in Costa Rica are as shown in the diagram and the world price of computers is $1200, how will opening the country to the possibility of buying computers in the world market affect consumer and producer surpluses in its domestic computer market?**

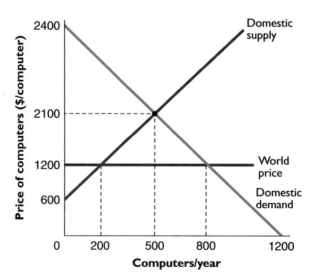

2  Adapted from B.D. Lesser (ed.), "Canada 'Creates' a Pulp and Paper Industry," in *Four Case Studies on Aspects of the Canadian Economy*, (Halifax: Nova Scotia Department of Education, 1977), pp. 1–2. See also Kenneth Norrie and Douglas Owram, *A History of the Canadian Economy*, 2nd ed., (Toronto: Harcourt Brace & Company Canada, Ltd., 1996), pp. 256–257, 323–324.

3  See "Softwood" at www.international.gc.ca for information about the Softwood Lumber Agreement (May 2008).

## WINNERS AND LOSERS FROM TRADE

If trade is so wonderful, why is there resistance to "free trade" and globalization? The reason, as we have already seen, is that, although trade can have net benefits, specific groups may not be better off. If those who are hurt by trade have sufficient political influence, they may be able to persuade politicians to enact policies that restrict the flow of goods and services across borders.

The supply-and-demand analyses shown in Figures 15.4 and 15.5 are useful in understanding who gains and who loses when an economy opens up to trade. Look first at Figure 15.4, which shows the market for computers in Costa Rica. When Costa Rica opens its computer market to international competition, Costa Rican consumers enjoy a larger quantity of computers at a lower price. Clearly, Costa Rican computer users benefit from the trade in computers and, in general, *domestic consumers of imported goods benefit from trade.* However, Costa Rican computer producers will not be so happy about opening their market to international competition. The fall in computer prices to the international level implies that less efficient domestic producers will go out of business, and those who remain will earn lower profits. Unemployment in the Costa Rican computer industry will rise and may persist over time, particularly if displaced computer workers cannot easily move to a new industry. Moreover, wages paid to Costa Rican computer workers also will fall, reflecting the lower relative price of computers. We see that, in general, trade hurts *domestic producers of imported goods. Opening the economy to trade makes it possible for consumers to compensate producers for their losses. However, if producers believe they actually will not be compensated, they will want international trade to be restricted.*

Consumers are helped, and producers hurt, when imports increase. The opposite conclusions apply for an increase in exports (see Figure 15.5). In the example of Costa Rica, an opening of the coffee market raises the domestic price of coffee to the world price and creates the opportunity for Costa Rica to export coffee. Domestic producers of coffee benefit from the increased market (they can now sell coffee abroad as well as at home) and from the higher price of their product. Employment and wages paid in the Costa Rican coffee sector will rise. In short, *domestic producers of exported goods benefit from trade.* Costa Rican coffee drinkers will be less enthusiastic, however, since they must now pay the higher world price of coffee and will therefore consume less. *Thus, trade hurts domestic consumers of exported goods.*

Trade increases the total economic surplus available to the economy. Indeed, unrestricted trade is an application of the *equilibrium principle*—markets in equilibrium leave no unexploited opportunities for individuals. Despite this, those who lose from trade may have good reason to believe they will not be compensated for their losses. They therefore have an incentive to generate political pressure to block or restrict trade. Table 15.1 summarizes who wins and who loses from international trade. In the next section, we will discuss the major types of policies used to restrict trade.

EQUILIBRIUM

**TABLE 15.1**
**Winners and Losers from Trade**

| **Winners** |
| --- |
| • Consumers of imported goods |
| • Producers of exported goods |
| **Losers** |
| • Consumers of exported goods |
| • Producers of imported goods |

## PROTECTIONIST POLICIES: TARIFFS AND QUOTAS

**protectionism** the view that trade is injurious and should be restricted

**tariff** a tax imposed on an imported good

**quota** a legal limit on the quantity of a good that may be imported

The view that trade is injurious and should be restricted is known as **protectionism.** Supporters of this view believe that the government should attempt to protect domestic markets from foreign suppliers by raising legal barriers to imports. Two of the most common types of such barriers are *tariffs* and *quotas.* A **tariff** is a tax imposed on an imported good. A **quota** is a legal limit on the quantity of a good that may be imported.

### Tariffs

The effects of tariffs and quotas can be explained using supply-and-demand diagrams. Suppose that Costa Rican computer makers, dismayed by the penetration of their market by imported computers, persuade their government to impose a tariff—that is, a tax—on every computer imported into the country. Computers produced in Costa Rica will be exempt from the tax. Figure 15.6 shows the likely effects of this tariff on the domestic Costa Rican computer market. The lower of the two horizontal lines in Figure 15.6(a) indicates the world price of computers, not including the tariff, is $1000 per computer. The higher of the two lines indicates the price Costa Rican consumers will actually pay for imported computers, including the tariff, as $1200 per computer. The vertical distance between the two lines equals the amount of the tariff that is imposed on each imported computer—here, $200 per computer.

From the point of view of domestic Costa Rican producers and consumers, the imposition of the tariff has the same effects as an equivalent increase in the world price

---

**FIGURE 15.6**

**The Market for Computers after the Imposition of an Import Tariff**

Imposing a tariff of $200 per imported computer increases the price of computers in Costa Rica from the world price ($1000) to the world price plus the tariff ($1200), represented by the upper horizontal line. Domestic production of computers rises from 1200 to 1600 per year. Domestic purchases of computers fall from 2800 to 2400 per year, and computer imports fall from 1600 to 800 per year. Compared to the alternative of free trade (Figure 15.4(b)), Costa Rican computer buyers lose $520 000 per year of consumer surplus and Costa Rican producers of computers gain $280 000 per year of producer surplus. The Costa Rican government collects revenue from the tariff equal to $160 000 per year, the area of the blue rectangle. The net effect of the tariff in the computer market is, thus, a reduction in total economic surplus of $80 000 per year.

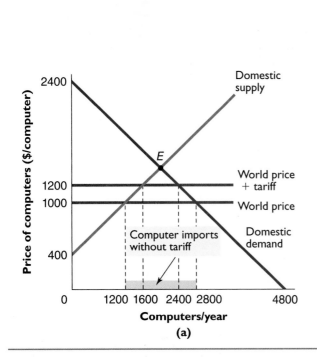

(a)

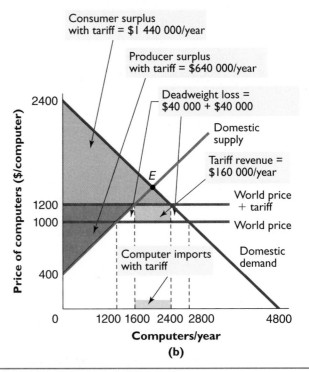

(b)

of computers. Because the price (including the tariff) of imported computers has risen, Costa Rican computer producers will be able to raise the price they charge for their computers to the world price plus the tariff, or $1200 per computer. Thus, the price Costa Rican consumers must pay, whether their computers are imported or not, equals $1200 per computer, represented by the upper horizontal line in Figure 15.6(a).

The $200 increase in the price of computers affects the quantities of computers supplied and demanded by Costa Ricans. Domestic computer producers, facing a higher price for computers, increase their production from 1200 to 1600 computers per year as seen in Figure 15.6(b). Costa Rican consumers, also reacting to the higher price, reduce their computer purchases from 2800 to 2400 per year. As a result, the number of imported computers, the difference between domestic purchases and domestic production, falls from 1600 to 800 per year.

Who are the winners and the losers from the tariff? Relative to having trade and no tariff, the winners are the domestic computer producers and the losers are Costa Rican consumers, who must now pay more for their computers. Another winner is the government, which collects revenue from the tariff. The blue area in Figure 15.6(b) shows the amount of revenue the government collects, equal to the quantity of computers imported after the imposition of the tariff, 800 per year, times the amount of the tariff, $200 per computer, for a total of $160 000 per year.

How does the tariff affect total economic surplus? From Figure 15.4(b), recall that computer buyers had a consumer surplus of $1 960 000 per year under free trade. In Figure 15.6(b), we see that imposition of the $200 tariff on computers results in a consumer surplus of only $1 440 000 per year, a decline of $520 000 per year. Similarly, we saw in Figure 15.4(b) that domestic computer sellers had a producer surplus of $360 000 per year in the absence of tariffs. Note in Figure 15.6(b), that the producer surplus increases to $640 000 per year with the imposition of the $200 tariff, a gain for producers of $280 000 per year. And note, finally, that in Figure 15.6(b) the government collects $160 000 per year in tariff revenue. Taking all these changes into account, the net effect of the imposition of the tariff is to cause a reduction in total economic surplus of $80 000 per year:

$$-\$520\,000/\text{year} + \$280\,000/\text{year} + \$160\,000/\text{year} = -\$80\,000/\text{year}$$

The reduction in total economic surplus is represented by the combined area of the two small white triangles at $40 000 each. Together, they represent the *deadweight loss* associated with the tariff. The deadweight loss is consistent with the concept of a deadweight loss developed in Chapter 7.

**If Costa Rica's supply and demand curves in its domestic computer market are as shown below, and buyers are currently able to import computers at the world price of $1200, how will the imposition of a tariff of $300 per computer affect total economic surplus?**

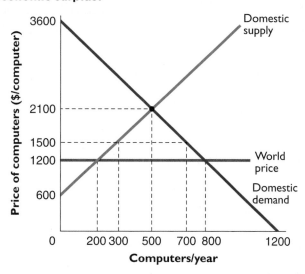

**E X E R C I S E   1 5 . 4**

ECONOMIC NATURALIST **15.2**

## Would Dalhousie University (in Halifax, Nova Scotia) exist today if tariffs had not existed?

Towards the end of the War of 1812–1814 between Britain and the U.S., a British force commanded by Lieutenant General John Coape Sherbrooke and Rear Admiral Edward Griffith occupied a section of Maine between the Penobscot and Saint Croix Rivers, governing the district until April 26, 1815. The end of the occupation left Governor Dalhousie in Halifax with a question: What was to be done with the tariff revenue that had been collected during the occupation? In those days, tariffs were the source of almost all local government revenue, but returning the money to the U.S. authorities was never seriously considered. In the end, Lord Dalhousie divided the funds between Garrison Library and Dalhousie College, which later became Dalhousie University. In effect then, a tariff, a trade barrier, was the source of the revenue that the British invested in educational infrastructure.

Lars Osberg

Tariffs were the major source of government revenue in Canada until the 20<sup>th</sup> century (partly because they are easy to administer) and, hence, much of the infrastructure on which Canada's early development depended was built with tariff revenue. Today, most government revenue in developed nations comes from individual and corporate income tax, sales tax, and property tax. However, collecting these types of taxes is difficult when the administrative infrastructure of government is poorly developed, so some less-developed countries still use tariffs as an important source of revenue. In such cases, the effect on aggregate output (i.e., the net cost of the tariffs) is the difference between the efficiency gains resulting from the improved infrastructure that is constructed using tariff revenues and the efficiency losses arising from impediments to trade.

### Quotas

An alternative to a tariff is a quota, or legal limit on the number or value of foreign goods that can be imported. A quota can be enforced by requiring importers to obtain a licence or permit for each good they bring into the country. The government distributes exactly the same number of permits as the number of goods that may be imported under the quota.

How does the imposition of a quota on, say, computers affect the domestic market for computers? The effect is shown in Figure 15.7, which is similar to Figure 15.6. As before, assume that at first there are no restrictions on trade. Consumers pay the world price for computers, and 1600 computers are imported each year as shown in Figure 15.7(a). Now suppose once more that domestic computer producers complain to the government about competition from foreign computer makers, and the government agrees to act. However, this time, instead of a tariff, the government imposes a quota on the number of computers that can be imported. For comparability with the tariff analyzed in Figure 15.6, let's assume that the quota permits the same level of imports as entered the country under the tariff: 800 computers per year. What effect does this policy have on the domestic market for computers?

After the imposition of the quota, the quantity of computers supplied to the Costa Rican market is the production of domestic firms plus the 800 imported computers allowed under the quota. Figure 15.7(a) shows the quantity of computers supplied inclusive of the quota. The total supply curve, labelled "Domestic supply plus quota," is the same as the domestic supply curve except for one change: for all prices above the world price of $1000 per computer, it is shifted 800 units to the right. (Even though the quota would allow foreign producers to sell 800 units at prices below $1000, none would do so, because they could get $1000 for them in the world market.) The domestic demand curve is the same as in Figure 15.6. Equilibrium in the domestic market for computers occurs at point *F* in Figure 15.7(a), the intersection of the supply curve including the quota and the domestic demand curve.

Relative to the initial situation with trade, the quota (1) raises the domestic price of computers by $200 per computer above the world price, (2) reduces domestic purchases of computers from 2800 to 2400 computers per year, (3) increases domestic production of computers from 1200 to 1600 computers per year, and (4) reduces imports from 1600 to 800 computers per year, the full amount permitted under the quota. Note, too, that in Figure 15.7(b) both consumer surplus and producer surplus are the same in the domestic computer market under a quota, as they were in that market under a tariff [Figure 15.6(b)]. So, like a tariff, the quota helps domestic producers by increasing their sales and the price they receive for their output, while hurting domestic consumers by forcing them to pay a higher price.

Under our assumption that the quota is set so as to permit the same level of imports as the tariff, the effects on the domestic market of the tariff and the quota are not only

---

**FIGURE 15.7**

**The Market for Computers after the Imposition of an Import Quota**

The figure shows the effects of the imposition of an import quota of 800 computers per year. The total supply of computers to the domestic economy is the domestic supply curve shifted to the right by 800 units (the amount of imports allowed under the quota). Market equilibrium occurs at point *F*. The effects of the quota are identical to those of the tariff analyzed in Figure 15.6. The domestic price rises from $1000 to $1200/computer, domestic production of computers rises from 1200 to 1600 computers/year, domestic purchases of computers fall from 2800 to 2400 computers/year, and computer imports fall from 1600 to 800 computers/year. Consumer and producer surpluses are the same under quotas as under tariffs. The tax revenue the government collected under the tariff goes instead as an economic rent to the holders of import licences. Like the tariff, the quota produces a deadweight loss of $80,000 per year.

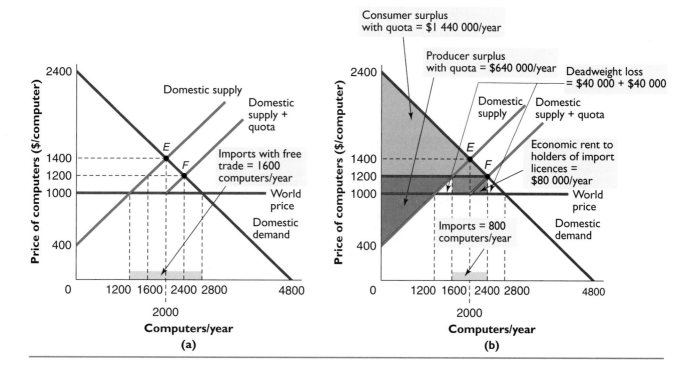

similar, they are *identical*. Comparing Figures 15.6 and 15.7, you can see that the two policies have precisely the same effects on the domestic price, domestic purchases, domestic production, and imports. Moreover, both create the same deadweight loss.

Although the market effects of a tariff and a quota are the same, there is one important difference between the two policies—a tariff generates revenue for the government, while a quota does not. With a quota, the revenue that would have gone to the government goes instead as an economic rent to those firms who hold the import licences. A holder of an import licence can purchase a computer at the world price of $1000 and resell it in the domestic market at a price of $1200, pocketing the difference. This difference is an economic rent, similar to a monopoly profit (see Chapter 8). As long as the number of licences is fixed, the economic rent cannot be competed away. Thus, with a tariff, the government collects the difference between the world price and the domestic market price of the good; with a quota, private firms or individuals collect that difference, in both cases $80 000 per year. Why then would the government ever impose a quota rather than a tariff? One possibility is that the distribution of import licences is a means of rewarding the government's political supporters.

Tariffs and quotas are not the only barriers to trade that governments erect. A government that wants to protect its domestic industry from foreign competition can also use "non-tariff barriers," such as creating health and safety regulations that foreign firms cannot satisfy. However, when does a country's sovereign right to control its own health and safety regulations conflict with its obligations under trade treaties to allow imports? How can one distinguish between regulations that legitimately protect health and those that are intended to prevent imports? European restrictions on genetically modified foods are an example. American exporters of genetically modified corn have protested against European bans on the imports of such products—bans strongly supported both by European farmers and some consumer advocacy groups. In this case, and in many others, the World Trade Organization, with headquarters in Geneva (see http://www.wto.org/) has been called in to arbitrate.

**www.wto.org**
**World Trade Organization**

---

> **BOX  15.1**
>
> ### Algebraic Approach to Trade Analysis
>
> This chapter provides a graphical analysis of international trade. For a discussion of how some of the same arguments can be presented algebraically, see Appendix 15A, An Algebraic Approach to Trade Analysis, on Connect.

## SUPPLY AND DEMAND: AN ANALYSIS OF FOREIGN EXCHANGE MARKETS

So far, our examples of trade in real goods (e.g., computers and coffee) have not involved money. In the real world, coffee producers who want computers would typically sell their coffee for money and use that money to buy the computers. International trade in goods and services functions as efficiently as it does because there is a parallel international trading system in the money that people use for transactions. For example, when a Canadian wants to buy a German good (e.g., a Porsche Cayman S[4]), he or she (who has Canadian dollars) and the German producer (who wants to be paid in euros), both depend on the foreign exchange markets where Canadian dollars and other currencies are traded.

---

4   The 2011 Porsche Cayman S accelerates from 0 to 100 km/hour in 5.2 seconds and has a top speed of 277km/hour.

Every day in financial markets, people in the U.K., Norway, India, and many other countries around the world use pounds, kroner, and rupees to buy and sell Canadian dollars. In the financial pages of your daily newspaper, you can read the rates at which one Canadian dollar exchanges for other currencies in these trades. For example, you might read that today one Canadian dollar is worth $0.9916 U.S. or $1.0934 Australian or 0.7065 euros; the financial pages provide the price of one Canadian dollar in terms of many other currencies. These prices are called **foreign exchange rates.** A *foreign exchange rate* is the price of one unit of a country's currency in terms of another country's currency and is determined in foreign exchange markets.

Analyzing the supply and demand for foreign exchange is a useful example of how competitive markets work because there are so many potential buyers and sellers, and foreign exchange markets adjust very quickly. As well, the foreign exchange rate is very important for the Canadian economy, so understanding how this market works is an important issue for any economics student. Nevertheless, there is a complication. When it comes to currencies, we can always express prices in two equivalent ways. We can either say that ten dimes equal a dollar or that one dime equals a tenth of a dollar. Saying it one way is just the flip side of the other; it is just a question of perspective, and the same is true of foreign currencies.

If you were to check the financial pages for the exchange rate of the Canadian dollar against the euro and find a quote of $1.4154 per euro, the exchange rate being expressed is the price of one euro in terms of Canadian dollars—one euro will cost $1.4154. But one could equally well see this as the price of one Canadian dollar in terms of euros (which we said earlier was €0.7065.) If it takes $1.4154 to buy one euro, then

$$€1 = \$1.4154.$$

If we divide both sides of the expression by 1.4154, then

$$\$1 = €0.7065,$$

which simply says that it takes 0.7065 euros to buy one Canadian dollar. Expressing the exchange rate one way answers the question, what's the price of one Canadian dollar? or, how many euros does it take to buy one Canadian dollar? which is just the flip side of the question, how many dollars does it take to buy one euro?

Whenever the exchange rate of one currency is stated in terms of another, a reciprocal exchange rate can be obtained.[5] A discussion that shifts from an exchange rate to its reciprocal and back again can become quite confusing. For example, one news commentator might say, "Tonight, the exchange rate is $1.4154." A few minutes later, the next commentator might say, "Tonight, the exchange rate is 0.7065 euros." It might not be clear to the viewer that both are quoting the same exchange rate. To avoid confusion on this point, in this textbook we will always be answering the question, what is the price of one Canadian dollar? Both commentators would agree that the price of one Canadian dollar is 0.7065 euros. So it is important to stick to only one perspective. In this text we will ask the question from the Canadian perspective—what is the price of one Canadian dollar?

Measured by the value of currency that is traded, the market in which U.S. and Canadian dollars are traded is the largest, whereas other markets (such as the market in which Japanese yen are exchanged for Canadian dollars) are much smaller. But the fundamental logic driving foreign exchange rates is the same around the world, so we can focus on a single market like the one in which euros and Canadian dollars are traded.

**foreign exchange rate** the price of one unit of a country's currency in terms of another country's currency; determined in foreign exchange markets

---

5  If you have ever purchased foreign currency, you know that a bank or currency broker charges a higher price when selling foreign currency than it offers when buying it from you. Bankers and currency brokers want to earn a net return for the services they provide, which they get from the spread between the buying and selling price. Since the spread is typically small, we will ignore it for now.

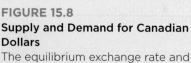

**FIGURE 15.8**
**Supply and Demand for Canadian Dollars**
The equilibrium exchange rate and quantity of dollars traded are given by the intersection of supply and demand.

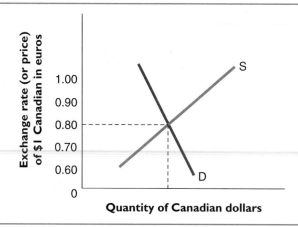

When using supply and demand to analyze foreign exchange markets, it is important to be clear about what is being measured along each axis of our graphs. In Figure 15.8, the quantity of Canadian dollars is measured along the horizontal axis. The exchange rate, or the price of one Canadian dollar in terms of euros, is measured along the vertical axis.

## THE SUPPLY OF CANADIAN DOLLARS IN FOREIGN EXCHANGE MARKETS

First, consider the supply of Canadian dollars to the market in which Canadian dollars and euros are traded. Who are the suppliers of Canadian dollars? Why do they want to supply Canadian dollars?

At any given time, the holders of Canadian dollars can use their dollars to buy Canadian goods and services, or Canadian financial assets. However, if they want to buy goods and services or financial assets in Europe, they must acquire euros before they can make these purchases. Whether Canadian tourists buy their euros before they leave or while they are cruising around France, Germany, Italy, and Spain, local people will only accept euros. Similarly, a Canadian financial investor who wants to buy a German company's shares or bonds will need to acquire euros to buy these assets. To obtain euros, they will *supply* Canadian dollars. Figure 15.8 displays a hypothetical supply curve for Canadian dollars. Notice that on the vertical axis, the price of a Canadian dollar is quoted in euros. The supply curve is upward sloping, showing that as price increases, a larger quantity of dollars is supplied.

Why does the supply curve slope upward? As any tourist knows, a low exchange rate means it is more expensive to have a good time while you are travelling—the lower the value of a Canadian dollar, the more Canadian dollars that are required to make any given purchase. If each Canadian dollar sold for only 0.25 euros, a European vacation would be very expensive indeed. A €100 hotel room in Paris is at the low end of the local market, but in Canadian dollars, it would cost $400, and many Canadians would look for a cheaper hotel (if they could find it). More important, many Canadians would decide that whatever the delights of Paris, it is just too expensive, and they would not go to Europe at all. When fewer Canadians travel, the quantity of Canadian dollars supplied to foreign exchange markets falls.

However, if each Canadian dollar were worth two euros, the same €100 hotel room would cost our traveller only $50 Canadian, and souvenirs and meals would be comparable bargains. Because the foreign exchange value (or price) of the Canadian dollar is higher, the fine wine and superb food of the best restaurants would look cheap to our fortunate traveller. More Canadians would travel to Europe and they would stay longer and buy more goods and services. To buy more, they would require more euros. To obtain more euros, they would increase the quantity of Canadian dollars supplied to the foreign exchange market. In general, the higher the price (expressed in euros) of one Canadian dollar, the greater the flow of Canadian tourists to Europe, the more each tourist buys, and the greater the quantity of Canadian dollars supplied to the foreign exchange market. That is why the supply curve of Figure 15.8 has a positive slope.

Tourism is one important reason for Canadians to supply Canadian dollars to foreign exchange markets, but there are many others. Canadians also want European goods and financial and real assets. To purchase them, Canadians must obtain euros by supplying Canadian dollars in a foreign exchange market. When the foreign exchange value (or price) of the dollar rises, Porsche sports cars and villas in the south of France cost fewer Canadian dollars, and, therefore, Canadians are more likely to purchase them, which means that the quantity of Canadian dollars supplied increases. Just as before, the supply curve in Figure 15.8 slopes upward.

## THE DEMAND FOR CANADIAN DOLLARS IN FOREIGN EXCHANGE MARKETS

Now consider the demand for Canadian dollars. Who are the demanders of Canadian dollars? Why would they want to buy Canadian dollars, and pay for them with euros?

Many Canadians travel abroad, but tourism is also a major industry in Canada. Whether it is skiing at Whistler, whale watching off Cape Breton or visiting Niagara Falls, many Europeans are drawn to Canada for an experience that they cannot get at home. Of course, Canadians want to be paid in Canadian dollars for car rentals, hotel rooms, and restaurant meals. German and French tourists thus have to pay with their euros for the Canadian dollars they buy in order to purchase the goods and services they want. The quantity of Canadian dollars they demand will depend on price per dollar, and when the exchange value of the Canadian dollar is low, vacations in Canada will seem like a great bargain to them.

The demand curve for Canadian dollars thus slopes down, because a lower exchange value (or price) for the dollar means that more European tourists will travel to Canada, stay longer, and buy more goods and services. To make more purchases, they will have to buy more dollars, which they will pay for with euros. A $150 hotel room in Toronto would only cost them €37.5 if the price of the Canadian dollar were 0.25 euros, so a Canadian vacation would be a "best buy," and more Europeans would take advantage of the bargain. On the other hand, if the exchange rate were to rise to two euros to the dollar, the same hotel room would cost them the equivalent of €300, and a Canadian vacation would be much less affordable.

Of course, tourism makes up only one part of the total demand for Canadian dollars. When Europeans buy Canadian goods (like wheat or aircraft) or Canadian assets (like Ontario bonds or Nova Scotia seafront properties) they need Canadian dollars to make their purchases. Therefore, the total demand for Canadian dollars is the sum of the dollars demanded by foreigners for all purchases of Canadian goods, services, financial assets, and real assets. But the basic logic is the same—a lower exchange rate (or the price of one Canadian dollar) will, other things being equal, increase the quantity of Canadian dollars demanded in foreign exchange markets.

When Canadians travel in Europe, they supply Canadian dollars to the foreign exchange market, and when Europeans travel in Canada, they demand Canadian dollars. The price matters to both, but Canadian tourists supply more dollars when the exchange rate is high, whereas European tourists demand more dollars when the exchange rate is low. It is the function of the foreign exchange market to bring supply and demand into equilibrium. Figure 15.8 shows the market for Canadian dollars in equilibrium at a price, or exchange rate, of 0.80 euros/Canadian dollar.

As Alfred Marshall said, like the two blades of a scissors, supply and demand *together* determine equilibrium. If tourism were the only reason for foreign exchange transactions, then equilibrium would occur when the supply of Canadian dollars (by Canadians travelling in Europe) is equal to the demand for Canadian dollars (by Europeans travelling in Canada). In the real world, there are many other reasons why Canadians want to supply Canadian dollars and why Europeans demand Canadian dollars—but in total, for all different types of transactions, the supply of and demand for Canadian dollars must balance in equilibrium.

## ECONOMIC NATURALIST   15.3

### Changing comparative advantage: The "Dutch Disease" comes to Canada

In Figure 15.3, we identified the potential for gains from trade when a country can exchange domestically produced goods for foreign-made goods at the international price ratio. When countries trade, global prices determine the consumption possibilities of each nation, and international trade enables each nation to consume a bundle of goods that is different from the bundle it produces at home. Nations can gain from trade because each nation's most efficient combination of goods in production can be different from the combination of goods that maximizes utility. So far, however, we have assumed a fixed ratio of prices in international markets and we have not addressed the question of what happens when international prices *change*.

We do not have to look very far for an example of the importance of the issue. Canada has a major

oil and gas industry and huge proven petroleum reserves. Most of Canada's proven petroleum reserves are in the Alberta oil sands (174 billion barrels) rather than in conventional reserves (only about 5.2 billion barrels), and extraction of oil from the oil sands requires significant investments of capital and labour.

Canada also uses capital and labour to produce a wide range of manufactured goods, from automobiles and airplanes to chocolates, paper, and furniture. Indeed, between 1994 and 2004, when the Canadian dollar was worth between US$0.65 and US$0.75, Canadian manufacturing firms found it highly profitable to export to the United States, and Canadian manufacturing provided many jobs.

**FIGURE 15.9**
**Oil Prices, 1993–2011**
The price of oil remained low and relatively stable throughout the 1990s. It spiked in 2008 and then dropped rapidly as the recession began. The price of oil then rose steadily during 2009–2011.
SOURCE: http://www.eia.gov/emeu/international/oilprice.html.

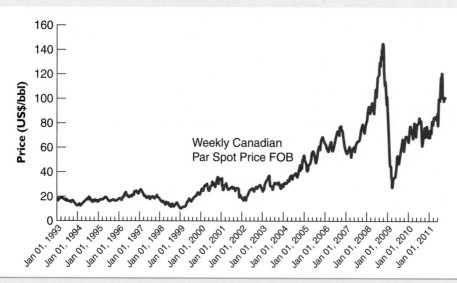

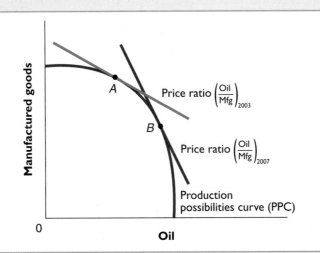

**FIGURE 15.10**

**The Effect of an Increase in the International Price of Oil**

An increase in the international price of oil relative to the price of manufactured goods is represented by the shift from the price ratio $(Oil/Mfg)_{2003}$ line to the price ratio $(Oil/Mfg)_{2007}$ line. The shift from point $A$ to point $B$ along the production possibilities curve portrays the resulting increase in production of oil and reduction of manufactured goods.

However, between 2004 and 2007, the price of oil increased dramatically, from US\$31/bbl to \$72. Since then, oil prices have been both volatile and upward bound, surging to over \$145 at one point during 2008 before dropping as the 2008 recession hit, and then recovering strongly during 2010 and hovering around \$100/bbl in 2011.[6] During this same period, the international prices of manufactured goods hardly budged. As a result, international relative prices, and Canada's comparative advantage, changed dramatically.[7] The huge new profits to be made in the development and production of oil and gas were signals from global markets that international prices were calling for a shift in the allocation of Canada's labour and capital. But how does the adjustment process happen?

Economists often use the term "the Dutch Disease" to describe this process and the role that the exchange rate plays in forcing shifts in production. In the 1950s, natural gas was discovered in Holland. Most of the new production was exported. To pay for this natural gas, foreign consumers had to buy Dutch guilders, which bid up the exchange value of the Dutch currency. Manufacturers in Holland, who had made reasonable profits at the old exchange rate, suddenly found they could not compete at the new, higher value of the Dutch guilder, and they laid off workers. However, the growth of the natural gas sector, and, more important, the expansion of services financed by natural gas revenues created new jobs at the same time as the rising value of the Dutch exchange rate pushed workers out of manufacturing

and into new areas of comparative advantage. Since Holland is a very small country, there were few geographic barriers to the mobility of resources between sectors.

Figure 15.10 provides a graphical picture of the process as it was experienced in Canada. The initial international price of oil relative to the price of manufactured goods in Canada in 2003 is represented by the slope of the price ratio $(Oil/Mfg)_{2003}$ line. Between 2003 and 2007, the value of the Canadian dollar against other currencies increased from an average value of US\$0.71 to near parity, as foreign purchasers increased their demand for Canadian dollars to buy Canadian oil and other resources. This caused employment in manufacturing to fall, while jobs in the oil industry increased. The higher price of oil relative to manufactured goods is reflected in the steeper slope of price ratio $(Oil/Mfg)_{2007}$ line. This caused production of oil to increase and production of manufactured goods to decrease, as shown by the movement from point $A$ to point $B$ on the production possibilities curve. As a result, employment in manufacturing decreased, while employment in the oil patch increased. However, unlike Holland, Canada is a country of vast distances, and the manufacturing plants that closed were often a long way from the oil patch jobs that opened up; reallocation between industrial sectors in Canada has often also required geographic mobility of labour over long distances.

6   See http://www.eia.gov/emeu/international/oilprice.html.

7   The shift in relative prices was not restricted to oil and gas, since the international price of many resource commodities (e.g., gold, copper) also rose substantially—but additional investment in production facilities for non-conventional oil was particularly important.

> **RECAP** ↑
>
> ## A SUPPLY-AND-DEMAND PERSPECTIVE ON TRADE
>
> - For a closed economy, domestic supply and demand for a good or service determine the equilibrium price and quantity of that good or service.
>
> - In an open economy, the price of a good or service traded on international markets equals the *world price*.
>
> - Generally, if the price of a good or service in a closed economy is lower than the world price and the economy opens to trade, the country will become a net exporter of that good or service. If the closed-economy price is higher than the world price and the economy opens to trade, the country will tend to become a net importer of the good or service.
>
> - Consumers of imported goods and producers of exported goods benefit from trade, while consumers of exported goods and producers of imported goods are hurt by trade.
>
> - The two most common types of trade barriers are *tariffs,* or taxes on imported goods, and *quotas*, legal limits on the quantity that can be imported.
>
> - Trade barriers reduce the overall size of the economic pie. Even though international trade can improve a nation's consumption possibilities, it can be difficult to achieve agreements that would liberalize international trade.
>
> - Supply and demand can be used to analyze changes in the values of currencies in foreign exchange markets. The supply and demand for a country's currency will determine the value of its currency against other currencies.

## SUMMARY

- The principle of comparative advantage argues that output is maximized when each nation specializes in the goods and services at which it is relatively most productive, and then trades with other nations to obtain the goods and services its citizens desire. **LO2**

- The production possibilities curve (PPC) of a country is a graph that describes the maximum amount of one good that can be produced at every possible level of production of the other good. At any point the slope of a PPC indicates the opportunity cost, in terms of foregone production of the good on the vertical axis, of increasing production of the good on the horizontal axis by one unit. The more of a good that is already being produced, the greater will be the opportunity cost of increasing production of that good still further. When an economy has many workers, the PPC has a smooth, outwardly bowed shape. **LO1**

- A country's *consumption possibilities* are the combinations of goods and services that might feasibly be consumed by its citizens. In a *closed economy* that does not trade with other countries, the citizens' consumption possibilities are identical to their production possibilities. But in an *open economy* that trades with other countries, consumption possibilities are typically greater than, and never less than, the economy's production possibilities. If an open economy's PPC is bowed outward, its consumption possibilities are described graphically by a downward-sloping line that just touches the PPC, and whose slope equals the amount of the good on the vertical axis that must be traded on an international market to obtain one unit of the good on the horizontal axis. A country achieves its highest consumption possibilities by producing at the point where the consumption possibilities line touches the PPC and then trading to obtain the most preferred point on the consumption possibilities line. LO2

■ In a closed economy, the relative price of a good or service is determined by the intersection of the supply curve of domestic producers and the demand curve of domestic consumers. In an open economy, the relative price of a good or service equals the world price—the price determined by supply and demand in the world economy. If the price of a good or service in a closed economy is greater than the world price, and the country opens its market to trade, it will become a net importer of that good or service. But if the closed-economy price is below the world price and the country opens itself to trade, it will become a net exporter of that good or service. LO3

■ Although trade maximizes total output and total economic surplus, some people—such as domestic producers of imported goods and domestic purchasers of exported goods—are hurt by liberalized international trade. LO4, LO6

■ Those hurt by trade may be able to induce the government to impose *protectionist* measures, such as tariffs or quotas. A *tariff* is a tax on an imported good that has the effect of raising the domestic price of the good. A higher domestic price increases domestic quantity supplied, reduces domestic quantity demanded, and reduces imports of the good. A *quota*, which is a legal limit on the amount of a good that may be imported, has the same effects as a tariff, except that the government collects no tax revenue. (The equivalent amount of revenue goes instead to those firms with the legal authority to import goods.) Under unrestricted trade, the benefits to winners from unrestricted trade exceed costs to losers so that it is possible in principle for everyone to be better off. Policies to assist those who are harmed by trade, such as assistance and training for workers idled by imports, help offset the adverse impacts of greater trade. LO7

■ Even though international trade can improve a nation's consumption possibilities, it can be difficult to achieve agreements that would liberalize international trade because: (1) A small nation may believe that its national sovereignty will be eroded if it makes an agreement with a large nation; (2) potential losers under liberalized international trade may believe that they will not be compensated for their losses; (3) a trading partner may believe that an agreement to liberalize international trade will restrict its ability to develop new industries by locking it into the existing pattern of comparative advantage. LO5

■ Currencies are traded in foreign exchange markets. For example, Canadians supply Canadian dollars to the foreign exchange market because they want to buy goods and services produced by other countries. Foreigners want Canadian dollars in order to buy Canadian goods and services. Supply and demand can be used to portray the resulting foreign exchange rate. LO8

## KEY TERMS

autarky (408)
closed economy (407)
consumption possibilities (408)

foreign exchange rate (423)
open economy (407)
protectionism (418)

quota (418)
tariff (418)
world price (412)

## REVIEW QUESTIONS

1. Why are production possibilities curves often bowed outward from the origin? **LO1**

2. What is meant by the *consumption possibilities* of a country? How are consumption possibilities related to production possibilities in a closed economy? in an open economy? **LO2**

3. True or false and explain: If a country is more productive in every sector than a neighbouring country, then there is no benefit in trading with the neighbouring country. **LO2**

4. Show graphically the effects of a tariff on imported automobiles on the domestic market for automobiles. Who is hurt by the tariff, and why? Who benefits, and why? **LO3, LO4, LO6**

5. Show graphically the effects of a quota on imported automobiles on the domestic market for automobiles. Who is hurt by the quota hurt, and who benefits? Explain. **LO7**

## PROBLEMS

Problems 1–5 refer to a small open economy whose production possibilities curve is as shown by the curve *ACGDB* in the diagram below.

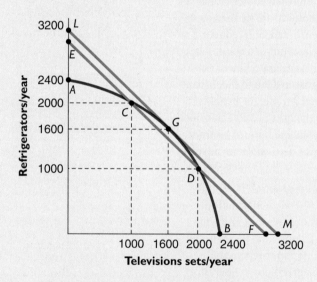

1. What is the maximum number of television sets this country can produce each year? What is the maximum number of refrigerators? **LO2**

2. If refrigerators and television sets can each be bought or sold for $500 in the world market, what is the maximum number of refrigerators this country can consume each year? The maximum number of television sets? How would your answers change if refrigerators and television sets both sold for $1000? **LO2**

3. If refrigerators and television sets both sell for $1000 in the world market, is it possible for this country to consume 1000 television sets per year and 2200 refrigerators? Could the country consume 1000 refrigerators each year and 2500 television sets? **LO2**

4. If refrigerators and television sets both sell for $1000 in the world market, how many units of each good will this country produce if it wants to maximize its consumption possibilities? **LO2**

5. If the world price of refrigerators rose to $1200 and the price of television sets remained $1000, how will this country alter the mix of the two goods it produces? How will it alter the mix of the two goods it consumes? **LO2**

6. A small, open economy is equally productive in producing coffee and tea—that is, for each additional kilogram of coffee it produces, it must sacrifice the production of exactly one kilogram of tea. What will this economy produce if the world price of coffee is 20-percent higher than that of tea? **LO2**

7. A developing economy requires 1000 hours of work to produce a television set and 10 hours of work to produce a bushel of corn. This economy has available a total of 1 000 000 hours of work per day. **LO1, LO2**

   a. Draw the PPC for daily output of the developing economy. Give numerical values for the PPC's vertical intercept, horizontal intercept, and slope. Relate the slope to the developing country's opportunity cost of producing each good. If this economy does not trade, what are its consumption possibilities?

   b. The developing economy is considering opening trade with a much larger, industrialized economy. The industrialized economy requires 10 hours of work to produce a television set and one hour of work to produce a bushel of corn. Show graphically how trading with the industrialized economy affects the developing economy's consumption possibilities. Is opening trade desirable for the developing economy?

8. Suppose that a Canadian worker can produce 1000 pairs of shoes or 10 industrial robots per year. For simplicity, assume there are no costs other than labour costs and firms earn zero profits. Initially, the Canadian economy is closed. The domestic price of shoes is $30 per pair, so a Canadian worker can earn $30 000 annually by working in the shoe industry. The domestic price of a robot is $3000, so a worker also can earn $30 000 annually working in the robot industry. Now suppose that Canada opens trade with the rest of the world. Foreign workers can produce 500 pairs of shoes or one robot per year. The world price of shoes after Canada opens its markets is $10 per pair, and the world price of robots is $5000. **LO2, LO5, LO6**

   a. Describe the new consumption possibilities curve for Canada.

   b. What do foreign workers earn annually, in dollars?

   c. When it opens to trade, which good will Canada import and which will it export?

   d. Find the real income of Canadian workers after the opening to trade, measured in (1) the number of pairs of shoes annual worker income will buy and (2) the number of robots annual worker income will buy. Compare this real income to the situation before the opening of trade.

   e. Does trading in goods produced by "cheap foreign labour" hurt Canadian workers?

   f. How might your conclusion in part *e* be modified in the short term if it is costly for workers to change industries? What policy response might help with this problem?

9. If the domestic supply and demand curves for toasters in Islandia are as shown in the diagram below and the world price of toasters is $18, how will opening the country to the possibility of buying toasters in the world market affect consumer and

producer surpluses in its domestic toaster market? **LO3, LO4, LO6**

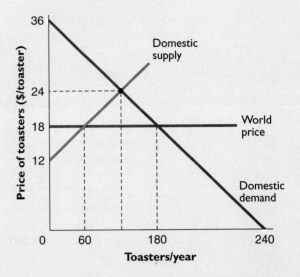

10. If Islandia's supply and demand curves in its domestic market for toasters are as shown in the diagram below, and buyers are currently able to import toasters at the world price of $18, how will the imposition of a tariff of $3 per toaster affect total economic surplus? **LO7**

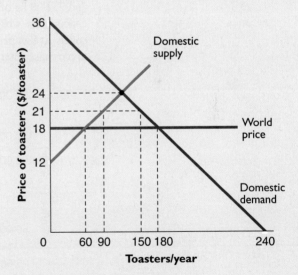

## ANSWERS TO IN-CHAPTER EXERCISES

**15.1** If Costa Rica produces at point *C* and can trade in the world market at the rate of 500 kg of coffee per computer, it can sell 500 computers for 25 000 kg of coffee. By so doing, Costa Rica can consume 125 000 kg of coffee and 500 computers per year (point *X* in the diagram). **LO2**

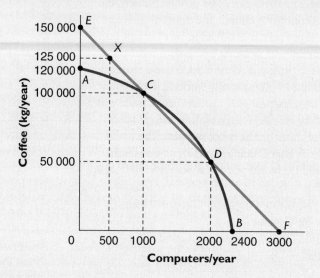

**15.2** At the point *Y* in the diagram, Costa Rica consumes 2500 computers per year and 25 000 kg of coffee. Costa Rica can go from *C* to *Y* by selling 75 000 kg of coffee in the world market at the world price of 0.02 computer per kilogram of coffee. At that price, its revenue from the sale of 75 000 kg of coffee will enable it to purchase 1500 computers for a total of 2500 computers. **LO2**

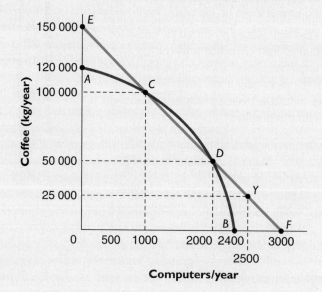

**15.3**   Domestic consumers and producers in the computer market each reap a surplus of $375 000 per year in the absence of trade (left panel), for a total economic surplus of $750 000. With trade, the country imports 600 computers per year at the world price of $1200 per computer. Computer buyers reap a consumer surplus of $960 000 per year, or $585 000 per year more than before trade. Computer sellers receive a producer surplus of $60 000 per year, or $315 000 less than before trade. The net gain in total economic surplus from trade is $270 000 per year. **LO4, LO6**

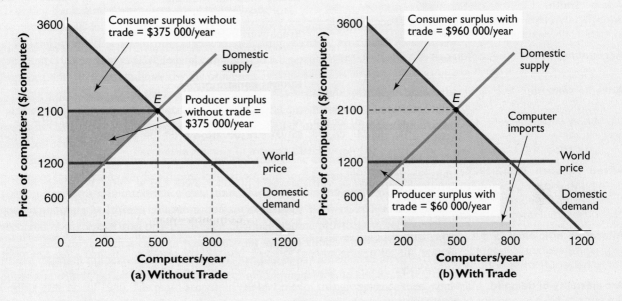

**15.4**   Total economic surplus without the tariff is $1 020 000 per year (left panel). With the tariff, consumer surplus falls by $225 000 per year, producer surplus rises by $75 000 per year, and government revenue rises by $120 000 per year. The net decrease in total economic surplus caused by the tariff is $30 000 per year. **LO7**

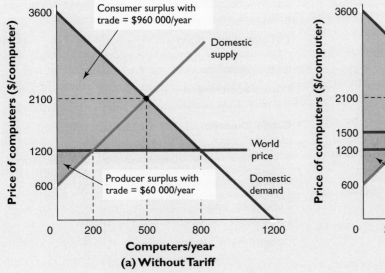
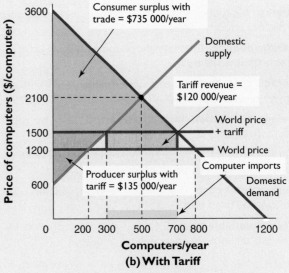

**Practise and learn online with Connect.**

# GLOSSARY

## A

**Absolute advantage.** The advantage of taking fewer hours to perform a task than another person does.

**Adam Smith.** (1723–1790) Scottish economist who wrote *The Wealth of Nations* (1776), probably the most influential economics book ever written

**Accounting profit.** The difference between a firm's total revenue and its explicit costs.

**Adverse selection.** The increase in average risk of the insured population that occurs when, at any given cost of insurance, people with a greater expectation of loss buy insurance while people with a lower expected value of claims choose not to buy insurance.

**Alfred Marshall (1842–1924).** An economist of the nineteenth and early twentieth centuries who published *Principles of Economics* (1890) and whose influence on economics continues to this day.

**Allocative efficiency.** occurs when it is impossible to reorganize economic resources so that at least one person is better off while nobody is worse off.

**Arc elasticity of demand.** Elasticity calculated between the endpoints of a segment of a demand curve.

**Asymmetric information.** Situations in which buyers and sellers are not equally well informed about the characteristics of goods and services for sale in the marketplace.

**Attainable point.** Any combination of goods that can be produced using currently available resources.

**Autarky.** A situation in which a country does not trade with other nations.

**Average benefit.** Total benefit of undertaking $n$ units of an activity divided by $n$.

**Average cost.** Total cost of undertaking $n$ units of an activity divided by $n$.

**Average fixed cost.** Total fixed cost divided by total output; fixed cost per unit of output.

**Average product.** Total output divided by total units of the variable factor of production.

**Average total cost.** The sum of average variable cost and average fixed cost.

**Average variable cost.** Total variable cost divided by total output; variable cost per unit of output.

## B

**Barrier to entry.** Any force that prevents firms from entering a new market.

**Basic elements of a game.** The players, the strategies available to each player, and the payoffs each player receives for each possible combination of strategies.

**Better-than-fair gamble.** A gamble whose expected value is positive.

**Breakeven income.** Under a negative income tax, the level of before-tax income at which a family's tax liability exactly offsets its initial tax credit.

**Budget constraint.** All commodity bundles whose total cost is exactly equal to the consumer's income; can be represented verbally, graphically, or algebraically.

**Buyer's reservation price.** See Demander's reservation price.

## C

**Capital.** Any durable inputs to the production process, such as tools, machinery, and buildings.

**Cartel.** A coalition of firms that agree to restrict output for the purpose of earning an economic profit.

**Ceteris paribus.** A Latin phrase meaning "all else equal."

**Change in demand.** A shift of the entire demand curve.

**Change in supply.** A shift of the entire supply curve.

**Change in quantity demanded.** A movement along the demand curve that occurs in response to a change in price.

**Change in quantity supplied.** A movement along the supply curve that occurs in response to a change in price.

**Circular flow diagram.** An illustration of exchange relationships in a monetary economy highlighting the mutual dependence of incomes and expenditures.

**Closed economy.** An economy that does not trade with the rest of the world.

**Coase theorem.** If, at no cost, people can negotiate the purchase and sale of the right to perform activities that cause externalities, they can arrive at surplus-maximizing solutions to the problems caused by externalities.

**Collective good.** A good or service that, to at least some degree, is nonrival but excludable.

**Commitment device.** A way of changing incentives so as to make otherwise empty threats or promises credible.

**Commitment problem.** A situation in which people cannot achieve their goals because of an inability to make credible threats or promises.

**Commons good.** A good for which nonpayers cannot easily be excluded and for which each unit consumed by one person means one fewer unit is available for others.

**Comparative advantage.** The advantage of having a lower opportunity cost of performing a task than another person does for the same task.

**Compensating wage differential.** A difference in the wage rate, negative or positive, that reflects the attractiveness of a job's working conditions.

**Complements.** A relationship between two goods such that an increase in the price of one causes a leftward shift in the demand curve for the other

**Composite good.** An amalgam of all goods available to a consumer except for one single good; the composite good represents all other bundles that could be bought with the income left after purchasing the single good.

**Constant (or parameter).** A quantity that is fixed in value.

**Constant returns to scale.** A situation in which long-run average cost does not change as scale changes.

**Consumer surplus.** The economic gain of the buyers of a product, as measured by the cumulative difference between their respective reservation prices and the price they actually paid.

**Consumption possibilities.** The combinations of goods and services that a country's citizens might feasibly consume.

**Costly-to-fake principle.** To communicate information credibly to a potential rival, a signal must be costly or difficult to fake.

**Cost-plus regulation.** A method of regulation under which the regulated firm is permitted to charge a price equal to its explicit costs of production plus a markup to cover the opportunity cost of resources provided by the firm's owners.

**Credible promise.** A promise to take an action that is in the promiser's interest to keep.

**Credible threat.** A threat to take an action that is in the threatener's interest to carry out.

**Cross-price elasticity of demand for two goods.** The percentage change in the quantity demanded of one good in response to a 1 percent change in the price of a second good.

## D

**Deadweight loss.** The reduction in economic surplus that results from adoption of policy.

**Decision tree (or game tree).** A diagram that describes the possible moves in a game, in sequence, and lists the payoffs that correspond to each possible combination of moves.

**Demand curve.** A curve or schedule showing the total quantity of a good of uniform quality that buyers want to buy at each price during a particular period of time provided that all other things are held constant.

**Demander's (or buyer's) reservation price.** The highest price a demander will offer in order to obtain a good or service.

**Dependent variable.** A variable in an equation whose value is determined by the value taken by another variable in the equation.

**Discount factor.** A coefficient used to discount a payment or receipt that occurs in the future to a present value.

**Diseconomies of scale.** A situation in which long-run average cost increases as a firm's output increases.

**Dominant strategy.** One that yields a higher payoff no matter what the other players in a game choose.

**Dominated strategy.** Any other strategy available to a player who has a dominant strategy.

## E

**Econometrics.** A branch of economics that involves the application of statistical techniques to economic data and the development of statistical techniques for analyzing such data.

**Economic (or excess) profit.** The difference between a firm's total revenue and the sum of its explicit and implicit costs.

**Economic loss.** An economic profit that is less than zero.

**Economic model.** A representation of economic reality that highlights particular variables and the relationships among them.

**Economic naturalist.** someone who uses insights from economics to help make sense of observations from everyday life.

**Economic profit.** The difference between a firm's total revenue and the sum of its explicit and implicit costs.

**Economic rent.** That part of the payment for a factor of production that exceeds the owner's reservation price, the price below which the owner would not supply the factor.

**Economic surplus.** The benefit of any action minus its cost.

**Economics.** The study of how people make choices under conditions of scarcity and of the results of those choices for society.

**Economies of scale.** A situation in which long-run average cost decreases as a firm's output increases.

**Efficient point.** Any combination of goods for which currently available resources do not allow an increase in the production of one good without a reduction in the production of the other.

**Elastic demand.** Price elasticity of demand that is greater than one.

**Elastic supply.** Supply is elastic if price elasticity of supply is greater than one.

**Employer discrimination.** An arbitrary preference by the employer for one group of workers over another.

**Entrepreneur.** A person who perceives an opportunity to make a profit and then takes the risks necessary to organize factors of production in order to realize that profit.

**Equation.** A mathematical expression that describes the relationship between two or more variables.

**Equilibrium.** A state of rest that occurs when all forces that act on all variables in a system are in balance, exactly offsetting each other so that none of the variables in the system has any tendency to change.

**Equilibrium price.** The price and quantity of a good at the intersection of the supply and demand curves for the good (also equilibrium quantity).

**Equilibrium quantity.** The price and quantity of a good at the intersection of the supply and demand curves for the good (also equilibrium price).

**Equity.** A state of impartiality and fairness.

**Excess demand.** The difference between the quantity supplied and the quantity demanded when the price of a good lies below the equilibrium price; leaves some buyers dissatisfied (also shortage).

**Excess supply.** The difference between the quantity supplied and the quantity demanded when the price of a good exceeds the equilibrium price; leaves some sellers dissatisfied (also surplus).

**Excise tax.** A tax charged on each unit of a good or service.

**Expected value of a gamble.** The sum of the possible outcomes multiplied by their respective probabilities.

**Explicit costs.** The actual payments a firm makes during a period of time to its factors of production and other suppliers.

**External benefit (or positive externality).** A benefit received by others that arises from an activity undertaken by an individual, firm, or other economic agent for which the agent is not compensated in the market price paid for the good or service involved.

**External cost (or negative externality).** A cost that arises from an activity undertaken by an individual, firm, or other economic agent and that is borne by others because the cost is not incorporated in market prices the agent pays.

**Externality.** An external cost or benefit of an activity.

## F

**Factor of production.** Resource used to produce output; falls into one of three categories—land, labour, or capital.

**Fair gamble.** A gamble whose expected value is zero.

**Fallacy of composition.** The argument that because something is true for a part, it also is true for the whole.

**Firm.** An organization that combines factors of production to produce a good or service or some combination of goods and services.

**Fixed cost.** Any cost that does not change when output changes.

**Fixed factor of production.** An input whose quantity cannot be altered in the short run.

**Foreign exchange rate.** The price of one unit of a country's currency in terms of another country's currency; determined in foreign exchange markets.

## G

**Game tree.** See Decision tree.

**Gini coefficient.** An index, which ranges between zero and one, of the amount of inequality in a population. When all persons have the same income (perfect equality), it equals zero. When only one person has all the income (perfect inequality), it equals one. Graphically, it can be represented as the ratio of the area between the Lorenz curve and the line of perfect equality to the area of the triangle below the line of perfect equality.

## H

**Head tax.** A tax that collects the same amount from every taxpayer.

**Human capital.** The skills produced by education, training, and experience that affect a worker's marginal product.

**Human capital theory.** A theory of pay determination stating that a worker's wage will be proportional to his or her stock of human capital.

**Hurdle method of price discrimination.** The practice by which a seller offers a discount to all buyers who overcome some obstacle.

## I

**Implicit costs.** All the firm's opportunity costs of the resources supplied by the firm's owners.

**Income effect.** The change in quantity demanded of a good that occurs because a change in the price of the good has changed the real income of the purchaser.

**Income elasticity of demand.** The percentage change in the quantity demanded of a good in response to a 1 percent change in income.

**Independent variable.** A variable in an equation whose value determines the value taken by another variable in the equation.

**Indifference curve.** Plots all the combinations of two goods that provide a consumer with the same satisfaction or utility; a consumer will be indifferent between any of the combinations included.

**Indifference map.** A graph of several indifference curves; the further the curve lies from the origin of the graph, the greater the level of utility it indicates.

**Indivisible cost.** The cost of an indivisible factor of production.

**Indivisible factor of production.** A factor of production that must be available in some minimum amount if a productive activity, even of minimal size, is to occur at all.

**Inefficient point.** Any combination of goods for which currently available resources enable an increase in the production of one good without a reduction in the production of the other.

**Inelastic demand.** Price elasticity of demand less than one.

**Inelastic supply.** Price elasticity of supply is less than one.

**Inferior good.** A good whose demand curve shifts leftward when the incomes of buyers increase. A good with a negative income elasticity of demand.

**Inputs.** Goods or services used in the process of producing a different good or service.

**Intermediate inputs.** Any inputs that are used up in the production process.

**Invisible hand.** Adam Smith's metaphor for his theory stating that under carefully specified circumstances, the actions of independent, self-interested buyers and sellers will result in the largest possible economic surplus.

## J

**John Maynard Keynes (1883-1946).** A British economist (whose surname is pronounced "Kains") whose *The General Theory of Employment, Interest and Money* (1936) is widely regarded as the seminal work in modern macroeconomics

## L

**Labour.** Physical or mental exertion by human beings to produce output.

**Labour union.** A group of workers who bargain collectively with employers for better wages and working conditions.

**Land.** Any naturally occurring resource used to produce output.

**Law of Demand.** Other things remaining equal, people will purchase a smaller quantity of any good or service they want as the price of purchasing one more unit of it increases.

**Law of diminishing marginal returns.** As equal increments of one input are added, there is a point beyond which the marginal product of that input will decrease, if technology and all other inputs are held constant.

**Law of diminishing marginal utility.** As consumption of a good increases beyond some point, the additional utility gained from an additional unit of the goods tends to decline.

**Lemons model.** George Akerlof's explanation of how asymmetric information tends to reduce the average quality of goods offered for sale.

**Long run.** A period of time of sufficient length that all the firm's factors of production are variable.

**Long-run average cost.** The lowest cost per unit that can be achieved for a given level of output when all factors of production, all costs, and the size of the firm are variable, but technology is constant.

**Lorenz curve.** A graph that orders the members of a population from poorest to richest; on the horizontal axis is the percentage of the population below a given income, and on the vertical axis the cumulative percentage of total income received by them.

**Luxury good.** A good with an income elasticity of demand greater than one; a subset of normal goods.

## M

**Macroeconomics.** The study of the performance of national economies and the policies that governments use to try to improve that performance.

**Marginal abatement cost.** The cost to a polluter of reducing GHG by one unit.

**Marginal benefit.** The increase in total benefit that results from carrying out one more unit of an activity.

**Marginal cost.** The increase in total cost incurred by producing one more unit of output.

**Marginal labour cost.** The amount by which a firm's total wage bill goes up if it hires an extra worker.

**Marginal product.** The increase in total output caused by an increase of one unit in the variable factor of production, holding technology and all other inputs constant.

**Marginal (physical) product of labour (MP).** The additional output a firm gets by employing one additional unit of labour.

**Marginal rate of substitution (MRS).** The absolute value of the slope of the indifference curve; the rate at which one good can be substituted for another while maintaining a constant level of utility.

**Marginal revenue.** The increase in total revenue obtained by producing and selling one more unit of output.

**Marginal utility.** The additional utility gained from consuming an additional unit of a good.

**Market.** The context in which potential buyers and sellers of a good or service can negotiate exchanges.

**Market equilibrium.** Occurs when all buyers and sellers are satisfied with their respective quantities at the market price.

**Market power.** A firm's ability to raise the price of a good without losing all its sales.

**Microeconomics.** The study of individual choice under scarcity and its implications for the behaviour of prices and quantities in individual markets.

**Minimum efficient quantity.** The smallest quantity of output that will achieve minimum long-run average cost.

**Monopolistic competition.** A market structure in which a large number of firms sell slightly differentiated products that are reasonably close substitutes for one another.

**Monopsony.** A market with only a single buyer.

**Moral hazard.** The tendency of people to exert less care or allocate fewer resources to prevent losses that are insured.

## N

**Nash equilibrium.** Any combination of strategies in which each player's strategy is his or her best choice, given the other players' strategies.

**Natural monopoly.** A monopoly that results from economies of scale.

**Negative externality.** See External cost.

**Negative income tax.** A system under which the government would grant every citizen a cash payment each year, financed by an additional tax on earned income.

**Network economy.** A reduction in the cost of providing a given quality of a product that occurs if the value of the product to individual users increases as more people join the network of users.

**Nominal price.** Absolute price of a good in dollar terms.

**Nonexcludable good.** A good that is difficult, or costly, to prevent nonpayers from consuming.

**Nonrival good.** A good whose consumption by one person does not diminish its availability for others.

**Normal good.** A good whose demand curve shifts rightward when the incomes of buyers increase. A good with a positive income elasticity of demand.

**Normal profit.** the opportunity cost of the resources supplied by the firm's owners; equal to accounting profit minus economic profit.

## O

**Observationally equivalent workers.** Workers of the same type; that is, with the same generally known personal characteristics (age, education, gender, work experience, race, ethnicity, etc.).

**Oligopoly.** A market in which there are only a few rival sellers

**Open economy.** An economy that trades with other countries.

**Opportunity cost.** The value of the next-best alternative that must be foregone in order to undertake the activity.

**Optimal combination of goods.** The affordable combination that yields the highest total utility.

## P

**Parameter.** See Constant.

**Payoff matrix.** A table that describes the payoffs in a game for each possible combination of strategies.

**Perfect hurdle.** One that completely segregates buyers whose reservation prices lie above some threshold from others whose reservation prices lie below it, imposing no cost on those who jump the hurdle.

**Perfectly competitive market.** A market in which no individual supplier has significant influence on the market price of the product.

**Perfectly discriminating monopolist.** A firm that charges each buyer exactly his or her reservation price.

**Perfectly elastic.** Price elasticity of demand is infinite.

**Perfectly elastic supply curve.** A supply curve whose elasticity with respect to price is infinite.

**Perfectly inelastic.** Price elasticity of demand is zero.

**Perfectly inelastic supply curve.** A supply curve whose elasticity with respect to price is zero.

**Point elasticity of demand.** Elasticity calculated at a specific point on a demand curve.

**Positional arms control agreement.** An agreement in which contestants attempt to limit mutually offsetting investments in performance enhancement.

**Positional arms race.** A series of mutually offsetting investments in performance enhancement that is stimulated by a positional externality.

**Positional externality.** Occurs when an increase in one person or firm's performance reduces the expected reward of another's in situations in which reward depends on relative performance.

**Positive economics.** Economic analysis offering cause-and-effect explanations of economic relationships; its propositions or hypotheses can, in principle, be confirmed or refuted by data; effectiveness of its predictions measurable by data.

**Positive externality.** See External benefit.

**Present value.** The current value of an amount paid or received in the future.

**Price ceiling.** A maximum allowable price, specified by law.

**Price discrimination.** The practice of charging different buyers different prices, not based on differences in cost of production, for essentially the same good or service.

**Price elasticity of demand.** The percentage change in the quantity demanded of a good that results from a 1 percent change in its price.

**Price elasticity of supply.** The percentage change in quantity supplied arising from a 1 percent change in price.

**Price floor.** A minimum allowable price, specified by law or regulation.

**Price setter.** A firm that can set its own price, recognizing that the price it sets will affect the quantity it can sell.

**Price taker.** A firm that has no influence over the price at which it sells its product.

**Prisoner's dilemma.** A game in which each player has a dominant strategy, and when each plays it, the resulting payoffs are smaller than if each had played a dominated strategy.

**Private good.** A good for which nonpayers can easily be excluded and for which each unit consumed by one person means one fewer unit is available for others.

**Producer surplus.** The economic gain of the sellers of a product, as measured by the cumulative difference between the price received and their respective reservation prices.

**Production function.** A technological relationship between inputs and outputs.

**Production possibilities curve.** A graph that describes the maximum amount of one good that can be produced for every possible level of production of the other good.

**Productive efficiency.** Occurs when an economy is using all of its economic resources in their technically most effective way

**Productivity.** Units of output per hour divided by units of input per hour.

**Profit.** The total revenue a firm receives from the sale of its product minus all costs, explicit and implicit, incurred in producing it.

**Profit-maximizing firm.** A firm whose primary goal is to maximize the difference between its total revenues and total costs.

**Progressive tax.** A tax in which the proportion of income paid in taxes rises as income rises.

**Proportional income tax.** A tax under which all taxpayers pay the same proportion of their incomes in taxes.

**Protectionism.** The view that trade is injurious and should be restricted.

**Public good.** A good or service that, to at least some degree, is both nonrival and nonexcludable.

**Pure monopoly.** A market in which there is only one supplier of a unique product with no close substitutes.

# Q

**Quantity demanded.** The total amount of a good of uniform quality purchased at a single, specific price by all buyers during a particular period of time.

**Quantity supplied.** The total amount of a good of uniform quality that all sellers are willing to produce and sell at a single, specific price, during a particular period of time.

**Quintile.** Each fifth of a group of individuals who are arranged in order of income, beginning with the lowest ranking fifth.

**Quota.** A legal limit on the quantity of a good that may be imported.

# R

**Rational decision maker.** Someone with clear objectives who behaves logically to achieve those objectives

**Rational spending rule.** The rule that in order to maximize the total utility a consumer can derive from a fixed budget, spending must be allocated across goods so that marginal utility per dollar is the same for each good.

**Real price.** Dollar price of a good relative to the average dollar price of all other goods and services.

**Regressive tax.** A tax under which the proportion of income paid in taxes declines as income rises.

**Rent-seeking.** The socially unproductive efforts of people or firms to win a prize.

**Repeated prisoner's dilemma.** A standard dilemma that confronts the same players repeatedly.

**Revenue.** The value of income received by a firm during a period of time in return for supplying goods and services

**Rise.** In a straight line, the vertical distance the straight line travels between any two points that corresponds to the horizontal distance (run). See Slope.

**Risk-averse person.** Someone who would refuse any fair gamble.

**Risk-neutral person.** Someone who would accept any gamble that is fair or better than fair.

**Rule for profit maximization.** Profits are maximized at the quantity of output where marginal revenue equals marginal cost.

**Run.** In a straight line, the horizontal distance that corresponds to the vertical distance the straight line travels between any two points (rise). See Slope.

# S

**Scale.** The size of a firm relative tzo other possible sizes of firms serving a particular market.

**Seller's reservation price.** See Supplier's reservation price.

**Shortage.** See Excess demand.

**Short run.** A period of time sufficiently short that at least one of the firm's factors of production cannot be varied.

**Short-run cost-minimizing quantity of output.** The quantity of output at which a factory reaches minimum average total cost.

**Short-run shutdown point.** A firm's minimum average variable cost; if price drops below minimum average variable cost, the firm will minimize its losses by shutting down.

**Side payment.** A payment made from one party to another in compensation for an external cost or benefit.

**Slope.** In a straight line, the ratio of the vertical distance the straight line travels between any two points (rise) to the corresponding horizontal distance (run).

**Spurious correlation.** A case in which two variables move together but are otherwise unrelated.

**Statistical discrimination.** The practice of making judgments about the quality of people, goods, or services based on the characteristics of the groups to which they belong.

**Substitutes.** A relationship between two goods such that an increase in the price of one causes a rightward shift in the demand curve for the other.

**Substitution effect.** The change in quantity demanded of a good whose relative price has changed while a consumer's real income is held constant.

**Sunk cost.** A cost that is beyond recovery at the moment a decision must be made.

**Supplier's (or seller's) reservation price.** The lowest price a supplier will accept in return for providing a good or service.

**Supply curve.** A curve or schedule showing the total quantity of a good that sellers want to sell at each price during a particular period of time, provided that all other things are held equal.

**Surplus.** See Excess supply.

## T

**Tariff.** A tax imposed on an imported good.

**Technical efficiency in production.** A condition that occurs when the least possible amounts of inputs are used to produce a given level of output.

**Technology.** The stock of knowledge, useful in producing goods and services, that is available to a society.

**Tit-for-tat.** A strategy for the repeated prisoner's dilemma in which players cooperate on the first move, then mimic their partner's last move on each successive move

**Total economic surplus.** The sum of all the individual economic surpluses gained by buyers and sellers who participate in the market.

**Total expenditure = total revenue.** The dollar amount consumers spend on a product is equal to the dollar amount sellers receive.

**Tragedy of the commons.** The tendency for a resource that has no price to be used until its marginal benefit falls to zero.

## U

**Ultimatum bargaining game.** One in which the first player has the power to confront the second player with a take-it-or-leave-it offer.

**Unattainable point.** Any combination of goods that cannot be produced using currently available resources.

**Unit elastic demand.** Price elasticity of demand equal to one.

**Utilitarianism.** A moral theory in which the right course of action is the one that results in the highest total utility.

**Util.** A unit of pleasure or utility obtained from an item.

**Utility.** The sense of well-being, satisfaction, or pleasure a person derives from consuming a good or service.

## V

**Value of marginal product of labour (VMP).** The dollar value of the additional output a firm gets by employing one additional unit of labour.

**Variable.** A quantity that is free to take a range of different values.

**Variable cost.** A cost that changes as the firm changes its output.

**Variable factor of production.** An input whose quantity can be altered in the short run.

**Vertical intercept.** In a straight line, the value taken by the dependent variable when the independent variable equals zero.

## W

**Welfare economics.** Economic analysis that is concerned not only with prediction or facts but also involves the evaluation of economic outcomes or situations according to ethical or value standards (which may be either explicit or implicit).

**Winner-take-all labour market.** A market in which small differences in human capital translate into large differences in pay.

**World price.** The price at which a good or service is traded on international markets.

# INDEX

monopolistic competition. *See also*
  imperfect competition
  cost-plus regulation in, 247–248
  deadweight loss in, 235–237
  defined, 219
  economies of scale and,
    223–228
  exclusive contracting in, 248
  fixed costs and, 223–228
  legislation and enforcement of,
    249–250
  market power and, 221–223,
    251–254
  patents and, 235–236
  perfectly discriminating
    monopolist in, 241
  price discrimination and,
    239–245
  public policy and, 245–250
  state management of, 245–247
monopoly. *See also* imperfect
    competition
  deadweight loss and, 235–237
  defined, 219
  distributive effect of, 237–238
  economies of scale and, 221–222,
    223–228
  graphical summary of, 233–234
  invisible hand in, 234–238
  marginal revenue under, 229–231
  market power sources, 221–223
  perfect vs. imperfect
    competition, 220
  perfectly discriminating
    monopolist, 241
  price discrimination and,
    239–245
  profit-maximizing rule under,
    231–233
  public policy and, 245–250
monopsony. *See also* imperfect
    competition
  defined, 338
  demand for labour and, 340–341
  marginal labour cost in, 338–339
  market power and, 340
  wage determination in, 337–341
moral hazard, 323
Mortensen, Dale, 311, 344
MP, 333. *See also* marginal physical
    product of labour (MP)
MRS. *See* marginal rate of
    substitution (MRS)
mutually beneficial exchange,
    187–189

## N

Nash equilibrium, 262–264
natural monopoly, 221–222,
    245–246. *See also* imperfect
    competition; monopoly
needs, 79
negative externality, 284
negative income tax (NIT), 377–380
neoclassical economics, 4

network economy, 222, 227n
"no free lunch," 5
nominal price, 88
nonexcludable good, 385, 386
nonrival good, 385, 386
normal good, 67, 102
normal profit, 162
normative economics, 13
North American Free Trade
    Agreement (NAFTA), 414–415

## O

observationally equivalent workers,
    335
oil prices, 88
oligopoly. *See also* imperfect
    competition
  cartel as, 266–267
  defined, 219
  game theory and, 261
  market, as, 250–251
  prisoner's dilemma and,
    266–267
*Ontario Human Rights Commission
    v. Zurich Insurance Co.*, 321n
open economy, 407
opportunity cost. *See also*
    production possibilities
  comparative advantage and,
    31–35
  decision pitfalls and, 7–9
  defined, 6–7
  increasing, principle of, 40, 42.
    *See also* diminishing marginal
    returns
  price and, 36–37
  productivity and, 33
  specialization and, 40
optimal combination of goods,
    82–83
Organization of Petroleum Exporting
    Countries (OPEC), 267
output market
  circular flow diagram and, 46
  monopoly and, 237–238
  perfectly competitive firm and,
    228–229
  price discrimination and,
    240–241
  profit-maximizing firm and,
    136–139, 228

## P

parameter, 22
patent, 222–223, 235–236
patents, 235–237
payoff matrix
  cartel agreement and, 267
  game theory and, 262–264
  prisoner's dilemma and, 265
perfect competition, 219. *See also*
    perfectly competitive market
perfect hurdle, 244
perfect information, 192, 310

perfectly competitive market
  defined, 185
  demand curve of, 186–187
  imperfect competition vs., 220
  mutually beneficial exchange
    and, 187–189
  preconditions for, 184–185
  price controls and, 193–202
  price takers and, 185
  reason to understand, 186
  wage determination in, 332–337
perfectly discriminating
    monopolist, 241
perfectly elastic, 101
perfectly elastic supply curve, 152
perfectly inelastic, 101
perfectly inelastic supply curve, 151
physical capital, 47
Pissarides, Christopher, 311, 344
point elasticity of demand, 99
positional arms race, 303
positional externalities
  defined, 303
  positional arms control
    agreement, 303–306
  positional arms race, 303
  relative performance payoff and,
    302–303
positive economics, 13
positive externality, 284
poverty, 366–369
  income inequality and, 368–369
  intensity, 367
  LICO and, 367
  unemployment rate and, 368
  wealth inequality, 370–372
PPC, 35. *See also* production
    possibilities
predatory pricing, 249
preferences, 276–278
present value, 347
price. *See also* demand curve;
    supply curve
  budget constraint, 113–116
  changes in, 62–70
  complements and, 66
  demand curve and, 56–57, 65–70
  discrimination in, 239–245
  elasticity of demand, of.
    *See* price elasticity of demand
  elasticity of supply and. *See*
    price elasticity of supply
  equilibrium and, 58–61, 68–70
  imperfect competition and, 220,
    229–234
  income effect and, 122–125
  indifference curves and, 113–125
  inputs and, 64
  labour demand curve and, 336
  market and, 53–70
  market demand and, 90–94
  market power and, 221–223
  nominal price, 88
  opportunity cost and, 36–37
  perfectly competitive market
    and, 186–187, 229